Classical Sociological Theory

Classical Sociological Theory

Third Edition

Edited by

Craig Calhoun, Joseph Gerteis, James Moody, Steven Pfaff, and Indermohan Virk

WILEY-BLACKWELL
A John Wiley & Sons, Ltd., Publication

This edition first published 2012
Editorial material and organization © 2012 John Wiley & Sons, Ltd

Edition history: Blackwell Publishing Ltd (1e, 2002 and 2e, 2007)

Wiley-Blackwell is an imprint of John Wiley & Sons formed by the merger of Wiley's global Scientific, Technical and Medical business with Blackwell Publishing.

Registered Office
John Wiley & Sons, Ltd, The Atrium, Southern Gate, Chichester, West Sussex, PO19 8SQ, United Kingdom

Editorial Offices
350 Main Street, Malden, MA 02148-5020, USA
9600 Garsington Road, Oxford, OX4 2DQ, UK
The Atrium, Southern Gate, Chichester, West Sussex, PO19 8SQ, UK

For details of our global editorial offices, for customer services, and for information about how to apply for permission to reuse the copyright material in this book please see our website at www.wiley.com/wiley-blackwell

The right of Craig Calhoun, Joseph Gerteis, James Moody, Steven Pfaff, and Indermohan Virk to be identified as the editors of the editorial material in this work has been asserted in accordance with the UK Copyright, Designs and Patents Act 1988.

All rights reserved. No part of this publication may be reproduced, stored in a retrieval system, or transmitted, in any form or by any means, electronic, mechanical, photocopying, recording or otherwise, except as permitted by the UK Copyright, Designs and Patents Act 1988, without the prior permission of the publisher.

Wiley also publishes its books in a variety of electronic formats. Some content that appears in print may not be available in electronic books.

Designations used by companies to distinguish their products are often claimed as trademarks. All brand names and product names used in this book are trade names, service marks, trademarks or registered trademarks of their respective owners. The publisher is not associated with any product or vendor mentioned in this book. This publication is designed to provide accurate and authoritative information in regard to the subject matter covered. It is sold on the understanding that the publisher is not engaged in rendering professional services. If professional advice or other expert assistance is required, the services of a competent professional should be sought.

Library of Congress Cataloging-in-Publication Data

Classical sociological theory / edited by Craig Calhoun ... [et al.].
    p. cm.
  Complements Contemporary sociological theory.
  Includes bibliographical references and index.
  ISBN 978-0-470-65567-2 (pbk.)
 1. Sociology–History. 2. Sociology–Philosophy.   I. Calhoun, Craig J., 1952–
 II. Contemporary sociological theory.
  HM435.C53 2012
  301'.01–dc23
                                                  2011036063

A catalogue record for this book is available from the British Library.

Set in 10.5/13pt Minion by SPi Publisher Services, Pondicherry, India
Printed and bound by CPI Group (UK) Ltd, Croydon, CR0 4YY

Contents

Notes on the Editors ix
Acknowledgments x

Introduction 1

Part I   Precursors to Sociological Theory 19

Introduction to Part I 21
1   Of the Natural Condition and the Commonwealth (from *Leviathan*) 30
    Thomas Hobbes
2   Of the Social Contract (from *The Social Contract*) 38
    Jean-Jacques Rousseau
3   What is Enlightenment? (from *Immanuel Kant, The Philosophy of Kant*) 50
    Immanuel Kant
4   The Wealth of Nations (from *The Wealth of Nations*) 55
    Adam Smith
5   The Theory of Moral Sentiments (from *The Theory of Moral Sentiments*) 67
    Adam Smith

Part II   The Sociological Theory of Alexis de Tocqueville 83

Introduction to Part II 85
6   The Old Régime and the French Revolution (from *The Old Régime and the French Revolution*) 94
    Alexis de Tocqueville
7   Influence of Democracy on the Feelings of the Americans (from *Democracy in America*) 103
    Alexis de Tocqueville

8   Tyranny of the Majority (from *Democracy in America*)   122
    Alexis de Tocqueville

Part III   The Sociological Theory of Karl Marx and Friedrich Engels   133

Introduction to Part III   135
9   The German Ideology (from *The German Ideology, Part One*)   142
    Karl Marx and Friedrich Engels
10 Economic and Philosophic Manuscripts of 1844
    (from *Collected Works, Volume 3*)   146
    Karl Marx
11 Manifesto of the Communist Party (from *Collected Works, Volume 6*)   156
    Karl Marx and Friedrich Engels
12 The Eighteenth Brumaire of Louis Bonaparte (from *Collected Works,
    Volume 11*)   172
    Karl Marx
13 Wage-Labour and Capital (from *Karl Marx: Selected Writings*)   182
    Karl Marx
14 Classes (from *Collected Works, Volume 37*)   190
    Karl Marx

Part IV   The Sociological Theory of Emile Durkheim   193

Introduction to Part IV   195
15 The Rules of Sociological Method (from *The Rules
    of Sociological Method*)   201
    Emile Durkheim
16 The Division of Labor in Society (from *The Division
    of Labor in Society*)   220
    Emile Durkheim
17 The Elementary Forms of the Religious Life (from *Elementary
    Forms of the Religious Life*)   243
    Emile Durkheim
18 Suicide (from *Suicide: A Study in Sociology*)   255
    Emile Durkheim

Part V   The Sociological Theory of Max Weber   265

Introduction to Part V   267
19 "Objectivity" in Social Science (from *The Methodology
    of the Social Sciences*)   273
    Max Weber

20	Basic Sociological Terms (from *The Theory of Social and Economic Organization*) Max Weber	280
21	The Protestant Ethic and the Spirit of Capitalism (from *Protestant Ethic and the Spirit of Capitalism With Other Writings on the Rise of the West*) Max Weber	291
22	The Distribution of Power within the Political Community: Class, Status, Party (from *From Max Weber: Essays in Sociology*) Max Weber	310
23	The Types of Legitimate Domination (from *The Theory of Social and Economic Organization*) Max Weber	320
24	Bureaucracy (from *Max Weber: Essays in Sociology*) Max Weber	328

Part VI Self and Society in Sociological Theory — 339

	Introduction to Part VI	341
25	The Self (from *Mind, Self and Society: From the Standpoint of a Social Behaviorist*) George Herbert Mead	347
26	The Stranger (from *Georg Simmel: On Individuality and Social Forms*) Georg Simmel	361
27	Group Expansion and the Development of Individuality (from *Georg Simmel: On Individuality and Social Forms*) Georg Simmel	366
28	The Dyad and the Triad (from *The Sociology of Georg Simmel*) Georg Simmel	382
29	Civilization and its Discontents (from *Civilization and its Discontents*) Sigmund Freud	396
30	The Souls of Black Folk (from *The Souls of Black Folk*) W. E. B. Du Bois	404
31	The Regulation of the Wishes (from *The Unadjusted Girl*) William I. Thomas	410

Part VII Critical Theory and the Sociology of Knowledge — 419

	Introduction to Part VII	421
32	Traditional and Critical Theory (from *Critical Theory: Selected Essays*) Max Horkheimer	425

33 The Work of Art in the Age of Mechanical Reproduction
    (from *Illuminations*)   441
    Walter Benjamin
34 The Culture Industry (from *The Dialectic of Enlightenment*)   465
    Max Horkheimer and Theodor W. Adorno
35 One-Dimensional Man (from *One-Dimensional Man: Studies
    in the Ideology of Advanced Industrial Society*)   478
    Herbert Marcuse

Part VIII   Structural-Functional Analysis   **487**

Introduction to Part VIII   489
36 The Position of Sociological Theory (from *The Position
    of Sociological Theory*)   495
    Talcott Parsons
37 An Outline of the Social System (from *Theories of Society*)   502
    Talcott Parsons
38 Manifest and Latent Functions (from *Social Theory
    and Social Structure*)   523
    Robert K. Merton
39 On Sociological Theories of the Middle Range (from *Social
    Theory and Social Structure*)   531
    Robert K. Merton

Index   543

Notes on the Editors

Craig Calhoun is University Professor of the Social Sciences at New York University and President of the Social Science Research Council. His books include *The Roots of Radicalism* (2011), *Nations Matter: Culture, History and the Cosmopolitan Dream* (2007), *Nationalism* (1997), and *Critical Social Theory: Culture, History, and the Challenge of Difference* (1995). For the Centennial of the American Sociological Association, he edited *Sociology in America: A History* (2006). He was also editor-in-chief of the *Oxford Dictionary of the Social Sciences* (2002), and he recently published the three volume collection *Possible Futures* (2011) looking at the financial crisis, its aftermath, and other global challenges.

Joseph Gerteis is Associate Professor of Sociology at the University of Minnesota, Twin Cities. His work explores the race, class and the complexities of American national identity in politics and social movements. He is author of *Class and the Color Line: Interracial Class Coalition in the Knights of Labor and the Populist Movement* (2007) and is co-investigator of the American Mosaic Project at the University of Minnesota.

James Moody is Robert O. Keohane Professor of Sociology at Duke University, Durham, North Carolina. His work examines social networks, with an emphasis on social cohesion, diffusion, and network dynamics.

Steven Pfaff is Associate Professor of Sociology at the University of Washington where he is also affiliated with European Studies. He has published articles in journals such the American Journal of Sociology, Theory & Society, Social Forces, Comparative Political Studies, and the Journal for the Scientific Study of Religion. His first monograph, *Exit-Voice Dynamics and the Collapse of East Germany* (2006), reflects his interests in comparative and historical sociology, political sociology, religion, and social movements.

Indermohan Virk is a lecturer in Sociology and Executive Director of the Patten Foundation at Indiana University. She teaches courses on sociological theory and race and ethnicity.

Acknowledgments

The editors and publisher gratefully acknowledge the permission granted to reproduce the copyright material in this book.

Chapter 1
Hobbes, Thomas, "Of the Natural Condition & the Commonwealth," pp. 183–190, 199, 223, 227–231 from Thomas Hobbes, *Leviathan*, ed. C.B. Macpherson. London: Penguin, 1968.

Chapter 2
Rousseau, Jean-Jacques "Of the Social Contract," Book I, from *The Social Contract*, 1762.

Chapter 3
Kant, Immanuel, "What Is Enlightenment?" pp. 132–139 from Immanuel Kant, *The Philosophy of Kant*, ed. Carl J. Friedrich. New York: Random House, The Modern Library, 1949 Copyright © 1949 by Random House, Inc. Used by permission of Random House, Inc.

Chapter 4
Smith, Adam, "Of the Division of Labor," from Adam Smith, *The Wealth of Nations*, 1776.

Chapter 5
Smith, Adam, "The Theory of Moral Sentiments," pp. 9–19, 23–26, 43–45, 50–53, 61–62 from Adam Smith, *The Theory of Moral Sentiments*, edited by D. D. Raphael and A.L. Macfie, Oxford University Press 1976. Reprinted with permission of Oxford University Press.

Chapter 6
de Tocqueville, Alexis, "The Old Regime and the French Revolution," pp. 19–21, 77–78, 80–81, 139, 140–142, 146, 147, 174, 175, 176–177, 179, 203, 204, 205, 209, 210 from Alexis de Tocqueville, *The Old Régime and the French Revolution*, translated by Stuart Gilbert. New York: Doubleday & Company, Inc., 1955 © 1955 by Doubleday, a division of Random House Inc. Used by permission of Doubleday, a division of Random House Inc.

Chapter 7
de Tocqueville, Alexis, "Influence of Democracy on the Feelings of the Americans" from Alexis de Tocqueville, *Democracy in America*: New York – J. & H.G. Langley 1840.

Chapter 8
de Tocqueville, Alexis. Democracy in America [Volume 1]. Translated by Henry Reeve. Third American Edition. New York: George Aldard. 1839.

Chapter 9
Marx, Karl and Engels, Friedrich "The German Ideology," pp. 41, 42, 46–47, 64–66 from Karl Marx and Friedrich Engels, *The German Ideology, Part One*, ed. C. J. Arthur. New York: International Publishers, 1996. Translation of Part I, Copyright © by International Publishers Co, Inc., 1947; revised translation of Part I © by Lawrence & Wishart, 1970. Reprinted by permission of International Publishers Inc.

Chapter 10
Marx, Karl, "Economic and Philosophic Manuscripts of 1844," pp. 270–282 from Karl Marx and Friedrich Engels, *Collected Works, Volume 3*. New York: International Publishers, 1975. Copyright © 1975. Reprinted by permission of International Publishers Inc.

Chapter 11
Marx, Karl and Engels, Friedrich, "Manifesto of the Communist Party," pp. 481–482, 485–506 from Karl Marx and Friedrich Engels, *Collected Works, Volume 6*. New York: International Publishers, 1975. Copyright © 1975. Reprinted by permission of International Publishers. Inc.

Chapter 12
Marx, Karl, "The Eighteenth Brumaire of Louis Bonaparte," pp.103–112, 194–197 from Karl Marx and Friedrich Engels, *Collected Works, Volume 11*. New York: International Publishers, 1975. Copyright © 1975. Reprinted by permission of International Publishers Inc.

Chapter 13
Marx, Karl, "Wage-Labour and Capital," pp. 249–250, 251–252, 255, 257–258, 258–259, 261–262, 263, 264, 265–266, 266–267, from David McLellan, ed., *Karl Marx:*

Selected Writings. Oxford: Oxford University Press, 1977. Copyright © 1977. This translation originally appeared in *MESW*, Vol. 1, pp. 79ff. (considerably modified). Reprinted by permission of Lawrence and Wishart Ltd.

Chapter 14
Marx, Karl, "Classes," pp.870–871 from Karl Marx and Friederich Engels, *Collected Works, Volume 37*. New York: International Publishers, 1975. Copyright © 1975. Reprinted by permission of International Publishers Inc.

Chapter 15
Durkheim, Emile, "The Rules of Sociological Method," pp.35–38, 50–59, 119–125, 127–132, 134–135 from Emile Durkheim, *The Rules of Sociological Method*, ed. Steven Lukes, trans. W.D. Halls. New York: Macmillan Publishers, Ltd., The Free Press, 1982. Copyright © 1982 by Steven Lukes. Translation, Copyright © 1982 by Macmillan Publishers, Ltd. Reprinted and edited with the permission of The Free Press, A Division of Simon & Schuster Adult Publishing Group and Palgrave Macmillan. All rights reserved.

Chapter 16
Durkheim, Emile, "The Division of Labor in Society," pp. 1–2, 24–29, 38–41, 60–63, 68–71, 83–85, 200–205, 301–306 from Emile Durkheim, *The Division of Labor in Society*, trans. by W.D. Halls. New York: Macmillan Publishers Ltd., The Free Press, 1984. Translation, Copyright © 1984 by Higher & Further Education Division, Macmillan Publishers, Ltd. Reprinted and edited with the permission of The Free Press, A Division of Simon & Schuster Adult Publishing Group and Palgrave Macmillan. All rights reserved.

Chapter 17
Durkheim, Emile, "The Elementary Forms of the Religious Life," pp.15–19, 21–22, 28–33, 467–475 from Emile Durkheim, *Elementary Forms of the Religious Life*, trans. Joseph W. Swain. New York: Simon & Schuster, Inc., The Free Press, 1965. Copyright © 1965 by The Free Press. Reprinted and edited with the permission of The Free Press, A Division of Simon & Schuster Adult Publishing Group, and Taylor & Francis Books UK. All rights reserved.

Chapter 18
Durkheim, Emile, "Anomic Suicide," pp. 246–258 from Emile Durkheim, *Suicide: A Study in Sociology*, ed. George Simpson, trans. John H. Spaulding and George Simpson. New York: Macmillan Publishing Co., Inc., The Free Press, 1951. Copyright © 1951 by The Free Press. Copyright © renewed 1979 by The Free Press. Reprinted with the permission of The Free Press, A Division of Simon & Schuster Adult Publishing Group. All rights reserved.

Chapter 19
Weber, Max, "'Objectivity' in Social Science," pp. 89–99, 110–112 from Max Weber, *The Methodology of the Social Sciences*, ed. and trans. Edward A. Shils and Henry

A. Finch. New York: Simon & Schuster, Inc., The Free Press, 1949. Copyright © 1949 by The Free Press. Copyright © renewed 1977 by Edward A. Shils. Reprinted and edited with the permission of The Free Press, A Division of Simon & Schuster Adult Publishing Group. All rights reserved.

Chapter 20
Weber, Max, "Basic Sociological Terms," pp.88–103, 107–117 from Max Weber, *The Theory of Social and Economic Organization*, ed. Talcott Parsons, trans. A. M. Henderson and Talcott Parsons. New York: Simon & Schuster, Inc., The Free Press, 1947. Copyright © 1947. Copyright © renewed 1975 by Talcott Parsons. Reprinted and edited with the permission of The Free Press, A Division of Simon & Schuster Adult Publishing Group. All rights reserved.

Chapter 21
Weber, Max, "The Protestant Ethic and the Spirit of Capitalism," from Max Weber, *Protestant Ethic and the Spirit of Capitalism With Other Writings on the Rise of the West* 4th edn, translated by Stephen Kalberg (2010) pp. 61–65, 69–79, 86, 151–159, published by Oxford University Press. Reprinted with permission of Oxford University Press.

Chapter 22
Weber, Max, "The Distribution of Power Within the Political Community: Class, Status, Party," pp. 180–195 from Max Weber, 'The Distribution of Power Within the Political Community: Class, Status, Party,' Politics Journal, 1949.

Chapter 23
Weber, Max, "The Types of Legitimate Domination" pp. 324–325, 328–330, 333–334, 341–343, 358–364, 367, 369–370 from Max Weber, *The Theory of Social and Economic Organization*, ed. Talcott Parsons, trans. A.M. Henderson and Talcott Parsons. New York: Simon & Schuster, Inc., The Free Press, 1947. Copyright © 1947. Copyright © renewed 1975 by Talcott Parsons. Reprinted and edited with the permission of The Free Press, A Division of Simon & Schuster Adult Publishing Group. All rights reserved.

Chapter 24
Weber, Max, "Bureaucracy," pp. 135–144, 149–158, 163–164, 173–178 from H.H. Gerth and C. Wright Mills, eds. and trans., *From Max Weber: Essays in Sociology*. New York: Oxford University Press, Inc., 1946. Copyright © 1946, 1958 by H. H. Gerth and C. Wright Mills. Used by permission of Oxford University Press.

Chapter 25
Mead, George Herbert, "The Self," pp. 135–144, 149–158, 163–164, 173–178 from George Herbert Mead, *Mind, Self and Society: From the Standpoint of a Social Behaviorist*, ed. Charles W. Morris. Chicago: University of Chicago Press, 1934.

Copyright © 1934 by University of Chicago Press. Reprinted by permission of The University of Chicago Press.

Chapter 26
Simmel, Georg, "The Stranger," pp. 143–149 from Georg Simmel, *Georg Simmel: On Individuality and Social Forms*, ed. Donald N. Levine. Chicago: University of Chicago Press, 1971. Copyright © 1971 by University of Chicago Press. Reprinted by permission of The University of Chicago Press.

Chapter 27
Simmel, Georg, "Group Expansion and the Development of Individuality," pp. 252–266, 268–274, 290–292 from Georg Simmel, *Georg Simmel: On Individuality and Social Forms*, ed. Donald N. Levine. Chicago: University of Chicago Press, 1971. Copyright © 1971 by University of Chicago Press. Reprinted by permission of The University of Chicago Press.

Chapter 28
Simmel, Georg, "The Dyad and the Triad," pp. 118–119, 122–127, 135–136, 138–139, 141–142, 145, 146–147, 148–149, 154–157, 159, 161–162, 167–169 from Kurt H. Wolff (trans/ed.), *The Sociology of Georg Simmel*. New York: The Free Press, 1950.

Chapter 29
Freud, Sigmund, "Civilization and its Discontents." From Sigmund Freud, *Civilization and its Discontents*, trans. James Strachey. New York: W.W. Norton & Company, Inc., 1961. Copyright © 1961 by James Strachey, renewed 1989 by Alix Strachey. Used by permission of W.W. Norton & Company, Inc. Sigmund Freud © Copyrights, The Institute of Psychoanalysis and The Hogarth Press for permission to quote from *The Standard Edition of the Complete Psychological Works of Sigmund Freud*. Reprinted by permission of The Random House Group Ltd.

Chapter 30
Du Bois, W.E.B, "The Souls of Black Folk." From W.E.B. Du Bois, *The Souls of Black Folk*. New York: Bantam Books, 1–9, 1989.

Chapter 31
Thomas, William I., "Definition of the Situation," pp. 41–46, 48–50, 54–57, 62, 64–66, 68–69 from William I Thomas, *The Unadjusted Girl*. Boston: Little, Brown, and Company, 1931.

Chapter 32
Horkheimer, Max, "Traditional and Critical Theory," pp.188–243 from Max Horkheimer, *Critical Theory: Selected Essays*. New York: Herder and Herder, Inc., 1972. English translation copyright © 1972 by Herder & Herder. Reprinted by

permission of The Copyright Clearance Center on behalf of The Continuum Publishing Group.

Chapter 33
Benjamin, Walter, "The Work of Art in the Age of Mechanical Reproduction," pp. 217–251 from Walter Benjamin, *Illuminations*, ed. Hannah Arendt, trans. Harry Zohn. New York: Schocken Books, 1969. Copyright © 1955 by Suhrkamp Verlag, Frankfurt a. M., English translation by Harry Zohn copyright © 1968 and renewed 1996 by Harcourt, Inc., reprinted by permission by Harcourt, Inc., and The Random House Group Ltd.

Chapter 34
Horkheimer, Max and W. Adorno, Theodor, "The Culture Industry: Enlightenment as Mass Deception," pp. 95–97, 99–100, 108–113, 115–117, 128–133, 135–136 from *The Dialectic of Enlightenment: Philosophical Fragments*, ed. Gunzelin Schmid Noerr, trans. by Edmund Jephcott. Standford: Stanford University Press, 2002. (c) 1944 by Social Studies Association, NY. New edition (c) S. Fisher Verlag GmbH, Frankfurt am Main 1969. Reprinted with permission of Stanford University Press.

Chapter 35
Marcuse, Herbert, "One-Dimensional Man," pp.1, 3–5, 7–8, 71–80, 82–83 from Herbert Marcuse, *One-Dimensional Man: Studies in the Ideology of Advanced Industrial Society*. Boston: Beacon Press, 1964. Copyright © 1964 by Herbert Marcuse. Reprinted by permission of Beacon Press, Boston.

Chapter 36
Parsons, Talcott, "The Position of Sociological Theory," pp. 156–163 from Talcott Parsons, "The Position of Sociological Theory." *American Sociological Review*, 13, 2. Washington: American Sociological Association, 1948.

Chapter 37
Parsons, Talcott, "An Outline of the Social System," pp. 36–43, 44–47, 70–72 from Talcott Parsons, Edward A. Shils, Kaspar D. Naegle, Jesse R. Pitts, eds., *Theories of Society*. New York: Simon & Schuster, The Free Press, 1961. Copyright © 1961 by The Free Press. Reprinted with the permission of The Free Press, A Division of Simon & Schuster Adult Publishing Group. All rights reserved.

Chapter 38
Merton, Robert K., "Manifest and Latent Functions," pp. 114–115, 117–122, 124–126 from Robert K. Merton, *Social Theory and Social Structure*. New York: Simon & Schuster, Inc., The Free Press, 1949. Copyright © 1949, 1957 by The Free Press. Copyright © renewed 1977, 1985 by Robert K. Merton. Reprinted and edited with the permission of The Free Press, A Division of Simon & Schuster Adult Publishing Group. All rights reserved.

Chapter 39
Merton, Robert K., "On Sociological Theories of the Middle Range," pp. 39–53 from Robert K. Merton, *Social Theory and Social Structure*. New York: Simon & Schuster, Inc., The Free Press, 1949. Copyright © 1949, 1957 by The Free Press. Copyright © renewed 1977, 1985 by Robert K. Merton. Reprinted and edited with the permission of The Free Press, A Division of Simon & Schuster Adult Publishing Group. All rights reserved.

Introduction

Sociology is the development of systematic knowledge about social life, the way it is organized, how it changes, its creation in social action, and its disruption and renewal in social conflict. Sociological theory is both a guide to sociological inquiry and an attempt to bring order to its results.

Sociological theory is not simply a collection of answers to questions about what society is like. It offers many answers, but it also offers help in posing better questions and developing inquiries that can answer them. Like all of science, thus, it is a process. It is always under development, responding to changes in our social lives and to improvements in our sociological knowledge. In this sense, the playwright and poet LeRoi Jones once compared writing and hunting. "Hunting is not those heads on the wall," he said.[1] He meant that hunting is an adventure; it is a project. Hunting is something one can do better or worse, but one can never know precisely what one will find. The same is true of writing, and of the pursuit of knowledge. Theory is our most developed way of organizing the knowledge we have, but that knowledge is never complete. Of necessity, therefore, theory is also a guide to new research and a way of organizing debates over what our partial knowledge tells us.

The adventure of sociological theory is relatively new – perhaps 200 years old at most.[2] But it is closely connected to a long history of social thought, extending back to the ancient world. Greek philosophers, Roman lawyers, and Jewish and Christian religious scholars all contributed significantly to the "prehistory" of sociological theory. They not only thought about society, they thought in systematic ways about what made it possible, how it could be made better, and what caused social order sometimes to collapse. Important social thinkers flourished also in the Muslim societies of Spain, North Africa, and Syria though they had only intermittent contact

Classical Sociological Theory, Third Edition. Edited by Craig Calhoun, Joseph Gerteis, James Moody, Steven Pfaff, and Indermohan Virk. Editorial material and organization © 2012 John Wiley & Sons, Ltd. Published 2012 by John Wiley & Sons, Ltd.

with thinkers in Christian Europe. Likewise, there were important achivements of social thought in China's Confucian tradition, in the Buddhist traditions that spread from India across Asia, and elsewhere in the world. Nonetheless, sociological theory did not develop until the modern era – mainly the 18th and 19th centuries. And it developed initially in Europe. The change that mattered most was the rise of science.

From Social Thought to Social Science

Science transformed the ways in which people understood the conditions of their own lives and relationships as well as the ways they understood astronomy or gravity.[3] At the most general level, and aside from any of its specific discoveries or theories, the scientific revolution centered in 17th-century Europe brought an emphasis on new learning. That is, researchers set out to gather as much knowledge as possible and especially as much empirical knowledge as possible, and to organize it as systematically as possible.

Many of the systems the early scientists developed for classifying knowledge have been abandoned or lost their distinctive influence, particularly where they were based on surface appearance rather than deeper underlying and causally significant relations. In a thousand different fields from astronomy to the study of moths, from the breeding of farm animals to the growth of the human population, the internal structure of human bodies to the way our sensory organs work, early scientists tried to see as objectively as possible, and to search as widely as possible for things to see. In most of these fields knowledge already existed. Modern science not only added to it, but also subjected it to questioning and tests. And it sought not just description and classification but explanation.

Partly as an inevitable consequence of this, science challenged the authority of traditions and venerable institutions including churches and governments. This was direct in some cases – famously that of Galileo – where scientific research produced results that contradicted old doctrines and the teachings of current religious authorities. The issue was not just whether the earth revolved around the sun or vice versa, but why planets and other astral bodies appeared to move as they did in the night sky. It was a question as old as the Greeks, and the Chinese had kept more detailed empirical records than any other society. But in early modern Europe asking why led to breakthroughs in explaining the patterns: the role of gravity, for example, changed not just how people thought about falling objects on earth but about the relations of planets and stars to each other. Copernicus and Newton joined in the quest to not only identify astronomical patterns accurately but also clarify the causal factors that produced them.

The same would be true as chemists asked not just what were the natural materials from which everything on earth was made, but why these combined in such different fashions, producing sometimes strong and useful materials and sometimes explosions. The same quest was behind the rise of evolutionary theory as, for example, Darwin sought to explain the emergence of new species of animals over time. And the social sciences grew as theorists asked not just what was going on – in wars, or markets, or changes in family life – but why. The answers always required a combination of empirical observation with theoretical conceptualization and analysis.

It became the general and pervasive view of scientists that the best knowledge was that based on logic and evidence. Relying on logic and evidence meant reasoning for oneself and looking at the world for oneself and thus potentially reasoning and looking anew. When early scientists stressed the importance of logic and rational thought on the one hand and empirical evidence on the other, they meant specifically to challenge the notion that we should simply believe what we are taught. They meant that even the most respected authorities and the most venerated traditions could sometimes be wrong. The starting points of science are to think for oneself, in the most rigorous way possible, and to trust the evidence of one's senses, especially when it is rooted in experiment or careful observation and demonstration and not casual everyday experience. This isn't the whole of science, however, not least because reason and evidence can come into conflict with each other. Much of the work of science is neither simple discovery of facts nor purely logical deductions. It is, on the one hand, difficult efforts to distinguish what is "objective" in fact from the language in which we state it or the specific (and often more or less artificial) circumstances under which we collect data (sometimes supplementing our senses with technology). And it is, on the other hand, efforts to discern logical order in enormously complex and always incomplete collections of facts.

This is something different from simply offering a summary of established facts. In the first place, facts always require interpretation, and making interpretation systematic is one of the main tasks of theory. In addition, knowledge advances by the process the philosopher of science Karl Popper called "conjecture and refutation."[4] That is, a scientist puts forward propositions about how the world works; these are initially conjectures, products of imagination as well as knowledge. They become the basis for hypotheses, and research and analysis confirm or reject them. But thinking about what might explain the facts we see always requires imagination. Equally, seeing patterns and connections in social life depends on imagination; theorists must try to see how things fit together. But refutation drives the development of knowledge forward as much as imagination. Refutation of an important hypothesis stimulates a rethinking of the whole pattern of knowledge that is organized by a theory.

Empirical research also depends on theory to specify the objects of its analysis: how do we know what constitutes a community, for example, or a religion? Appealing to common sense doesn't solve the problem. Common sense is generally formed on the basis of a particular religion or a particular experience of community – and this is a source of bias if one is seeking knowledge of religion or community in general, in all social contexts. Even more basically, concepts are like lenses that enable us to see phenomena. Take the concept "self-fulfilling prophecy," developed by the American sociologist Robert Merton in the mid-20th century.[5] This calls our attention to a common aspect of human actions that may take place in many different contexts and which we wouldn't otherwise relate to each other. Aided by the concept, we can easily see the commonality among teachers' predictions of students' future success or failure in school, the labeling of criminals (who then find it hard to get legitimate jobs), and the comments of famous securities analysts on TV about what stocks are likely to go up or down. In none of these cases is the outcome of the predictions independent of the predictions themselves.

Theories also contain propositions, statements about how the world works. As communities grow larger, one prominent sociological proposition holds, they will become more internally differentiated. Any factual proposition like this can be tested by turning it into a hypothesis – a prediction – and by specifying facts that would count as refuting it. In this case, research seems so far mostly to confirm the growth/differentiation correlation (though there are exceptions and qualifications). Another proposed correlation is that as science and rationalization advance in modern societies, religion will decline; this secularization hypothesis is more controversial. In some societies the decline is evident, in others less so. But even where most people still say they are religious, both the content of religious teaching and the place of religion in people's lives have often changed. This suggests one reason why theories grow complicated. It is impossible to get a serious grasp on the relationship between science and religion without considering that each refers to many different things, and that many other features of social reality shape the relations between them. Politics, for example, may change the relationship between science and religion, leading some to back one against the other, defining legal boundaries between the two, or joining specific versions of each in a sense of national identity. Theories provide frameworks for relating different research results to each other and developing explanations: community relationships organize less of social life as markets expand; professionals perform services that were once the province of family, friends, and neighbors; and governments and corporations grow stronger and more formally organized. These changes also, of course, give a new context to religion. One of the most important things theory does is offer a systematic account of the overall workings of social life within which one can place specific topics. It is important to be systematic – to rely on theory rather than just vague assumptions – partly because this enables one to correct assumptions when new research challenges them.

Theory is concerned with the development of concepts with which to grasp social life, with identifying patterns in social relations and social action, with producing explanations for both specific features of life in society and changes in overall forms of society. It is thus an indispensable part of sociology, crucial to its standing as a science. At the same time, sociological theory is more than a tool for sociologists. It is also a crucial basis for reflection on social life, informing moral deliberations and public decisions. This is true first because sociological theory – along with the rest of social science – enables us to understand specific events, institutions, and social trends. It is a different thing, for example, to experience living in a city and to have a theoretical understanding of why cities have grown to enormous size. Secondly, sociological theory helps us to see the connections among different events, institutions, and trends. It helps us answer questions like how changes in gender roles and relations affect families, schools, workplaces, and politics. It helps us to see general patterns in social life – differences and similarities among countries, for example, or among historical periods. Thirdly, sociological theory helps us relate personal life to society. This is important at all scales from interpersonal relations like love or friendship to large-scale patterns in economy, government, or culture. Sociological theory helps us to see to what extent we can choose the conditions we live under – and also to what extent our choices are shaped by our backgrounds and other social factors. It helps us literally to judge what is possible and what is not, and what are the likely consequences of different courses of action.

Sociological theory does not tell us what parties to vote for, what religion to profess – if any – or what moral values are right. But it does enable us to make systematic and informed judgments about what policies will promote the values we hold dear and which will be likely to undermine them. Among its main contributions is assistance in being systematic in assessing social phenomena and proposals for social change. It also helps us to be systematic in working out our own ideas, to see when there are tensions between different values we hold. In many cases, sociological theory does not settle arguments, but helps us to see more deeply what is at stake in them. Take the idea that people are basically rational actors making decisions on the basis of self-interest. Sociological theory includes explorations of how much of social life can be explained in these terms – and this leads to at least partial explanations of phenomena, like marriage decisions, that people usually insist have nothing to do with such strategic analysis. Sociological theory also explores the ways in which culture shapes ideas of what is rational, what is of interest, and even what the self is like. It explores how being embedded in networks of social relations or in institutions such as a church or a business corporation may shape what kinds of actions we choose. And it considers whether in addition to strategic interests people are moved by emotions such as anger and love or sentiments such as sympathy for others.

Thinking about social relationships is basic to having them. Creating a family involves not just biological reproduction but embracing the idea of family, and the development of social roles. All human societies that we know of differentiate their members on the basis of gender, age, and kinship or descent. These distinctions help to organize social life; they are also charged with moral significance. Thinking about social life, in short, is part of how we create it.

Like a family, an army, a city, a religion, a kingdom, or a nation must be imagined and made the object of thought in order to exist as such. This does not mean that it will be well or systematically understood (and indeed, many social factors influence us without our ever being aware of them). The thought that helps a city to exist may name it, but not grasp why its population grows. It will probably include some understanding of its governance, of who belongs in it by right and who is tolerated as an outsider, and of the place of markets or temples within it. All of these and likely many other features of the city will be the objects of reflection by its members – and perhaps by others, such as invaders who would conquer it. As language is used to coordinate human action, both social life and social thought may grow more complex. Thought about society is a basic part of human culture, in short, whether in mythic or scientific or purely practical forms.

Social thought developed in the context of religion as people explored the ultimate meaning of their life together and the moral norms that guided it. It developed in law as people sought to resolve the practical problems of organizing social life. Eventually political inquiry came to explore what kind of society a particular form of government produced – or conversely, what sort of government a given form of society could support. Ideas about what would constitute a good society developed out of each of these traditions, and have been a part of philosophy since its earliest phases. Alongside this large question people posed more specific ones about family, friendship, and ways to organize armies or religious communities. Should there be more hierarchy or more equality? Must men and women be kept sharply distinct or should they be allowed similar roles? Is freedom compatible with unity? Some of these general reflections on social life were remarkably insightful and still repay study. But they did not add up to sociological theory.

To do so, they had to meet two basic criteria. First, they had to offer empirical claims that could be the basis of either tests (and thereby confirmation, correction, or improvement) or comparisons among theories (and thereby judgment as to which more accurately grasped social reality). In this sense, the idea of theory is embedded in the notion of science and the specifically scientific use of empirical observations. Second, theories were not *sociological* theories unless they focused on social life as a specific and distinct object of study. In the simplest sense, sociological theories needed to be about society, in its own right, and not simply as an adjunct of religion, law, or politics. Of course, just what society was or is could be debated. Early sociological theorists tended to assume that it meant more or less the same thing as nation – so one spoke of French society or English society. But it also meant local communities, voluntary organizations, interpersonal relationships, and public communication. It included culture and social action as well as social structure. Society only began to command the attention of theorists during the 17th and 18th centuries.

The Idea of Society and the Roots of Sociological Theory

Society – social action and relationships and organizations – came to the fore not simply as an intellectual development but in response to enormous changes in social life itself. Among the many changes, four stand out as especially significant for the development of sociological theory:

1. **The rise of individualism.** Individualism may seem the opposite of a concern for society, but it did not mean the absence of society so much as a different way of organizing and thinking about it.[6] Conceived as the product of individual thought and action, or judged on the criterion of how well it meets individuals'

needs, society looks different from when it is approached as ordered according to divine law or dictated by kings.

Individualism's most important early appearance was in religion. Especially in the Protestant Reformation, the notion became widespread that people should read the Bible for themselves (not leave that to priests), pray in terms they made up for themselves (not simply by official prayers handed down by the church), and develop a personal relationship with God. These ideas had an influence on the rise of science, which was also rooted in modern individualism and also helped to undermine traditional authorities.

Individualism had a similar impact in social life and on thinking about society, introducing a shift from inherited (or ascribed) to chosen (or achieved) relationships. Individualism led people to think for themselves about social relationships and social organizations, not simply accept those which had been passed down from earlier ages. This was reflected in changing commitments to family and community. Increasingly, these social relationships were approached as objects of personal choice. Migration away from rural communities reflected individuals pursuit of economic gain, and an urban economy open to strangers from the countryside or even other countries encouraged individual decisions to relocate. Perhaps even more dramatically, marriages were increasingly understood as personal relationships, ideally founded on love between individuals, rather than mainly alliances between broader kin groups.

Sometimes an exaggerated individualism makes people think that personal choice decides everything. But of course this isn't true. Individual desires and decisions are shaped by social influences, both conscious and unconscious, from advertising to friends and family to religion and national culture. In addition, the very institutions and social structures that give individuals the capacity to act – like markets and voluntary organizations – also constrain their actions.

The idea that individual relationships ought to be products of choice suggested also that social relationships in general could be chosen. In the 17th and 18th century, theorists borrowed the idea of contract from economic life (and from the Biblical notion of a covenant between God and His chosen people) to describe social life generally.[7] Thomas Hobbes, John Locke, and Jean-Jacques Rousseau were among the most important early "social contract" theorists. They sought to describe how society could come into being on the basis of a contract among individuals – and to use reasoning about what sorts of social arrangements free people would agree to as a way to analyze whether actually existing social organization was just. Early social contract theory focused mostly on political questions, but it contributed to the rise of sociological theory by approaching the question of what political arrangements were legitimate through examination of how social relations might come into being. Locke and Rousseau especially distinguished society from government and gave it priority.

Emphasizing individual responsibility in religion and in the choice of relationships was also linked to a positive value in everyday, ordinary personal life. Christianity had tended previously to exalt the spiritual and otherworldly. During the early modern period, Christian thinkers placed a new emphasis on how religion could guide personal life; marriage, family, and work thus all gained positive value, because affairs of this world were not seen merely as preparation for the hereafter. This suggested also that individuals should apply themselves to building a better society here on earth, not simply waiting for salvation after death. As the poet William Blake put it, "I will not cease from mental fight, Nor shall my sword sleep in my hand, Till we have built Jerusalem, In England's green and pleasant land."[8]

2. **The rise of modern states.** There had long been kings and other sorts of rulers, of course. What changed with modernity was the capacity of states to regulate and shape different aspects of social life.[9] States built roads, raised citizen armies, operated schools and prisons, and collected taxes to pay for all these and other activities. At one level, thus, states helped to organize societies. At another level, though, states were distinct from society. This was made evident in a distinctive modern phenomenon – revolution.[10]

Revolution involved "the people" rising up to change the political institutions under which they lived, and often to try to reorganize society more generally. Blake suggested something of the underlying idea in suggesting that Englishmen should build a New Jerusalem. Among other things the English, American, and French Revolutions all signaled a change in how people thought about the legitimacy of government. It was not enough to know that a king was the oldest son of his father or that he claimed divine right to rule. People demanded evidence that government ruled in the best interests of the people. But who were the people? Revolutionary thought signaled also the growing prominence of a new idea, the nation, understood as the group of people and the cultural identity that endured as governments came and went. The idea of nation deeply influenced the idea of society, suggesting that it should be understood as a bounded, internally organized population at the level of a country.[11] This concept proved extremely influential, although in fact social organization was always both more local and more international than a nation-state centered concept of society suggested.

Through the modern era, states took on more and more functions, from providing schools to building roads and organizing unemployment benefits. States organized systems of money and security services like police. This meant they played bigger social roles and were themselves complex social organizations. Where to limit state action became controversial; many argued that states should not intervene in matters of religion, family, or markets."

The distinction of state from society was affirmed in the concept of "civil society" – that is, society that was a free product of relations among private persons.[12] Contract was a model for those relations, but not the only one. Friendship, religious community, and the self-governance of medieval guilds and cities also offered models. During the 18th and early 19th centuries, several theorists responded to a growing importance for civil society. They laid part of the foundation for sociological theory in emphasizing how much of human life was organized at a level between the interior privacy of intimate family life (or indeed, the inner personality of the individual) and the exterior direction of the state. Society was the crucial middle ground in which relationships could not be explained entirely by either psychology or by politics. And, as the Scot Adam Ferguson wrote, society had its own history, distinct from that of politics.[13]

3. **The development of large-scale markets, capitalism and modern industry.** One crucial thing that people did in "civil society" was to pursue material interests and well-being. The pace of economic change in the late 18th and early 19th centuries was so rapid and its impact so great that contemporaries borrowed the previously political idea of revolution to describe it: the industrial revolution.[14]

The industrial revolution was actually felt first in agriculture; rapidly rising farm productivity meant that large nonagricultural populations could be supported by relatively few farmers. This shaped both the decline of rural villages and the rise of cities. Both phenomena called attention to the idea of society, as people questioned whether the economic changes were good for social relations. One enduring sociological theme reflects this: the distinction of community from association or civil society, in which the former reflects the image of small scale, tight-knit, and directly interpersonal relations in villages or small towns while the latter reflects the image of impersonal, looser relationships in the city, and the loss of direct ties to indirect ones through markets, media, and formal organizations.[15]

The transformation of productivity by division of labor, factories, and technology was a crucial feature of the late 18th and early 19th centuries in Britain and took place slightly later in other European countries, America, and eventually much of the world. It not only had sociological effects (e.g., on community) but was itself a sociological as well as an economic phenomenon. It contributed to the rise of the idea of society most crucially through two notions: the division of labor and the market. Adam Smith was influential in establishing the importance of both, and thus counts as a founder of sociology as well as economics.[16]

In his famous book, *The Wealth of Nations*, Smith described the division of labor as a social process, and one basic to growing productivity.[17] Instead of combining a number of skills in the person of one craftsman, this involved training workers to be specialists in each. Therefore, instead of a pin maker, there was someone who straightened wire, someone who sharpened its point, someone who made a head, and someone who attached it. In addition, crucially, there was also an entrepreneur or manager who organized and supervised the process. As individuals, each of these people might be less skilled than the former pin maker (and all but the manager would be paid less), but together they could produce more and cheaper pins. This made for economic efficiency. It also demonstrated, however, how different people with different jobs were in fact dependent on each other in a larger social organization – something true of society on a large scale as well as each workplace. For pin making, the necessary social organization was produced by entrepreneurs and managers. For society at large, one might think the government had the same role and in fact many people thought and still think just this. But Smith argued that government was not the only way to achieve social organization on a large scale. At least equally important (and often more efficient) was the market.

Insofar as people operated as buyers and sellers (of their labor and managerial ingenuity as well as of physical goods), the market operated through the law of supply and demand to condition each to behave efficiently. Much more could be produced on the basis of a social division of labor mediated by the market than by individuals or families aiming at self-subsistence. Trade, combined with socially organized production like factories, could thus increase the total supply of goods, helping to overcome scarcity; self-interest could be harnessed therefore to create public benefits. Smith suggested that individual people were led to create social value, as if by an "invisible hand." In other words, the market was self-organizing (at least so long as participants in it were relatively equal to each other). Smith emphasized this point not only to show its economic importance but also to illustrate how relationships among ordinary people, rather than decisions of the king or laws enforced by the state, could provide for social order.

4. **European exploration of the rest of the world and the trade, war, and colonization that followed in its wake.** Economic expansion was among the most important forces driving European exploration of the rest of the globe. This also had roots in religion, however, as missionaries sought to convert nonbelievers to Christianity. It was shaped by state-building as European kings and later republics sought to expand their power through empires. It was even a product of science, as explorers sought to prove the world round and to discover new biological species even while also serving economic and political employers. Exploration – and exploitation – were also both influences on – and influenced by – early social science. Theorists provided accounts of the inferiority of non-European peoples. They provided justifications for colonial rule. But they also learned enormously, most importantly about culture, about differences in forms of social organization, and about the complex manner in which different ways of life are held together.

The 18th century French social theorist, the Baron of Montesquieu, thus helped to pave the way for sociology. He asked why different countries had different legal and political systems, and sought the answer in cultural differences that he called "the spirit" behind laws.[18] Montesquieu, like most of his contemporaries, combined prejudice with fact, speculating for example, that warm climates made some people naturally lazy and thus in need of more despotic rule. But he was also part of a broad current of European thought that first recognized that social conditions were not natural and immutable partly through seeing how many different sorts of social institutions there were in the rest of the world. Instead of conceptualizing this through the notion of social contract, Montesquieu emphasized the way in which culture knits together a whole package of knowledge, beliefs, practices, and values.

Although Europeans often tried to impose their culture – and political, economic, and religious practices – on the people they colonized elsewhere in the world, they also tried to understand them. This became a powerful inducement to the development of sociological theory and social science generally. Some developed evolutionary theories to try to explain differences in social organization as the product of growth or progress. Indeed, some of these theorists came before and influenced Darwin's biological theory of evolution; some joined the two, like Herbert Spencer – simultaneously a sociologist and a biologist and the coiner of the term "survival of the fittest." Eventually many social scientists became critics of colonialism, and sought to point out that difference did not always mean either superiority or inferiority.

European expansion into the rest of the world had material effects that were also important influences on the rise of social theory. Wealth extracted from other lands and long-distance trade contributed to the growth of capitalism; the need to administer far-flung colonies contributed to the development of more scientific approaches to government and formal organizations. The idea of America figured prominently. In the beginning, wrote John Locke, all the world was America.[19] He meant that the entire world was organized in the minimalist fashion he thought typical of the aboriginal Native Americans with low population density, no large-scale centralized government, and no intensive use of the land (he had tribes in mind, not the Inca or Aztec empires). He thought this made European occupation legitimate. Both the confrontation with small-scale, non-state-centered societies elsewhere and the development of transnational empires helped counterbalance the tendency to equate society with nation-state. For later theorists, the significance of America (as of other settler societies such as Australia) was to dramatize the experiment of creating new social forms completely by choice, with little inheritance behind them. In the 1830s, for example, the Frenchman Alexis de Tocqueville visited the United States to learn about Europe's future. This lay, he thought, with democracy, which he understood as a society based on free individualistic choice and relatively social equality. His account, *Democracy in America*, became a classic of sociological theory, taking up the question (following Montesquieu) of what social and culture conditions made stable democratic government possible – and what might make it collapse into anarchy or tyranny.[20]

Sociological theory was born, in short, in reflection on both momentous changes in Europe and the pattern of similarities and differences discerned among human societies around the world. Science offered a new method for developing knowledge; both social change and the confrontation with social difference made ordinary people, business leaders, and government officials all seek new knowledge about society. The changes and the confrontations with difference were often disruptive, but by their very disruptions called attention to the issue of how society worked.

The 20th Century: Synthesis and Critique

World War I marked a watershed in sociological theory. Marxist internationalism, for example, confronted the power of nationalism. The optimism of 19th century evolutionism and faith in progress was deeply challenged. Several of the great founders of modern sociology – like Weber and Durkheim – lived through the war and struggled after it with a growing concern for the fate of modern society.

At the same time, the World War itself signaled – albeit ironically – a new level of interconnections among the different European countries and between affairs in Europe and elsewhere. In Russia, for example, World War I was a precipitating factor in the communist revolution of 1917. This introduced a new kind of East-West split, no longer between Occident and Orient but between capitalist and communist countries. Much of the rest of 20th century history was shaped by it. World War I also marked the emergence of the United States as a global military power, entering the war late but decisively. And the nature of the war itself revealed that power depended on the ability to mobilize industry, transport systems, and a wide variety of citizens. Success in war, in other words, depended on social organization and not only that of the military itself.

Perhaps it is not surprising that after the war the United States also began to emerge more prominently as a force in sociological theory. Indeed, an American, Talcott Parsons, sought to pick up the projects of the great classical sociological theorists of Europe and synthesize them into a new social theory. At the heart of his conception was the effort to reconcile social action and social structure, the ways in which people could make choices about their lives and the ways in which all of social life depended on underlying patterns that were beyond individual choice. In some ways, Parsons' sociological theory mirrored a basic issue in the developing self-understanding of the Western, non-communist societies. Capitalism and democracy both presented the importance of individuals and their choices as basic to modern life. "Free enterprise," consumer choice, and open elections were basic to the idea of speaking of the "free world" – as opposed to communism. Parsons embraced that idea, but at the same time recognized how incomplete it was. If choice – by both managers and consumers – was basic to capitalism, so was the idea of the market as a self-regulating system. If open elections were basic to democracy, so was the concentration of power in the state bureaucracy (rather, for example, than independent feudal lords).

These concerns were not unique to Talcott Parsons. Many social theorists took on the challenge of trying effectively to relate action to structure. For some, like Karl Mannheim, the question was to what extent ideas reflected the social positions of those who espoused them. Mannheim asked whether intellectuals in some sense might occupy a special social position that enabled them to be more objective. For others, like George Herbert Mead, the question was how the individual might come into being as a result of social processes, through communication with others and through a recognition of how he or she fit into the large patterns of social interaction. We only gain full individuality, Mead suggested, when we can see ourselves at least in part as others see us – and for this we need social learning. At the same time, in the words of another great American sociologist, Charles Horton Cooley, "self and society are twinborn."[21] Imagining individuals as existing before and separate from society misunderstands both. But, society cannot make individuals in any shape; human nature is recalcitrant, limiting the options and pressing in specific directions.

Sigmund Freud made this point as strongly as anyone in the early 20th century.[22] Not only did nature matter, though, human beings were internally complex creatures, driven by conflicting tendencies, wants, and needs. Emotions mattered alongside reason and often in conflict with it.

Talcott Parsons, in his synthesis, approached personality, culture, and society as quasi-autonomous systems, three different levels in the analysis of human life. Many of his critics charged that he smoothed out the conflicts and contradictions in each, and thus presented more harmony and consensus than was accurate. Perhaps this was most visible in the contrast between his presentation of the economy as working "functionally" to supply the needs of everyone and of all different parts of society and Marx's account of class conflict and the inherent contradictions and recurrent crises of capitalism. Likewise, in terms of personality, though Parsons was deeply influenced by Freud, he emphasized the ideal of full and successful integration of the personality more than the inevitability of internal conflicts. Though he drew on Weber, he emphasized the capacity of culture to integrate human societies and guide evolution more than he did the cultural contradictions of modern life, the ways in which rationalization undermined creative individual spirit or consumerism granted people choice but reduced its meaning. Weber, after all, had talked gloomily of an "iron cage" in which capitalism and bureaucracy started out by creating individual opportunity and effective social organization and ultimately trapped people in a social system without spirit.

The Second World War and the Great Depression that preceded it seemed to many to point out the merit in Weber's pessimism. Max Horkheimer, Theodore Adorno, and colleagues based initially at Frankfurt's Institute for Social Research combined influences from Weber, Marx, and Freud (among other sources) to produce a "critical theory." This aimed at understanding the ways in which rationalization could turn against reason and the limits to both capitalist development and bureaucratic states. The critical theorists were particularly influential in analyzing the rise of fascism, an ideology which combined heavy emphases on science and technology with an effort to restore "nature" and "spirit" to modern life. Adorno organized a research team to study the social factors – like a repressive work environment – that contributed to an "authoritarian personality" which made people want to join movements like fascism. Critical theory which examined the rationalization of modern life produced not only Parsons' functional social system, but also a reduction of human choices to consumer options and a loss of capacity to advance liberty by transforming institutions. Part of the problem was that people found it hard to grasp that they had the capacity to remake the social world – not as individuals, but as members of social movements, creators of culture, and citizens in democratic society.

Sociological theory was often divided between those who stressed the successes of social integration and those who emphasized its limits and failures, and the importance of conflict to how society really worked. Parsons and other 20th century theorists drew on Durkheim and many 19th century theorists to produce a new sociological theory that shared an emphasis on how the whole of society could be greater than the sum of its parts, and how the needs of each part for the others encouraged "functional integration." This theory has proved powerful in accounting for many of the ways in which society does indeed coalesce despite diversity and differentiation. Like economic theories of the market as an "invisible hand," this sociological functionalism suggests that freely formed relationships can be self-regulating. But the functionalists didn't say very much about the extent to which power and violence determined how the system got started, who was wealthy, who was protected, and who was vulnerable. Their critics did a much better job with pointing out the "visible hand" of corporate power, military power, and other ways in which some social actors could control others or prosper at their expense. The critics also stressed the ways in which history was not simple progress but a story of conflicts and crises. Where functionalists tended to approach conflict as the breakdown of social relations, others drew on Georg Simmel who had pointed out that conflict was itself socially organized, a form of social relations.

These criticisms would become increasingly powerful in the last third of the 20th century and remain basic to the debates that define contemporary sociological theory. We will turn to many of them in the second volume of this anthology. Functionalism and closely related theories dominated sociological discussions until the 1960s. Increasing controversy over them was linked to other controversies that came to the fore in the 1960s, over poverty, race, war, and new kinds of international domination and exploitation. There has been no group of theories since that has ever attained comparable hegemony over the field as a whole – and the field has suffered some disunity as a result, as well as being opened to new creativity. The functionalist synthesis was not the last word in sociological theory, but it remains enormously influential. To stress only functional integration and not power may be one-sided, but such integration is nonetheless of vital importance.

Conclusion

It is not easy to say when sociological theory started. As we have seen, ideas from the ancient world and especially from the 17th and 18th centuries made an important contribution. But it was only in the 19th century that sociological theory gained autonomy from other theories which had privileged politics or economics or indeed, law or religion. August Comte coined the name sociology in the 1830s. He and his contemporary de Tocqueville were more clearly sociologists than their forebears Montesquieu and Rousseau (though both of the earlier writers did develop sociological theories). Likewise, Karl Marx built on the work of Adam Smith as well as on theorists of civil society like G.W.F. Hegel. But Marx's work is more specifically sociological, concerned with capitalism not only as an economic system but as a social formation, a kind of society with specific forms of power relations, cities, culture, and social movements. The creation of sociological theory does not end with the mid-19th century theorists like Comte, de Tocqueville, and Marx who pioneered the mixture of scientific observation and rational analysis that would be basic. Indeed, it was a generation of successors who came of age in the 1890s who exerted the most enduring influence on the institutionalization of sociological theory within universities.[23] Emile Durkheim and Max Weber are the most important of these. And of course, the development of sociological theory continued in the 20th century and continues now in the 21st. Many of the themes are rooted in the social changes of the early modern era. The division of labor that Adam Smith analyzed was a basic starting point for Emile Durkheim's theory of social solidarity. Both remain key influences on contemporary theorists. The question of division of labor is being rethought in the contexts of global organization of production and new technologies that shift dramatically the relationships between knowledge and industrial production.

Similarly, the work of Max Weber has been described as a dialogue with the ghost of Karl Marx. Weber saw much truth in Marx's analysis of capitalism, but also thought it one-sided, and insisted on the importance of religion and culture in ways contrary to Marx. Both are influential today among the theorists who ask how the globalization of economic activity will affect – or be affected by – cultures and religions around the world. The story of the development of sociological theory, in short, is one in which progress in the creation of new theory does not necessarily make older theory obsolete. On the contrary, some of the great classical sociological theories remain both influential and relevant today. They represent brilliant intellectual achievements and we learn much by thinking with the scholars who created them. They also offer signposts in intellectual argument, helping us to identify where later thinkers stand on basic questions by how they identify with or challenge earlier thinkers. Sometimes, too, social change makes us see new lessons in old theories. Marx's work is perhaps the extreme case here, partly because its later use has been so heavily shaped by politics.

Because Marx's theory was an influence on communism – indeed, taken as a sort of sacred text for communism – many assumed that the post-1989 collapse of communism made Marx's work irrelevant and for a time it lost prestige. As attention turned to globalization, however, and as globalization pitted different social interests against each other in a variety of conflicts, new readers found much of interest in Marx's theory. As early as 1848, for example, he and his collaborator Friedrich Engels discerned tendencies that seemed new to others a hundred and fifty years later: "exploitation of the world market has given a cosmopolitan character to production and consumption in every country. [...] All old-established national industries have been destroyed or are daily being destroyed. [...] In place of the old local and national seclusion and self-sufficiency, we have intercourse in every direction, universal interdependence of nations. And as in material, so also in intellectual production. The intellectual creations of individual nations become common property."[24]

This was prescient, but it was not the last word. As we noted at the beginning of this introductory essay, there is no last word. Theory is not the correct answer to all our questions. It offers many answers, but all of them provisional, all of them subject to revision and improvement on the basis of new evidence. Science is about asking questions. Some of these are new questions, some are old ones that have puzzled theorists as long as theory has existed. What is the relationship between the individual and society? Between creative action and seemingly stable structures of relations? How does growth in economies or populations or knowledge itself change society? What, with de Tocqueville, are the social and cultural conditions for democracy? What, with Durkheim, are the social and cultural conditions for solidarity and moral order? Can religion guide social life in the future as much as it did at some times in the past? Are strong local communities necessarily undermined by global economic competition?

Sociological theorists have made great strides in answering these and other pressing questions, and also great strides in figuring out why they are hard to answer conclusively. Theories such as those excerpted in the rest of this book are indispensable tools for grappling with basic questions in social life. That life is always part structure – to be analyzed as objectively as possible, and part action, to be understood in terms of reasons and possibilities. Theory, in other words, guides not just our search for right answers, but our search for right actions. Our actions will change the world for better or worse, and we will still need theory to understand it.

NOTES

1. In *The Fiction of LeRoi Jones/Amiri Baraka* (Chicago: Chicago Review Press; orig. 1964). Jones later changed his name to Amiri Baraka claiming a closer relationship with his African heritage.
2. There is no altogether satisfactory history of sociological theory. Several textbooks that cover much of its development are listed in the bibliography. For a serious account of the key modern theorists, see Lewis Coser, *Masters of Sociological Thought* (New York: Harcourt Brace Jovanovich, 1977); for a somewhat lighter review, see Randall Collins and Makowsky, *Discovery of Society* (New York: McGraw-Hill, rev. ed., 1997). For more depth on specific theorists, see George Ritzer, ed.: *The Blackwell Companion to the Major Social Theorists* (Cambridge, MA: Blackwell, 2011). For a more historical account, see Tom Bottomore and Robert Nisbet, eds., *A History of Sociological Analysis* (New York: Basic Books, 1978).
3. There are many histories of modern science; a readable and authoritative one is Brian Silver, *The Ascent of Science* (Oxford: Oxford University Press, 1997); to situate the rise of science in Western intellectual history more generally, see Jacob Bronowski and Bruce Mazlish, *The Western Intellectual Tradition, from Leonardo to Hegel* (New York: Harper Collins 1986).
4. Popper, Karl R., *Conjectures and Refutations: The Growth of Scientific Knowledge* (London: Routledge, 1992).
5. Robert K. Merton, *Social Theory and Social Structure* (Glencoe, IL: Free Press, 1957).
6. On the early history of individualism as a sociological concept, see Steven Lukes, *Individualism* (Oxford: Blackwell, 1973).
7. See David Zaret, *The Heavenly Contract* (Chicago: University of Chicago Press, 1985) and C.B. MacPherson, *The Political Theory of Possessive Individualism* (Cambridge: Cambridge University Press, 1976).
8. William Blake, "The New Jerusalem," in *The Complete Poetry and Prose of William Blake* (New York: Anchor, 1982).

9   For sociological accounts of the rise of the modern state, see Anthony Giddens, *The Nation-State and Violence* (Berkeley: University of California Press, 1984); Michael Mann, *The Sources of Social Power*, vols. 1 and 2 (Cambridge: Cambridge University Press, 1983, 1993), Gianfranco Poggi, *The State: Its Nature, Development, and Progress* (Stanford: Stanford University Press, 1991).

10 On the specific place of revolutions within the early modern era, see Jack Goldstone, *Revolution and Rebellion in the Early Modern World*, (Berkeley: University of California Press, 1991).

11 See Craig Calhoun, *Nationalism* (Minneapolis: University of Minnesota Press, 1997) and "Nationalism, Political Community, and the Representation of Society: Or, Why Feeling at Home Is Not a Substitute for Public Space," *European Journal of Social Theory*, Vol. 2 (1999) No. 2, pp. 217–31.

12 See Jean Cohen and Andrew Arato, *The Political Theory of Civil Society* (Cambridge, MA: MIT Press, 1992); also John Keane, *Civil Society* (Stanford: Stanford University Press, 1999); Adam Seligman, *Civil Society*. (New York: Free Press, 1992); Craig Calhoun, "Public Sphere/Civil Society: History of the Concepts" *International Encyclopedia of Social and Behavioral Sciences* (Amsterdam: Elsevier, 2001).

13 *An Essay on the History of Civil Society* (Cambridge: Cambridge University Press, 1996; orig. 1767).

14 The term "industrial revolution" was first used by French writers in the early 19th century and rapidly appropriated into English thought; Raymond Williams, *Culture and Society, 1780–1950* (Harmondsworth: Penguin, 1958).

15 The classic sociological account of this contrast is Ferdinand Toennies, *Community and Association/Gemeinschaft und Gesellschaft* (New Brunswick, NJ: Transaction Publishers, 1988; orig. 1887). Toennies term 'gesellschaft' should arguably be translated as 'civil society'.

16 See David A. Reissman, *Adam Smith's Sociological Economics* (London: Croom Helm, 1976).

17 Adam Smith, *An Inquiry into the Nature and causes of the Wealth of Nations* (Chicago: University of Chicago Press, 1977; orig. 1776).

18 Charles Louis de Secondat, Baron de Montesquieu, *The Spirit of Laws* (Berkeley: University of California Press, 1978; orig. 1748).

19 John Locke, *Second Treatise on Government* (Englewood Cliffs, NJ: Prentice-Hall, 1952; orig. 1690).

20 Alexis de Tocqueville, *Democracy in America* (New York: Harper, 2000; orig. 1840, 1844).

21 C.H. Cooley, *Social Organization* (New York: Scribners, 1902).

22 See, notably, *Civilization and its Discontents* (New York: Norton, 1961; orig. 1930).

23 See H. Stuart Hughes, *Consciousness and Society: The Reorientation of European Social Thought, 1890–1930* (New York: Knopf, 1961) and Talcott Parsons, *The Structure of Social Action* (Glencoe: Free Press, 1967; orig. 1937).

24 Karl Marx and Friedrich Engels, *Manifesto of the Communist Party*, pp. 477–519 in *Collected Works* (New York: International Publishers, 1976), p. 488.

Chapter 1

Of the Natural Condition and the Commonwealth [1651]

Thomas Hobbes

Of the *Naturall Condition* of Mankind, as concerning their Felicity, and Misery

Nature hath made men so equall, in the faculties of body, and mind; as that though there bee found one man sometimes manifestly stronger in body, or of quicker mind then another; yet when all is reckoned together, the difference between man, and man, is not so considerable, as that one man can thereupon claim to himselfe any benefit, to which another may not pretend, as well as he. For as to the strength of body, the weakest has strength enough to kill the strongest, either by secret machination, or by confederacy with others, that are in the same danger with himself.

And as to the faculties of the mind, (setting aside the arts grounded upon words, and especially that skill of proceeding upon generall, and infallible rules, called Science; which very few have, and but in few things; as being not a native faculty, born with us; nor attained, (as Prudence,) while we look after somewhat els,) I find yet a greater equality amongst men, than that of strength. For Prudence, is but Experience; which equall time, equally bestowes on all men, in those things they equally apply themselves unto. That which may perhaps make such equality incredible, is but a vain conceipt of ones owne wisdome, which almost all men think they have in a greater degree, than the Vulgar; that is, than all men but themselves, and a few others, whom by Fame, or for concurring with themselves, they approve.

For such is the nature of men, that howsoever they may acknowledge many others to be more witty, or more eloquent, or more learned; Yet they will hardly believe there be many so wise as themselves: For they see their own wit at hand, and other mens at a distance. But this proveth rather that men are in that point equall, than unequall. For there is not ordinarily a greater signe of the equall distribution of any thing, than that every man is contented with his share.

From this equality of ability, ariseth equality of hope in the attaining of our Ends. And therefore if any two men desire the same thing, which neverthelesse they cannot both enjoy, they become enemies; and in the way to their End, (which is principally their owne conservation, and sometimes their delectation only,) endeavour to destroy, or subdue one an other. And from hence it comes to passe, that where an Invader hath no more to feare, than an other mans single power; if one plant, sow, build, or possesse a convenient Seat, others may probably be expected to come prepared with forces united, to dispossesse, and deprive him, not only of the fruit of his labour, but also of his life, or liberty. And the Invader again is in the like danger of another.

And from this diffidence of one another, there is no way for any man to secure himselfe, so reasonable, as Anticipation; that is, by force, or wiles, to master the persons of all men he can, so long, till he see no other power great enough to endanger him: And this is no more than his own conservation requireth, and is generally allowed. Also because there be some, that taking pleasure in contemplating their own power in the acts of conquest, which they pursue farther than their security requires; if others, that otherwise would be glad to be at ease within modest bounds, should not by invasion increase their power, they would not be able, long time, by standing only on their defence, to subsist. And by consequence, such augmentation of dominion over men, being necessary to a mans conservation, it ought to be allowed him.

Againe, men have no pleasure, (but on the contrary a great deale of griefe) in keeping company, where there is no power able to over-awe them all. For every man looketh that his companion should value him, at the same rate he sets upon himselfe: And upon all signes of contempt, or undervaluing, naturally endeavours, as far as he dares (which amongst them that have no common power, to keep them in quiet, is far enough to make them destroy each other,) to extort a greater value from his contemners, by dommage; and from others, by the example.

So that in the nature of man, we find three principall causes of quarrell. First, Competition; Secondly, Diffidence; Thirdly, Glory.

The first, maketh men invade for Gain; the second, for Safety; and the third, for Reputation. The first use Violence, to make themselves Masters of other mens persons, wives, children, and cattell; the second, to defend them; the third, for trifles, as a word, a smile, a different opinion, and any other signe of undervalue, either direct in their Persons, or by reflexion in their Kindred, their Friends, their Nation, their Profession, or their Name.

Hereby it is manifest, that during the time men live without a common Power to keep them all in awe, they are in that condition which is called Warre; and such a warre, as is of every man, against every man. For WARRE, consisteth not in Battell onely, or the act of fighting; but in a tract of time, wherein the Will to contend by Battell is sufficiently known: and therefore the notion of *Time*, is to be considered in the nature of Warre; as it is in the nature of Weather. For as the nature of Foule weather, lyeth not in a showre or two of rain; but in an inclination thereto of many dayes together: So the nature of War, consisteth not in actuall fighting; but in the known disposition thereto, during all the time there is no assurance to the contrary. All other time is PEACE.

Whatsoever therefore is consequent to a time of Warre, where every man is Enemy to every man; the same is consequent to the time, wherein men live without other security, than what their own strength, and their own invention shall furnish them withall. In such condition, there is no place for Industry; because the fruit thereof is uncertain: and consequently no Culture of the Earth; no Navigation, nor use of the commodities that may be imported by Sea; no commodious Building; no Instruments of moving, and removing such things as require much force; no Knowledge of the face of the Earth; no account of Time; no Arts; no Letters; no Society; and which is worst of all, continuall feare, and danger of violent death; And the life of man, solitary, poore, nasty, brutish, and short.

It may seem strange to some man, that has not well weighed these things; that Nature should thus dissociate, and render men apt to invade, and destroy one another: and he may therefore, not trusting to this Inference, made from the Passions, desire perhaps to have the same confirmed by Experience. Let him therefore consider with himselfe, when taking a journey, he armes himselfe, and seeks to go well accompanied; when going to sleep, he locks his dores; when even in his house he locks his chests; and this when he knows there bee Lawes, and publike Officers, armed, to revenge all injuries shall bee done him; what opinion he has of his fellow subjects, when he rides armed; of his fellow Citizens, when he locks his dores; and of his children, and servants, when he locks his chests. Does he not there as much accuse mankind by his actions, as I do by my words? But neither of us accuse mans nature in it. The Desires, and other Passions of man, are in themselves no Sin. No more are the Actions, that proceed from those Passions, till they know a Law that forbids them: which till Lawes be made they cannot know: nor can any Law be made, till they have agreed upon the Person that shall make it.

It may peradventure be thought, there was never such a time, nor condition of warre as this; and I believe it was never generally so, over all the world: but there are many places, where they live so now. For the savage people in many places of *America*, except the government of small Families, the concord whereof dependeth on naturall lust, have no government at all; and live at this day in that brutish manner, as I said before. Howsoever, it may be perceived what manner of life there would be, where there were no common Power to feare; by the manner of life, which men that have formerly lived under a peacefull government, use to degenerate into, in a civill Warre.

But though there had never been any time, wherein particular men were in a condition of warre one against another; yet in all times, Kings, and Persons of

Soveraigne authority, because of their Independency, are in continuall jealousies, and in the state and posture of Gladiators; having their weapons pointing, and their eyes fixed on one another; that is, their Forts, Garrisons, and Guns upon the Frontiers of their Kingdomes; and continuall Spyes upon their neighbours; which is a posture of War. But because they uphold thereby, the Industry of their Subjects; there does not follow from it, that misery, which accompanies the Liberty of particular men.

To this warre of every man against every man, this also is consequent; that nothing can be Unjust. The notions of Right and Wrong, Justice and Injustice have there no place. Where there is no common Power, there is no Law: where no Law, no Injustice. Force, and Fraud, are in warre the two Cardinall vertues. Justice, and Injustice are none of the Faculties neither of the Body, nor Mind. If they were, they might be in a man that were alone in the world, as well as his Senses, and Passions. They are Qualities, that relate to men in Society, not in Solitude. It is consequent also to the same condition, that there be no Propriety, no Dominion, no *Mine* and *Thine* distinct; but onely that to be every mans that he can get; and for so long, as he can keep it. And thus much for the ill condition, which man by meer Nature is actually placed in; though with a possiblity to come out of it, consisting partly in the Passions, partly in his Reason.

The Passions that encline men to Peace, are Feare of Death; Desire of such things as are necessary to commodious living; and a Hope by their Industry to obtain them. And Reason suggesteth convenient Articles of Peace, upon which men may be drawn to agreement. These Articles, are they, which otherwise are called the Lawes of Nature: whereof I shall speak more particularly, in the two following Chapters.

Of the first and second *Naturall Lawes*

The right of nature, which Writers commonly call *Jus Naturale*, is the Liberty each man hath, to use his own power, as he will himselfe, for the preservation of his own Nature; that is to say, of his own Life; and consequently, of doing any thing, which in his own Judgement, and Reason, hee shall conceive to be the aptest means thereunto.

By LIBERTY, is understood, according to the proper signification of the word, the absence of externall Impediments: which Impediments, may oft take away part of a mans power to do what hee would; but cannot hinder him from using the power left him, according as his judgement, and reason shall dictate to him.

A Law of Nature, (*Lex Naturalis,*) is a Precept, or generall Rule, found out by Reason, by which a man is forbidden to do, that, which is destructive of his life, or taketh away the means of preserving the same; and to omit, that, by which he thinketh it may be best preserved. For though they that speak of this subject, use to confound *Jus,* and *Lex, Right* and *Law*; yet they ought to be distinguished; because RIGHT, consisteth in liberty to do, or to forbeare; Whereas LAW, determineth, and bindeth to one of them: so that Law, and Right, differ as much, as Obligation, and Liberty; which in one and the same matter are inconsistent.

And because the condition of Man, (as hath been declared in the precedent Chapter) is a condition of Warre of every one against every one; in which case every one is governed by his own Reason; and there is nothing he can make use of, that may not be a help unto him, in preserving his life against his enemyes; It followeth, that in such a condition, every man has a Right to every thing; even to one anothers body. And therefore, as long as this naturall Right of every man to every thing endureth, there can be no security to any man, (how strong or wise soever he be,) of living out the time, which Nature ordinarily alloweth men to live. And consequently it is a precept, or generall rule of Reason, *That every man, ought to endeavour Peace, as farre as he has hope of obtaining it; and when he cannot obtain it, that he may seek, and use, all helps, and advantages of Warre.* The first branch of which Rule, containeth the first, and Fundamentall Law of Nature; which is, *to seek Peace, and follow it.* The Second, the summe of the Right of Nature; which is, *By all means we can, to defend our selves.*

From this Fundamentall Law of Nature, by which men are commanded to endeavour Peace, is derived this second Law; *That a man be willing, when others are so too, as farre-forth, as for Peace, and defence of himselfe he shall think it necessary, to lay down this right to all things; and be contented with so much liberty against other men, as he would allow other men against himselfe.* For as long as every man holdeth this Right, of doing any thing he liketh; so long are all men in the condition of Warre. But if other men will not lay down their Right, as well as he; then there is no Reason for any one, to devest himselfe of his: For that were to expose himselfe to Prey, (which no man is bound to) rather than to dispose himselfe to Peace. This is that Law of the Gospell; *Whatsoever you require that others should do to you, that do ye to them.* And that Law of all men, *Quod tibi fieri non vis, alteri ne feceris.*

[…]

A Covenant not to defend my selfe from force, by force, is alwayes voyd. For (as I have shewed before) no man can transferre, or lay down his Right to save himselfe from Death, Wounds, and Imprisonment, (the avoyding whereof is the onely End of laying down any Right, and therefore the promise of not resisting force, in no Covenant transferreth any right; nor is obliging. For though a man may Covenant thus, *Unlesse I do so, or so, kill me*; he cannot Covenant thus, *Unlesse I do so, or so, I will not resist you, when you come to kill me.* For man by nature chooseth the lesser evill, which is danger of death in resisting; rather than the greater, which is certain and present death in not resisting. And this is granted to be true by all men, in that they lead Criminals to Execution, and Prison, with armed men, notwithstanding that such Criminals have consented to the Law, by which they are condemned.

[…]

Of the Causes, Generation, and Definition of a *Common-wealth*

The finall Cause, End, or Designe of men, (who naturally love Liberty, and Dominion over others,) in the introduction of that restraint upon themselves, (in which wee see them live in Common-wealths,) is the foresight of their own preservation, and of a more contented life thereby; that is to say, of getting themselves out from that miserable condition of Warre, which is necessarily consequent (as hath been shewn) to the naturall Passions of men, when there is no visible Power to keep them in awe, and tye them by feare of punishment to the performance of their Covenants, and observation of those Lawes of Nature set down in the fourteenth and fifteenth Chapters.

[…]

The only way to erect such a Common Power, as may be able to defend them from the invasion of Forraigners, and the injuries of one another, and thereby to secure them in such sort, as that by their owne industrie, and by the fruites of the Earth, they may nourish themselves and live contentedly; is, to conferre all their power and strength upon one Man, or upon one Assembly of men, that may reduce all their Wills, by plurality of voices, unto one Will: which is as much as to say, to appoint one man, or Assembly of men, to beare their Person; and every one to owne, and acknowledge himselfe to be Author of whatsoever he that so beareth their Person, shall Act, or cause to be Acted, in those things which concerne the Common Peace and Safetie; and therein to submit their Wills, every one to his Will, and their Judgements, to his Judgment. This is more than Consent, or Concord; it is a reall Unitie of them all, in one and the same Person, made by Covenant of every man with every man, in such manner, as if every man should say to every man, *I Authorise and give up my Right of Governing my selfe, to this Man, or to this Assembly of men, on this condition, that thou give up thy Right to him, and Authorise all his Actions in like manner*. This done, the Multitude so united in one Person, is called a COMMON-WEALTH, in latine CIVITAS. This is the Generation of that great LEVIATHAN, or rather (to speake more reverently) of that *Mortall God*, to which wee owe under the *Immortall God*, our peace and defence. For by this Authoritie, given him by every particular man in the Common-Wealth, he hath the use of so much Power and Strength conferred on him, that by terror thereof, he is inabled to forme the wills of them all, to Peace at home, and mutuall ayd against their enemies abroad. And in him consisteth the Essence of the Common-wealth; which (to define it,) is *One Person, of whose Acts a great Multitude, by mutuall Covenants one with another, have made themselves every one the Author, to the end he may use the strength and means of them all, as he shall think expedient, for their Peace and Common Defence.*

And he that carryeth this Person, is called SOVERAIGNE, and said to have *Soveraigne Power*; and every one besides, his SUBJECT.

The attaining to this Soveraigne Power, is by two wayes. One, by Naturall force; as when a man maketh his children, to submit themselves, and their children to his government, as being able to destroy them if they refuse; or by Warre subdueth his enemies to his will, giving them their lives on that condition. The other, is when men agree amongst themselves, to submit to some Man, or Assembly of men, voluntarily, on confidence to be protected by him against all others. This later, may be called a Politicall Common-wealth or Commonwealth by *Institution*; and the former, a Commonwealth by *Acquisition*. […]

Of the *Rights* of Soveraignes by Institution

A *Common-wealth* is said to be *Instituted*, when a *Multitude* of men do Agree, and *Covenant, every one, with every one,* that to whatsoever *Man,* or *Assembly of Men,* shall be given by the major part, the *Right* to *Present* the Person of them all, (that is to say, to be their *Representative*;) every one, as well he that *Voted for it,* as he that *Voted against it,* shall *Authorise* all the Actions and Judgements, of that Man, or Assembly of men, in the same manner, as if they were his own, to the end, to live peaceably amongst themselves, and be protected against other men.

From this Institution of a Common-wealth are derived all the *Rights*, and *Facultyes* of him, or them, on whom the Soveraigne Power is conferred by the consent of the People assembled.

First, because they Covenant, it is to be understood, they are not obliged by former Covenant to any thing repugnant hereunto. And Consequently they that have already Instituted a Commonwealth, being thereby bound by Covenant, to own the Actions, and Judgements of one, cannot lawfully make a new Covenant, amongst themselves, to be obedient to any other, in any thing whatsoever, without his permission. And therefore, they that are subjects to a Monarch, cannot without his leave cast off Monarchy, and return to the confusion of a disunited Multitude; nor transferre their Person from him that beareth it, to another Man, or other Assembly of men: for they are bound, every man to every man, to Own, and be reputed Author of all, that he that already is their Soveraigne, shall do, and judge fit to be done: so that any one man dissenting, all the rest should break their Covenant made to that man, which is injustice: and they have also every man given the Soveraignty to him that beareth their Person; and therefore if they depose him, they take from him that which is his own, and so again it is injustice. Besides, if he that attempteth to depose his Soveraign, be killed, or punished by him for such attempt, he is author of his own punishment, as being by the Institution, Author of all his Soveraign shall do: And because it is injustice for a man to do any thing, for which he may be punished by his own authority, he is also upon that title, unjust. And whereas some men have pretended for their disobedience to their Soveraign, a new Covenant, made, not with men, but with God; this also is unjust: for there is no Covenant with God, but by mediation of some body that representeth Gods Person; which none doth but Gods Lieutenant, who hath the Soveraignty under God. But this pretence of Covenant with God, is so evident a lye, even in the pretenders own consciences, that it is not onely an act of an unjust, but also of a vile, and unmanly disposition.

Secondly, Because the Right of bearing the Person of them all, is given to him they make Soveraigne, by Covenant onely of one to another, and not of him to any of them; there can happen no breach of Covenant on the part of the Soveraigne; and consequently none of his Subjects, by any pretence of forfeiture, can be freed from his Subjection. That he which is made Soveraigne maketh no Covenant with his Subjects beforehand, is manifest; because either he must make it with the whole multitude, as one party to the Covenant; or he must make a severall Covenant with every man. With the whole, as one party, it is impossible; because as yet they are not one Person: and if he make so many severall Covenants as there be men, those Covenants after he hath the Soveraignty are voyd, because what act soever can be pretended by any one of them for breach thereof, is the act both of himselfe, and of all the rest, because done in the Person, and by the Right of every one of them in particular. Besides, if any one, or more of them, pretend a breach of the Covenant made by the Soveraigne at his Institution; and others, or one other of his Subjects, or himselfe alone, pretend there was no such breach, there is in this case, no Judge to decide the controversie: it returns therefore to the Sword again; and every man recovereth the right of Protecting himselfe by his own strength, contrary to the designe they had in the Institution. It is therefore in vain to grant Soveraignty by way of precedent Covenant. The opinion that any Monarch receiveth his Power by Covenant, that is to say on Condition, proceedeth from want of understanding this easie truth, that Covenants being but words, and breath, have no force to oblige, contain, constrain, or protect any man, but what it has from the publique Sword; that is, from the untyed hands of that Man, or Assembly of men that hath the Soveraignty, and whose actions are avouched by them all, and performed by the strength of them all, in him united. But when an Assembly of men is made Soveraigne; then no man imagineth any such Covenant to have past in the Institution; for no man is so dull as to say, for example, the People of *Rome*, made a Covenant with the Romans, to hold the Soveraignty on such or such conditions; which not performed, the Romans might lawfully depose the Roman People. That men see not the reason to be alike in a Monarchy, and in a Popular Government, proceedeth from the ambition of some, that are kinder to the government of an Assembly, whereof they may hope to participate, than of Monarchy, which they despair to enjoy.

[...]

Part I

Precursors to Sociological Theory

Introduction to Part I
1 Of the Natural Condition and the Commonwealth
2 Of the Social Contract
3 What is Enlightenment?
4 The Wealth of Nations
5 The Theory of Moral Sentiments

Introduction to Part I

The word "sociology" was coined by Auguste Comte in the 1830s, but the idea of sociology had been developing for more than a century. Indeed, sociological theory drew on an intellectual heritage stretching back to the Hebrew Bible, Ancient Greece, and Rome, and the birth of Christianity. The roots of modern sociological theory may be traced to changes starting in the 17th century that built on these traditional philosophical foundations.

The Idea of Society

One set of changes had to do with the very idea of society itself. Today it seems obvious to think society exists and is important. We may define it as a functional system, or the product of meaningful interaction among individuals, or the sum of social institutions. But though there are debates over definition, there is a widespread agreement about the importance of the ways in which people are related to each other from love and friendship, family and community through large-scale organizations like schools, businesses and governments to the growing social connections linking the whole world. For society to become the focus of attention and the object of a new science, however, people had to see the world in somewhat different ways.

First, there had to be a separation of the idea of society from government. Early modern thinkers emphasized all the links connecting the members of society to each other, including the culture they shared, the markets in which they exchanged goods, and their communication networks. They distinguished these social relations from control by kings or government officials. This is the basis of the idea of civil society,

Classical Sociological Theory, Third Edition. Edited by Craig Calhoun, Joseph Gerteis, James Moody, Steven Pfaff, and Indermohan Virk. Editorial material and organization © 2012 John Wiley & Sons, Ltd. Published 2012 by John Wiley & Sons, Ltd.

which remains prominent today. When we say there is a "civil society" response to an emergency or social problem, we mean that churches and synagogues, non-governmental organizations, and volunteer groups responded – as distinct from government agencies. This distinction is rooted directly in the 17th- and 18th-century rise of the idea of society at least partially independent of government.

Second, there had to be an idea that what happened in society was valuable in itself. Early modern thinkers developed the idea that members of society had common interests, that these were morally important, and that social relations should be organized to advance them. Some used the term "commonwealth" to emphasize the connection between the way people were socially organized and their economic productivity and capacity to improve their quality of life. Both sociology and economics grew in part out of this shift in perspective. We see it, for example, in the reading from Adam Smith (and later Durkheim) on the importance of the division of labor. But the change in perspective was not simply a matter of noticing the importance of social organization; it was also a matter of valuing ordinary life. In the Middle Ages, for example, many religious thinkers argued that people should focus only on God, heaven and hell, and salvation – rather than on improving the quality of worldly life. This changed within religious thought as more people looked to the Bible and prayer for guidance in everyday affairs such as family life. Eventually, theories about this worldly social life became more secular and less theological.

Almost as important, an explicit place for the rights of subjects appears in political thought, as we see a shift from the complete rights of kings to the notion that rulers had an obligation to serve the interests of the people they ruled. This was an important basis for the theory that revolution could be just, which was important to the founding of the United States and the transformation of France in the late 18th century. The idea of a social contract traces this shift in thought from Hobbes to Rousseau.

Third, the idea of "the people" had to develop in a new way. For democracy to be possible, for example, it had to be possible for "the people" to express their collective opinions – whether through voting or in other ways, from protest demonstrations to petitions. This required a strong idea of "the people" such as that embodied in the United States Constitution, which begins, "We the people of the United States, in order to form a more perfect union, [...]" This opening sentence only makes sense if one believes that "the people" can act collectively to make a Constitution, which depends on the cultural idea that the people can be identified and have a common interest. This was shaped in the early modern notions of nation and citizenship, which defined membership in "the people" and also stressed their common rights, interests, and obligations.

These three core ideas remain influential throughout the modern era: society is distinct from government, ordinary social life is valuable, and large numbers of people can achieve enough social solidarity to make it meaningful to speak of "the people" as the basis for democracy. These ideas changed actual social life, and also gave rise to sociology as the scientific field for studying social life. But in addition to the rise of this new idea of society, the 17th and 18th centuries also saw the rise of new ideas about science and human reason. These are also important for the invention of sociology.

Enlightenment and Science

This second set of basic changes is often summed up in the idea of an "Age of Enlightenment," stretching from the middle of the 17th century through the 18th. This description was familiar to 18th-century thinkers themselves, who saw themselves as bringing the light of science, systematic analysis, and new ideas to the shadowy realms of tradition and ignorance. They expected the "light of reason" to illuminate a path of human progress, clarifying both the ways things worked objectively in the world and the values human beings should rightly hold. Like the idea of society, the Enlightenment directly shaped practical projects like the American and French Revolutions, not least by promoting the belief that human beings could choose the social conditions of their own lives, based on reason, rather than simply accepting the institutions they had inherited.

The Enlightenment is a label for a collection of partially separate ideas such as science, the exercise of individual reason, tolerance of difference, and equality of rights (including notably for women, who had previously been excluded from most public life and began in this period the long struggle for equality). The reading below from Immanuel Kant is among the most influential of all accounts of the Enlightenment, but it is a summary written near the end of the Age of Enlightenment – by which time most leading European thinkers considered themselves "enlightened." Earlier thinkers like Baruch Spinoza (1632–77) and René Descartes (1596–1650) had seemed much more revolutionary. When their ideas began to attract a growing range of followers in the 17th century, this was widely understood as a direct challenge to religion. Spinoza, for example, argued there should be tolerance for people who held contrary religious beliefs – and many thought this amounted to saying that sinful error should be accepted. Descartes held that the basis for certain knowledge started with human reason (famously, he wrote, "I think therefore I am"). Although he held this was consistent with the biblical notion that God gave human beings the capacity for independent reason, many others thought this was an attack on the authority of the Bible.

Theories like those of Spinoza and Descartes suggested that individuals should think for themselves and that reason was often a better basis for judgment than tradition. These "rationalist" ideas were soon complemented with the "empiricist" idea that evidence for the truth should be found in observations of the material world. Descartes' contemporary Francis Bacon (1561–1626) had suggested this, but the idea really caught on with the dramatic growth in scientific knowledge that made the 17th century an age of scientific revolution. The father of modern physics, Isaac Newton (1642–1727), was among its most important figures. But both reason *and* the search for empirical evidence – the hallmarks of science – were applied immediately not only to physics, chemistry, and medicine but to the project of understanding social life: how markets worked, what government was best, whether population growth would lead to famine, and so forth.

Throughout the modern era, some religious thinkers have remained uncomfortable with the rise of science. Others have sought to re-examine religious questions in the light of science. Both religious thought itself and the place of religion in the world have changed. But this did not necessarily mean an abandonment of religion. Immanuel Kant himself wrote a book arguing for "religion within the limits of reason alone." He meant that it wasn't necessary to rely on mysterious revelations, but rather that the reason with which God had endowed human beings was sufficient. Certainly many religious leaders disagreed, but most religious leaders did place more emphasis on the exercise of individual reason.

A variety of other social changes helped the Enlightenment spread its message of reason and reliance on empirical evidence. One of the most important was the printing press, which allowed a much wider distribution of books. With this came growth in literacy and education, which helped the rise of reason. Already in the era of the Protestant Reformation, more Christians had begun to read the Bible for themselves, and think for themselves about its meaning, not simply rely on the teachings of religious authorities. This same sort of emphasis on individual reason was extended more widely to more questions.

The idea of individual rights was grounded largely in the notion that every individual could exercise reason for himself or herself. This was a key basis for the growing claims that women should have equal rights, because they too could reason independently (whatever their other physical differences from men). The ideas of "human rights" coupled the emphasis on reason with equality. Because every human being had the capacity for reason, each deserved respect and had basic rights (such as life, liberty, and the pursuit of happiness, according to the US Declaration of Independence, or those listed in the Declaration of the Rights of Man by the French Revolutionaries). The American Revolutionary hero Tom Paine wrote famously of the importance of common sense, the age of reason, and the rights of man. This inspired both the idea of independence for America and the idea of creating a democratic government to ensure the independence and freedom of Americans inside the new country. If Paine spoke of the Rights of Man, however, he was quickly answered by Mary Wollstonecraft's *Vindication of the Rights of Woman* (1792). Wollstonecraft was indignant at the failure to recognize women equally, but she had faith that eventually women's rights would be recognized because this was, literally, only reasonable.

The example of equal rights for women reminds us that simply declaring rights doesn't mean effectively realizing them, and that there are a variety of influential social forces, besides the exercise of reason. Sociology has been shaped both by the emphasis on independent reason – as sociologists have sought to use logic and evidence to understand society scientifically – and by the effort to understand those other social forces, from emotions to tradition to commitments to family or community or nation to the exercise of power. The Enlightenment encouraged a belief in progress based on the exercise of reason, but while many sociologists have believed in progress, most have also studied the limits or impediments to it and some have questioned whether it is as inevitable as the Enlightenment theorists imagined.

Already in the later years of the Age of Enlightenment, there were questioning voices. Mary Wollstonecraft's daughter Mary Shelley, wrote the novel *Frankenstein* with its theme of a scientist who overreaches himself by seeking to create life. Her work was part of a Romantic movement which complemented and sometimes countered the Enlightenment faith in reason with more emphasis on tradition, emotions, and above all nature. Rousseau was a formative influence on this movement which, not surprisingly, found many of its later leaders among poets and musicians. This too shaped sociology, for the scientific researchers found that the evidence suggested that society was not simply the result of rational decisions by its members.

Authors and Readings

We start our section with two examples from the Social Contract tradition, representing opposing ends of the tradition. Hobbes was born in Westport, England and entered Oxford at 15. After graduating he served as a tutor to the Cavendish family and traveled widely, exchanging ideas with the intellectuals of his age (including Descartes and Galileo). His first publication was a translation of Thucydides (1628), but it was reading Euclid that ultimately convinced Hobbes that matters of political philosophy needed similar axiomatic treatment. He wrote *Leviathan or the Matter, Form and Power of a Commonwealth, Ecclesiastical and Civil* in 1651.

Hobbes was often personally fearful and lived amid civil war; he made fear and the need for caution key themes in his theory. He takes as his starting point that people are by nature equal – in the sense that even the strongest can be overtaken by coalitions of others; and that skill in one area is outweighed by the skills and strengths of others. In the state of nature, the hypothetical time before government, people are characterized by "First Competition; Secondly, Diffidence (that is mistrust); Thirdly, Glory" (*Leviathan* I, 13). People are by nature competitors trying to gain at others' expense. This leads to living in a continual state of war, where the fruits of one's labor are never ensured from theft by others. This means, according to Hobbes, that "In such a condition, there is no place for Industry; because the fruit thereof is uncertain; and consequently no Culture of the Earth; [...] no Arts; no Letters; no Society; and, which is worst of all, continuall feare, and danger of violent death; And the life of man, solitary, poore, nasty, brutish, and short" (*Leviathan* I, 13). He arrives at this conclusion deductively, from the basic point that, without restraint, people try to take what they can from others. That we all lock our doors at night is all the evidence Hobbes needs to confirm the initial premise, then his conclusion follows from his rigorous application of the deductive method borrowed from geometry.

Hobbes sees only the power of the *commonwealth* as the solution to the problem of the state of nature. Driven by our natural passions to a self-destructive state of war, civilized survival requires a power to check the passions and create order. This power must have the ability to control others through force, since "Covenants, without the Sword, are but Words," which lack the power necessary to enforce order. Hobbes sees this power arising when people give themselves completely to "one Man, or upon one Assembly of men, that may reduce all their Wills, by plurality of voices, unto one Will" (*Leviathan* 2, 17). This is done by each transferring their rights to the leader, which creates the *sovereign*. So long as all give their rights similarly, all are bound to the leader (or leadership body) similarly. Note the sovereign rules completely, as the covenant is among all subjects, not between the subjects and the sovereign, and thus there can be no breach of contract by the sovereign (*Leviathan*, I, 18). It is interesting to note that this model does, however, generate power from the subjects rather than God. It is in the covenant of people with each other that the Sovereign's power derives, not from the divine right of kings.

The views of human nature, rights, and the sovereign are very different for Jean-Jacques Rousseau (1712–78). Born in Geneva, Rousseau lived most of his life in Paris. He was influenced by an idealized memory of the smaller community of Geneva but he also remembered being driven out by the city's Calvinist leaders who found his theories scandalous. He promoted new approaches to music and education as well as social theory. In all of his work, however, he emphasized the importance of nature – both individual human nature (with its inner voice) and outside nature. In his theory of education, for example, he advocated raising children in the countryside so they would be close to nature but also discover their distinctive inner selves without the distractions and pressures to conform typical of urban society.

Rousseau was passionate about the exercise of individual reason, but in unconventional ways he burst on the scene by writing the winning essay in a contest calling for discourses on progress in the arts and science. Shockingly, he argued that progress in science actually brought humanity unhappiness by separating people from nature. Rousseau argued that much of what was widely accepted as progress in society in fact brought alienation, separation of people not only from nature but from their inner, natural selves (Karl Marx was greatly influenced by Rousseau when he took up this theme in the 19th century; it has been recurrently important in sociology).

Rousseau placed great emphasis on inner reflection to discover the truth, for example, and less on conforming to accepted standards of logic. We see something of this in the reading here where he presents two different ideas about how the common will of the people may be found. One, the "will of all," is more superficial, based on the aggregation of separate, self-interested individual wills (as in voting or opinion polls). The other, "general will," is more basic, he suggests, but cannot be measured in such mechanistic ways. Each of us has within us, however, a capacity to see this light.

Though many later thinkers have found the logic of Rousseau's writings difficult, they have been profoundly influential. This is partly because he was a wonderful writer and his work is a pleasure to read even if hard sometimes to pin down. But even more, his influence stems from the powerful way in which he established the ideas of freedom and equality as basic to modern thought. "Man is born free," Rousseau wrote, "yet everywhere he is in chains," limited by the arbitrary conventions of society and the exercise of power. Nature is given by God to all humanity, yet private property divides it and erects boundaries to exclude. How is this possible? Can it be just? The questions remain basic.

Immanuel Kant (1724–1804) admired Rousseau enormously and kept a bust of the earlier thinker in his study. He lived his whole life in Konigsberg, a Prussian city in the north of Germany (that after the Second World War was acquired by Russia and resettled as Kaliningrad). He took walks on such a regular schedule that townspeople were said to set their watches by him (and the very spread of watches was part of the era's more general concern for orderly, precise social life). Though he never traveled, Kant was intensely curious about the rest of the world, reading reports from explorers and missionaries. He sought to develop an intellectual approach that would be valid for all humanity, based on the universal character of reason rather than the differences among cultures.

Kant took up the core Rousseauian themes of freedom and equality, but emphasized overwhelmingly the link of each to the basic idea of the individual exercise of reason. One of the founders of the largely German philosophical school called "idealism," he argued that secure human knowledge and morality came not from external imposition but from the inherent capacities of the human mind. Ideas like time and space, Kant suggested, do not come to us as material facts; they are mental categories we need in order to understand material reality.

Kant examined almost every philosophical topic, from mathematics (pure reason) to law and aesthetic judgment (different forms of practical reason). He was concerned to see reason used to settle human conflicts rather than force and imagined progress leading to an era of perpetual peace. He argued that morality needed to be achieved on the basis of human beings' free will because we consider actions properly moral when they are chosen, not forced. This meant that morality was to be pursued by cultivating human capacity for reason rather than limiting human freedom.

Kant also pioneered what he called "critique," a philosophical approach to examining the conditions of actual and apparent knowledge. When he wrote a "critique of pure reason," he therefore didn't attack pure reason; he asked how it was possible and urged his reader to try to grasp the underlying, most basic foundations of thought. Too much of what passed for knowledge, he thought, was merely belief accepted out of habit. We need to look critically at such beliefs in pursuit of the truth. This notion influenced all of sociology (and most of modern thought); it was also especially influential for the "critical theorists" we examine later. This notion of basic foundations for knowledge and the pursuit of pure truth became basic to modern science – but also basic to the versions of "modernity" attacked in the late 20th century by those who sometimes called themselves "postmodernists." It was too easy, they argued, for this idea of perfect knowledge to become the enemy of freedom, especially if it encouraged governments to develop top-down master plans for how society should be organized.

Adam Smith (1723–90) was a central figure in what is often called the Scottish Enlightenment. Part of the broader European Enlightenment, the Scottish thinkers were distinctive in several ways. One was that they were more skeptical than Kant and most of the Germans about the capacities of unaided reason, and more attentive to the ways in which human beings – and human societies – learned from the accumulated trial and error of history. One of their greatest theorists, David Hume, had provoked Kant to take on his quest for secure foundations of knowledge by severely questioning the limits of abstract reason and arguing that for many crucial questions – like the nature of cause and effect – we have no choice but to rely on inductions from empirical evidence that can never be entirely conclusive. Another, Adam Ferguson, helped to introduce the idea of civil society and also anticipated later evolutionary theory, by holding that history revealed a pattern of improvements in social organization, reflecting among other things growth in productive capacity by which human societies sustained themselves in relation to nature and each other.

Smith focused on questions of moral philosophy, arguing that humans would be bound together by natural sympathies and that human sentiments included benevolent dispositions as well as sources of conflict. But much more famously, he helped to create modern economics, as well as sociology, with his book *The Wealth of Nations* (1776). The selection printed here on the division of labor was widely influential. Smith wrote more generally about the extent to which markets created order and produced collective benefits even when the motivations of individual participants were entirely selfish. First, he suggested, markets taught sensible behavior by a kind of external conditioning: they rewarded buying cheap and selling dear and they punished the opposite. Second, markets led people with different skills or properties to cooperate through exchange, thus not only circulating goods effectively but boosting production Third, markets did all this without anyone being in charge and directing them. And this was the key point: markets were self-regulating. They were proof, Smith suggested, that it was not necessary to rely on kings or governments to establish all the conditions of social life. Markets could be self-regulating. This is what he meant by saying they worked as though led by an "invisible hand." There were emergent properties of market structure and process that were not the results of any plan or intention. Studying such emergent properties of social organization has remained a key theme for sociology.

The common wealth, Smith suggested, could be better achieved by freeing individuals to compete in self-regulating markets than by central planning or restrictions on trade. Of course, markets could become imbalanced and fail in self-regulation – Smith argued that competition only worked among human individuals, not large corporations, because the participants had to be relatively equal. And there were some things, like national defense, that were best provided by government because they needed central authority. But Smith's points were not only about markets for their own sake. Markets were simply one of the best examples of social self-regulation that went on throughout society – as people found partners to marry, decided how many children to have, wrote books (for the "marketplace of ideas") and so forth. Most of civil society could be self-regulating, not only markets – as long as there was freedom for individuals to make their own decisions and at least substantial equality, though not perfect equality since individuals needed to learn from the decisions they made and this meant that some had to win and some lose.

SELECTED BIBLIOGRAPHY

Baumgold, Deborah. 2010. *Contract Theory in Historical Context: Essays on Grotius, Hobbes and Locke.* Leiden: Brill. (A nice overview of contract theory.)

Gay, Peter 1996. *The Enlightenment: An Interpretation.* New York: Norton, rev. ed. (Still perhaps the best overview.)

Israel, Jonathan I. 2001. *Radical Enlightenment.* Oxford: Oxford University Press. (Excellent on Descartes, Spinoza, and the early pre-Kantian Enlightenment).

Kuehn, Manfred 2001. *Kant: A Biography.* Cambridge: Cambridge University Press. (An exceptionally good biography that also introduces Kant's theory and situates it in the Age of Enlightenment.)

Maneat, Pierre 1996. *Tocqueville and the Nature of Democracy.* Lanham, MD: Rowman & Littlefleld Publishers. (Perhaps the best general introduction.)

Pope, Whitney and Lucetta Pope. 1986. *Alexis de Tocqueville: His Social and Political Theory.* Beverly Hills, CA: Sage. (Helpful in the connections of Tocqueville to sociology.)

Reisman, David A. 1976. *Adam Smith's Sociological Economics.* London: Croom Helm. (An excellent study showing how the sociological and economic dimensions of Smith's work are intertwined.)

Schmidt, James (ed.) 1996. *What Is Enlightenment? Eighteenth Century Answers and Twentieth Century Questions.* Berkeley, CA: University of California Press. (Situates Kant in relation to several contemporaries asking similar questions and also shows why those remain current questions today.)

Shklar, Judith 1969. *Men and Citizens: A Study of Rousseau's Social Theory.* Cambridge: Cambridge University Press. (Still one of the best accounts.)

Winch, Donald 1978. *Adam Smith's Politics.* Cambridge: Cambridge University Press. (A broader study than the title implies, contesting narrow readings of Smith as "just" an economist.)

Zunz, Olivier and Alan S. Kahan (eds.). 2002. *The Tocqueville Reader.* Oxford: Blackwell. (Selections from Tocqueville with an introduction that shows the development of his thought.)

Chapter 2

Of the Social Contract [1762]

Jean-Jacques Rousseau

Man is born free; and everywhere he is in chains. One thinks himself the master of others, and still remains a greater slave than they. How did this change come about? I do not know. What can make it legitimate? That question I think I can answer.

If I took into account only force, and the effects derived from it, I should say: "As long as a people is compelled to obey, and obeys, it does well; as soon as it can shake off the yoke, and shakes it off, it does still better; for, regaining its liberty by the same right as took it away, either it is justified in resuming it, or there was no justification for those who took it away." But the social order is a sacred right which is the basis of all other rights. Nevertheless, this right does not come from nature, and must therefore be founded on conventions. Before coming to that, I have to prove what I have just asserted.

The First Societies

The most ancient of all societies, and the only one that is natural, is the family: and even so the children remain attached to the father only so long as they need him for their preservation. As soon as this need ceases, the natural bond is dissolved. The children, released from the obedience they owed to the father, and the father, released from the care he owed his children, return equally to independence. If they remain united, they continue so no longer naturally, but voluntarily; and the family itself is then maintained only by convention.

This common liberty results from the nature of man. His first law is to provide for his own preservation, his first cares are those which he owes to himself; and, as soon

Rousseau, Jean-Jacques "Of the Social Contract," Book I, from *The Social Contract*, 1762.

Classical Sociological Theory, Third Edition. Edited by Craig Calhoun, Joseph Gerteis, James Moody, Steven Pfaff, and Indermohan Virk. Editorial material and organization © 2012 John Wiley & Sons, Ltd. Published 2012 by John Wiley & Sons, Ltd.

as he reaches years of discretion, he is the sole judge of the proper means of preserving himself, and consequently becomes his own master.

The family then may be called the first model of political societies: the ruler corresponds to the father, and the people to the children; and all, being born free and equal, alienate their liberty only for their own advantage. The whole difference is that, in the family, the love of the father for his children repays him for the care he takes of them, while, in the State, the pleasure of commanding takes the place of the love which the chief cannot have for the peoples under him.

Grotius denies that all human power is established in favour of the governed, and quotes slavery as an example. His usual method of reasoning is constantly to establish right by fact.[1] It would be possible to employ a more logical method, but none could be more favourable to tyrants.

It is then, according to Grotius, doubtful whether the human race belongs to a hundred men, or that hundred men to the human race: and, throughout his book, he seems to incline to the former alternative, which is also the view of Hobbes. On this showing, the human species is divided into so many herds of cattle, each with its ruler, who keeps guard over them for the purpose of devouring them.

As a shepherd is of a nature superior to that of his flock, the shepherds of men, i.e., their rulers, are of a nature superior to that of the peoples under them. Thus, Philo tells us, the Emperor Caligula reasoned, concluding equally well either that kings were gods, or that men were beasts.

The reasoning of Caligula agrees with that of Hobbes and Grotius. Aristotle, before any of them, had said that men are by no means equal naturally, but that some are born for slavery, and others for dominion.

Aristotle was right; but he took the effect for the cause. Nothing can be more certain than that every man born in slavery is born for slavery. Slaves lose everything in their chains, even the desire of escaping from them: they love their servitude, as the comrades of Ulysses loved their brutish condition.[2] If then there are slaves by nature, it is because there have been slaves against nature. Force made the first slaves, and their cowardice perpetuated the condition.

I have said nothing of King Adam, or Emperor Noah, father of the three great monarchs who shared out the universe, like the children of Saturn, whom some scholars have recognised in them. I trust to getting due thanks for my moderation; for, being a direct descendant of one of these princes, perhaps of the eldest branch, how do I know that a verification of titles might not leave me the legitimate king of the human race? In any case, there can be no doubt that Adam was sovereign of the world, as Robinson Crusoe was of his island, as long as he was its only inhabitant; and this empire had the advantage that the monarch, safe on his throne, had no rebellions, wars, or conspirators to fear.

The Right of the Strongest

The strongest is never strong enough to be always the master, unless he transforms strength into right, and obedience into duty. Hence the right of the strongest, which, though to all seeming meant ironically, is really laid down as a fundamental principle.

But are we never to have an explanation of this phrase? Force is a physical power, and I fail to see what moral effect it can have. To yield to force is an act of necessity, not of will – at the most, an act of prudence. In what sense can it be a duty?

Suppose for a moment that this so-called "right" exists. I maintain that the sole result is a mass of inexplicable nonsense. For, if force creates right, the effect changes with the cause: every force that is greater than the first succeeds to its right. As soon as it is possible to disobey with impunity, disobedience is legitimate; and, the strongest being always in the right, the only thing that matters is to act so as to become the strongest. But what kind of right is that which perishes when force fails? If we must obey perforce, there is no need to obey because we ought; and if we are not forced to obey, we are under no obligation to do so. Clearly, the word "right" adds nothing to force: in this connection, it means absolutely nothing.

Obey the powers that be. If this means yield to force, it is a good precept, but superfluous: I can answer for its never being violated. All power comes from God, I admit; but so does all sickness: does that mean that we are forbidden to call in the doctor? A brigand surprises me at the edge of a wood: must I not merely surrender my purse on compulsion; but, even if I could withhold it, am I in conscience bound to give it up? For certainly the pistol he holds is also a power.

Let us then admit that force does not create right, and that we are obliged to obey only legitimate powers. In that case, my original question recurs.

Slavery

Since no man has a natural authority over his fellow, and force creates no right, we must conclude that conventions form the basis of all legitimate authority among men.

If an individual, says Grotius, can alienate his liberty and make himself the slave of a master, why could not a whole people do the same and make itself subject to a king? There are in this passage plenty of ambiguous words which would need explaining; but let us confine ourselves to the word *alienate*. To alienate is to give or to sell. Now, a man who becomes the slave of another does not give himself; he sells himself, at the least for his subsistence: but for what does a people sell itself? A king is so far from furnishing his subjects with their subsistence that he gets his own only from them; and, according to Rabelais, kings do not live on nothing. Do subjects then give their persons on condition that the king takes their goods also? I fail to see what they have left to preserve.

It will be said that the despot assures his subjects civil tranquillity. Granted; but what do they gain, if the wars his ambition brings down upon them, his insatiable avidity, and the vexations conduct of his ministers press harder on them than their own dissensions would have done? What do they gain, if the very tranquillity they enjoy is one of their miseries? Tranquillity is found also in dungeons; but is that enough to make them desirable places to live in? The Greeks imprisoned in the cave of the Cyclops lived there very tranquilly, while they were awaiting their turn to be devoured.

To say that a man gives himself gratuitously, is to say what is absurd and inconceivable; such an act is null and illegitimate, from the mere fact that he who does it is out of his mind. To say the same of a whole people is to suppose a people of madmen; and madness creates no right.

Even if each man could alienate himself, he could not alienate his children: they are born men and free; their liberty belongs to them, and no one but they has the right to dispose of it. Before they come to years of discretion, the father can, in their name, lay down conditions for their preservation and well-being, but he cannot give them irrevocably and without conditions: such a gift is contrary to the ends of nature, and exceeds the rights of paternity. It would therefore be necessary, in order to legitimise an arbitrary government, that in every generation the people should be in a position to accept or reject it; but, were this so, the government would be no longer arbitrary.

To renounce liberty is to renounce being a man, to surrender the rights of humanity and even its duties. For him who renounces everything no indemnity is possible. Such a renunciation is incompatible with man's nature; to remove all liberty from his will is to remove all morality from his acts. Finally, it is an empty and contradictory convention that sets up, on the one side, absolute authority, and, on the other, unlimited obedience. Is it not clear that we can be under no obligation to a person from whom we have the right to exact everything? Does not this condition alone, in the absence of equivalence or exchange, in itself involve the nullity of the act? For what right can my slave have against me, when all that he has belongs to me, and, his right being mine, this right of mine against myself is a phrase devoid of meaning?

Grotius and the rest find in war another origin for the so-called right of slavery. The victor having, as they hold, the right of killing the vanquished, the latter can buy back his life at the price of his liberty; and this convention is the more legitimate because it is to the advantage of both parties.

But it is clear that this supposed right to kill the conquered is by no means deducible from the state of war. Men, from the mere fact that, while they are living in their primitive independence, they have no mutual relations stable enough to constitute either the state of peace or the state of war, cannot be naturally enemies. War is constituted by a relation between things, and not between persons; and, as the state of war cannot arise out of simple personal relations, but only out of real relations, private war, or war of man with man, can exist neither in the state of nature, where there is no constant property, nor in the social state, where everything is under the authority of the laws.

Individual combats, duels and encounters, are acts which cannot constitute a state; while the private wars, authorised by the Establishments of Louis IX, King of France, and suspended by the Peace of God, are abuses of feudalism, in itself an absurd system if ever there was one, and contrary to the principles of natural right and to all good polity.

War then is a relation, not between man and man, but between State and State, and individuals are enemies only accidentally, not as men, nor even as citizens,[3] but as soldiers; not as members of their country, but as its defenders. Finally, each State can have for enemies only other States, and not men; for between things disparate in nature there can be no real relation.

Furthermore, this principle is in conformity with the established rules of all times and the constant practice of all civilised peoples. Declarations of war are intimations less to powers than to their subjects. The foreigner, whether king, individual, or people, who robs, kills or detains the subjects, without declaring war on the prince, is not an enemy, but a brigand. Even in real war, a just prince, while laying hands, in the enemy's country, on all that belongs to the public, respects the lives and goods of individuals: he respects rights on which his own are founded. The object of the war being the destruction of the hostile State, the other side has a right to kill its defenders, while they are bearing arms; but as soon as they lay them down and surrender, they cease to be enemies or instruments of the enemy, and become once more merely men, whose life no one has any right to take. Sometimes it is possible to kill the State without killing a single one of its members; and war gives no right which is not necessary to the gaining of its object. These principles are not those of Grotius: they are not based on the authority of poets, but derived from the nature of reality and based on reason.

The right of conquest has no foundation other than the right of the strongest. If war does not give the conqueror the right to massacre the conquered peoples, the right to enslave them cannot be based upon a right which does not exist. No one has a right to kill an enemy except when he cannot make him a slave, and the right to enslave him cannot therefore be derived from the right to kill him. It is accordingly an unfair exchange to make him buy at the price of his liberty his life, over which the victor holds no right. Is it not clear that there is a vicious circle in founding the right of life and death on the right of slavery, and the right of slavery on the right of life and death?

Even if we assume this terrible right to kill everybody, I maintain that a slave made in war, or a conquered people, is under no obligation to a master, except to obey him as far as he is compelled to do so. By taking an equivalent for his life, the victor has not done him a favour; instead of killing him without profit, he has killed him usefully. So far then is he from acquiring over him any authority in addition to that of force, that the state of war continues to subsist between them: their mutual relation is the effect of it, and the usage of the right of war does not imply a treaty of peace. A convention has indeed been made; but this convention, so far from destroying the state of war, presupposes its continuance.

So, from whatever aspect we regard the question, the right of slavery is null and void, not only as being illegitimate, but also because it is absurd and meaningless. The words *slave* and *right* contradict each other, and are mutually exclusive. It will always be equally foolish for a man to say to a man or to a people: "I make with you a convention wholly at your expense and wholly to my advantage; I shall keep it as long as I like, and you will keep it as long as I like."

That We Must Always Go Back to a First Convention

Even if I granted all that I have been refuting, the friends of despotism would be no better off. There will always be a great difference between subduing a multitude and ruling a society. Even if scattered individuals were successively enslaved by one man, however numerous they might be, I still see no more than a master and his slaves, and certainly not a people and its ruler; I see what may be termed an aggregation, but not an association; there is as yet neither public good nor body politic. The man in question, even if he has enslaved half the world, is still only an individual; his interest, apart from that of others, is still a purely private interest. If this same man comes to die, his empire, after him, remains scattered and without unity, as an oak falls and dissolves into a heap of ashes when the fire has consumed it.

A people, says Grotius, can give itself to a king. Then, according to Grotius, a people is a people before it gives itself. The gift is itself a civil act, and implies public deliberation. It would be better, before examining the act by which a people gives itself to a king, to examine that by which it has become a people; for this act, being necessarily prior to the other, is the true foundation of society.

Indeed, if there were no prior convention, where, unless the election were unanimous, would be the obligation on the minority to submit to the choice of the majority? How have a hundred men who wish for a master the right to vote on behalf of ten who do not? The law of majority voting is itself something established by convention, and presupposes unanimity, on one occasion at least.

The Social Compact

I suppose men to have reached the point at which the obstacles in the way of their preservation in the state of nature show their power of resistance to be greater than the resources at the disposal of each individual for his maintenance in that state. That primitive condition can then subsist no longer; and the human race would perish unless it changed its manner of existence.

But, as men cannot engender new forces, but only unite and direct existing ones, they have no other means of preserving themselves than the formation, by aggregation, of a sum of forces great enough to overcome the resistance. These they have to bring into play by means of a single motive power, and cause to act in concert.

This sum of forces can arise only where several persons come together: but, as the force and liberty of each man are the chief instruments of his self-preservation, how can he pledge them without harming his own interests, and neglecting the care he owes to himself? This difficulty, in its bearing on my present subject, may be stated in the following terms:

> The problem is to find a form of association which will defend and protect with the whole common force the person and goods of each associate, and in which each, while uniting himself with all, may still obey himself alone, and remain as free as before.

This is the fundamental problem of which the *Social Contract* provides the solution.

The clauses of this contract are so determined by the nature of the act that the slightest modification would make them vain and ineffective; so that, although they have perhaps never been formally set forth, they are everywhere the same and everywhere tacitly admitted and recognised, until, on the violation of the social compact, each regains his original rights and resumes his natural liberty, while losing the conventional liberty in favour of which he renounced it.

These clauses, properly understood, may be reduced to one – the total alienation of each associate, together with all his rights, to the whole community; for, in the first place, as each gives himself absolutely, the conditions are the same for all; and, this being so, no one has any interest in making them burdensome to others.

Moreover, the alienation being without reserve, the union is as perfect as it can be, and no associate has anything more to demand: for, if the individuals retained certain rights, as there would be no common superior to decide between them and the public, each, being on one point his own judge, would ask to be so on all; the state of nature would thus continue, and the association would necessarily become inoperative or tyrannical.

Finally, each man, in giving himself to all, gives himself to nobody; and as there is no associate over whom he does not acquire the same right as he yields others over himself, he gains an equivalent for everything he loses, and an increase of force for the preservation of what he has.

If then we discard from the social compact what is not of its essence, we shall find that it reduces itself to the following terms:

> Each of us puts his person and all his power in common under the supreme direction of the general will, and, in our corporate capacity, we receive each member as an indivisible part of the whole.

At once, in place of the individual personality of each contracting party, this act of association creates a moral and collective body, composed of as many members as the assembly contains votes, and receiving from this act its unity, its common identity, its life and its will. This public person, so formed by the union of all other persons formerly took the name of *city*,⁴ and now takes that of *Republic* or *body politic*; it is called by its members *State* when passive, *Sovereign* when active, and *Power* when compared with others like itself. Those who are associated in it take collectively the name of *people*, and severally are called *citizens*, as sharing in the sovereign power, and *subjects*, as being under the laws of the State. But these terms are often confused and taken one for another: it is enough to know how to distinguish them when they are being used with precision.

The Sovereign

This formula shows us that the act of association comprises a mutual undertaking between the public and the individuals, and that each individual, in making a contract, as we may say, with himself, is bound in a double capacity; as a member of the Sovereign he is bound to the individuals, and as a member of the State to the Sovereign. But the maxim of civil right, that no one is bound by undertaking made to himself, does not apply in this case; for there is a great difference between incurring an obligation to yourself and incurring one to a whole of which you form a part.

Attention must further be called to the fact that public deliberation, while competent to bind all the subjects to the Sovereign, because of the two different capacities in which each of them may be regarded, cannot, for the opposite reason, bind the Sovereign to itself; and that it is consequently against the nature of the body politic for the Sovereign to impose on itself a law which it cannot infringe. Being able to regard itself in only one capacity, it is in the position of an individual who makes a contract with himself; and this makes it clear that there neither is nor can be any kind of fundamental law binding on the body of the people – not even the social contract itself. This does not mean that the body politic cannot enter into undertakings with others, provided the contract is not infringed by them; for in relation to what is external to it, it becomes a simple being, an individual.

But the body politic or the Sovereign, drawing its being wholly from the sanctity of the contract, can never bind itself, even to an outsider, to do anything derogatory to the original act, for instance, to alienate any part of itself, or to submit to another Sovereign. Violation of the act by which it exists would be self-annihilation; and that which is itself nothing can create nothing.

As soon as this multitude is so united in one body, it is impossible to offend against one of the members without attacking the body, and still more to offend against the body without the members resenting it. Duty and interest therefore equally oblige the two contracting parties to give each other help; and the same men should seek to combine, in their double capacity, all the advantages dependent upon that capacity.

Again, the Sovereign, being formed wholly of the individuals who compose it, neither has nor can have any interest contrary to theirs; and consequently the sovereign power need give no guarantee to its subjects, because it is impossible for the body to wish to hurt all its members. We shall also see later on that it cannot hurt any in particular. The Sovereign, merely by virtue of what it is, is always what it should be.

This, however, is not the case with the relation of the subjects to the Sovereign, which, despite the common interest, would have no security that they would fulfil their undertakings, unless it found means to assure itself of their fidelity.

In fact, each individual, as a man, may have a particular will contrary or dissimilar to the general will which he has as a citizen. His particular interest may speak to him quite differently from the common interest: his absolute and naturally independent existence may make him look upon what he owes to the common cause as a gratuitous contribution, the loss of which will do less harm to others than the payment of it is burdensome to himself; and, regarding the moral person which constitutes the State as a *persona ficta*, because not a man, he may wish to enjoy the rights of citizenship without being ready to fulfil the duties of a subject. The continuance of such an injustice could not but prove the undoing of the body politic.

In order then that the social compact may not be an empty formula, it tacitly includes the undertaking, which alone can give force to the rest, that whoever refuses to obey the general will shall be compelled to do so by the whole body. This means nothing less than that he will be forced to be free; for this is the condition which, by giving each citizen to his country, secures him against all personal dependence. In this lies the key to the working of the political machine; this alone legitimises civil undertakings, which, without it, would be absurd, tyrannical, and liable to the most frightful abuses.

The Civil State

The passage from the state of nature to the civil state produces a very remarkable change in man, by substituting justice for instinct in his conduct, and giving his actions the morality they had formerly lacked. Then only, when the voice of duty takes the place of physical impulses and right of appetite, does man, who so far had considered only himself, find that he is forced to act on different principles, and to consult his reason before listening to his inclinations. Although, in this state, he deprives himself of some advantages which he got from nature, he gains in return others so great, his faculties are so stimulated and developed, his ideas so extended, his feelings so ennobled, and his whole soul so uplifted, that, did not the abuses of this new condition often degrade him below that which he left, he would be bound to bless continually the happy moment which took him from it for ever, and, instead of a stupid and unimaginative animal, made him an intelligent being and a man.

Let us draw up the whole account in terms easily commensurable. What man loses by the social contract is his natural liberty and an unlimited right to everything he tries to get and succeeds in getting; what he gains is civil liberty and the proprietorship of all he possesses. If we are to avoid mistake in weighing one against the other, we must clearly distinguish natural liberty, which is bounded only by the strength of the individual, from civil liberty, which is limited by the general will; and possession, which is merely the effect of force or the right of the first occupier, from property, which can be founded only on a positive title.

We might, over and above all this, add, to what man acquires in the civil state, moral liberty, which alone makes him truly master of himself; for the mere impulse of appetite is slavery, while obedience to a law which we prescribe to ourselves is liberty. But I have already said too much on this head, and the philosophical meaning of the word liberty does not now concern us.

Real Property

Each member of the community gives himself to it, at the moment of its foundation, just as he is, with all the resources at his command, including the goods he possesses. This act does not make possession, in changing hands, change its nature, and become property in the hands of the Sovereign; but, as the forces of the city are incomparably greater than those of an individual, public possession is also, in fact, stronger and more irrevocable, without being any more legitimate, at any rate from the point of view of foreigners. For the State, in relation to its members, is master of all their goods by the social contract, which, within the State, is the basis of all rights; but, in relation to other powers, it is so only by the right of the first occupier, which it holds from its members.

The right of the first occupier, though more real than the right of the strongest, becomes a real right only when the right of property has already been established. Every man has naturally a right to everything he needs; but the positive act which makes him proprietor of one thing excludes him from everything else. Having his share, he ought to keep to it, and can have no further right against the community. This is why the right of the first occupier, which in the state of nature is so weak, claims the respect of every man in civil society. In this right we are respecting not so much what belongs to another as what does not belong to ourselves.

In general, to establish the right of the first occupier over a plot of ground, the following conditions are necessary: first, the land must not yet be inhabited; secondly, a man must occupy only the amount he needs for his subsistence; and, in the third place, possession must be taken, not by an empty ceremony, but by labour and cultivation, the only sign of proprietorship that should be respected by others, in default of a legal title.

In granting the right of first occupancy to necessity and labour, are we not really stretching it as far as it can go? Is it possible to leave such a right unlimited? Is it to be enough to set foot on a plot of common ground, in order to be able to call yourself at once the master of it? Is it to be enough that a man has the strength to expel others for a moment, in order to establish his right to prevent them from ever returning? How can a man or a people seize an immense territory and keep it from the rest of the world except by a punishable usurpation, since all others are being robbed, by such an act, of the place of habitation and the means of subsistence which nature gave them in common? When Nunez Balboa, standing on the sea-shore, took possession of the South Seas and the whole of South America in the name of the crown of Castile, was that enough to dispossess all their actual inhabitants, and to shut out from them all the princes of the world? On such a showing, these ceremonies are idly multiplied, and the Catholic King need only take possession all at once, from his apartment, of the whole universe, merely making a subsequent reservation about what was already in the possession of other princes.

We can imagine how the lands of individuals, where they were contiguous and came to be united, became the public territory, and how the right of Sovereignty, extending from the subjects over the lands they held, became at once real and personal. The possessors were thus made more dependent, and the forces at their command used to guarantee their fidelity. The advantage of this does not seem to have been felt by ancient monarchs, who called themselves Kings of the Persians, Scythians, or Macedonians, and seemed to regard themselves more as rulers of men than as masters of a country. Those of the present day more cleverly call themselves Kings of France, Spain, England, etc.: thus holding the land, they are quite confident of holding the inhabitants.

The peculiar fact about this alienation is that, in taking over the goods of individuals, the community, so far from despoiling them, only assures them legitimate possession, and changes usurpation into a true right and enjoyment into proprietorship. Thus the possessors, being regarded as depositories of the public good, and having their rights respected by all the members of the State and maintained against foreign aggression by all its forces, have, by a cession which benefits both the public and still more themselves, acquired, so to speak, all that they gave up. This paradox may easily be explained by the distinction between the rights which the Sovereign and the proprietor have over the same estate, as we shall see later on.

It may also happen that men begin to unite one with another before they possess anything, and that, subsequently occupying a tract of country which is enough for all, they enjoy it in common, or share it out among themselves, either equally or according to a scale fixed by the Sovereign. However the acquisition be made, the right which each individual has to his own estate is always subordinate to the right which the community has over all: without this, there would be neither stability in the social tie, nor real force in the exercise of Sovereignty.

I shall end this chapter and this book by remarking on a fact on which the whole social system should rest: i.e., that, instead of destroying natural inequality, the fundamental compact substitutes, for such physical inequality as nature may have set up between men, an equality that is moral and legitimate, and that men, who may be unequal in strength or intelligence, become every one equal by convention and legal right.[5]

NOTES

1 "Learned inquiries into public right are often only the history of past abuses; and troubling to study them too deeply is a profitless infatuation" (*Essay on the Interests of France in Relation to its Neighbours*, by the Marquis d'Argenson). This is exactly what Grotius has done.
2 See a short treatise of Plutarch's entitled *That Animals Reason*.
3 The Romans, who understood and respected the right of war more than any other nation on earth, carried their scruples on this head so far that a citizen was not allowed to serve as a volunteer without engaging himself expressly against the enemy, and against such and such an enemy by name. A legion in which the younger Cato was seeing his first service under Popilius having been reconstructed, the elder Cato wrote to Popilius that, if he wished his son to continue serving under him, he must administer to him a new military oath, because, the first having been annulled, he was no longer able to bear arms against the enemy. The same Cato wrote to his son telling him to take great care not to go into battle before taking this new oath. I know that the siege of Clusium and other isolated events can be quoted against me; but I am citing laws and customs. The Romans are the people that least often transgressed its laws; and no other people has had such good ones.
4 The real meaning of this word has been almost wholly lost in modern times; most people mistake a town for a city, and a townsman for a citizen. They do not know that houses make a town, but citizens a city. The same mistake long ago cost the Carthaginians dear.

I have never read of the title of citizens being given to the subjects of any prince, not even the ancient Macedonians or the English of today, though they are nearer liberty than any one else. The French alone everywhere familiarly adopt the name of citizens, because, as can be seen from their dictionaries, they have no idea of its meaning; otherwise they would be guilty in usurping it, of the crime of *lèse-majesté*: among them, the name expresses a virtue, and not a right. When Bodin spoke of our citizens and townsmen, he fell into a bad blunder in taking the one class for the other. M. d'Alembert has avoided the error, and, in his article on Geneva, has clearly distinguished the four orders of men (or even five, counting mere foreigners) who dwell in our town, of which two only compose the Republic. No other French writer, to my knowledge, has understood the real meaning of the word citizen.

5 Under bad governments, this equality is only apparent and illusory: it serves only to keep the pauper in his poverty and the rich man in the position he has usurped. In fact, laws are always of use to those who possess and harmful to those who have nothing: from which it follows that the social state is advantageous to men only when all have something and none too much.

Chapter 3

What is Enlightenment? [1784]

Immanuel Kant

Enlightenment is man's leaving his self-caused immaturity. Immaturity is the incapacity to use one's intelligence without the guidance of another. Such immaturity is self-caused if it is not caused by lack of intelligence, but by lack of determination and courage to use one's intelligence without being guided by another. *Sapere Aude!* (Have the courage to use your own intelligence!) is therefore the motto of the enlightenment.

Through laziness and cowardice a large part of mankind, even after nature has freed them from alien guidance, gladly remain immature. It is because of laziness and cowardice that it is so easy for others to usurp the role of guardians. It is so comfortable to be a minor! If I have a book which provides meaning for me, a pastor who has conscience for me, a doctor who will judge my diet for me and so on, then I do not need to exert myself. I do not have any need to think; if I can pay, others will take over the tedious job for me. The guardians who have kindly undertaken the supervision will see to it that by far the largest part of mankind, including the entire "beautiful sex," should consider the step into maturity, not only as difficult but as very dangerous.

After having made their domestic animals dumb and having carefully prevented these quiet creatures from daring to take any step beyond the lead-strings to which they have fastened them, these guardians then show them the danger which threatens them, should they attempt to walk alone. Now this danger is not really so very great; for they would presumably learn to walk after some stumbling. However, an example of this kind intimidates and frightens people out of all further attempts.

Kant, Immanuel, "What Is Enlightenment?" pp. 132–139 from Immanuel Kant, *The Philosophy of Kant*, ed. Carl J. Friedrich. New York: Random House, The Modern Library, 1949 Copyright © 1949 by Random House, Inc. Used by permission of Random House, Inc.

Classical Sociological Theory, Third Edition. Edited by Craig Calhoun, Joseph Gerteis, James Moody, Steven Pfaff, and Indermohan Virk. Editorial material and organization © 2012 John Wiley & Sons, Ltd. Published 2012 by John Wiley & Sons, Ltd.

It is difficult for the isolated individual to work himself out of the immaturity which has become almost natural for him. He has even become fond of it and for the time being is incapable of employing his own intelligence, because he has never been allowed to make the attempt. Statutes and formulas, these mechanical tools of a serviceable use, or rather misuse, of his natural faculties, are the ankle-chains of a continuous immaturity. Whoever threw it off would make an uncertain jump over the smallest trench because he is not accustomed to such free movement. Therefore there are only a few who have pursued a firm path and have succeeded in escaping from immaturity by their own cultivation of the mind.

But it is more nearly possible for a public to enlighten itself: this is even inescapable if only the public is given its freedom. For there will always be some people who think for themselves, even among the self-appointed guardians of the great mass who, after having thrown off the yoke of immaturity themselves, will spread about them the spirit of a reasonable estimate of their own value and of the need for every man to think for himself. It is strange that the very public, which had previously been put under this yoke by the guardians, forces the guardians thereafter to keep it there if it is stirred up by a few of its guardians who are themselves incapable of all enlightenment. It is thus very harmful to plant prejudices, because they come back to plague those very people who themselves (or whose predecessors) have been the originators of these prejudices. Therefore a public can only arrive at enlightenment slowly. Through revolution, the abandonment of personal despotism may be engendered and the end of profit-seeking and domineering oppression may occur, but never a true reform of the state of mind. Instead, new prejudices, just like the old ones, will serve as the guiding reins of the great, unthinking mass.

All that is required for this enlightenment is *freedom*; and particularly the least harmful of all that may be called freedom, namely, the freedom for man to make *public use* of his reason in all matters. But I hear people clamor on all sides: Don't argue! The officer says: Don't argue, drill! The tax collector: Don't argue, pay! The pastor: Don't argue, believe! (Only a single lord in the world says: *Argue*, as much as you want to and about what you please, *but obey*!) Here we have restrictions on freedom everywhere. Which restriction is hampering enlightenment, and which does not, or even promotes it? I answer: The *public use* of a man's reason must be free at all times, and this alone can bring enlightenment among men: while the private use of a man's reason may often be restricted rather narrowly without thereby unduly hampering the progress of enlightenment.

I mean by the public use of one's reason, the use which a scholar makes of it before the entire reading public. Private use I call the use which he may make of this reason in a civic post or office. For some affairs which are in the interest of the commonwealth a certain mechanism is necessary through which some members of the commonwealth must remain purely passive in order that an artificial agreement with the government for the public good be maintained or so that at least the destruction of the good be prevented. In such a situation it is not permitted to argue; one must obey. But in so far as this unit of the machine considers himself as a member of the entire commonwealth, in fact even of world society; in other words, he considers himself in the quality of a scholar who is addressing the true public through his writing, he may indeed argue without the affairs suffering for which he is employed partly as a passive member. Thus it would be very harmful if an officer who, given an order by his superior, should start, while in the service, to argue concerning the utility or appropriateness of that command. He must obey, but he cannot equitably be prevented from making observations as a scholar concerning the mistakes in the military service nor from submitting these to the public for its judgment. The citizen cannot refuse to pay the taxes imposed upon him. Indeed, a rash criticism of such taxes, if they are the ones to be paid by him, may be punished as a scandal which might cause general resistance. But the same man does not act contrary to the duty of a citizen if, as a scholar, he utters publicly his thoughts against the undesirability or even the injustice of such taxes. Likewise a clergyman is obliged to teach his pupils and his congregation according to the doctrine of the church which he serves, for he has been accepted on that condition. But as a scholar, he has full freedom, in fact, even the obligation, to communicate to the public all his diligently examined and well-intentioned thoughts concerning erroneous points in that doctrine and concerning proposals regarding the better institution of religious and ecclesiastical matters. There is nothing in this for which the conscience could be blamed. For what he teaches according to his office as one authorized by the church, he presents as something in regard to which he has no latitude to teach according to his own preference. ... He will say: Our church teaches this or that, these are the proofs which are employed for it. In this way he derives all possible practical benefit for his congregation from rules which he would not himself subscribe to with full conviction. But he may nevertheless undertake the presentation of these rules because it is not entirely inconceivable that truth may be contained in them. In any case, there is nothing directly contrary to inner religion to be found in such doctrines. For, should he believe that the latter was not the case he could not administer his office in good conscience; he would have to resign it. Therefore the use which an employed teacher makes of his reason before his congregation is merely a private use since such a gathering is always only domestic, no matter how large. As a priest (a member of an organization) he is not free and ought not to be, since he is executing someone else's mandate. On the other hand, the scholar speaking through his writings to the true public which is the world, like the clergyman making public use of his reason, enjoys an unlimited freedom to employ his own reason and to speak in his own person. For to suggest that the guardians of the people in spiritual matters should always be immature minors is a non-sense which would mean perpetuating forever existing non-sense.

But should a society of clergymen, for instance an ecclesiastical assembly, be entitled to commit itself by oath to a certain unalterable doctrine in order to perpetuate an endless guardianship over each of its members and through them over the people? I answer that this is quite inconceivable. Such a contract which would be concluded in order to keep humanity forever from all further enlightenment is absolutely impossible, even should it be confirmed by the highest authority through parliaments and the most solemn peace treaties. An age cannot conclude a pact and take an oath upon it to commit the succeeding age to a situation in which it would be impossible for the latter to enlarge even its most important knowledge, to eliminate error and altogether to progress in enlightenment. Such a thing would be a crime against human nature, the original destiny of which consists in such progress. Succeeding generations are entirely justified in discarding such decisions as unauthorized and criminal. The touchstone of all this to be agreed upon as a law for people is to be found in the question whether a people could impose such a law upon itself. Now it might be possible to introduce a certain order for a definite short period as if in anticipation of a better order. This would be true if one permitted at the same time each citizen and especially the clergyman to make his criticisms in his quality as a scholar. ... In the meantime, the provisional order might continue until the insight into the particular matter in hand has publicly progressed to the point where through a combination of voices (although not, perhaps, of all) a proposal may be brought to the crown. Thus those congregations would be protected which had agreed to (a changed religious institution) according to their own ideas and better understanding, without hindering those who desired to allow the old institutions to continue. ...

A man may postpone for himself, but only for a short time, enlightening himself regarding what he ought to know. But to resign from such enlightenment altogether either for his own person or even more for his descendants means to violate and to trample underfoot the sacred rights of mankind. Whatever a people may not decide for themselves, a monarch may even less decide for the people, for his legislative reputation rests upon his uniting the entire people's will in his own. If the monarch will only see to it that every true or imagined reform (of religion) fits in with the civil order, he had best let his subjects do what they consider necessary for the sake of their salvation; that is not his affair. His only concern is to prevent one subject from hindering another by force, to work according to each subject's best ability to determine and to promote his salvation. In fact, it detracts from his majesty if he interferes in such matters and subjects to governmental supervision the writings by which his subjects seek to clarify their ideas (concerning religion). This is true whether he does it from his own highest insight, for in this case he exposes himself to the reproach: *Caesar non est supra grammaticos*; it is even more true when he debases his highest power to support the spiritual despotism of some tyrants in his state against the rest of his subjects.

The question may now be put: Do we live at present in an enlightened age? The answer is: No, but in an age of enlightenment. Much still prevents men from being placed in a position or even being placed into position to use their own minds securely and well in matters of religion. But we do have very definite indications that this field of endeavor is being opened up for men to work freely and reduce gradually the hindrances preventing a general enlightenment and an escape from self-caused immaturity. In this sense, this age is the age of enlightenment and the age of Frederick (the Great).

A prince should not consider it beneath him to declare that he believes it to be his duty not to prescribe anything to his subjects in matters of religion but to leave to them complete freedom in such things. In other words, a prince who refuses the conceited title of being "tolerant" is himself enlightened. He deserves to be praised by his grateful contemporaries and descendants as the man who first freed humankind of immaturity, at least as far as the government is concerned and who permitted everyone to use his own reason in all matters of conscience. Under his rule, venerable clergymen could, regardless of their official duty, set forth their opinions and views even though they differ from the accepted doctrine here and there; they could do so in the quality of scholars, freely and publicly. The same holds even more true of every other person who is not thus restricted by official duty. This spirit of freedom is spreading even outside (the country of Frederick the Great) to places where it has to struggle with the external hindrances imposed by a government which misunderstands its own position. For an example is illuminating them which shows that such freedom (public discussion) need not cause the slightest worry regarding public security and the unity of the commonwealth. Men raise themselves by and by out of backwardness if one does not purposely invent artifices to keep them down.

I have emphasized the main point of enlightenment, that is of man's release from his self-caused immaturity, primarily *in matters of religion*. I have done this because our rulers have no interest in playing the guardian of their subjects in matters of arts and sciences. Furthermore immaturity in matters of religion is not only most noxious but also most dishonorable. But the point of view of a head of state who favors freedom in the arts and sciences goes even farther; for he understands that there is no danger in legislation permitting his subjects to make *public* use of their own reason and to submit *publicly* their thoughts regarding a better framing of such laws together with a frank criticism of existing *legislation*. We have a shining example of this; no prince excels him whom we admire. Only he who is himself enlightened does not fear spectres when he at the same time has a well-disciplined army at his disposal as a guarantee of public peace. Only he can say what (the ruler of a) free state dare not say: *Argue as much as you want and about whatever you want but obey*! Thus we see here as elsewhere an unexpected turn in human affairs just as we observe that almost everything therein is paradoxical. A great degree of civic freedom seems to be advantageous for the freedom of the *spirit* of the people and yet it establishes impassable limits. A lesser degree of such civic freedom provides additional space in which the spirit of a people can develop to its full capacity. Therefore nature has cherished, within its hard shell, the germ of the inclination and need for free *thought*. This free thought gradually acts upon the mind of the people and they gradually become more capable of acting in freedom. Eventually, the government is also influenced by this free thought and thereby it treats man, who is now more than a machine, according to this dignity.

Chapter 4

The Wealth of Nations [1776]
Adam Smith

Of the Division of Labour

The greatest improvement in the productive powers of labour, and the greater part of the skill, dexterity, and judgment with which it is any where directed, or applied, seem to have been the effects of the division of labour.

The effects of the division of labour, in the general business of society, will be more easily understood, by considering in what manner it operates in some particular manufactures. It is commonly supposed to be carried furthest in some very trifling ones; not perhaps that it really is carried further in them than in others of more importance: but in those trifling manufactures which are destined to supply the small wants of but a small number of people, the whole number of workmen must necessarily be small; and those employed in every different branch of the work can often be collected into the same workhouse, and placed at once under the view of the spectator. In those great manufactures, on the contrary, which are destined to supply the great wants of the great body of the people, every different branch of the work employs so great a number of workmen, that it is impossible to collect them all into the same workhouse. We can seldom see more, at one time, than those employed in one single branch. Though in such manufactures, therefore, the work may really be divided into a much greater number of parts, than in those of a more trifling nature, the division is not near so obvious, and has accordingly been much less observed.

Smith, Adam, "Of the Division of Labor," from Adam Smith, *The Wealth of Nations*, 1776

Classical Sociological Theory, Third Edition. Edited by Craig Calhoun, Joseph Gerteis, James Moody, Steven Pfaff, and Indermohan Virk. Editorial material and organization © 2012 John Wiley & Sons, Ltd. Published 2012 by John Wiley & Sons, Ltd.

To take an example, therefore, from a very trifling manufacture; but one in which the division of labour has been very often taken notice of, the trade of the pin-maker; a workman not educated to this business (which the division of labour has rendered a distinct trade), nor acquainted with the use of the machinery employed in it (to the invention of which the same division of labour has probably given occasion), could scarce, perhaps, with his utmost industry, make one pin in a day, and certainly could not make twenty. But in the way in which this business is now carried on, not only the whole work is a peculiar trade, but it is divided into a number of branches, of which the greater part are likewise peculiar trades. One man draws out the wire, another straights it, a third cuts it, a fourth points it, a fifth grinds it at the top for receiving the head; to make the head requires two or three distinct operations; to put it on, is a peculiar business, to whiten the pins is another; it is even a trade by itself to put them into the paper; and the important business of making a pin is, in this manner, divided into about eighteen distinct operations, which, in some manufactories, are all performed by distinct hands, though in others the same man will sometimes perform two or three of them. I have seen a small manufactory of this kind where ten men only were employed, and where some of them consequently performed two or three distinct operations. But though they were very poor, and therefore but indifferently accommodated with the necessary machinery, they could, when they exerted themselves, make among them about twelve pounds of pins in a day. There are in a pound upwards of four thousand pins of a middling size. Those ten persons, therefore, could make among them upwards of forty-eight thousand pins in a day. Each person, therefore, making a tenth part of forty-eight thousand pins, might be considered as making four thousand eight hundred pins in a day. But if they had all wrought separately and independently, and without any of them having been educated to this peculiar business, they certainly could not each of them have made twenty, perhaps not one pin in a day; that is, certainly, not the two hundred and fortieth, perhaps not the four thousand eight hundredth part of what they are at present capable of performing, in consequence of a proper division and combination of their different operations.

In every other art and manufacture, the effects of the division of labour are similar to what they are in this very trifling one; though, in many of them, the labour can neither be so much subdivided, nor reduced to so great a simplicity of operation. The division of labour, however, so far as it can be introduced, occasions, in every art, a proportionable increase of the productive powers of labour. The separation of different trades and employments from one another, seems to have taken place, in consequence of this advantage. This separation too is generally carried furthest in those countries which enjoy the highest degree of industry and improvement; what is the work of one man in a rude state of society, being generally that of several in an improved one. In every improved society, the farmer is generally nothing but a farmer; the manufacturer, nothing but a manufacturer. The labour too which is necessary to produce any one complete manufacture, is almost always divided among a great number of hands. How many different trades are employed in each branch of the linen and woollen manufactures, from the growers of the flax and the wool, to the bleachers and smoothers of the linen, or to the dyers and dressers of the cloth! The nature of agriculture, indeed, does not admit of so many subdivisions of labour, nor of so complete a separation of one business from another, as manufactures. It is impossible to separate so entirely, the business of the grazier from that of the corn-farmer, as the trade of the carpenter is commonly separated from that of the smith. The spinner is almost always a distinct person from the weaver; but the ploughman, the harrower, the sower of the seed, and the reaper of the corn, are often the same. The occasions for those different sorts of labour returning with the different seasons of the year, it is impossible that one man should be constantly employed in any one of them. This impossibility of making so complete and entire a separation of all the different branches of labour employed in agriculture, is perhaps the reason why the improvement of the productive powers of labour in this art, does not always keep pace with their improvement in manufactures. The most opulent nations, indeed, generally excel all their neighbours in agriculture as well as in manufactures; but they are commonly more distinguished by their superiority in the latter than in the former. Their lands are in general better cultivated, and having more labour and expence bestowed upon them, produce more in proportion to the extent and natural fertility of the ground. But this superiority of produce is seldom much more than in proportion to the superiority of labour and expence. In agriculture, the labour of the rich country is not always much more productive than that of the poor; or, at least, it is never so much more productive, as it commonly is in manufactures. The corn of the rich country, therefore, will not always, in the same degree of goodness, come cheaper to market than that of the poor. The corn of Poland, in the same degree of goodness, is as cheap as that of France, notwithstanding the superior opulence and improvement of the latter country. The corn of France is, in the corn provinces, fully as good, and in most years nearly about the same price with the corn of England, though, in opulence and improvement, France is perhaps inferior to England. The corn-lands of England, however, are better cultivated than those of France, and the corn-lands of France are said to be much better cultivated than those of Poland. But though the poor country, notwithstanding the inferiority of its cultivation, can, in some measure, rival the rich in the cheapness and goodness of its corn, it can pretend to no such competition in its manufactures; at least if those manufactures suit the soil, climate, and situation of the rich country. The silks of France are better and cheaper than those of England, because the silk manufacture, at least under the present high duties upon the importation of raw silk, does not so well suit the climate of England as that of France. But the hard-ware and the coarse woollens of England are beyond all comparison superior to those of France, and much cheaper too in the same degree of goodness. In Poland there are said to be scarce any manufactures of any kind, a few of those coarser household manufactures excepted, without which no country can well subsist.

This great increase of the quantity of work, which, in consequence of the division of labour, the same number of people are capable of performing, is owing to three different circumstances; first, to the increase of dexterity in every particular workman; secondly, to the saving of the time which is commonly lost in passing from one species of work to another; and lastly, to the invention of a great number of machines which facilitate and abridge labour, and enable one man to do the work of many.

First, the improvement of the dexterity of the workman necessarily increases the quantity of the work he can perform; and the division of labour, by reducing every man's business to some one simple operation, and by making this operation the sole employment of his life, necessarily increases very much the dexterity of the workman. A common smith, who, though accustomed to handle the hammer, has never been used to make nails, if upon some particular occasion he is obliged to attempt it, will scarce, I am assured, be able to make above two or three hundred nails in a day, and those too very bad ones. A smith who has been accustomed to make nails, but whose sole or principal business has not been that of a nailer, can seldom with his utmost diligence make more than eight hundred or a thousand nails in a day. I have seen several boys under twenty years of age who had never exercised any other trade but that of making nails, and who, when they exerted themselves, could make, each of them, upwards of two thousand three hundred nails in a day. The making of a nail, however, is by no means one of the simplest operations. The same person blows the bellows, stirs or mends the fire as there is occasion, heats the iron, and forges every part of the nail: In forging the head too he is obliged to change his tools. The different operations into which the making of a pin, or of a metal button, is subdivided, are all of them much more simple, and the dexterity of the person, of whose life it has been the sole business to perform them, is usually much greater. The rapidity with which some of the operations of those manufactures are performed, exceeds what the human hand could, by those who had never seen them, be supposed capable of acquiring.

Secondly, the advantage which is gained by saving the time commonly lost in passing from one sort of work to another, is much greater than we should at first view be apt to imagine it. It is impossible to pass very quickly from one kind of work to another, that is carried on in a different place, and with quite different tools. A country weaver, who cultivates a small farm, must lose a good deal of time in passing from his loom to the field, and from the field to his loom. When the two trades can be carried on in the same workhouse, the loss of time is no doubt much less. It is even in this case, however, very considerable. A man commonly saunters a little in turning his hand from one sort of employment to another. When he first begins the new work he is seldom very keen and hearty; his mind, as they say, does not go to it, and for some time he rather trifles than applies to good purpose. The habit of sauntering and of indolent careless application, which is naturally, or rather necessarily acquired by every country workman who is obliged to change his work and his tools every half hour, and to apply his hand in twenty different ways almost every day of his life; renders him almost always slothful and lazy, and incapable of any vigorous application even on the most pressing occasions. Independent, therefore, of this deficiency in point of dexterity, this cause alone must always reduce considerably the quantity of work which he is capable of performing.

Thirdly, and lastly, every body must be sensible how much labour is facilitated and abridged by the application of proper machinery. It is unnecessary to give any example. I shall only observe, therefore, that the invention of all those machines by which labour is so much facilitated and abridged, seems to have been originally owing to the division of labour. Men are much more likely to discover easier and readier methods of attaining any object, when the whole attention of their minds is directed towards that single object, than when it is dissipated among a great variety of things. But in consequence of the division of labour, the whole of every man's attention comes naturally to be directed towards some one very simple object. It is naturally to be expected, therefore, that some one or other of those who are employed in each particular branch of labour should soon find out easier and readier methods of performing their own particular work, wherever the nature of it admits of such improvement. A great part of the machines made use of in those manufactures in which labour is most subdivided, were originally the inventions of common workmen, who, being each of them employed in some very simple operation, naturally turned their thoughts towards finding out easier and readier methods of performing it. Whoever has been much accustomed to visit such manufactures, must frequently have been shewn very pretty machines, which were the inventions of such workmen, in order to facilitate and quicken their own particular part of the work. In the first fire-engines, a boy was constantly employed to open and shut alternately the communication between the boiler and the cylinder, according as the piston either ascended or descended. One of those boys, who loved to play with his companions, observed that, by tying a string from the handle of the valve which opened this communication to another part of the machine, the valve would open and shut without his assistance, and leave him at liberty to divert himself with his play-fellows. One of the greatest improvements that has been made upon this machine, since it was first invented, was in this manner the discovery of a boy who wanted to save his own labour.

All the improvements in machinery, however, have by no means been the inventions of those who had occasion to use the machines. Many improvements have been made by the ingenuity of the makers of the machines, when to make them became the business of a peculiar trade; and some by that of those who are called philosophers or men of speculation, whose trade it is not to do any thing, but to observe every thing; and who, upon that account, are often capable of combining together the powers of the most distant and dissimilar objects. In the progress of society, philosophy or speculation becomes, like every other employment, the principal or sole trade and occupation of a particular class of citizens. Like every other employment too, it is subdivided into a great number of different branches, each of which affords occupation to a peculiar tribe or class of philosophers; and this subdivision of employment in philosophy, as well as in every other business, improves dexterity, and saves time. Each individual becomes more expert in his own peculiar branch, more work is done upon the whole, and the quantity of science is considerably increased by it.

It is the great multiplication of the productions of all the different arts, in consequence of the division of labour, which occasions, in a well-governed society, that universal opulence which extends itself to the lowest ranks of the people. Every workman has a great quantity of his own work to dispose of beyond what he himself has occasion for; and every other workman being exactly in the same situation, he is enabled to exchange a great quantity of his own goods for a great quantity, or, what comes to the same thing, for the price of a great quantity of theirs. He supplies them abundantly with what they have occasion for, and they accommodate him as amply with what he has occasion for, and a general plenty diffuses itself through all the different ranks of the society.

Observe the accommodation of the most common artificer or day-labourer in a civilized and thriving country, and you will perceive that the number of people of whose industry a part, though but a small part, has been employed in procuring him this accommodation, exceeds all computation. The woollen coat, for example, which covers the day-labourer, as coarse and rough as it may appear, is the produce of the joint labour of a great multitude of workmen. The shepherd, the sorter of the wool, the wool-comber or carder, the dyer, the scribbler, the spinner, the weaver, the fuller, the dresser, with many others, must all join their different arts in order to complete even this homely production. How many merchants and carriers, besides, must have been employed in transporting the materials from some of those workmen to others who often live in a very distant part of the country! How much commerce and navigation in particular, how many ship-builders, sailors, sail-makers, rope-makers, must have been employed in order to bring together the different drugs made use of by the dyer, which often come from the remotest corners of the world! What a variety of labour too is necessary in order to produce the tools of the meanest of those workmen! To say nothing of such complicated machines as the ship of the sailor, the mill of the fuller, or even the loom of the weaver, let us consider only what a variety of labour is requisite in order to form that very simple machine, the shears with which the shepherd clips the wool. The miner, the builder of the furnace for smelting the ore, the feller of the timber, the burner of the charcoal to be made use of in the smelting-house, the brick-maker, the brick-layer, the workmen who attend the furnace, the mill-wright, the forger, the smith, must all of them join their different arts in order to produce them. Were we to examine, in the same manner, all the different parts of his dress and household furniture, the coarse linen shirt which he wears next his skin, the shoes which cover his feet, the bed which he lies on, and all the different parts which compose it, the kitchen-grate at which he prepares his victuals, the coals which he makes use of for that purpose, dug from the bowels of the earth, and brought to him perhaps by a long sea and a long land carriage, all the other utensils of his kitchen, all the furniture of his table, the knives and forks, the earthen or pewter plates upon which he serves up and divides his victuals, the different hands employed in preparing his bread and his beer, the glass window which lets in the heat and the light, and keeps out the wind and the rain, with all the knowledge and art requisite for preparing that beautiful and happy invention, without which these northern parts of the world could scarce have afforded a very comfortable habitation, together with the tools of all the different workmen employed in producing those different conveniencies; if we examine, I say, all these things, and consider what a variety of labour is employed about each of them, we shall be sensible that without the assistance and co-operation of many thousands, the very meanest person in a civilized country could not be provided, even according to, what we very falsely imagine, the easy and simple manner in which he is commonly accommodated. Compared, indeed, with the more extravagant luxury of the great, his accommodation must no doubt appear extremely simple and easy; and yet it may be true, perhaps, that the accommodation of an European prince does not always so much exceed that of an industrious and frugal peasant, as the accommodation of the latter exceeds that of many an African king, the absolute master of the lives and liberties of ten thousand naked savages.

Of the Principle Which Gives Occasion to the Division of Labour

This division of labour, from which so many advantages are derived, is not originally the effect of any human wisdom, which foresees and intends that general opulence to which it gives occasion. It is the necessary, though very slow and gradual, consequence of a certain propensity in human nature which has in view no such extensive utility; the propensity to truck, barter, and exchange one thing for another.

Whether this propensity be one of those original principles in human nature, of which no further account can be given; or whether, as seems more probable, it be the necessary consequence of the faculties of reason and speech, it belongs not to our present subject to enquire. It is common to all men, and to be found in no other race of animals, which seem to know neither this nor any other species of contracts. Two greyhounds, in running down the same hare, have sometimes the appearance of acting in some sort of concert. Each turns her towards his companion, or endeavours to intercept her when his companion turns her towards himself. This, however, is not the effect of any contract, but of the accidental concurrence of their passions in the same object at that particular time. Nobody ever saw a dog make a fair and deliberate exchange of one bone for another with another dog. Nobody ever saw one animal by its gestures and natural cries signify to another, this is mine, that yours; I am willing to give this for that. When an animal wants to obtain something either of a man or of another animal, it has no other means of persuasion but to gain the favour of those whose service it requires. A puppy fawns upon its dam, and a spaniel endeavours by a thousand attractions to engage the attention of its master who is at dinner, when it wants to be fed by him. Man sometimes uses the same arts with his brethren, and when he has no other means of engaging them to act according to his inclinations, endeavours by every servile and fawning attention to obtain their good will. He has not time, however, to do this upon every occasion. In civilized society he stands at all times in need of the co-operation and assistance of great multitudes, while his whole life is scarce sufficient to gain the friendship of a few persons. In almost every other race of animals each individual, when it is grown up to maturity, is entirely independent, and in its natural state has occasion for the assistance of no other living creature. But man has almost constant occasion for the help of his brethren, and it is in vain for him to expect it from their benevolence only. He will be more likely to prevail if he can interest their self-love in his favour, and shew them that it is for their own advantage to do for him what he requires of them. Whoever offers to another a bargain of any kind, proposes to do this. Give me that which I want, and you shall have this which you want, is the meaning of every such offer; and it is in this manner that we obtain from one another the far greater part of those good offices which we stand in need of. It is not from the benevolence of the butcher, the brewer, or the baker, that we expect our dinner, but from their regard to their own interest. We address ourselves, not to their humanity but to their self-love, and never talk to them of our own necessities but of their advantages. Nobody but a beggar chuses to depend chiefly upon the benevolence of his fellow-citizens. Even a beggar does not depend upon it entirely. The charity of well-disposed people, indeed, supplies him with the whole fund of his subsistence. But though this principle ultimately provides him with all the necessaries of life which he has occasion for, it neither does nor can provide him with them as he has occasion for them. The greater part of his occasional wants are supplied in the same manner as those of other people, by treaty, by barter, and by purchase. With the money which one man gives him he purchases food. The old cloaths which another bestows upon him he exchanges for other old cloaths which suit him better, or for lodging, or for food, or for money, with which he can buy either food, cloaths, or lodging, as he has occasion.

As it is by treaty, by barter, and by purchase, that we obtain from one another the greater part of those mutual good offices which we stand in need of, so it is this same trucking disposition which originally gives occasion to the division of labour. In a tribe of hunters or shepherds a particular person makes bows and arrows, for example, with more readiness and dexterity than any other. He frequently exchanges them for cattle or for venison with his companions; and he finds at last that he can in this manner get more cattle and venison, than if he himself went to the field to catch them. From a regard to his own interest, therefore, the making of bows and arrows grows to be his chief business, and he becomes a sort of armourer. Another excels in making the frames and covers of their little huts or moveable houses. He is accustomed to be of use in this way to his neighbours, who reward him in the same manner with cattle and with venison, till at last he finds it his interest to dedicate himself entirely to this employment, and to become a sort of house-carpenter. In the same manner a third becomes a smith or a brazier; a fourth a tanner or dresser of hides or skins, the principal part of the clothing of savages. And thus the certainty of being able to exchange all that surplus part of the produce of his own labour, which is over and above his own consumption, for such parts of the produce of other men's labour as he may have occasion for, encourages every man to apply himself to a particular occupation, and to cultivate and bring to perfection whatever talent or genius he may possess for that particular species of business.

The difference of natural talents in different men is, in reality, much less than we are aware of; and the very different genius which appears to distinguish men of different professions, when grown up to maturity, is not upon many occasions so much the cause, as the effect of the division of labour. The difference between the most dissimilar characters, between a philosopher and a common street porter, for example, seems to arise not so much from nature, as from habit, custom, and education. When they came into the world, and for the first six or eight years of their existence, they were, perhaps, very much alike, and neither their parents nor playfellows could perceive any remarkable difference. About that age, or soon after, they come to be employed in very different occupations. The difference of talents comes then to be taken notice of, and widens by degrees, till at last the vanity of the philosopher is willing to acknowledge scarce any resemblance. But without the disposition to truck, barter, and exchange, every man must have procured to himself every necessary and conveniency of life which he wanted. All must have had the same duties to perform, and the same work to do, and there could have been no such difference of employment as could alone give occasion to any great difference of talents.

As it is this disposition which forms that difference of talents, so remarkable among men of different professions, so it is this same disposition which renders that difference useful. Many tribes of animals acknowledged to be all of the same species, derive from nature a much more remarkable distinction of genius, than what, antecedent to custom and education, appears to take place among men. By nature a philosopher is not in genius and disposition half so different from a street porter, as a mastiff is from a greyhound, or a greyhound from a spaniel, or this last from a shepherd's dog. Those different tribes of animals, however, though all of the same species, are of scarce any use to one another. The strength of the mastiff is not in the least supported either by the swiftness of the greyhound, or by the sagacity of the spaniel, or by the docility of the shepherd's dog. The effects of those different geniuses and talents, for want of the power or disposition to barter and exchange, cannot be brought into a common stock, and do not in the least contribute to the better accommodation and conveniency of the species. Each animal is still obliged to support and defend itself, separately and independently, and derives no sort of advantage from that variety of talents with which nature has distinguished its fellows. Among men, on the contrary, the most dissimilar geniuses are of use to one another; the different produces of their respective talents, by the general disposition to truck, barter, and exchange, being brought, as it were, into a common stock, where every man may purchase whatever part of the produce of other men's talents he has occasion for.

[...]

Of Restraints upon the Importation from Foreign Countries of Such Goods as Can Be Produced at Home

By restraining, either by high duties, or by absolute prohibitions, the importation of such goods from foreign countries as can be produced at home, the monopoly of the home market is more or less secured to the domestic industry employed in producing them. ... The variety of goods of which the importation into Great

Britain is prohibited, either absolutely, or under certain circumstances, greatly exceeds what can easily be suspected by those who are not well acquainted with the laws of the customs.

That this monopoly of the home-market frequently gives great encouragement to that particular species of industry which enjoys it, and frequently turns towards that employment a greater share of both the labour and stock of the society than would otherwise have gone to it, cannot be doubted. But whether it tends either to increase the general industry of the society, or to give it the most advantageous direction, is not, perhaps, altogether so evident.

The general industry of the society never can exceed what the capital of the society can employ. As the number of workmen that can be kept in employment by any particular person must bear a certain proportion to his capital, so the number of those that can be continually employed by all the members of a great society, must bear a certain proportion to the whole capital of that society, and never can exceed that proportion. No regulation of commerce can increase the quantity of industry in any society beyond what its capital can maintain. It can only divert a part of it into a direction into which it might not otherwise have gone; and it is by no means certain that this artificial direction is likely to be more advantageous to the society than that into which it would have gone of its own accord.

Every individual is continually exerting himself to find out the most advantageous employment for whatever capital he can command. It is his own advantage, indeed, and not that of the society, which he has in view. But the study of his own advantage naturally, or rather necessarily leads him to prefer that employment which is most advantageous to the society.

First, every individual endeavours to employ his capital as near home as he can, and consequently as much as he can in the support of domestic industry; provided always that he can thereby obtain the ordinary, or not a great deal less than the ordinary profits of stock.

[…]

Secondly, every individual who employs his capital in the support of domestic industry, necessarily endeavours so to direct that industry, that its produce may be of the greatest possible value.

The produce of industry is what it adds to the subject or materials upon which it is employed. In proportion as the value of this produce is great or small, so will likewise be the profits of the employer. But it is only for the sake of profit that any man employs a capital in the support of industry; and he will always, therefore, endeavour to employ it in the support of that industry of which the produce is likely to be of the greatest value, or to exchange for the greatest quantity either of money or of other goods.

But the annual revenue of every society is always precisely equal to the exchangeable value of the whole annual produce of its industry, or rather is precisely the same thing with that exchangeable value. As every individual, therefore, endeavours as much as he can both to employ his capital in the support of domestic industry, and so to direct that industry that its produce may be of the greatest value; every individual necessarily labours to render the annual revenue of the society as great as he can. He generally, indeed, neither intends to promote the public interest, nor knows how much he is promoting it. By preferring the support of domestic to that of foreign industry, he intends only his own security; and by directing that industry in such a manner as its produce may be of the greatest value, he intends only his own gain, and he is in this, as in many other cases, led by an invisible hand to promote an end which was no part of his intention. Nor is it always the worse for the society that it was no part of it. By pursuing his own interest he frequently promotes that of the society more effectually than when he really intends to promote it. I have never known much good done by those who affected to trade for the public good. It is an affectation, indeed, not very common among merchants, and very few words need be employed in dissuading them from it.

What is the species of domestic industry which his capital can employ, and of which the produce is likely to be of the greatest value, every individual, it is evident, can, in his local situation, judge much better than any statesman or lawgiver can do for him. The statesman, who should attempt to direct private people in what manner they ought to employ their capitals, would not only load himself with a most unnecessary attention, but assume an authority which could safely be trusted, not only to no single person, but to no council or senate whatever, and which would nowhere be so dangerous in the hands of a man who had folly and presumption enough to fancy himself fit to exercise it.

To give the monopoly of the home-market to the produce of domestic industry, in any particular art or manufacture, is in some measure to direct private people in what manner they ought to employ their capitals, and must, in almost all cases, be either a useless or a hurtful regulation. If the produce of domestic can be brought there as cheap as that of foreign industry, the regulation is evidently useless. If it cannot, it must generally be hurtful. It is the maxim of every prudent master of a family, never to attempt to make at home what it will cost him more to make than to buy. The taylor does not attempt to make his own shoes, but buys them of the shoemaker. The shoemaker does not attempt to make his own clothes, but employs a taylor. The farmer attempts to make neither the one nor the other, but employs those different artificers. All of them find it for their interest to employ their whole industry in a way in which they have some advantage over their neighbours, and to purchase with a part of its produce, or what is the same thing, with the price of a part of it, whatever else they have occasion for.

What is prudence in the conduct of every private family, can scarce be folly in that of a great kingdom. If a foreign country can supply us with a commodity cheaper than we ourselves can make it, better buy it of them with some part of the produce of our own industry, employed in a way in which we have some advantage. The general industry of the country, being always in proportion to the capital which employs it, will not thereby be diminished, no more than that of the above-mentioned artificers; but only left to find out the way in which it can be employed with the greatest advantage. It is certainly not employed to the greatest advantage, when it is thus directed towards an object which it can buy cheaper than it can make. The value of its annual produce is certainly more or less diminished, when it is thus turned away from producing commodities evidently of more value than the commodity which it is directed to produce. According to the supposition, that commodity could be purchased from foreign countries cheaper than it can be made at home. It could, therefore, have been purchased with a part only of the commodities, or, what is the same thing, with a part only of the price of the commodities, which the industry employed by an equal capital would have produced at home, had it been left to follow its natural course. The industry of the country, therefore, is thus turned away from a more, to a less advantageous employment, and the exchangeable value of its annual produce, instead of being increased, according to the intention of the lawgiver, must necessarily be diminished by every such regulation.

[…]

Chapter 5

The Theory of Moral Sentiments [1776]
Adam Smith

Of the Sense of Propriety

Of Sympathy

How selfish soever man may be supposed, there are evidently some principles in his nature, which interest him in the fortune of others, and render their happiness necessary to him, though he derives nothing from it except the pleasure of seeing it. Of this kind is pity or compassion, the emotion which we feel for the misery of others, when we either see it, or are made to conceive it in a very lively manner. That we often derive sorrow from the sorrow of others, is a matter of fact too obvious to require any instances to prove it; for this sentiment, like all the other original passions of human nature, is by no means confined to the virtuous and humane, though they perhaps may feel it with the most exquisite sensibility. The greatest ruffian, the most hardened violator of the laws of society, is not altogether without it.

As we have no immediate experience of what other men feel, we can form no idea of the manner in which they are affected, but by conceiving what we ourselves should feel in the like situation. Though our brother is upon the rack, as long as we ourselves are at our ease, our senses will never inform us of what he suffers. They never did, and never can, carry us beyond our own person, and it is by the imagination only that we can form any conception of what are his sensations. Neither can that faculty help us to this any other way, than by representing to us what would be our own, if we were in his case. It is the impressions of our own senses only, not those of his, which our imaginations copy. By the imagination we place ourselves in his situation, we conceive ourselves enduring all the same torments, we enter as it were into his body, and become in some measure the same person with him, and thence form some idea of his sensations, and even feel something which, though weaker in degree, is not altogether unlike them. His agonies, when they are thus brought home to ourselves, when we have thus adopted and made them our own, begin at last to affect us, and we then tremble and shudder at the thought of what he feels. For as to be in pain or distress of any kind excites the most excessive sorrow, so to conceive or to imagine that we are in it, excites some degree of the same emotion, in proportion to the vivacity or dulness of the conception.

That this is the source of our fellow-feeling for the misery of others, that it is by changing places in fancy with the sufferer, that we come either to conceive or to be affected by what he feels, may be demonstrated by many obvious observations, if it should not be thought sufficiently evident of itself. When we see a stroke aimed and just ready to fall upon the leg or arm of another person, we naturally shrink and draw back our own leg or our own arm; and when it does fall, we feel it in some measure, and are hurt by it as well as the sufferer. The mob, when they are gazing at a dancer on the slack rope, naturally writhe and twist and balance their own bodies, as they see him do, and as they feel that they themselves must do if in his situation. Persons of delicate fibres and a weak constitution of body complain, that in looking on the sores and ulcers which are exposed by beggars in the streets, they are apt to feel an itching or uneasy sensation in the correspondent part of their own bodies. The horror which they conceive at the misery of those wretches affects that particular part in themselves more than any other; because that horror arises from conceiving what they themselves would suffer, if they really were the wretches whom they are looking upon, and if that particular part in themselves was actually affected in the same miserable manner. The very force of this conception is sufficient, in their feeble frames, to produce that itching or uneasy sensation complained of. Men of the most robust make, observe that in looking upon sore eyes they often feel a very sensible soreness in their own, which proceeds from the same reason; that organ being in the strongest man more delicate, than any other part of the body is in the weakest.

Neither is it those circumstances only, which create pain or sorrow, that call forth our fellow-feeling. Whatever is the passion which arises from any object in the person principally concerned, an analogous emotion springs up, at the thought of his situation, in the breast of every attentive spectator. Our joy for the deliverance of those heroes of tragedy or romance who interest us, is as sincere as our grief for their distress, and our fellow-feeling with their misery is not more real than that with their happiness. We enter into their gratitude towards those faithful friends who did not desert them in their difficulties; and we heartily go along with their resentment against those perfidious traitors who injured, abandoned, or deceived them. In every passion of which the mind of man is susceptible, the emotions of the by-stander always correspond to what, by bringing the case home to himself, he imagines should be the sentiments of the sufferer.

Pity and compassion are words appropriated to signify our fellow-feeling with the sorrow of others. Sympathy, though its meaning was, perhaps, originally the same, may now, however, without much impropriety, be made use of to denote our fellow-feeling with any passion whatever.

Upon some occasions sympathy may seem to arise merely from the view of a certain emotion in another person. The passions, upon some occasions, may seem to be transfused from one man to another, instantaneously, and antecedent to any knowledge of what excited them in the person principally concerned. Grief and joy, for example, strongly expressed in the look and gestures of any one, at once affect the spectator with some degree of a like painful or agreeable emotion. A smiling face is, to every body that sees it, a cheerful object; as a sorrowful countenance, on the other hand, is a melancholy one.

This, however, does not hold universally, or with regard to every passion. There are some passions of which the expressions excite no sort of sympathy, but before we are acquainted with what gave occasion to them, serve rather to disgust and provoke us against them. The furious behaviour of an angry man is more likely to exasperate us against himself than against his enemies. As we are unacquainted with his provocation, we cannot bring his case home to ourselves, nor conceive any thing like the passions which it excites. But we plainly see what is the situation of those with whom he is angry, and to what violence they may be exposed from so enraged an adversary. We readily, therefore, sympathize with their fear or resentment, and are immediately disposed to take part against the man from whom they appear to be in so much danger.

If the very appearances of grief and joy inspire us with some degree of the like emotions, it is because they suggest to us the general idea of some good or bad fortune that has befallen the person in whom we observe them: and in these passions this is sufficient to have some little influence upon us. The effects of grief and joy terminate in the person who feels those emotions, of which the expressions do not, like those of resentment, suggest to us the idea of any other person for whom we are concerned, and whose interests are opposite to his. The general idea of good or bad fortune, therefore, creates some concern for the person who has met with it, but the general idea of provocation excites no sympathy with the anger of the man who has received it. Nature, it seems, teaches us to be more averse to enter into this passion, and, till informed of its cause, to be disposed rather to take part against it.

Even our sympathy with the grief or joy of another, before we are informed of the cause of either, is always extremely imperfect. General lamentations, which express nothing but the anguish of the sufferer, create rather a curiosity to inquire into his situation, along with some disposition to sympathize with him, than any actual sympathy that is very sensible. The first question which we ask is, What has befallen you? Till this be answered, though we are uneasy both from the vague idea of his misfortune, and still more from torturing ourselves with conjectures about what it may be, yet our fellow-feeling is not very considerable.

Sympathy, therefore, does not arise so much from the view of the passion, as from that of the situation which excites it. We sometimes feel for another, a passion of which he himself seems to be altogether incapable; because, when we put ourselves in his case, that passion arises in our breast from the imagination, though it does not in his from the reality. We blush for the impudence and rudeness of another, though he himself appears to have no sense of the impropriety of his own behaviour; because we cannot help feeling with what confusion we ourselves should be covered, had we behaved in so absurd a manner.

[...]

Of the Pleasure of mutual Sympathy

But whatever may be the cause of sympathy, or however it may be excited, nothing pleases us more than to observe in other men a fellow-feeling with all the emotions of our own breast; nor are we ever so much shocked as by the appearance of the contrary. Those who are fond of deducing all our sentiments from certain refinements of self-love, think themselves at no loss to account, according to their own principles, both for this pleasure and this pain. Man, say they, conscious of his own weakness, and of the need which he has for the assistance of others, rejoices whenever he observes that they adopt his own passions, because he is then assured of that assistance; and grieves whenever he observes the contrary, because he is then assured of their opposition. But both the pleasure and the pain are always felt so instantaneously, and often upon such frivolous occasions, that it seems evident that neither of them can be derived from any such self-interested consideration. A man is mortified when, after having endeavoured to divert the company, he looks round and sees that nobody laughs at his jests but himself. On the contrary, the mirth of the company is highly agreeable to him, and he regards this correspondence of their sentiments with his own as the greatest applause.

Neither does his pleasure seem to arise altogether from the additional vivacity which his mirth may receive from sympathy with theirs, nor his pain from the disappointment he meets with when he misses this pleasure; though both the one and the other, no doubt, do in some measure. When we have read a book or poem so often that we can no longer find any amusement in reading it by ourselves, we can still take pleasure in reading it to a companion. To him it has all the graces of novelty; we enter into the surprise and admiration which it naturally excites in him, but which it is no longer capable of exciting in us; we consider all the ideas which it presents rather in the light in which they appear to him, than in that in which they appear to ourselves, and we are amused by sympathy with his amusement which thus enlivens our own. On the contrary, we should be vexed if he did not seem to be entertained with it, and we could no longer take any pleasure in reading it to him. It is the same case here. The mirth of the company, no doubt, enlivens our own mirth, and their silence, no doubt, disappoints us. But though this may contribute both to the pleasure which we derive from the one, and to the pain which we feel from the other, it is by no means the sole cause of either; and this correspondence of the sentiments of others with our own appears to be a cause of pleasure, and the want of it a cause of pain, which cannot be accounted for in this manner. The sympathy, which my friends express with my joy, might, indeed, give me pleasure by enlivening that joy: but that which they express with my grief could give me none, if it served only to enliven that grief. Sympathy, however, enlivens joy and alleviates grief. It enlivens joy by presenting another source of satisfaction; and it alleviates grief by insinuating into the heart almost the only agreeable, sensation which it is at that time capable of receiving.

It is to be observed accordingly, that we are still more anxious to communicate to our friends our disagreeable than our agreeable passions, that we derive still more satisfaction from their sympathy with the former than from that with the latter, and that we are still more shocked by the want of it.

How are the unfortunate relieved when they have found out a person to whom they can communicate the cause of their sorrow? Upon his sympathy they seem to disburthen themselves of a part of their distress: he is not improperly said to share it with them. He not only feels a sorrow of the same kind with that which they feel, but as if he had derived a part of it to himself, what he feels seems to alleviate the weight of what they feel. Yet by relating their misfortunes they in some measure renew their grief. They awaken in their memory the remembrance of those circumstances which occasioned their affliction. Their tears accordingly flow faster than before, and they are apt to abandon themselves to all the weakness of sorrow. They take pleasure, however, in all this, and, it is evident, are sensibly relieved by it; because the sweetness of his sympathy more than compensates the bitterness of that sorrow, which, in order to excite this sympathy, they had thus enlivened and renewed. The cruelest insult, on the contrary, which can be offered to the unfortunate, is to appear to make light of their calamities. To seem not to be affected with the joy of our companions is but want of politeness; but not to wear a serious countenance when they tell us their afflictions, is real and gross inhumanity.

Love is an agreeable; resentment, a disagreeable passion; and accordingly we are not half so anxious that our friends should adopt our friendships, as that they should enter into our resentments. We can forgive them though they seem to be little affected with the favours which we may have received, but lose all patience if they seem indifferent about the injuries which may have been done to us: nor are we half so angry with them for not entering into our gratitude, as for not sympathizing with our resentment. They can easily avoid being friends to our friends, but can hardly avoid being enemies to those with whom we are at variance. We seldom resent their being at enmity with the first, though upon that account we may sometimes affect to make an awkward quarrel with them; but we quarrel with them in good earnest if they live in friendship with the last. The agreeable passions of love and joy can satisfy and support the heart without any auxiliary pleasure. The bitter and painful emotions of grief and resentment more strongly require the healing consolation of sympathy.

As the person who is principally interested in any event is pleased with our sympathy, and hurt by the want of it, so we, too, seem to be pleased when we are able to sympathize with him, and to be hurt when we are unable to do so. We run not only to congratulate the successful, but to condole with the afflicted; and the pleasure which we find in the conversation of one whom in all the passions of his heart we can entirely sympathize with, seems to do more than compensate the painfulness of that sorrow with which the view of his situation affects us. On the contrary, it is always disagreeable to feel that we cannot sympathize with him, and instead of being pleased with this exemption from sympathetic pain, it hurts us to find that we cannot share his uneasiness. If we hear a person loudly lamenting his misfortunes, which, however, upon bringing the case home to ourselves, we feel, can produce no such violent effect upon us, we are shocked at his grief; and, because we cannot enter into it, call it pusillanimity and weakness. It gives us the spleen, on the other hand, to see another too happy or too much elevated, as we call it, with any little piece of good fortune. We are disobliged even with his joy; and, because we cannot go along with it, call it levity and folly. We are even put out of humour if our companion laughs louder or longer at a joke than we think it deserves; that is, than we feel that we ourselves could laugh at it.

Of the manner in which we judge of the propriety or impropriety of the affections of other men, by their concord or dissonance with our own

When the original passions of the person principally concerned are in perfect concord with the sympathetic emotions of the spectator, they necessarily appear to this last just and proper, and suitable to their objects; and, on the contrary, when, upon bringing the case home to himself, he finds that they do not coincide with what he feels, they necessarily appear to him unjust and improper, and unsuitable to the causes which excite them. To approve of the passions of another, therefore, as suitable to their objects, is the same thing as to observe that we entirely sympathize with them; and not to approve of them as such, is the same thing as to observe that we do not entirely sympathize with them. The man who resents the injuries that have been done to me, and observes that I resent them precisely as he does, necessarily approves of my resentment. The man whose sympathy keeps time to my grief, cannot but admit the reasonableness of my sorrow. He who admires the same poem, or the same picture, and admires them exactly as I do, must surely allow the justness of my admiration. He who laughs at the same joke, and laughs along with me, cannot well deny the propriety of my laughter. On the contrary, the person who, upon these different occasions, either feels no such emotion as that which I feel, or feels none that bears any proportion to mine, cannot avoid disapproving my sentiments on account of their dissonance with his own. If my animosity goes beyond what the indignation of my friend can correspond to; if my grief exceeds what his most tender compassion can go along with; if my admiration is either too high or too low to tally with his own; if I laugh loud and heartily when he only smiles, or, on the contrary, only smile when he laughs loud and heartily; in all these cases, as soon as he comes from considering the object, to observe how I am affected by it, according as there is more or less disproportion between his sentiments and mine, I must incur a greater or less degree of his disapprobation: and upon all occasions his own sentiments are the standards and measures by which he judges of mine.

To approve of another man's opinions is to adopt those opinions, and to adopt them is to approve of them. If the same arguments which convince you convince me likewise, I necessarily approve of your conviction; and if they do not, I necessarily disapprove of it: neither can I possibly conceive that I should do the one without the other. To approve or disapprove, therefore, of the opinions of others is acknowledged, by every body, to mean no more than to observe their agreement or disagreement with our own. But this is equally the case with regard to our approbation or disapprobation of the sentiments or passions of others.

There are, indeed, some cases in which we seem to approve without any sympathy or correspondence of sentiments, and in which, consequently, the sentiment of approbation would seem to be different from the perception of this coincidence. A little attention, however, will convince us that even in these cases our approbation is ultimately founded upon a sympathy or correspondence of this kind. I shall give an instance in things of a very frivolous nature, because in them the judgments of mankind are less apt to be perverted by wrong systems. We may often approve of a jest, and think the laughter of the company quite just and proper, though we ourselves do not laugh, because, perhaps, we are in a grave humour, or happen to have our attention engaged with other objects. We have learned, however, from experience, what sort of pleasantry is upon most occasions capable of making us laugh, and we observe that this is one of that kind. We approve, therefore, of the laughter of the company, and feel that it is natural and suitable to its object; because, though in our present mood we cannot easily enter into it, we are sensible that upon most occasions we should very heartily join in it.

The same thing often happens with regard to all the other passions. A stranger passes by us in the street with all the marks of the deepest affliction; and we are immediately told that he has just received the news of the death of his father. It is impossible that, in this case, we should not approve of his grief. Yet it may often happen, without any defect of humanity on our part, that, so far from entering into the violence of his sorrow, we should scarce conceive the first movements of concern upon his account. Both he and his father, perhaps, are entirely unknown to us, or we happen to be employed about other things, and do not take time to picture out in our imagination the different circumstances of distress which must occur to him. We have learned, however, from experience, that such a misfortune naturally excites such a degree of sorrow, and we know that if we took time to consider his situation, fully and in all its parts, we should, without doubt, most sincerely sympathize with him. It is upon the consciousness of this conditional sympathy, that our approbation of his sorrow is founded, even in those cases in which that sympathy does not actually take place; and the general rules derived from our preceding experience of what our sentiments would commonly correspond with, correct upon this, as upon many other occasions, the impropriety of our present emotions.

The sentiment or affection of the heart from which any action proceeds, and upon which its whole virtue or vice must ultimately depend, may be considered under two different aspects, or in two different relations; first, in relation to the cause which excites it, or the motive which gives occasion to it; and secondly, in relation to the end which it proposes, or the effect which it tends to produce.

In the suitableness or unsuitableness, in the proportion or disproportion which the affection seems to bear to the cause or object which excites it, consists the propriety or impropriety, the decency or ungracefulness of the consequent action.

In the beneficial or hurtful nature of the effects which the affection aims at, or tends to produce, consists the merit or demerit of the action, the qualities by which it is entitled to reward, or is deserving of punishment.

Philosophers have, of late years, considered chiefly the tendency of affections, and have given little attention to the relation which they stand in to the cause which excites them. In common life, however, when we judge of any person's conduct, and of the sentiments which directed it, we constantly consider them under both these aspects. When we blame in another man the excesses of love, of grief, of resentment, we not only consider the ruinous effects which they tend to produce, but the little occasion which was given for them. The merit of his favourite, we say, is not so great, his misfortune is not so dreadful, his provocation is not so extraordinary, as to justify so violent a passion. We should have indulged, we say; perhaps, have approved of the violence of his emotion, had the cause been in any respect proportioned to it.

When we judge in this manner of any affection, as proportioned or disproportioned to the cause which excites it, it is scarce possible that we should make use of any other rule or canon but the correspondent affection in ourselves. If, upon bringing the case home to our own breast, we find that the sentiments which it gives occasion to, coincide and tally with our own, we necessarily approve of them as proportioned and suitable to their objects; if otherwise, we necessarily disapprove of them, as extravagant and out of proportion.

Every faculty in one man is the measure by which he judges of the like faculty in another. I judge of your sight by my sight, of your ear by my ear, of your reason by my reason, of your resentment by my resentment, of your love by my love. I neither have, nor can have, any other way of judging about them.

[…]

Of the amiable and respectable virtues

Upon these two different efforts, upon that of the spectator to enter into the sentiments of the person principally concerned, and upon that of the person principally concerned, to bring down his emotions to what the spectator can go along with, are founded two different sets of virtues. The soft, the gentle, the amiable virtues, the virtues of candid condescension and indulgent humanity, are founded upon the one: the great, the awful and respectable, the virtues of self-denial, of self-government, of that command of the passions which subjects all the movements of our nature to what our own dignity and honour, and the propriety of our own conduct require, take their origin from the other.

How amiable does he appear to be, whose sympathetic heart seems to reecho all the sentiments of those with whom he converses, who grieves for their calamities, who resents their injuries, and who rejoices at their good fortune! When we bring home to ourselves the situation of his companions, we enter into their gratitude, and feel what consolation they must derive from the tender sympathy of so affectionate a friend. And for a contrary reason, how disagreeable does he appear to be, whose hard and obdurate heart feels for himself only, but is altogether insensible to the happiness or misery of others! We enter, in this case too, into the pain which his presence must give to every mortal with whom he converses, to those especially with whom we are most apt to sympathize, the unfortunate and the injured.

On the other hand, what noble propriety and grace do we feel in the conduct of those who, in their own case, exert that recollection and self-command which constitute the dignity of every passion, and which bring it down to what others can enter into! We are disgusted with that clamorous grief, which, without any delicacy, calls upon our compassion with sighs and tears and importunate lamentations. But we reverence that reserved, that silent and majestic sorrow, which discovers itself only in the swelling of the eyes, in the quivering of the lips and cheeks, and in the distant, but affecting, coldness of the whole behaviour. It imposes the like silence upon us. We regard it with respectful attention, and watch with anxious concern over our whole behaviour, lest by any impropriety we should disturb that concerted tranquillity, which it requires so great an effort to support.

The insolence and brutality of anger, in the same manner, when we indulge its fury without check or restraint, is, of all objects, the most detestable. But we admire that noble and generous resentment which governs its pursuit of the greatest injuries, not by the rage which they are apt to excite in the breast of the sufferer, but by the indignation which they naturally call forth in that of the impartial spectator; which allows no word, no gesture, to escape it beyond what this more equitable sentiment would dictate; which never, even in thought, attempts any greater vengeance, nor desires to inflict any greater punishment, than what every indifferent person would rejoice to see executed.

And hence it is, that to feel much for others and little for ourselves, that to restrain our selfish, and to indulge our benevolent affections, constitutes the perfection of human nature; and can alone produce among mankind that harmony of sentiments and passions in which consists their whole grace and propriety. As to love our neighbour as we love ourselves is the great law of Christianity, so it is the great precept of nature to love ourselves only as we love our neighbour, or what comes to the same thing, as our neighbour is capable of loving us.

As taste and good judgment, when they are considered as qualities which deserve praise and admiration, are supposed to imply a delicacy of sentiment and an acuteness of understanding not commonly to be met with; so the virtues of sensibility and self-command are not apprehended to consist in the ordinary, but in the uncommon degrees of those qualities. The amiable virtue of humanity requires, surely, a sensibility, much beyond what is possessed by the rude vulgar of mankind. The great and exalted virtue of magnanimity undoubtedly demands much more than that degree of self-command, which the weakest of mortals is capable of exerting. As in the common degree of the intellectual qualities, there is no abilities; so in the common degree of the moral, there is no virtue. Virtue is excellence, something uncommonly great and beautiful, which rises far above what is vulgar and ordinary. The amiable virtues consist in that degree of sensibility which surprises by its exquisite and unexpected delicacy and tenderness. The awful and respectable, in that degree of self-command which astonishes by its amazing superiority over the most ungovernable passions of human nature.

There is, in this respect, a considerable difference between virtue and mere propriety; between those qualities and actions which deserve to be admired and celebrated, and those which simply deserve to be approved of. Upon many occasions, to act with the most perfect propriety, requires no more than that common and ordinary degree of sensibility or self-command which the most worthless of mankind are possest of, and sometimes even that degree is not necessary. Thus, to give a very low instance, to eat when we are hungry, is certainly, upon ordinary occasions, perfectly right and proper, and cannot miss being approved of as such by every body. Nothing, however, could be more absurd than to say it was virtuous.

On the contrary, there may frequently be a considerable degree of virtue in those actions which fall short of the most perfect propriety; because they may still approach nearer to perfection than could well be expected upon occasions in which it was so extremely difficult to attain it: and this is very often the case upon those occasions which require the greatest exertions of self-command. There are some situations which bear so hard upon human nature, that the greatest degree of self-government, which can belong to so imperfect a creature as man, is not able to stifle, altogether, the voice of human weakness, or reduce the violence of the passions to that pitch of moderation, in which the impartial spectator can entirely enter into them. Though in those cases, therefore, the behaviour of the sufferer fall short of the most perfect propriety, it may still deserve some applause, and even in a certain sense, may be denominated virtuous. It may still manifest an effort of generosity and magnanimity of which the greater part of men are incapable; and though it fails of absolute perfection, it may be a much nearer approximation towards perfection, than what, upon such trying occasions, is commonly either to be found or to be expected.

In cases of this kind, when we are determining the degree of blame or applause which seems due to any action, we very frequently make use of two different standards. The first is the idea of complete propriety and perfection, which, in those difficult situations, no human conduct ever did, or ever can come up to; and in comparison with which the actions of all men must for ever appear blameable and imperfect. The second is the idea of that degree of proximity or distance from this complete perfection, which the actions of the greater part of men commonly arrive at. Whatever goes beyond this degree, how far soever it may be removed from absolute perfection, seems to deserve applause; and whatever falls short of it, to deserve blame.

It is in the same manner that we judge of the productions of all the arts which address themselves to the imagination. When a critic examines the work of any of the great masters in poetry or painting, he may sometimes examine it by an idea of perfection, in his own mind, which neither that nor any other human work will ever come up to;

and as long as he compares it with this standard, he can see nothing in it but faults and imperfections. But when he comes to consider the rank which it ought to hold among other works of the same kind, he necessarily compares it with a very different standard, the common degree of excellence which is usually attained in this particular art; and when he judges of it by this new measure, it may often appear to deserve the highest applause, upon account of its approaching much nearer to perfection than the greater part of those works which can be brought into competition with it.

[…]

Of the Effects of Prosperity and Adversity upon the Judgment of Mankind with regard to the Propriety of Action; and why it is more easy to obtain their Approbation in the one state than in the other

That though our sympathy with sorrow is generally a more lively sensation than our sympathy with joy, it commonly falls much more short of the violence of what is "naturally" felt by the person principally concerned

Our sympathy with sorrow, though not more real, has been more taken notice of than our sympathy with joy. The word sympathy, in its most proper and primitive signification, denotes our fellow-feeling with the sufferings, not that with the enjoyments, of others. A late ingenious and subtile philosopher thought it necessary to prove, by arguments, that we had a real sympathy with joy, and that congratulation was a principle of human nature. Nobody, I believe, ever thought it necessary to prove that compassion was such.

First of all, our sympathy with sorrow is, in some sense, more universal than that with joy. Though sorrow is excessive, we may still have some fellow-feeling with it. What we feel does not, indeed, in this case, amount to that complete sympathy, to that perfect harmony and correspondence of sentiments which constitutes approbation. We do not weep, and exclaim, and lament, with the sufferer. We are sensible, on the contrary, of his weakness and of the extravagance of his passion, and yet often feel a very sensible concern upon his account. But if we do not entirely enter into, and go along with, the joy of another, we have no sort of regard or fellow-feeling for it. The man who skips and dances about with that intemperate and senseless joy which we cannot accompany him in, is the object of our contempt and indignation.

Pain besides, whether of mind or body, is a more pungent sensation than pleasure, and our sympathy with pain, though it falls greatly short of what is naturally felt by the sufferer, is generally a more lively and distinct perception than our sympathy with pleasure, though this last often approaches more nearly, as I shall shew immediately, to the natural vivacity of the original passion.

Over and above all this, we often struggle to keep down our sympathy with the sorrow of others. Whenever we are not under the observation of the sufferer, we endeavour, for our own sake, to suppress it as much as we can, and we are not always successful. The opposition which we make to it, and the reluctance with which we yield to it, necessarily oblige us to take more particular notice of it. But we never have occasion to make this opposition to our sympathy with joy. If there is any envy in the case, we never feel the least propensity towards it; and if there is none, we give way to it without any reluctance. On the contrary, as we are always ashamed of our own envy, we often pretend, and sometimes really wish to sympathize with the joy of others, when by that disagreeable sentiment we are disqualified from doing so. We are glad, we say, on account of our neighbour's good fortune, when in our hearts, perhaps, we are really sorry. We often feel a sympathy with sorrow when we would wish to be rid of it; and we often miss that with joy when we would be glad to have it. The obvious observation, therefore, which it naturally falls in our way to make, is, that our propensity to sympathize with sorrow must be very strong, and our inclination to sympathize with joy very weak.

Notwithstanding this prejudice, however, I will venture to affirm, that, when there is no envy in the case, our propensity to sympathize with joy is much stronger than our propensity to sympathize with sorrow; and that our fellow-feeling for the agreeable emotion approaches much more nearly to the vivacity of what is naturally felt by the persons principally concerned, than that which we conceive for the painful one.

[…]

Of the origin of Ambition; and of the distinction of Ranks

It is because mankind are disposed to sympathize more entirely with our joy than with our sorrow, that we make parade of our riches, and conceal our poverty. Nothing is so mortifying as to be obliged to expose our distress to the view of the public, and to feel, that though our situation is open to the eyes of all mankind, no mortal conceives for us the half of what we suffer. Nay, it is chiefly from this regard to the sentiments of mankind, that we pursue riches and avoid poverty. For to what purpose is all the toil and bustle of this world? what is the end of avarice and ambition, of the pursuit of wealth, of power, and preheminence? Is it to supply the necessities of nature? The wages of the meanest labourer can supply them. We see that they afford him food and clothing, the comfort of a house, and of a family. If we examined his oeconomy with rigour, we should find that he spends a great part of them upon conveniencies, which may be regarded as superfluities, and that, upon extraordinary occasions, he can give something even to vanity and distinction. What then is the cause of our aversion to his situation, and why should those who have been educated in the higher ranks of life, regard it as worse than death, to be reduced to live, even without labour, upon the same simple fare with him, to dwell under the same lowly roof, and to be clothed in the same humble attire? […] The rich man glories in his riches, because he feels that they naturally draw upon him the attention of the world, and that mankind are disposed to go along with him in all those agreeable emotions with which the advantages of his situation so readily inspire him. At the thought of this, his heart seems to swell and dilate itself within him, and he is fonder of his wealth, upon this account, than for all the other advantages it procures him. The poor man, on the contrary, is ashamed of his poverty. He feels that it either places him out of the sight of mankind, or, that if they take any notice of him, they have, however, scarce any fellow-feeling with the misery and distress which he suffers. He is mortified upon both accounts; for though to be overlooked, and to be disapproved of, are things entirely different, yet as obscurity covers us from the daylight of honour and approbation, to feel that we are taken no notice of, necessarily damps the most agreeable hope, and disappoints the most ardent desire, of human nature. The poor man goes out and comes in unheeded, and when in the midst of a crowd is in the same obscurity as if shut up in his own hovel. […] The man of rank and distinction, on the contrary, is observed by all the world. Every body is eager to look at him, and to conceive, at least by sympathy, that joy and exultation with which his circumstances naturally inspire him. His actions are the objects of the public care. Scarce a word, scarce a gesture, can fall from him that is altogether neglected. […] It is this, which, notwithstanding the restraint it imposes, notwithstanding the loss of liberty with which it is attended, renders greatness the object of envy, and compensates, in the opinion of mankind, all that toil, all that anxiety, all those mortifications which must be undergone in the pursuit of it; and what is of yet more consequence, all that leisure, all that ease, all that careless security, which are forfeited for ever by the acquisition.

When we consider the condition of the great, in those delusive colours in which the imagination is apt to paint it, it seems to be almost the abstract idea of a perfect and happy state. It is the very state which, in all our waking dreams and idle reveries, we had sketched out to ourselves as the final object of all our desires. We feel, therefore, a peculiar sympathy with the satisfaction of those who are in it. We favour all their inclinations, and forward all their wishes. What pity, we think, that any thing should spoil and corrupt so agreeable a situation! […] Every calamity that befals them, every injury that is done them, excites in the breast of the spectator ten times more compassion and resentment than he would have felt, had the same things happened to other men. […]

Upon this disposition of mankind, to go along with all the passions of the rich and the powerful, is founded the distinction of ranks, and the order of society. Our obsequiousness to our superiors more frequently arises from our admiration for the advantages of their situation, than from any private expectations of benefit from their good-will. Their benefits can extend but to a few; but their fortunes interest almost every body. We are eager to assist them in completing a system of happiness that approaches so near to perfection; and we desire to serve them for their own sake, without any other recompense but the vanity or the honour of obliging them. Neither is our deference to their inclinations founded chiefly, or altogether, upon a regard to the utility of such submission, and to the order of society, which is best supported by it. Even when the order of society seems to require that we should oppose them, we can hardly bring ourselves to do it. That kings are the servants of the people, to be obeyed, resisted, deposed, or punished, as the public conveniency may require, is the doctrine of reason and philosophy;

but it is not the doctrine of Nature. Nature would teach us to submit to them for their own sake, to tremble and bow down before their exalted station, to regard their smile as a reward sufficient to compensate any services, and to dread their displeasure, though no other evil were to follow from it, as the severest of all mortifications. To treat them in any respect as men, to reason and dispute with them upon ordinary occasions, requires such resolution, that there are few men whose magnanimity can support them in it, unless they are likewise assisted by familiarity and acquaintance. The strongest motives, the most furious passions, fear, hatred, and resentment, are scarce sufficient to balance this natural disposition to respect them: and their conduct must, either justly or unjustly, have excited the highest degree of all those passions, before the bulk of the people can be brought to oppose them with violence, or to desire to see them either punished or deposed. Even when the people have been brought this length, they are apt to relent every moment, and easily relapse into their habitual state of deference to those whom they have been accustomed to look upon as their natural superiors. They cannot stand the mortification of their monarch. Compassion soon takes the place of resentment, they forget all past provocations, their old principles of loyalty revive, and they run to re-establish the ruined authority of their old masters, with the same violence with which they had opposed it. The death of Charles I. brought about the Restoration of the royal family. Compassion for James II. when he was seized by the populace in making his escape on ship-board, had almost prevented the Revolution, and made it go on more heavily than before.

[…]

Of the corruption of our moral sentiments, which is occasioned by this disposition to admire the rich and the great, and to despise or neglect persons of poor and mean condition

This disposition to admire, and almost to worship, the rich and the powerful, and to despise, or, at least, to neglect persons of poor and mean condition, though necessary both to establish and to maintain the distinction of ranks and the order of society, is, at the same time, the great and most universal cause of the corruption of our moral sentiments. That wealth and greatness are often regarded with the respect and admiration which are due only to wisdom and virtue; and that the contempt, of which vice and folly are the only proper objects, is often most unjustly bestowed upon poverty and weakness, has been the complaint of moralists in all ages.

We desire both to be respectable and to be respected. We dread both to be contemptible and to be contemned. But, upon coming into the world, we soon find that wisdom and virtue are by no means the sole objects of respect; nor vice and folly, of contempt. We frequently see the respectful attentions of the world more strongly directed towards the rich and the great, than towards the wise and the virtuous. We see frequently the vices and follies of the powerful much less despised than the poverty and weakness of the innocent. To deserve, to acquire, and to enjoy the respect and admiration of mankind, are the great objects of ambition and emulation. Two different roads are presented to us, equally leading to the attainment of this so much desired object; the one, by the study of wisdom and the practice of virtue; the other, by the acquisition of wealth and greatness. Two different characters are presented to our emulation; the one, of proud ambition and ostentatious avidity; the other, of humble modesty and equitable justice. Two different models, two different pictures, are held out to us, according to which we may fashion our own character and behaviour; the one more gaudy and glittering in its colouring; the other more correct and more exquisitely beautiful in its outline: the one forcing itself upon the notice of every wandering eye; the other, attracting the attention of scarce any body but the most studious and careful observer. They are the wise and the virtuous chiefly, a select, though, I am afraid, but a small party, who are the real and steady admirers of wisdom and virtue. The great mob of mankind are the admirers and worshippers, and, what may seem more extraordinary, most frequently the disinterested admirers and worshippers, of wealth and greatness.

[...]

Part II

The Sociological Theory of Alexis de Tocqueville

Introduction to Part II
6   The Old Régime and the French Revolution
7   Influence of Democracy on the Feelings of the Americans
8   Tyranny of the Majority

Introduction to Part II

Life and Works

Like his contemporaries Karl Marx and Friedrich Engels, Alexis de Tocqueville (1805–59) was not merely a toiler in the archives or a lecture-hall gladiator but an active partisan in the great social and political conflicts of his day (Aron, 1968). Although a child of aristocratic privilege, his was not an upbringing marked by certainty and ease. His family, of an ancient noble house in Normandy, was deeply scarred by the French Revolution and the Reign of Terror. His parents narrowly escaped and fled into exile while relatives fell to the guillotine. In his political sociology, Tocqueville appreciated the constitutional role of the nobility under the pre-revolutionary old regime and insisted on the social importance of responsible and stabilizing élite classes. Yet Tocqueville was neither a reactionary nor a snob (inheriting the title of count in 1836, he refused to use it) and came to regard aristocratic politics in the modern age as nostalgic and vain. The young Tocqueville studied law and began his political career in 1830, serving as a parliamentary deputy in the new regime dubbed the "July monarchy" after the month in which a popular uprising put an end to the reign of King Charles X whose Bourbon dynasty had been restored after the fall of Napoleon's military dictatorship. The new government was headed by another royal, Louis-Philippe. His regime promised liberal reforms and constitutional monarchy, though only a small fraction of the male population was entitled to vote, corruption was endemic, and government was conducted largely for the benefit of the wealthy business class (the "bourgeoisie"). Generally dissatisfied with this state of affairs, Tocqueville built a political reputation as a principled liberal

Classical Sociological Theory, Third Edition. Edited by Craig Calhoun, Joseph Gerteis, James Moody, Steven Pfaff, and Indermohan Virk. Editorial material and organization © 2012 John Wiley & Sons, Ltd. Published 2012 by John Wiley & Sons, Ltd.

and cautious reformer. In parliament and in his writings he became a voice for the abolition of slavery, the promotion of free trade, and indirect rule in an Algeria recently conquered by France. As a parliamentarian, and later as a government minister, Tocqueville explained that he wished to govern "in a regular, moderate, conservative, and quite constitutional way" (*Recollections*, p. 228). As it turned out, however, Tocqueville's tenure in government came in the midst of a revolution in which such principles had little chance to prevail.

Tocqueville was rescued from a conventional career in 1831. A great opportunity had arisen when he and Gustave de Beaumont (1802–66), a fellow parliamentarian and life-long friend, were offered a government commission to tour the United States and draft a report on the state of prisons in the young republic. The result was an intellectually fertile journey in which the two budding scholars traveled across antebellum America and explored its political institutions, economy, values, and social relations. During their nine months in America, they proved erudite and curious tourists, traveling almost everywhere, north and south, east and west. They had little difficulty arranging interviews with many of the republic's great men, including John Quincy Adams, Andrew Jackson, and Daniel Webster. They attended political rallies, town meetings, and a Fourth of July parade; they traveled on steamboats, and slept in a log cabin. Upon their return, the friends quickly composed a book on the penitentiary system in the United States and its relevance for France. However, Tocqueville's notes and observations, combined with assiduous research, bore much greater fruit in his masterwork *Democracy in America*, published in two volumes in 1835 and 1840.

The brilliance and originality of the book made Tocqueville famous. It announced that democracy was an irresistible force in modern times and that political and social equality were the great issues of the age that no political system could avoid. For sure, these themes were on everyone's mind in the middle of the 19th century but Tocqueville offered novel insights into how democratic revolution could be accommodated without violent upheavals, ruinous populism, or the recourse to tyranny to uphold order. Rather, deliberate institutional reform could make peaceful, progressive democratic politics possible without descent into mob rule and the dispossession of the élites. Provocatively, Tocqueville's analysis identified the strength of the American republic in what Europeans would regard as its apparent weaknesses: its limited scope of government, decentralization, egalitarianism, and deference to local civil society. While Tocqueville saw much to admire in both the institutions and practices of the American republic, his book was no uncritical celebration. Slavery and its attendant racism violated the libertarian principles of the republic and threatened sectional warfare between North and South. The very egalitarianism of American public culture often led to coarseness and anti-intellectual prejudice. And Tocqueville was deeply worried that rapid economic growth might dangerously increase material inequality among Americans, threatening the equality that was the ideological and practical foundation of their system of government. The book became a sensation in France and remains a foundational work of political theory and political sociology.

Tocqueville was in Paris when the revolution of February 1848 erupted, leading swiftly to the collapse of Louis-Philippe's monarchy. He was elected as a delegate to the new constituent assembly and participated in the drafting of the constitution for the Second Republic (the first had been that established during the first French revolution in the 1790s). The new government was divided between the socialists, who called for a "democratic and social republic," and the "party of order," representing a coalition of aristocratic and bourgeois forces. Social tensions mounted, resulting in the June insurrection of 1848 in which the Parisian proletariat, led by the socialists, clashed with regular army troops in bloody street battles. With the insurgents defeated, Tocqueville was made Minister of Foreign Affairs in a new government and took part in the drafting of a revised constitution. In the midst of the crisis, Tocqueville insisted that his cherished principles of freedom of the press and political association should be suspended in Paris until law and order could be restored. Nevertheless, stability proved elusive and in the direct, popular elections held for president in December 1848 the candidate favored by Tocqueville and his allies was defeated by Louis Bonaparte, the former emperor Napoleon's nephew, and a cunning populist. Bonaparte campaigned skillfully against the republic, demanded the right to run for an unconstitutional second term of office, and secured the support of the army. In December 1851, Bonaparte and his supporters engineered a coup d'état. A year later, he abolished the republic and declared a second Napoleonic empire.

Tocqueville opposed Bonaparte and with the triumph of his dictatorship, his political career was over. After a brief period of imprisonment, Tocqueville was allowed to return to his chateau in Normandy. During the years remaining to him, Tocqueville wrote his political memoirs (unpublished until the end of the 19th century) and, vexed by France's apparent inability to evolve toward constitutional democracy began a study that would probe the origins of France's political turbulence. He resolved that the best way to understand a new society is to visit the old one in its grave. He accomplished this through extensive scholarly research in the records of the pre-1789 monarchy – the "old regime." In the state archives he found a "mine of information" and documents that were "a living memorial to the spirit of the old regime" (Tocqueville, 1955: ix). The result was *The Old Régime and the French Revolution*, published in 1856. In it, he explored the origins of the failure of the French monarchy in 1789 and sought causes for France's decades of conflict, instability, war, and revolution. Above all, it was a pioneering work of historical sociology that explored how long-term structural changes in economy and society influenced politics, examined the enduring role of political institutions, and identified the centralization of state power as the dominant trend in French history.

Tocqueville planned to write a second volume of *The Old Régime and the French Revolution* but his rapidly declining health denied him the chance. In his Norman retreat he enjoyed the company of his wife, Marie Motley, an Englishwoman he had married in 1835. The marriage, though apparently a contented one, remained childless. Shortly before his death, the sickly Tocqueville entreated his old friend

Beaumont to join him and his ailing wife at his chateau, a request which his oldest and best friend honored. Following his death, Madam de Tocqueville and Beaumont organized Tocqueville's papers and recollections, making possible their subsequent publication.

Social Theory

Tocqueville's fascinating political memoir of the 1848 revolution and its aftermath, *Recollections*, provides enduring insights into how he understood comparative and historical social science. In explaining events like those that roiled France from 1848 to 1851, Tocqueville was not content to employ the traditional descriptive and narrative methods of a historian. For sure, idiosyncratic factors such as the blunders of clumsy political leaders, miscalculations by interested parties, and unfortunate events played their part but these were only the "accidents" that rendered the underlying "disease" fatal. He made clear that we should be concerned explicitly with the problem of causation and hoped to identify general social mechanisms that might be operating in particular times and places.

In understanding the structural and constitutional vulnerability that puts states at risk of collapse, Tocqueville thought that we should analyze "antecedent facts, the nature of institutions, turn of mind and the state of mores [that] are the materials from which chance composes those impromptu events that surprise and terrify us" (Tocqueville, 1987: 62). In colorful terms, he was laying out the foundations of what we would now call a social-scientific approach to comparative and historical inquiry. Indeed, that basic set of preoccupations that Tocqueville considered in the case of 1848 – long-term structural transformation, institutions, political culture, and popular values – are the reoccurring themes upon which Tocqueville built his theory and which found expression in his two most important works, *Democracy in America* and *The Old Régime and the French Revolution*, both of which are excerpted in this volume.

The outlines of Tocqueville's social theory are contained in his masterpiece, *Democracy in America*. In it, he makes clear that the modern age has unleashed the power of individualism – the demand by individuals of all social classes for social autonomy and political voice. This individualism poses a threat to society because it can unbridle selfishness and so cripple the capacity for collective action among citizens, so that experiments in democracy fail. Should revolution lead to chaos and conflict, frightened and confused citizens will then all too often cry for a despotic solution such as a return to monarchy or their rescue by a charismatic dictator. Democracies face a dilemma: self-interest is a basic feature of the sort of progressive, market-oriented society that is the foundation for democratic politics but the spirit of possessive individualism easily fosters egoism and selfish preferences that make management of common affairs difficult. Traditional society avoided these pitfalls by binding people to each other in a dense web of social obligations. In aristocratic polities, the members of hierarchically-organized status groups have mutual obligations. The nobility serves as patrons and protectors of common interests. But in democratic societies, inherited status weakens, replaced by universal claims to rights. Yet the remaining obligations among people are few and self-interest undermines public service. With its citizens disengaged and egotistical, public goods cannot be achieved and democratic government fails. Did this mean that democratic government was doomed to surrender to authoritarianism?

Tocqueville was convinced that democratic government could flourish, as it appeared it had in antebellum America. He proclaimed, "The Americans have combated by free institutions the tendency of equality to keep men asunder, and they have subdued it." In the place of an extensive state bureaucracy, government led by public-minded notables and propelled by civic associations achieved robust social order and provided most of the public goods Americans demanded. America's limited government and federal system avoided the tyranny of the majority that can result from a strong, elected government favoring only its own supporters. Its decentralization and restricted scope meant that citizens had to rely on local initiatives that unleashed their self-interest in service of the public good. Its constitution protected the rights of political minorities and wisely disestablished religion, permitting a flourishing of clubs and civic groups as well as vital, self-organizing religious denominations.

But how had Americans balanced the competing claims of egalitarianism and autonomy with the need for social order? The answer, Tocqueville claimed, resided above all in the institutions of the American republic that encouraged what we would now call *locally-focused collective action*. Tocqueville proposed that because the United States had a weak central government and substantial decentralization, people expected little from the federal state and concerned themselves largely with local and regional affairs. In this context, people were compelled to engage in local collective action to achieve both private interests and public goods. Thus American institutions provided strong incentives for citizens to collaborate and try to establish trustworthy reputations that would help propel their efforts. Subsequent theorists have referred to the social ties among people, the mutual expectations they generate, and the trust that facilitates collective action among them as *social capital*. While Tocqueville did not employ this term he was one of the foundational thinkers that informed that theory.

Tocqueville proposed that *civic associations*, that is, voluntary organizations that promote a collective good, were the true foundation of the American polity and made its institutions effective. Associations made it possible for citizens to appeal to government, select favorable public officials, and see to it that the political parties addressed their needs. Moreover, these practices of civic life were the school for effective democracy. People who were "educated" through civic association were easier to mobilize politically, paid more attention to public affairs, and reached more informed opinions – all leading to the exercise of "enlightened" self-interest. Freedom of the press and a thriving print capitalism also helped by making information cheap and readily accessible, making it easier for citizens to coordinate their interests, find like-minded people, and stay apprised of public affairs. American institutions reinforced in the élite the need to appeal for the support of the common people. Americans elected officials at all levels of government. Tocqueville thought that this practice compelled citizens to interact in matters of common interest and engage in public affairs. Yes, Americans formed political parties as they did in Europe, but at the local level Tocqueville saw that party organizations were weak and largely ineffective without the cooperation of interest organizations that mobilized groups of citizens. As one of many examples of the effect of American institutions, Tocqueville pointed to the practice of electing local officials and judges rather than having them appointed by governors and senior bureaucrats. This, he thought, made officialdom dependent on the goodwill of the governed, promoted political moderation, and encouraged public-spirited interest in local affairs.

Even though the formal structures of their polity seemed weak, they empowered citizens. As their weak and limited national government did (and could do) so little for them, citizens were forced to rely on their own civic engagement to pursue local goals. They founded their own organizations to advance their agendas – including manufacturing and agrarian associations, immigrants' mutual-aid societies, unions, business-improvement groups, charities and benevolent societies, social clubs, and moral reform societies such as the abolitionists and temperance advocates. Even religion, which Tocqueville generally saw as an obstacle to moderate and rational self-government in Europe, promoted democracy in America through its congregational and local organization. As with the rest of American life, religion was based on voluntary collective action in denominations rather than in established churches, making it practical, worldly, and interested in civic affairs.

Tocqueville drew general lessons from his study of the American case. Tocqueville offered the proposition that the greater the degree of social equality in a society, the more it must develop civic associations to avoid authoritarianism. He posited that in centralized states with extensive state capacities and a professional bureaucracy, government initiatives would dominate public affairs and crowd out civic groups. If such societies tried to democratize rapidly, they would likely fail as their citizens had so little experience in handling civic affairs and were accustomed to the moderation and limited aims required of plural government. Tocqueville thought he saw this tendency in his native France. However, where government avoided excessive centralization and permitted civic associations, citizens would take the lead in fostering new economic, social, and cultural developments. The result would be a vital, dynamic, and cooperative society that would be prepared for democracy. The implications are important: constitutionally limited government and strong civic associations may help to overcome the democratic dilemma facing all modernizing states. More generally, Tocqueville built upon the liberal tradition in political thought to provide an account of how the practice of voluntary, local civic activism could provide the basis for a robust social order without a Hobbesian state.

Tocqueville returned to the same basic theme of the tension between social order and equality in *The Old Régime and the French Revolution*. In this study of the causes and consequences of the French revolution of 1789, Tocqueville wanted to explore why an evolution toward constitutional monarchy and pluralism (such as had occurred in England) had not occurred in monarchial France. He was puzzled as to why the revolutions, whose leaders initially favored gradual and limited reform, unleashed a radical transformation of society that obliterated existing institutions, massively increased the power of the state, and initiated two decades of conflict, civil war, invasion, and the eventual dictatorship of Napoleon.

Tocqueville traced long-term structural transformations and probed the social psychology of rebellion and revolution. He used primary source materials from the French state archives to fuel his inquiry. He found that France had undergone steady improvement in its economy and state capacities over the course of the 18th century. But rather than satisfy public opinion, these improvements only stoked the demand for more extensive reform. Tocqueville argued that periods of sustained economic growth and social progress had a paradoxical tendency to increase political discontent. This *crisis of rising expectations* became acute for the population of a country when, after a sustained period of improving conditions, a sudden reversal was experienced. Even though the resulting situation would tend to impose circumstances that were less severe than they had been in the past, citizens would have come to expect more and would no longer be satisfied by conditions that failed to meet their expectations. In this way, the economic difficulties and the acute fiscal crisis that the monarchy confronted in the late 1780s provoked a level of élite conflict and popular unrest that Tocqueville considered quite out of proportion with the objective grievances held by most French subjects. As he observed, "a grievance comes to appear intolerable once the possibility of removing it crosses men's minds" (p. 177).

In the midst of a growing sense of crisis, the French monarchy pledged itself to reform. But its opponents took these reforms as a sign of weakness while radicals were disappointed that they were too limited and moderate. As the government and its supporters grew politically weaker, its opponents gained popularity. The relaxation of political control expanded the political opportunities available to the king's diverse opponents. Though the government urgently sought to institute reforms it could not satisfy growing demands for action. Confidence in the monarchy collapsed and financial catastrophe loomed, providing the revolutionaries with their chance. Many of France's traditional institutions and practices were regarded by the growing class of urban intellectuals as chaotic, inefficient, and corrupt. Tocqueville posited that certain social conditions promoted intellectual radicalism. When opportunities for education expanded faster than social opportunities and when intellectuals had no route into government or public responsibility, radicalism would flourish. In the case of French intellectuals, they had been nourished on the idealism of the Enlightenment but were excluded from government and the highest levels of French society by its aristocratic caste system. Their social position nourished their resentment but also encouraged their idealism since their ideas were unburdened by the practical obligations of governing. Meanwhile, France's traditional political and social élite, the nobility, jealously guarded its privileges while its real economic status declined relative to the bourgeoisie. By the end of the century, the nobility – the social class most important for the stability of the old regime – was politically isolated and demoralized. In the midst of the revolutionary upheaval from 1789, the moderate and aristocratic reformers were swept away by radicals promising universal citizenship, equality before the law, and a new, unified French nation. While their idealism inspired many, they proved inexperienced and incapable in governing the country, provoking civil conflict, war, and economic difficulty. In time, they too were swept away by a military dictatorship promising to retain the achievements of the revolution while restoring order and stability.

For Tocqueville, the greatest irony of the French revolution was that while rationalization and centralization of the state administration and the institution of legal equality (that is, the abolition of the feudal system) were its greatest achievements, gradual movement toward precisely those aims had already been underway in the old regime prior to 1789. Hence, in identifying long-term structural changes that had undermined the social foundation of the monarchy, the crisis of rising expectations that resulted from a weak state's inability to manage demands for continual improvement, and the rise of a class of radical intellectuals, Tocqueville uncovered general social mechanisms that helped unravel the "dark and sinister enigma" of the revolution and its legacy.

Continuing Relevance

In sociology, Tocqueville's interrogation of possessive individualism and the decay of traditional status groups has been taken up by many subsequent theorists, among them Emile Durkheim (see Part IV). However, Tocqueville has also become an icon among many thinkers concerned with explaining American society and politics. For some, he has become a crucial theorist in explaining why the United States has a less centralized government and a less generous welfare state than most other modern democracies. They tend to cite Tocqueville to point to the genius of American institutions and a political culture that favors individualism, voluntarism, and self-interested action over collectivism and state control. For others, Tocqueville serves as continuing reminder of the tensions at the heart of the American democratic experiment, including its racial boundaries and social inequalities, as well as its smugness, populism, and self-satisfaction. In the political instrumentalization of Tocqueville, however, his contributions as a pioneering comparative and historical social scientist and social theorist are often lost.

The continuing influence of Tocqueville's social theory is nowhere more evident than in the work of Harvard political scientist Robert Putnam. In his books on the effectiveness of local government in Italy and on the decay of social capital in the United States, Putnam has built on Tocqueville's theory of civic associations as the basis of effective democratic government. In a provocative book entitled *Bowling Alone* (2000), Putnam argued that American democracy was imperiled by growing social isolation and disengagement from civic affairs in recent decades. While

Putnam's claims have been controversial, his work has revitalized the study of civil society and social capital pioneered by Tocqueville.

Tocqueville also continues to be employed in the comparative and historical analysis of politics and society. His insights into the mechanics of civic associationalism and the institutions that foster good government and public-spirited collective action remain trenchant. And his ideas can be applied to understanding revolutionary upheavals in the modern world. Tocqueville famously noted, "For it is not always when things are going from bad to worse that revolutions break out. On the contrary, it oftener happens that when a people has put up with an oppressive rule over a long period without protest suddenly finds the government relaxing its pressure, it takes up arms against it. Thus the social order overthrown by a revolution is almost always better than the one immediately preceding it, and experiences teaches us that, generally speaking, the most perilous moment for a bad government is when it seeks to mend its ways" (Tocqueville, 1955: 176–7). This insight seems as true today as it was a century and a half ago. And his insights into the social dynamics operating in revolutionary episodes seem to help explain not only France's revolutions, but also subsequent events such as the Russian revolution of 1917, the fall of the Iranian shah in 1979, and the 1989–91 collapse of communism in Eastern Europe and the Soviet Union. As a theorist that experienced intimately the social dislocation and political upheavals that often accompany economic development and democratization, Tocqueville offers much as we analyze contemporary societies struggling to accommodate increasing equality while maintaining order.

SELECTED BIBLIOGRAPHY

Aron, Raymond. 1968. *Main Currents in Sociological Thought.* Vol. I. Translated by Richard Howard and Helen Weaver. New York: Anchor.

Putnam, Robert. 2000. *Bowling Alone: The Collapse and Revival of American Community.* New York: Simon & Schuster.

Tocqueville, Alexis de. 1955 [1856]. *The Old Régime and the French Revolution.* Translated by Stuart Gilbert. New York: Doubleday.

_____. 1987. *Recollections: The French Revolution of 1848.* Edited by J.P. Taylor and A.P. Kerr. New Brunswick, NJ: Transaction Press.

_____. 2000 [1835–1840]. *Democracy in America.* Translated and edited by Harvey C. Mansfield and Delba Winthrop. Chicago and London: The University of Chicago Press.

Chapter 6

The Old Régime and the French Revolution [1856]

Alexis de Tocqueville

What did the French Revolution and Accomplish?

[…]

The aim of the Revolution was not, as once was thought, to destroy the authority of the Church and religious faith in general. Appearances notwithstanding, it was essentially a movement for political and social reform and, as such, did not aim at creating a state of permanent disorder in the conduct of public affairs or (as one of its opponents bitterly remarked) at "methodizing anarchy." On the contrary, it sought to increase the power and jurisdiction of the central authority. Nor was it intended, as some have thought, to change the whole nature of our traditional civilization, to arrest its progress, or even to make any vital change in the principles basic to the structure of society in the Western World. If we disregard various incidental developments which briefly modified its aspect at different periods and in different lands, and study it as it was essentially, we find that the chief permanent achievement of the French Revolution was the suppression of those political institutions, commonly described as feudal, which for many centuries had held unquestioned sway in most European countries. The Revolution set out to replace them with a new social and political order, at once simple and more uniform, based on the concept of the equality of all men.

de Tocqueville, Alexis, "The Old Regime and the French Revolution," pp. 19–21, 77–78, 80–81, 139, 140–142, 146, 147, 174, 175, 176–177, 179, 203, 204, 205, 209, 210 from Alexis de Tocqueville, *The Old Régime and the French Revolution*, translated by Stuart Gilbert. New York: Doubleday & Company, Inc., 1955 © 1955 by Doubleday, a division of Random House Inc. Used by permission of Doubleday, a division of Random House Inc.

Classical Sociological Theory, Third Edition. Edited by Craig Calhoun, Joseph Gerteis, James Moody, Steven Pfaff, and Indermohan Virk. Editorial material and organization © 2012 John Wiley & Sons, Ltd. Published 2012 by John Wiley & Sons, Ltd.

This in itself was enough to constitute a thorough-paced revolution since, apart from the fact that the old feudal institutions still entered into the very texture of the religious and political institutions of almost the whole of Europe, they had also given rise to a host of ideas, sentiments, manners, and customs which, so to speak, adhered to them. Thus nothing short of a major operation was needed to excise from the body politic these accretions and to destroy them utterly. The effect was to make the Revolution appear even more drastic than it actually was; since what it was destroying affected the entire social system.

Radical though it may have been, the Revolution made far fewer changes than is generally supposed, as I shall point out later. What in point of fact it destroyed, or is in process of destroying – for the Revolution is still operative – may be summed up as everything in the old order that stemmed from aristocratic and feudal institutions, was in any way connected with them, or even bore, however faintly, their imprint. The only elements of the old régime that it retained were those which had always been foreign to its institutions and could exist independently of them. [...]

Such then was the achievement of the Revolution, and it may appear surprising that even the most clear sighted contemporaries should have missed the point of an event whose purport seems so clear to us today. Even Burke failed to understand it. "You wish to correct the abuses of your government," he said to the French, "but why invent novelties? Why not return to your old traditions? Why not confine yourselves to a resumption of your ancient liberties? Or, if it was not possible to recover the obliterated features of your original constitution, why not look towards England? There you would have found the ancient common law of Europe." Burke did not see that what was taking place before his eyes was a revolution whose aim was precisely to abolish that "ancient common law of Europe," and that there could be no question of putting the clock back.

But why did the storm that was gathering over the whole of Europe break in France and not elsewhere, and why did it acquire certain characteristics in France which were either absent in similar movements in other countries, or if present, assumed quite different forms? [...]

How France had become the Country in which Men were most like each other

One of the things which cannot fail to strike an attentive student of the social system under the old order is that it had two quite contradictory aspects. On the one hand, we get an impression that the people composing it, at least those belonging to the upper and the middle classes – the only ones that is to say who catch the eye – were all exactly like each other. Nevertheless, we also find that this seemingly homogeneous mass was still divided within itself into a great number of watertight compartments, small, self-contained units, each of which watched vigilantly over its own interests and took no part in the life of the community at large.

If we bear in mind the number of these minute gradings and the fact that nowhere else in the world were citizens less inclined to join forces and stand by each other in emergencies, we can see how it was that a successful revolution could tear down the whole social structure almost in the twinkling of an eye. All the flimsy barriers between the various compartments were instantaneously laid low, and out of the ruins there arose a social order closer knit and less differentiated, perhaps, than any that the Western World had ever known.

I have pointed out how local differences between the various provinces had long since been obliterated throughout practically the entire kingdom; this had greatly contributed to making Frenchmen everywhere so much like each other. Behind such diversities as still existed the unity of the nation was making itself felt, sponsored by that new conception: "the same laws for all." For as the eighteenth century advances, we find an ever increasing number of edicts, Orders in Council, and royal mandates imposing the same regulations and the same procedures on all parts of the kingdom. Not only the governing class but also the governed endorsed this concept of a standardized legislative system valid everywhere. Indeed, it underlies all the successive projects of reform put forward during the three decades preceding the Revolution. Two centuries earlier any such projects would have been quite literally unthinkable.

Not only did the provinces come to resemble each other more and more, but within each province members of the various classes (anyhow those above the lowest social stratum) became ever more alike, differences of rank notwithstanding. This is borne out conspicuously by the *cahiers* (written instructions given to the deputies) presented by the different Orders at the meeting of the Estates-General in 1789. Allowing for the fact that the parties who drew up these memoranda had strongly conflicting interests, they seem remarkably alike in tenor.

[…]

Education and a similar style of living had already obliterated many of the distinctions between the two classes. The bourgeois was as cultivated as the nobleman and his enlightenment came from the same source. Both had been educated on literary and philosophic lines, for Paris, now almost the sole fountainhead of knowledge for the whole of France, had cast the minds of all in the same mold and given them the same equipment. No doubt it was still possible at the close of the eighteenth century to detect shades of difference in the behavior of the aristocracy and that of the bourgeoisie; for nothing takes longer to acquire than the surface polish which is called good manners. But basically all who ranked above the common herd were of a muchness; they had the same ideas, the same habits, the same tastes, the same kinds of amusements; read the same books and spoke in the same way. They differed only in their rights.

I doubt if this leveling-up process was carried so far in any other country, even in England, where the different classes, though solidly allied by common interests, still differed in mentality and manners. For political freedom, though it has the admirable effect of creating reciprocal ties and a feeling of solidarity between all the members of a nation, does not necessarily make them resemble each other. It is only government by a single man that in the long run irons out diversities and makes each member of a nation indifferent to his neighbor's lot.

[…]

How Towards the Middle of the Eighteenth Century Men of Letters took the Lead in Politics and the Consequences of this New Development

[…]

The political programs advocated by our eighteenth-century writers varied so much that any attempt to synthesize them or deduce a single coherent theory of government from them would be labor lost. Nonetheless, if, disregarding details, we look to the directive ideas, we find that all these various systems stemmed from a single concept of a highly general order, their common source, and that our authors took this as their premise before venturing on their personal, often somewhat eccentric solutions of the problem of good government. Thus, though their ways diverged in the course of their researches, their starting point was the same in all cases; and this was the belief that what was wanted was to replace the complex of traditional customs governing the social order of the day by simple, elementary rules deriving from the exercise of the human reason and natural law.

[…]

It was not by mere chance that our eighteenth-century thinkers as a body enounced theories so strongly opposed to those that were still regarded as basic to the social order; they could hardly be expected to do otherwise when they contemplated the world around them. The sight of so many absurd and unjust privileges, whose evil effects were increasingly felt on every hand though their true causes were less and less understood, urged or, rather, forced them towards a concept of the natural equality of all men irrespective of social rank. When they saw so many ridiculous, ramshackle institutions, survivals of an earlier age, which no one had attempted to co-ordinate or to adjust to modern conditions and which seemed destined to live on despite the fact that they had ceased to have any present value, it was natural enough that thinkers of the day should come to loathe everything that savored of the past and should desire to remold society on entirely new lines, traced by each thinker in the sole light of reason.

Their very way of living led these writers to indulge in abstract theories and generalizations regarding the nature of government, and to place a blind confidence in these. For living as they did, quite out of touch with practical politics, they lacked the experience which might have tempered their enthusiasms. Thus they completely failed to perceive the very real obstacles in the way of even the most praiseworthy reforms, and to gauge the perils involved in even the most salutary revolutions. That they should not have had the least presentiment of these dangers was only to be expected, since as a result of the total absence of any political freedom, they had little acquaintance with the realities of public life, which, indeed, was *terra incognita* to them. Taking no personal part in it and unable to see what was being done by others in that field, they lacked even the superficial acquaintance with such matters which comes to those who live under a free régime, can see what is happening, and hear the voice of public opinion even though they themselves take no part whatever in the government of the country. As a result, our literary men became much bolder in their speculations, more addicted to general ideas and systems, more contemptuous of the wisdom of the ages, and even more inclined to trust their individual reason than most of those who have written books on politics from a philosophic angle.

When it came to making themselves heard by the masses and appealing to their emotions, this very ignorance served them in good stead. If the French people had still played an active part in politics (through the Estates-General) or even if they had merely continued to concern themselves with the day-to-day administration of affairs through the provincial assemblies, we may be sure that they would not have let themselves be carried away so easily by the ideas of the writers of the day; any experience, however slight, of public affairs would have made them chary of accepting the opinions of mere theoreticians.

Similarly if, like the English, they had succeeded in gradually modifying the spirit of their ancient institutions without destroying them, perhaps they would not have been so prompt to clamor for a new order. As it was, however, every Frenchman felt he was being victimized; his personal freedom, his money, his self-respect, and the amenities of his daily life were constantly being tampered with on the strength of some ancient law, some medieval usage, or the remnants of some antiquated servitude. Nor did he see any constitutional remedy for this state of affairs; it seemed as if the choice lay between meekly accepting everything or destroying the whole system.

Nevertheless, in the nation-wide debacle of freedom we had preserved one form of it; we could indulge, almost without restriction, in learned discussions on the origins of society, the nature of government, and the essential rights of man. All who were chafing under the yoke of the administration enjoyed these literary excursions into politics; indeed, the taste for them spread even into sections of the community whose temperaments or upbringing would have normally discouraged them from abstract speculations. [...]

Thus the philosopher's cloak provided safe cover for the passions of the day and the political ferment was canalized into literature, the result being that our writers now became the leaders of public opinion and played for a while the part which normally, in free countries, falls to the professional politician. And as things were, no one was in a position to dispute their right to leadership.

[...]

Thus alongside the traditional and confused, not to say chaotic, social system of the day there was gradually built up in men's minds an imaginary ideal society in which all was simple, uniform, coherent, equitable, and rational in the full sense of the term. It was this vision of the perfect State that fired the imagination of the masses and little by little estranged them from the here-and-now. Turning away from the real world around them, they indulged in dreams of a far better one and ended up by living, spiritually, in the ideal world thought up by the writers.

[…]

When we closely study the French Revolution we find that it was conducted in precisely the same spirit as that which gave rise to so many books expounding theories of government in the abstract. Our revolutionaries had the same fondness for broad generalizations, cut-and-dried legislative systems, and a pedantic symmetry; the same contempt for hard facts: the same taste for reshaping institutions on novel, ingenious, original lines; the same desire to reconstruct the entire constitution according to the rules of logic and a preconceived system instead of trying to rectify its faulty parts. The result was nothing short of disastrous; for what is a merit in the writer may well be a vice in the statesman and the very qualities which go to make great literature can lead to catastrophic revolutions.

[…]

A study of comparative statistics makes it clear that in none of the decades immediately following the Revolution did our national prosperity make such rapid forward strides as in the two preceding it. Only the thirty-seven years of constitutional monarchy, which were for us a time of peace and plenty, are in any way comparable in this respect with the reign of Louis XVI.

At first sight it seems hard to account for this steady increase in the wealth of the country despite the as yet unremedied shortcomings of the administration and the obstacles with which industry still had to contend. Indeed, many of our politicians, being unable to explain it, have followed the example of Molière's physician, who declared that no sick man could recover "against the rules of medicine" – and simply denied its existence. That France could prosper and grow rich, given the inequality of taxation, the vagaries of local laws, internal customs barriers, feudal rights, the trade corporations, the sales of offices, and all the rest, may well seem hardly credible. Yet the fact remains that the country did grow richer and living conditions improved throughout the land, and the reason was that though the machinery of government was ramshackle, ill regulated, inefficient, and though it tended to hinder rather than to further social progress, it had two redeeming features which sufficed to make it function and made for national prosperity. Firstly, though the government was no longer despotic, it still was powerful and capable of maintaining order everywhere; and secondly, the nation possessed an upper class that was the freest, most enlightened of the day and a social system under which every man could get rich if he set his mind to it and keep intact the wealth he had acquired.

[…]

It is a singular fact that this steadily increasing prosperity, far from tranquilizing the population, everywhere promoted a spirit of unrest. The general public became more and more hostile to every ancient institution, more and more discontented; indeed, it was increasingly obvious that the nation was heading for a revolution.

Moreover, those parts of France in which the improvement in the standard of living was most pronounced were the chief centers of the revolutionary movement.

[…]

Thus it was precisely in those parts of France where there had been most improvement that popular discontent ran highest. This may seem illogical – but history is full of such paradoxes. For it is not always when things are going from bad to worse that revolutions break out. On the contrary, it oftener happens that when a people which has put up with an oppressive rule over a long period without protest suddenly finds the government relaxing its pressure, it takes up arms against it. Thus the social order overthrown by a revolution is almost always better than the one immediately preceding it, and experience teaches us that, generally speaking, the most perilous moment for a bad government is one when it seeks to mend its ways. Only consummate statecraft can enable a King to save his throne when after a long spell of oppressive rule he sets to improving the lot of his subjects. Patiently endured so long as it seemed beyond redress, a grievance comes to appear intolerable once the possibility of removing it crosses men's minds. For the mere fact that certain abuses have been remedied draws attention to the others and they now appear more galling; people may suffer less, but their sensibility is exacerbated. At the height of its power feudalism did not inspire so much hatred as it did on the eve of its eclipse.

[…]

Thus it was that *rentiers*, merchants, manufacturers, businessmen, and financiers – the section of the community usually most averse to violent political changes, warm supporters of the existing government, whatever it may be, and essentially law-abiding even when they despise or dislike the laws – now proved to be the most strenuous and determined advocates of reform. What they demanded most vociferously was nothing short of a radical change in the entire financial administration of the country, and they failed to realize that a change so revolutionary would spell the downfall of the constitution as a whole. It is hard to see how a catastrophe could have been averted. On the one hand was a nation in which the love of wealth and luxury was daily spreading; on the other a government that while constantly fomenting this new passion, at the same time I frustrated it – and by this fatal inconsistency was sealing its own doom.

[…]

How, given the facts set forth in the preceding chapters, the Revolution was a foregone conclusion

[…]

When we remember that it was in France that the feudal system, while retaining the characteristics which made it so irksome to, and so much resented by, the masses, had most completely discarded all that could benefit or protect them, we may feel less surprise at the fact that France was the place of origin of the revolt destined so violently to sweep away the last vestiges of that ancient European institution.

Similarly, if we observe how the nobility after having lost their political rights and ceased, to a greater extent than in any other land of feudal Europe, to act as leaders of the people had nevertheless not only retained but greatly increased their fiscal immunities and the advantages accruing to them individually; and if we also note how, while ceasing to be the ruling class, they had remained a privileged, closed group, less and less (as I have pointed out) an aristocracy and more and more a caste – if we bear these facts in mind, it is easy to see why the privileges enjoyed by this small section of the community seemed so unwarranted and so odious to the French people and why they developed that intense jealousy of the "upper class" which rankles still today.

Finally, when we remember that the nobility had deliberately cut itself off both from the middle class and from the peasantry (whose former affection it had alienated) and had thus become like a foreign body in the State: ostensibly the high command of a great army, but actually a corps of officers without troops to follow them – when we keep this in mind, we can easily understand why the French nobility, after having so far weathered every storm, was stricken down in a single night.

[…]

In no other country of Europe had all political thought been so thoroughly and for so long stifled as in France; in no other country had the private citizen become so completely out of touch with public affairs and so unused to studying the course of events, so much so that not only had the average Frenchman no experience of "popular movements" but he hardly understood what "the people" meant. Bearing this in mind, we may find it easier to understand why the nation as a whole could launch out into a sanguinary revolution, with those very men who stood to lose most by it taking the lead and clearing the ground for it.

Since no free institutions and, as a result, no experienced and organized political parties existed any longer in France, and since in the absence of any political groups of this sort the guidance of public opinion, when its first stirrings made themselves felt, came entirely into the hands of the philosophers, that is to say the intellectuals, it was only to be expected that the directives of the Revolution should take the form of abstract principles, highly generalized theories, and that political realities would be largely overlooked. Thus, instead of attacking only such laws as seemed objectionable, the idea developed that *all* laws indiscriminately must be abolished and a wholly new system of government, sponsored by these writers, should replace the ancient French constitution.

[…]

Actually there had existed under the old régime a host of institutions which had quite a "modern" air and, not being incompatible with equality, could easily be embodied in the new social order and all these institutions offered remarkable facilities to despotism. They were hunted for among the wreckage of the old order and duly salvaged. These institutions had formerly given rise to customs, usages, ideas, and prejudices tending to keep men apart, and thus make them easier to rule. They were revived and skillfully exploited; centralization was built up anew, and in the process all that had once kept it within bounds was carefully eliminated. Thus there arose, within a nation that had but recently laid low its monarchy, a central authority with powers wider, stricter, and more absolute than those which any French King had ever wielded. Rash though this venture may have been, it was carried through with entire success for the good reason that people took into account only what was under their eyes and forgot what they had seen before. Napoleon fell but the more solid parts of his achievement lasted on; his government died, but his administration survived, and every time that an attempt is made to do away with absolutism the most that could be done has been to graft the head of Liberty onto a servile body.

[...]

To those who study it as an isolated phenomenon the French Revolution can but seem a dark and sinister enigma; only when we view it in the light of the events preceding it can we grasp its true significance. And, similarly, without a clear idea of the old régime, its laws, its vices, its prejudices, its shortcomings, and its greatness, it is impossible to comprehend the history of the sixty years following its fall.

Chapter 7

Influence of Democracy on the Feelings of the Americans [1840]

Alexis de Tocqueville

Why Democratic Nations Show a More Ardent and Enduring Love of Equality than of Liberty

The first and most intense passion which is engendered by the equality of conditions is, I need hardly say, the love of that same equality. My readers will therefore not be surprised that I speak of it before all others.

Everybody has remarked, that in our time, and especially in France, this passion for equality is every day gaining ground in the human heart. It has been said a hundred times that our contemporaries are far more ardently and tenaciously attached to equality than to freedom; but, as I do not find that the causes of the fact have been sufficiently analyzed, I shall endeavour to point them out.

It is possible to imagine an extreme point at which freedom and equality would meet and be confounded together. Let us suppose that all the members of the community take a part in the government, and that each one of them has an equal right to take a part in it. As none is different from his fellows, none can exercise a tyrannical power: men will be perfectly free, because they will all be entirely equal; and they will all be perfectly equal, because they will be entirely free. To this ideal state democratic nations tend. Such is the completest form that equality can assume upon earth; but there are a thousand others which, without being equally perfect, are not less cherished by those nations.

de Tocqueville, Alexis, "Influence of Democracy on the Feelings of the Americans" from Alexis de Tocqueville, *Democracy in America*: New York – J. & H.G. Langley 1840.

The principle of equality may be established in civil society, without prevailing in the political world. Equal rights may exist of indulging in the same pleasures, of entering the same professions, of frequenting the same places – in a word, of living in the same manner and seeking wealth by the same means, although all men do not take an equal share in the government.

A kind of equality may even be established in the political world, though there should be no political freedom there. A man may be the equal of all his countrymen save one, who is the master of all without distinction, and who selects equally from among them all the agents of his power.

Several other combinations might be easily imagined, by which very great equality would be united to institutions more or less free, or even to institutions wholly without freedom.

Although men cannot become absolutely equal unless they be entirely free, and consequently equality, pushed to its furthest extent, may be confounded with freedom, yet there is good reason for distinguishing the one from the other. The taste which men have for liberty, and that which they feel for equality, are, in fact, two different things; and I am not afraid to add, that, among democratic nations, they are two unequal things.

Upon close inspection, it will be seen that there is in every age some peculiar and preponderating fact with which all others are connected; this fact almost always gives birth to some pregnant idea or some ruling passion, which attracts to itself, and bears away in its course, all the feelings and opinions of the time: it is like a great stream, toward which each of the surrounding rivulets seem to flow.

Freedom has appeared in the world at different times and under various forms; it has not been exclusively bound to any social-condition, and it is not confined to democracies. Freedom cannot, therefore, form the distinguishing characteristic of democratic ages. The peculiar and preponderating fact which marks those ages as its own is the equality of conditions; the ruling passion of men in those periods is the love of this equality. Ask not what singular charm the men of democratic ages find in being equal, or what special reasons they may have for clinging so tenaciously to equality rather than to the other advantages which society holds out to them: equality is the distinguishing characteristic of the age they live in; that, of itself, is enough to explain that they prefer it to all the rest.

But independently of this reason there are several others, which will at all times habitually lead men to prefer equality to freedom.

If a people could ever succeed in destroying, or even in diminishing, the equality which prevails in its own body, this could only be accomplished by long and laborious efforts. Its social condition must be modified, its laws abolished, its opinions superseded, its habits changed, its manners corrupted. But political liberty is more easily lost; to neglect to hold it fast, is to allow it to escape.

Men therefore not only cling to equality because it is dear to them; they also adhere to it because they think it will last for ever.

That political freedom may compromise in its excesses the tranquillity, the property, the lives of individuals, is obvious to the narrowest and most unthinking minds. But, on the contrary, none but attentive and clear-sighted men perceive the perils with which equality threatens us, and they commonly avoid pointing them out. They know that the calamities they apprehend are remote, and flatter themselves that they will only fall upon future generations, for which the present generation takes but little thought. The evils which freedom sometimes brings with it are immediate; they are apparent to all, and all are more or less affected by them. The evils which extreme equality may produce are slowly disclosed; they creep gradually into the social frame; they are only seen at intervals, and at the moment at which they become most violent, habit already causes them to be no longer felt.

The advantages which freedom brings are only shown by length of time; and it is always easy to mistake the cause in which they originate. The advantages of equality are instantaneous, and they may constantly be traced from their source.

Political liberty bestows exalted pleasures, from time to time, upon a certain number of citizens. Equality every day confers a number of small enjoyments on every man. The charms of equality are every instant felt, and are within the reach of all: the noblest hearts are not insensible to them, and the most vulgar souls exult in them. The passion which equality engenders must therefore be at once strong and general. Men cannot enjoy political liberty unpurchased by some sacrifices, and they never obtain it without great exertions. But the pleasures of equality are self-proffered: each of the petty incidents of life seems to occasion them, and in order to taste them nothing is required but to live.

Democratic nations are at all times fond of equality, but there are certain epochs at which the passion they entertain for it swells to the height of fury. This occurs at the moment when the old social system, long menaced, completes its own destruction after a last intestine struggle, and when the barriers of rank are at length thrown down. At such times men pounce upon equality as their booty, and they cling to it as to some precious treasure which they fear to lose. The passion for equality penetrates on every side into men's hearts, expands there, and fills them entirely. Tell them not that by this blind surrender of themselves to an exclusive passion, they risk their dearest interests: they are deaf. Show them not freedom escaping from their grasp, while they are looking another way: they are blind – or rather, they can discern but one sole object to be desired in the universe.

What I have said is applicable to all democratic nations: what I am about to say concerns the French alone. Among most modern nations, and especially among all those of the continent of Europe, the taste and the idea of freedom only began to exist and to extend itself at the time when social conditions were tending to equality, and as a consequence of that very equality. Absolute kings were the most efficient levellers of ranks among their subjects. Among these nations equality preceded freedom: equality was therefore a fact of some standing, when freedom was still a novelty: the one had already created customs, opinions, and laws belonging to it, when the other, alone and for the first time, came into actual existence. Thus the latter was still only an affair of opinion and of taste, while the former had already crept into the habits of the people, possessed itself of their manners, and given a particular turn to the smallest actions in their lives. Can it be wondered that the men of our own time prefer the one to the other?

I think that democratic communities have a natural taste for freedom: left to themselves, they will seek it, cherish it, and view any privation of it with regret. But for equality, their passion is ardent, insatiable, incessant, invincible: they call for equality in freedom; if they cannot obtain that, they still call for equality in slavery. They will endure poverty, servitude, barbarism – but they will not endure aristocracy.

This is true at all times, and especially true in our own. All men and all powers seeking to cope with this irresistible passion, will be overthrown and destroyed by it. In our age, freedom cannot be established without it, and despotism itself cannot reign without its support.

Of Individualism in Democratic Countries

I have shown how it is that in ages of equality every man seeks for his opinions within himself: I am now about to show how it is that, in the same ages, all his feelings are turned toward himself alone. *Individualism* is a novel expression to which a novel idea has given birth. Our fathers were only acquainted with egotism. Egotism is a passionate and exaggerated love of self, which leads a man to connect everything with his own person, and to prefer himself to everything in the world. Individualism is a mature and calm feeling, which disposes each member of the community to sever himself from the mass of his fellow-creatures, and to draw apart with his family and his friends so that, after he has thus formed a little circle of his own, he willingly leaves society at large to itself. Egotism originates in blind instinct: individualism proceeds from erroneous judgement more than from depraved feelings; it originates as much in the deficiencies of the mind as in the perversity of the heart.

Egotism blights the germ of all virtue: Individualism, at first, only saps the virtues of public life; but, in the long run, it attacks and destroys all others, and is at length absorbed in downright egotism. Egotism is a vice as old as the world, which does not belong to one form of society more than to another: individualism is of democratic origin, and it threatens to spread in the same ratio as the equality of conditions.

Among aristocratic nations, as families remain for centuries in the same condition, often on the same spot, all generations become as it were contemporaneous. A man almost always knows his forefathers, and respects them: he thinks he already sees his remote descendants, and he loves them. He willingly imposes duties on himself toward the former and the latter; and he will frequently sacrifice his personal gratifications to those who went before and to those who will come after him.

Aristocratic institutions have, moreover, the effect of closely binding every man to several of his fellow-citizens. As the classes of an aristocratic people are strongly marked and permanent, each of them is regarded by its own members as a sort of lesser country, more tangible and more cherished than the country at large. As in aristocratic communities all the citizens occupy fixed positions, one above the other, the result is that each of them always sees a man above himself whose patronage is necessary to him, and below himself another man whose co-operation he may claim.

Men living in aristocratic ages are therefore almost always closely attached to something placed out of their own sphere, and they are often disposed to forget themselves. It is true that in those ages the notion of human fellowship is faint, and that men seldom think of sacrificing themselves for mankind; but they often sacrifice themselves for other men. In democratic ages, on the contrary, when the duties of each individual to the race are much more clear, devoted service to any one man becomes more rare; the bond of human affection is extended, but it is relaxed.

Among democratic nations new families are constantly springing up, others are constantly falling away, and all that remain change their condition; the woof of time is every instant broken, and the track of generations effaced. Those who went before are soon forgotten; of those who will come after no one has any idea: the interest of man is confined to those in close propinquity to himself.

As each class approximates to other classes, and intermingles with them, its members become indifferent and as strangers to one another. Aristocracy had made a chain of all the members of the community, from the peasant to the king: democracy breaks that chain, and severs every link of it.

As social conditions become more equal, the number of persons increases who, although they are neither rich enough nor powerful enough to exercise any great influence over their fellow-creatures, have nevertheless acquired or retained sufficient education and fortune to satisfy their own wants. They owe nothing to any man, they expect nothing from any man; they acquire the habit of always considering themselves as standing alone, and they are apt to imagine that their whole destiny is in their own hands.

Thus not only does democracy make every man forget his ancestors, but it hides his descendants, and separates his contemporaries, from him; it throws him back for ever upon himself alone, and threatens in the end to confine him entirely within the solitude of his own heart.

[...]

That the Americans Combat the Effects of Individualism by Free Institutions

Despotism, which is of a very timorous nature, is never more secure of continuance than when it can keep men asunder; and all its influence is commonly exerted for that purpose. No vice of the human heart is so acceptable to it as egotism: a despot easily forgives his subjects for not loving him, provided they do not love each other. He does not ask them to assist him in governing the state; it is enough that they do not aspire to govern it themselves. He stigmatizes as turbulent and unruly spirits those who would combine their exertions to promote the prosperity of the community; and, perverting the natural meaning of words, he applauds as good citizens those who have no sympathy for any but themselves.

Thus the vices which despotism engenders are precisely those which equality fosters. These two things mutually and perniciously complete and assist each other. Equality places men side by side, unconnected by any common tie; despotism raises barriers to keep them asunder: the former predisposes them not to consider their fellow-creatures, the latter makes general indifference a sort of public virtue.

Despotism then, which is at all times dangerous, is more particularly to be feared in democratic ages. It is easy to see that in those same ages men stand most in need of freedom. When the members of a community are forced to attend to public affairs, they are necessarily drawn from the circle of their own interests, and snatched at times from self-observation. As soon as a man begins to treat of public affairs in public, he begins to perceive that he is not so independent of his fellow-men as he had at first imagined, and that, in order to obtain their support, he must often lend them his co-operation.

When the public is supreme, there is no man who does not feel the value of public good will, or who does not endeavour to court it by drawing to himself the esteem and affection of those among whom he is to live. Many of the passions which congeal and keep asunder human hearts, are then obliged to retire and hide below the surface. Pride must be dissembled; disdain dares not break out; egotism fears its own self. Under a free government, as most public offices are elective, the men, whose elevated minds or aspiring hopes are too closely circumscribed in private life, constantly feel that they cannot do without the population that surrounds them. Men learn at such times to think of their fellow-men from ambitious motives; and they frequently find it, in a manner, their interest to forget themselves.

I may here be met by an objection derived from electioneering intrigues, the meannesses of candidates, and the calumnies of their opponents. These are opportunities for animosity, which occur the oftener, the more frequent elections become. Such evils are doubtless great, but they are transient; whereas the benefits which attend them remain. The desire of being elected may lead some men for a time to violent hostility; but this same desire leads all men in the long run mutually to support each other; and, if it happens that an election accidentally severs two friends, the electoral system brings a multitude of citizens permanently together, who would always have remained unknown to each other. Freedom engenders private animosities, but despotism gives birth to general indifference.

The Americans have combated by free institutions the tendency of equality to keep men asunder, and they have subdued it. The legislators of America did not suppose that a general representation of the whole nation would suffice to ward off a disorder at once so natural to the frame of democratic society, and so fatal: they also thought that it would be well to infuse political life into each portion of the territory, in order to multiply to an infinite extent opportunities of acting in concert, for all the members of the community, and to make them constantly feel their mutual dependance on each other. The plan was a wise one. The general affairs of a country only engage the attention of leading politicians, who assemble from time to time in the same places; and as they often lose sight of each other afterward, no lasting ties are established between them. But if the object be to have the local affairs of a district conducted by the men who reside there, the same persons are always in contact, and they are, in a manner, forced to be acquainted, and to adapt themselves to one another.

It is difficult to draw a man out of his own circle to interest him in the destiny of the state, because he does not clearly understand what influence the destiny of the state can have upon his own lot. But if it be proposed to make a road cross the end of his estate, he will see at a glance that there is a connexion between this small public affair and his greatest private affairs; and he will discover, without its being shown to him, the close tie which unites private to general interest. Thus, far more may be done by entrusting to the citizens the administration of minor affairs than by surrendering to them the control of important ones, toward interesting them in the public welfare, and convincing them that they constantly stand in need one of the other in order to provide for it. A brilliant achievement may win for you the favour of a people at one stroke; but to earn the love and respect of the population which surrounds you, a long succession of little services rendered and of obscure good deeds – a constant habit of kindness, and an established reputation for disinterestedness – will be required. Local freedom, then, which leads a great number of citizens to value the affection of their neighbours and of their kindred, perpetually brings men together, and forces them to help one another, in spite of the propensities which sever them.

In the United States the more opulent citizens take great care not to stand aloof from the people; on the contrary, they constantly keep on easy terms with the lower classes: they listen to them, they speak to them every day. They know that the rich in democracies always stand in need of the poor; and that in democratic ages you attach a poor man to you more by your manner than by benefits conferred. The magnitude of such benefits, which sets off the difference of conditions, causes a secret irritation to those who reap advantage from them; but the charm of simplicity of manners is almost irresistible: their affability carries men away, and even their want of polish is not always displeasing. This truth does not take root at once in the minds of the rich. They generally resist it as long as the democratic revolution lasts, and they do not acknowledge it immediately after that revolution is accomplished. They are very ready to do good to the people, but they still choose to keep them at arm's length; they think that is sufficient, but they are mistaken. They might spend fortunes thus without warming the hearts of the population around them; – that population does not ask them for the sacrifice of their money, but of their pride.

It would seem as if every imagination in the United States were upon the stretch to invent means of increasing the wealth and satisfying the wants of the public. The best informed inhabitants of each district constantly use their information to discover new truths which may augment the general prosperity; and, if they have made any such discoveries, they eagerly surrender them to the mass of the people.

When the vices and weaknesses, frequently exhibited by those who govern in America, are closely examined, the prosperity of the people occasions – but improperly occasions – surprise. Elected magistrates do not make the American democracy flourish; it flourishes because the magistrates are elective.

It would be unjust to suppose that the patriotism and the zeal which every American displays for the welfare of his fellow-citizens are wholly insincere.

Although private interest directs the greater part of human actions in the United States, as well as elsewhere, it does not regulate them all. I must say that I have often seen Americans make great and real sacrifices to the public welfare; and I have remarked a hundred instances in which they hardly ever failed to lend faithful support to each other. The free institutions which the inhabitants of the United States possess, and the political rights of which they make so much use, remind every citizen, and in a thousand ways, that he lives in society. They every instant impress upon his mind the notion that it is the duty as well as the interest of men to make themselves useful to their fellow-creatures; and as he sees no particular ground of animosity to them, since he is never either their master or their slave, his heart readily leans to the side of kindness. Men attend to the interests of the public, first by necessity, afterward, by choice: what was intentional becomes an instinct; and by dint of working for the good of one's fellow-citizens, the habit and the taste for serving them is at length acquired.

Many people in France consider equality of conditions as one evil, and political freedom as a second. When they are obliged to yield to the former, they strive at least to escape from the latter. But I contend, that in order to combat the evils which equality may produce, there is only one effectual remedy – namely, political freedom.

Of the Use Which the Americans Make of Public Associations in Civil Life

I do not propose to speak of those political associations by the aid of which men endeavour to defend themselves against the despotic influence of a majority, or against the aggressions of regal power. That subject I have already treated. If each citizen did not learn, in proportion as he individually becomes more feeble and consequently more incapable of preserving his freedom single handed, to combine with his fellow-citizens for the purpose of defending it, it is clear that tyranny would unavoidably increase together with equality.

Those associations only which are formed in civil life, without reference to political objects, are here adverted to. The political associations which exist in the United States are only a single feature in the midst of the immense assemblage of associations in that country. Americans of all ages, all conditions, and all dispositions, constantly form associations. They have not only commercial and manufacturing companies, in which all take part, but associations of a thousand other kinds – religious, moral, serious, futile, extensive or restricted, enormous or diminutive. The Americans make associations to give entertainments, to found establishments for education, to build inns, to construct churches, to diffuse books, to send missionaries to the antipodes; and in this manner they found hospitals, prisons, and schools. If it be proposed to advance some truth, or to foster some feeling by the encouragement of a great example, they form a society. Wherever, at the head of some new undertaking, you see the government in France, or a man of rank in England, in the United States you will be sure to find an association.

I met with several kinds of associations in America, of which I confess I had no previous notion; and I have often admired the extreme skill with which the inhabitants of the United States succeed in proposing a common object to the exertions of a great many men, and in getting them voluntarily to pursue it.

I have since travelled over England, whence the Americans have taken some of their laws and many of their customs; and it seemed to me that the principle of association was by no means so constantly or so adroitly used in that country. The English often perform great things singly; whereas the Americans form associations for the smallest undertakings. It is evident that the former people consider association as a powerful means of action, but the latter seem to regard it as the only means they have of acting.

Thus the most democratic country on the face of the earth is that in which men have in our time carried to the highest perfection the art of pursuing in common the object of their common desires, and have applied this new science to the greatest number of purposes. Is this the result of accident? or is there in reality any necessary connexion between the principle of association and that of equality?

Aristocratic communities always contain, among a multitude of persons who by themselves are powerless, a small number of powerful and wealthy citizens, each of whom can achieve great undertakings single-handed. In aristocratic societies men do not need to combine in order to act, because they are strongly held together. Every wealthy and powerful citizen constitutes the head of a permanent and compulsory association, composed of all those who are dependant upon him, or whom he makes subservient to the execution of his designs.

Among democratic nations, on the contrary, all the citizens are independent and feeble; they can do hardly anything by themselves, and none of them can oblige his fellow-men to lend him their assistance. They all, therefore, fall into a state incapacity, if they do not learn voluntarily to help each other. If men living in democratic countries had no right and no inclination to associate for political purposes, their independence would be in great jeopardy; but they might long preserve their wealth and their cultivation: whereas if they never acquired the habit of forming associations in ordinary life, civilization itself would be endangered. A people among which individuals should lose the power of achieving great things single-handed, without acquiring the means of producing them by united exertions, would soon relapse into barbarism.

Unhappily, the same social condition which renders associations so necessary to democratic nations, renders their formation more difficult among those nations than among all others. When several members of an aristocracy agree to combine, they easily succeed in doing so: as each of them brings great strength to the partnership, the number of its members may be very limited; and when the members of an association are limited in number, they may easily become mutually acquainted, understand each other, and establish fixed regulations. The same opportunities do not occur among democratic nations, where the associated members must always be very numerous for their association to have any power.

I am aware that many of my countrymen are not in the least embarrassed by this difficulty. They contend that the more enfeebled and incompetent the citizens become, the more able and active the Government ought to be rendered, in order that society at large may execute what individuals can no longer accomplish. They believe this answers the whole difficulty, but I think they are mistaken.

A Government might perform the part of some of the largest American companies; and several States, members of the Union, have already attempted it: but what political power could ever carry on the vast multitude of lesser undertakings which the American citizens perform every day, with the assistance of the principle of association? It is easy to foresee that the time is drawing near when man will be less and less able to produce, of himself alone, the commonest necessaries of life. The task of the governing power will therefore perpetually increase, and its very efforts will extend it every day. The more it stands in the place of associations, the more will individuals, losing the notion of combining together, require its assistance: these are causes and effects which unceasingly engender each other. Will the administration of the country ultimately assume the management of all the manufactures, which no single citizen is able to carry on? And if a time at length arrives, when, in consequence of the extreme subdivision of landed property, the soil is split into an infinite number of parcels, so that it can only be cultivated by companies of husbandmen, will it be necessary that the head of the government should leave the helm of state to follow the plough? The morals and the intelligence of a democratic people would be as much endangered as its business and manufactures, if the government ever wholly usurped the place of private companies.

Feelings and opinions are recruited, the heart is enlarged, and the human mind is developed by no other means than by the reciprocal influence of men upon each other. I have shown that these influences are almost null in democratic countries; they must therefore be artificially created, and this can only be accomplished by associations.

When the members of an aristocratic community adopt a new opinion, or conceive a new sentiment, they give it a station, as it were, beside themselves, upon the lofty platform where they stand; and opinions or sentiments so conspicuous to the eyes of the multitude are easily introduced into the minds or hearts of all around. In democratic countries the governing power alone is naturally in a condition to act in this manner; but it is easy to see that its action is always inadequate, and often dangerous. A government can no more be competent to keep alive and to renew the circulation of opinions and feelings among a great people, than to manage all the speculations of productive industry. No sooner does a government attempt to go beyond its political sphere and to enter upon this new track, than it exercises, even unintentionally, an insupportable tyranny; for a government can only dictate strict rules, the opinions which it favours are rigidly enforced, and it is never easy to discriminate between its advice and its commands. Worse still will be the case if the government really believes itself interested in preventing all circulation of ideas; it will then stand motionless, and oppressed by the heaviness of voluntary torpor. Governments therefore should not be the only active powers: associations ought, in democratic nations, to stand in lieu of those powerful private individuals whom the equality of conditions has swept away.

As soon as several of the inhabitants of the United States have taken up an opinion or a feeling which they wish to promote in the world, they look out for mutual assistance; and as soon as they have found each other out, they combine. From that moment they are no longer isolated men, but a power seen from afar, whose actions serve for an example, and whose language is listened to. The first time I heard in the United States that a hundred thousand men had bound themselves publicly to abstain from spirituous liquors, it appeared to me more like a joke than a serious engagement; and I did not at once perceive why these temperate citizens could not content themselves with drinking water by their own firesides. I at last understood that these hundred thousand Americans, alarmed by the progress of drunkenness around them, had made up their minds to patronise temperance. They acted just in the same way as a man of high rank who should dress very plainly, in order to inspire the humbler orders with a contempt of luxury. It is probable, that if these hundred thousand men had lived in France, each of them would singly have memorialized the government to watch the public houses all over the kingdom.

Nothing, in my opinion, is more deserving of our attention than the intellectual and moral associations of America. The political and industrial associations of that country strike us forcibly; but the others elude our observation, or if we discover them, we understand them imperfectly, because we have hardly ever seen anything of the kind. It must, however, be acknowledged that they are as necessary to the American people as the former, and perhaps more so.

In democratic countries the science of association is the mother of science; the progress of all the rest depends upon the progress it has made.

Among the laws which rule human societies there is one which seems to be more precise and clear than all others. If men are to remain civilized, or to become so, the art of associating together must grow and improve, in the same ratio in which the equality of conditions is increased.

Of the Relation Between Public Associations and Newspapers

When men are no longer united among themselves by firm and lasting ties, it is impossible to obtain the co-operation of any great number of them, unless you can persuade every man whose concurrence you require that his private interest obliges him voluntarily to unite his exertions to the exertions of all the rest. This can only be habitually and conveniently effected by means of a newspaper; nothing but a newspaper can drop the same thought, into a thousand minds at the same moment. A newspaper is an adviser who does not require to be sought, but who comes of his own accord, and talks to you briefly every day of the common weal, without distracting you from your private affairs.

Newspapers therefore become more necessary in proportion as men become more equal, and individualism more to be feared. To suppose that they only serve to protect freedom would be to diminish their importance: they maintain civilization. I shall not deny that in democratic countries newspapers frequently lead the citizens to launch together in very ill-digested schemes; but if there were no newspapers there would be no common activity. The evil which they produce is therefore much less than that which they cure.

The effect of a newspaper is not only to suggest the same purpose to a great number of persons, but also to furnish means for executing in common the designs which they may have singly conceived. The principal citizens who inhabit an aristocratic country discern each other from afar; and if they wish to unite their forces, they move toward each other, drawing a multitude of men after them. It frequently happens, on the contrary, in democratic countries, that a great number of men who wish or who want to combine cannot accomplish it, because as they are very insignificant and lost amid the crowd, they cannot see, and know not where to find, one another. A newspaper then takes up the notion or the feeling which had occurred simultaneously, but singly, to each of them. All are then immediately guided toward this beacon; and these wandering minds, which had long sought each other in darkness, at length meet and unite.

The newspaper brought them together, and the newspaper is still necessary to keep them united. In order that an association among a democratic people should have any power, it must be a numerous body. The persons of whom it is composed are therefore scattered over a wide extent, and each of them is detained in the place of his domicil by the narrowness of his income, or by the small unremitting exertions by which he earns it. Means then must be found to converse every day without seeing each other, and to take steps in common without having met. Thus hardly any democratic association can do without newspapers.

There is consequently a necessary connexion between public associations and newspapers: newspapers make associations, and associations make newspapers; and if it has been correctly advanced that associations will increase in number as the conditions of men become more equal, it is not less certain that the number of newspapers increases in proportion to that of associations. Thus it is in America that we find at the same time the greatest number of associations and of newspapers.

This connexion between the number of newspapers and that of associations, leads us to the discovery of a further connexion between the state of the periodical press and the form of the administration in a country; and shows that the number of newspapers must diminish or increase among a democratic people, in proportion as its administration is more or less centralized. For, among democratic nations, the exercise of local powers cannot be entrusted to the principal members of the community, as in aristocracies. Those powers must either be abolished, or placed in the hands of very large numbers of men, who then in fact constitute an association permanently established by law, for the purpose of administering the affairs of a certain extent of territory; and they require a journal, to bring to them every day, in the midst of their own minor concerns, some intelligence of the state of their public weal. The more numerous local powers are, the greater is the number of men in whom they are vested by law; and, as this want is hourly felt, the more profusely do newspapers abound.

The extraordinary subdivision of administrative power has much more to do with the enormous number of American newspapers, than the great political freedom of the country and the absolute liberty of the press. If all the inhabitants of the Union had the suffrage – but a suffrage which should only extend to the choice of their legislators in Congress – they would require but few newspapers, because they would only have to act together on a few very important, but very rare, occasions. But within the pale of the great association of the nation, lesser associations have been established by law in every county, every city, and indeed in every village, for the purposes of local administration. The laws of the country thus compel every American to co-operate every day of his life with some of his fellow-citizens for a common purpose, and each one of them requires a newspaper to inform him what all the others are doing.

I am of opinion that a democratic people,[1] without any national representative assemblies, but with a great number of small local powers, would have in the end more newspapers than another people governed by a centralized administration and an elective legislation. What best explains to me the enormous circulation of the daily press in the United States, is that among the Americans I find the utmost national freedom combined with local freedom of every kind.

There is a prevailing opinion in France and England that the circulation of newspapers would be indefinitely increased by removing the taxes which have been laid upon the press. This is a very exaggerated estimate of the effects of such a reform. Newspapers increase in numbers, not only according to their cheapness, but according to the more or less frequent want which a great number of men may feel for intercommunication and combination.

In like manner I should attribute the increasing influence of the daily press to causes more general than those by which it is commonly explained. A newspaper can only subsist on the condition of publishing sentiments or principles common to a large number of men. A newspaper therefore always represents an association which is composed of its habitual readers. This association may be more or less defined, more or less restricted, more or less numerous; but the fact that the newspaper keeps alive, is a proof that at least the germ of such an association exists in the minds of its readers.

This leads me to a last reflection, with which I shall conclude this chapter. The more equal the conditions of men become, and the less strong men individually are, the more easily do they give way to the current of the multitude, and the more difficult is it for them to adhere by themselves to an opinion which the multitude discard. A newspaper represents an association; it may be said to address each of its readers in the name of all the others, and to exert its influence over them in proportion to their individual weakness. The power of the newspaper press must therefore increase as the social conditions of men become more equal.

Connexion of Civil and Political Associations

There is only one country on the face of the earth where the citizens enjoy unlimited freedom of association for political purposes. This same country is the only one in the world where the continual exercise of the right of association has been introduced into civil life, and where all the advantages which civilization can confer are procured by means of it.

In all the countries where political associations are prohibited, civil associations are rare. It is hardly probable that this is the result of accident; but the inference should rather be, that there is a natural, and perhaps a necessary, connexion between these two kinds of associations.

Certain men happen to have a common interest in some concern, either a commercial undertaking is to be managed, or some speculation in manufactures to be tried; they meet, they combine, and thus by degrees they become familiar with the principle of association. The greater is the multiplicity of small affairs, the more do men, even without knowing it, acquire facility in prosecuting great undertakings in common.

Civil associations, therefore, facilitate political association: but on the other hand, political association singularly strengthens and improves associations for civil purposes. In civil life every man may, strictly speaking, fancy that he can provide for his own wants; in politics, he can fancy no such thing. When a people, then, have any knowledge of public life, the notion of association, and the wish to coalesce, present themselves every day to the minds of the whole community: whatever natural repugnance may restrain men from acting in concert, they will always be ready to combine for the sake of a party. Thus political life makes the love and practice of association more general; it imparts a desire of union, and teaches the means of combination to numbers of men who would have always lived apart.

Politics not only give birth to numerous associations, but to associations of great extent. In civil life it seldom happens that any one interest draws a very large number of men to act in concert; much skill is required to bring such an interest into existence: but in politics opportunities present themselves every day. Now it is solely in great associations that the general value of the principle of association is displayed. Citizens who are individually powerless, do not very clearly anticipate the strength which they may acquire by uniting together; it must be shown to them in order to be understood. Hence it is often easier to collect a multitude for a public purpose than a few persons; a thousand citizens do not see what interest they have in combining together – ten thousand will be perfectly aware of it. In politics men combine for great undertakings; and the use they make of the principle of association in important affairs practically teaches them that it is their interest to help each other in those of less moment. A political association draws a number of individuals at the same time out of their own circle; however they may be naturally kept asunder by age, mind, and fortune, it places them nearer together and brings them into contact. Once met, they can always meet again.

Men can embark in few civil partnerships without risking a portion of their possessions; this is the case with all manufacturing and trading companies. When men are as yet but little versed in the art of association, and are unacquainted with its principal rules, they are afraid, when first they combine in this manner, of buying their experience dear. They therefore prefer depriving themselves of a powerful instrument of success, to running the risks which attend the use of it. They are, however, less reluctant to join political associations, which appear to them to be without danger, because they adventure no money in them. But they cannot belong to these associations for any length of time without finding out how order is maintained among a large number of men, and by what contrivance they are made to advance, harmoniously and methodically, to the same object. Thus they learn to surrender their own will to that of all the rest, and to make their own exertions subordinate to the common impulse – things which it is not less necessary to know in civil than in political associations. Political associations may therefore be considered as large free-schools, where all the members of the community go to learn the general theory of association.

But even if political association did not directly contribute to the progress of civil association, to destroy the former would be to impair the latter. When citizens can only meet in public for certain purposes, they regard such meetings as a strange proceeding of rare occurrence, and they rarely think at all about it. When they are allowed to meet freely for all purposes, they ultimately look upon public association as the universal, or in a manner the sole, means which men can employ to accomplish the different purposes they may have in view. Every new want instantly revives the notion. The art of association then becomes, as I have said before, the mother of action, studied and applied by all.

When some kinds of associations are prohibited and others allowed, it is difficult to distinguish the former from the latter beforehand. In this state of doubt men abstain from them altogether, and a sort of public opinion passes current, which tends to cause any association whatsoever to be regarded as a bold and almost an illicit enterprise.[2]

It is therefore chimerical to suppose that the spirit of association, when it is repressed on some one point, will nevertheless display the same vigor on all others; and that if men be allowed to prosecute certain undertakings in common, that is quite enough for them eagerly to set about them. When the members of a community are allowed and accustomed to combine for all purposes, they will combine as readily for the lesser as for the more important ones; but if they are only allowed to combine for small affairs, they will be neither inclined nor able to effect it. It is in vain that you will leave them entirely free to prosecute their business on joint-stock account: they will hardly care to avail themselves of the rights you have granted to them; and, after having exhausted your strength in vain efforts to put down prohibited associations, you will be surprised that you cannot persuade men to form the associations you encourage.

I do not say that there can be no civil associations in a country where political association is prohibited; for men can never live in society without embarking in some common undertakings; but I maintain that in such a country civil associations will always be few in number, feebly planned, unskilfully managed, that they will never form any vast designs, or that they will fail in the execution of them.

This naturally leads me to think that freedom of association in political matters is not so dangerous to public tranquillity as is supposed; and that possibly, after having agitated society for some time, it may strengthen the State in the end. In democratic countries political associations are, so to speak, the only powerful persons who aspire to rule the State. Accordingly, the governments of our time look upon associations of this kind just as sovereigns in the middle ages regarded the great vassals of the crown: they entertain a sort of instinctive abhorrence of them, and they combat them on all occasions. They bear, on the contrary, a natural good-will to civil associations, because they readily discover that, instead of directing the minds of the community to public affairs, these institutions serve to divert them from such reflections; and that, by engaging them more and more in the pursuit of objects which cannot be attained without public tranquillity, they deter them from revolutions. But these governments do not attend to the fact, that political associations tend amazingly to multiply and facilitate those of a civil character, and that in avoiding a dangerous evil they deprive themselves of an efficacious remedy.

When you see the Americans freely and constantly forming associations for the purpose of promoting some political principle, of raising one man to the head of affairs, or of wresting power from another, you have some difficulty in understanding that men so independent do not constantly fall into the abuse of freedom. If, on the other hand, you survey the infinite number of trading companies which are in operation in the United States, and perceive that the Americans are on every side unceasingly engaged in the execution of important and difficult plans, which the slightest revolution would throw into confusion, you will readily comprehend why people so well employed are by no means tempted to perturb the State, nor to destroy that public tranquillity by which they all profit.

Is it enough to observe these things separately, or should we not discover the hidden tie which connects them? In their political associations, the Americans of all conditions, minds, and ages, daily acquire a general taste for association, and grow accustomed to the use of it. There they meet together in large numbers, they converse, they listen to each other, and they are mutually stimulated to all sorts of undertakings. They afterward transfer to civil life the notions they have thus acquired, and make them subservient to a thousand purposes. Thus it is by the enjoyment of a dangerous freedom that the Americans learn the art of rendering the dangers of freedom less formidable.

If a certain moment in the existence of a nation be selected, it is easy to prove that political associations perturb the State, and paralyze productive industry: but take the whole life of a people, and it may perhaps be easy to demonstrate that freedom of association in political matters is favourable to the prosperity and even to the tranquillity of the community.

I said in the former part of this work, "The unrestrained liberty of political associations cannot be entirely assimilated to the liberty of the press. The one is at the same time less necessary and more dangerous than the other. A nation may confine it within certain limits without ceasing to be mistress of itself; and it may sometimes be obliged to do so in order to maintain its own authority." And further on I added: "It cannot be denied that the unrestrained liberty of association for political purposes is the last degree of liberty which a people is fit for. If it does not throw them into anarchy, it perpetually brings them, as it were, to the verge of it." Thus I do not think that a nation is always at liberty to invest its citizens with an absolute right of association for political purposes; and I doubt whether, in any country or in any age, it be wise to set no limits to freedom of association.

A certain nation, it is said, could not maintain tranquillity in the community, cause the laws to be respected, or establish a lasting government, if the right of association were not confined within narrow limits. These blessings are doubtless invaluable; and I can imagine that, to acquire or to preserve them, a nation may impose upon itself severe temporary restrictions: but still it is well that the nation should know at what price these blessings are purchased. I can understand that it may be advisable to cut off a man's arm in order to save his life; but it would be ridiculous to assert that he will be as dexterous as he was before he lost it.

The Americans Combat Individualism by the Principle of Interest Rightly Understood

When the world was managed by a few rich and powerful individuals, these persons loved to entertain a lofty idea of the duties of man. They were fond of professing that it is praiseworthy to forget oneself, and that good should be done without hope of reward, as it is by the Deity himself. Such were the standard opinions of that time in morals.

I doubt whether men were more virtuous in aristocratic ages than in others; but they were incessantly talking of the beauties of virtue, and its utility was only studied in secret. But since the imagination takes less lofty flights and every man's thoughts are centered in himself, moralists are alarmed by this idea of self-sacrifice, and they no longer venture to present it to the human mind. They therefore content themselves with inquiring whether the personal advantage of each member of the community does not consist in working for the good of all; and when they have hit upon some point on which private interest and public interest meet and amalgamate, they are eager to bring it into notice. Observations of this kind are gradually multiplied: what was only a single remark becomes a general principle; and it is held as a truth that man serves himself in serving his fellow-creatures, and that his private interest is to do good.

I have already shown, in several parts of this work, by what means the inhabitants of the United States almost always manage to combine their own advantage with that of their fellow-citizens: my present purpose is to point out the general rule which enables them to do so. In the United States hardly anybody talks of the beauty of virtue; but they maintain that virtue is useful, and prove it every day. The American moralists do not profess that men ought to sacrifice themselves for their fellow-creatures *because* it is noble to make such sacrifices; but they boldly aver that such sacrifices are as necessary to him who imposes them upon himself, as to him for whose sake they are made.

They have found out that in their country and their age man is brought home to himself by an irresistible force; and losing all hope of stopping that force, they turn all their thoughts to the direction of it. They therefore do not deny that every man may follow his own interest; but they endeavour to prove that it is the interest of every man to be virtuous. I shall not here enter into the reasons they allege, which would divert me from my subject: suffice it to say that they have convinced their fellow-countrymen.

Montaigne said long ago, "Were I not to follow the straight road for its straightness, I should follow it for having found by experience that in the end it is commonly the happiest and most useful track." The doctrine of interest rightly understood is not then new, but among the Americans of our time it finds universal acceptance: it has become popular there; you may trace it at the bottom of all their actions, you will remark it in all they say. It is as often to be met with on the lips of the poor man as of the rich. In Europe the principle of interest is much grosser than it is in America, but at the same time it is less common, and especially it is less avowed; among us men still constantly feign great abnegation which they no longer feel.

The Americans, on the contrary, are fond of explaining almost all the actions of their lives by the principle of interest rightly understood; they show with complacency how an enlightened regard for themselves constantly prompts them to assist each other, and inclines them willingly to sacrifice a portion of their time and property to the welfare of the State. In this respect I think they frequently fail to do themselves justice; for in the United States, as well as elsewhere, people are sometimes seen to give way to those disinterested and spontaneous impulses which are natural to man: but the Americans seldom allow that they yield to emotions of this kind; they are more anxious to do honour to their philosophy than to themselves.

I might here pause, without attempting to pass a judgement on what I have described. The extreme difficulty of the subject would be my excuse, but I shall not avail myself of it; and I had rather that my readers, clearly perceiving my object, should refuse to follow me, than that I should leave them in suspense.

The principle of interest rightly understood is not a lofty one, but it is clear and sure. It does not aim at mighty objects, but it attains without excessive exertion all those at which it aims. As it lies within the reach of all capacities, every one can without difficulty apprehend and retain it. By its admirable conformity to human weaknesses, it easily obtains great dominion; nor is that dominion precarious, since the principle checks one personal interest by another, and uses, to direct the passions, the very same instrument which excites them.

The principle of interest rightly understood produces no great acts of self-sacrifice, but it suggests daily small acts of self-denial. By itself it cannot suffice to make a man virtuous, but it disciplines a number of citizens in habits of regularity, temperance, moderation, foresight, self-command; and, if it does not lead men straight to virtue by the will, it gradually draws them in that direction by their habits. If the principle of interest rightly understood were to sway the whole moral world, extraordinary virtues would doubtless be more rare; but I think that gross depravity would then also be less common. The principle of interest rightly understood perhaps prevents some men from rising far above the level of mankind; but a great number of other men, who were falling far below it, are caught and restrained by it. Observe some few individuals, they are lowered by it; survey mankind, it is raised.

I am not afraid to say, that the principle of interest rightly understood appears to me the best suited of all philosophical theories to the wants of the men of our time, and that I regard it as their chief remaining security against themselves. Toward it, therefore, the minds of the moralists of our age should turn; even should they judge it to be incomplete, it must nevertheless be adopted as necessary.

I do not think upon the whole that there is more egotism among us than in America; the only difference is, that there it is enlightened – here it is not. Every American will sacrifice a portion of his private interests to preserve the rest; we would fain preserve the whole, and oftentimes the whole is lost. Every body I see about me seems bent on teaching his contemporaries, by precept and example, that what is useful is never wrong. Will nobody undertake to make them understand how what is right may be useful?

No power upon earth can prevent the increasing equality of conditions from inclining the human mind to seek out what is useful, or from leading every member of the community to be wrapped up in himself. It must therefore be expected that personal interest will become more than ever the principal, if not the sole, spring of men's actions; but it remains to be seen how each man will understand his personal interest. If the members of a community, as they become more equal, become more ignorant and coarse, it is difficult to foresee to what pitch of stupid excesses their egotism may lead them; and no one can foretel into what disgrace and wretchedness they would plunge themselves, lest they should have to sacrifice something of their own well-being to the prosperity of their fellow-creatures.

I do not think that the system of interest, as it is professed in America, is, in all its parts, self-evident; but it contains a great number of truths so evident, that men, if they are but educated, cannot fail to see them. Educate, then, at any rate; for the age of implicit self-sacrifice and instinctive virtues is already flitting far away from us, and the time is fast approaching when freedom, public peace, and social order itself will not be able to exist without education.

NOTES

1. I say a *democratic people:* the administration of an aristocratic people may be the reverse of centralized, and yet the want of newspapers be little felt, because local powers are then rested in the hands of a very small number of men, who either act apart, or who know each other and can easily meet and come to an understanding.
2. This is more especially true when the executive government has a discretionary power of allowing or prohibiting associations. When certain associations are simply prohibited by law, and the courts of justice have to punish infringements of that law, the evil is far less considerable. Then every citizen knows beforehand pretty nearly what he has to expect. He judges himself before he is judged by the law, and, abstaining from prohibited associations, he embarks in those which are legally sanctioned. It is by these restrictions that all free nations have always admitted that the right of association might be limited. But if the legislature should invest a man with a power of ascertaining beforehand which associations are dangerous and which are useful, and should authorise him to destroy all associations in the bud or to allow them to be formed, as nobody would be able to foresee in what cases associations might be established and in what cases they would be put down, the spirit of association would be entirely paralyzed. The former of these laws would only assail certain associations; the latter would apply to society itself, and inflict an injury upon it. I can conceive that a regular government may have recourse to the former, but I do not concede that any government has the right of enacting the latter.

Chapter 8

Tyranny of the Majority [1840]

Alexis de Tocqueville

Unlimited Power of the Majority in the United States, and its Consequences

[…]

The very essence of democratic government consists in the absolute sovereignty of the majority; for there is nothing in democratic states which is capable of resisting it. Most of the American Constitutions have sought to increase this natural strength of the majority by artificial means.[1]

The legislature is, of all political institutions, the one which is most easily swayed by the wishes of the majority. The Americans determined that the members of the legislature should be elected by the people immediately, and for a very brief term, in order to subject them, not only to the general convictions, but even to the daily passions of their constituents. The members of both Houses are taken from the same class in society, and are nominated in the same manner; so that the modifications of the legislative bodies are almost as rapid and quite as irresistible as those of a single assembly. It is to a legislature thus constituted, that almost all the authority of the Government has been entrusted.

But while the law increased the strength of those authorities which of themselves were strong, it enfeebled more and more those which were naturally weak. It deprived the representatives of the executive of all stability and independence; and by subjecting them completely to the caprices of the legislature, it robbed them of the slender

---

de Tocqueville, Alexis. *Democracy in America* [Volume 1]. Translated by Henry Reeve. Third American Edition. New York: George Aldard. 1839.

Classical Sociological Theory, Third Edition. Edited by Craig Calhoun, Joseph Gerteis, James Moody, Steven Pfaff, and Indermohan Virk. Editorial material and organization © 2012 John Wiley & Sons, Ltd. Published 2012 by John Wiley & Sons, Ltd.

influence which the nature of a democratic government might have allowed them to retain. In several States, the judicial power was also submitted to the elective discretion of the majority; and in all of them its existence was made to depend on the pleasure of the legislative authority, since the representatives were empowered annually to regulate the stipend of the judges.

Custom, however, has done even more than law. A proceeding which will in the end set all the guarantees of representative government at nought, is becoming more and more general in the United States: it frequently happens that the electors, who choose a delegate, point out a certain line of conduct to him, and impose upon him a certain number of positive obligations which he is pledged to fulfil. With the exception of the tumult, this comes to the same thing as if the majority of the populace held its deliberations in the market-place.

Several other circumstances concur in rendering the power of the majority in America, not only preponderant, but irresistible. The moral authority of the majority is partly based upon the notion, that there is more intelligence and more wisdom in a great number of men collected together than in a single individual, and that the quantity of legislators is more important than their quality. The theory of equality is in fact applied to the intellect of man; and human pride is thus assailed in its last retreat, by a doctrine which the minority hesitate to admit, and in which they very slowly concur. Like all other powers, and perhaps more than all other powers, the authority of the many requires the sanction of time; at first it enforces obedience by constraint; but its laws are not respected until they have long been maintained.

The right of governing society, which the majority supposes itself to derive from its superior intelligence, was introduced into the United States by the first settlers: and this idea, which would be sufficient of itself to create a free nation, has now been amalgamated with the manners of the people, and the minor incidents of social intercourse.

The French, under the old monarchy, held it for a maxim, (which is still a fundamental principle of the English Constitution,) that the King could do no wrong; and if he did wrong, the blame was imputed to his advisers. This notion was highly favorable to habits of obedience; and it enabled the subject to complain of the law, without ceasing to love and honor the lawgiver. The Americans entertain the same opinion with respect to the majority.

The moral power of the majority is founded upon yet another principle, which is, that the interests of the many are to be preferred to those of the few. It will readily be perceived that the respect here professed for the rights of the majority must naturally increase or diminish according to the state of parties. When a nation is divided into several irreconcileable factions, the privilege of the majority is often overlooked, because it is intolerable to comply with its demands.

If there existed in America a class of citizens whom the legislating majority sought to deprive of exclusive privileges, which they had possessed for ages, and to bring down from an elevated station to the level of the ranks of the multitude, it is probable that the minority would be less ready to comply with its laws. But as the United States were colonized by men holding an equal rank among themselves, there is as yet no natural or permanent source of dissension between the interests of its different inhabitants.

There are certain communities in which the persons who constitute the minority can never hope to draw over the majority to their side, because they must then give up the very point which is at issue between them. Thus, an aristocracy can never become a majority while it retains its exclusive privileges, and it cannot cede its privileges without ceasing to be an aristocracy.

In the United States, political questions cannot be taken up in so general and absolute a manner; and all parties are willing to recognise the rights of the majority, because they all hope to turn those rights to their own advantage at some future time. The majority therefore in that country exercises a prodigious actual authority, and a moral influence which is scarcely less preponderant; no obstacles exist which can impede, or so much as retard its progress, or which can induce it to heed the complaints of those whom it crushes upon its path. This state of things is fatal in itself and dangerous for the future.

[…]

Tyranny of the Majority

[…]

I hold it to be an impious and an execrable maxim that, politically speaking, a people has a right to do whatsoever it pleases; and yet I have asserted that all authority originates in the will of the majority. Am I, then, in contradiction with myself?

A general law – which bears the name of Justice – has been made and sanctioned, not only by a majority of this or that people, but by a majority of mankind. The rights of every people are consequently confined within the limits of what is just. A nation may be considered in the light of a jury which is empowered to represent society at large, and to apply the great and general law of Justice. Ought such a jury, which represents society, to have more power than the society in which the laws it applies originate?

When I refuse to obey an unjust law, I do not contest the right which the majority has of commanding, but I simply appeal from the sovereignty of the people to the sovereignty of mankind. It has been asserted that a people can never entirely outstep the boundaries of justice and of reason in those affairs which are more peculiarly its own; and that consequently full power may fearlessly be given to the majority by which it is represented. But this language is that of a slave.

A majority taken collectively may be regarded as a being whose opinions, and most frequently whose interests, are opposed to those of another being, which is styled a minority. If it be admitted that a man, possessing absolute power, may misuse that power by wronging his adversaries, why should a majority not be liable to the same reproach? Men are not apt to change their characters by agglomeration; nor does their patience in the presence of obstacles increase with the consciousness of their strength.[2] And for these reasons I can never willingly invest any number of my fellow creatures with that unlimited authority which I should refuse to any one of them.

I do not think that it is possible to combine several principles in the same government, so as at the same time to maintain freedom, and really to oppose them to one another. The form of government which is usually termed *mixed* has always appeared to me to be a mere chimera. Accurately speaking, there is no such thing as a mixed government, (with the meaning usually given to that word,) because in all communities some one principle of action may be discovered, which preponderates over the others. England in the last century, which has been more especially cited as an example of this form of government, was in point of fact an essentially aristocratic state, although it comprised very powerful elements of democracy: for the laws and customs of the country were such, that the aristocracy could not but preponderate in the end, and subject the direction of public affairs to its own will. The error arose from too much attention being paid to the actual struggle which was going on between the nobles and the people, without considering the probable issue of the contest, which was in reality the important point. When a community really has a mixed government, that is to say, when it is equally divided between two adverse principles, it must either pass through a revolution, or fall into complete dissolution.

I am therefore of opinion that some one social power must always be made to predominate over the others; but I think that liberty is endangered when this power is checked by no obstacles which may retard its course, and force it to moderate its own vehemence.

Unlimited power is in itself a bad and dangerous thing; human beings are not competent to exercise it with discretion; and God alone can be omnipotent, because his wisdom and his justice are always equal to his power. But no power upon earth is so worthy of honor for itself, or of reverential obedience to the rights which it represents, that I would consent to admit its uncontrolled and all-predominant authority. When I see that the right and the means of absolute command are conferred on a people or upon a king, upon an aristocracy or a democracy, a monarchy or a republic, I recognize the germ of tyranny, and I journey onward to a land of more hopeful institutions.

In my opinion the main evil of the present democratic institutions of the United States does not arise, as is often asserted in Europe, from their weakness, but from their overpowering strength; and I am not so much alarmed at the excessive liberty which reigns in that country, as at the very inadequate securities which exist against tyranny.

When an individual or a party is wronged in the United States, to whom can he apply for redress? If to public opinion, public opinion constitutes the majority; if to the legislature, it represents the majority, and implicitly obeys its instructions; if to the executive power, it is appointed by the majority and remains a passive tool in its hands; the public troops consist of the majority under arms; the jury is the majority invested with the right of hearing judicial cases; and in certain States even the judges are elected by the majority. However iniquitous or absurd the evil of which you complain may be, you must submit to it as well as you can.[3]

If, on the other hand, a legislative power could be so constituted as to represent the majority without necessarily being the slave of its passions; an executive, so as to retain a certain degree of uncontrolled authority; and a judiciary, so as to remain independent of the two other powers; a government would be formed which would still be democratic, without incurring any risk of tyrannical abuse.

I do not say that tyrannical abuses frequently occur in America at the present day; but I maintain that no sure barrier is established against them, and that the causes which mitigate the government are to be found in the circumstances and the manners of the country more than in its laws.

[...]

Power Exercised by the Majority in America Upon Opinion

[...]

It is in the examination of the display of public opinion in the United States, that we clearly perceive how far the power of the majority surpasses all the powers with which we are acquainted in Europe. Intellectual principles exercise an influence which is so invisible and often so inappreciable, that they baffle the toils of oppression. At the present time the most absolute monarchs in Europe are unable to prevent certain notions, which are opposed to their authority, from circulating in secret throughout their dominions, and even in their courts. Such is not the case in America; so long as the majority is still undecided, discussion is carried on; but as soon as its decision is irrevocably pronounced, a submissive silence is observed; and the friends, as well as the opponents of the measure, unite in assenting to its propriety. The reason of this is perfectly clear: no monarch is so absolute as to combine all the powers of society in his own hands, and to conquer all opposition, with the energy of a majority, which is invested with the right of making and of executing the laws.

The authority of a king is purely physical, and it controls the actions of the subject without subduing his private will; but the majority possesses a power which is physical and moral at the same time; it acts upon the will as well as upon the actions of men, and it represses not only alt contest, but all controversy.

I know no country in which there is so little true independence of mind and freedom of discussion as in America. In any constitutional state in Europe every sort of religious and political theory may be advocated and propagated abroad; for there is no country in Europe so subdued by any single authority, as not to contain citizens who are ready to protect the man who raises his voice in the cause of truth, from the consequences of his hardihood. If he is unfortunate enough to live under an absolute government, the people is upon his side; if he inhabits a free country, he may find a shelter behind the authority of the throne, if be require one. The aristocratic part of society supports him in some countries, and the democracy in others. But in a nation where democratic institutions exist, organized like those of the United States, there is but one sole authority, one single element of strength and of success, with nothing beyond it.

In America, the majority raises very formidable barriers to the liberty of opinion: within these barriers an author may write whatever he pleases, but he will repent it if he ever step beyond them. Not that he is exposed to the terrors of an auto-da-fé, but he is tormented by the slights and persecutions of daily obloquy. His political career is closed for ever, since he has offended the only authority which is able to promote his success. Every sort of compensation, even that of celebrity, is refused to him. Before he published his opinions, he imagined that he held them in common with many others; but no sooner has he declared them openly, than he is loudly censured by his overbearing opponents, while those who think, without having the courage to speak, like him, abandon him in silence. He yields at length, oppressed by the daily efforts he has been making, and he subsides into silence as if he was tormented by remorse for having spoken the truth.

Fetters and headsmen were the coarse instruments which tyranny formerly employed; but the civilization of our age has refined the arts of despotism, which seemed however to have been sufficiently perfected before. The excesses of monarchical power had devised a variety of physical means of oppression; the democratic republics of the present day have rendered it as entirely an affair of the mind, as that will which it is intended to coerce. Under the absolute sway of an individual despot, the body was attacked in order to subdue the soul; and the soul escaped the blows which were directed against it, and rose superior to the attempt; but such is not the course adopted by tyranny in democratic republics; there the body is left free, and the soul is enslaved. The sovereign can no longer say, "You shall think as I do on pain of death;" but he says, "You are free to think differently from me, and to retain your life, your property, and all that you possess; but if such be your determination, you are henceforth an alien among your people. You may retain your civil rights, but they will be useless to you, for you will never be chosen by your fellow-citizens, if you solicit their suffrages; and they will affect to scorn you, if you solicit their esteem. You will remain among men, but you will be deprived of the rights of mankind. Your fellow-creatures will shun you like an impure being; and those who are most persuaded of your innocence will abandon you too, lest they should be shunned in their turn. Go in peace! I have given you your life, but it is an existence incomparably worse than death."

Absolute monarchies have thrown an odium upon despotism; let us beware lest democratic republics should restore oppression, and should render it less odious and less degrading in the eyes of the many, by making it still more onerous to the few.

Works have been published in the proudest nations of the Old World, expressly intended to censure the vices and deride the follies of the time; Labruyère inhabited the palace of Louis XIV. when he composed his chapter upon the Great, and Molière criticized the courtiers in the very pieces which were acted before the Court. But the ruling power in the United States is not to be made game of; the smallest reproach irritates its sensibility, and the slightest joke which has any foundation in truth renders it indignant; from the style of its language to the more solid virtues of its character, everything must be made the subject of encomium. No writer, whatever be bis eminence, can escape from this tribute of adulation to his fellow-citizens. The majority lives in the perpetual exercise of self applause; and there are certain truths which the Americans can only learn from strangers or from experience.

If great writers have not at present existed in America, the reason is very simply given in these facts; there can be no literary genius without freedom of opinion, and freedom of opinion does not exist in America. The Inquisition has never been able to prevent a vast number of anti-religious books from circulating in Spain. The empire of the majority succeeds much better in the United States, since it actually removes the wish of publishing them. Unbelievers are to be met with in America, but, to say the truth, there is no public organ of infidelity. Attempts have been made by some governments to protect the morality of nations by prohibiting licentious books. In the United States no one is punished for this sort of works, but no one is induced to write them; not because all the citizens are immaculate in their manners, but because the majority of the community is decent and orderly.

In these cases the advantages derived from the exercise of this power are unquestionable; and I am simply discussing the nature of the power itself. This irresistible authority is a constant fact, and its beneficent exercise is an accidental occurrence.

Effects of the Tyranny of the Majority Upon the National Character of the Americans

[...]

The tendencies which I have just alluded to are as yet very slightly perceptible in political society; but they already begin to exercise an unfavorable influence upon the national character of the Americans. I am inclined to attribute the singular paucity of distinguished political characters to the ever-increasing activity of the despotism of the majority in the United States.

When the American Revolution broke out, they arose in great numbers; for public opinion then served, not to tyrannize over, but to direct the exertions of individuals. Those celebrated men took a full part in the general agitation of mind common at that period, and they attained a high degree of personal fame, which was reflected back upon the nation, but which was by no means borrowed from it.

In absolute governments, the great nobles who are nearest to the throne flatter the passions of the sovereign, and voluntarily truckle to his caprices. But the mass of the nation does not degrade itself by servitude; it often submits from weakness, from habit, or from ignorance, and sometimes from loyalty. Some nations have been known to sacrifice their own desires to those of the sovereign with pleasure and with pride; thus exhibiting a sort of independence in the very act of submission. These peoples are miserable, but they are not degraded. There is a great difference between doing what one does not approve, and feigning to approve what one does; the one is the necessary case of a weak person, the other befits the temper of a lacquey.

In free countries, where every one is more or less called upon to give his opinion in the affairs of state; in democratic republics, where public life is incessantly commingled with domestic affairs, where the sovereign authority is accessible on every side, and where its attention can almost always be attracted by vociferation, more persons are to be met with who speculate upon its foibles, and live at the cost of its passions, than in absolute monarchies. Not because men are naturally worse in these States than elsewhere, but the temptation is stronger, and of easier access at the same time. The result is a far more extensive debasement of the characters of citizens.

Democratic republics extend the practice of currying favor with the many, and they introduce it into a great number of classes at once: this is one of the most serious reproaches that can be addressed to them. In democratic States organized on the principles of the American republics, this is more especially the case, where the authority of the majority is so absolute and so irresistible, that a man must give up his rights as a citizen, and almost abjure his quality as a human being, if he intends to stray from the track which it lays down.

In that immense crowd which throngs the avenues to power in the United States, I found very few men who displayed any of that manly candor, and that masculine independence of opinion which frequently distinguished the Americans in former times, and which constitute the leading feature in distinguished characters wheresoever they may be found. It seems, at first sight, as if all the minds of the Americans were formed upon one model, so accurately do they correspond in their manner of judging. A stranger does, indeed, sometimes meet with Americans who dissent from these rigorous formularies; with men who deplore the defects of the laws, the mutability and the ignorance of democracy; who even go so far as to observe the evil tendencies which impair the national character, and to point out such remedies as it might be possible to apply; but no one is there to hear these things beside yourself, and you, to whom these secret reflections are confided, are a stranger and a bird of passage. They are very ready to communicate truths which are useless to you, but they continue to hold a different language in public.

If even these lines are read in America, I am well assured of two things: in the first place, that all who peruse them will raise their voices to condemn me; and in the second place, that very many of them will acquit me at the bottom of their conscience.

[...]

I have heard of patriotism in the United States, and it is a virtue which may be found among the people, but never among the leaders of the people. This may be explained by analogy; despotism debases the oppressed, much more than the oppressor; in absolute monarchies the king has often great virtues, but the courtiers are invariably servile. It is true that the American courtiers do not say, 'Sire,' or 'Your Majesty' – a distinction without a difference. They are forever talking of the natural intelligence of the populace they serve; they do not debate the question as to which of the virtues of their master is pre-eminently worthy of admiration; for they assure him that he possesses all the virtues under heaven without having acquired them, or without caring to acquire them: they do not give him their daughters and their wives to be raised at his pleasure to the rank of his concubines, but, by sacrificing their opinions, they prostitute themselves. Moralists and philosophers in America are not obliged to conceal their opinions under the veil of allegory; but, before they venture upon a harsh truth, they say, 'We are aware that the people which we are addressing is too superior to all the weaknesses of human nature to lose the command of its temper for an instant; and we should not hold this language if we were not speaking to men, whom their virtues and their intelligence render more worthy of freedom than all the rest of the world.'

It would have been impossible for the sycophants of Louis XIV. to flatter more dexterously. For my part, I am persuaded that in all governments, whatever their nature may be, servility will cower to force, and adulation will cling to power. The only means of preventing men from degrading themselves, is to invest no one with that unlimited authority which is the surest method of debasing them.

The Greatest Dangers of the American Republics Proceed from the Unlimited Power of the Majority

[...]

Governments usually fall a sacrifice to impotence or to tyranny. In the former case their power escapes from them: it is wrested from their grasp in the latter. Many observers who have noticed the anarchy of democratic States, have imagined that the government of those States was naturally weak and impotent. The truth is, that when once hostilities are begun between parties, the government loses its control over society. But I do not think that a democratic power is naturally without resources: say rather, that it is almost always by the abuse of its force, and the misemployment of its resources, that a democratic government fails. Anarchy is almost always produced by its tyranny or its mistakes, but not by its want of strength.

It is important not to confound stability with force, or the greatness of a thing with its duration. In democratic republics, the power which directs[4] society is not stable; for it often changes hands and assumes a new direction. But whichever way it turns, its force is almost irresistible. The Governments of the American republics appear to me to be as much centralized as those of the absolute monarchies of Europe, and more energetic than they are. I do not, therefore, imagine that they will perish from weakness.[5]

If ever the free institutions of America are destroyed, that event may be attributed to the unlimited authority of the majority, which may at some future time urge the minorities to desperation, and oblige them to have recourse to physical force. Anarchy will then be the result, but it will have been brought about by despotism.

Mr. Hamilton expresses the same opinion in the Federalist, No. 51. "It is of great importance in a republic not only to guard the society against the oppression of its rulers, but to guard one part of the society against the injustice of the other part. Justice is the end of government. It is the end of civil society. It ever has been, and ever will be pursued until it be obtained, or until liberty be lost in the pursuit. In a society, under the forms of which the stronger faction can readily unite and oppress the weaker, anarchy may as truly be said to reign as in a state of nature, where the weaker individual is not secured against the violence of the stronger: and as in the latter state even the stronger individuals are prompted by the uncertainty of their condition to submit to a government which may protect the weak as well as themselves, so in the former state will the more powerful factions be gradually induced by a like motive to wish for a government which will protect all parties, the weaker as well as the more powerful. It can be little doubted, that if the State of Rhode Island was separated from the Confederacy and left to itself, the insecurity of rights under the popular form of government within such narrow limits, would be displayed by such reiterated oppressions of the factious majorities, that some power altogether independent of the people would soon be called for by the voice of the very factions whose misrule had proved the necessity of it."

Jefferson has also thus expressed himself in a letter to Madison:[6] "The executive power in our Government is not the only, perhaps not even the principal object of my solicitude. The tyranny of the legislature is really the danger most to be feared, and will continue to be so for many years to come. The tyranny of the executive power will come in its turn, but at a more distant period."

I am glad to cite the opinion of Jefferson upon this subject rather than that of another, because I consider him to be the most powerful advocate democracy has ever sent forth.

NOTES

1. We observed in examining the Federal Constitution that the efforts of the legislators of the Union had been diametrically opposed to the present tendency. The consequence has been that the Federal Government is more independent in its sphere than that of the States. But the Federal Government scarcely ever interferes in any but external affairs; and the governments of the States are in reality the authorities which direct society in America.
2. No one will assert that a people cannot forcibly wrong another people: but parties may be looked upon as lesser nations within a greater one, and they are aliens to each other: if therefore it be admitted that a nation can act tyrannically towards another nation, it cannot be denied that a party may do the same towards another party.
3. A striking instance of the excesses which may be occasioned by the despotism of the majority occurred at Baltimore in the year 1812. At that time the war was very popular in Baltimore. A journal which had taken the other side of the question excited the indignation of the inhabitants by its opposition. The populace assembled, broke the printing-presses, and attacked the houses of the newspaper editors. The militia was called out, but no one obeyed the call; and the only means of saving the poor wretches who were threatened by the frenzy of the mob, was to throw them into prison as common malefactors. But even this precaution was ineffectual; the mob collected again during the night; the magistrates again made a vain attempt to call out the militia; the prison was forced, one of the newspaper editors was killed upon the spot, and the others were left for dead: the guilty parties were acquitted by the jury when they were brought to trial.

    I said one day to an inhabitant of Pennsylvania, "Be so good as to explain to me how it happens, that in a State founded by Quakers, and celebrated for its toleration, freed Blacks are not allowed to exercise civil rights. They pay the taxes: is it not fair that they should have a vote?"

    "You insult us," replied my informant, "if you imagine that our legislators could have committed so gross an act of injustice and intolerance."

"What, then, the Blacks possess the right of voting in this country?"

"Without the smallest doubt."

"How comes it, then, that at the polling-booth this morning I did not perceive a single Negro in the whole meeting?"

"This is not the fault of the law; the Negroes have an undisputed right of voting: but they voluntarily abstain from making their appearance."

"A very pretty piece of modesty on their parts!" rejoined I.

"Why, the truth is, that they are not disinclined to vote, but they are afraid of being maltreated; in this country the law is sometimes unable to maintain its authority without the support of the majority. But in this case the majority entertains very strong prejudices against the Blacks, and the magistrates are unable to protect them in the exercise of their legal privileges."

"What, then, the majority claims the right not only of making the laws, but of breaking the laws it has made?"

4 This power may be centred in an assembly, in which case it will be strong without being stable; or it may be centred in an individual, in which case it will be less strong, but more stable.

5 I presume that it is scarcely necessary to remind the reader here, as well as throughout the remainder of this chapter, that I am speaking not of the Federal Government, but of the several Governments of each State which the majority controls at its pleasure.

6 15th March, 1789.

Part III

The Sociological Theory of Karl Marx and Friedrich Engels

Introduction to Part III

9 The German Ideology

10 Economic and Philosophic Manuscripts of 1844

11 Manifesto of the Communist Party

12 The Eighteenth Brumaire of Louis Bonaparte

13 Wage-Labour and Capital

14 Classes

Part II

The Sociological Theory of Karl Marx and Friedrich Engels

Introduction to Part III

Although he is conventionally regarded as one of the "founding fathers" of modern sociology, Karl Marx (1818–83) was never a professional academic. Nor was he directly a part of the nascent field of sociology in his day. Instead Marx was trained as a philosopher and saw himself as an economist and social critic. His enduring legacy in sociology comes about because of the way that his work brought a theoretical focus to empirical social analysis. Marx provided a way to understand the connection between the concrete economic relationships among people and the broad patterns of social order that emerge from them in specific eras – an argument now known as "historical materialism." In developing historical materialism as a theoretical system, Marx and his collaborator Friedrich Engels (1820–95) laid the foundation of what was to become a Marxist school of sociological thought and analysis. Marx continues to fascinate not only because of his brilliance as a philosopher and social scientist, but because he represents the epitome of the scholar-activist, the social critic who is, to paraphrase Marx's own words in the *Theses on Feurbach*, not content with criticizing the world but is resolved to change it.

Marx's Life and Intellectual Outlook

Karl Marx was born in Trier, a commercial city in western Germany near the border of France, in 1818. He was the son of a prosperous merchant family and attended university (first in Bonn, and then in Berlin) in order to study law. Marx soon shifted his interest to philosophy, eventually earning a doctorate at Jena. Abandoning the

Classical Sociological Theory, Third Edition. Edited by Craig Calhoun, Joseph Gerteis, James Moody, Steven Pfaff, and Indermohan Virk. Editorial material and organization © 2012 John Wiley & Sons, Ltd. Published 2012 by John Wiley & Sons, Ltd.

idea of a university career, Marx became a political journalist and a member of a radical philosophical circle known as the "Young Hegelians." In 1842, he met Friedrich Engels, who would become his friend, collaborator, and life-long benefactor. The two intellectuals resolved to dedicate their lives to the cause of revolutionary socialism. Owing to press censorship and political repression in the Prussian dominions, Marx, now married, moved to Paris. There he met many of the most important literary and political figures of his day. His continuing political journalism led to his being charged with high treason by the Prussian government in 1844. In 1845, under pressure from Prussia, the French government banished Marx from Paris as well and he moved to Brussels, then briefly to Cologne. Marx finally settled in London in 1849, at the age of 31. Engels settled in the industrial center of Manchester, where he spent nearly two decades managing his family's industrial concerns.

Throughout his career Marx was strenuously engaged both in the development of a philosophical system based on the principle of negative critique of existing social conditions and as political activist, journalist, and agitator. Early in his career, Marx rejected the idea that liberal reform, that is the gradual political emancipation and right to political participation in a democratic state, would be enough to redress the social crisis and gross inequalities of the capitalist system. For Marx, the mistake of liberal political theory was that it assumed that a particular class – the bourgeoisie – would claim political and social rights, and then extend them to the rest of society. According to Marx, this was a mistake, because it missed the real material foundation of such rights in the power that adheres to the ownership of property. Thus, bourgeois democracy depends on the possession of rights that actually reside only in property. In Western countries at least, the abolition of slavery meant that workers were formally free under law, but according to Marx, this was an empty reality so long as real power flowed from economic possession. While Marx advocated the extension of suffrage and other democratic rights, he never considered these the goals of political struggle, only a means by which a revolutionary transformation of society might be achieved.

Alongside Engels, Marx became involved in an organization known as the Communist League, which advocated radical socialism as an answer to the social and political crises created by the industrial revolution in Europe. In February 1848, while living in Brussels, Marx and Engels published the *Manifesto of the Communist Party*, a call to arms for a great working-class social revolution and one of the most important political and social tracts ever written. A brilliant polemical essay, the *Manifesto* sketched out a philosophy of world history as the struggle between contending social classes. This class struggle could only be resolved through putting an end to the alienation between people created by the institution of private property. In timely fashion, revolutionary insurrections grew out of economic crisis and social unrest in France in February and in Germany in March 1848. Marx and Engels returned to Germany and took an active part in the revolution, editing a radical Cologne newspaper and involving themselves in political (and in the case of Engels, military) struggles.

Marx and Engels' flight to England followed the collapse of the revolution and the triumph of reactionary forces in Germany and France. Marx began to devote his energy to the full-time study of economics, spending long hours in the public reading room of the British Museum. Marx was supported largely by generous payments made by Engels, though he was also a journalistic contributor to many publications, including the *New York Daily Tribune*. Many of Marx's essays on such subjects as the collapse of the second French republic, the consequences of British imperialism in India, and slavery and the Civil War in the United States are recognized as masterpieces of political journalism. In 1864, Marx helped to found the first international socialist movement, the International Working Men's Association in London. In 1867, Marx published the crowning achievement of his life's work, *Capital*, a radical critique of the science of economics and an indictment of the material basis of bourgeois society. In the following years, Marx labored on a second and third volume (which remained uncompleted) while Engels wrote the influential explanatory treatise *Socialism: Utopian and Scientific* (1880). Marx remained an active force in steering the political affairs of the international socialist movement until his death in London in 1883. Following Marx's death, Engels went on to write *The Origin of the Family, Private Property, and the State* (1884), which extended historical materialism into the realm of the family and sexual relations. Engels now played the role of the leading intellectual in the socialist movement until his own death in 1895.

Marx's Philosophy and Social Thought

Marx's philosophical system was influenced, first and foremost, by the work of the prominent philosopher Georg Wilhelm Friedrich Hegel and his followers. However, Marx's thought also had a more practical and empirically engaged dimension than did Hegel's. This can be seen in Marx's ongoing dialogue and critique of the early science of economics, which provided the core themes of his sociological thought. Marx objected to the overly abstract and ideal conception of the world represented by Hegel's philosophy. For Marx, Hegel's discussion of "spirit" as the force driving the history of the world was an abstract mystification of the actual force in world history: an active humanity making and unmaking the material world. Marx also rejected Hegel's claims about the role of the state; rather than civil society growing out of the state, the state springs from society.

Marx's material analysis has radical implications for how we understand knowledge. For Marx, humanity's objective economic activity is the base upon which ideas and institutions are balanced. As a result, ideas cannot be understood in isolation, but rather only in direct relation to the social context within which they were born. In the *German Ideology* (excerpted here) Marx noted, "The production of ideas, of conceptions, of consciousness, is directly interwoven with material activity and material intercourse of men and appear at this stage as the direct efflux of their material behavior." In other words, it is not ideas that determine the material world, but rather the other way around. Marx called this "turning Hegel over on his head."

Nevertheless, Marx adopted much from the method, if not the content, of Hegel's philosophy, including the dialectical mode of logic. Simply put, "dialectic" refers to a process of change in human society where the contradictions contained in a given idea or era produce a change that can be seen as its negation. Where Hegel focused on the dialectical relation of ideas, Marx's dialectic was based on social relations of the material world, analyzing the way that opposing forces produce contradiction and conflict. So, for example, increasing exploitation of workers by the capitalists may have the consequence of causing workers to become more militant. In the face of this militancy, the capitalists may become more exploitative and repressive in order to crush their resistance. This may inadvertently help the workers to realize that only a complete revolution against existing conditions can be their salvation. Marx argued that social analysts must be aware of the reciprocal economic relationships among social actors and the broader social structure that results from them. Because economic relationships shift over history, Marx contended that we must understand present reality in relation to its past and its future.

Marx used social criticism as his standard form of social analysis. Marx defined criticism as the "radical negation of social reality." Instead of accepting existing social relations on face value, Marx subjected them to analysis. In rejecting Hegel's idealization of the state, for example, Marx provides a searing critique of calls for state-led development as an alternative to market forces and proclaims the proletariat as the social force destined to negate the existing order and replace it with another. For Marx and his followers, the purpose of social critique was to measure society's claims about itself against the reality of its operations. This focus is apparent in Engels' early classic, *The Condition of the Working Class in England in 1844*, an attempt based on an empirical survey of existing conditions to critique the idealized claims of the proponents of capitalist development. Hegel had remarked, "Periods of bliss are history's blank pages." As is dazzlingly presented in Marx's celebrated essay *The Eighteenth Brumaire of Louis Bonaparte*, excerpted below, in his own analysis of historical events, Marx's attention was focused on periods of conflict. Marx understood processes of social change in terms of the clash of opposing interests and the material forces that determine them.

Like Hegel, Marx saw human history as one of estrangement and conflict. And Marx broke with the economists by arguing for what we might see today as *sociology* of economic relations. Marx tried to reveal in his posthumously published *Economic and Philosophical Manuscripts of 1844* (excerpted below) that the cause of this was not alienation from an abstract "spirit," but a deeply human process, involving social estrangement and material dispossession. Marx argued that the foundation of society was humankind's joint involvement in free, productive, and creative work. However, for Marx the history of civilization revealed the progressive coercion of human labor and the dispossession of the product of labor from its producers. Driven by greed and need, creative work had become wage labor, the motives for which did not speak to the creative capacity that is essential to what it means to be human. For Marx, work had become inhuman in a literal sense – it contradicted human nature. Hence, the working classes were being both materially dispossessed and estranged from their own human nature as people. Marx suggested the image of the capitalist as a sort of vampire that literally drains away the productive life of the worker objectified in the goods that his labor has created.

Although this tendency was apparent throughout human history, it had become accelerated under industrial capitalism. Yet hope was not lost. Marx regarded capitalism as a system of *creative destruction*, as a force that provokes epochal social change. In the *Communist Manifesto* (excerpted here), Marx and Engels reveal how the forces of production unleashed by capitalism were sweeping away the old world while a new one was still in the making. Marx and Engels observed that in the modern world "Everything solid melts into air," including old ways of life, beliefs, and social relations, dissolving under the pressure of material transformation. In view of the technological achievements and scientific spirit of the industrial revolution this was not altogether bad. Marx's analysis of capitalist production led him to conclude that the system was inherently unstable, destructive, and exploitative. In time, it would become an obstacle to human progress. But the new industrial technology and productivity unleashed by capitalism offered a way out by freeing man from the shackles of subsistence and ignorance through universal enlightenment and prosperity. Revolution would achieve this by liberating the workers and putting the ownership of the means of production in their own hands thereby abolishing the exploiting class.

Marx's monumental contribution was to lay out a systematic theory of the capitalist economy, its genesis, and its tendency toward crisis. As reflected in the essay "Wage Labour and Capital," included in this volume, Marx tried to show that the roots of all profit in the capitalist system could be traced to the extraction of surplus value from human labor. As capitalist competition increased, the owners of capital would be compelled by falling profit margins to attempt to increase the exploitation of workers. Capitalists would oversupply the market with commodities for which there were insufficient buyers. A cycle of boom and bust would result, and industrial depressions become ever more frequent and destructive occurrences. At the same time, as the scale of production increased and workers were herded together into factories and industrial cities, they would begin to see themselves as members of the same social class with the same objective interests. In time, they would reject their increasing misery, band together as a political force, and overturn the capitalist system (though note that Marx began to recognize that economic differentiation was producing a more complex class system, not a polarized one, in his later work; see the fragment on "Classes" included in this volume). In the place of private ownership of capital, social ownership of capital would be introduced. Gradually, the need for a coercive administration of economy and society would vanish as solidarity and cooperation replaced estrangement and competition. Marx suggested that the capitalist system of production so riddled with contradictions and contending aims and the growing solidarity of the working classes were so evidently apparent that the final crisis of capitalism and the great proletarian revolution was practically inevitable.

Marx envisioned the great social revolution as an opportunity to end humankind's self-alienation and make the Enlightenment dream of a "positive humanism" a reality. In the new world of the future, human beings would become conscious producers and be free to engage in creative pursuits beyond the coercive dictates of the labor market. And once the estrangement of humankind from himself and from his product was eliminated, there was no longer a need for a state whose real purpose was the enforcement of this alienation. Marx's practical utopianism was thus not merely a scientific response to the irrationalities of the capitalist system, but also an ethical vision of human emancipation and self-realization.

Marx's Legacy

Marx's thought endures in importance because of its search for objective, material causes, its focus on conflict as a basic social mechanism, and its effort to apply scientific reason in the analysis of social life. In contrast to many social philosophies, Marx's theories yield testable propositions that allow rigorous evaluation and even falsification. Marx's influence can be clearly observed in a number of sociological traditions. Max Weber, in particular, was impressed by Marx's thought and saw much of his own work as inspired by his effort to falsify Marxist thought (see Part V).

Despite his contribution to empirical social science, it is only by considering the ethical appeal of Marx's thought that we can understand why it became the foundation not only of a school of sociological and historical analysis, but also of the modern socialist movement. Marx offered a way to understand society framed in a morally empowering language that savaged the half-hearted and incremental reforms that were endorsed by many in Western societies and unflinchingly took the side of the oppressed. In both its brilliance and menace Marx's thought represents a thorough indictment of capitalist modernity – the only theoretical system to offer such a complete repudiation of existing society and radical call to arms. The Critical Theory of the Frankfurt School was directly inspired by this element of Marx's thought (see Part V).

Over the century and a half since Marx and Engels began their work, their radical rejection of the status quo and indictment of exploitation have had enormous influence, sometimes for the good of society, and often for its devastating harm. Workers, women, colonized peoples, and other marginalized and dispossessed groups have seen in Marx and Engels' theory a diagnosis of their oppression and a set of conceptual weapons in their struggles. Despite its unyielding radicalism, their theory helped to inform reformist politics such as those of the European social democracies that have achieved some of the world's most humane societies. However, for much of the 20th century, Marx's thought was also used to promote dogmatism, intolerance, and a dangerous strain of militant utopianism in which radical ends were thought to justify any ghastly means that might be used to achieve them. Marxism became a rigid and confining ideology that, at its worst, justified the reign of tyrants and the exercise of mass murder against those deemed as obstacles to the final triumph of the revolution.

In contemporary social science Marxian concepts are of continuing relevance, even if many of the specific propositions and predictions that Marx and his followers made have been shown to be mistaken. Few today would argue that the capitalist system is so inherently flawed that it must collapse. Most would agree that profits are generated not only by extracting labor power, but also by investment in technology and human capital. In most Western nations and some industrializing nations around the world working people are not worse off, as Marx predicted, but substantially better off than they were in the 19th century. Rather than growing ever larger and more militant, in most developed nations the industrial "proletariat" is an ever-smaller fraction of the workforce as the service sector grows and new industries such as information technology, health care, and biosciences expand. Moreover, as personal investment becomes common and workers are obliged to invest in stock and bond markets to secure their retirement, the meaning of "ownership" of productive means is no longer so clear. And although Marx rejected the possibility of liberal reform, working-class movements did succeed in many countries in improving their living standards and asserting political rights without overturning the system. At the same time, however, alienation is still felt. Today many workers would understand and agree with Marx's comment that in their occupations – which should be a satisfying and creative experience – they are often treated like expendable commodities. Moreover, the dislocation and alarm that many people experience now in an age of economic globalization, deep and prolonged recessions, the naked power and privilege of business and banking élites, commodity fetishism, and persistent inequality and social insecurity will continue to stimulate Marxian analysis.

SELECTED BIBLIOGRAPHY

Aron, Raymond. 1968. *Main Currents in Sociological Thought. Volume 1*. Garden City, NY: Anchor Books. (This volume contains a very long chapter on Marx that introduces the thinker's specifically sociological relevance.)

Avineri, Schlomo. 1968. *The Social and Political Thought of Karl Marx*. London: Cambridge University Press. (This volume offers an excellent general introduction to the work of Marx.)

Hunt, Tristram. 2009. *Marx's General: The Revolutionary Life of Friedrich Engels*. New York: Metropolitan Books. (The fascinating story of the man who willingly played "second fiddle" to Marx, which makes a convincing case for Engels' central contribution to the theory of historical materialism.)

McClellan, David. 1973. *Karl Marx: His Life and Thought*. New York: Harper and Row (An important intellectual biography of Marx.)

McClellan, David. 1974. *The Thought of Karl Marx: An Introduction*. New York: Harper & Row. (A basic introduction to Marx's work.)

Postone, Moishe. 1993. *Time, Labor and Social Domination*. London: Cambridge University Press. (A reevaluation of Marx's contribution to critical theory.)

Tucker, Robert C. (ed.). 1978. *The Marx-Engels Reader*. Second edition. New York: W.W. Norton & Company. (An indispensable volume that includes an excellent introduction and very good selection of key readings.)

Chapter 9

The German Ideology [1845]

Karl Marx and Friedrich Engels

Hitherto men have constantly made up for themselves false conceptions about themselves, about what they are and what they ought to be. They have arranged their relationships according to their ideas of God, of normal man, etc. The phantoms of their brains have got out of their hands. They, the creators, have bowed down before their creations. Let us liberate them from the chimeras, the ideas, dogmas, imaginary beings under the yoke of which they are pining away. Let us revolt against the rule of thoughts. Let us teach men, says one, to exchange these imaginations for thoughts which correspond to the essence of man; says the second, to take up a critical attitude to them; says the third, to knock them out of their heads; and – existing reality will collapse.

[…]

First Premises of Materialist Method

The premises from which we begin are not arbitrary ones, not dogmas, but real premises from which abstraction can only be made in the imagination. They are the real individuals, their activity and the material conditions under which they live, both those which they find already existing and those produced by their activity. These premises can thus be verified in a purely empirical way.

Marx, Karl and Engels, Friedrich "The German Ideology," pp. 41, 42, 46–47, 64–66 from Karl Marx and Friedrich Engels, *The German Ideology, Part One*, ed. C. J. Arthur. New York: International Publishers, 1996. Translation of Part I, Copyright © by International Publishers Co, Inc., 1947; revised translation of Part I © by Lawrence & Wishart, 1970. Reprinted by permission of International Publishers Inc.

Classical Sociological Theory, Third Edition. Edited by Craig Calhoun, Joseph Gerteis, James Moody, Steven Pfaff, and Indermohan Virk. Editorial material and organization © 2012 John Wiley & Sons, Ltd. Published 2012 by John Wiley & Sons, Ltd.

The first premise of all human history is, of course, the existence of living human individuals. Thus the first fact to be established is the physical organisation of these individuals and their consequent relation to the rest of nature. Of course, we cannot here go either into the actual physical nature of man, or into the natural conditions in which man finds himself – geological, oreohydrographical, climatic and so on. The writing of history must always set out from these natural bases and their modification in the course of history through the action of men.

Men can be distinguished from animals by consciousness, by religion or anything else you like. They themselves begin to distinguish themselves from animals as soon as they begin to *produce* their means of subsistence, a step which is conditioned by their physical organisation. By producing their means of subsistence men are indirectly producing their actual material life.

The way in which men produce their means of subsistence depends first of all on the nature of the actual means of subsistence they find in existence and have to reproduce. This mode of production must not be considered simply as being the production of the physical existence of the individuals. Rather it is a definite form of activity of these individuals, a definite form of expressing their life, a definite *mode of life* on their part. As individuals express their life, so they are. What they are, therefore, coincides with their production, both with *what* they produce and with *how* they produce. The nature of individuals thus depends on the material conditions determining their production.

[...]

The fact is, therefore, that definite individuals who are productively active in a definite way enter into these definite social and political relations. Empirical observation must in each separate instance bring out empirically, and without any mystification and speculation, the connection of the social and political structure with production. The social structure and the State are continually evolving out of the life-process of definite individuals, but of individuals, not as they may appear in their own or other people's imagination, but as they *really* are; i.e. as they operate, produce materially, and hence as they work under definite material limits, presuppositions and conditions independent of their will.

The production of ideas, of conceptions, of consciousness, is at first directly interwoven with the material activity and the material intercourse of men, the language of real life. Conceiving, thinking, the mental intercourse of men, appear at this stage as the direct efflux of their material behaviour. The same applies to mental production as expressed in the language of politics, laws, morality, religion, metaphysics, etc. of a people. Men are the producers of their conceptions, ideas, etc. – real, active men, as they are conditioned by a definite development of their productive forces and of the intercourse corresponding to these, up to its furthest forms. Consciousness can never be anything else than conscious existence, and the existence of men is their actual life-process. If in all ideology men and their circumstances appear upside-down as in a *camera obscura*, this phenomenon arises just as much from their historical life-process as the inversion of objects on the retina does from their physical life-process.

[...]

Ruling Class and Ruling Ideas

The ideas of the ruling class are in every epoch the ruling ideas, i.e. the class which is the ruling *material* force of society is at the same time its ruling *intellectual* force. The class which has the means of material production at its disposal, has control at the same time over the means of mental production, so that thereby, generally speaking, the ideas of those who lack the means of mental production are subject to it. The ruling ideas are nothing more than the ideal expression of the dominant material relationships, the dominant material relationships grasped as ideas; hence of the relationships which make the one class the ruling one, therefore, the ideas of its dominance. The individuals composing the ruling class possess among other things consciousness, and therefore think. Insofar, therefore, as they rule as a class and determine the extent and compass of an epoch, it is self-evident that they do this in its whole range, hence among other things rule also as thinkers, as producers of ideas, and regulate the production and distribution of the ideas of their age: thus their ideas are the ruling ideas of the epoch. For instance, in an age and in a country where royal power, aristocracy, and bourgeoisie are contending for mastery and where, therefore, mastery is shared, the doctrine of the separation of powers proves to be the dominant idea and is expressed as an "eternal law".

The division of labour ... as one of the chief forces of history up till now, manifests itself also in the ruling class as the division of mental and material labour, so that inside this class one part appears as the thinkers of the class (its active, conceptive ideologists, who make the perfecting of the illusion of the class about itself their chief source of livelihood), while the others' attitude to these ideas and illusions is more passive and receptive, because they are in reality the active members of this class and have less time to make up illusions and ideas about themselves. Within this class this cleavage can even develop into a certain opposition and hostility between the two parts, which, however, in the case of a practical collision, in which the class itself is endangered, automatically comes to nothing, in which case there also vanishes the semblance that the ruling ideas were not the ideas of the ruling class and had a power distinct from the power of this class. The existence of revolutionary ideas in a particular period presupposes the existence of a revolutionary class; about the premises for the latter sufficient has already been said ...

If now in considering the course of history we detach the ideas of the ruling class from the ruling class itself and attribute to them an independent existence, if we confine ourselves to saying that these or those ideas were dominant at a given time, without bothering ourselves about the conditions of production and the producers of these ideas, if we thus ignore the individuals and world conditions which are the source of the ideas, we can say, for instance, that during the time that the aristocracy was dominant, the concepts honour, loyalty, etc. were dominant, during the dominance of the bourgeoisie the concepts freedom, equality, etc. The ruling class itself on the whole imagines this to be so. This conception of history, which is common to all historians, particularly since the eighteenth century, will necessarily come up against the phenomenon that increasingly abstract ideas hold sway, i.e. ideas which increasingly take on the form of universality. For each new class which puts itself in the place of one ruling before it, is compelled, merely in order to carry through its aim, to represent its interest as the common interest of all the members of society, that is, expressed in ideal form: it has to give its ideas the form of universality, and represent them as the only rational, universally valid ones. The class making a revolution appears from the very start, if only because it is opposed to a *class*, not as a class but as the representative of the whole of society; it appears as the whole mass of society confronting the one ruling class. It can do this because, to start with, its interest really is more connected with the common interest of all other non-ruling classes, because under the pressure of hitherto existing conditions its interest has not yet been able to develop as the particular interest of a particular class. Its victory, therefore, benefits also many individuals of the other classes which are not winning a dominant position, but only insofar as it now puts these individuals in a position to raise themselves into the ruling class. When the French bourgeoisie overthrew the power of the aristocracy, it thereby made it possible for many proletarians to raise themselves above the proletariat, but only insofar as they become bourgeois. Every new class, therefore, achieves its hegemony only on a broader basis than that of the class ruling previously, whereas the opposition of the non-ruling class against the new ruling class later develops all the more sharply and profoundly. Both these things determine the fact that the struggle to be waged against this new ruling class, in its turn, aims at a more decided and radical negation of the previous conditions of society than could all previous classes which sought to rule.

This whole semblance, that the rule of a certain class is only the rule of certain ideas, comes to a natural end, of course, as soon as class rule in general ceases to be the form in which society is organised, that is to say, as soon as it is no longer necessary to represent a particular interest as general or the "general interest" as ruling.

Chapter 10

Economic and Philosophic Manuscripts of 1844

Karl Marx

We have proceeded from the premises of political economy. We have accepted its language and its laws. We presupposed private property, the separation of labour, capital and land, and of wages, profit of capital and rent of land – likewise division of labour, competition, the concept of exchange-value, etc. On the basis of political economy itself, in its own words, we have shown that the worker sinks to the level of a commodity and becomes indeed the most wretched of commodities; that the wretchedness of the worker is in inverse proportion to the power and magnitude of his production; that the necessary result of competition is the accumulation of capital in a few hands, and thus the restoration of monopoly in a more terrible form; and that finally the distinction between capitalist and land rentier, like that between the tiller of the soil and the factory worker, disappears and that the whole of society must fall apart into the two classes – the *property owners* and the propertyless *workers*.

Political economy starts with the fact of private property; it does not explain it to us. It expresses in general, abstract formulas the *material* process through which private property actually passes, and these formulas it then takes for *laws*. It does not *comprehend* these laws, i.e., it does not demonstrate how they arise from the very nature of private property. Political economy throws no light on the cause of the division between labour and capital, and between capital and land. When, for example, it defines the relationship of wages to profit, it takes the interest of the capitalists to be the ultimate cause, i.e., it takes for granted what it is supposed to explain. Similarly, competition comes in everywhere. It is explained from external

Marx, Karl, "Economic and Philosophic Manuscripts of 1844," pp. 270–282 from Karl Marx and Friedrich Engels, *Collected Works, Volume 3*. New York: International Publishers, 1975. Copyright © 1975. Reprinted by permission of International Publishers Inc.

Classical Sociological Theory, Third Edition. Edited by Craig Calhoun, Joseph Gerteis, James Moody, Steven Pfaff, and Indermohan Virk. Editorial material and organization © 2012 John Wiley & Sons, Ltd. Published 2012 by John Wiley & Sons, Ltd.

circumstances. As to how far these external and apparently accidental circumstances are but the expression of a necessary course of development, political economy teaches us nothing. We have seen how exchange itself appears to it as an accidental fact. The only wheels which political economy sets in motion are *greed* and the *war amongst the greedy – competition*.

Precisely because political economy does not grasp the way the movement is connected, it was possible to oppose, for instance, the doctrine of competition to the doctrine of monopoly, the doctrine of the freedom of the crafts to the doctrine of the guild, the doctrine of the division of landed property to the doctrine of the big estate – for competition, freedom of the crafts and the division of landed property were explained and comprehended only as accidental, premeditated and violent consequences of monopoly, of the guild system, and of feudal property, not as their necessary, inevitable and natural consequences.

Now, therefore, we have to grasp the intrinsic connection between private property, avarice, the separation of labour, capital and landed property; the connection of exchange and competition, of value and the devaluation of men, of monopoly and competition, etc. – we have to grasp this whole estrangement connected with the *money* system.

Do not let us go back to a fictitious primordial condition as the political economist does, when he tries to explain. Such a primordial condition explains nothing; it merely pushes the question away into a grey nebulous distance. The economist assumes in the form of a fact, of an event, what he is supposed to deduce – namely, the necessary relationship between two things – between, for example, division of labour and exchange. Thus the theologian explains the origin of evil by the fall of man; that is, he assumes as a fact, in historical form, what has to be explained.

We proceed from an *actual* economic fact.

The worker becomes all the poorer the more wealth he produces, the more his production increases in power and size. The worker becomes an ever cheaper commodity the more commodities he creates. The *devaluation* of the world of men is in direct proportion to the *increasing value* of the world of things. Labour produces not only commodities: it produces itself and the worker as a *commodity* – and this at the same rate at which it produces commodities in general.

This fact expresses merely that the object which labour produces – labour's product – confronts it as *something alien*, as a *power independent* of the producer. The product of labour is labour which has been embodied in an object, which has become material: it is the *objectification* of labour. Labour's realisation is its objectification. Under these economic conditions this realisation of labour appears as *loss of realisation* for the workers; objectification as *loss of the object and bondage to it*; appropriation as *estrangement, as alienation*.

So much does labour's realisation appear as loss of realisation that the worker loses realisation to the point of starving to death. So much does objectification appear as loss of the object that the worker is robbed of the objects most necessary not only for his life but for his work. Indeed, labour itself becomes an object which he can obtain only with the greatest effort and with the most irregular interruptions.

So much does the appropriation of the object appear as estrangement that the more objects the worker produces the less he can possess and the more he falls under the sway of his product, capital.

All these consequences are implied in the statement that the worker is related to the *product of his labour* as to an *alien* object. For on this premise it is clear that the more the worker spends himself, the more powerful becomes the alien world of objects which he creates over and against himself, the poorer he himself – his inner world – becomes, the less belongs to him as his own. It is the same in religion. The more man puts into God, the less he retains in himself. The worker puts his life into the object; but now his life no longer belongs to him but to the object. Hence, the greater this activity, the more the worker lacks objects. Whatever the product of his labour is, he is not. Therefore the greater this product, the less is he himself. The *alienation* of the worker in his product means not only that his labour becomes an object, an *external* existence, but that it exists *outside him*, independently, as something alien to him, and that it becomes a power on its own confronting him. It means that the life which he has conferred on the object confronts him as something hostile and alien.

Let us now look more closely at the *objectification*, at the production of the worker; and in it at the *estrangement*, the *loss* of the object, of his product.

The worker can create nothing without *nature*, without the *sensuous external world*. It is the material on which his labour is realised, in which it is active, from which and by means of which it produces.

But just as nature provides labour with [the] *means of life* in the sense that labour cannot *live* without objects on which to operate, on the other hand, it also provides the *means of life* in the more restricted sense, i.e., the means for the physical subsistence of the *worker* himself.

Thus the more the worker by his labour *appropriates* the external world, sensuous nature, the more he deprives himself of *means of life* in two respects: first, in that the sensuous external world more and more ceases to be an object belonging to his labour – to be his labour's *means of life*; and secondly, in that it more and more ceases to be *means of life* in the immediate sense, means for the physical subsistence of the worker.

In both respects, therefore, the worker becomes a servant of his object, first, in that he receives an *object of labour*, i.e., in that he receives *work*; and secondly, in that he receives *means of subsistence*. This enables him to exist, first, as a *worker*, and, second, as a *physical subject*. The height of this servitude is that it is only as a *worker* that he can maintain himself as a *physical subject*, and that it is only as a *physical subject* that he is a worker.

(According to the economic laws the estrangement of the worker in his object is expressed thus: the more the worker produces, the less he has to consume; the more values he creates, the more valueless, the more unworthy he becomes; the better formed his product, the more deformed becomes the worker; the more civilised his object, the more barbarous becomes the worker; the more powerful labour becomes, the more powerless becomes the worker; the more ingenious labour becomes, the less ingenious becomes the worker and the more he becomes nature's servant.)

*Political economy conceals the estrangement inherent in the nature of labour by not considering the **direct** relationship between the **worker** (labour) and production.* It is true that labour produces wonderful things for the rich – but for the worker it produces privation. It produces palaces – but for the worker, hovels. It produces beauty – but for the worker, deformity. It replaces labour by machines, but it throws one section of the workers back to a barbarous type of labour, and it turns the other section into a machine. It produces intelligence – but for the worker, stupidity, cretinism.

The direct relationship of labour to its products is the relationship of the worker to the objects of his production. The relationship of the man of means to the objects of production and to production itself is only a *consequence* of this first relationship – and confirms it. We shall consider this other aspect later. When we ask, then, what is the essential relationship of labour we are asking about the relationship of the *worker* to production.

Till now we have been considering the estrangement; the alienation of the worker only in one of its aspects, i.e., the worker's *relationship to the products of his labour*. But the estrangement is manifested not only in the result but in the *act of production*, within the *producing activity* itself. How could the worker come to face the product of his activity as a stranger, were it not that in the very act of production he was estranging himself from himself? The product is after all but the summary of the activity, of production. If then the product of labour is alienation, production itself must be active alienation, the alienation of activity, the activity of alienation. In the estrangement of the object of labour is merely summarised the estrangement, the alienation, in the activity of labour itself.

What, then, constitutes the alienation of labour?

First, the fact that labour is *external* to the worker, i.e., it does not belong to his intrinsic nature; that in his work, therefore, he does not affirm himself but denies himself, does not feel content but unhappy, does not develop freely his physical and mental energy but mortifies his body and ruins his mind. The worker therefore only feels himself outside his work, and in his work feels outside himself. He feels at home when he is not working, and when he is working he does not feel at home. His labour is therefore not voluntary, but coerced; it is *forced labour*. It is therefore not the satisfaction of a need; it is merely a *means* to satisfy needs external to it. Its alien character emerges clearly in the fact that as soon as no physical or other compulsion exists, labour is shunned like the plague. External labour, labour in which man alienates himself, is a labour of self-sacrifice, of mortification. Lastly, the external character of labour for the worker appears in the fact that it is not his own, but someone else's, that it does not belong to him, that in it he belongs, not to himself, but to another. Just as in religion the spontaneous activity of the human imagination, of the human brain and the human heart, operates on the individual independently of him – that is, operates as an alien, divine or diabolical activity – so is the worker's activity not his spontaneous activity. It belongs to another; it is the loss of his self.

As a result, therefore, man (the worker) only feels himself freely active in his animal functions – eating, drinking, procreating, or at most in his dwelling and in dressing-up, etc.; and in his human functions he no longer feels himself to be anything but an animal. What is animal becomes human and what is human becomes animal.

Certainly eating, drinking, procreating, etc., are also genuinely human functions. But taken abstractly, separated from the sphere of all other human activity and turned into sole and ultimate ends, they are animal functions.

We have considered the act of estranging practical human activity, labour, in two of its aspects. (1) The relation of the worker to the *product of labour* as an alien object exercising power over him. This relation is at the same time the relation to the sensuous external world, to the objects of nature, as an alien world inimically opposed to him. (2) The relation of labour to the *act of production* within the *labour* process. This relation is the relation of the worker to his own activity as an alien activity not belonging to him; it is activity as suffering, strength as weakness, begetting as emasculating, the worker's *own* physical and mental energy, his personal life – for what is life but activity? – as an activity which is turned against him, independent of him and not belonging to him. Here we have *self-estrangement* as previously we had the estrangement of the *thing*.

We have still a third aspect of *estranged labour* to deduce from the two already considered.

Man is a species-being, not only because in practice and in theory he adopts the species (his own as well as those of other things) as his object, but – and this is only another way of expressing it – also because he treats himself as the actual, living species; because he treats himself as a *universal* and therefore a free being.

The life of the species, both in man and in animals, consists physically in the fact that man (like the animal) lives on inorganic nature; and the more universal man (or the animal) is, the more universal is the sphere of inorganic nature on which he lives. Just as plants, animals, stones, air, light, etc., constitute theoretically a part of human consciousness, partly as objects of natural science, partly as objects of art – his spiritual inorganic nature, spiritual nourishment which he must first prepare to make palatable and digestible – so also in the realm of practice they constitute a part of human life and human activity. Physically man lives only on these products of nature, whether they appear in the form of food, heating, clothes, a dwelling, etc. The universality of man appears in practice precisely in the universality which makes all nature his *inorganic* body – both inasmuch as nature is (1) his direct means of life, and (2) the material, the object, and the instrument of his life activity. Nature is man's *inorganic body* – nature, that is, insofar as it is not itself human body. Man *lives* on nature – means that nature is his *body*, with which he must remain in continuous interchange if he is not to die. That man's physical and spiritual life is linked to nature means simply that nature is linked to itself, for man is a part of nature.

In estranging from man (1) nature, and (2) himself, his own active functions, his life activity, estranged labour estranges the *species* from man. It changes for him the *life of the species* into a means of individual life. First it estranges the life of the species and individual life, and secondly it makes individual life in its abstract form the purpose of the life of the species, likewise in its abstract and estranged form.

For labour, *life activity, productive life* itself, appears to man in the first place merely as a *means* of satisfying a need – the need to maintain physical existence. Yet the productive life is the life of the species. It is life-engendering life. The whole character of a species – its species-character – is contained in the character of its life activity; and free, conscious activity is man's species-character. Life itself appears only as a *means to life*.

The animal is immediately one with its life activity. It does not distinguish itself from it. It is *its life activity*. Man makes his life activity itself the object of his will and of his consciousness. He has conscious life activity. It is not a determination with which he directly merges. Conscious life activity distinguishes man immediately from animal life activity. It is just because of this that he is a species-being. Or it is only because he is a species-being that he is a conscious being, i.e., that his own life is an object for him. Only because of that is his activity free activity. Estranged labour reverses this relationship, so that it is just because man is a conscious being that he makes his life activity, his *essential being*, a mere means to his *existence*.

In creating a *world of objects* by his practical activity, in his *work upon* inorganic nature, man proves himself a conscious species-being, i.e., as a being that treats the species as its own essential being, or that treats itself as a species-being. Admittedly animals also produce. They build themselves nests, dwellings, like the bees, beavers, ants, etc. But an animal only produces what it immediately needs for itself or its young. It produces one-sidedly, whilst man produces universally. It produces only under the dominion of immediate physical need, whilst man produces even when he is free from physical need and only truly produces in freedom therefrom. An animal produces only itself, whilst man reproduces the whole of nature. An animal's product belongs immediately to its physical body, whilst man freely confronts his product. An animal forms objects only in accordance with the standard and the need of the species to which it belongs, whilst man knows how to produce in accordance with the standard of every species, and knows how to apply everywhere the inherent standard to the object. Man therefore also forms objects in accordance with the laws of beauty.

It is just in his work upon the objective world, therefore, that man really proves himself to be a *species-being*. This production is his active species-life. Through this production, nature appears as *his* work and his reality. The object of labour is, therefore, the *objectification of man's species-life*; for he duplicates himself not only, as in consciousness, intellectually, but also actively, in reality, and therefore he sees himself in a world that he has created. In tearing away from man the object of his production, therefore, estranged labour tears from him his *species-life*, his real objectivity as a member of the species, and transforms his advantage over animals into the disadvantage that his inorganic body, nature, is taken away from him.

Similarly, in degrading spontaneous, free activity to a means, estranged labour makes man's species-life a means to his physical existence.

The consciousness which man has of his species is thus transformed by estrangement in such a way that species [-life] becomes for him a means.

Estranged labour turns thus:

(3) *Man's species-being*, both nature and his spiritual species-property, into a being *alien* to him, into a *means* for his *individual existence*. It estranges from man his own body, as well as external nature and his spiritual aspect, his *human* aspect.

(4) An immediate consequence of the fact that man is estranged from the product of his labour, from his life activity, from his species-being is the *estrangement of man from man*. When man confronts himself, he confronts the *other* man. What applies to a man's relation to his work, to the product of his labour and to himself, also holds of a man's relation to the other man, and to the other man's labour and object of labour.

In fact, the proposition that man's species-nature is estranged from him means that one man is estranged from the other, as each of them is from man's essential nature.

The estrangement of man, and in fact every relationship in which man [stands] to himself, is realised and expressed only in the relationship in which a man stands to other men.

Hence within the relationship of estranged labour each man views the other in accordance with the standard and the relationship in which he finds himself as a worker.

We took our departure from a fact of political economy – the estrangement of the worker and his product. We have formulated this fact in conceptual terms as *estranged, alienated* labour. We have analysed this concept – hence analysing merely a fact of political economy.

Let us now see, further, how the concept of estranged, alienated labour must express and present itself in real life.

If the product of labour is alien to me, if it confronts me as an alien power, to whom, then, does it belong?

If my own activity does not belong to me, if it is an alien, a coerced activity, to whom, then, does it belong?

To a being *other* than myself.

Who is this being?

The *gods*? To be sure, in the earliest times the principal production (for example, the building of temples, etc., in Egypt, India and Mexico) appears to be in the service of the gods, and the product belongs to the gods. However, the gods on their own were never the lords of labour. No more was *nature*. And what a contradiction it would be if, the more man subjugated nature by his labour and the more miracles of the gods were rendered superfluous by the miracles of industry, the more man were to renounce the joy of production and the enjoyment of the product to please these powers.

The *alien* being, to whom labour and the product of labour belongs, in whose service labour is done and for whose benefit the product of labour is provided, can only be *man* himself.

If the product of labour does not belong to the worker, if it confronts him as an alien power, then this can only be because it belongs to some *other man than the worker*. If the worker's activity is a torment to him, to another it must give *satisfaction* and pleasure. Not the gods, not nature, but only man himself can be this alien power over man.

We must bear in mind the previous proposition that man's relation to himself only becomes for him *objective* and *actual* through his relation to the other man. Thus, if the product of his labour, his labour objectified, is for him an *alien, hostile* powerful object independent of him, then his position towards it is such that someone else is master of this object, someone who is alien, hostile, powerful and independent of him. If he treats his own activity as an unfree activity, then he treats it as an activity performed in the service, under the dominion, the coercion, and the yoke of another man.

Every self-estrangement of man, from himself and from nature, appears in the relation in which he places himself and nature to men other than and differentiated from himself. For this reason religious self-estrangement necessarily appears in the relationship of the layman to the priest, or again to a mediator, etc., since we are here dealing with the intellectual world. In the real practical world self-estrangement can only become manifest through the real practical relationship to other men. The medium through which estrangement takes place is itself *practical*. Thus through estranged labour man not only creates his relationship to the object and to the act of production as to powers that are alien and hostile to him; he also creates the relationship in which other men stand to his production and to his product, and the relationship in which he stands to these other men. Just as he creates his own production as the loss of his reality, as his punishment; his own product as a loss, as a product not belonging to him; so he creates the domination of the person who does not produce over production and over the product. Just as he estranges his own activity from himself, so he confers upon the stranger an activity which is not his own.

We have until now considered this relationship only from the standpoint of the worker and later we shall be considering it also from the standpoint of the non-worker.

Through *estranged, alienated labour*, then, the worker produces the relationship to this labour of a man alien to labour and standing outside it. The relationship of the worker to labour creates the relation to it of the capitalist (or whatever one chooses to call the master of labour). *Private property* is thus the product, the result, the necessary consequence, of *alienated labour*, of the external relation of the worker to nature and to himself.

Private property thus results by analysis from the concept of *alienated labour*, i.e., of *alienated man*, of estranged labour, of estranged life, of *estranged* man.

True, it is as a result of the *movement of private property* that we have obtained the concept of *alienated labour* (*of alienated life*) in political economy. But analysis of this concept shows that though private property appears to be the reason, the cause of alienated labour, it is rather its consequence, just as the gods are *originally* not the cause but the effect of man's intellectual confusion. Later this relationship becomes reciprocal.

Only at the culmination of the development of private property does this, its secret, appear again, namely, that on the one hand it is the *product* of alienated labour, and that on the other it is the *means* by which labour alienates itself, the *realisation of this alienation*.

This exposition immediately sheds light on various hitherto unsolved conflicts.

(1)   Political economy starts from labour as the real soul of production; yet to labour it gives nothing, and to private property everything. Confronting this contradiction, Proudhon has decided in favour of labour against private property. We understand, however, that this apparent contradiction is the contradiction of *estranged labour* with itself, and that political economy has merely formulated the laws of estranged labour.

We also understand, therefore, that *wages* and *private property* are identical. Indeed, where the product, as the object of labour, pays for labour itself, there the wage is but a necessary consequence of labour's estrangement. Likewise, in the wage of labour, labour does not appear as an end in itself but as the servant of the wage. We shall develop this point later, and meanwhile will only draw some conclusions.

An enforced *increase of wages* (disregarding all other difficulties, including the fact that it would only be by force, too, that such an increase, being an anomaly, could be maintained) would therefore be nothing but better *payment for the slave*, and would not win either for the worker or for labour their human status and dignity.

Indeed, even the *equality of wages*, as demanded by Proudhon, only transforms the relationship of the present-day worker to his labour into the relationship of all men to labour. Society is then conceived as an abstract capitalist.

Wages are a direct consequence of estranged labour, and estranged labour is the direct cause of private property. The downfall of the one must therefore involve the downfall of the other.

(2)   From the relationship of estranged labour to private property it follows further that the emancipation of society from private property, etc., from servitude, is expressed in the *political* form of the *emancipation of the workers*; not that *their* emancipation alone is at stake, but because the emancipation of the workers contains universal human emancipation – and it contains this, because the whole of human servitude is involved in the relation of the worker to production, and all relations of servitude are but modifications and consequences of this relation.

Just as we have derived the concept of *private property* from the concept of *estranged, alienated labour* by *analysis*, so we can develop every *category* of political economy with the help of these two factors; and we shall find again in each category, e.g., trade, competition, capital, money, only a *particular* and *developed expression* of these first elements.

Before considering this phenomenon, however, let us try to solve two other problems.

(1)   To define the general *nature of private property*, as it has arisen as a result of estranged labour, in its relation to *truly human* and *social property*.

(2) We have accepted the *estrangement of labour*, its *alienation*, as a fact, and we have analysed this fact. How, we now ask, does *man* come to *alienate*, to estrange, his *labour*? How is this estrangement rooted in the nature of human development? We have already gone a long way to the solution of this problem by *transforming* the question of the *origin of private property* into the question of the relation of *alienated labour* to the course of humanity's development. For when one speaks of *private property*, one thinks of dealing with something external to man. When one speaks of labour, one is directly dealing with man himself. This new formulation of the question already contains its solution.

As to (1): The general nature of private property and its relation to truly human property.

Alienated labour has resolved itself for us into two components which depend on one another, or which are but different expressions of one and the same relationship. *Appropriation* appears as *estrangement*, as *alienation*; and *alienation* appears as *appropriation, estrangement* as truly *becoming a citizen*.

We have considered the one side – *alienated* labour in relation to the worker himself, i.e., the *relation of alienated labour to itself*. The product, the necessary outcome of this relationship, as we have seen, is the *property relation of the non-worker to the worker and to labour*. Private property, as the material, summary expression of alienated labour, embraces both relations – the *relation of the worker to labour and to the product of his labour and to the non-worker*, and the relation of the *non-worker to the worker and to the product of his labour*.

Having seen that in relation to the worker who *appropriates* nature by means of his labour, this appropriation appears as estrangement, his own spontaneous activity as activity for another and as activity of another, vitality as a sacrifice of life, production of the object as loss of the object to an alien power, to an *alien* person – we shall now consider the relation to the worker, to labour and its object of this person who is *alien* to labour and the worker.

First it has to be noted that everything which appears in the worker as an *activity of alienation, of estrangement*, appears in the non-worker as a *state of alienation, of estrangement*.

Secondly, that the worker's *real, practical attitude* in production and to the product (as a state of mind) appears in the non-worker confronting him as a *theoretical* attitude.

Thirdly, the non-worker does everything against the worker which the worker does against himself; but he does not do against himself what he does against the worker.

Let us look more closely at these three relations.[1]

NOTE

1 At this point the first manuscript breaks off unfinished. – Ed.

Chapter 11

Manifesto of the Communist Party [1848]

Karl Marx and Friedrich Engels

A spectre is haunting Europe – the spectre of Communism. All the Powers of old Europe have entered into a holy alliance to exorcise this spectre: Pope and Czar, Metternich and Guizot, French Radicals and German police-spies.

Where is the party in opposition that has not been decried as Communistic by its opponents in power? Where the Opposition that has not hurled back the branding reproach of Communism, against the more advanced opposition parties, as well as against its reactionary adversaries?

Two things result from this fact:

I. Communism is already acknowledged by all European Powers to be itself a Power.

II. It is high time that Communists should openly, in the fact of the whole world, publish their views, their aims, their tendencies, and meet this nursery tale of the Spectre of Communism with a Manifesto of the party itself.

To this end, Communists of various nationalities have assembled in London, and sketched the following Manifesto, to be published in the English, French, German, Italian, Flemish and Danish languages.

I Bourgeois and Proletarians[1]

The history of all hitherto existing society is the history of class struggles.

Freeman and slave, patrician and plebeian, lord and serf, guild-master and journeyman, in a word, oppressor and oppressed, stood in constant opposition

Marx, Karl and Engels, Friedrich, "Manifesto of the Communist Party," pp.481–482, 485–506 from *Karl Marx and Friedrich Engels, Collected Works, Volume 6.* New York: International Publishers, 1975. Copyright © 1975. Reprinted by permission of International Publishers. Inc.

Classical Sociological Theory, Third Edition. Edited by Craig Calhoun, Joseph Gerteis, James Moody, Steven Pfaff, and Indermohan Virk. Editorial material and organization © 2012 John Wiley & Sons, Ltd. Published 2012 by John Wiley & Sons, Ltd.

to one another, carried on an uninterrupted, now hidden, now open fight, a fight that each time ended, either in a revolutionary re-constitution of society at large, or in the common ruin of the contending classes.

In the earlier epochs of history, we find almost everywhere a complicated arrangement of society into various orders, a manifold gradation of social rank. In ancient Rome we have patricians, knights, plebeians, slaves; in the Middle Ages, feudal lords, vassals, guild-masters, journeymen, apprentices, serfs; in almost all of these classes, again, subordinate gradations.

The modern bourgeois society that has sprouted from the ruins of feudal society has not done away with class antagonisms. It has but established new classes, new conditions of oppression, new forms of struggle in place of the old ones.

Our epoch, the epoch of the bourgeoisie, possesses, however, this distinctive feature: it has simplified the class antagonisms. Society as a whole is more and more splitting up into two great hostile camps, into two great classes directly facing each other: Bourgeoisie and Proletariat.

From the serfs of the Middle Ages sprang the chartered burghers of the earliest towns. From these burgesses the first elements of the bourgeoisie were developed.

The discovery of America, the rounding of the Cape, opened up fresh ground for the rising bourgeoisie. The East-Indian and Chinese markets, the colonisation of America, trade with the colonies, the increase in the means of exchange and in commodities generally, gave to commerce, to navigation, to industry, an impulse never before known, and thereby, to the revolutionary element in the tottering feudal society, a rapid development.

The feudal system of industry, under which industrial production was monopolised by closed guilds, now no longer sufficed for the growing wants of the new markets. The manufacturing system took its place. The guild-masters were pushed on one side by the manufacturing middle class; division of labour between the different corporate guilds vanished in the face of division of labour in each single workshop.

Meantime the markets kept ever growing, the demand ever rising. Even manufacture no longer sufficed. Thereupon, steam and machinery revolutionised industrial production. The place of manufacture was taken by the giant, Modern Industry, the place of the industrial middle class, by industrial millionaires, the leaders of whole industrial armies, the modern bourgeois.

Modern industry has established the world market, for which the discovery of America paved the way. This market has given an immense development to commerce, to navigation, to communication by land. This development has, in its turn, reacted on the extension of industry; and in proportion as industry, commerce, navigation, railways extended, in the same proportion the bourgeoisie developed, increased its capital, and pushed into the background every class handed down from the Middle Ages.

We see, therefore, how the modern bourgeoisie is itself the product of a long course of development, of a series of revolutions in the modes of production and of exchange.

Each step in the development of the bourgeoisie was accompanied by a corresponding political advance of that class. An oppressed class under the sway of the feudal nobility, an armed and self-governing association in the medieval commune;[2] here independent urban republic (as in Italy and Germany), there taxable "third estate" of the monarchy (as in France), afterwards, in the period of manufacture proper, serving either the semi-feudal or the absolute monarchy as a counterpoise against the nobility, and, in fact, cornerstone of the great monarchies in general, the bourgeoisie has at last, since the establishment of Modern Industry and of the world market, conquered for itself, in the modern representative State, exclusive political sway. The executive of the modern State is but a committee for managing the common affairs of the whole bourgeoisie.

The bourgeoisie, historically, has played a most revolutionary part.

The bourgeoisie, wherever it has not the upper hand, has put an end to all feudal, patriarchal, idyllic relations. It has pitilessly torn asunder the motpley feudal ties that bound man to his "natural superiors", and has left remaining no other nexus between man and man than naked self-interest, than callous "cash payment". It has drowned the most heavenly ecstasies of religious fervour, of chivalrous enthusiasm, of philistine sentimentalism, in the icy water of egotistical calculation. It has resolved personal worth into exchange value, and in place of the numberless indefeasible chartered freedoms, has set up that single, unconscionable freedom – Free Trade. In one word, for exploitation, veiled by religious and political illusions, it has substituted naked, shameless, direct, brutal exploitation.

The bourgeoisie has stripped of its halo every occupation hitherto honoured and looked up to with reverent awe. It has converted the physician, the lawyer, the priest, the poet, the man of science, into its paid wage-labourers.

The bourgeoisie has torn away from the family its sentimental veil, and has reduced the family relation to a mere money relation.

The bourgeoisie has disclosed how it came to pass that the brutal display of vigour in the Middle Ages, which Reactionists so much admire, found its fitting complement in the most slothful indolence. It has been the first to show what man's activity can bring about. It has accomplished wonders for surpassing Egyptian pyramids, Roman aqueducts, and Gothic cathedrals; it has conducted expeditions that put in the shade all former Exoduses of nations and crusades.

The bourgeoisie cannot exist without constantly revolutionising the instruments of production, and thereby the relations of production, and with them the whole relations of society. Conservation of the old modes of production in unaltered form, was, on the contrary, the first condition of existence for all earlier industrial classes. Constant revolutionising of production, uninterrupted disturbance of all social conditions, everlasting uncertainty and agitation distinguish the bourgeois epoch from all earlier ones. All fixed, fast-frozen relations, with their train of ancient and venerable prejudices and opinions, are swept away, all new-formed ones become antiquated before they can ossify. All that is solid melts into air, all that is holy is profaned, and man is at last compelled to face with sober senses, his real conditions of life, and his relations with his kind.

The need of a constantly expanding market for its products chases the bourgeoisie over the whole surface of the globe. It must nestle everywhere, settle everywhere, establish connexions everywhere.

The bourgeoisie has through its exploitation of the world market given a cosmopolitan character to production and consumption in every country. To the great chagrin of Reactionists, it has drawn from under the feet of industry the national ground on which it stood. All old-established national industries have been destroyed or are daily being destroyed. They are dislodged by new industries, whose introduction becomes a life and death question for all civilised nations, by industries that no longer work up indigenous raw material, but raw material drawn from the remotest zones; industries whose products are consumed, not only at home, but in every quarter of the globe. In place of the old wants, satisfied by the productions of the country, we find new wants, requiring for their satisfaction the products of distant lands and climes. In place of the old local and national seclusion and self-sufficiency, we have intercourse in every direction, universal inter-dependence of nations. And as in material, so also in intellectual production. The intellectual creations of individual nations become common property. National one-sidedness and narrow-mindedness become more and more impossible, and from the numerous national and local literatures, there arises a world literature.

The bourgeoisie, by the rapid improvements of all instruments of production, by the immensely facilitated means of communication, draws all, even the most barbarian, nations into civilisation. The cheap prices of its commodities are the heavy artillery with which it batters down all Chinese walls, with which it forces the barbarians' intensely obstinate hatred of foreigners to capitulate. It compels all nations, on pain of extinction, to adopt the bourgeois mode of production; it compels them to introduce what it calls civilisation into their midst, i.e., to become bourgeois themselves. In one word, it creates a world after its own image.

The bourgeoisie has subjected the country to the rule of the towns. It has created enormous cities, has greatly increased the urban population as compared with the rural, and has thus rescued a considerable part of the population from the idiocy of rural life. Just as it has made the country dependent on the towns, so it has made barbarian and semi-barbarian countries dependent on the civilised ones, nations of peasants on nations of bourgeois, the East on the West.

The bourgeoisie keeps more and more doing away with the scattered state of the population, of the means of production, and of property. It has agglomerated population, centralised means of production, and has concentrated property in a few hands. The necessary consequence of this was political centralisation. Independent, or but loosely connected provinces with separate interests, laws, governments and systems of taxation, become lumped together into one nation, with one government, one code of laws, one national class-interest, one frontier and one customs-tariff.

The bourgeoisie, during its rule of scarce one hundred years, has created more massive and more colossal productive forces than have all preceding generations together. Subjection of Nature's forces to man, machinery, application of chemistry to industry and agriculture, steam-navigation, railways, electric telegraphs, clearing of whole continents for cultivation, canalisation of rivers, whole populations conjured out of the ground – what earlier century had even a presentiment that such productive forces slumbered in the lap of social labour?

We see then: the means of production and of exchange, on whose foundation the bourgeoisie built itself up, were generated in feudal society. At a certain stage in the development of these means of production and of exchange, the conditions under which feudal society produced and exchanged, the feudal organisation of agriculture and manufacturing industry, in one word, the feudal relations of property became no longer compatible with the already developed productive forces; they became so many fetters. They had to be burst asunder; they were burst asunder.

Into their place stepped free competition, accompanied by a social and political constitution adapted to it, and by the economical and political sway of the bourgeois class.

A similar movement is going on before our own eyes. Modern bourgeois society with its relations of production, of exchange and of property, a society that has conjured up such gigantic means of production and of exchange, is like the sorcerer, who is no longer able to control the powers of the nether world whom he has called up by his spells. For many a decade past the history of industry and commerce is but the history of the revolt of modern productive forces against modern conditions of production, against the property relations that are the conditions for the existence of the bourgeoisie and of its rule. It is enough to mention the commercial crises that by their periodical return put on its trial, each time more threateningly, the existence of the entire bourgeois society. In these crises a great part not only of the existing products, but also of the previously created productive forces, are periodically destroyed. In these crises there breaks out an epidemic that, in all earlier epochs, would have seemed an absurdity – the epidemic of over-production. Society suddenly finds itself put back into a state of momentary barbarism; it appears as if a famine, a universal war of devastation had cut off the supply of every means of subsistence; industry and commerce seem to be destroyed; and why? Because there is too much civilisation, too much means of subsistence, too much industry, too much commerce. The productive forces at the disposal of society no longer tend to further the development of the conditions of bourgeois property; on the contrary, they have become too powerful for these conditions, by which they are fettered, and so soon as they overcome these fetters, they bring disorder into the whole of bourgeois society, endanger the existence of bourgeois property. The conditions of bourgeois society are too narrow to comprise the wealth created by them. And how does the bourgeoisie get over these crises? On the one hand by enforced destruction of a mass of productive forces; on the other, by the conquest of new markets, and by the more thorough exploitation of the old ones. That is to say, by paving the way for more extensive and more destructive crises, and by diminishing the means whereby crises are prevented.

The weapons with which the bourgeoisie felled feudalism to the ground are now turned against the bourgeoisie itself.

But not only has the bourgeoisie forged the weapons that bring death to itself; it has also called into existence the men who are to wield those weapons – the modern working class – the proletarians.

In proportion as the bourgeoisie, i.e., capital, is developed, in the same proportion is the proletariat, the modern working class, developed – a class of labourers, who live only so long as they find work, and who find work only so long as their labour increases capital. These labourers, who must sell themselves piecemeal, are a commodity, like every other article of commerce, and are consequently exposed to all the vicissitudes of competition, to all the fluctuations of the market.

Owing to the extensive use of machinery and to division of labour, the work of the proletarians has lost all individual character, and, consequently, all charm for the workman. He becomes an appendage of the machine, and it is only the most simple, most monotonous, and most easily acquired knack, that is required of him. Hence, the cost of production of a workman is restricted, almost entirely, to the means of subsistence that he requires for his maintenance, and for the propagation of his race. But the price of a commodity, and therefore also of labour, is equal to its cost of production. In proportion, therefore, as the repulsiveness of the work increases, the wage decreases. Nay more, in proportion as the use of machinery and division of labour increases, in the same proportion the burden of toil also increases, whether by prolongation of the working hours, by increase of the work exacted in a given time or by increased speed of the machinery, etc.

Modern industry has converted the little workshop of the patriarchal master into the great factory of the industrial capitalist. Masses of labourers, crowded into the factory, are organised like soldiers. As privates of the industrial army they are placed under the command of a perfect hierarchy of officers and sergeants. Not only are they slaves of the bourgeois class, and of the bourgeois State; they are daily and hourly enslaved by the machine, by the overlooker, and, above all, by the individual bourgeois manufacturer himself. The more openly this despotism proclaims gain to be its end and aim, the more petty, the more hateful and the more embittering it is.

The less the skill and exertion of strength implied in manual labour, in other words, the more modern industry becomes developed, the more is the labour of men superseded by that of women. Differences of age and sex have no longer any distinctive social validity for the working class. All are instruments of labour, more or less expensive to use, according to their age and sex.

No sooner is the exploitation of the labourer by the manufacturer, so far, at an end, and he receives his wages in cash, than he is set upon by the other portions of the bourgeoisie, the landlord, the shopkeeper, the pawnbroker, etc.

The lower strata of the middle class – the small tradespeople, shopkeepers, and retired tradesmen generally, the handicraftsmen and peasants – all these sink gradually into the proletariat, partly because their diminutive capital does not suffice for the scale on which Modern Industry is carried on, and is swamped in the competition with the large capitalists, partly because their specialised skill is rendered worthless by new methods of production. Thus the proletariat is recruited from all classes of the population.

The proletariat goes through various stages of development. With its birth begins its struggle with the bourgeoisie. At first the contest is carried on by individual labourers, then by the workpeople of a factory, then by the operatives of one trade, in one locality, against the individual bourgeois who directly exploits them. They direct their attacks not against the bourgeois conditions of production, but against the instruments of production themselves, they destroy imported wares that compete with their labour, they smash to pieces machinery, they set factories ablaze, they seek to restore by force the vanished status of the workman of the Middle Ages.

At this stage the labourers still form an incoherent mass scattered over the whole country, and broken up by their mutual competition. If anywhere they unite to form more compact bodies, this is not yet the consequence of their own active union, but of the union of the bourgeoisie, which class, in order to attain its own political ends, is compelled to set the whole proletariat in motion, and is moreover yet, for a time, able to do so. At this stage, therefore, the proletarians do not fight their enemies, but the enemies of their enemies, the remnants of absolute monarchy, the landowners, the non-industrial bourgeois, the petty bourgeoisie. Thus the whole historical movement is concentrated in the hands of the bourgeoisie; every victory so obtained is a victory for the bourgeoisie.

But with the development of industry the proletariat not only increases in number; it becomes concentrated in greater masses, its strength grows, and it feels that strength more. The various interests and conditions of life within the ranks of the proletariat are more and more equalised, in proportion as machinery obliterates all distinctions of labour, and nearly everywhere reduces wages to the same low level. The growing competition among the bourgeois, and the resulting commercial crises, make the wages of the workers ever more fluctuating. The unceasing improvement of machinery, ever more rapidy developing, makes their livelihood more and more precarious; the collisions between individual workmen and individual bourgeois take more and more the character of collisions between two classes. Thereupon the workers begin to form combinations (Trades' Unions) against the bourgeois; they club together in order to keep up the rate of wages; they found permanent associations in order to make provision beforehand for these occasional revolts. Here and there the contest breaks out into riots.

Now and then the workers are victorious, but only for a time. The real fruit of their battles lies, not in the immediate result, but in the ever-expanding union of the workers. This union is helped on by the improved means of communication that are created by modern industry and that place the workers of different localities in contact with one another. It was just this contact that was needed to centralise the numerous local struggles, all of the same character, into one national struggle between classes. But every class struggle is a political struggle. And that union, to attain which the burghers of the Middle Ages, with their miserable highways, required centuries, the modern proletarians, thanks to railways, achieve in a few years.

This organisation of the proletarians into a class, and consequently into a political party, is continually being upset again by the competition between the workers themselves. But it ever rises up again, stronger, firmer, mightier. It compels legislative recognition of particular interests of the workers, by taking advantage of the divisions among the bourgeoisie itself. Thus the ten-hours' bill in England was carried.

Altogether collisions between the classes of the old society further, in many ways, the course of development of the proletariat. The bourgeoisie finds itself involved in a constant battle. At first with the aristocracy; later on, with those portions of the bourgeoisie itself, whose interests have become antagonistic to the progress of industry; at all times, with the bourgeoisie of foreign countries. In all these battles it sees itself compelled to appeal to the proletariat, to ask for its help, and thus, to drag it into the political arena. The bourgeoisie itself, therefore, supplies the proletariat with its own elements of political and general education, in other words, it furnishes the proletariat with weapons for fighting the bourgeoisie.

Further, as we have already seen, entire sections of the ruling classes are, by the advance of industry, precipitated into the proletariat, or are at least threatened in their conditions of existence. These also supply the proletariat with fresh elements of enlightenment and progress.

Finally, in times when the class struggle nears the decisive hour, the process of dissolution going on within the ruling class, in fact within the whole range of old society, assumes such a violent, glaring character, that a small section of the ruling class cuts itself adrift, and joins the revolutionary class, the class that holds the future in its hands. Just as, therefore, at an earlier period, a section of the nobility went over to the bourgeoisie, so now a portion of the bourgeoisie goes over to the proletariat, and in particular, a portion of the bourgeois ideologists, who have raised themselves to the level of comprehending theoretically the historical movement as a whole.

Of all the classes that stand face to face with the bourgeoisie today, the proletariat alone is a really revolutionary class. The other classes decay and finally disappear in the fact of Modern Industry; the proletariat is its special and essential product.

The lower middle class, the small manufacturer, the shopkeeper, the artisan, the peasant, all these fight against the bourgeoisie, to save from extinction their existence as fractions of the middle class. They are therefore not revolutionary, but conservative. Nay more, they are reactionary, for they try to roll back the wheel of history. If by chance they are revolutionary, they are so only in view of their impending transfer into the proletariat, they thus defend not their present, but their future interests, they desert their own standpoint to place themselves at that of the proletariat.

The "dangerous class", the social scum, that passively rotting mass thrown off by the lowest layers of old society may, here and there, be swept into the movement by a proletarian revolution; its conditions of life, however, prepare it far more for the part of a bribed tool of reactionary intrigue.

In the conditions of the proletariat, those of old society at large are already virtually swamped. The proletarian is without property; his relation to his wife and children has no longer anything in common with the bourgeois family relations;

modern industrial labour, modern subjection to capital, the same in England as in France, in America as in Germany, has stripped him of every trace of national character. Law, morality, religion, are to him so many bourgeois prejudices, behind which lurk in ambush just as many bourgeois interests.

All the preceding classes that got the upper hand, sought to fortify their already acquired status by subjecting society at large to their conditions of appropriation. The proletarians cannot become masters of the productive forces of society, except by abolishing their own previous mode of appropriation, and thereby also every other previous mode of appropriation. They have nothing of their own to secure and to fortify; their mission is to destroy all previous securities for, and insurances of, individual property.

All previous historical movements were movements of minorities, or in the interest of minorities. The proletarian movement is the self-conscious, independent movement of the immense majority, in the interest of the immense majority. The proletariat, the lowest stratum of our present society, cannot stir, cannot raise itself up, without the whole superincumbent strata of official society being sprung into the air.

Though not in substance, yet in form, the struggle of the proletariat with the bourgeoisie is at first a national struggle. The proletariat of each country must, of course, first of all settle matters with its own bourgeoisie.

In depicting the most general phases of the development of the proletariat, we traced the more or less veiled civil war, raging within existing society, up to the point where that war breaks out into open revolution, and where the violent overthrow of the bourgeoisie lays the foundation for the sway of the proletariat.

Hitherto, every form of society has been based, as we have already seen, on the antagonism of oppressing and oppressed classes. But in order to oppress a class, certain conditions must be assured to it under which it can, at least, continue its slavish existence. The serf, in the period of serfdom, raised himself to membership in the commune, just as the petty bourgeois, under the yoke of feudal absolutism, managed to develop into a bourgeois. The modern labourer, on the contrary, instead of rising with the progress of industry, sinks deeper and deeper below the conditions of existence of his own class. He becomes a pauper, and pauperism develops more rapidly than population and wealth. And here it becomes evident, that the bourgeoisie is unfit any longer to be the ruling class in society, and to impose its conditions of existence upon society as an over-riding law. It is unfit to rule because it is incompetent to assure an existence to its slave within his slavery, because it cannot help letting him sink into such a state, that it has to feed him, instead of being fed by him. Society can no longer live under this bourgeoisie, in other words, its existence is no longer compatible with society.

The essential condition for the existence, and for the sway of the bourgeois class, is the formation and augmentation of capital; the condition for capital is wage-labour. Wage-labour rests exclusively on competition between the labourers. The advance of industry, whose involuntary promoter is the bourgeoisie, replaces the isolation of the labourers, due to competition, by their revolutionary combination, due to association. The development of Modern Industry, therefore, cuts from under its feet the very foundation on which the bourgeoisie produces and appropriates products. What the bourgeoisie, therefore, produces, above all, is its own grave-diggers. Its fall and victory of the proletariat are equally inevitable.

II Proletarians and Communists

In what relation do the Communists stand to the proletarians as a whole?

The Communists do not form a separate party opposed to other working-class parties.

They have no interests separate and apart from those of the proletariat as a whole.

They do not set up any sectarian principles of their own, by which to shape and mould the proletarian movement.

The Communists are distinguished form the other working-class parties by this only: 1. In the national struggles of the proletarians of the different countries, they point out and bring to the front the common interests of the entire proletariat, independently of all nationality. 2. In the various stages of development which the struggle of the working class against the bourgeoisie has to pass through, they always and everywhere represent the interests of the movement as a whole.

The Communists, therefore, are on the one hand, practically, the most advanced and resolute section of the working-class parties of every country, that section which pushes forward all others; on the other hand, theoretically, they have over the great mass of the proletariat the advantage of clearly understanding the line of march, the conditions, and the ultimate general results of the proletarian movement.

The immediate aim of the Communists is the same as that of all the other proletarian parties: formation of the proletariat into a class, overthrow of the bourgeois supremacy, conquest of political power by the proletariat.

The theoretical conclusions of the Communists are in no way based on ideas or principles that have been invented, or discovered by this or that would-be universal reformer.

They merely express, in general terms, actual relations springing from an existing class struggle, from a historical movement going on under our very eyes. The abolition of existing property relations is not at all a distinctive feature of Communism.

All property relations in the past have continually been subject to historical change consequent upon the change in historical conditions.

The French Revolution, for example, abolished feudal property in favour of bourgeois property.

The distinguishing feature of Communism is not the abolition of property generally, but the abolition of bourgeois property. But modern bourgeois private property is the final and most complete expression of the system of producing and appropriating products, that is based on class antagonisms, on the exploitation of the many by the few.

In this sense, the theory of the Communists may be summed up in the single sentence: Abolition of private property.

We Communists have been reproached with the desire of abolishing the right of personally acquiring property as the fruit of a man's own labour, which property is alleged to be the groundwork of all personal freedom, activity and independence.

Hard-won, self-acquired, self-earned property! Do you mean the property of the petty artisan and of the small peasant, a form of property that preceded the bourgeois form? There is no need to abolish that; the development of industry has to a great extent already destroyed it, and is still destroying it daily.

Or do you mean modern bourgeois private property?

But does wage-labour create any property for the labourer? Not a bit. It creates capital, i.e., that kind of property which exploits wage-labour, and which cannot increase except upon condition of begetting a new supply of wage-labour for fresh exploitation. Property, in its present form, is based on the antagonism of capital and wage-labour. Let us examine both sides of this antagonism.

To be a capitalist is to have not only a purely personal, but a social *status* in production. Capital is a collective product, and only by the united action of many members, nay, in the last resort, only by the united action of all members of society, can it be set in motion.

Capital is, therefore, not a personal, it is a social power.

When, therefore, capital is converted into common property, into the property of all members of society, personal property is not thereby transformed into social property. It is only the social character of the property that is changed. It loses its class character.

Let us now take wage-labour.

The average price of wage-labour is the minimum wage, i.e., that quantum of the means of subsistence, which is absolutely requisite to keep the labourer in bare existence as a labourer. What, therefore, the wage-labourer appropriates by means of his labour, merely suffices to prolong and reproduce a bare existence. We by no means intend to abolish this personal appropriation of the products of labour, an appropriation that is made for the maintenance and reproduction of human life, and that leaves no surplus wherewith to command the labour of others. All that we want to do away with is the miserable character of this appropriation, under which the labourer lives merely to increase capital, and is allowed to live only in so far as the interest of the ruling class requires it.

In bourgeois society, living labour is but a means to increase accumulated labour. In Communist society, accumulated labour is but a means to widen, to enrich, to promote the existence of the labourer.

In bourgeois society, therefore, the past dominates the present; in Communist society, the present dominates the past. In bourgeois society capital is independent and has individuality, while the living person is dependent and has no individuality.

And the abolition of this state of things is called by the bourgeois, abolition of individuality and freedom! And rightly so. The abolition of bourgeois individuality, bourgeois independence, and bourgeois freedom is undoubtedly aimed at.

By freedom is meant, under the present bourgeois conditions of production, free trade, free selling and buying.

But if selling and buying disappears, free selling and buying disappears also. This talk about free selling and buying, and all the other "brave words" of our bourgeoisie about freedom in general, have a meaning, if any, only in contrast with restricted selling and buying, with the fettered traders of the Middle Ages, but have no meaning when opposed to the Communistic abolition of buying and selling, of the bourgeois conditions of production, and of the bourgeoisie itself.

You are horrified at our intending to do away with private property. But in your existing society, private property is already done away with for nine-tenths of the population; its existence for the few is solely due to its non-existence in the hands of those nine-tenths. You reproach us, therefore, with intending to do away with a form of property, the necessary condition for whose existence is the non-existence of any property for the immense majority of society.

In one word, you reproach us with intending to do away with your property. Precisely so; that is just what we intend.

From the moment when labour can no longer be converted into capital, money, or rent, into a social power capable of being monopolised, i.e., from the moment when individual property can no longer be transformed into bourgeois property, into capital, from that moment, you say, individuality vanishes.

You must, therefore, confess that by "individual" you mean no other person than the bourgeois, than the middle-class owner of property. This person must, indeed, be swept out of the way, and made impossible.

Communism deprives no man of the power to appropriate the products of society; all that it does is to deprive him of the power to subjugate the labour of others by means of such appropriation.

It has been objected that upon the abolition of private property all work will cease, and universal laziness will overtake us.

According to this, bourgeois society ought long ago to have gone to the dogs through sheer idleness; for those of its members who work, acquire nothing, and those who acquire anything, do not work. The whole of this objection is but another expression of the tautology: that there can no longer be any wage-labour when there is no longer any capital.

All objections urged against the Communistic mode of producing and appropriating material products, have, in the same way, been urged against the Communistic modes of producing and appropriating intellectual products. Just as, to the bourgeois, the disappearance of class property is the disappearance of production itself, so the disappearance of class culture is to him identical with the disappearance of all culture.

That culture, the loss of which he laments, is, for the enormous majority, a mere training to act as a machine.

But don't wrangle with us so long as you apply, to our intended abolition of bourgeois property, the standard of your bourgeois notions of freedom, culture, law, &c. Your very ideas are but the outgrowth of the conditions of your bourgeois production and bourgeois property, just as your jurisprudence is but the will of your class made into a law for all, a will, whose essential character and direction are determined by the economical conditions of existence of your class.

The selfish misconception that induces you to transform into eternal laws of nature and of reason, the social forms springing from your present mode of production and form of property – historical relations that rise and disappear in the progress of production – this misconception you share with every ruling class that has preceded you. What you see clearly in the case of ancient property, what you admit in the case of feudal property, you are of course forbidden to admit in the case of your own bourgeois form of property.

Abolition of the family! Even the most radical flare up at this infamous proposal of the Communists.

On what foundation is the present family, the bourgeois family, based? On capital, on private gain. In its completely developed form this family exists only among the bourgeoisie. But this state of things finds its complement in the practical absence of the family among the proletarians, and in public prostitution.

The bourgeois family will vanish as a matter of course when its complement vanishes, and both will vanish with the vanishing of capital.

Do you charge us with wanting to stop the exploitation of children by their parents? To this crime we plead guilty.

But, you will say, we destroy the most hallowed of relations, when we replace home education by social.

And your education! Is not that also social, and determined by the social conditions under which you educate, by the intervention, direct or indirect, of society, by means of schools, &c.? The Communists have not invented the intervention of society in education; they do but seek to alter the character of that intervention, and to rescue education from the influence of the ruling class.

The bourgeois clap-trap about the family and education, about the hallowed corelation of parent and child, becomes all the more disgusting, the more, by the action of Modern Industry, all family ties among the proletarians are torn asunder, and their children transformed into simple articles of commerce and instruments of labour.

But you Communists would introduce community of women, screams the whole bourgeoisie in chorus.

The bourgeois sees in his wife a mere instrument of production. He hears that the instruments of production are to be exploited in common, and, naturally, can come to no other conclusion than that the lot of being common to all will likewise fall to the women.

He has not even a suspicion that the real point aimed at is to do away with the status of women as mere instruments of production.

For the rest, nothing is more ridiculous than the virtuous indignation of our bourgeois at the community of women which, they pretend, is to be openly and officially established by the Communists. The Communists have no need to introduce community of women; it has existed almost from time immemorial.

Our bourgeois, not content with having the wives and daughters of their proletarians at their disposal, not to speak of common prostitutes, take the greatest pleasure in seducing each other's wives.

Bourgeois marriage is in reality a system of wives in common and thus, at the most, what the Communists might possibly be reproached with, is that they desire to introduce, in substitution for a hypocritically concealed, an openly legalised community of women. For the rest, it is self-evident that the abolition of the present system of production must bring with it the abolition of the community of all women springing from that system, i.e., of prostitution both public and private.

The Communists are further reproached with desiring to abolish countries and nationality.

The working men have no country. We cannot take from them what they have not got. Since the proletariat must first of all acquire political supremacy, must rise to be the leading class of the nation, must constitute itself *the* nation, it is, so far, itself national, though not in the bourgeois sense of word.

National differences and antagonism between peoples are daily more and more vanishing, owing to the development of the bourgeoisie, to freedom of commerce, to the world market, to uniformity in the mode of production and in the conditions of life corresponding thereto.

The supremacy of the proletariat will cause them to vanish still faster. United action, of the leading civilised countries at least, is one of the first conditions for the emancipation of the proletariat.

In proportion as the exploitation of one individual by another is put an end to, the exploitation of one nation by another will also be put an end to. In proportion as the antagonism between classes within the nation vanishes, the hostility of one nation to another will come to an end.

The charges against communism made from a religious, a philosophical, and, generally, from an ideological standpoint, are not deserving of serious examination.

Does it require deep intuition to comprehend that man's ideas, views and conceptions, in one word, man's consciousness, changes with every change in the conditions of his material existence, in his social relations and in his social life?

What else does the history of ideas prove, than that intellectual production changes its character in proportion as material production is changed? The ruling ideas of each age have ever been the ideas of its ruling class.

When people speak of ideas that revolutionise society, they do but express the fact, that within the old society, the elements of a new one have been created, and that the dissolution of the old ideas keeps even pace with the dissolution of the old conditions of existence.

When the ancient world was in its last throes, the ancient religions were overcome by Christianity. When Christian ideas succumbed in the 18th century to rationalist ideas, feudal society fought its death battle with the then revolutionary bourgeoisie. The ideas of religious liberty and freedom of conscience merely gave expression to the sway of free competition within the domain of knowledge.

"Undoubtedly," it will be said, 'religious, moral, philosophical and juridical ideas have been modified in the course of historical development. But religion, morality, philosophy, political science, and law, constantly survived this change.

"There are, besides, eternal truths, such as Freedom, Justice, etc., that are common to all states of society. But communism abolishes eternal truths, it abolishes all religion and all morality, instead of constituting them on a new basis; it therefore acts in contradiction to all past historical experience."

What does this accusation reduce itself to? The history of all past society has consisted in the development of class antagonisms, antagonisms that assumed different forms at different epochs.

But whatever form they may have taken, one fact is common to all past ages, *viz.*, the exploitation of one part of society by the other. No wonder, then, that the social consciousness of past ages, despite all the multiplicity and variety it displays, moves within certain common forms, or general ideas, which cannot completely vanish except with the total disappearance of class antagonisms.

The Communist revolution is the most radical rupture with traditional property relations; no wonder that its development involves the most radical rupture with traditional ideas.

But let us have done with the bourgeois objections to Communism.

We have seen above, that the first step in the revolution by the working class is to raise the proletariat to the position of ruling class, to win the battle of democracy.

The proletariat will use its political supremacy to wrest, by degrees, all capital from the bourgeoisie, to centralise all instruments of production in the hands of the State, i.e., of the proletariat organised as the ruling class; and to increase the total of productive forces as rapidly as possible.

Of course, in the beginning, this cannot be effected except by means of despotic inroads on the rights of property, and on the conditions of bourgeois production; by means of measures, therefore, which appear economically insufficient and untenable, but which, in the course of the movement, outstrip themselves, necessitate further inroads upon the old social order, and are unavoidable as a means of entirely revolutionising the mode of production.

These measures will of course be different in different countries.

Nevertheless in the most advanced countries, the following will be pretty generally applicable:

1   Abolition of property in land and application of all rents of land to public purposes.
2   A heavy progressive or graduated income tax.
3   Abolition of all right of inheritance.
4   Confiscation of the property of all emigrants and rebels.

5   Centralisation of credit in the hands of the State, by means of a national bank with State capital and an exclusive monopoly.
6   Centralisation of the means of communication and transport in the hands of the State.
7   Extension of factories and instruments of production owned by the State; the bringing into cultivation of waste-lands, and the improvement of the soil generally in accordance with a common plan.
8   Equal liability of all to labour. Establishment of industrial armies, especially for agriculture.
9   Combination of agriculture with manufacturing industries; gradual abolition of the distinction between town and country, by a more equable distribution of the population over the country.
10 Free education for all children in public schools. Abolition of children's factory labour in its present form. Combination of education with industrial production. &c., &c.

When, in the course of development, class distinctions have disappeared, and all production has been concentrated in the hands of a vast association of the whole nation, the public power will lose its political character. Political power, properly so called, is merely the organised power of one class for oppressing another. If the proletariat during its contest with the bourgeoisie is compelled, by the force of circumstances, to organise itself as a class, if, by means of a revolution, it makes itself the ruling class, and, as such, sweeps away by force the old conditions of production, then it will, along with these conditions, have swept away the conditions for the existence of class antagonisms and of classes generally, and will thereby have abolished its own supremacy as a class.

In place of the old bourgeois society, with its classes and class antagonisms, we shall have an association, in which the free development of each is the condition for the free development of all.

NOTES

1   By bourgeoisie is meant the class of modern Capitalists, owners of the means of social production and employers of wage-labour. By proletariat, the class of modern wage-labourers who, having no means of production of their own, are reduced to selling their labour-power in order to live. [*Note by Engels to the English edition of 1888.*]
2   This was the name given their urban communities by the townsmen of Italy and France, after they had purchased or wrested their initial rights of self-government from their feudal lords. [*Note by Engels to the German edition of 1890.*]

Chapter 12

The Eighteenth Brumaire of Louis Bonaparte [1852]

Karl Marx

Hegel remarks somewhere that all facts and personages of great importance in world history occur, as it were, twice. He forgot to add: the first time as tragedy, the second as farce. Caussidière for Danton, Louis Blanc for Robespierre, the Montagne of 1848 to 1851 for the Montagne of 1793 to 1795, the Nephew for the Uncle. And the same caricature occurs in the circumstances attending the second edition of the eighteenth Brumaire!

    Men make their own history, but they do not make it just as they please; they do not make it under circumstances chosen by themselves, but under circumstances directly encountered, given and transmitted from the past. The tradition of all the dead generations weighs like a nightmare on the brain of the living. And just when they seem engaged in revolutionising themselves and things, in creating something that has never yet existed, precisely in such periods of revolutionary crisis they anxiously conjure up the spirits of the past to their service and borrow from them names, battle-cries and costumes in order to present the new scene of world history in this time-honoured disguise and this borrowed language. Thus Luther donned the mask of the Apostle Paul, the revolution of 1789 to 1814 draped itself alternately as the Roman Republic and the Roman Empire, and the revolution of 1848 knew nothing better to do than to parody, now 1789, now the revolutionary tradition of 1793 to 1795. In like manner a beginner who has learnt a new language always translates it back into his mother tongue, but he has assimilated the spirit of the new

Marx, Karl, "The Eighteenth Brumaire of Louis Bonaparte," pp.103–112, 194–197 from Karl Marx and Friedrich Engels, *Collected Works, Volume 11*. New York: International Publishers, 1975. Copyright © 1975. Reprinted by permission of International Publishers Inc.

Classical Sociological Theory, Third Edition. Edited by Craig Calhoun, Joseph Gerteis, James Moody, Steven Pfaff, and Indermohan Virk. Editorial material and organization © 2012 John Wiley & Sons, Ltd. Published 2012 by John Wiley & Sons, Ltd.

language and can freely express himself in it only when he finds his way in it without recalling the old and forgets his native tongue in the use of the new.

Consideration of this world-historical necromancy reveals at once a salient difference. Camille Desmoulins, Danton, Robespierre, Saint-Just, Napoleon, the heroes as well as the parties and the masses of the old French Revolution, performed the task of their time in Roman costume and with Roman phrases, the task of unchaining and setting up modern *bourgeois* society. The first ones knocked the feudal basis to pieces and mowed off the feudal heads which had grown on it. The other created inside France the conditions under which free competition could first be developed, the parcelled landed property exploited and the unchained industrial productive forces of the nation employed; and beyond the French borders he everywhere swept the feudal institutions away, so far as was necessary to furnish bourgeois society in France with a suitable up-to-date environment on the European Continent. The new social formation once established, the antediluvian Colossi disappeared and with them resurrected Romanity – the Brutuses, Gracchi, Publicolas, the tribunes, the senators, and Caesar himself. Bourgeois society in its sober reality had begotten its true interpreters and mouthpieces in the Says, Cousins, Royer-Collards, Benjamin Constants and Guizots; its real commanders sat behind the counter, and the hog-headed Louis XVIII was its political chief. Wholly absorbed in the production of wealth and in peaceful competitive struggle, it no longer comprehended that ghosts from the days of Rome had watched over its cradle. But unheroic as bourgeois society is, it nevertheless took heroism, sacrifice, terror, civil war and battles of peoples to bring it into being. And in the classically austere traditions of the Roman Republic its gladiators found the ideals and the art forms, the self-deceptions that they needed in order to conceal from themselves the bourgeois limitations of the content of their struggles and to maintain their passion on the high plane of great historical tragedy. Similarly, at another stage of development, a century earlier, Cromwell and the English people had borrowed speech, passions and illusions from the Old Testament for their bourgeois revolution. When the real aim had been achieved, when the bourgeois transformation of English society had been accomplished, Locke supplanted Habakkuk.

Thus the resurrection of the dead in those revolutions served the purpose of glorifying the new struggles, not of parodying the old; of magnifying the given task in imagination, not of feeling from its solution in reality; of finding once more the spirit of revolution, not of making its ghost walk about again.

From 1848 to 1851 only the ghost of the old revolution walked about, from Marrast, the *républicain en gants jaunes*,[1] who disguised himself as the old Bailly, down to the adventurer who hides his commonplace repulsive features under the iron death mask of Napoleon. An entire people, which had imagined that by means of a revolution it had imparted to itself an accelerated power of motion, suddenly finds itself set back into a defunct epoch and, in order that no doubt as to the relapse may be possible, the old dates arise again, the old chronology, the old names, the old edicts, which had long become a subject of antiquarian erudition, and the old myrmidons of the law, who had seemed long decayed. The nation feels like that mad

Englishman in Bedlam who fancies that he lives in the times of the ancient Pharoahs and daily bemoans the hard labour that he must perform in the Ethiopian mines as a gold digger, immured in this subterranean prison, a dimly burning lamp fastened to his head, the overseer of the slaves behind him with a long whip, and at the exits a confused welter of barbarian mercenaries, who understand neither the forced labourers in the mines nor one another, since they speak no common language. "And all this is expected of me," sighs the mad Englishman, "of me, a free-born Briton, in order to make gold for the old Pharoahs." "In order to pay the debts of the Bonaparte family," sighs the French nation. The Englishman, so long as he was in his right mind, could not get rid of the fixed idea of making gold. The French, so long as they were engaged in revolution, could not get rid of the memory of Napoleon, as the election of December 10 proved. They hankered to return from the perils of revolution to the fleshpots of Egypt, and December 2, 1851 was the answer. They have not only a caricature of the old Napoleon, they have the old Napoleon himself, caricatured as he must appear in the middle of the nineteenth century.

The social revolution of the nineteenth century cannot draw its poetry from the past, but only from the future. It cannot begin with itself before it has stripped off all superstition about the past. Earlier revolutions required recollections of past world history in order to dull themselves to their own content. In order to arrive at its own content, the revolution of the nineteenth century must let the dead bury their dead.[2] There the words went beyond the content; here the content goes beyond the words.

The February revolution was a surprise attack, a *taking* of the old society *unawares*, and the people proclaimed this unexpected *coup de main* as a deed of historic importance, ushering in the new epoch. On December 2 the February revolution is conjured away by a cardsharper's trick, and what seems overthrown is no longer the monarchy but the liberal concessions that were wrung from it by centuries of struggle. Instead of *society* having conquered a new content for itself, it seems that the *state* only returned to its oldest form, to the shamelessly simple domination of the sabre and the cowl. This is the answer to the *coup de main* of February 1848, given by the *coup de tête*[3] of December 1851. Easy come, easy go. Meanwhile the intervening time has not passed by unused. During the years 1848 to 1851 French society made up, and that by an abbreviated because revolutionary method, for the studies and experiences which, in a regular, so to speak, textbook course of development, would have had to precede the February revolution, if it was to be more than a ruffling of the surface. Society now seems to have fallen back behind its point of departure; it has in truth first to create for itself the revolutionary point of departure, the situation, the relations, the conditions under which alone modern revolution becomes serious.

Bourgeois revolutions, like those of the eighteenth century, storm swiftly from success to success, their dramatic effects outdo each other, men and things seem set in sparkling brilliants, ecstasy is the everyday spirit, but they are short-lived, soon they have attained their zenith, and a long crapulent depression seizes society before it learns soberly to assimilate the results of its storm-and-stress period. On the other hand, proletarian revolutions, like those of the nineteenth century, criticise themselves constantly, interrupt themselves continually in their own course, come back to the apparently accomplished in order to begin it afresh, deride with unmerciful thoroughness the inadequacies, weaknesses and paltrinesses of their first attempts, seem to throw down their adversary only in order that he may draw new strength from the earth and rise again, more gigantic, before them, and recoil again and again from the indefinite prodigiousness of their own aims, until a situation has been created which makes all turning back impossible, and the conditions themselves cry out:

> Hic Rhodus, hic salta!
> Here is the rose, here dance!

For the rest, every fairly competent observer, even if he had not followed the course of French development step by step, must have had a presentiment that an unheard-of fiasco was in store for the revolution. It was enough to hear the self-complacent howl of victory with which Messieurs the Democrats congratulated each other on the beneficial consequences of the second Sunday in May 1852. In their minds the second Sunday in May 1852 had become a fixed idea, a dogma, like the day on which Christ should reappear and the millennium begin, in the minds of the Chiliasts. As ever, weakness had taken refuge in a belief in miracles, fancied the enemy overcome when it had only conjured him away in imagination, and lost all understanding of the present in a passive glorification of the future in store for it and of the deeds it had *in petto*[4] but which it merely did not want as yet to make public. Those heroes who seek to disprove their proven incapacity by offering each other their sympathy and getting together in a crowd had tied up their bundles, collected their laurel wreaths in advance and were just then engaged in discounting on the exchange market the republics *in partibus*[5] for which they had already providently organised the government personnel with all the calm of their unassuming disposition. December 2 struck them like a thunderbolt from a clear sky, and the peoples that in periods of pusillanimous depression gladly let their inward apprehension be drowned out by the loudest bawlers will have perhaps convinced themselves that the times are past when the cackle of geese could save the Capitol.

The Constitution, the National Assembly, the dynastic parties, the blue and the red republicans, the heroes of Africa, the thunder from the platform, the sheet lightning of the daily press, the entire literature, the political names and the intellectual reputations, the civil law and the penal code, the *liberté, égalité, fraternité* and the second Sunday in May 1852 – all has vanished like a phantasmagoria before the spell of a man whom even his enemies do not make out to be a magician. Universal suffrage seems to have survived only for a moment, in order that with its own hand it may make its last will and testament before the eyes of all the world and declare in the name of the people itself: "All that comes to birth is fit for overthrow, as nothing worth."[6]

It is not enough to say, as the French do, that their nation was taken unawares. A nation and a woman are not forgiven the unguarded hour in which the first adventurer that came along could violate them. The riddle is not solved by such turns of speech, but merely formulated differently. It remains to be explained how a nation of thirty-six million can be surprised and delivered unresisting into captivity by three swindlers.

Let us recapitulate in general outline the phases that the French Revolution went through from February 24, 1848 to December 1851.

Three main periods are unmistakable: *the February period*; May 4, 1848 to May 28, 1849: *the period of the constitution of the republic* or *of the Constituent National Assembly*, May 28, 1849 to December 2, 1851: *the period of the constitutional republic* or *of the Legislative National Assembly*.

The *first period*, from February 24, or the overthrow of Louis Philippe, to May 4, 1848, the meeting of the Constituent Assembly, the *February period* proper, may be described as the *prologue* to the revolution. Its character was officially expressed in the fact that the government improvised by it declared itself that it was *provisional* and, like the government, everything that was mooted, attempted or enunciated during this period proclaimed itself to be only *provisional*. Nothing and nobody ventured to lay claim to the right of existence and of real action. All the elements that had prepared or determined the revolution, the dynastic opposition, the republican bourgeoisie, the democratic-republican petty bourgeoisie and the Social-Democratic workers, provisionally found their place in the February *government*.

It could not be otherwise. The February days originally aimed at an electoral reform, by which the circle of the politically privileged among the possessing class itself was to be widened and the exclusive domination of the finance aristocracy overthrown. When it came to the actual conflict, however, when the people mounted the barricades, the National Guard maintained a passive attitude, the army offered no serious resistance and the monarchy ran away, the republic appeared to be a matter of course. Every party construed it in its own way. Having secured it arms in hand, the proletariat impressed its stamp upon it and proclaimed it to be a *social republic*. There was thus indicated the general content of the contradiction to everything that, with the material available, with the degree of education attained by the masses, under the given circumstances and relations, could be immediately realised in practice. On the other hand, the claims of all the remaining elements that had collaborated in the February revolution were recognised by the lion's share that they obtained in the government. In no period do we, therefore, find a more confused mixture of high-flown phrases and actual uncertainty and clumsiness, of more enthusiastic striving for innovation and more thorough domination of the old routine, of more apparent harmony of the whole of society and more profound estrangement of its elements. While the Paris proletariat still revelled in the vision of the wide prospects that had opened before it and indulged in earnest discussions on social problems, the old forces of society had grouped themselves, rallied, reflected and found unexpected support in the mass of the nation, the peasants and petty bourgeois, who all at once stormed on to the political stage, after the barriers of the July monarchy had fallen.

The *second period*, from May 4, 1848 to the end of May 1849, is the period of the *constitution*, the *foundation*, *of the bourgeois republic*. Directly after the February days not only had the dynastic opposition been surprised by the republicans and the republicans by the Socialists, but all France by Paris. The National Assembly, which met on May 4, 1848, had emerged from the national elections and represented the nation. It was a living protest against the aspirations of the February days and was to reduce the results of the revolution to the bourgeois scale. In vain the Paris proletariat, which immediately grasped the character of this National Assembly, attempted on May 15, a few days after it met, forcibly to negate its existence, to dissolve it, to disintegrate again into its constituent parts the organic form in which the proletariat was threatened by the reacting spirit of the nation. As is known, May 15 had no other result save that of removing Blanqui and his comrades, that is, the real leaders of the proletarian party, from the public stage for the entire duration of the cycle we are considering.

The *bourgeois monarchy* of Louis Philippe can be followed only by a *bourgeois republic*, that is to say, whereas a limited section of the bourgeoisie ruled in the name of the king, the whole of the bourgeoisie will now rule on behalf of the people. The demands of the Paris proletariat are utopian nonsense, to which an end must be put. To this declaration of the Constituent National Assembly the Paris proletariat replied with the *June insurrection*, the most colossal event in the history of European civil wars. The bourgeois republic triumphed. On its side stood the finance aristocracy, the industrial bourgeoisie, the middle class, the petty bourgeois, the *army*, the lumpenproletariat organised as the Mobile Guard, the intellectuals, the clergy and the rural population. On the side of the Paris proletariat stood none but itself. More than 3,000 insurgents were butchered after the victory, and 15,000 were deported without trial. With this defeat the proletariat recedes into the *background* of the revolutionary stage. It attempts to press forward again on every occasion, as soon as the movement appears to make a fresh start, but with ever decreased expenditure of strength and always slighter results. As soon as one of the social strata situated above it gets into revolutionary ferment, the proletariat enters into an alliance with it and so shares all the defeats that the different parties suffer, one after another. But these subsequent blows become the weaker, the greater the surface of society over which they are distributed. The more important leaders of the proletariat in the Assembly and in the press successively fall victim to the courts, and ever more equivocal figures come to head it. In part it throws itself into *doctrinaire experiments, exchange banks and workers' associations, hence into a movement in which it renounces the revolutionising of the old world by means of the latter's own great, combined resources, and seeks, rather, to achieve its salvation behind society's back, in private fashion, within its limited conditions of existence, and hence necessarily suffers shipwreck*. It seems to be unable either to rediscover revolutionary greatness in itself or to win new energy from the connections newly entered into, until *all classes* with which it contended in June themselves lie prostrate beside it. But at least it succumbs with the honours of the great, world-historic struggle; not only France, but all Europe trembles at the June earthquake, while the ensuing defeats of the upper classes are so cheaply bought that they require barefaced exaggeration by the victorious party to be able to pass for events at all, and become the more ignominious the further the defeated party is from the proletarian party.

The defeat of the June insurgents, to be sure, had indeed prepared and levelled the ground on which the bourgeois republic could be founded and built up, but it had shown at the same time that in Europe the questions at issue are other than that of "republic or monarchy". It had revealed that here *bourgeois republic* signifies the unlimited despotism of one class over other classes. It had proved that in countries with an old civilisation, with a developed formation of classes, with modern conditions of production and with an intellectual consciousness in which all traditional ideas have been dissolved by the work of centuries, *the republic* signifies *in general only the political form of the revolutionising of bourgeois society* and not its *conservative form of life*, as, for example, in the United States of North America, where, though classes already exist, they have not yet become fixed, but continually change and interchange their component elements in constant flux, where the modern means of production, instead of coinciding with a stagnant surplus population, rather compensate for the relative deficiency of heads and hands, and where, finally, the feverish, youthful movement of material production, which has to make a new world its own, has left neither time nor opportunity for abolishing the old spirit world.

During the June days all classes and parties had united in the *Party of Order* against the proletarian class as the *Party of Anarchy*, of socialism, of communism. They had "saved" society from "*the enemies of society*". They had given out the watch-words of the old society, "*property, family, religion, order*", to their army as passwords and had proclaimed to the counter-revolutionary crusaders: "By this sign thou shalt conquer!" From this moment, as soon as one of the numerous parties which had gathered under this sign against the June insurgents seeks to hold the revolutionary battlefield in its own class interest, it goes down before the cry: "property, family, religion, order." Society is saved just as often as the circle of its rulers contracts, as a more exclusive interest is maintained against a wider one. Every demand of the simplest bourgeois financial reform, of the most ordinary liberalism, of the most formal republicanism, of the most shallow democracy, is simultaneously castigated as an "attempt on society" and stigmatised as "socialism". And, finally, the high priests of "religion and order" themselves are driven with kicks from their Pythian tripods, hauled out of their beds in the darkness of night, put in prisonvans, thrown into dungeons or sent into exile; their temple is razed to the ground, their mouths are sealed, their pens broken, their law torn to pieces in the name of religion, of property, of the family, of order. Bourgeois fanatics for order are shot down on their balconies by mobs of drunken soldiers, their domestic sanctuaries profaned, their houses bombarded for amusement – in the name of property, of the family, of religion and of order. Finally, the scum of bourgeois society forms the *holy phalanx of order* and the hero Krapülinski[7] installs himself in the Tuileries as the "*saviour of society*". …

As the executive authority which has made itself an independent power, Bonaparte feels it to be his mission to safeguard "bourgeois order". But the strength of this bourgeois order lies in the middle class. He looks on himself, therefore, as the representative of the middle class and issues decrees in this sense. Nevertheless, he is somebody solely due to the fact that he has broken the political power of this middle class and daily breaks it anew. Consequently, he looks on himself as the adversary of the political and literary power of the middle class. But by protecting its material power, he generates its political power anew. The cause must accordingly be kept alive; but the effect, where it manifests itself, must be done away with. But this cannot pass off without slight confusions of cause and effect, since in their interaction both lose their distinguishing features. New decrees that obliterate the border line. As against the bourgeoisie, Bonaparte looks on himself, at the same time, as the representative of the peasants and of the people in general, who wants to make the lower classes of the people happy within the framework of bourgeois society. New decrees that cheat the "true Socialists" of their statecraft in advance. But, above all, Bonaparte looks on himself as the chief of the Society of December 10, as the representative of the lumpenproletariat, to which he himself, his entourage, his government and his army belong, and whose price consideration is to benefit itself and draw California lottery prizes from the state treasury. And he vindicates his position as chief of the Society of December 10 with decrees, without decrees and despite decrees.

This contradictory task of the man explains the contradictions of his government, the confused, blind to-ing and fro-ing which seeks now to win, now to humiliate first one class and then another and arrays all of them uniformly against him, whose practical uncertainty forms a highly comical contrast to the imperious, categorical style of the government decrees, a style which is faithfully copied from the uncle.

Industry and trade, hence the business affairs of the middle class, are to prosper in hothouse fashion under the strong government. The grant of innumerable railway concessions. But the Bonapartist lumpenproletariat is to enrich itself. The initiated play *tripotage*[8] on the *bourse* with the railway concessions. But no capital is forthcoming for the railways. Obligation of the Bank to make advances on railway shares. But, at the same time, the Bank is to be exploited for personal ends and therefore must be cajoled. Release of the Bank from the obligation to publish its report weekly. Leonine agreement of the Bank with the government. The people are to be given employment. Initiation of public works. But the public works increase the obligations of the people in respect of taxes. Hence reduction of the taxes by an onslaught on the *rentiers*, by conversion of the five per cent bonds to four-and-a-half per cent. But, once more the middle class must receive a *douceur*.[9] Therefore doubling of the wine tax for the people, who buy it *en détail*,[10] and halving of the wine tax for the middle class, who drink it *en gros*.[11] Dissolution of the actual workers' associations, but promises of miracles of association in the future. The peasants are to be helped. Mortgage banks that expedite their getting into debt and accelerate the concentration of property. But these banks are to be used to make money out of the confiscated estates of the House of Orleans. No capitalist wants to agree to this condition, which is not in the decree, and the mortgage bank remains a mere decree, etc., etc.

Bonapart would like to appear as the patriarchal benefactor of all classes. But he cannot give to one class without taking from another. Just as at the time of the Fronde it was said of the Duke of Guise that he was the most *obligeant* man in France because he had turned all his estates into his partisans' obligations to him, so Bonaparte would fain be the most *obligeant* man in France and turn all the property, all the labour of France into a personal obligation to himself. He would like to steal the whole of France in order to be able to make a present of her to France or, rather, in order to be able to buy France anew with French money, for as the chief of the Society of December 10 he must needs buy what ought to belong to him. And all the state institutions, the Senate, the Council of State, the legislative body, the Legion of Honour, the soldiers' medals, the wash-houses, the public works, the railways, the *état-major*[12] of the National guard excluding privates, and the confiscated estates of the House of Orleans – all become parts of the institution of purchase. Every place in the army and in the government machine becomes a means of purchase. But the most important feature of this process, whereby France is taken in order to be given back, is the percentages that find their way into the pockets of the head and the members of the Society of December 10 during the transaction. The witticism with which Countess L.,[13] the mistress of M. de Morny, characterised the confiscation of the Orleans estates: "*C'est le premier vol*[14] *de l'aigle*"[15] is applicable to every flight of this *eagle*, which is more like a *raven*. He himself and his adherents call out to one another daily like that Italian Carthusian admonishing the miser who, with boastful display, counted up the goods on which he could yet live for years to come: "*Tu fai conto sopra i beni, bisogna prima far il conto sopra gli anni.*"[16] Lest they make a mistake in the years, they count the minutes. A gang of shady characters push their way forward to the court, into the ministries, to the head of the administration and the army, a crowd of the best of whom it must be said that no one knows whence he comes, a noisy, disreputable, rapacious bohème that crawls into braided coast with the same grotesque dignity as the high dignitaries of Soulouque. One can visualise clearly this upper stratum of the Society of December 10, if one reflects that *Véron-Crevel*[17] is its preacher of morals and *Granier de Cassagnac* its thinker. When Guizot, at the time of his ministry, utilised this Granier on a hole-and-corner newspaper against the dynastic opposition, he used to boast of him with the quip: "*C'est le roi des drôles*," "he is the king of buffoons."[18] One would do wrong to recall the Regency or Louis XV in connection with Louis Bonaparte's court and clique. For "often already, France has experienced a government of *hommes entretenus.*"[19,20]

Driven by the contradictory demands of his situation and being at the same time, like a conjurer, under the necessity of keeping the public gaze fixed on himself, as Napoleon's substitute, by springing constant surprises, that is to say, under the necessity of executing a coup d'état *en miniature* every day, Bonaparte throws the entire bourgeois economy into confusion, violates everything that seemed inviolable to the revolution of 1848, makes some tolerant of revolution, others desirous of revolution, and produces actual anarchy in the name of order, while at the same time stripping its halo from the entire state machine, profanes it and makes it at once loathsome and ridiculous. The cult of the Holy Coat of Trier he duplicates in Paris with the cult of the Napoleonic imperial mantle. But when the imperial mantle finally falls on the shoulders of Louis Bonaparte, the Bronze statue of Napoleon will crash from the top of the Vendôme Column.

NOTES

1. Republican in yellow gloves.
2. Cf. Matthew 8:22.
3. Rash act.
4. In reserve.
5. *In partibus infidelium* – literally: in parts inhabited by infidels. The words are added to the title of Roman Catholic bishops holding purely nominal dioceses in non-Christian countries. In the figurative sense they mean: "not really existing".
6. Goethe, *Faust*, Erster Teil, "Studierzimmer".
7. *Krapülinski* – one of the main characters in Heine's poem "Zwei Ritter" (*Romanzero*). Here Marx alludes to Louis Bonaparte.
8. Hanky-panky.
9. Sop.
10. Retail.
11. Wholesale.
12. General Staff.
13. Lehon.
14. *Vol* means flight and theft.
15. "It is the first flight (theft) of the eagle."
16. "Thou contest thy goods, thou shouldst first count thy years."
17. In this novel *Cousine Bette*, Blazac delineates the thoroughly dissolute Parisian philistine in Crevel, a character based on Dr Véron, owner of the *Constitutionnel*.
18. Quoted in the article by Dupont "Chronique de l'Interieur", *Voix du Proscrit*, No. 8. December 15, 1850.
19. The words quoted are those of Madame Girardin.
20. *Hommes entretenus*: kept men. The 1852 edition further has: "and Cato, who took his life to be able to associate with heroes in the Elysian Fields! Poor Cato!"

Chapter 13

Wage-Labour and Capital [1847]

Karl Marx

[...]

[...] What are wages? How are they determined?

If workers were asked: "How much are your wages?" one would reply: "I get a mark a day from my employer"; another, "I get two marks," and so on. According to the different trades to which they belong, they would mention different sums of money which they receive from their respective employers for the performance of a particular piece of work, for example, weaving a yard of linen or type-setting a printed sheet. In spite of the variety of their statements, they would all agree on one point: wages are the sum of money paid by the capitalist for a particular labour time or for a particular output of labour.

The capitalist, it seems, therefore, buys their labour with money. They sell him their labour for money. For the same sum with which the capitalist has bought their labour, for example, two marks, he could have bought two pounds of sugar or a definite amount of any other commodity. The two marks, with which he bought two pounds of sugar, are the price of the two pounds of sugar. The two marks, with which he bought twelve hours' use of labour, are the price of twelve hours' labour. Labour, therefore, is a commodity, neither more nor less than sugar. The former is measured by the clock, the latter by the scales.

The workers exchange their commodity, labour, for the commodity of the capitalist, for money, and this exchange takes place in a definite ratio. So much

Marx, Karl, "Wage-Labour and Capital," pp. 249–250, 251–252, 255, 257–258, 258–259, 261–262, 263, 264, 265–266, 266–267, from David McLellan, ed., *Karl Marx: Selected Writings*. Oxford: Oxford University Press, 1977. Copyright © 1977. This translation originally appeared in *MESW*, Vol. 1, pp. 79ff. (considerably modified). Reprinted by permission of Lawrence and Wishart Ltd.

Classical Sociological Theory, Third Edition. Edited by Craig Calhoun, Joseph Gerteis, James Moody, Steven Pfaff, and Indermohan Virk. Editorial material and organization © 2012 John Wiley & Sons, Ltd. Published 2012 by John Wiley & Sons, Ltd.

money for so much labour. For twelve hours' weaving, two marks. And do not the two marks represent all the other commodities which I can buy for two marks? In fact, therefore, the worker has exchanged his commodity, labour, for other commodities of all kinds and that in a definite ratio. By giving him two marks, the capitalist has given him so much meat, so much clothing, so much fuel, light, etc., in exchange for his day's labour. Accordingly, the two marks express the ratio in which labour is exchanged for other commodities, the exchange value of his labour. The exchange value of a commodity, reckoned in money, is what is called its price. Wages are only a special name for the price of labour, for the price of this peculiar commodity which has no other repository than human flesh and blood.

Let us take any worker, say, a weaver. The capitalist supplies him with the loom and yarn. The weaver sets to work and the yarn is converted into linen. The capitalist takes possession of the linen and sells it, say, for twenty marks. Now are the wages of the weaver a share in the linen, in the twenty marks, in the product of his labour? By no means. Long before the linen is sold, perhaps long before its weaving is finished, the weaver has received his wages. The capitalist, therefore, does not pay these wages with the money which he will obtain from the linen, but with money already in reserve. Just as the loom and the yarn are not the product of the weaver to whom they are supplied by his employer, so likewise with the commodities which the weaver receives in exchange for his commodity, labour. It was possible that his employer found no purchaser at all for his linen. It was possible that he did not get even the amount of the wages by its sale. It is possible that he sells it very profitably in comparison with the weaver's wages. All that has nothing to do with the weaver. The capitalist buys the labour of the weaver with a part of his available wealth, of his capital, just as he has bought the raw material – the yarn – and the instrument of labour – the loom – with another part of his wealth. After he has made these purchases, and these purchases include the labour necessary for the production of linen, he produces only with the raw materials and instruments of labour belonging to him. For the latter include now, true enough, our good weaver as well, who has as little share in the product or the price of the product as the loom has.

Wages are, therefore, not the worker's share in the commodity produced by him. Wages are the part of already existing commodities with which the capitalist buys for himself a definite amount of productive labour.

Labour is, therefore, a commodity which its possessor, the wage-worker, sells to capital. Why does he sell it? In order to live.

[…]

Wages, as we have seen, are the price of a definite commodity, of labour. Wages are, therefore, determined by the same laws that determine the price of every other commodity. The question, therefore, is, how is the price of a commodity determined?

By competition between buyers and sellers, by the relation of inquiry to delivery, of demand to supply. Competition, by which the price of a commodity is determined, is three-sided.

The same commodity is offered by various sellers. With goods of the same quality, the one who sells most cheaply is certain of driving the others out of the field and securing the greatest sale for himself. Thus, the sellers mutually contend among themselves for sales, for the market. Each of them desires to sell, to sell as much as possible and, if possible, to sell alone, to the exclusion of the other sellers. Hence, one sells cheaper than another. Consequently, competition takes place among the sellers, which depresses the price of the commodities offered by them.

But competition also takes place among the buyers, which in its turn causes the commodities offered to rise in price.

Finally competition occurs between buyers and sellers; the former desire to buy as cheaply as possible, the latter to sell as dearly as possible. The result of this competition between buyers and sellers will depend upon how the two above-mentioned sides of the competition are related, that is, whether the competition is stronger in the army of buyers or in the army of sellers. Industry leads two armies into the field against each other, each of which again carries on a battle within its own ranks, among its own troops. The army whose troops beat each other up the least gains the victory over the opposing host.

[...]

Now, the same general laws that regulate the price of commodities in general of course also regulate wages, the price of labour.

Wages will rise and fall according to the relation of supply and demand, according to the turn taken by the competition between the buyers of labour, the capitalists, and the sellers of labour, the workers. The fluctuations in wages correspond in general to the fluctuations in prices of commodities. Within these fluctuations, however, the price of labour will be determined by the cost of production, by the labour time necessary to produce this commodity – labour power.

What, then, is the cost of production of labour?

It is the cost required for maintaining the worker as a worker and of developing him into a worker.

The less the period of training, therefore, that any work requires the smaller is the cost of production of the worker and the lower is the price of his labour, his wages. In those branches of industry in which hardly any period of apprenticeship is required and where the mere bodily existence of the worker suffices, the cost necessary for his production is almost confined to the commodities necessary for keeping him alive and capable of working. The price of his labour will, therefore, be determined by the price of the necessary means of subsistence.

Another consideration, however, also comes in. The manufacturer in calculating his cost of production and, accordingly, the price of the products takes into account the wear and tear of the instruments of labour. If, for example, a machine costs him 1,000 marks and wears out in ten years, he adds 100 marks annually to the price of the commodities so as to be able to replace the worn-out machine by a new one at the end of ten years. In the same way, in calculating the cost of production of simple labour, there must be included the cost of reproduction, whereby the race of workers is enabled to multiply and to replace worn-out workers by new ones. Thus the depreciation of the worker is taken into account in the same way as the depreciation of the machine.

The cost of production of simple labour, therefore, amounts to the cost of existence and reproduction of the worker. The price of this cost of existence and reproduction constitutes wages. Wages so determined are called the wage minimum. This wage minimum, like the determination of the price of commodities by the cost of production in general, does not hold good for the single individual but for the species. Individual workers, millions of workers, do not get enough to be able to exist and reproduce themselves; but the wages of the whole working class level down, within their fluctuations, to this minimum.

[…]

What takes place in the exchange between capitalist and wage-worker?

The worker receives means of subsistence in exchange for his labour, but the capitalist receives in exchange for his means of subsistence labour, the productive activity of the worker, the creative power whereby the worker not only replaces what he consumes but gives to the accumulated labour a greater value than it previously possessed. The worker receives a part of the available means of subsistence from the capitalist. For what purpose do these means of subsistence serve him? For immediate consumption. As soon, however, as I consume the means of subsistence, they are irretrievably lost to me unless I use the time during which I am kept alive by them in order to produce new means of subsistence, in order during consumption to create by my labour new values in place of the values which perish in being consumed. But it is just this noble reproductive power that the worker surrenders to the capitalist in exchange for means of subsistence received. He has, therefore, lost it for himself.

[…]

Does a worker in a cotton factory produce merely cotton textiles? No, he produces capital. He produces values which serve afresh to command his labour and by means of it to create new values.

Capital can only increase by exchanging itself for labour power, by calling wage labour to life. The labour of the wage-worker can only be exchanged for capital by increasing capital, by strengthening the power whose slave it is. Hence, increase of capital is increase of the proletariat, that is, of the working class.

The interests of the capitalist and those of the worker are, therefore, one and the same, assert the bourgeois and their economists. Indeed! The worker perishes if capital does not employ him. Capital perishes if it does not exploit labour, and in order to exploit it, it must buy it. The faster capital intended for production, productive capital, increases, the more, therefore, industry prospers, the more the bourgeoisie enriches itself and the better business is, the more workers does the capitalist need, the more dearly does the worker sell himself.

The indispensable condition for a tolerable situation of the worker is, therefore, the fastest possible growth of productive capital.

But what is the growth of productive capital? Growth of the power of accumulated labour over living labour. Growth of the domination of the bourgeoisie over the working class. If wage labour produces the wealth of others that rules over it, the power that is hostile to it, capital, then the means of employment, that is, the means of subsistence, flow back to it from this hostile power, on condition that it makes itself afresh into a part of capital, into the lever which hurls capital anew into an accelerated movement of growth.

To say that the interests of capital and those of the workers are one and the same is only to say that capital and wage labour are two sides of one and the same relation. The one conditions the other, just as usurer and squanderer condition each other.

As long as the wage-worker is a wage-worker his lot depends upon capital. That is the much-vaunted community of interests between worker and capitalist.

[...]

In addition, we recall that, in spite of the fluctuations in prices of commodities, the average price of every commodity, the ratio in which it is exchanged for other commodities, is determined by its cost of production. Hence the overreachings within the capitalist class necessarily balance one another. The improvement of machinery, new application of natural forces in the service of production, enable a larger amount of products to be created in a given period of time with the same amount of labour and capital, but not by any means a larger amount of exchange values. If, by the use of the spinning jenny, I can turn out twice as much yarn in an hour as before its invention, say, one hundred pounds instead of fifty, then in the long run I will receive for these hundred pounds no more commodities in exchange than formerly for the fifty pounds, because the cost of production has fallen by one-half, or because I can deliver double the product at the same cost.

Finally, in whatever proportion the capitalist class, the bourgeoisie, whether of one country or of the whole world market, shares the net profit of production within itself, the total amount of this net profit always consists only of the amount by which, on the whole, accumulated labour has been increased by direct labour. This total amount grows, therefore, in the proportion in which labour augments capital, that is, in the proportion in which profit rises in comparison with wages.

We see, therefore, that even if we remain within the relation of capital and wage labour, the interests of capital and the interests of wage labour are diametrically opposed.

A rapid increase of capital is equivalent to a rapid increase of profit. Profit can only increase rapidly if the exchange value of labour, if relative wages, decrease just as rapidly. Relative wages can fall although real wages rise simultaneously with nominal wages, with the money value of labour, if they do not rise, however, in the same proportion as profit. If, for instance, in times when business is good, wages rise by five per cent, profit on the other hand by thirty per cent, then the comparative, the relative wages, have not increased but decreased.

Thus if the income of the worker increases with the rapid growth of capital, the social gulf that separates the worker from the capitalist increases at the same time, and the power of capital over labour, the dependence of labour on capital, likewise increases at the same time.

To say that the worker has an interest in the rapid growth of capital is only to say that the more rapidly the worker increases the wealth of others, the richer will be the crumbs that fall to him, the greater is the number of workers that can be employed and called into existence, the more can the mass of slaves dependent on capital be increased.

We have thus seen that:

Even the most favourable situation for the working class, the most rapid possible growth of capital, however much it may improve the material existence of the worker, does not remove the antagonism between his interests and the interests of the bourgeoisie, the interests of the capitalists. Profit and wages remain as before in inverse proportion.

If capital is growing rapidly, wages may rise; the profit of capital rises incomparably more rapidly. The material position of the worker has improved, but at the cost of his social position. The social gulf that divides him from the capitalist has widened.

Finally:

To say that the most favourable condition for wage labour is the most rapid possible growth of productive capital is only to say that the more rapidly the working class increases and enlarges the power that is hostile to it, the wealth that does not belong to it and that rules over it, the more favourable will be the conditions under which it is allowed to labour anew at increasing bourgeois wealth, at enlarging the power of capital, content with forging for itself the golden chains by which the bourgeoisie drags it in its train.

[...]

If, on the whole, the productive capital of bourgeois society grows, a more manifold accumulation of labour takes place. The capitals increase in number and extent. The numerical increase of the capitals increases the competition between the capitalists. The increasing extent of the capitals provides the means for bringing more powerful labour armies with more gigantic instruments of war into the industrial battlefield.

One capitalist can drive another from the field and capture his capital only by selling more cheaply. In order to be able to sell more cheaply without ruining himself, he must produce more cheaply, that is, raise the productive power of labour as much as possible. But the productive power of labour is raised, above all, by a greater division of labour, by a more universal introduction and continual improvement of machinery. The greater the labour army among whom labour is divided, the more gigantic the scale on which machinery is introduced, the more does the cost of production proportionately decrease, the more fruitful is labour. Hence, a general rivalry arises among the capitalists to increase the division of labour and machinery and to exploit them on the greatest possible scale.

[...]

However, the privileged position of our capitalist is not of long duration; other competing capitalists introduce the same machines, the same division of labour, introduce them on the same or on a larger scale, and this introduction will become so general that the price of linen is reduced not only below its old, but below its new cost of production.

The capitalists find themselves, therefore, in the same position relative to one another as before the introduction of the new means of production, and if they are able to supply by these means double the production at the same price, they are now forced to supply the double product below the old price. On the basis of this new cost of production, the same game begins again. More division of labour, more machinery, enlarged scale of exploitation of machinery and division of labour. And again competition brings the same counteraction against this result.

We see how in this way the mode of production and the means of production are continually transformed, revolutionized, how the division of labour is necessarily followed by greater division of labour, the application of machinery by still greater application of machinery, work on a large scale by work on a still larger scale.

[...]

If now we picture to ourselves this feverish simultaneous agitation on the whole world market, it will be comprehensible how the growth, accumulation, and concentration of capital results in an uninterrupted division of labour, and in the application of new and the perfecting of old machinery precipitately and on an ever more gigantic scale.

But how do these circumstances, which are inseparable from the growth of productive capital, affect the determination of wages?

The greater division of labour enables one worker to do the work of five, ten, or twenty; it therefore multiplies competition among the workers fivefold, tenfold, or twentyfold. The workers do not only compete by one selling himself cheaper than another; they compete by one doing the work of five, ten, twenty; and the division of labour, introduced by capital and continually increased, compels the workers to compete among themselves in this way.

Further, as the division of labour increases, labour is simplified. The special skill of the worker becomes worthless. He becomes transformed into a simple, monotonous productive force that does not have to use intense bodily or intellectual faculties. His labour becomes a labour that anyone can perform. Hence, competitors crowd upon him on all sides, and besides we remind the reader that the more simple and easily learned the labour is, the lower the cost of production needed to master it, the lower do wages sink, for, like the price of every other commodity, they are determined for by the cost of production.

[...]

Let us sum up: The more productive capital grows, the more the division of labour and the application of machinery expands. The more the division of labour and the application of machinery expands, the more competition among the workers expands and the more their wages contract.

In addition, the working class gains recruits from the higher strata of society also; a mass of petty industrialists and small rentiers are hurled down into its ranks and have nothing better to do than urgently stretch out their arms alongside those of the workers. Thus the forest of uplifted arms demanding work becomes ever thicker, while the arms themselves become ever thinner.

That the small industrialist cannot survive in a contest one of the first conditions of which is to produce on an ever greater scale, that is, precisely to be a large and not a small industrialist, is self-evident.

That the interest on capital decreases in the same measure as the mass and number of capitals increase, as capital grows; that, therefore, the small rentier can no longer live on his interest but must throw himself into industry, and, consequently, help to swell the ranks of the small industrialists and thereby of candidates for the proletariat – all this surely requires no further explanation.

Finally, as the capitalists are compelled, by the movement described above, to exploit the already existing gigantic means of production on a larger scale and to set in motion all the mainsprings of credit to this end, there is a corresponding increase in industrial earthquakes, in which the trading world can only maintain itself by sacrificing a part of wealth, of products and even of productive forces to the gods of the nether world – in a word, crises increase. They become more frequent and more violent, if only because, as the mass of production, and consequently the need for extended markets, grows, the world market becomes more and more contracted, fewer and fewer new markets remain available for exploitation, since every preceding crisis has subjected to world trade a market hitherto unconquered or only superficially exploited. But capital does not live only on labour. A lord, at once aristocratic and barbarous, it drags with it into the grave the corpses of its slaves, whole hecatombs of workers who perish in the crises. Thus we see: if capital grows rapidly, competition among the workers grows incomparably more rapidly, that is, the means of employment, the means of subsistence, of the working class decrease proportionately so much the more, and, nevertheless, the rapid growth of capital is the most favourable condition for wage labour.

Chapter 14

Classes [1867]

Karl Marx

The owners merely of labour power, owners of capital, and land-owners, whose respective sources of income are wages, profit and ground rent, in other words, wage labourers, capitalists and landowners, constitute then three big classes of modern society based upon the capitalist mode of production.

In England, modern society is indisputably most highly and classically developed in economic structure. Nevertheless, even here the stratification of classes does not appear in its pure form. Middle and intermediate strata even here obliterate lines of demarcation everywhere (although incomparably less in rural districts than in the cities). However, this is immaterial for our analysis. We have seen that the continual tendency and law of development of the capitalist mode of production is more and more to divorce the means of production from labour, and more and more to concentrate the scattered means of production into large groups, thereby transforming labour into wage labour and the means of production into capital. And to this tendency, on the other hand, corresponds the independent separation of landed property from capital and labour, or the transformation of all landed property into the form of landed property corresponding to the capitalist mode of production.

The first question to be answered is this: What constitutes a class? – and the reply to this follows naturally from the reply to another question, namely: What makes wage labourers, capitalists and landlords constitute the three great social classes?

Marx, Karl, "Classes," pp.870–871 from Karl Marx and Friederich Engels, *Collected Works, Volume 37*. New York: International Publishers, 1975. Copyright © 1975. Reprinted by permission of International Publishers Inc.

Classical Sociological Theory, Third Edition. Edited by Craig Calhoun, Joseph Gerteis, James Moody, Steven Pfaff, and Indermohan Virk. Editorial material and organization © 2012 John Wiley & Sons, Ltd. Published 2012 by John Wiley & Sons, Ltd.

At first glance – the identity of revenues and sources of revenue. There are three great social groups whose members, the individuals forming them, live on wages, profit and ground rent respectively, on the realisation of their labour power, their capital, and their landed property.

However, from this standpoint, physicians and officials, e.g., would also constitute two classes, for they belong to two distinct social groups, the members of each of these groups receiving their revenue from one and the same source. The same would also be true of the infinite fragmentation of interest and rank into which the division of social labour splits labourers as well as capitalists and landlords – the latter, e.g., into owners of vineyards, farm owners, owners of forests, mine owners and owners of fisheries.

[Here the manuscript breaks off.]

Chapter 15

The Rules of Sociological Method [1895]

Emile Durkheim

The proposition which states that social facts must be treated as things – the proposition which is at the very basis of our method – is among those which have stirred up the most opposition. It was deemed paradoxical and scandalous for us to assimilate to the realities of the external world those of the social world. This was singularly to misunderstand the meaning and effect of this assimilation, the object of which was not to reduce the higher forms of being to the level of lower ones but, on the contrary, to claim for the former a degree of reality at least equal to that which everyone accords to the latter. Indeed, we do not say that social facts are material things, but that they are things just as are material things, although in a different way.

What indeed is a thing? The thing stands in opposition to the idea, just as what is known from the outside stands in opposition to what is known from the inside. A thing is any object of knowledge which is not naturally penetrable by the understanding. It is all that which we cannot conceptualise adequately as an idea by the simple process of intellectual analysis. It is all that which the mind cannot understand without going outside itself, proceeding progressively by way of observation and experimentation from those features which are the most external and the most immediately accessible to those which are the least visible and the most profound. To treat facts of a certain order as things is therefore not to place them in this or that

---

Durkheim, Emile, "The Rules of Sociological Method," pp.35–38, 50–59, 119–125, 127–132, 134–135 from Emile Durkheim, *The Rules of Sociological Method*, ed. Steven Lukes, trans. W.D. Halls. New York: Macmillan Publishers, Ltd., The Free Press, 1982. Copyright © 1982 by Steven Lukes. Translation, Copyright © 1982 by Macmillan Publishers, Ltd. Reprinted and edited with the permission of The Free Press, A Division of Simon & Schuster Adult Publishing Group and Palgrave Macmillan. All rights reserved.

Classical Sociological Theory, Third Edition. Edited by Craig Calhoun, Joseph Gerteis, James Moody, Steven Pfaff, and Indermohan Virk. Editorial material and organization © 2012 John Wiley & Sons, Ltd. Published 2012 by John Wiley & Sons, Ltd.

category of reality; it is to observe towards them a certain attitude of mind. It is to embark upon the study of them by adopting the principle that one is entirely ignorant of what they are, that their characteristic properties, like the unknown causes upon which they depend, cannot be discovered by even the most careful form of introspection.

The terms being so defined, our proposition, far from being a paradox, might almost pass for a truism if it were not too often still unrecognised in those sciences which deal with man, and above all in sociology. Indeed, in this sense it may be said that any object of knowledge is a thing, except perhaps for mathematical objects. Regarding the latter, since we construct them ourselves, from the most simple to the most complex, it is enough to look within ourselves and to analyse internally the mental process from which they arise, in order to know what they are. But as soon as we consider facts *per se*, when we undertake to make a science of them, they are of necessity unknowns for us, *things* of which we are ignorant, for the representations that we have been able to make of them in the course of our lives, since they have been made without method and uncritically, lack any scientific value and must be discarded. The facts of individual psychology themselves are of this nature and must be considered in this light. Indeed, although by definition they are internal to ourselves, the consciousness that we have of them reveals to us neither their inmost character nor their origin. Consciousness allows us to know them well up to a certain point, but only in the same way as our senses make us aware of heat or light, sound or electricity. It gives us muddled impressions of them, fleeting and subjective, but provides no clear, distinct notions or explanatory concepts. This is precisely why during this century an objective psychology has been founded whose fundamental rule is to study mental facts from the outside, namely as things. This should be even more the case for social facts, for consciousness cannot be more capable of knowing them than of knowing its own existence.[1] It will be objected that, since they have been wrought by us, we have only to become conscious of ourselves to know what we have put into them and how we shaped them. Firstly, however, most social institutions have been handed down to us already fashioned by previous generations; we have had no part in their shaping; consequently it is not by searching within ourselves that we can uncover the causes which have given rise to them. Furthermore, even if we have played a part in producing them, we can hardly glimpse, save in the most confused and often even the most imprecise way, the real reasons which have impelled us to act, or the nature of our action. Already, even regarding merely the steps we have taken personally, we know very inaccurately the relatively simple motives that govern us. We believe ourselves disinterested, whereas our actions are egoistic; we think that we are commanded by hatred whereas we are giving way to love, that we are obedient to reason whereas we are the slaves of irrational prejudices, etc. How therefore could we possess the ability to discern more clearly the causes, of a different order of complexity, which inspire the measures taken by the collectivity? For at the very least each individual shares in only an infinitesimally small part of them; we have a host of fellow-fashioners, and what is occurring in their different consciousnesses eludes us.

Thus our rule implies no metaphysical conception, no speculation about the innermost depth of being. What it demands is that the sociologist should assume the state of mind of physicists, chemists and physiologists when they venture into an as yet unexplored area of their scientific field. As the sociologist penetrates into the social world he should be conscious that he is penetrating into the unknown. He must feel himself in the presence of facts governed by laws as unsuspected as those of life before the science of biology was evolved. He must hold himself ready to make discoveries which will surprise and disconcert him. Yet sociology is far from having arrived at this degree of intellectual maturity. While the scientist who studies physical nature feels very keenly the resistances that it proffers, ones which he has great difficulty in overcoming, it really seems as if the sociologist operates among things immediately clear to the mind, so great is the ease with which he seems to resolve the most obscure questions. In the present state of the discipline, we do not really know the nature of the principal social institutions, such as the state or the family, property rights or contract, punishment and responsibility. We are virtually ignorant of the causes upon which they depend, the functions they fulfil, and their laws of evolution. It is as if, on certain points, we are only just beginning to perceive a few glimmers of light. Yet it suffices to glance through works of sociology to see how rare is any awareness of this ignorance and these difficulties. Not only is it deemed mandatory to dogmatise about every kind of problem at once, but it is believed that one is capable, in a few pages or sentences, of penetrating to the inmost essence of the most complex phenomena. This means that such theories express, not the facts, which could not be so swiftly fathomed, but the preconceptions of the author before he began his research. Doubtless the idea that we form of collective practices, of what they are, or what they should be, is a factor in their development. But this idea itself is a fact which, in order to be properly established, needs to be studied from the outside. For it is important to know not the way in which a particular thinker individually represents a particular institution, but the conception that the group has of it. This conception is indeed the only socially effective one. But it cannot be known through mere inner observation, since it is not wholly and entirely within any one of us; one must therefore find some external signs which make it apparent. Furthermore, it did not arise from nothing: it is itself the result of external causes which must be known in order to be able to appreciate its future role. Thus, no matter what one does, it is always to the same method that one must return. [...]

What is a Social Fact?

Before beginning the search for the method appropriate to the study of social facts it is important to know what are the facts termed "social".

The question is all the more necessary because the term is used without much precision. It is commonly used to designate almost all the phenomena that occur within society, however little social interest of some generality they present. Yet under this heading there is, so to speak, no human occurrence that cannot be called social. Every individual drinks, sleeps, eats, or employs his reason, and society has every interest in seeing that these functions are regularly exercised. If therefore these facts were social ones, sociology would possess no subject matter peculiarly its own, and its domain would be confused with that of biology and psychology.

However, in reality there is in every society a clearly determined group of phenomena separable, because of their distinct characteristics, from those that form the subject matter of other sciences of nature.

When I perform my duties as a brother, a husband or a citizen and carry out the commitments I have entered into, I fulfil obligations which are defined in law and custom and which are external to myself and my actions. Even when they conform to my own sentiments and when I feel their reality within me, that reality does not cease to be objective, for it is not I who have prescribed these duties; I have received them through education. Moreover, how often does it happen that we are ignorant of the details of the obligations that we must assume, and that, to know them, we must consult the legal code and its authorised interpreters! Similarly the believer has discovered from birth, ready fashioned, the beliefs and practices of his religious life; if they existed before he did, it follows that they exist outside him. The system of signs that I employ to express my thoughts, the monetary system I use to pay my debts, the credit instruments I utilise in my commercial relationships, the practices I follow in my profession, etc., all function independently of the use I make of them. Considering in turn each member of society, the foregoing remarks can be repeated for each single one of them. Thus there are ways of acting, thinking and feeling which possess the remarkable property of existing outside the consciousness of the individual.

Not only are these types of behaviour and thinking external to the individual, but they are endued with a compelling and coercive power by virtue of which, whether he wishes it or not, they impose themselves upon him. Undoubtedly when I conform to them of my own free will, this coercion is not felt hardly at all, since it is unnecessary. None the less it is intrinsically a characteristic of these facts; the proof of this is that it asserts itself as soon as I try to resist. If I attempt to violate the rules of law they react against me so as to forestall my action, if there is still time. Alternatively, they annul it or make my action conform to the norm if it is already accomplished but capable of being reversed; or they cause me to pay the penalty for it if it is irreparable. If purely moral rules are at stake, the public conscience restricts any act which infringes them by the surveillance it exercises over the conduct of citizens and by the special punishments it has at its disposal. In other cases the constraint is less violent; nevertheless, it does not cease to exist. If I do not conform to ordinary conventions, if in my mode of dress I pay no heed to what is customary in my country and in my social class, the laughter I provoke, the social distance at which I am kept, produce, although in a more mitigated form, the same results as any real penalty. In other cases, although it may be indirect, constraint is no less effective. I am not forced to speak French with my compatriots, nor to use the legal currency, but it is impossible for me to do otherwise. If I tried to escape the necessity, my attempt would fail miserably. As an industrialist nothing prevents me from working with the processes and methods of the previous century, but if I do I will most certainly ruin myself. Even when in fact I can struggle free from these rules and successfully break them, it is never without being forced to fight against them. Even if in the end they are overcome, they make their constraining power sufficently felt in the resistance that they afford. There is no innovator, even a fortunate one, whose ventures do not encounter opposition of this kind.

Here, then, is a category of facts which present very special characteristics: they consist of manners of acting, thinking and feeling external to the individual, which are invested with a coercive power by virtue of which they exercise control over him. Consequently, since they consist of representations and actions, they cannot be confused with organic phenomena, nor with psychical phenomena, which have no existence save in and through the individual consciousness. Thus they constitute a new species and to them must be exclusively assigned the term *social*. It is appropriate, since it is clear that, not having the individual as their substratum, they can have none other than society, either political society in its entirety or one of the partial groups that it includes – religious denominations, political and literary schools, occupational corporations, etc. Moreover, it is for such as these alone that the term is fitting, for the word "social" has the sole meaning of designating those phenomena which fall into none of the categories of facts already constituted and labelled. They are consequently the proper field of sociology. It is true that this word "constraint", in terms of which we define them, is in danger of infuriating those who zealously uphold out-and-out individualism. Since they maintain that the individual is completely autonomous, it seems to them that he is diminished every time he is made aware that he is not dependent on himself alone. Yet since it is indisputable today that most of our ideas and tendencies are not developed by ourselves, but come to us from outside, they can only penetrate us by imposing themselves upon us. This is all that our definition implies. Moreover, we know that all social constraints do not necessarily exclude the individual personality.[2]

Yet since the examples just cited (legal and moral rules, religious dogmas, financial systems, etc.) consist wholly of beliefs and practices already well established, in view of what has been said it might be maintained that no social fact can exist except where there is a well defined social organisation. But there are other facts which do not present themselves in this already crystallised form but which also possess the same objectivity and ascendancy over the individual. These are what are called social "currents". Thus in a public gathering the great waves of enthusiasm, indignation and pity that are produced have their seat in no one individual consciousness. They come to each one of us from outside and can sweep us along in spite of ourselves. If perhaps I abandon myself to them I may not be conscious of the pressure that they are exerting upon me, but that pressure makes its presence felt immediately I attempt to struggle against them. If an individual tries to pit himself against one of these collective manifestations, the sentiments that he is rejecting will be turned against him. Now if this external coercive power asserts itself so acutely in cases of resistance, it must be because it exists in the other instances cited above without our being conscious of it. Hence we are the victims of an illusion which leads us to believe we have ourselves produced what has been imposed upon us externally. But if the willingness with which we let ourselves be carried along disguises the pressure we have undergone, it does not eradicate it. Thus air does not cease to have weight, although we no longer feel that weight. Even when we have individually and spontaneously shared in the common emotion, the impression we have experienced is utterly different from what we would have felt if we had been alone. Once the assembly has broken up and these social influences have ceased to act upon us, and we are once more on our own, the emotions we have felt seem an alien phenomenon, one in which we no longer recognise ourselves. It is then we perceive that we have undergone the emotions much more than generated them. These emotions may even perhaps fill us with horror, so much do they go against the grain. Thus individuals who are normally perfectly harmless may, when gathered together in a crowd, let themselves be drawn into acts of atrocity. And what we assert about these transitory outbreaks likewise applies to those more lasting movements of opinion which relate to religious, political, literary and artistic matters, etc., and which are constantly being produced around us, whether throughout society or in a more limited sphere.

Moreover, this definition of a social fact can be verified by examining an experience that is characteristic. It is sufficient to observe how children are brought up. If one views the facts as they are and indeed as they have always been, it is patently obvious that all education consists of a continual effort to impose upon the child ways of seeing, thinking and acting which he himself would not have arrived at spontaneously. From his earliest years we oblige him to eat, drink and sleep at regular hours, and to observe cleanliness, calm and obedience; later we force him to learn how to be mindful of others, to respect customs and conventions, and to work, etc. If this constraint in time ceases to be felt it is because it gradually gives rise to habits, to inner tendencies which render it superfluous; but they supplant the constraint only because they are derived from it. It is true that, in Spencer's view, a rational education should shun such means and allow the child complete freedom to do what he will. Yet as this educational theory has never been put into practice among any known people, it can only be the personal expression of a *desideratum* and not a fact which can be established in contradiction to the other facts given above. What renders these latter facts particularly illuminating is that education sets out precisely with the object of creating a social being. Thus there can be seen, as in an abbreviated form, how the social being has been fashioned historically. The pressure to which the child is subjected unremittingly is the same pressure of the social environment which seeks to shape him in its own image, and in which parents and teachers are only the representatives and intermediaries.

Thus it is not the fact that they are general which can serve to characterise sociological phenomena. Thoughts to be found in the consciousness of each individual and movements which are repeated by all individuals are not for this reason social facts. If some have been content with using this characteristic in order to define them it is because they have been confused, wrongly, with what might be termed their individual incarnations. What constitutes social facts are the beliefs, tendencies and practices of the group taken collectively. But the forms that these collective states may assume when they are "refracted" through individuals are things of a different kind. What irrefutably demonstrates this duality of kind is that these two categories of facts frequently are manifested dissociated from each other. Indeed some of these ways of acting or thinking acquire, by dint of repetition, a sort of consistency which, so to speak, separates them out, isolating them from the particular events which reflect them. Thus they assume a shape, a tangible form peculiar to them and constitute a reality *sui generis* vastly distinct from the individual facts which manifest that reality. Collective custom does not exist only in a state of immanence in the successive actions which it determines, but, by a privilege without example in the biological kingdom, expresses itself once and for all in a formula repeated by word of mouth, transmitted by education and even enshrined in the written word. Such are the origins and nature of legal and moral rules, aphorisms and popular sayings, articles of faith in which religious or political sects epitomise their beliefs, and standards of taste drawn up by literary schools, etc. None of these modes of acting and thinking are to be found wholly in the application made of them by individuals, since they can even exist without being applied at the time.

Undoubtedly this state of dissociation does not always present itself with equal distinctiveness. It is sufficient for dissociation to exist unquestionably in the numerous important instances cited, for us to prove that the social fact exists separately from its individual effects. Moreover, even when the dissociation is not immediately observable, it can often be made so with the help of certain methodological devices. Indeed it is essential to embark on such procedures if one wishes to refine out the social fact from any amalgam and so observe it in its pure state. Thus certain currents of opinion, whose intensity varies according to the time and country in which they occur, impel us, for example, towards marriage or suicide, towards higher or lower birth-rates, etc. Such currents are plainly social facts. At first sight they seem inseparable from the forms they assume in individual cases. But statistics afford us a means of isolating them. They are indeed not inaccurately represented by rates of births, marriages and suicides, that is, by the result obtained after dividing the average annual total of marriages, births, and voluntary homicides by the number of persons of an age to marry, produce children, or commit suicide.[3] Since each one of these statistics includes without distinction all individual cases, the individual circumstances which may have played some part in producing the phenomenon cancel each other out and consequently do not contribute to determining the nature of the phenomenon. What it expresses is a certain state of the collective mind.

That is what social phenomena are when stripped of all extraneous elements. As regards their private manifestations, these do indeed having something social about them, since in part they reproduce the collective model. But to a large extent each one depends also upon the psychical and organic constitution of the individual, and on the particular circumstances in which he is placed. Therefore they are not phenomena which are in the strict sense sociological. They depend on both domains at the same time, and could be termed socio-psychical. They are of interest to the sociologist without constituting the immediate content of sociology. The same characteristic is to be found in the organisms of those mixed phenomena of nature studied in the combined sciences such as biochemistry.

It may be objected that a phenomenon can only be collective if it is common to all the members of society, or at the very least to a majority, and consequently, if it is general. This is doubtless the case, but if it is general it is because it is collective (that is, more or less obligatory); but it is very far from being collective because it is general. It is a condition of the group repeated in individuals because it imposes itself upon them. It is in each part because it is in the whole, but far from being in the whole because it is in the parts. This is supremely evident in those beliefs and practices which are handed down to us ready fashioned by previous generations. We accept and adopt them because, since they are the work of the collectivity and one that is centuries old, they are invested with a special authority that our education has taught us to recognise and respect. It is worthy of note that the vast majority of social phenomena come to us in this way. But even when the social fact is partly due to our direct co-operation, it is no different in nature. An outburst of collective emotion in a gathering does not merely express the sum total of what individual feelings share in common, but is something of a very different order, as we have demonstrated. It is a product of shared existence, of actions and reactions called into play between the consciousnesses of individuals. If it is echoed in each one of them it is precisely by virtue of the special energy derived from its collective origins. If all hearts beat in unison, this is not as a consequence of a spontaneous, pre-established harmony; it is because one and the same force is propelling them in the same direction. Each one is borne along by the rest.

We have therefore succeeded in delineating for ourselves the exact field of sociology. It embraces one single, well defined group of phenomena. A social fact is identifiable through the power of external coercion which it exerts or is capable of exerting upon individuals. The presence of this power is in turn recognisable because of the existence of some pre-determined sanction, or through the resistance that the fact opposes to any individual action that may threaten it. However, it can also be defined by ascertaining how widespread it is within the group, provided that, as noted above, one is careful to add a second essential characteristic; this is, that it exists independently of the particular forms that it may assume in the process of spreading itself within the group. In certain cases this latter criterion can even be more easily applied than the former one. The presence of constraint is easily ascertainable when it is manifested externally through some direct reaction of society, as in the case of law, morality, beliefs, customs and even fashions. But when constraint is merely indirect, as with that exerted by an economic organisation, it is not always so clearly discernible. Generality combined with objectivity may then be easier to establish. Moreover, this second definition is simply another formulation of the first one: if a mode of behaviour existing outside the consciousnesses of individuals becomes general, it can only do so by exerting pressure upon them.[4]

However, one may well ask whether this definition is complete. Indeed the facts which have provided us with its basis are all *ways of functioning*: they are "physiological" in nature. But there are also collective *ways of being*, namely, social facts of an "anatomical" or morphological nature. Sociology cannot dissociate itself from what concerns the substratum of collective life. Yet the number and nature of the elementary parts which constitute society, the way in which they are articulated, the degree of coalescence they have attained, the distribution of population over the earth's surface, the extent and nature of the network of communications, the design of dwellings, etc., do not at first sight seem relatable to ways of acting, feeling or thinking.

Yet, first and foremost, these various phenomena present the same characteristic which has served us in defining the others. These ways of being impose themselves upon the individual just as do the ways of acting we have dealt with. In fact, when we wish to learn how a society is divided up politically, in what its divisions consist and the degree of solidarity that exists between them, it is not through physical inspection and geographical observation that we may come to find this out: such divisions are social, although they may have some physical basis. It is only through public law that we can study such political organisation, because this law is what determines its nature, just as it determines our domestic and civic relationships. The organisation is no less a form of compulsion. If the population clusters together in our cities instead of being scattered over the rural areas, it is because there exists a trend of opinion, a collective drive which imposes this concentration upon individuals. We can no more choose the design of our houses than the cut of our clothes – at least, the one is as much obligatory as the other. The communication network forcibly prescribes the direction of internal migrations or commercial exchanges, etc., and even their intensity. Consequently, at the most there are grounds for adding one further category to the list of phenomena already enumerated as bearing the distinctive stamp of a social fact. But as that enumeration was in no wise strictly exhaustive, this addition would not be indispensable.

Moreover, it does not even serve a purpose, for these ways of being are only ways of acting that have been consolidated. A society's political structure is only the way in which its various component segments have become accustomed to living with each other. If relationships between them are traditionally close, the segments tend to merge together; if the contrary, they tend to remain distinct. The type of dwelling imposed upon us is merely the way in which everyone around us and, in part, previous generations, have customarily built their houses. The communication network is only the channel which has been cut by the regular current of commerce and migrations, etc., flowing in the same direction. Doubtless if phenomena of a morphological kind were the only ones that displayed this rigidity, it might be thought that they constituted a separate species. But a legal rule is no less permanent an arrangement than an architectural style, and yet it is a "physiological" fact. A simple moral maxim is certainly more malleable, yet it is cast in forms much more rigid than a mere professional custom or fashion. Thus there exists a whole range of gradations which, without any break in continuity, join the most clearly delineated structural facts to those free currents of social life which are not yet caught in any definite mould. This therefore signifies that the differences between them concern only the degree to which they have become consolidated. Both are forms of life at varying stages of crystallisation. It would undoubtedly be advantageous to reserve the term "morphological" for those social facts which relate to the social substratum, but only on condition that one is aware that they are of the same nature as the others. Our definition will therefore subsume all that has to be defined if it states:

> *A social fact is any way of acting, whether fixed or not, capable of exerting over the individual an external constraint;*

or:

> which is general over the whole of a given society whilst having an existence of its own, independent of its individual manifestation.[5]

Rules for the Explanation of Social Facts

Most sociologists believe they have accounted for phenomena once they have demonstrated the purpose they serve and the role they play. They reason as if phenomena existed solely for this role and had no determining cause save a clear or vague sense of the services they are called upon to render. This is why it is thought that all that is needful has been said to make them intelligible when it has been established that these services are real and that the social need they satisfy has been demonstrated. Thus Comte relates all the drive for progress of the human species to this basic tendency, "which directly impels man continually to improve his condition in all respects", whereas Spencer relates it to the need for greater happiness. It is by virtue of this principle that Spencer explains the formation of society as a function of the advantages which flow from co-operation, the institution of government by the utility which springs from regulating military co-operation, and the transformations which the family has undergone from the need for a more perfect reconciliation of the interests of parents, children and society.

But this method confuses two very different questions. To demonstrate the utility of a fact does not explain its origins, nor how it is what it is. The uses which it serves presume the specific properties characteristic of it, but do not create it. Our need for things cannot cause them to be of a particular nature; consequently, that need scannot produce them out of nothing, conferring in this way existence upon them. They spring from causes of another kind. The feeling we have regarding their utility can stimulate us to set these causes in motion and draw upon the effects they bring in their train, but it cannot conjure up these results out of nothing. This proposition is self-evident so long as only material or even psychological phenomena are being considered. It would also not be disputed in sociology if the social facts, because of their total lack of material substance, did not appear – wrongly, moreover – bereft of intrinsic reality. Since we view them as purely mental configurations, provided they are found to be useful, as soon as the idea of them occurs to us they seem to be self-generating. But since each fact is a force which prevails over the force of the individual and possesses its own nature, to bring a fact into existence it cannot suffice to have merely the desire or the will to engender it. Prior forces must exist, capable of producing this firmly established force, as well as natures capable of producing this special nature. Only under these conditions can facts be created. To revive the family spirit where it has grown weak, it is not enough for everybody to realise its advantages; we must set directly in operation those causes which alone can engender it. To endow a government with the authority it requires, it is not enough to feel the need for this. We must address ourselves to the sole sources from which all authority is derived: the establishment of traditions, a common spirit, etc. For this we must retrace our steps farther back along the chain of cause and effect until we find a point at which human action can effectively intervene.

What clearly demonstrates the duality of these two avenues of research is that a fact can exist without serving any purpose, either because it has never been used to further any vital goal or because, having once been of use, it has lost all utility but continues to exist merely through force of custom. There are even more instances of such survivals in society than in the human organism. There are even cases where a practice or a social institution changes its functions without for this reason changing its nature. The rule of *is pater est quem justae nuptiae declarant* has remained substantially the same in our legal code as it was in ancient Roman law. But while its purpose was to safeguard the property rights of the father over children born of his legitimate wife, it is much more the rights of the children that it protects today. The swearing of an oath began by being a kind of judicial ordeal before it became simply a solemn and impressive form of attestation. The religious dogmas of Christianity have not changed for centuries, but the role they play in our modern societies is no longer the same as in the Middle Ages. Thus words serve to express new ideas without their contexture changing. Moreover, it is a proposition true in sociology as in biology, that the organ is independent of its function, i.e. while staying the same it can serve different ends. Thus the causes which give rise to its existence are independent of the ends it serves.

Yet we do not mean that the tendencies, needs and desires of men never actively intervene in social evolution. On the contrary, it is certain that, according to the way they make an impact upon the conditions on which a fact depends, they can hasten or retard development. Yet, apart from the fact that they can never create something out of nothing, their intervention itself, regardless of its effects, can only occur by virtue of efficient causes. Indeed, a tendency cannot, even to this limited extent, contribute to the production of a new phenomenon unless it is itself new, whether constituted absolutely or arising from some transformation of a previous tendency. For unless we postulate a truly providential harmony established beforehand, we could not admit that from his origins man carried within him in potential all the tendencies whose opportuneness would be felt as evolution progressed, each one ready to be awakened when the circumstances called for it. Furthermore, a tendency is also a thing; thus it cannot arise or be modified for the sole reason that we deem it useful. It is a force possessing its own nature. For that nature to come into existence or be changed, it is not enough for us to find advantage in this occurring. To effect such changes causes must come into play which require them physically.

For example, we have explained the constant development of the social division of labour by showing that it is necessary in order for man to sustain himself in the new conditions of existence in which he is placed as he advances in history. We have therefore attributed to the tendency which is somewhat improperly termed the instinct of self-preservation an important role in our explanation. But in the first place the tendency alone could not account for even the most rudimentary form of specialisation. It can accomplish nothing if the conditions on which this phenomenon depends are not already realised, that is, if individual differences have not sufficiently increased through the progressive state of indetermination of the common consciousness and hereditary influences. The division of labour must even have begun already to occur for its utility to be perceived and its need to be felt. The mere development of individual differences, implying a greater diversity of tastes and abilities, had necessarily to bring about this first consequence. Moreover, the instinct of self-preservation did not come by itself and without cause to fertilise this first germ of specialisation. If it directed first itself and then us into this new path, it is because the course it followed and caused us to follow beforehand was as if blocked. This was because the greater intensity of the struggle for existence brought about by the greater concentration of societies rendered increasingly difficult the survival of those individuals who continued to devote themselves to more unspecialised tasks. Thus a change of direction was necessary. On the other hand if it turned itself, and for preference turned our activity, towards an ever increasing division of labour, it was also because it was the path of least resistance. The other possible solutions were emigration, suicide or crime. Now, on average, the ties that bind us to our country, to life and to feeling for our fellows are stronger and more resistant sentiments than the habits which can deter us from narrower specialisation. Thus these habits had inevitably to give ground as every advance occurred. Thus, since we are ready to allow for human needs in sociological explanations, we need not revert, even partially, to teleology. For these needs can have no influence over social evolution unless they themselves evolve, and the changes through which they pass can only be explained by causes which are in no way final.

What is even more convincing than the foregoing argument is the study of how social facts work out in practice. Where teleology rules, there rules also a fair margin of contingency, for there are no ends – and even fewer means – which necessarily influence all men, even supposing they are placed in the same circumstances. Given the same environment, each individual, according to his temperament, adapts himself to it in the way he pleases and which he prefers to all others. The one will seek to change it so that it better suits his needs; the other will prefer to change himself and to moderate his desires. Thus to arrive at the same goal, many different routes can be, and in reality are, followed. If then it were true that historical development occurred because of ends felt either clearly or obscurely, social facts would have to present an infinite diversity and all comparison would almost be impossible. But the opposite is true. Undoubtedly external events, the links between which constitute the superficial part of social life, vary from one people to another. Yet in this way each individual has his own history, although the bases of physical and social organisation remain the same for all. If, in fact, one comes even a little into contact with social phenomena, one is on the contrary surprised at the outstanding regularity with which they recur in similar circumstances. Even the most trivial and apparently most puerile practices are repeated with the most astonishing uniformity. A marriage ceremony, seemingly purely symbolic, such as the abduction of the bride-to-be, is found to be identical everywhere that a certain type of family exists, which itself is lined to a whole political organisation. The most bizarre customs, such as the "couvade", the levirate, exogamy, etc. are to be observed in the most diverse peoples and are symptomatic of a certain social state. The right to make a will appears at a specific phase of history and, according to the severity of the restrictions which limit it, we can tell at what stage of social evolution we have arrived. It would be easy to multiply such examples. But the widespread character of collective forms would be inexplicable if final causes held in sociology the preponderance attributed to them.

Therefore when one undertakes to explain a social phenomenon the efficient cause which produces it and the function it fulfils must be investigated separately. We use the word "function" in preference to "end" or "goal" precisely because social phenomena generally do not exist for the usefulness of the results they produce. We must determine whether there is a correspondence between the fact being considered and the general needs of the social organism, and in what this correspondence consists, without seeking to know whether it was intentional or not. All such questions of intention are, moreover, too subjective to be dealt with scientifically.

Not only must these two kinds of problems be dissociated from each other, but it is generally appropriate to deal with the first kind before the second. This order of precedence corresponds to that of the facts. It is natural to seek the cause of a phenomenon before attempting to determine its effects. This method is all the more logical because the first question, once resolved, will often help to answer the second. Indeed, the solid link which joins cause to effect is of a reciprocal character which has not been sufficiently recognised. Undoubtedly the effect cannot exist without its cause, but the latter, in turn, requires its effect. It is from the cause that the effect derives its energy, but on occasion it also restores energy to the cause and consequently cannot disappear without the cause being affected.[6] For example, the social reaction which constitutes punishment is due to the intensity of the collective sentiments that crime offends. On the other hand it serves the useful function of maintaining those sentiments at the same level of intensity, for they could not fail to weaken if the offences committed against them remained unpunished. Likewise, as the social environment becomes more complex and unstable, traditions and accepted beliefs are shaken and take on a more indeterminate and flexible character, whilst faculties of reflection develop. These same faculties are indispensable for societies and individuals to adapt themselves to a more mobile and complex environment. As men are obliged to work more intensively, the products of their labour become more numerous and better in quality; but this increase in abundance and quality of the products is necessary to compensate for the effort that this more considerable labour entails. Thus, far from the cause of social phenomena consisting of a mental anticipation of the function they are called upon to fulfil, this function consists on the contrary, in a number of cases at least, in maintaining the pre-existent cause from which the phenomena derive. We will therefore discover more easily the function if the cause is already known.

If we must proceed only at a second stage to the determination of the function, it is none the less necessary for the complete explanation of the phenomenon. Indeed, if the utility of a fact is not what causes its existence, it must generally be useful to continue to survive. If it lacks utility, that very reason suffices to make it harmful, since in that case it requires effort but brings in no return. Thus if the general run of social phenomena had this parasitic character, the economy of the organism would be in deficit, and social life would be impossible. Consequently, to provide a satisfactory explanation of social life we need to show how the phenomena which are its substance come together to place society in harmony with itself and with the outside world. Undoubtedly the present formula which defines life as a correspondence between the internal and the external environments is only approximate. Yet in general it remains true; thus to explain a fact which is vital, it is not enough to show the cause on which it depends. We must also – at least in most cases – discover the part that it plays in the establishment of that general harmony.

Having distinguished between these two questions, we must determine the method whereby they must be resolved.

At the same time as being teleological, the method of explanation generally followed by sociologists is essentially psychological. The two tendencies are closely linked. Indeed, if society is only a system of means set up by men to achieve certain ends, these ends can only be individual, for before society existed there could only exist individuals. It is therefore from the individual that emanate the ideas and needs which have determined the formation of societies. If it is from him that everything comes, it is necessarily through him that everything must be explained. Moreover, in society there is nothing save individual consciousnesses, and it is consequently in these that is to be found the source of all social evolution. Thus sociological laws can only be a corollary of the more general laws of psychology. The ultimate explanation of collective life will consist in demonstrating how it derives from human nature in general, either by direct deduction from it without any preliminary observation, or by establishing links after having observed human nature. [...]

But such a method is not applicable to sociological phenomena unless one distorts their nature. For proof of this we need only refer to the definition we have given. Since their essential characteristic is the power they possess to exert outside pressure on individual consciousnesses, this shows that they do not derive from these consciousnesses and that consequently sociology is not a corollary of psychology. This constraining power attests to the fact that they express a nature different from our own, since they only penetrate into us by force or at the very least by bearing down more or less heavily upon us. If social life were no more than an extension of the individual, we would not see it return to its origin and invade the individual consciousness so precipitately. The authority to which the individual bows when he acts, thinks or feels socially dominates him to such a degree because it is a product of forces which transcend him and for which he consequently cannot account. It is not from within himself that can come the external pressure which he undergoes; it is therefore not what is happening within himself which can explain it. It is true that we are not incapable of placing constraints upon ourselves; we can restrain our tendencies, our habits, even our instincts, and halt their development by an act of inhibition. But inhibitive movements must not be confused with those which make up social constraint. The process of inhibitive movements is centrifugal; but the latter are centripetal. The former are worked out in the individual consciousness and then tend to manifest themselves externally; the latter are at first external to the individual, whom they tend afterwards to shape from the outside in their own image. Inhibition is, if one likes, the means by which social constraint produces its psychical effects, but is not itself that constraint.

Now, once the individual is ruled out, only society remains. It is therefore in the nature of society itself that we must seek the explanation of social life. We can conceive that, since it transcends infinitely the indivdual both in time and space, it is capable of imposing upon him the ways of acting and thinking that it has consecrated by its authority. This pressure, which is the distinctive sign of social facts, is that which all exert upon each individual.

But it will be argued that since the sole elements of which society is composed are individuals, the primary origin of sociological phenomena cannot be other than psychological. Reasoning in this way, we can just as easily establish that biological phenomena are explained analytically by inorganic phenomena. It is indeed certain that in the living cell there are only molecules of crude matter. But they are in association, and it is this association which is the cause of the new phenomena which characterise life, even the germ of which it is impossible to find in a single one of these associated elements. This is because the whole does not equal the sum of its parts; it is something different, whose properties differ from those displayed by the parts from which it is formed. Association is not, as has sometimes been believed, a phenomenon infertile in itself, which consists merely in juxtaposing externally facts already given and properties already constituted. On the contrary, is it not the source of all the successive innovations that have occurred in the course of the general evolution of things? What differences exist between the lower organisms and others, between the organised living creature and the mere protoplasm, between the latter and the inorganic molecules of which it is composed, if it is not differences in association? All these beings, in the last analysis, split up into elements of the same nature; but these elements are in one place juxtaposed, in another associated. Here they are associated in one way, there in another. We are even justified in wondering whether this law does not even extend to the mineral world, and whether the differences which separate inorganic bodies do not have the same origin.

By virtue of this principle, society is not the mere sum of individuals, but the system formed by their association represents a specific reality which has its own characteristics. Undoubtedly no collective entity can be produced if there are no individual consciousnesses: this is a necessary but not a sufficient condition. In addition, these consciousnesses must be associated and combined, but combined in a certain way. It is from this combination that social life arises and consequently it is this combination which explains it. By aggregating together, by interpenetrating, by fusing together, individuals give birth to a being, psychical if you will, but one which constitutes a psychical individuality of a new kind.[7] Thus it is in the nature of that individuality and not in that of its component elements that we must search for the proximate and determining causes of the facts produced in it. The group thinks, feels and acts entirely differently from the way its members would if they were isolated. If therefore we begin by studying these members separately, we will understand nothing about what is taking place in the group. In a word, there is between psychology and sociology the same break in continuity as there is between biology and the physical and chemical sciences. Consequently every time a social phenomenon is directly explained by a psychological phenomenon, we may rest assured that the explanation is false.

Some will perhaps argue that, although society, once formed, is the proximate cause of social phenomena, the causes which have determined its formation are of a psychological nature. They may concede that, when individuals are associated together, their association may give rise to a new life, but claim that this can only take place for individual reasons. But in reality, as far as one can go back in history, the fact of association is the most obligatory of all, because it is the origin of all other obligations. By reason of my birth, I am obligatorily attached to a given people. It may be said that later, once I am an adult, I acquiesce in this obligation by the mere fact that I continue to live in my own country. But what does that matter? Such acquiescence does not remove its imperative character. Pressure accepted and undergone with good grace does not cease to be pressure. Moreover, how far does such acceptance go? Firstly, it is forced, for in the immense majority of cases it is materially and morally impossible for us to shed our nationality; such a rejection is even generally declared to be apostasy. Next, the acceptance cannot relate to the past, when I was in no position to accept, but which nevertheless determines the present. I did not seek the education I received; yet this above all else roots me to my native soil. Lastly, the acceptance can have no moral value for the future, in so far as this is unknown. I do not even know all the duties which one day may be incumbent upon me in my capacity as a citizen. How then could I acquiesce in them in advance? Now, as we have shown, all that is obligatory has its origins outside the individual. Thus, provided one does not place oneself outside history, the fact of association is of the same character as the others and is consequently explicable in the same way. Furthermore, as all societies are born of other societies, with no break in continuity, we may be assured that in the whole course of social evolution there has not been a single time when individuals have really had to consult together to decide whether they would enter into collective life together, and into one sort of collective life rather than another. Such a question is only possible when we go back to the first origins of any society. But the solutions, always dubious, which can be brought to such problems could not in any case affect the method whereby the facts given in history must be treated. We have therefore no need to discuss them.

Yet our thought would be singularly misinterpreted if the conclusion was drawn from the previous remarks that sociology, in our view, should not even take into account man and his faculties. On the contrary, it is clear that the general characteristics of human nature play their part in the work of elaboration from which social life results. But it is not these which produce it or give it its special form: they only make it possible. Collective representations, emotions and tendencies have not as their causes certain states of consciousness in individuals, but the conditions under which the body social as a whole exists. Doubtless these can be realised only if individual natures are not opposed to them. But these are simply the indeterminate matter which the social factor fashions and transforms. Their contribution is made up exclusively of very general states, vague and thus malleable predispositions which of themselves could not assume the definite and complex forms which characterise social phenomena, if other agents did not intervene.

What a gulf, for example, between the feelings that man experiences when confronted with forces superior to his own and the institution of religion with its beliefs and practices, so multifarious and complicated, and its material and moral organisation! What an abyss between the psychical conditions of sympathy which two people of the same blood feel for each other, and that hotchpotch of legal and moral rules which determine the structure of the family, personal relationships, and the relationship of things to persons, etc.! We have seen that even when society is reduced to an unorganised crowd, the collective sentiments which arise within it can not only be totally unlike, but even opposed to, the average sentiments of the individuals in it. How much greater still must be the gap when the pressure exerted upon the individual comes from a normal society, where, to the influence exerted by his contemporaries, is added that of previous generations and of tradition! A purely psychological explanation of social facts cannot therefore fail to miss completely all that is specific, i.e. social, about them.

What has blinkered the vision of many sociologists to the insufficiency of this method is the fact that, taking the effect for the cause, they have very often highlighted as causal conditions for social phenomena certain psychical states, relatively well defined and specific, but which in reality are the consequence of the phenomena. Thus it has been held that a certain religiosity is innate in man, as is a certain minimum of sexual jealousy, filial piety of fatherly affection, etc., and it is in these that explanations have been sought for religion, marriage and the family. But history shows that these inclinations, far from being inherent in human nature, are either completely absent under certain social conditions or vary so much from one society to another that the residue left after eliminating all these differences, and which alone can be considered of psychological origin, is reduced to something vague and schematic, infinitely removed from the facts which have to be explained. Thus these sentiments result from the collective organisation and are far from being at the basis of it. It has not even been proved at all that the tendency to sociability was originally a congenital instinct of the human race. It is much more natural to see in it a product of social life which has slowly become organised in us, because it is an observable fact that animals are sociable or otherwise, depending on whether their environmental conditions force them to live in common or cause them to shun such a life. And even then we must add that a considerable gap remains between these well determined tendencies and social reality. [...]

Hence we arrive at the following rule: *The determining cause of a social fact must be sought among antecedent social facts and not among the states of the individual consciousness.* Moreover, we can easily conceive that all that has been stated above applies to the determination of the function as well as the cause of a social fact. Its function can only be social, which means that it consists in the production of socially useful effects. Undoubtedly it can and indeed does happen that it has repercussions which also serve the individual. But this happy result is not the immediate rationale for its existence. Thus we can complement the preceding proposition by stating: *The function of a social fact must always be sought in the relationship that it bears to some social end.*

It is because sociologists have often failed to acknowledge this rule and have considered sociological phenomena from too psychological a viewpoint that their theories appear to many minds too vague, too ethereal and too remote from the distinctive nature of the things which sociologists believe they are explaining. The historian, in particular, who has a close contact with social reality cannot fail to feel strongly how these too general interpretations are incapable of being linked to the facts. In part, this has undoubtedly produced the mistrust that history has often manifested towards sociology. Assuredly this does not mean that the study of psychological facts is not indispensable to the sociologist. If collective life does not derive from individual life, the two are none the less closely related. If the latter cannot explain the former, it can at least render its explanation easier. Firstly, as we have shown, it is undeniably true that social facts are produced by an elaboration *sui generis* of psychological facts. But in addition this action is itself not dissimilar to that which occurs in each individual consciousness and which progressively transforms the primary elements (sensations, reflexes, instincts) of which the consciousness was originally made up. Not unreasonably has the claim been made that the ego is itself a society, just as is the organism, although in a different way. For a long time psychologists have demonstrated the absolute importance of the factor of *association* in the explanation of mental activity. Thus a psychological education, even more than a biological one, constitutes a necessary preparation for the sociologist. But it can only be of service to him if, once he has acquired it, he frees himself from it, going beyond it by adding a specifically sociological education. He must give up making psychology in some way the focal point of his operations, the point of departure to which he must always return after his adventurous incursions into the social world. He must establish himself at the very heart of social facts in order to observe and confront them totally, without any mediating factor, while calling upon the science of the individual only for a general preparation and, if needs be, for useful suggestions.[8]

NOTES

1. It can be seen that to concede this proposition it is unnecessary to maintain that social life is made up of anything save representations. It is sufficient to posit that representations, whether individual or collective, cannot be studied scientifically unless they are studied objectively.
2. Moreover, this is not to say that all constraint is normal.
3. Suicides do not occur at any age, nor do they occur at all ages of life with the same frequency.
4. It can be seen how far removed this definition of the social fact is from that which serves as the basis for the ingenious system of Tarde. We must first state that our research has nowhere led us to corroboration of the preponderant influence that Tarde attributes to

imitation in the genesis of collective facts. Moreover, from this definition, which is not a theory but a mere résumé of the immediate data observed, it seems clearly to follow that imitation does not always express, indeed never expresses, what is essential and characteristic in the social fact. Doubtless every social fact is imitated and has, as we have just shown, a tendency to become generalised, but this is because it is social, i.e. obligatory. Its capacity for expansion is not the cause but the consequence of its sociological character. If social facts were unique in bringing about this effect, imitation might serve, if not to explain them, at least to define them. But an individual state which impacts on others none the less remains individual. Moreover, one may speculate whether the term "imitation" is indeed appropriate to designate a proliferation which occurs through some coercive influence. In such a single term very different phenomena, which need to be distinguished, are confused.

5 This close affinity of life and structure, organ and function, can be readily established in sociology because there exists between these two extremes a whole series of intermediate stages, immediately observable, which reveal the link between them. Biology lacks this methodological resource. But one may believe legitimately that sociological inductions on this subject are applicable to biology and that, in organisms as in societies, between these two categories of facts only differences in degree exist.

6 We would not wish to raise questions of general philosophy which would be inappropriate here. However, we note that, if more closely studied, this reciprocity of cause and effect could provide a means of reconciling scientific mechanism with the teleology implied by the existence and, above all, the persistence of life.

7 In this sense and for these reasons we can and must speak of a collective consciousness distinct from individual consciousnesses. To justify this distinction there is no need to hypostatise the collective consciousness; it is something special and must be designated by a special term, simply because the states which constitute it differ specifically from those which make up individual consciousnesses. This specificity arises because they are not formed from the same elements. Individual consciousnesses result from the nature of the organic and psychical being taken in isolation, collective consciousnesses from a plurality of beings of this kind. The results cannot therefore fail to be different, since the component parts differ to this extent. Our definition of the social fact, moreover, did no more than highlight, in a different way, this demarcation line.

8 Psychical phenomena can only have social consequences when they are so closely linked to social phenomena that the actions of both are necessarily intermingled. This is the case for certain socio-psychical phenomena. Thus a public official is a social force, but at the same time he is an individual. The result is that he can employ the social force he commands in a way determined by his individual nature and thereby exert an influence on the constitution of society. This is what occurs with statesmen and, more generally, with men of genius. The latter, although they do not fulfil a social role, draw from the collective sentiments of which they are the object an authority which is itself a social force, one which they can to a certain extent place at the service of their personal ideas. But it can be seen that such cases are due to individual chance and consequently cannot affect the characteristics which constitute the social species, which alone is the object of science. The limitation on the principle enunciated above is therefore not of great importance to the sociologist.

Part IV

The Sociological Theory of Emile Durkheim

Introduction to Part IV

15 The Rules of Sociological Method

16 The Division of Labor in Society

17 The Elementary Forms of the Religious Life

18 Suicide

Introduction to Part IV

Along with Karl Marx and Max Weber, Emile Durkheim (1858–1917) is one of the influential classical theorists in sociology. Of the three, Durkheim was the only one to actually hold a chair in the discipline, and he was the author of some of the most programmatic statements about what sociology was and how it should be done. Durkheim's key theoretical contribution lies in his claim that social phenomena are *sui generis* realities that can only be explained by other social facts.

Durkheim's modern legacy is somewhat odd in the sense that his work is now considered central to sociologists of very different theoretical inclinations. Although Durkheim has recently come to be associated with positivism in sociology, his work also addresses important philosophical and cultural questions. Durkheim's theoretical writings have had wide-ranging influence on social anthropology, criminology, and studies of education, religion, and social movements. To some degree, Durkheim's reputation suffered due to the reaction against functionalism (see Part VII in this volume), with which Durkheim's name has come to be associated in the English-speaking world. The recent renewal of "neofunctionalism" and analysis has brought interested readers again to Durkheim's work.

Durkheim's Life and Intellectual Context

Durkheim was born in Épinal, France in 1858 and grew up in a traditional Jewish family, which was part of the long-established Jewish community of Alsace-Lorraine. His father was the rabbi of the town and, in fact, Durkheim's family had a long

Classical Sociological Theory, Third Edition. Edited by Craig Calhoun, Joseph Gerteis, James Moody, Steven Pfaff, and Indermohan Virk. Editorial material and organization © 2012 John Wiley & Sons, Ltd. Published 2012 by John Wiley & Sons, Ltd.

rabbinical tradition. In keeping with this tradition, Durkheim was expected to devote himself to religious studies. In general, Durkheim and his siblings were brought up in an austere atmosphere, with a strong sense of duty and moral discipline.

Durkheim's early education began at a rabbinical school. However, he soon decided against this course of study and switched to the local school. Durkheim was a serious student, and decided at an early age that he wanted to pursue higher education. After graduation, he moved to Paris in order to prepare for the entrance exam for the École Normale Supérieure, the most distinguished college in France. After two failed attempts, he was admitted to the École in 1879. He experienced intense anxiety about the academic competition there and he feared failure. At the same time, however, the École provided a setting for exhilarating intellectual discussions, and Durkheim thrived on these. In the course of his studies at the École, Durkheim became critical of its educational approach, which he found to be "too humanistic and literary, and too hostile to scientific attitudes" (Lukes, 1972: 52–3). Initially interested in psychology and philosophy, he soon turned his attention to the study of morality and society, and finally to sociology.

At the École, Durkheim's intellectual development was shaped by the ideas of two neo-Kantian scholars, Renouvier and Boutroux. In particular, Durkheim was persuaded by Renouvier's commitment to rationalism, his central concern with the scientific study of morality, his anti-utilitarianism, and his advocacy of secular education. From Boutroux, Durkheim derived the principle that each science is irreducible to that of the preceding one, a principle that was to shape Durkheim's own conceptualization of the distinctive subject matter and methodology of sociology. Under Boutroux's guidance, he also engaged in a close reading of Auguste Comte, the inventor of the term "sociology." Methodologically, Durkheim was influenced by the historian Fustel de Coulanges, an advocate of the scientific method and a believer in the importance of religion in social life.

Following graduation, Durkheim taught philosophy at several provincial schools from 1882 to 1887. By this time, he had also settled on a topic for his doctoral thesis: the relation between individualism and socialism. He later recast the idea as the relation between the individual and society, and, finally, between individual personality and social solidarity. Although still quite abstract and philosophical, these ideas eventually spawned *The Division of Labor in Society*. By the time he completed the first draft of this work in 1886, Durkheim had committed himself to the establishment of the new science of sociology.

In this intellectual commitment, Durkheim was indebted to Comte's advocacy of scientific methods for the study of society. Although profound, this debt was not received uncritically by Durkheim. He believed that while Comte correctly identified "the social" as the object of sociology, Comte's work still amounted more to philosophical contemplation of humanity in general rather than the study of any specific society. Although Comte coined the term "sociology" in 1822, the discipline itself was just becoming established in Durkheim's lifetime, and it was still struggling for recognition in the academic world. In his search for examples of sociology at work, Durkheim turned his attention to Germany. He spent the academic year 1885–6 visiting several German universities, where he became impressed with the German contribution to the emerging science of sociology.

In this respect, he found Herbert Spencer's earlier application of an organic analogy to societies a more satisfactory explanatory tool. The idea had become current in the work of many prominent German social thinkers. Organicism is based on the premise that the laws governing the functioning and evolution of animal organisms provide a model for a natural science of society. Durkheim was also impressed with the scientific study of morality that he encountered in Germany, for instance the work of social economists such as Wagner and Schmoller. However, it was the work of Wilhelm Wundt that Durkheim considered to be the greatest contribution to the sociological treatment of morality. Durkheim's articles on German social science and philosophy attracted public attention, and in 1887 he was appointed to teach the first university course in social science at the University of Bordeaux. At that time, the appointment of a social scientist to the predominantly humanist Faculty of Letters was in itself quite a significant event.

Durkheim's fifteen years at Bordeaux were extremely productive. In addition to numerous reviews and articles, he published *The Division of Labor* as well as *The Rules of Sociological Method* and *Suicide*. Durkheim's lectures on sociological subjects further staked the claim for sociology as a discipline. In addition, Durkheim founded *L'Année Sociologique* (1898–1913), the first social science journal in France. These intellectual projects brought upon Durkheim charges of "sociological imperialism" (see Lukes, 1972: 103). While he was largely able to overcome opposition from his colleagues in Bordeaux, for a time these charges kept him from a professorship in Paris, something to which he had aspired.

Although Durkheim held a strong antipathy for politics, he made two exceptions: the Dreyfus Affair and the First World War. It was Durkheim's involvement in the Dreyfus Affair that eventually brought him an appointment in Paris. In 1894, a Jewish staff officer named Captain Alfred Dreyfus was court-martialed for selling secrets to the German Embassy in Paris. When a later review of the case under a new chief of counter-intelligence found Dreyfus to be innocent, it became a public scandal. It was in the course of the public debate following this controversy that Durkheim published his only study addressing contemporary politics. The article, "Individualism and Intellectuals," published in 1898, responded to those who accused the intellectuals supporting Dreyfus's case of provoking individualism and anarchy. Durkheim argued in this article for a concept he called "moral individualism." Properly understood, individualism was not the same thing as pure egotism, Durkheim argued.

Following the Dreyfus Affair, Durkheim's continued involvement in public debates led to his appointment in Paris. In 1902, he was appointed to a position in education at the Sorbonne. Although he became a full professor in 1906, it was not until 1913 that he was named Chair in "Education and Sociology." Durkheim's intellectual interests during his Paris years were the sociology of morality, knowledge, and religion. Following the outbreak of the First World War, Durkheim immersed himself in the war effort. By this time, his health had begun to decline, and he suffered a further blow with the death of his son in the war. Durkheim died in 1917 at the age of 59.

Durkheim's Work

Of the large body of work that Durkheim produced, the most influential are the four major books that were published during his lifetime: *The Division of Labor, The Rules of Sociological Method, Suicide,* and *The Elementary Forms of the Religious Life.* In these books, Durkheim developed some of his principal intellectual ideas. One project that he committed himself to was the establishment of sociology as a discipline. His goal was to provide a firm definition of the field and a scientific basis for its study. A second concern of Durkheim's was the issue of social integration in society. Durkheim wondered about the sources and nature of moral authority as an integrating force in society, as well as the rise of individualism. Finally, Durkheim held a strong interest in the practical implications of social-scientific knowledge.

Durkheim intended *The Rules* as a programmatic statement about the cause of sociology as a discipline, which must have its own distinctive subject matter and methodology. Substantively, the domain of sociology must necessarily be "social facts" that are "external to individuals." Methodologically, sociologists must strive for objectivity by studying "social facts as things," that is, through empirical investigation. In demarcating the explanatory method of sociology from that of psychology, Durkheim proposed that sociology must focus on macro-level causal analysis, relating social causes to social effects. In addition to a causal analysis, he suggested that sociology must undertake a functional explanation of a social fact in terms of the needs of a social "organism."

Durkheim intended his book *Suicide* to be an example of his method. Durkheim took the suicide rate as an example of a social fact, and attempted to explain scientifically the variations in that rate. The suicide rate is an interesting example for several reasons. First, it is "external to individuals." Durkheim did not attempt to explain the inner feelings of someone contemplating suicide, nor even the causes of individual suicides. Instead, he examined variations in the suicide rate. What caused these variations? He argued that under different social conditions, different causes produced patterns of suicides. In modern societies, the most important cause was a disconnection of people from social bonds – resulting either from isolation or from disorienting changes in society at large.

In *The Division of Labor,* Durkheim confronted the basic question of what holds modern society together. Using an evolutionary approach, his central thesis in the book was that the increasing division of labor in modern societies was taking the place of the *conscience collective* – the moral consensus or collective conscience – that marked traditional societies. Despite this, social cohesion still operates, but in a different way. Durkheim characterizes the social integration that results from the division of labor in modern societies as "organic solidarity," a solidarity born out of mutual need. This was quickly replacing the "mechanical solidarity" typical of simpler societies. The term "organic" referred to the functional interconnectedness of elements in society, similar to the way that the parts of an organism are functionally connected. In modern societies, we may not feel morally or culturally connected to those around us. But as the division of labor increases, we are more than ever functionally connected by our mutual needs.

The Elementary Forms of the Religious Life marked an explicitly cultural turn in Durkheim's work. It was ostensibly a study of Totemism, a "primitive and simple religion" of the aboriginal people of Australia. Durkheim picked this example because he believed that the simplest religions offered the purest examples of the essential elements of religious life. More broadly, Durkheim contributed in this work to a general theory of religion and the sociology of knowledge. *The Elementary Forms* can be seen as the study of collective representations, a concept that increasingly came to replace that of the *conscience collective* in Durkheim's work. In this direction, Durkheim traced the social origins and the social functions of religious beliefs. As the embodiment of collective ideals, religion is reinforced through ceremonials and rituals. Durkheim also advanced a sociological theory of knowledge that addresses old philosophical questions, such as the origin of categories of thought and action.

In doing so, he wanted to unite two philosophical claims that seemed to be opposed to one another. On the one hand, there was the claim that categories are constructed out of human experience. On the other hand, there was the claim that categories are logically prior to experience. Durkheim suggested that categories are collective representations; that is, categories are the product of society. To the extent people collectively constitute society, our categories of knowledge can be said to be human creations. But because society is a *sui generis* phenomenon, they are prior to the experience of any particular person.

Durkheim's Legacy

By the turn of the century, Durkheim's hard work had paid off. Sociology had gained considerable popularity in Europe and the United States, and in France, Durkheim's vision of the discipline was well entrenched. Many of his students pursued his intellectual ideas in their own work. His nephew and collaborator Marcel Mauss studied reciprocity in the form of gift giving, and the notion of the person or "self"; Holbwachs did research on working-class consumption and collective memory; Bouglé studied caste.

Ironically, in recent decades Durkheim's methodology has been far more influential in America and Britain than in France. The British anthropologist Alfred Radcliffe-Brown first introduced Durkheim's ideas to the English-speaking world. Radcliffe-Brown also helped stimulate interest in Durkheim's writings in the United States. However, this interest became more widespread in the United States through the work of Talcott Parsons and Robert Merton.

Nevertheless, Durkheim's ideas influenced several major theoretical movements in the 20th century. They were strongly present in the emergence of "structuralism" through the work of Jean Piaget and Claude Lévi-Strauss. Alexander (1988) points to the often-unacknowledged debt that the recent cultural revival in social theory owes to the ideas of Durkheim, for instance in the work of Ferdinand de Saussure, Michel Foucault (see Part V of *Contemporary Sociological Theory*), and Clifford Geertz, as well as Peter Berger, Robert Bellah, and others.

SELECTED BIBLIOGRAPHY

Alexander, Jeffrey (ed.). 1988. *Durkheimian Sociology: Cultural Studies*. Cambridge: Cambridge University Press. (An excellent collection of essays on the contribution of Durkheim's work to cultural analysis and the study of religion.)

Bellah, Robert (ed.). 1973. *Émile Durkheim on Morality and Society, Selected Writings*. Chicago, IL: University of Chicago Press. (This volume includes a good introduction on morality and religion.)

Fenton, Steve with Robert Reiner and Ian Hamnett. 1984. *Durkheim and Modern Sociology*. Cambridge: Cambridge University Press. (A useful book for the general reader, organized around key sociological themes.)

Giddens, Anthony. 1978. *Émile Durkheim*. New York: Viking Press. (A short but useful introduction to Durkheim's work.)

Jones, Robert. 1986. *Émile Durkheim: An Introduction to Four Major Works*. Masters of Social Theory, Vol. 2. Beverly Hills, CA: Sage Publications. (A good summary of Durkheim's major work.)

La Capra, Dominick. 1972. *Émile Durkheim: Sociologist and Philosopher*. Ithaca, NY: Cornell University Press. (A general introductory book with chapters devoted to Durkheim's important writings.)

Lukes, Steven. 1972. *Émile Durkheim: His Life and Work*. New York: Harper & Row. (One of the most detailed and authoritative interpretations of Durkheim's work.)

Lukes, Steven. 1982. "Introduction." *The Rules of Sociological Method*. New York: Free Press. (A good discussion of Durkheim's ideas on sociology as a science.)

Nisbet, Robert. 1974. *The Sociology of Émile Durkheim*. New York: Oxford University Press. (A good general introduction, but controversial for its treatment of Durkheim as a conservative.)

Pickering, W.S.F. 1984. *Durkheim's Sociology of Religion: Themes and Theories*. London: Routledge. (A valuable source for further reading on Durkheim's theory of religion.)

Thompson, Kenneth. 1982. *Émile Durkheim*. New York: Tavistock Publications. (A comprehensive summary and critique of Durkheim's work.)

Traugott, Mark. (ed.). 1978. *Émile Durkheim on Institutional Analysis*. Chicago, IL: University of Chicago Press. (For those interested in a further reading of Durkheim's work, an interesting collection of his writings.)

Wallwork, Ernest. 1972. *Durkheim: Morality and Milieu*. Cambridge, MA: Harvard University Press. (A more specialized discussion of Durkheim's moral philosophy.)

Wolff, Kurt (ed.). 1960. *Émile Durkheim, 1858–1917*. Columbus, OH: Ohio State University Press. (An early collection of essays on various themes related to Durkheim's work.)

Chapter 16

The Division of Labor in Society [1893]

Emile Durkheim

The Problem

Although the division of labour is not of recent origin, it was only at the end of the last century that societies began to become aware of this law, to which up to then they had submitted almost unwittingly. Undoubtedly even from antiquity several thinkers had perceived its importance. Yet Adam Smith was the first to attempt to elaborate the theory of it. Moreover, it was he who first coined the term, which social science later lent to biology.

Nowadays the phenomenon has become so widespread that it catches everyone's attention. We can no longer be under any illusion about the trends in modern industry. It involves increasingly powerful mechanisms, large-scale groupings of power and capital, and consequently an extreme division of labour. Inside factories, not only are jobs demarcated, becoming extremely specialised, but each product is itself a speciality entailing the existence of others. Adam Smith and John Stuart Mill persisted in hoping that agriculture at least would prove an exception to the rule, seeing in it the last refuge of small-scale ownership. Although in such a matter we must guard against generalising unduly, nowadays it appears difficult to deny that the main branches of the agricultural industry are increasingly swept along in the

Durkheim, Emile, "The Division of Labor in Society," pp. 1–2, 24–29, 38–41, 60–63, 68–71, 83–85, 200–205, 301–306 from Emile Durkheim, *The Division of Labor in Society*, trans. by W.D. Halls. New York: Macmillan Publishers Ltd., The Free Press, 1984. Translation, Copyright © 1984 by Higher & Further Education Division, Macmillan Publishers, Ltd. Reprinted and edited with the permission of The Free Press, A Division of Simon & Schuster Adult Publishing Group and Palgrave Macmillan. All rights reserved.

Classical Sociological Theory, Third Edition. Edited by Craig Calhoun, Joseph Gerteis, James Moody, Steven Pfaff, and Indermohan Virk. Editorial material and organization © 2012 John Wiley & Sons, Ltd. Published 2012 by John Wiley & Sons, Ltd.

general trend. Finally, commerce itself contrives ways to follow and reflect, in all their distinctive nuances, the boundless diversity of industrial undertakings. Although this evolution occurs spontaneously and unthinkingly, those economists who study its causes and evaluate its results, far from condemning such diversification or attacking it, proclaim its necessity. They perceive in it the higher law of human societies and the condition for progress.

Yet the division of labour is not peculiar to economic life. We can observe its increasing influence in the most diverse sectors of society. Functions, whether political, administrative or judicial, are becoming more and more specialised. The same is true in the arts and sciences. [...]

The Function of the Division of Labour

We have not merely to investigate whether, in these kinds of societies, there exists a social solidarity arising from the division of labour. This is a self-evident truth, since in them the division of labour is highly developed and it engenders solidarity. But above all we must determine the degree to which the solidarity it produces contributes generally to the integration of society. Only then shall we learn to what extent it is necessary, whether it is an essential factor in social cohesion, or whether, on the contrary, it is only an ancillary and secondary condition for it. To answer this question we must therefore compare this social bond to others, in order to measure what share in the total effect must be attributed to it. To do this it is indispensable to begin by classifying the different species of social solidarity.

However, social solidarity is a wholly moral phenomenon which by itself is not amenable to exact observation and especially not to measurement. To arrive at this classification, as well as this comparison, we must therefore substitute for this internal datum, which escapes us, an external one which symbolises it, and then study the former through the latter.

That visible symbol is the law. Indeed where social solidarity exists, in spite of its non-material nature, it does not remain in a state of pure potentiality, but shows its presence through perceptible effects. Where it is strong it attracts men strongly to one another, ensures frequent contacts between them, and multiplies the opportunities available to them to enter into mutual relationships. To state the position precisely, at the point we have now reached it is not easy to say whether it is social solidarity that produces these phenomena or, on the contrary, whether it is the result of them. Likewise it is a moot point whether men draw closer to one another because of the strong effects of social solidarity, or whether it is strong because men *have* come closer together. However, for the moment we need not concern ourselves with clarifying this question. It is enough to state that these two orders of facts are linked, varying with each other simultaneously and directly. The more closely knit the members of a society, the more they maintain various relationships either with one another or with the group collectively. For if they met together rarely, they would not be mutually dependent, except sporadically and somewhat weakly. Moreover, the number of these relationships is necessarily proportional to that of the legal rules that determine them. In fact, social life, wherever it becomes lasting, inevitably tends to assume a definite form and become organised. Law is nothing more than this very organisation in its most stable and precise form. Life in general within a society cannot enlarge in scope without legal activity simultaneously increasing in proportion. Thus we may be sure to find reflected in the law all the essential varieties of social solidarity.

It may certainly be objected that social relationships can be forged without necessarily taking on a legal form. Some do exist where the process of regulation does not attain such a level of consolidation and precision. This does not mean that they remain indeterminate; instead of being regulated by law they are merely regulated by custom. Thus law mirrors only a part of social life and consequently provides us with only incomplete data with which to resolve the problem. What is more, it is often the case that custom is out of step with the law. It is repeatedly stated that custom tempers the harshness of the law, corrects the excesses that arise from its formal nature, and is even occasionally inspired with a very different ethos. Might then custom display other kinds of social solidarity than those expressed in positive law?

But such an antithesis only occurs in wholly exceptional circumstances. For it to occur law must have ceased to correspond to the present state of society and yet, although lacking any reason to exist, is sustained through force of habit. In that event, the new relationships that are established in spite of it will become organised, for they cannot subsist without seeking to consolidate themselves. Yet, being at odds with the old law, which persists, and not succeeding in penetrating the legal domain proper, they do not rise beyond the level of custom. Thus opposition breaks out. But this can only happen in rare, pathological cases, and cannot even continue without becoming dangerous. Normally custom is not opposed to law; on the contrary, it forms the basis for it. It is true that sometimes nothing further is built upon this basis. There may exist social relationships governed only by that diffuse form of regulation arising from custom. But this is because they lack importance and continuity, excepting naturally those abnormal cases just mentioned. Thus if types of social solidarity chance to exist which custom alone renders apparent, these are assuredly of a very secondary order. On the other hand the law reproduces all those types that are essential, and it is about these alone that we need to know.

Should we go further and assert that social solidarity does not consist entirely in its visible manifestations; that these express it only partially and imperfectly; that beyond law and custom there exists an inner state from which solidarity derives; and that to know it in reality we must penetrate to its heart, without any intermediary? But in science we can know causes only through the effects that they produce. In order to determine the nature of these causes more precisely science selects only those results that are the most objective and that best lend themselves to quantification. Science studies heat through the variations in volume that changes in temperature cause in bodies, electricity through its physical and chemical effects, and force through movement. Why should social solidarity prove an exception?

Moreover, what remains of social solidarity once it is divested of its social forms? What imparts to it its specific characteristics is the nature of the group whose unity it ensures, and this is why it varies according to the types of society. It is not the same within the family as within political societies. We are not attached to our native land in the same way as the Roman was to his city or the German to his tribe. But since such differences spring from social causes, we can only grasp them through the differences that the social effects of solidarity present to us. Thus if we neglect the differences, all varieties become indistinguishable, and we can perceive no more than that which is common to all varieties, that is, the general tendency to sociability, a tendency that is always and everywhere the same and is not linked to any particular social type. But this residual element is only an abstraction, for sociability *per se* is met with nowhere. What exists and what is really alive are the special forms of solidarity – domestic, professional, national, that of the past and that of today, etc. Each has its own special nature. Hence generalities can in any case only furnish a very incomplete explanation of the phenomenon, since they necessarily allow to escape what is concrete and living about it.

Thus the study of solidarity lies within the domain of sociology. It is a social fact that can only be thoroughly known through its social effects. If so many moralists and psychologists have been able to deal with this question without following this method, it is because they have avoided the difficulty. They have divested the phenomenon of everything that is more specifically social about it, retaining only the psychological core from which it develops. It is certain that solidarity, whilst being pre-eminently a social fact, is dependent upon our individual organism. In order to be capable of existing it must fit our physical and psychological constitution. Thus, at the very least, we can content ourselves with studying it from this viewpoint. But in that case we shall perceive only that aspect of it which is the most indistinct and the least special. Strictly speaking, this is not even solidarity itself, but only what makes it possible.

Even so, such an abstract study cannot yield very fruitful results. For, so long as it remains in the state of a mere predisposition of our psychological nature, solidarity is something too indefinite to be easily understood. It remains an intangible virtuality too elusive to observe. To take on a form that we can grasp, social outcomes must provide an external interpretation of it. Moreover, even in such an indeterminate state, it depends on social conditions that explain it, and cannot consequently be detached from them. This is why some sociological perspectives are not infrequently to be found mixed up with these purely psychological analyses. For example, some mention is made of the influence of the *gregarious state* on the formation of social feeling in general; or the main social relationships on which sociability most obviously depends are rapidly sketched out. Undoubtedly such additional considerations, introduced unsystematically as examples and at random as they suggest themselves, cannot suffice to cast much light on the social nature of solidarity. Yet at least they demonstrate that the sociological viewpoint must weigh even with the psychologists.

Thus our method is clearly traced out for us. Since law reproduces the main forms of social solidarity, we have only to classify the different types of law in order to be able to investigate which types of social solidarity correspond to them. It is already likely that one species of law exists which symbolises the special solidarity engendered by the division of labour. Once we have made this investigation, in order to judge what part the division of labour plays it will be enough to compare the number of legal rules which give it expression with the total volume of law.

To undertake this study we cannot use the habitual distinctions made by jurisprudents. Conceived for the practice of law, from this viewpoint they can be very convenient, but science cannot be satisfied with such empirical classifications and approximations. The most widespread classification is that which divides law into public and private law. Public law is held to regulate the relationships of the individual with the state, private law those of individuals with one another. Yet when we attempt to define these terms closely, the dividing line, which appeared at first sight to be so clear-cut, disappears. All law is private, in the sense that always and everywhere individuals are concerned and are its actors. Above all, however, all law is public, in the sense that it is a social function, and all individuals are, although in different respects, functionaries of society. The functions of marriage and parenthood, etc. are not spelt out or organised any differently from those of ministers or legislators. Not without reason did Roman law term guardianship a *munus publicum*. Moreover, what is the state? Where does it begin, where does it end? The controversial nature of this question is well known. It is unscientific to base such a fundamental classification on such an obscure and inadequately analysed idea.

In order to proceed methodically, we have to discover some characteristic which, whilst essential to juridical phenomena, is capable of varying as they vary. Now, every legal precept may be defined as a rule of behaviour to which sanctions apply. Moreover, it is clear that the sanctions change according to the degree of seriousness attached to the precepts, the place they occupy in the public consciousness, and the role they play in society. Thus it is appropriate to classify legal rules according to the different sanctions that are attached to them.

These are of two kinds. The first consist essentially in some injury, or at least some disadvantage imposed upon the perpetrator of a crime. Their purpose is to do harm to him through his fortune, his honour, his life, his liberty, or to deprive him of some object whose possession he enjoys. These are said to be repressive sanctions, such as those laid down in the penal code. It is true that those that appertain to purely moral rules are of the same character. Yet such sanctions are administered in a diffuse way by everybody without distinction, whilst those of the penal code are applied only through the mediation of a definite body – they are organised. As for the other kind of sanctions, they do not necessarily imply any suffering on the part of the perpetrator, but merely consist in *restoring the previous state of affairs*, re-establishing relationships that have been disturbed from their normal form. This is done either by forcibly redressing the action impugned, restoring it to the type from which it has deviated, or by annulling it, that is depriving it of all social value. Thus legal rules must be divided into two main species, according to whether they relate to repressive, organised sanctions, or to ones that are purely restitutory. The first group covers all penal law; the second, civil law, commercial law, procedural law, administrative and constitutional law, when any penal rules which may be attached to them have been removed.

Let us now investigate what kind of social solidarity corresponds to each of these species. [...]

Mechanical Solidarity, or Solidarity by Similarities

The totality of beliefs and sentiments common to the average members of a society forms a determinate system with a life of its own. It can be termed the collective or common consciousness. Undoubtedly the substratum of this consciousness does not consist of a single organ. By definition it is diffused over society as a whole, but nonetheless possesses specific characteristics that make it a distinctive reality. In fact it is independent of the particular conditions in which individuals find themselves. Individuals pass on, but it abides. It is the same in north and south, in large towns and in small, and in different professions. Likewise it does not change with every generation but, on the contrary, links successive generations to one another. Thus it is something totally different from the consciousnesses of individuals, although it is only realised in individuals. It is the psychological type of society, one which has its properties, conditions for existence and mode of development, just as individual types do, but in a different fashion. For this reason it has the right to be designated by a special term. It is true that the one we have employed above is not without ambiguity. Since the terms "collective" and "social" are often taken as synonyms, one is inclined to believe that the collective consciousness is the entire social consciousness, that is, co-terminous with the psychological life of society, whereas, particularly in higher societies, it constitutes only a very limited part of it. Those functions that are judicial, governmental, scientific or industrial – in short, all the specific functions – appertain to the psychological order, since they consist of systems of representation and action. However, they clearly lie outside the common consciousness. To avoid a confusion[1] that has occurred it would perhaps be best to invent a technical expression which would specifically designate the sum total of social similarities. However, since the use of a new term, when it is not absolutely necessary, is not without its disadvantages, we shall retain the more generally used expression, "collective (or common) consciousness", but always keeping in mind the restricted sense in which we are employing it.

Thus, we may state that an act is criminal when it offends the strong, well-defined states of the collective consciousness.[2]

This proposition, taken literally, is scarcely disputed, although usually we give it a meaning very different from the one it should have. It is taken as if it expressed, not the essential characteristics of the crime, but one of its repercussions. We well know that crime offends very general sentiments, but ones that are strongly held. But it is believed that their generality and strength spring from the criminal nature of the act, which consequently still remains wholly to be defined. It is not disputed that any criminal act excites universal disapproval, but it is taken for granted that this results from its criminal nature. Yet one is then hard put to it to state what is the nature of this criminality. Is it in a particularly serious form of immorality? I would concur, but this is to answer a question by posing another, by substituting one term for another. For what *is* immorality is precisely what we want to know – and particularly that special form of immorality which society represses by an organised system of punishments, and which constitutes criminality. Clearly it can only derive from one or several characteristics common to all varieties of crime. Now the only characteristic to satisfy that condition refers to the opposition that exists between crime of any kind and certain collective sentiments. It is thus the opposition which, far from deriving from the crime, constitutes the crime. In other words, we should not say that an act offends the common consciousness because it is criminal, but that it is criminal because it offends that consciousness. We do not condemn it because it is a crime, but it is a crime because we condemn it. As regards the intrinsic nature of these feelings, we cannot specify what that is. They have very diverse objects, so that they cannot be encompassed within a single formula. They cannot be said to relate to the vital interests of society or to a minimum of justice. All such definitions are inadequate. But by the mere fact that a sentiment, whatever may be its origin and purpose, is found in every consciousness and endowed with a certain degree of strength and precision, every act that disturbs it is a crime. Present-day psychology is increasingly turning back to Spinoza's idea that things are good because we like them, rather than that we like them because they are good. What is primary is the tendency and disposition: pleasure and pain are only facts derived from this. The same holds good for social life. An act is socially evil because it is rejected by society. But, it will be contended, are there no collective sentiments that arise from the pleasure or pain that society feels when it comes into contact with their objects? This is doubtless so, but all such sentiments do not originate in this way. Many, if not the majority, derive from utterly different causes. Anything that obliges our activity to take on a definite form can give rise to habits that result in dispositions which then have to be satisfied. Moreover, these dispositions alone are truly fundamental. The others are only special forms of them and are more determinate. Thus to find charm in a particular object, collective sensibility must already have been constituted in such a way as to be able to appreciate it. If the corresponding sentiments are abolished, an act most disastrous for society will not only be capable of being tolerated, but honoured and held up as an example. Pleasure cannot create a disposition out of nothing; it can only link to a particular end those dispositions that already exist, provided that end is in accordance with their original nature. [...]

Thus our analysis of punishment has substantiated our definition of crime. We began by establishing inductively that crime consisted essentially in an act contrary to strong, well-defined states of the common consciousness. We have just seen that in effect all the characteristics of punishment derive from the nature of crime. Thus the rules sanctioned by punishment are the expression of the most essential social similarities.

We can therefore see what kind of solidarity the penal law symbolises. In fact we all know that a social cohesion exists whose cause can be traced to a certain conformity of each individual consciousness to a common type, which is none other than the psychological type of society. Indeed under these conditions all members of the group are not only individually attracted to one another because they resemble one another, but they are also linked to what is the condition for the existence of this collective type, that is, to the society that they form by coming together. Not only do fellow-citizens like one another, seeking one another out in preference to foreigners, but they love their country. They wish for it what they would wish for themselves, they care that it should be lasting and prosperous, because without it a whole area of their psychological life would fail to function smoothly. Conversely, society insists upon its citizens displaying all these basic resemblances because it is a condition for its own cohesion. Two consciousnesses exist within us: the one comprises only states that are personal to each one of us, characteristic of us as individuals, whilst the other comprises states that are common to the whole of society.[3] The former represents only our individual personality, which it constitutes; the latter represents the collective type and consequently the society without which it would not exist. When it is an element of the latter determining our behaviour, we do not act with an eye to our own personal interest, but are pursuing collective ends. Now, although distinct, these two consciousnesses are linked to each other, since in the end they constitute only one entity, for both have one and the same organic basis. Thus they are solidly joined together. This gives rise to a solidarity *sui generis* which, deriving from resemblances, binds the individual directly to society. We propose to term this solidarity mechanical. It does not consist merely in a general, indeterminate attachment of the individual to the group, but is also one that concerts their detailed actions. Indeed, since such collective motives are the same everywhere, they produce everywhere the same effects. Consequently, whenever they are brought into play all wills spontaneously move as one in the same direction.

It is this solidarity that repressive law expresses, at least in regard to what is vital to it. Indeed the acts which such law forbids and stigmatises as crimes are of two kinds: either they manifest directly a too violent dissimilarity between the one who commits them and the collective type; or they offend the organ of the common consciousness. In both cases the force shocked by the crime and that rejects it is thus the same. It is a result of the most vital social similarities, and its effect is to maintain the social cohesion that arises from these similarities. It is that force which the penal law guards against being weakened in any way. At the same time it does this by insisting upon a minimum number of similarities from each one of us, without which the individual would be a threat to the unity of the body social, and by enforcing respect for the symbol which expresses and epitomises these resemblances, whilst simultaneously guaranteeing them.

By this is explained why some acts have so frequently been held to be criminal, and punished as such, without in themselves being harmful to society. Indeed, just like the individual type, the collective type has been fashioned under the influence of very diverse causes, and even of random events. A product of historical development, it bears the mark of those circumstances of every kind through which society has lived during its history. It would therefore be a miracle if everything to be found in it were geared to some useful end. Some elements, more or less numerous, cannot fail to have been introduced into it which are unrelated to social utility. Among the dispositions and tendencies the individual has received from his ancestors or has developed over time there are certainly many that serve no purpose, or that cost more than the benefits they bring. Undoubtedly most of these are not harmful, for if they were, in such conditions the individual could not live. But there are some that persist although lacking in all utility. Even those that do undisputedly render a service are frequently of an intensity disproportionate to their usefulness, because that intensity derives in part from other causes. The same holds good for collective emotions. Every act that disturbs them is not dangerous in itself, or at least is not so perilous as the condemnation it earns. However, the reprobation such acts incur is not without reason. For, whatever the origin of these sentiments, once they constitute a part of the collective type, and particularly if they are essential elements in it, everything that serves to undermine them at the same time undermines social cohesion and is prejudicial to society. In their origin they had no usefulness but, having survived it, it becomes necessary for them to continue despite their irrationality. This is generally why it is good that acts that offend these sentiments should not be tolerated. Doubtless, by reasoning in the abstract it can indeed be shown that there are no grounds for a society to prohibit the eating of a particular kind of meat, an action inoffensive in itself. But once an abhorrence of this food has become an integral part of the common consciousness it cannot disappear without social bonds becoming loosened, and of this the healthy individual consciousness is vaguely aware.[4]

The same is true of punishment. Although it proceeds from an entirely mechanical reaction and from an access of passionate emotion, for the most part unthinking, it continues to play a useful role. But that role is not the one commonly perceived. It does not serve, or serves only very incidentally, to correct the guilty person or to scare off any possible imitators. From this dual viewpoint its effectiveness may rightly be questioned; in any case it is mediocre. Its real function is to maintain inviolate the cohesion of society by sustaining the common consciousness in all its vigour. If that consciousness were thwarted so categorically, it would necessarily lose some of its power, were an emotional reaction from the community not forthcoming to make good that loss. Thus there would result a relaxation in the bonds of social solidarity. The consciousness must therefore be conspicuously reinforced the moment it meets with opposition. The sole means of doing so is to give voice to the unanimous aversion that the crime continues to evoke, and this by an official act, which can only mean suffering inflicted upon the wrongdoer. Thus, although a necessary outcome of the causes that give rise to it, this suffering is not a gratuitous act of cruelty. It is a sign indicating that the sentiments of the collectivity are still unchanged, that the communion of minds sharing the same beliefs remains absolute, and in this way the injury that the crime has inflicted upon society is made good. This is why it is right to maintain that the criminal should suffer in proportion to his crime, and why theories that deny to punishment any expiatory character appear, in the minds of many, to subvert the social order. In fact such theories could only be put into practice in a society from which almost every trace of the common consciousness has been expunged. Without this necessary act of satisfaction what is called the moral consciousness could not be preserved. Thus, without being paradoxical, we may state that punishment is above all intended to have its effect upon honest people. Since it serves to heal the wounds inflicted upon the collective sentiments, it can only fulfil this role where such sentiments exist, and in so far as they are active. Undoubtedly, by forestalling in minds already distressed any further weakening of the collective psyche, punishment can indeed prevent such attacks from multiplying. But such a result, useful though it is, is merely a particular side-effect. In short, to visualise an exact idea of punishment, the two opposing theories that have been advanced must be reconciled: the one sees in punishment an expiation, the other conceives it as a weapon for the defence of society. Certainly it does fulfil the function of protecting society, but this is because of its expiatory nature. Moreover, if it must be expiatory, this is not because suffering redeems error by virtue of some mystic strength or another, but because it cannot produce its socially useful effect save on this one condition.[5] [...]

Solidarity Arising from the Division of Labour, or Organic Solidarity

The very nature of the restitutory sanction is sufficient to show that the social solidarity to which that law corresponds is of a completely different kind.

The distinguishing mark of this sanction is that it is not expiatory, but comes down to a mere *restoration of the "status quo ante"*. Suffering in proportion to the offence is not inflicted upon the one who has broken the law or failed to acknowledge it; he is merely condemned to submit to it. If certain acts have already been performed, the judge restores them to what they should be. He pronounces what the law is, but does not talk of punishment. Damages awarded have no penal character: they are simply a means of putting back the clock so as to restore the past, so far as possible, to its normal state. It is true that Tarde believed that he had discovered a kind of civil penal law in the awarding of costs, which are always borne by the losing party. Yet taken in this sense the term has no more than a metaphorical value. For there to be punishment there should at least be some proportionality between the punishment and the wrong, and for this one would have to establish exactly the degree of seriousness of the wrong. In fact the loser of the case pays its costs even when his intentions were innocent and he is guilty of nothing more than ignorance. The reasons for this rule therefore seem to be entirely different. Since justice is not administered free, it seems equitable that the costs should be borne by the one who has occasioned them. Moreover, although it is possible that the prospect of such costs may stop the overhasty litigant, this is not enough for them to be considered a punishment. The fear of ruin that is normally consequent upon idleness and neglect may cause the businessman to be energetic and diligent. Yet ruin, in the exact connotation of the term, is not the penal sanction for his shortcomings.

Failure to observe these rules is not even sanctioned by a diffused form of punishment. The plaintiff who has lost his case is not disgraced, nor is his honour impugned. We can even envisage these rules being different from what they are without any feeling of repugnance. The idea that murder can be tolerated sets us up in arms, but we very readily accept that the law of inheritance might be modified, and many even conceive that it could be abolished. At least it is a question that we are not unwilling to discuss. Likewise, we agree without difficulty that the laws regarding easements or usufruct might be framed differently, or that the mutual obligations of buyer and vendor might be determined in another way, and that administrative functions might be allocated according to different principles. Since these prescriptions do not correspond to any feeling within us, and as generally we do not know their scientific justification, since this science does not yet exist, they have no deep roots in most of us. Doubtless there are exceptions. We do not tolerate the idea that an undertaking entered into that is contrary to morals or obtained either by violence or fraud can bind the contracting parties. Thus when public opinion is faced with cases of this kind it shows itself less indifferent than we have just asserted, and it adds its disapprobation to the legal sanction, causing it to weigh more heavily. This is because there are no clear-cut partitions between the various domains of moral life. On the contrary, they form a continuum, and consequently adjacent areas exist where different characteristics may be found at one and the same time. Nevertheless the proposition we have enunciated remains true in the overwhelming majority of cases. It demonstrates that rules where sanctions are restitutory either constitute no part at all of the collective consciousness, or subsist in it in only a weak state. Repressive law corresponds to what is the heart and centre of the common consciousness. Purely moral rules are already a less central part of it. Lastly, restitutory law springs from the farthest zones of consciousness and extends well beyond them. The more it becomes truly itself, the more it takes its distance.

This characteristic is moreover evinced in the way that it functions. Whereas repressive law tends to stay diffused throughout society, restitutory law sets up for itself ever more specialised bodies: consular courts, and industrial and administrative tribunals of every kind. Even in its most general sector, that of civil law, it is brought into use only by special officials – magistrates, lawyers, etc., who have been equipped for their role by a very special kind of training.

But although these rules are more or less outside the collective consciousness, they do not merely concern private individuals. If this were the case, restitutory law would have nothing in common with social solidarity, for the relationships it regulates would join individuals to one another without their being linked to society. They would be mere events of private life, as are, for instance, relationships of friendship. Yet it is far from the case that society is absent from this sphere of legal activity. Generally it is true that it does not intervene by itself and of its own volition: it must be solicited to do so by the parties concerned. Yet although it has to be invoked, its intervention is none the less the essential cog in the mechanism, since it alone causes that mechanism to function. It is society that declares what the law is, through its body of representatives.

However, it has been maintained that this role is in no way an especially social one, but comes down to being that of a conciliator of private interests. Consequently it has been held that any private individual could fulfil it, and that if society adopted it, this was solely for reasons of convenience. Yet it is wholly inaccurate to make society a kind of third-party arbitrator between the other parties. When it is induced to intervene it is not to reconcile the interests of individuals. It does not investigate what may be the most advantageous solution for the protagonists, nor does it suggest a compromise. But it does apply to the particular case submitted to it the general and traditional rules of the law. Yet the law is pre-eminently a social matter, whose object is absolutely different from the interests of the litigants. The judge who examines a divorce petition is not concerned to know whether this form of separation is really desirable for the husband and wife, but whether the causes invoked for it fall into one of the categories stipulated by law.

Yet to assess accurately the importance of the intervention by society it must be observed not only at the moment when the sanction is applied, or when the relationship that has been upset is restored, but also when it is instituted.

Social action is in fact necessary either to lay a foundation for, or to modify, a number of legal relationships regulated by this form of law, and which the assent of the interested parties is not adequate enough either to institute or alter. Of this nature are those relationships in particular that concern personal status. Although marriage is a contract, the partners can neither draw it up nor rescind it at will. The same holds good for all other domestic relationships, and *a fortiori* for all those regulated by administrative law. It is true that obligations that are properly contractual can be entered into or abrogated by the mere will to agreement of the parties. Yet we must bear in mind that, if a contract has binding force, it is society which confers that force. Let us assume that it does not give its blessing to the obligations that have been contracted; these then become pure promises possessing only moral authority.[6] Every contract therefore assumes that behind the parties who bind each other, society is there, quite prepared to intervene and to enforce respect for any undertakings entered into. Thus it only bestows this obligatory force upon contracts that have a social value in themselves, that is, those that are in conformity with the rules of law. We shall even occasionally see that its intervention is still more positive. It is therefore present in every relationship determined by restitutory law, even in ones that appear the most completely private, and its presence, although not felt, at least under normal conditions, is no less essential.

Since the rules where sanctions are restitutory do not involve the common consciousness, the relationships that they determine are not of the sort that affect everyone indiscriminately. This means that they are instituted directly, not between the individual and society, but between limited and particular elements in society, which they link to one another. Yet on the other hand, since society is not absent it must necessarily indeed be concerned to some extent, and feel some repercussions. Then, depending upon the intensity with which it feels them, it intervenes at a greater or lesser distance, and more or less actively, through the mediation of special bodies whose task it is to represent it. These relationships are therefore very different from those regulated by repressive law, for the latter join directly, without any intermediary, the individual consciousness to that of society, that is, the individual himself to society. [...]

(1) The first kind links the individual directly to society without any intermediary. With the second kind he depends upon society because he depends upon the parts that go to constitute it.

(2) In the two cases, society is not viewed from the same perspective. In the first, the term is used to denote a more or less organised society composed of beliefs and sentiments common to all the members of the group: this is the collective type. On the contrary, in the second case the society to which we are solidly joined is a system of different and special functions united by definite relationships. Moreover, these two societies are really one. They are two facets of one and the same reality, but which none the less need to be distinguished from each other.

(3) From this second difference there arises another which will serve to allow us to characterise and delineate the features of these two kinds of solidarity.

The first kind can only be strong to the extent that the ideas and tendencies common to all members of the society exceed in number and intensity those that appertain personally to each one of those members. The greater this excess, the more active this kind of society is. Now what constitutes our personality is that which each one of us possesses that is peculiar and characteristic, what distinguishes it from others. This solidarity can therefore only increase in inverse relationship to the personality. As we have said, there is in the consciousness of each one of us two consciousnesses: one that we share in common with our group in its entirety, which is consequently not ourselves, but society living and acting within us; the other that, on the contrary, represents us alone in what is personal and distinctive about us, what makes us an individual.[7] The solidarity that derives from similarities is at its *maximum* when the collective consciousness completely envelops our total consciousness, coinciding with it at every point. At that moment our individuality is zero. That individuality cannot arise until the community fills us less completely. Here there are two opposing forces, the one centripetal, the other centrifugal, which cannot increase at the same time. We cannot ourselves develop simultaneously in two so opposing directions. If we have a strong inclination to think and act for ourselves we cannot be strongly inclined to think and act like other people. If the ideal is to create for ourselves a special, personal image, this cannot mean to be like everyone else. Moreover, at the very moment when this solidarity exerts its effect, our personality, it may be said by definition, disappears, for we are no longer ourselves, but a collective being.

The social molecules that can only cohere in this one manner cannot therefore move as a unit save in so far as they lack any movement of their own, as do the molecules of inorganic bodies. This is why we suggest that this kind of solidarity should be called mechanical. The word does not mean that the solidarity is produced by mechanical and artificial means. We only use this term for it by analogy with the cohesion that links together the elements of raw materials, in contrast to that which encompasses the unity of living organisms. What finally justifies the use of this term is the fact that the bond that thus unites the individual with society is completely analogous to that which links the thing to the person. The individual consciousness, considered from this viewpoint, is simply a dependency of the collective type, and follows all its motions, just as the object possessed follows those which its owner imposes upon it. In societies where this solidarity is highly developed the individual does not belong to himself; he is literally a thing at the disposal of society. Thus, in these same social types, personal rights are still not yet distinguished from 'real' rights.

The situation is entirely different in the case of solidarity that brings about the division of labour. Whereas the other solidarity implies that individuals resemble one another, the latter assumes that they are different from one another. The former type is only possible in so far as the individual personality is absorbed into the collective personality; the latter is only possible if each one of us has a sphere of action that is peculiarly our own, and consequently a personality. Thus the collective consciousness leaves uncovered a part of the individual consciousness, so that there may be established in it those special functions that it cannot regulate. The more extensive this free area is, the stronger the cohesion that arises from this solidarity. Indeed, on the one hand each one of us depends more intimately upon society the more labour is divided up, and on the other, the activity of each one of us is correspondingly more specialised, the more personal it is. Doubtless, however circumscribed that activity may be, it is never completely original. Even in the exercise of our profession we conform to usages and practices that are common to us all within our corporation. Yet even in this case, the burden that we bear is in a different way less heavy than when the whole of society bears down upon us, and this leaves much more room for the free play of our initiative. Here, then, the individuality of the whole grows at the same time as that of the parts. Society becomes more effective in moving in concert, at the same time as each of its elements has more movements that are peculiarly its own. This solidarity resembles that observed in the higher animals. In fact each organ has its own special characteristics and autonomy, yet the greater the unity of the organism, the more marked the individualisation of the parts. Using the analogy, we propose to call 'organic' the solidarity that is due to the division of labour. [...]

The Causes

Thus it is in certain variations of the social environment that we must seek the cause that explains the progress of the division of labour.

In fact we have seen that the organised structure, and consequently the division of labour, develops regularly as the segmentary structure vanishes. It is therefore this disappearance that is the cause of this development; alternatively, the latter may be the cause of the former. This last hypothesis is not acceptable, for we know that the segmentary arrangement is an insurmountable obstacle to the division of labour and that the arrangement must have disappeared, at least in part, for the division of labour to be able to appear. It can only do so when the arrangement no longer exists. Undoubtedly once the division of labour exists it can contribute to speeding up its disappearance, but it only becomes apparent after the segmentary arrangement has partly receded. The effect reacts upon the cause, but does not in consequence cease to be an effect. Thus the reaction that it exerts is a secondary one. The increase in the division of labour is therefore due to the fact that the social segments lose their individuality, that the partitions dividing them become more permeable. In short, there occurs between them a coalescence that renders the social substance free to enter upon new combinations.

But the disappearance of this type can only bring about this result for the following reason. It is because there occurs a drawing together of individuals who were separated from one another, or at least they draw more closely together than they had been. Hence movements take place between the parts of the social mass which up to then had no reciprocal effect upon one another. The more the alveolar system is developed, the more the relationships in which each one of us is involved become enclosed within the limits of the alveola to which we belong. There are, as it were, moral vacuums between the various segments. On the other hand these vacuums fill up as the system levels off. Social life, instead of concentrating itself in innumerable small foci that are distinct but alike, becomes general. Social relationships – more exactly we should say intra-social relationships – consequently become more numerous, since they push out beyond their original boundaries on all sides. Thus the division of labour progresses the more individuals there are who are sufficiently in contact with one another to be able mutually to act and react upon one another. If we agree to call dynamic or moral density this drawing together and the active exchanges that result from it, we can say that the progress of the division of labour is in direct proportion to the moral or dynamic density of society.

But this act of drawing together morally can only bear fruit if the real distance between individuals has itself diminished, in whatever manner. Moral density cannot therefore increase without physical density increasing at the same time, and the latter can serve to measure the extent of the former. Moreover, it is useless to investigate which of the two has influenced the other; it suffices to realise that they are inseparable.

The progressive increase in density of societies in the course of their historical development occurs in three main ways:

(1) Whilst lower societies spread themselves over areas that are relatively vast in comparison with the number of individuals that constitute them, amongst more advanced peoples the population is continually becoming more concentrated. Spencer says: "If we contrast the populousness of regions inhabited by wild tribes with the populousness of equal regions in Europe; or if we contrast the density of population in England under the Heptarchy with its present density; we see that besides the growth produced by union of groups there has gone an interstitial growth."

The changes wrought successively in the industrial life of nations demonstrate how general this transformation is. The activity of nomadic tribes, whether hunters or shepherds, entails in fact the absence of any kind of concentration and dispersion over as wide an area as possible. Agriculture, because it is of necessity a settled existence, already presumes a certain drawing together of the social tissues, but one still very incomplete, since between each family tracts of land are interposed. In the city, although the condensation process was greater, yet houses did not adjoin one another, for joined building was not known in Roman law. This was invented on our own soil and demonstrates that the social ties have become tighter.[8] Moreover, from their origins European societies have seen their density increase continuously in spite of a few cases of temporary regression.

(2) The formation and development of towns are a further symptom, even more characteristic, of the same phenomenon. The increase in average density can be due solely to the physical increase in the birth rate and can consequently be reconciled with a very weak concentration of people, and the very marked maintenance of the segmentary type of society. But towns always result from the need that drives individuals to keep constantly in the closest possible contact with one another. They are like so many points where the social mass is contracting more strongly than elsewhere. They cannot therefore multiply and spread out unless the moral density increases. Moreover, we shall see that towns recruit their numbers through migration to them, which is only possible to the extent that the fusion of social segments is far advanced.

So long as the social organisation is essentially segmentary, towns do not exist. There are none in lower societies; they are not met with among the Iroquois, nor among the primitive German tribes. The same was true for the primitive populations of Italy. "The peoples of Italy," states Marquardt, "originally used not to live in towns, but in family or village communities (*pagi*), over which farms (*vici*, οἶχοί) were scattered." Yet after a fairly short period of time the town made its appearance. Athens and Rome were or became towns, and the same transformation was accomplished throughout Italy. In our Christian societies the town appears from the very beginning, for those that the Roman Empire had left behind did not disappear with it. Since then, they have not ceased to grow and multiply. The tendency of country dwellers to flow into the towns, so general in the civilised world, is only a consequence of this movement. But this phenomenon does not date from the present day: from the seventeenth century onwards it preoccupied statesmen.

Because societies generally start with an agricultural period we have occasionally been tempted to regard the development of urban centres as a sign of old age and decadence. But we must not lose sight of the fact that this agricultural phase is the shorter the more societies belong to a higher type. Whilst in Germany, among the American Indians and among all primitive peoples, it lasts as long as do these peoples themselves, in Rome or Athens it ceases fairly early on, and in France we may say that this agricultural state has never existed in a pure form. Conversely, urban life begins very early on, and consequently extends itself more. The regularly quicker acceleration of this development demonstrates that, far from constituting a kind of pathological phenomenon, it derives from the very nature of the higher social species. Even supposing therefore that today this movement has reached threatening proportions for our societies, which perhaps have no longer sufficient flexibility to adapt to it, it will not cease to continue, either through them, or after them, and the social types to be formed after our own will probably be distinguished by a more rapid and more complete regression of agricultural society.

(3) Finally, there is the number and speed of the means of communication and transmission. By abolishing or lessening the vacuums separating social segments, these means increase the density of society. Moreover, there is no need to demonstrate that they are the more numerous and perfect the higher the type of society.

Since this visible and measurable symbol reflects the variations in what we have termed moral density,[9] we can substitute this symbol for the latter in the formula that we have put forward. We must, moreover, repeat here what we were saying earlier. If society, in concentrating itself, determines the development of the division of labour, the latter in its turn increases the concentration of society. But this is of no consequence, for the division of labour remains the derived action, and consequently the advances it makes are due to a parallel progress in social density, whatever may be the cause of this progress. This all we wished to establish.

But this factor is not the only one.

If the concentration of society produces this result, it is because it multiplies intrasocial relationships. But these will be even more numerous if the total number of members in a society also becomes larger. If it includes more individuals, as well as their being in closer contact, the effect will necessarily be reinforced. Social volume has therefore the same influence over the division of labour as density.

In fact, societies are generally more voluminous the more advanced they are and consequently labour is more divided up in them. Spencer says that, 'Societies, like living bodies, begin as germs – originate from masses which are extremely minute in comparison with the masses some of them eventually reach. That out of small wandering hordes such as the lowest races now form, have arisen the largest societies, is a conclusion not to be contested.'

What we have said about the segmentary constitution makes this unquestionably true. We know in fact that societies are formed by a certain number of segments of unequal size that overlap with one another. These moulds are not artificial creations, particularly in the beginning. Even when they have become conventional they imitate and reproduce so far as possible the forms of natural arrangement that preceded them. Many ancient societies are maintained in this form. The largest among these subdivisions, those that include the others, correspond to the nearest lower social type. Likewise, among the segments of which they in turn are made up, the most extensive are the remains of the type that comes directly below the preceding one, and so on. Among the most advanced peoples we find traces of the most primitive social organisation. Thus the tribe is made up of an aggregate of hordes or clans; the nation (the Jewish nation, for example) and the city, of an aggregate of tribes; the city, in its turn, with the villages that are subordinate to it, is one element that enters into the most complex societies, etc. The social volume therefore cannot fail to grow, since each species is made up of a replication of societies of the immediately preceding species.

Yet there are exceptions. The Jewish nation, before the conquest, was probably more voluminous than the Roman city of the fourth century; yet it was of a lower species. China and Russia are much more populous than the most civilised nations in Europe. Consequently among these same peoples the division of labour did not develop in proportion to the social volume. This is because the growth in volume is not necessarily a mark of superiority if the density does not grow at the same time and in the same proportion. A society can reach very large dimensions because it contains a very large number of segments, whatever may be the nature of these. If therefore the largest of them only reproduces societies of a very inferior type, the segmentary structure will remain very pronounced, and in consequence the social organisation will be little advanced. An aggregate of clans, even if immense, ranks below the smallest society that is organised, since the latter has already gone through those stages of evolution below which the aggregate has remained. Likewise if the number of social units has some influence over the division of labour, it is not through itself and of necessity, but because the number of social relationships increases generally with the number of individuals. To obtain this result it is not enough for the society to comprise a large number of persons, but they must be in fairly intimate contact so as to act and react upon one another. If on the other hand they are separated by environments that are mutually impenetrable, only very rarely, and with difficulty, can they establish relationships, and everything occurs as if the number of people was small. An increase in social volume therefore does not always speed up the progress of the division of labour, but only when the mass condenses at the same time and to the same degree. Consequently it is, one may say, only an additional factor. Yet, when joined to the first factor, it extends the effects by an action peculiarly its own, and thus requires to be distinguished from it.

We can therefore formulate the following proposition:

The division of labour varies in direct proportion to the volume and density of societies and if it progresses in a continuous manner over the course of social development it is because societies become regularly more dense and generally more voluminous.

At all times, it is true, it has been clearly understood that there was a relationship between these two orders of facts. This is because, for functions to specialise even more, there must be additional co-operating elements, which must be grouped close enough together to be able to co-operate. Yet in societies in this condition we usually see hardly more than the means by which the division of labour is developed, and not the cause of this development. The cause is made to depend upon individual aspirations towards wellbeing and happiness, which can be the better satisfied when societies are more extensive and more condensed. The law we have just established is completely different. We state, not that the growth and condensation of societies *permit* a greater division of labour, but that they *necessitate* it. It is not the instrument whereby that division is brought about; but it is its determining cause.[10] [...]

The Anomic Division of Labour

Although Auguste Comte recognised that the division of labour is a source of solidarity, he does not appear to have perceived that this solidarity is *sui generis* and is gradually substituted for that which social similarities engender. This is why, noticing that these similarities are very blurred where the functions are very specialised, he saw in this process of disappearance a morbid phenomenon, a threat to social cohesion, due to excessive specialisation. He explained in this way the fact of the lack of co-ordination which sometimes accompanies the development of the division of labour. Yet since we have established that the weakening of the collective consciousness is a normal phenomenon, we could not make it the cause of the abnormal phenomena we are at present studying. If in certain cases organic solidarity is not all that is needful, it is certainly not because mechanical solidarity has lost ground, but because all the conditions of existence for the former have not been realised.

Indeed we know that wherever it is to be observed, we meet at the same time a regulatory system sufficiently developed to determine the mutual relationships between functions. For organic solidarity to exist it is not enough for there to be a system of organs necessary to one another that feel their solidarity in a general way. The manner in which they should co-operate, if not on every kind of occasion when they meet, at least in the most common circumstances, must be predetermined. Otherwise, a fresh struggle would be required each time in order to bring them into a state of equilibrium with one another, for the conditions for this equilibrium can only be found by a process of trial and error, in the course of which each party treats the other as an opponent as much as an auxiliary. Such conflicts would therefore break out continually, and in consequence solidarity would be hardly more than virtual, and the mutual obligations would have to be negotiated anew in their entirety for each individual case. It will be objected that contracts exist. But firstly, not every social relationship is capable of assuming this legal form. Moreover, we know that a contract is not sufficient in itself, but supposes a regulatory system that extends and grows more complicated just as does contractual life itself. Moreover, the ties originating in this way are always of short duration. The contract is only a truce, and a fairly precarious one at that; it suspends hostilities only for a while. Doubtless, however precise the regulatory system may be, it will always leave room for much dispute. But it is neither necessary nor even possible for social life to be without struggle. The role of solidarity is not to abolish competition but to moderate it.

Moreover, in the normal state, these rules emerge automatically from the division of labour; they are, so to speak, its prolongation. Certainly if the division of labour only brought together individuals who unite for a brief space of time with a view to the exchange of personal services, it could not give rise to any regulatory process. But what it evokes are functions, that is, definite ways of acting that are repeated identically in given circumstances, since they relate to the general unchanging conditions of social life. The relationships entertained between these functions cannot therefore fail to arrive at the same level of stability and regularity. There are certain ways of reacting upon one another which, being more in accordance with the nature of things, are repeated more often and become habits. Then the habits, as they grow in strength, are transformed into rules of conduct. The past predetermines the future. In other words, there exists a certain allocation of rights and duties that is established by usage and that ends up by becoming obligatory. Thus the rule does not set up the state of mutual dependence in which the solidly linked organs are to be found, but only serves to express it in a perceptible, definite way, as a function of a given situation. Likewise the nervous system, far from dominating the evolution of the organism, as was once believed, is a result of it. The nerve tracts are probably only the paths along which have passed the wave-like movements and stimuli exchanged between the various organs. They are the channels that life has dug for itself by always flowing in the same direction, and the ganglions would only be the place where several of these paths intersect. It is because they have failed to recognise this aspect of the phenomenon that certain moralists have charged the division of labour with not producing real solidarity. They have seen in it only individual exchanges, ephemeral combinations, without a past, just as they also have no tomorrow, in which the individual is abandoned to his own devices. They have not perceived that slow task of consolidation, that network of ties that gradually becomes woven of its own accord and that makes organic solidarity something that is permanent.

Now, in all the cases we have described above, this regulatory process either does not exist or is not related to the degree of development of the division of labour. Nowadays there are no longer any rules that fix the number of economic undertakings, and in each branch of industry production is not regulated in such a way that it remains exactly at the level of consumption. Moreover, we do not wish to draw from this fact any practical conclusion. We do not maintain that restrictive legislation is necessary. We have not to weigh here the advantages and disadvantages. What is certain is that this lack of regulation does not allow the functions to perform regularly and harmoniously. The economists show, it is true, that harmony is re-established by itself when necessary, thanks to the increase or decrease in prices, which, according to the need, stimulates or slows production. But in any case it is not re-established in this way until after breaks in equilibrium and more or less prolonged disturbances have occurred. Moreover, such disturbances are naturally all the more frequent the more specialised the functions, for the more complex an organisation is, the more the necessity for extensive regulation is felt.

The relationships between capital and labour have up to now remained in the same legal state of indeterminacy. The contract for the hiring of services occupies in our legal codes a very small place, particularly when we consider the diversity and complexity of the relationships it is called upon to regulate. Moreover, we need emphasise no further the deficiencies that all peoples feel at the present time and that they are attempting to remedy.

Methodological rules are to science what rules of law and morality are to conduct. They direct the thinking of the scientist just as the latter govern the actions of men. Yet if every science has its method, the order that is established is entirely an internal one. The method co-ordinates the procedures followed by scientists who are studying the same science, but not their relationships externally. There are hardly any disciplines that harmonise the efforts of the different sciences towards a common goal. This is especially true of the moral and social sciences, for the mathematical, physical, chemical and even biological sciences do not seem to such an extent foreign to one another. But the jurist, the psychologist, the anthropologist, the economist, the statistician, the linguist, the historian – all these go about their investigations as if the various orders of facts that they are studying formed so many independent worlds. Yet in reality these facts interlock with one another at every point. Consequently the same should occur for the corresponding sciences. This is how there has arisen the anarchy that has been pinpointed – moreover, not without some exaggeration – in science generally, but that is above all true for these special sciences. Indeed they afford the spectacle of an aggregate of disconnected parts that fail to co-operate with one another. If they therefore form a whole lacking in unity, it is not because there is no adequate view of their similarities, it is because they are not organised.

These various examples are therefore varieties of the same species. In all these cases, if the division of labour does not produce solidarity it is because the relationships between the organs are not regulated; it is because they are in a state of *anomie*.

But from where does this state spring?

Since a body of rules is the definite form taken over time by the relationships established spontaneously between the social functions, we may say *a priori* that a state of *anomie* is impossible wherever organs solidly linked to one another are in sufficient contact, and in sufficiently lengthy contact. Indeed, being adjacent to one another, they are easily alerted in every situation to the need for one another and consequently they experience a keen, continuous feeling of their mutual dependence. For the same reason, exchanges between them occur easily; being regular, they occur frequently; they regulate themselves and time gradually effects the task of consolidation. Finally, because the slightest reaction can be felt throughout, the rules formed in this way bear the mark of it, that is, they foresee and fix in some detail the conditions of equilibrium. Yet if, on the other hand, some blocking environment is interposed between them, only stimuli of a certain intensity can communicate from one organ to another. Contacts being rare, they are not repeated often enough to take on a determinate form. Each time the procedure is again one of trial and error. The paths along which pass the wave-like movements can no longer become definite channels because the waves themselves are too intermittent. If at least some rules are successfully constituted, these are general and vague, for in these conditions only the most general outlines of the phenomena can be fixed. The same is true of closeness of contact: whilst it is sufficient, it is too recent or has lasted too short a while.[11]

Very generally this condition of contiguity is realised by the nature of things. For a function cannot distribute itself between two or more parts of an organism unless these parts are more or less in contact. Moreover, once labour is divided up, as they have need of one another, they tend naturally to reduce the distance that separates them. This is why, as one rises in the animal scale, one sees organs growing closer together and, as Spencer puts it, insinuating themselves into one another's interstices. But a coincidence of exceptional circumstances can cause it to be otherwise.

This is what occurs in the cases with which we are dealing at present. So long as the segmentary type of society is strongly marked, there are roughly as many economic markets as there are different segments. In consequence, each one of them is very limited. The producers, being very close to the consumers, can easily estimate the extent of the needs that have to be satisfied. The equilibrium is therefore established without difficulty and production is regulated by itself. On the contrary, as the organised type of society develops, the fusion of the various segments entails the fusion of the markets into one single market, which embraces almost all of society. It even extends beyond and tends to become universal, for the barriers between peoples are lowered at the same time as those that separate the segments within each one of them. The result is that each industry produces for consumers who are dispersed over the length and breadth of the country, or even the whole world. The contact is therefore no longer sufficient. The producer can no longer keep the whole market within his purview, not even mentally. He can no longer figure out to himself its limits, since it is, so to speak, unlimited. Consequently production lacks any check or regulation. It can only proceed at random, and in the course of so doing it is inevitable that the yardstick is wrong, either in one way or the other. Hence the crises that periodically disturb economic functions. The increase in those local and limited crises represented by bankruptcies is likely to be an effect of the same cause.

As the market becomes more extensive, large-scale industry appears. The effect of it is to transform the relationship between employers and workers. The greater fatigue occasioned to the nervous system, linked to the contagious influence of large urban areas, causes the needs of the workers to increase. Machine work replaces that of the man, manufacturing that of the small workshop. The worker is regimented, removed for the whole day from his family. He lives ever more apart from the person who employs him, etc. These new conditions of industrial life naturally require a new organisation. Yet because these transformations have been accomplished with extreme rapidity the conflicting interests have not had time to strike an equilibrium.[12]

NOTES

1 Such a confusion is not without its dangers. Thus it is occasionally asked whether the individual consciousness varies with the collective consciousness. Everything depends on the meaning assigned to the term. If it represents social similarities, the variation, as will be seen, is one of inverse relationship. If it designates the entire psychological life of society, the relationship is direct. Hence the need to draw a distinction.

2   We shall not go into the question as to whether the collective consciousness is like that of the individual. For us this term merely designates the sum total of social similarities, without prejudice to the category by which this system of phenomena must be defined.
3   In order to simplify our exposition we assume that the individual belongs to only one society. In fact we form a part of several groups and there exist in us several collective consciousnesses; but this complication does not in any way change the relationship we are establishing.
4   This does not mean that a penal rule should nonetheless be retained because at some given moment it corresponded to a particular collective feeling. The rule has no justification unless the feeling is still alive and active. If it has disappeared or grown weak nothing is so vain or even counter-productive as to attempt to preserve it artificially by force. It may even happen to become necessary to fight against a practice that was common once, but is no longer so, one that militates against the establishment of new and essential practices. But we need not enter into this problem of a casuistic nature.
5   In saying that punishment, as it is, has a reason for its existence we do not mean that it is perfect and cannot be improved upon. On the contrary, it is only too plain that, since it is produced by purely mechanical causes, it can only be very imperfectly attuned to its role. The justification can only be a rough and ready one.
6   Even that moral authority derives from custom, and hence from society.
7   Nevertheless these two consciousnesses are not regions of ourselves that are "geographically" distinct, for they interpenetrate each other at every point.
8   By reasoning in this way we do not mean that the increase in density is the result of economic changes. The two facts have a mutual conditioning effect upon each other, and this suffices for the presence of the one to attest to the presence of the other.
9   However, there are special cases of an exceptional kind, where material density and moral density are perhaps not entirely in proportion.
10 On this point we can again rely upon the authority of Comte. "I need only," he says, "point now to the progressive increase in density of our species as an ultimate general factor helping to regulate the effective rapidity of social movement. First, therefore, one may freely recognise that this influence contributes a great deal, above all at the beginning, in determining for human labour as a whole its increasingly specialised division, which is necessarily incompatible with a small number of people co-operating together. *Moreover, by a more intimate and less well-known property, although of even greater importance, such a densifying process directly and very powerfully stimulates the swifter development in social evolution*, either by stimulating individuals to put forth fresh efforts using refined methods, in order to ensure for themselves an existence which otherwise would become more difficult, or by obliging society also to react with greater energy and persistence, and in more concerted fashion, struggling against the increasedly powerful upsurge of particular divergences. On both counts we see that here it is not a question of the absolute increase in the number of individuals, but above all of the more intense competition between them in a given area" (*Cours de philosophie positive*, vol. IV, p. 455).
11 There is, however, one case where *anomie* can occur, although the contiguity is sufficient. This is when the necessary regulation can only be established at the expense of transformations that the social structure is no longer capable of carrying out, for the malleability of societies is not indefinite. When it has reached its limit, even necessary changes are impossible.
12 Let us nevertheless remember that this antagonism is not due wholly to the speed of these transformations, but to a considerable extent to the still too great inequality in the external conditions of the struggle. Over this factor time has no effect.

Chapter 17

The Elementary Forms of the Religious Life [1912]

Emile Durkheim

We cannot arrive at an understanding of the most recent religions except by following the manner in which they have been progressively composed in history. In fact, historical analysis is the only means of explanation which it is possible to apply to them. It alone enables us to resolve an institution into its constituent elements, for it shows them to us as they are born in time, one after another. On the other hand, by placing every one of them in the condition where it was born, it puts into our hands the only means we have of determining the causes which gave rise to it. Every time that we undertake to explain something human, taken at a given moment in history – be it a religious belief, a moral precept, a legal principle, an aesthetic style or an economic system – it is necessary to commence by going back to its most primitive and simple form, to try to account for the characteristics by which it was marked at that time, and then to show how it developed and became complicated little by little, and how it became that which it is at the moment in question. One readily understands the importance which the determination of the point of departure has for this series of progressive explanations, for all the others are attached to it. It was one of Descartes's principles that the first ring has a predominating place in the chain of scientific truths. But there is no question of placing at the foundation of the science of religions an idea elaborated after the Cartesian manner, that is to say, a logical concept, a pure possibility, constructed simply by force of thought. What we must find is a concrete reality, and historical and ethnological observation alone can reveal that to us. But even if this cardinal conception is obtained by a different process than that of Descartes, it remains true that it is destined to have a considerable influence on the whole series of propositions which the science establishes. Biological evolution has been conceived quite differently ever since it has been known that monocellular beings do exist. In the same way, the arrangement of religious facts is explained quite differently, according as we put naturism, animism or some other religious form at the beginning of the evolution. Even the most specialized scholars, if they are unwilling to confine themselves to a task of pure erudition, and if they desire to interpret the facts which they analyse, are obliged to choose one of these hypotheses, and make it their starting-point. Whether they desire it or not, the questions which they raise necessarily take the following form: how has naturism or animism been led to take this particular form, here or there, or to enrich itself or impoverish itself in such and such a fashion? Since it is impossible to avoid taking sides on this initial problem, and since the solution given is destined to affect the whole science, it must be attacked at the outset: this is what we propose to do.

Besides this, outside of these indirect reactions, the study of primitive religions has of itself an immediate interest which is of primary importance.

If it is useful to know what a certain particular religion consists in, it is still more important to know what religion in general is. This is the problem which has aroused the interest of philosophers in all times; and not without reason, for it is of interest to all humanity. Unfortunately, the method which they generally employ is purely dialectic: they confine themselves to analysing the idea which they make for themselves of religion, except as they illustrate the results of this mental analysis by examples borrowed from the religions which best realize their ideal. But even if this method ought to be abandoned, the problem remains intact, and the great service of philosophy is to have prevented its being suppressed by the disdain of scholars. Now it is possible to attack it in a different way. Since all religions can be compared to each other, and since all are species of the same class, there are necessarily many elements which are common to all. We do not mean to speak simply of the outward and visible characteristics which they all have equally, and which make it possible to give them a provisional definition from the very outset of our researches; the discovery of these apparent signs is relatively easy, for the observation which it demands does not go beneath the surface of things. But these external resemblances suppose others which are profound. At the foundation of all systems of beliefs and of all cults there ought necessarily to be a certain number of fundamental representations or conceptions and of ritual attitudes which, in spite of the diversity of forms which they have taken, have the same objective significance and fulfil the same functions everywhere. These are the permanent elements which constitute that which is permanent and human in religion; they form all the objective contents of the idea which is expressed when one speaks of *religion* in general. How is it possible to pick them out?

Surely it is not by observing the complex religions which appear in the course of history. Every one of these is made up of such a variety of elements that it is very difficult to distinguish what is secondary from what is principal, the essential from the accessory. Suppose that the religion considered is like that of Egypt, India or the classical antiquity. It is a confused mass of many cults, varying according to the locality, the temples, the generations, the dynasties, the invasions, etc. Popular superstitions are there confused with the purest dogmas. Neither the thought nor the activity of the religion is evenly distributed among the believers; according to the men, the environment and the circumstances, the beliefs as well as the rites are thought of in different ways. Here they are priests, there they are monks, elsewhere they are laymen; there are mystics and rationalists, theologians and prophets, etc. In these conditions it is difficult to see what is common to all. In one or another of these systems it is quite possible to find the means of making a profitable study of some particular fact which is specially developed there, such as sacrifice or prophecy, monasticism or the mysteries; but how is it possible to find the common foundation of the religious life underneath the luxuriant vegetation which covers it? How is it possible to find, underneath the disputes of theology, the variations of ritual, the multiplicity of groups and the diversity of individuals, the fundamental states characteristic of religious mentality in general?

Things are quite different in the lower societies. The slighter development of individuality, the small extension of the group, the homogeneity of external circumstances, all contribute to reducing the differences and variations to a minimum. The group has an intellectual and moral conformity of which we find but rare examples in the more advanced societies. Everything is common to all. Movements are stereotyped; everybody performs the same ones in the same circumstances, and this conformity of conduct only translates the conformity of thought. Every mind being drawn into the same eddy, the individual type nearly confounds itself with that of the race. And while all is uniform, all is simple as well. Nothing is deformed like these myths, all composed of one and the same theme which is endlessly repeated, or like these rites made up of a small number of gestures repeated again and again. Neither the popular imagination nor that of the priests has had either the time or the means of refining and transforming the original substance of the religious ideas and practices; these are shown in all their nudity, and offer themselves to an examination, it requiring only the slightest effort to lay them open. That which is accessory or secondary, the development of luxury, has not yet come to hide the principal elements.[1] All is reduced to that which is indispensable, to that without which there could be no religion. But that which is indispensable is also that which is essential, that is to say, that which we must know before all else.

Primitive civilizations offer privileged cases, then, because they are simple cases. That is why, in all fields of human activity, the observations of ethnologists have frequently been veritable revelations, which have renewed the study of human institutions. For example, before the middle of the nineteenth century, everybody was convinced that the father was the essential element of the family; no one had dreamed that there could be a family organization of which the paternal authority was not the keystone. But the discovery of Bachofen came and upset this old conception. Up to very recent times it was regarded as evident that the moral and legal relations of kindred were only another aspect of the psychological relations which result from a common descent; Bachofen and his successors, MacLennan,

Morgan and many others still laboured under this misunderstanding. But since we have become acquainted with the nature of the primitive clan, we know that, on the contrary, relationships cannot be explained by consanguinity. To return to religions, the study of only the most familiar ones had led men to believe for a long time that the idea of god was characteristic of everything that is religious. Now the religion which we are going to study presently is, in a large part, foreign to all idea of divinity; the forces to which the rites are there addressed are very different from those which occupy the leading place in our modern religions, yet they aid us in understanding these latter forces. So nothing is more unjust than the disdain with which too many historians still regard the work of ethnographers. Indeed, it is certain that ethnology has frequently brought about the most fruitful revolutions in the different branches of sociology. It is for this same reason that the discovery of unicellular beings, of which we just spoke, has transformed the current idea of life. Since in these very simple beings, life is reduced to its essential traits, these are less easily misunderstood.

But primitive religions do not merely aid us in disengaging the constituent elements of religion; they also have the great advantage that they facilitate the explanation of it. Since the facts there are simpler, the relations between them are more apparent. The reasons with which men account for their acts have not yet been elaborated and denatured by studied reflection; they are nearer and more closely related to the motives which have really determined these acts.

[...]

But our study is not of interest merely for the science of religion. In fact, every religion has one side by which it overlaps the circle of properly religious ideas, and there, the study of religious phenomena gives a means of renewing the problems which, up to the present, have only been discussed among philosophers.

For a long time it has been known that the first systems of representations with which men have pictured to themselves the world and themselves were of religious origin. There is no religion that is not a cosmology at the same time that it is a speculation upon divine things. If philosophy and the sciences were born of religion, it is because religion began by taking the place of the sciences and philosophy. But it has been less frequently noticed that religion has not confined itself to enriching the human intellect, formed beforehand, with a certain number of ideas; it has contributed to forming the intellect itself. Men owe to it not only a good part of the substance of their knowledge, but also the form in which this knowledge has been elaborated.

At the roots of all our judgments there are a certain number of essential ideas which dominate all our intellectual life, they are what philosophers since Aristotle have called the categories of the understanding: ideas of time, space,[2] class, number, cause, substance, personality, etc. They correspond to the most universal properties of things. They are like the solid frame which encloses all thought; this does not seem to be able to liberate itself from them without destroying itself, for it seems that we cannot think of objects that are not in time and space, which have no number, etc. Other ideas are contingent and unsteady; we can conceive of their being unknown to a man, a society or an epoch; but these others appear to be nearly inseparable from the normal working of the intellect. They are like the framework of the intelligence. Now when primitive religious beliefs are systematically analysed, the principal categories are naturally found. They are born in religion and of religion; they are a product of religious thought. [...]

The fundamental proposition of the apriorist theory is that knowledge is made up of two sorts of elements, which cannot be reduced into one another, and which are like two distinct layers superimposed one upon the other.[3] Our hypothesis keeps this principle intact. In fact, that knowledge which is called empirical, the only knowledge of which the theorists of empiricism have made use in constructing the reason, is that which is brought into our minds by the direct action of objects. It is composed of individual states which are completely explained[4] by the psychical nature of the individual. If, on the other hand, the categories are, as we believe they are, essentially collective representations, before all else, they should show the mental states of the group; they should depend upon the way in which this is founded and organized, upon its morphology, upon its religious, moral and economic institutions, etc. So between these two sorts of representations there is all the difference which exists between the individual and the social, and one can no more derive the second from the first than he can deduce society from the individual, the whole from the part, the complex from the simple.[5] Society is a reality *sui generis*; it has its own peculiar characteristics, which are not found elsewhere and which are not met with again in the same form in all the rest of the universe. The representations which express it have a wholly different contents from purely individual ones and we may rest assured in advance that the first add something to the second.

Even the manner in which the two are formed results in differentiating them. Collective representations are the result of an immense co-operation, which stretches out not only into space but into time as well; to make them, a multitude of minds have associated, united and combined their ideas and sentiments; for them, long generations have accumulated their experience and their knowledge. A special intellectual activity is therefore concentrated in them which is infinitely richer and complexer than that of the individual. From that one can understand how the reason has been able to go beyond the limits of empirical knowledge. It does not owe this to any vague mysterious virtue but simply to the fact that according to the well-known formula, man is double. There are two beings in him: an individual being which has its foundation in the organism and the circle of whose activities is therefore strictly limited, and a social being which represents the highest reality in the intellectual and moral order that we can know by observation – I mean society. This duality of our nature has as its consequence in the practical order, the irreducibility of a moral ideal to a utilitarian motive, and in the order of thought, the irreducibility of reason to individual experience. In so far as he belongs to society, the individual transcends himself, both when he thinks and when he acts.

This same social character leads to an understanding of the origin of the necessity of the categories. It is said that an idea is necessary when it imposes itself upon the mind by some sort of virtue of its own, without being accompanied by any proof. It contains within it something which constrains the intelligence and which leads to its acceptance without preliminary examination. The apriorist postulates this singular quality, but does not account for it; for saying that the categories are necessary because they are indispensable to the functioning of the intellect is simply repeating that they are necessary. But if they really have the origin which we attribute to them, their ascendancy no longer has anything surprising in it. They represent the most general relations which exist between things; surpassing all our other ideas in extension, they dominate all the details of our intellectual life. If men did not agree upon these essential ideas at every moment, if they did not have the same conception of time, space, cause, number, etc., all contact between their minds would be impossible, and with that, all life together. Thus society could not abandon the categories to the free choice of the individual without abandoning itself. If it is to live there is not merely need of a satisfactory moral conformity, but also there is a minimum of logical conformity beyond which it cannot safely go. For this reason it uses all its authority upon its members to forestall such dissidences. Does a mind ostensibly free itself from these forms of thought? It is no longer considered a human mind in the full sense of the word, and is treated accordingly. That is why we feel that we are no longer completely free and that something resists, both within and outside ourselves, when we attempt to rid ourselves of these fundamental notions, even in our own conscience. Outside of us there is public opinion which judges us; but more than that, since society is also represented inside of us, it sets itself against these revolutionary fancies, even inside of ourselves; we have the feeling that we cannot abandon them if our whole thought is not to cease being really human. This seems to be the origin of the exceptional authority which is inherent in the reason and which makes us accept its suggestions with confidence. It is the very authority of society,[6] transferring itself to a certain manner of thought which is the indispensable condition of all common action. The necessity with which the categories are imposed upon us is not the effect of simple habits whose yoke we could easily throw off with a little effort; nor is it a physical or metaphysical necessity, since the categories change in different places and times; it is a special sort of moral necessity which is to the intellectual life what moral obligation is to the will.[7]

But if the categories originally only translate social states, does it not follow that they can be applied to the rest of nature only as metaphors? If they were made merely to express social conditions, it seems as though they could not be extended to other realms except in this sense. Thus in so far as they aid us in thinking of the physical or biological world, they have only the value of artificial symbols, useful practically perhaps, but having no connection with reality. Thus we come back, by a different road, to nominalism and empiricism.

But when we interpret a sociological theory of knowledge in this way, we forget that even if society is a specific reality it is not an empire within an empire; it is a part of nature, and indeed its highest representation. The social realm is a natural realm which differs from the others only by a greater complexity. Now it is impossible that nature should differ radically from itself in the one case and the other in regard to that which is most essential. The fundamental relations that exist between things – just that which it is the function of the categories to express – cannot be essentially dissimilar in the different realms. If they are more clearly disengaged in the social world, it is nevertheless impossible that they should not be found elsewhere, though in less pronounced forms. Society makes them more manifest but it does not have a monopoly upon them. That is why ideas which have been elaborated on the model of social things can aid us in thinking of another department of nature. It is at least true that if these ideas play the rôle of symbols when they are thus turned aside from their original signification, they are well-founded symbols. If a sort of artificiality enters into them from the mere fact that they are constructed concepts, it is an artificiality which follows nature very closely and which is constantly approaching it still more closely.[8] From the fact that the ideas of time, space, class, cause or personality are constructed out of social elements, it is not necessary to conclude that they are devoid of all objective value. On the contrary, their social origin rather leads to the belief that they are not without foundation in the nature of things.[9]

Thus renovated, the theory of knowledge seems destined to unite the opposing advantages of the two rival theories, without incurring their inconveniences. It keeps all the essential principles of the apriorists; but at the same time it is inspired by that positive spirit which the empiricists have striven to satisfy. It leaves the reason its specific power, but it accounts for it and does so without leaving the world of observable phenomena. It affirms the duality of our intellectual life, but it explains it, and with natural causes. The categories are no longer considered as primary and unanalysable facts, yet they keep a complexity which falsifies any analysis as ready as that with which the empiricists content themselves. They no longer appear as very simple notions which the first comer can very easily arrange from his own personal observations and which the popular imagination has unluckily complicated, but rather they appear as priceless instruments of thought which the human groups have laboriously forged through the centuries and where they have accumulated the best of their intellectual capital.[10] A complete section of the history of humanity is resumed therein. This is equivalent to saying that to succeed in understanding them and judging them, it is necessary to resort to other means than those which have been in use up to the present. To know what these conceptions which we have not made ourselves are really made of, it does not suffice to interrogate our own consciousnesses; we must look outside of ourselves, it is history that we must observe, there is a whole science which must be formed, a complex science which can advance but slowly and by collective labour, and to which the present work brings some fragmentary contributions in the nature of an attempt. [...]

But, it is said, what society is it that has thus made the basis of religion? Is it the real society, such as it is and acts before our very eyes, with the legal and moral organization which it has laboriously fashioned during the course of history? This is full of defects and imperfections. In it, evil goes beside the good, injustice often reigns supreme, and the truth is often obscured by error. How could anything so crudely organized inspire the sentiments of love, the ardent enthusiasm and the spirit of abnegation which all religions claim of their followers? These perfect beings which are gods could not have taken their traits from so mediocre, and sometimes even so base, a reality.

But, on the other hand, does someone think of a perfect society, where justice and truth would be sovereign, and from which evil in all its forms would be banished for ever? No one would deny that this is in close relations with the religious sentiment; for, they would say, it is towards the realization of this that all religions strive. But that society is not an empirical fact, definite and observable; it is a fancy, a dream with which men have lightened their sufferings, but in which they have never really lived. It is merely an idea which comes to express our more or less obscure aspirations towards the good, the beautiful and the ideal. Now these aspirations have their roots in us; they come from the very depths of our being; then there is nothing outside of us which can account for them. Moreover, they are already religious in themselves; thus it would seem that the ideal society presupposes religion, far from being able to explain it.

But, in the first place, things are arbitrarily simplified when religion is seen only on its idealistic side: in its way, it is realistic. There is no physical or moral ugliness, there are no vices or evils which do not have a special divinity. There are gods of theft and trickery, of lust and war, of sickness and of death. Christianity itself, howsoever high the idea which it has made of the divinity may be, has been obliged to give the spirit of evil a place in its mythology. Satan is an essential piece of the Christian system; even if he is an impure being, he is not a profane one. The antigod is a god, inferior and subordinated, it is true, but nevertheless endowed with extended powers; he is even the object of rites, at least of negative ones. Thus religion, far from ignoring the real society and making abstraction of it, is in its image; it reflects all its aspects, even the most vulgar and the most repulsive. All is to be found there, and if in the majority of cases we see the good victorious over evil, life over death, the powers of light over the powers of darkness, it is because reality is not otherwise. If the relation between these two contrary forces were reversed, life would be impossible; but, as a matter of fact, it maintains itself and even tends to develop.

But if, in the midst of these mythologies and theologies, we see reality clearly appearing, it is none the less true that it is found there only in an enlarged, transformed and idealized form. In this respect, the most primitive religions do not differ from the most recent and the most refined. For example, we have seen how the Arunta place at the beginning of time a mythical society whose organization exactly reproduces that which still exists to-day; it includes the same clans and phratries, it is under the same matrimonial rules and it practises the same rites. But the personages who compose it are ideal beings, gifted with powers and virtues to which common mortals cannot pretend. Their nature is not only higher, but it is different, since it is at once animal and human. The evil powers there undergo a similar metamorphosis: evil itself is, as it were, made sublime and idealized. The question now raises itself of whence this idealization comes.

Some reply that men have a natural faculty for idealizing, that is to say, of substituting for the real world another different one, to which they transport themselves by thought. But that is merely changing the terms of the problem; it is not resolving it or even advancing it. This systematic idealization is an essential characteristic of religions. Explaining them by an innate power of idealization is simply replacing one word by another which is the equivalent of the first; it is as if they said that men have made religions because they have a religious nature. Animals know only one world, the one which they perceive by experience, internal as well as external. Men alone have the faculty of conceiving the ideal, of adding something to the real. Now where does this singular privilege come from? Before making it an initial fact or a mysterious virtue which escapes science, we must be sure that it does not depend upon empirically determinable conditions.

The explanation of religion which we have proposed has precisely this advantage, that it gives an answer to this question. For our definition of the sacred is that it is something added to and above the real: now the ideal answers to this same definition; we cannot explain one without explaining the other. In fact, we have seen that if collective life awakens religious thought on reaching a certain degree of intensity, it is because it brings about a state of effervescence which changes the conditions of psychic activity. Vital energies are over-excited, passions more active, sensations stronger; there are even some which are produced only at this moment. A man does not recognize himself; he feels himself transformed and consequently he transforms the environment which surrounds him. In order to account for the very particular impressions which he receives, he attributes to the things with which he is in most direct contact properties which they have not, exceptional powers and virtues which the objects of every-day experience do not possess. In a word, above the real world where his profane life passes he has placed another which, in one sense, does not exist except in thought, but to which he attributes a higher sort of dignity than to the first. Thus, from a double point of view it is an ideal world.

The formation of the ideal world is therefore not an irreducible fact which escapes science; it depends upon conditions which observation can touch; it is a natural product of social life. For a society to become conscious of itself and maintain at the necessary degree of intensity the sentiments which it thus attains, it must assemble and concentrate itself. Now this concentration brings about an exaltation of the mental life which takes form in a group of ideal conceptions where is portrayed the new life thus awakened; they correspond to this new set of psychical forces which is added to those which we have at our disposition for the daily tasks of existence. A society can neither create itself nor recreate itself without at the same time creating an ideal. This creation is not a sort of work of supererogation for it, by which it would complete itself, being already formed; it is the act by which it is periodically made and remade. Therefore when some oppose the ideal society to the real society, like two antagonists which would lead us in opposite directions, they materialize and oppose abstractions. The ideal society is not outside of the real society; it is a part of it. Far from being divided between them as between two poles which mutually repel each other, we cannot hold to one without holding to the other. For a society is not made up merely of the mass of individuals who compose it, the ground which they occupy, the things which they use and the movements which they perform, but above all is the idea which it forms of itself. It is undoubtedly true that it hesitates over the manner in which it ought to conceive itself; it feels itself drawn in divergent directions. But these conflicts which break forth are not between the ideal and reality, but between two different ideals, that of yesterday and that of to-day, that which has the authority of tradition and that which has the hope of the future. There is surely a place for investigating whence these ideals evolve; but whatever solution may be given to this problem it still remains that all passes in the world of the ideal.

Thus the collective ideal which religion expresses is far from being due to a vague innate power of the individual, but it is rather at the school of collective life that the individual has learned to idealize. It is in assimilating the ideals elaborated by society that he has become capable of conceiving the ideal. It is society which, by leading him within its sphere of action, had made him acquire the need of raising himself above the world of experience and has at the same time furnished him with the means of conceiving another. For society has constructed this new world in constructing itself, since it is society which this expresses. Thus both with the individual and in the group, the faculty of idealizing has nothing mysterious about it. It is not a sort of luxury which a man could get along without, but a condition of his very existence. He could not be a social being, that is to say, he could not be a man, if he had not acquired it. It is true that in incarnating themselves in individuals, collective ideals tend to individualize themselves. Each understands them after his own fashion and marks them with his own stamp; he suppresses certain elements and adds others. Thus the personal ideal disengages itself from the social ideal in proportion as the individual personality develops itself and becomes an autonomous source of action. But if we wish to understand this aptitude, so singular in appearance, of living outside of reality, it is enough to connect it with the social conditions upon which it depends.

Therefore it is necessary to avoid seeing in this theory of religion a simple restatement of historical materialism: that would be misunderstanding our thought to an extreme degree. In showing that religion is something essentially social, we do not mean to say that it confines itself to translating into another language the material forms of society and its immediate vital necessities. It is true that we take it as evident that social life depends upon its material foundation and bears its mark, just as the mental life of an individual depends upon his nervous system and in fact his whole organism. But collective consciousness is something more than a mere epiphenomenon of its morphological basis, just as individual consciousness is something more than a simple efflorescence of the nervous system. In order that the former may appear, a synthesis *sui generis* of particular consciousnesses is required. Now this synthesis has the effect of disengaging a whole world of sentiments, ideas and images which, once born, obey laws all their own. They attract each other, repel each other, unite, divide themselves, and multiply, though these combinations are not commanded and necessitated by the condition of the underlying reality. The life thus brought into being even enjoys so great an independence that it sometimes indulges in manifestations with no purpose or utility of any sort, for the mere pleasure of affirming itself. We have shown that this is often precisely the case with ritual activity and mythological thought. [...]

Thus there is something eternal in religion which is destined to survive all the particular symbols in which religious thought has successively enveloped itself. There can be no society which does not feel the need of upholding and reaffirming at regular intervals the collective sentiments and the collective ideas which make its unity and its personality. Now this moral remaking cannot be achieved except by the means of reunions, assemblies and meetings where the individuals, being closely united to one another, reaffirm in common their common sentiments; hence come ceremonies which do not differ from regular religious ceremonies, either in their object, the results which they produce, or the processes employed to attain these results. What essential difference is there between an assembly of Christians celebrating the principal dates of the life of Christ, or of Jews remembering the exodus from Egypt or the promulgation of the decalogue, and a reunion of citizens commemorating the promulgation of a new moral or legal system or some great event in the national life?

If we find a little difficulty to-day in imagining what these feasts and ceremonies of the future could consist in, it is because we are going through a stage of transition and moral mediocrity. The great things of the past which filled our fathers with enthusiasm do not excite the same ardour in us, either because they have come into common usage to such an extent that we are unconscious of them, or else because they no longer answer to our actual aspirations; but as yet there is nothing to replace them. We can no longer impassionate ourselves for the principles in the name of which Christianity recommended to masters that they treat their slaves humanely, and, on the other hand, the idea which it has formed of human equality and fraternity seems to us to-day to leave too large a place for unjust inequalities. Its pity for the outcast seems to us too Platonic; we desire another which would be more practicable; but as yet we cannot clearly see what it should be or how it could be realized in facts. In a word, the old gods are growing old or already dead, and others are not yet born. This is what rendered vain the attempt of Comte with the old historic souvenirs artificially revived: it is life itself, and not a dead past, which can produce a living cult. But this state of incertitude and confused agitation cannot last for ever. A day will come when our societies will know again those hours of creative effervescence, in the course of which new ideas arise and new formulae are found which serve for a while as a guide to humanity; and when these hours shall have been passed through once, men will spontaneously feel the need of reliving them from time to time in thought, that is to say, of keeping alive their memory by means of celebrations which regularly reproduce their fruits.

NOTES

1 But that is not equivalent to saying that all luxury is lacking to the primitive cults. On the contrary, we shall see that in every religion there are beliefs and practices which do not aim at strictly utilitarian ends. This luxury is indispensable to the religious life; it is at its very heart. But it is much more rudimentary in the inferior religions than in the others, so we are better able to determine its reason for existence here.
2 We say that time and space are categories because there is no difference between the rôle played by these ideas in the intellectual life and that which falls to the ideas of class or cause.
3 Perhaps some will be surprised that we do not define the apriorist theory by the hypothesis of innateness. But this conception really plays a secondary part in the doctrine. It is a simple way of stating the impossibility of reducing rational knowledge to empirical data. Saying that the former is innate is only a positive way of saying that it is not the product of experience, such as it is ordinarily conceived.

4   At least, in so far as there are any representations which are individual and hence wholly empirical. But there are in fact probably none where the two elements are not found closely united.

5   This irreducibility must not be taken in any absolute sense. We do not wish to say that there is nothing in the empirical representations which shows rational ones, nor that there is nothing in the individual which could be taken as a sign of social life. If experience were completely separated from all that is rational, reason could not operate upon it; in the same way, if the psychic nature of the individual were absolutely opposed to the social life, society would be impossible. A complete anlysis of the categories should seek these germs of rationality even in the individual consciousness. All that we wish to establish here is that between these indistinct germs of reason and the reason properly so called, there is a difference comparable to that which separates the properties of the mineral elements out of which a living being is composed from the characteristic attributes of life after this has once been constituted.

6   It has frequently been remarked that social disturbances result in multiplying mental disturbances. This is one more proof that logical discipline is a special aspect of social discipline. The first gives way as the second is weakened.

7   There is an analogy between this logical necessity and moral obligation, but there is not an actual identity. To-day society treats criminals in a different fashion than subjects whose intelligence only is abnormal; that is a proof that the authority attached to logical rules and that inherent in moral rules are not of the same nature, in spite of certain similarities. They are two species of the same class. It would be interesting to make a study on the nature and origin of this difference, which is probably distinguished between the deranged and the delinquent. We confine ourselves to signalizing this question. By this example, one may see the number of problems which are raised by the analysis of these notions which generally pass as being elementary and simple, but which are really of an extreme complexity.

8   The rationalism which is imminent in the sociological theory of knowledge is thus midway between the classical empiricism and apriorism. For the first, the categories are purely artificial constructions; for the second, on the contrary, they are given by nature; for us, they are in a sense a work of art, but of an art which imitates nature with a perfection capable of increasing unlimitedly.

9   For example, that which is at the foundation of the category of time is the rhythm of social life; but if there is a rhythm in collective life, one may rest assured that there is another in the life of the individual, and more generally, in that of the universe. The first is merely more marked and apparent than the others. In the same way, we shall see that the notion of class is founded on that of the human group. But if men form natural groups, it can be assumed that among things there exist groups which are at once analogous and different. Classes and species are natural groups of things.

If it seems to many minds that a social origin cannot be attributed to the categories without depriving them of all speculative value, it is because society is still too frequently regarded as something that is not natural; hence it is concluded that the representations which express it express nothing in nature. But the conclusion is not worth more than the premise.

10 This is how it is legitimate to compare the categories to tools; for on its side, a tool is material accumulated capital. There is a close relationship between the three ideas of tool, category and institution.

Chapter 18

Suicide [1897]

Emile Durkheim

[...]

II

No living being can be happy or even exist unless his needs are sufficiently proportioned to his means. In other words, if his needs require more than can be granted, or even merely something of a different sort, they will be under continual friction and can only function painfully. Movements incapable of production without pain tend not to be reproduced. Unsatisfied tendencies atrophy, and as the impulse to live is merely the result of all the rest, it is bound to weaken as the others relax.

In the animal, at least in a normal condition, this equilibrium is established with automatic spontaneity because the animal depends on purely material conditions. All the organism needs is that the supplies of substance and energy constantly employed in the vital process should be periodically renewed by equivalent quantities; that replacement be equivalent to use. When the void created by existence in its own resources is filled, the animal, satisfied, asks nothing further. Its power of reflection is not sufficiently developed to imagine other ends than those implicit in its physical nature. On the other hand, as the work demanded of each organ itself

---

Durkheim, Emile, "Anomic Suicide," pp. 246–258 from Emile Durkheim, *Suicide: A Study in Sociology*, ed. George Simpson, trans. John H. Spaulding and George Simpson. New York: Macmillan Publishing Co., Inc., The Free Press, 1951. Copyright © 1951 by The Free Press. Copyright © renewed 1979 by The Free Press. Reprinted with the permission of The Free Press, A Division of Simon & Schuster Adult Publishing Group. All rights reserved.

Classical Sociological Theory, Third Edition. Edited by Craig Calhoun, Joseph Gerteis, James Moody, Steven Pfaff, and Indermohan Virk. Editorial material and organization © 2012 John Wiley & Sons, Ltd. Published 2012 by John Wiley & Sons, Ltd.

depends on the general state of vital energy and the needs of organic equilibrium, use is regulated in turn by replacement and the balance is automatic. The limits of one are those of the other; both are fundamental to the constitution of the existence in question, which cannot exceed them.

This is not the case with man, because most of his needs are not dependent on his body or not to the same degree. Strictly speaking, we may consider that the quantity of material supplies necessary to the physical maintenance of a human life is subject to computation, though this be less exact than in the preceding case and a wider margin left for the free combinations of the will; for beyond the indispensable minimum which satisfies nature when instinctive, a more awakened reflection suggests better conditions, seemingly desirable ends craving fulfillment. Such appetites, however, admittedly sooner or later reach a limit which they cannot pass. But how determine the quantity of well-being, comfort or luxury legitimately to be craved by a human being? Nothing appears in man's organic nor in his psychological constitution which sets a limit to such tendencies. The functioning of individual life does not require them to cease at one point rather than at another; the proof being that they have constantly increased since the beginnings of history, receiving more and more complete satisfaction, yet with no weakening of average health. Above all, how establish their proper variation with different conditions of life, occupations, relative importance of services, etc.? In no society are they equally satisfied in the different stages of the social hierarchy. Yet human nature is substantially the same among all men, in its essential qualities. It is not human nature which can assign the variable limits necessary to our needs. They are thus unlimited so far as they depend on the individual alone. Irrespective of any external regulatory force, our capacity for feeling is in itself an insatiable and bottomless abyss.

But if nothing external can restrain this capacity, it can only be a source of torment to itself. Unlimited desires are insatiable by definition and insatiability is rightly considered a sign of morbidity. Being unlimited, they constantly and infinitely surpass the means at their command; they cannot be quenched. Inextinguishable thirst is constantly renewed torture. It has been claimed, indeed, that human activity naturally aspires beyond assignable limits and sets itself unattainable goals. But how can such an undetermined state be any more reconciled with the conditions of mental life than with the demands of physical life? All man's pleasure in acting, moving and exerting himself implies the sense that his efforts are not in vain and that by walking he has advanced. However, one does not advance when one walks toward no goal, or – which is the same thing – when his goal is infinity. Since the distance between us and it is always the same, whatever road we take, we might as well have made the motions without progress from the spot. Even our glances behind and our feeling of pride at the distance covered can cause only deceptive satisfaction, since the remaining distance is not proportionately reduced. To pursue a goal which is by definition unattainable is to condemn oneself to a state of perpetual unhappiness. Of course, man may hope contrary to all reason, and hope has its pleasures even when unreasonable. It may sustain him for a time; but it cannot survive the repeated disappointments of experience indefinitely. What more can the future offer him than the past, since he can never reach a tenable condition nor even approach the glimpsed ideal? Thus, the more one has, the more one wants, since satisfactions received only stimulate instead of filling needs. Shall action as such be considered agreeable? First, only on condition of blindness to its uselessness. Secondly, for this pleasure to be felt and to temper and half veil the accompanying painful unrest, such unending motion must at least always be easy and unhampered. If it is interfered with only restlessness is left, with the lack of ease which it, itself, entails. But it would be a miracle if no insurmountable obstacle were never encountered. Our thread of life on these conditions is pretty thin, breakable at any instant.

To achieve any other result, the passions first must be limited. Only then can they be harmonized with the faculties and satisfied. But since the individual has no way of limiting them, this must be done by some force exterior to him. A regulative force must play the same role for moral needs which the organism plays for physical needs. This means that the force can only be moral. The awakening of conscience interrupted the state of equilibrium of the animal's dormant existence; only conscience, therefore, can furnish the means to re-establish it. Physical restraint would be ineffective; hearts cannot be touched by physio-chemical forces. So far as the appetites are not automatically restrained by physiological mechanisms, they can be halted only by a limit that they recognize as just. Men would never consent to restrict their desires if they felt justified in passing the assigned limit. But, for reasons given above, they cannot assign themselves this law of justice. So they must receive it from an authority which they respect, to which they yield spontaneously. Either directly and as a whole, or through the agency of one of its organs, society alone can play this moderating role; for it is the only moral power superior to the individual, the authority of which he accepts. It alone has the power necessary to stipulate law and to set the point beyond which the passions must not go. Finally, it alone can estimate the reward to be prospectively offered to every class of human functionary, in the name of the common interest.

As a matter of fact, at every moment of history there is a dim perception, in the moral consciousness of societies, of the respective value of different social services, the relative reward due to each, and the consequent degree of comfort appropriate on the average to workers in each occupation. The different functions are graded in public opinion and a certain coefficient of well-being assigned to each, according to its place in the hierarchy. According to accepted ideas, for example, a certain way of living is considered the upper limit to which a workman may aspire in his efforts to improve his existence, and there is another limit below which he is not willingly permitted to fall unless he has seriously demeaned himself. Both differ for city and country workers, for the domestic servant and the day-laborer, for the business clerk and the official, etc. Likewise the man of wealth is reproved if he lives the life of a poor man, but also if he seeks the refinements of luxury overmuch. Economists may protest in vain; public feeling will always be scandalized if an individual spends too much wealth for wholly superfluous use, and it even seems that this severity relaxes only in times of moral disturbance.[1] A genuine regimen exists, therefore, although not always legally formulated, which fixes with relative precision the maximum degree of ease of living to which each social class may legitimately aspire. However, there is nothing immutable about such a scale. It changes with the increase or decrease of collective revenue and the changes occurring in the moral ideas of society. Thus what appears luxury to one period no longer does so to another; and the well-being which for long periods was granted to a class only by exception and supererogation, finally appears strictly necessary and equitable.

Under this pressure, each in his sphere vaguely realizes the extreme limit set to his ambitions and aspires to nothing beyond. At least if he respects regulations and is docile to collective authority, that is, has a wholesome moral constitution, he feels that it is not well to ask more. Thus, an end and goal are set to the passions. Truly, there is nothing rigid nor absolute about such determination. The economic ideal assigned each class of citizens is itself confined to certain limits, within which the desires have free range. But it is not infinite. This relative limitation and the moderation it involves make men contented with their lot while stimulating them moderately to improve it; and this average contentment causes the feeling of calm, active happiness, the pleasure in existing and living which characterizes health for societies as well as for individuals. Each person is then at least, generally speaking, in harmony with his condition, and desires only what he may legitimately hope for as the normal reward of his activity. Besides, this does not condemn man to a sort of immobility. He may seek to give beauty to his life; but his attempts in this direction may fail without causing him to despair. For, loving what he has and not fixing his desire solely on what he lacks, his wishes and hopes may fail of what he has happened to aspire to, without his being wholly destitute. He has the essentials. The equilibrium of his happiness is secure because it is defined, and a few mishaps cannot disconcert him.

But it would be of little use for everyone to recognize the justice of the hierarchy of functions established by public opinion, if he did not also consider the distribution of these functions just. The workman is not in harmony with his social position if he is not convinced that he has his desserts. If he feels justified in occupying another, what he has would not satisfy him. So it is not enough for the average level of needs for each social condition to be regulated by public opinion, but another, more precise rule, must fix the way in which these conditions are open to individuals. There is no society in which such regulation does not exist. It varies with times and places. Once it regarded birth as the almost exclusive principle of social classification; today it recognizes no other inherent inequality than hereditary fortune and merit. But in all these various forms its object is unchanged. It is also only possible, everywhere, as a restriction upon individuals imposed by superior authority, that is, by collective authority. For it can be established only by requiring of one or another group of men, usually of all, sacrifices and concessions in the name of the public interest.

Some, to be sure, have thought that this moral pressure would become unnecessary if men's economic circumstances were only no longer determined by heredity. If inheritance were abolished, the argument runs, if everyone began life with equal resources and if the competitive struggle were fought out on a basis of perfect equality, no one could think its results unjust. Each would instinctively feel that things are as they should be.

Truly, the nearer this ideal equality were approached, the less social restraint will be necessary. But it is only a matter of degree. One sort of heredity will always exist, that of natural talent. Intelligence, taste, scientific, artistic, literary or industrial ability, courage and manual dexterity are gifts received by each of us at birth, as the heir to wealth receives his capital or as the nobleman formerly received his title and function. A moral discipline will therefore still be required to make those less favored by nature accept the lesser advantages which they owe to the chance of birth. Shall it be demanded that all have an equal share and that no advantage be given those more useful and deserving? But then there would have to be a discipline far stronger to make these accept a treatment merely equal to that of the mediocre and incapable.

But like the one first mentioned, this discipline can be useful only if considered just by the peoples subject to it. When it is maintained only by custom and force, peace and harmony are illusory; the spirit of unrest and discontent are latent; appetites superficially restrained are ready to revolt. This happened in Rome and Greece when the faiths underlying the old organization of the patricians and plebeians were shaken, and in our modern societies when aristocratic prejudices began to lose their old ascendancy. But this state of upheaval is exceptional; it occurs only when society is passing through some abnormal crisis. In normal conditions the collective order is regarded as just by the great majority of persons. Therefore, when we say that an authority is necessary to impose this order on individuals, we certainly do not mean that violence is the only means of establishing it. Since this regulation is meant to restrain individual passions, it must come from a power which dominates individuals; but this power must also be obeyed through respect, not fear.

It is not true, then, that human activity can be released from all restraint. Nothing in the world can enjoy such a privilege. All existence being a part of the universe is relative to the remainder; its nature and method of manifestation accordingly depend not only on itself but on other beings, who consequently restrain and regulate it. Here there are only differences of degree and form between the mineral realm and the thinking person. Man's characteristic privilege is that the bond he accepts is not physical but moral; that is, social. He is governed not by a material environment brutally imposed on him, but by a conscience superior to his own, the superiority of which he feels. Because the greater, better part of his existence transcends the body, he escapes the body's yoke, but is subject to that of society.

But when society is disturbed by some painful crisis or by beneficent but abrupt transitions, it is momentarily incapable of exercising this influence; thence come the sudden rises in the curve of suicides which we have pointed out above.

In the case of economic disasters, indeed, something like a declassification occurs which suddenly casts certain individuals into a lower state than their previous one. Then they must reduce their requirements, restrain their needs, learn greater self-control. All the advantages of social influence are lost so far as they are concerned; their moral education has to be recommenced. But society cannot adjust them instantaneously to this new life and teach them to practice the increased self-repression to which they are unaccustomed. So they are not adjusted to the condition forced on them, and its very prospect is intolerable; hence the suffering which detaches them from a reduced existence even before they have made trial of it.

It is the same if the source of the crisis is an abrupt growth of power and wealth. Then, truly, as the conditions of life are changed, the standard according to which needs were regulated can no longer remain the same; for it varies with social resources, since it largely determines the share of each class of producers. The scale is upset; but a new scale cannot be immediately improvised. Time is required for the public conscience to reclassify men and things. So long as the social forces thus freed have not regained equilibrium, their respective values are unknown and so all regulation is lacking for a time. The limits are unknown between the possible and the impossible, what is just and what is unjust, legitimate claims and hopes and those which are immoderate. Consequently, there is no restraint upon aspirations. If the disturbance is profound, it affects even the principles controlling the distribution of men among various occupations. Since the relations between various parts of society are necessarily modified, the ideas expressing these relations must change. Some particular class especially favored by the crisis is no longer resigned to its former lot, and, on the other hand, the example of its greater good fortune arouses all sorts of jealousy below and about it. Appetites, not being controlled by a public opinion, become disoriented, no longer recognize the limits proper to them. Besides, they are at the same time seized by a sort of natural erethism simply by the greater intensity of public life. With increased prosperity desires increase. At the very moment when traditional rules have lost their authority, the richer prize offered these appetites stimulates them and makes them more exigent and impatient of control. The state of de-regulation or anomy is thus further heightened by passions being less disciplined, precisely when they need more disciplining.

But then their very demands make fulfillment impossible. Overweening ambition always exceeds the results obtained, great as they may be, since there is no warning to pause here. Nothing gives satisfaction and all this agitation is uninterruptedly maintained without appeasement. Above all, since this race for an unattainable goal can give no other pleasure but that of the race itself, if it is one, once it is interrupted the participants are left empty-handed. At the same time the struggle grows more violent and painful, both from being less controlled and because competition is greater. All classes contend among themselves because no established classification any longer exists. Effort grows, just when it becomes less productive. How could the desire to live not be weakened under such conditions?

This explanation is confirmed by the remarkable immunity of poor countries. Poverty protects against suicide because it is a restraint in itself. No matter how one acts, desires have to depend upon resources to some extent; actual possessions are partly the criterion of those aspired to. So the less one has the less he is tempted to extend the range of his needs indefinitely. Lack of power, compelling moderation, accustoms men to it, while nothing excites envy if no one has superfluity. Wealth, on the other hand, by the power it bestows, deceives us into believing that we depend on ourselves only. Reducing the resistance we encounter from objects, it suggests the possibility of unlimited success against them. The less limited one feels, the more intolerable all limitation appears. Not without reason, therefore, have so many religions dwelt on the advantages and moral value of poverty. It is actually the best school for teaching self-restraint. Forcing us to constant self-discipline, it prepares us to accept collective discipline with equanimity, while wealth, exalting the individual, may always arouse the spirit of rebellion which is the very source of immorality. This, of course, is no reason why humanity should not improve its material condition. But though the moral danger involved in every growth of prosperity is not irremediable, it should not be forgotten.

III

If anomy never appeared except, as in the above instances, in intermittent spurts and acute crisis, it might cause the social suicide-rate to vary from time to time, but it would not be a regular, constant factor. In one sphere of social life, however – the sphere of trade and industry – it is actually in a chronic state.

For a whole century, economic progress has mainly consisted in freeing industrial relations from all regulation. Until very recently, it was the function of a whole system of moral forces to exert this discipline. First, the influence of religion was felt alike by workers and masters, the poor and the rich. It consoled the former and taught them contentment with their lot by informing them of the providential nature of the social order, that the share of each class was assigned by God himself, and by holding out the hope for just compensation in a world to come in return for the inequalities of this world. It governed the latter, recalling that worldly interests are not man's entire lot, that they must be subordinate to other and higher interests, and that they should therefore not be pursued without rule or measure. Temporal power, in turn, restrained the scope of economic functions by its supremacy over them and by the relatively subordinate role it assigned them. Finally, within the business world proper, the occupational groups, by regulating salaries, the price of products and production itself, indirectly fixed the average level of income on which needs are partially based by the very force of circumstances. However, we do not mean to propose this organization as a model. Clearly it would be inadequate to existing societies without great changes. What we stress is its existence, the fact of its useful influence, and that nothing today has come to take its place.

Actually, religion has lost most of its power. And government, instead of regulating economic life, has become its tool and servant. The most opposite schools, orthodox economists and extreme socialists, unite to reduce government to the role of a more or less passive intermediary among the various social functions. The former wish to make it simply the guardian of individual contracts; the latter leave it the task of doing the collective bookkeeping, that is, of recording the demands of consumers, transmitting them to producers, inventorying the total revenue and distributing it according to a fixed formula. But both refuse it any power to subordinate other social organs to itself and to make them converge toward one dominant aim. On both sides nations are declared to have the single or chief purpose of achieving industrial prosperity; such is the implication of the dogma of economic materialism, the basis of both apparently opposed systems. And as these theories merely express the state of opinion, industry, instead of being still regarded as a means to an end transcending itself, has become the supreme end of individuals and societies alike. Thereupon the appetites thus excited have become freed of any limiting authority. By sanctifying them, so to speak, this apotheosis of well-being has placed them above all human law. Their restraint seems like a sort of sacrilege. For this reason, even the purely utilitarian regulation of them exercised by the industrial world itself through the medium of occupational groups has been unable to persist. Ultimately, this liberation of desires has been made worse by the very development of industry and the almost infinite extension of the market. So long as the producer could gain his profits only in his immediate neighborhood, the restricted amount of possible gain could not much overexcite ambition. Now that he may assume to have almost the entire world as his customer, how could passions accept their former confinement in the face of such limitless prospects?

Such is the source of the excitement predominating in this part of society, and which has thence extended to the other parts. There, the state of crisis and anomy is constant and, so to speak, normal. From top to bottom of the ladder, greed is aroused without knowing where to find ultimate foothold. Nothing can calm it, since its goal is far beyond all it can attain. Reality seems valueless by comparison with the dreams of fevered imaginations; reality is therefore abandoned, but so too is possibility abandoned when it in turn becomes reality. A thirst arises for novelties, unfamiliar pleasures, nameless sensations, all of which lose their savor once known. Henceforth one has no strength to endure the least reverse. The whole fever subsides and the sterility of all the tumult is apparent, and it is seen that all these new sensations in their infinite quantity cannot form a solid foundation of happiness to support one during days of trial. The wise man, knowing how to enjoy achieved results without having constantly to replace them with others, finds in them an attachment to life in the hour of difficulty. But the man who has always pinned all his hopes on the future and lived with his eyes fixed upon it, has nothing in the past as a comfort against the present's afflictions, for the past was nothing to him but a series of hastily experienced stages. What blinded him to himself was his expectation always to find further on the happiness he had so far missed. Now he is stopped in his tracks; from now on nothing remains behind or ahead of him to fix his gaze upon. Weariness alone, moreover, is enough to bring disillusionment, for he cannot in the end escape the futility of an endless pursuit.

We may even wonder if this moral state is not principally what makes economic catastrophes of our day so fertile in suicides. In societies where a man is subjected to a healthy discipline, he submits more readily to the blows of chance. The necessary effort for sustaining a little more discomfort costs him relatively little, since he is used to discomfort and constraint. But when every constraint is hateful in itself, how can closer constraint not seem intolerable? There is no tendency to resignation in the feverish impatience of men's lives. When there is no other aim but to outstrip constantly the point arrived at, how painful to be thrown back! Now this very lack of

Table 18.1 Suicides per million persons of different occupations

	Trade	Transportation	Industry	Agriculture	Liberal* professions
France (1878–87)†	440	.....	340	240	300
Switzerland (1876)	664	1,514	577	304	558
Italy (1866–76)	277	152.6	80.4	26.7	618‡
Prussia (1883–90)	754	.....	456	315	832
Bavaria (1884–91)	465	.....	369	153	454
Belgium (1886–90)	421	.....	160	160	100
Wurttemberg (1873–8)	273	.....	190	206	...
Saxony (1878)		341.59§		71.17	...

* When statistics distinguish several different sorts of liberal occupations, we show as a specimen the one in which the suicide-rate is highest.
† From 1826 to 1880 economic functions seem less affected (see *Compte-rendu* of 1880); but were occupational statistics very accurate?
‡ This figure is reached only by men of letters.
§ Figure represents Trade, Transportation and Industry combined for Saxony.

organization characterizing our economic condition throws the door wide to every sort of adventure. Since imagination is hungry for novelty, and ungoverned, it gropes at random. Setbacks necessarily increase with risks and thus crises multiply, just when they are becoming more destructive.

Yet these dispositions are so inbred that society has grown to accept them and is accustomed to think them normal. It is everlastingly repeated that it is man's nature to be eternally dissatisfied, constantly to advance, without relief or rest, toward an indefinite goal. The longing for infinity is daily represented as a mark of moral distinction, whereas it can only appear within unregulated consciences which elevate to a rule the lack of rule from which they suffer. The doctrine of the most ruthless and swift progress has become an article of faith. But other theories appear parallel with those praising the advantages of instability, which, generalizing the situation that gives them birth, declare life evil, claim that it is richer in grief than in pleasure and that it attracts men only by false claims. Since this disorder is greatest in the economic world, it has most victims there.

Industrial and commercial functions are really among the occupations which furnish the greatest number of suicides (see table 18.1). Almost on a level with the liberal professions, they sometimes surpass them; they are especially more afflicted than agriculture, where the old regulative forces still make their appearance felt most and where the fever of business has least penetrated. Here is best recalled what was once the general constitution of the economic order. And the divergence would be yet greater if, among the suicides of industry, employers were distinguished from workmen, for the former are probably most stricken by the state of anomy. The enormous rate of those with independent means (720 per million) sufficiently shows that the possessors of most comfort suffer most. Everything that enforces subordination attenuates the effects of this state. At least the horizon of the lower classes is limited by those above them, and for this same reason their desires are more modest. Those who have only empty space above them are almost inevitably lost in it, if no force restrains them.

Anomy, therefore, is a regular and specific factor in suicide in our modern societies; one of the springs from which the annual contingent feeds. So we have here a new type to distinguish from the others. It differs from them in its dependence, not on the way in which individuals are attached to society, but on how it regulates them. Egoistic suicide results from man's no longer finding a basis for existence in life; altruistic suicide, because this basis for existence appears to man situated beyond life itself. The third sort of suicide, the existence of which has just been shown, results from man's activity's lacking regulation and his consequent sufferings. By virtue of its origin we shall assign this last variety the name of *anomic suicide*.

Certainly, this and egoistic suicide have kindred ties. Both spring from society's insufficient presence in individuals. But the sphere of its absence is not the same in both cases. In egoistic suicide it is deficient in truly collective activity, thus depriving the latter of object and meaning. In anomic suicide, society's influence is lacking in the basically individual passions, thus leaving them without a check-rein. In spite of their relationship, therefore, the two types are independent of each other. We may offer society everything social in us, and still be unable to control our desires; one may live in an anomic state without being egoistic, and vice versa. These two sorts of suicide therefore do not draw their chief recruits from the same social environments; one has its principal field among intellectual careers, the world of thought – the other, the industrial or commercial world.

NOTE

1 Actually, this is a purely moral reprobation and can hardly be judicially implemented. We do not consider any reestablishment of sumptuary laws desirable or even possible.

Chapter 19

"Objectivity" in Social Science [1904]

Max Weber

We have in abstract economic theory an illustration of those synthetic constructs which have been designated as "*ideas*" of historical phenomena. It offers us an ideal picture of events on the commodity-market under conditions of a society organized on the principles of an exchange economy, free competition and rigorously rational conduct. This conceptual pattern brings together certain relationships and events of historical life into a complex, which is conceived as an internally consistent system. Substantively, this construct in itself is like a *utopia* which has been arrived at by the analytical accentuation of certain elements of reality. Its relationship to the empirical data consists solely in the fact that where market-conditioned relationships of the type referred to by the abstract construct are discovered or suspected to exist in reality to some extent, we can make the *characteristic* features of this relationship pragmatically *clear* and *understandable* by reference to an *ideal-type*. This procedure can be indispensable for heuristic as well as expository purposes. The ideal typical concept will help to develop our skill in imputation in *research*: it *is* no "hypothesis" but it offers guidance to the construction of hypotheses. It is not a *description* of reality but it aims to give unambiguous means of expression to such a description. It is thus the "idea" of the *historically* given modern society, based on an exchange economy, which is developed for us by quite the same logical principles as are used in constructing the idea of the medieval "city economy" as a "genetic" concept. When we do this, we construct the concept "city economy" not as an average of the economic

Weber, Max, "'Objectivity' in Social Science," pp. 89–99, 110–112 from Max Weber, *The Methodology of the Social Sciences*, ed. and trans. Edward A. Shils and Henry A. Finch. New York: Simon & Schuster, Inc., The Free Press, 1949. Copyright © 1949 by The Free Press. Copyright © renewed 1977 by Edward A. Shils. Reprinted and edited with the permission of The Free Press, A Division of Simon & Schuster Adult Publishing Group. All rights reserved.

Classical Sociological Theory, Third Edition. Edited by Craig Calhoun, Joseph Gerteis, James Moody, Steven Pfaff, and Indermohan Virk. Editorial material and organization © 2012 John Wiley & Sons, Ltd. Published 2012 by John Wiley & Sons, Ltd.

structures actually existing in all the cities observed but as an *ideal-type*. An ideal type is formed by the one-sided *accentuation* of one or more points of view and by the synthesis of a great many diffuse, discrete, more or less present and occasionally absent *concrete individual* phenomena, which are arranged according to those one-sidedly emphasized viewpoints into a unified *analytical* construct (*Gedankenbild*). In its conceptual purity, this mental construct (*Gedankenbild*) cannot be found empirically anywhere in reality. It is a *utopia*. Historical research faces the task of determining in each individual case the extent to which this ideal-construct approximates to or diverges from reality, to what extent for example, the economic structure of a certain city is to be classified as a "city-economy." When carefully applied, those concepts are particularly useful in research and exposition. In very much the same way one can work the "idea" of "handicraft" into a utopia by arranging certain traits, actually found in an unclear, confused state in the industrial enterprises of the most diverse epochs and countries, into a consistent ideal-construct by an accentuation of their essential tendencies. This ideal-type is then related to the idea (*Gedankenausdruck*) which one finds expressed there. One can further delineate a society in which all branches of economic and even intellectual activity are governed by maxims which appear to be applications of the same principle which characterizes the ideal-typical "handicraft" system. Furthermore, one can juxtapose alongside the ideal-typical "handicraft" system the antithesis of a correspondingly ideal-typical capitalistic productive system, which has been abstracted out of certain features of modern large-scale industry. On the basis of this, one can delineate the utopia of a "capitalistic" culture, i.e., one in which the governing principle is the investment of private capital. This procedure would accentuate certain individual concretely diverse traits of modern material and intellectual culture in its unique aspects into an ideal construct which from our point of view would be completely self-consistent. This would then be the delineation of an *"idea"* of *capitalistic culture*. We must disregard for the moment whether and how this procedure could be carried out. It is possible, or rather, it must be accepted as certain that numerous, indeed a very great many, utopias of this sort can be worked out, of which *none* is like another, and *none* of which can be observed in empirical reality as an actually existing economic system, but *each* of which however claims that it is a representation of the "idea" of capitalistic culture. *Each* of these can claim to be a representation of the "idea" of capitalistic culture to the extent that it has really taken certain traits, meaningful in their essential features, from the empirical reality of our culture and brought them together into a unified ideal-construct. For those phenomena which interest us as cultural phenomena are interesting to us with respect to very different kinds of evaluative ideas to which we relate them. Inasmuch as the "points of view" from which they can become significant for us are very diverse, the most varied criteria can be applied to the selection of the traits which are to enter into the construction of an ideal-typical view of a particular culture.

What is the significance of such ideal-typical constructs for an *empirical* science, as we wish to constitute it? Before going any further, we should emphasize that the idea of an ethical *imperative*, of a "model" of what "ought" to exist is to be carefully distinguished from the analytical construct, which is "ideal" in the strictly logical sense of the term. It is a matter here of constructing relationships which our imagination accepts as plausibly motivated and hence as "objectively possible" and which appear as *adequate* from the nomological standpoint.

Whoever accepts the proposition that the knowledge of historical reality can or should be a "presuppositionless" copy of "objective" facts, will deny the value of the ideal-type. [...] Every conscientious examination of the conceptual elements of historical exposition shows however that the historian, as soon as he attempts to go beyond the bare establishment of concrete relationships and to determine the *cultural* significance of even the simplest individual event in order to "characterize" it, *must* use concepts which are precisely and unambiguously definable only in the form of ideal types. Or are concepts such as "individualism," "imperialism," "feudalism," "mercantilism," "conventional," etc., and innumerable concepts of like character by means of which we seek analytically and empathically to understand reality constructed substantively by the "presuppositionless" *description* of some concrete phenomenon or through the abstract synthesis of those traits which are *common* to numerous concrete phenomena? Hundreds of words in the historian's vocabulary are ambiguous constructs created to meet the unconsciously felt need for adequate expression and the meaning of which is only concretely felt but not clearly thought out. In a great many cases, particularly in the field of descriptive political history, their ambiguity has not been prejudicial to the clarity of the presentation. It is sufficient that in each case the reader should *feel* what the historian had in mind; or, one can content one's self with the idea that the author used a *particular* meaning of the concept with special reference to the concrete case at hand. The greater the need however for a sharp appreciation of the significance of a cultural phenomenon, the more imperative is the need to operate with unambiguous concepts which are not only particularly but also systematically defined. [...]

In this function especially, the ideal-type is an attempt to analyze historically unique configurations or their individual components by means of genetic concepts. Let us take for instance the concepts "church" and "sect." They may be broken down purely classificatorily into complexes of characteristics whereby not only the distinction between them but also the content of the concept must constantly remain fluid. If however I wish to formulate the concept of "sect" genetically, e.g., with reference to certain important cultural significances which the "sectarian spirit" has had for modern culture, certain characteristics of both become *essential* because they stand in an adequate causal relationship to those influences. However, the concepts thereupon become ideal-typical in the sense that they appear in full conceptual *integrity* either not at all or only in individual instances. Here as elsewhere every concept which is not purely classificatory diverges from reality. But the discursive nature of our knowledge, i.e., the fact that we comprehend reality only through a chain of intellectual modifications postulates such a conceptual shorthand. Our imagination can often dispense with explicit conceptual formulations as a means of *investigation*. But as regards exposition, to the extent that it wishes to be unambiguous, the use of precise formulations in the sphere of cultural analysis is in many cases absolutely necessary. Whoever disregards it entirely must confine himself to the formal aspect of cultural phenomena, e.g., to legal history. The universe of legal norms is naturally clearly definable and is valid (in the *legal* sense!) for historical reality. But social science in our sense is concerned with practical *significance*. This significance however can very often be brought unambiguously to mind only by relating the empirical data to an ideal limiting case. If the historian (in the widest sense of the word) rejects an attempt to construct such ideal types as a "theoretical construction," i.e., as useless or dispensable for his concrete heuristic purposes, the inevitable consequence is either that he consciously or unconsciously uses other similar concepts without formulating them verbally and elaborating them logically or that he remains stuck in the realm of the vaguely "felt."

Nothing, however, is more dangerous than the *confusion* of theory and history stemming from naturalistic prejudices. This confusion expresses itself firstly in the belief that the "true" content and the essence of historical reality is portrayed in such theoretical constructs or secondly, in the use of these constructs as a pro-crustean bed into which history is to be forced or thirdly, in the hypostatization of such "ideas" as real "forces" and as a "true" reality which operates behind the passage of events and which works itself out in history.

This latter danger is especially great since we are also, indeed primarily, accustomed to understand by the "ideas" of an epoch the thoughts or ideals which dominated the mass or at least an historically decisive number of the persons living in that epoch itself, and who were therefore significant as components of its culture. Now there are two aspects to this: in the first place, there are certain relationships between the "idea" in the sense of a tendency of practical or theoretical thought and the "idea" in the sense of the ideal-*typical* portrayal of an epoch constructed as a heuristic device. An ideal type of certain situations, which can be abstracted from certain characteristic social phenomena of an epoch, might – and this is indeed quite often the case – have also been present in the minds of the persons living in that epoch as an ideal to be striven for in practical life or as a maxim for the regulation of certain social relationships. [...]

The relationship between the logical structure of the conceptual system in which we present such "ideas" and what is immediately given in empirical reality naturally varies considerably. It is relatively simple in cases in which one or a few easily formulated theoretical main principles as for instance Calvin's doctrine of predestination or clearly definable ethical postulates govern human conduct and produce historical effects, so that we can analyze the "idea" into a hierarchy of ideas which can be logically derived from those theses. It is of course easily overlooked that however important the significance even of the purely logically persuasive force of ideas – Marxism is an outstanding example of this type of force – nonetheless empirical-historical events occurring in men's minds must be understood as primarily *psychologically* and not logically conditioned. The ideal-typical character of such syntheses of historically effective ideas is revealed still more clearly when those fundamental main principles and postulates no longer survive in the minds of those individuals who are still dominated by ideas which were logically or associatively derived from them because the "idea" which was historically and originally fundamental has either died out or has in general achieved wide diffusion only for its broadest implications. The basic fact that the synthesis is an "idea" which *we* have created emerges even more markedly when those fundamental main principles have either only very imperfectly or not at all been raised to the level of explicit consciousness or at least have not taken the form of explicitly elaborated complexes of ideas. When we adopt this procedure, as it very often happens and must happen, we are concerned in these ideas, e.g., the "liberalism" of a certain period or "Methodism" or some intellectually unelaborated variety of "socialism," with a *pure* ideal type of much the same character as the synthetic "principles" of economic epochs in which we had our point of departure. The more inclusive the relationships to be presented, and the more many-sided their cultural *significance* has been, the *more* their comprehensive systematic exposition in a conceptual system approximates the character of an ideal type, and the less is it possible to operate with *one* such concept. In such situations the frequently repeated attempts to discover ever *new* aspects of significance by the construction of new ideal-typical concepts is all the more natural and unavoidable. All expositions for example of the "essence" of Christianity are ideal types enjoying only a necessarily very relative and problematic validity when they are intended to be regarded as the historical portrayal of empirically existing facts. On the other hand, such presentations are of great value for research and of high systematic value for expository purposes when they are used as conceptual instruments for *comparison* with and the *measurement* of reality. They are indispensable for this purpose.

There is still another even more complicated significance implicit in such ideal-typical presentations. They regularly seek to be, or are unconsciously, ideal-types not only in the *logical* sense but also in the *practical* sense, i.e., they are *model types* which – in our illustration – contain what, from the point of view of the expositor, *should* be and what *to him* is "essential" in Christianity *because it is enduringly valuable*. If this is consciously or – as it is more frequently – unconsciously the case, they contain ideals *to* which the expositor *evaluatively* relates Christianity. These ideals are tasks and ends towards which he orients his "idea" of Christianity and which naturally can and indeed doubtless always will differ greatly from the values which other persons, for instance, the early Christians, connected with Christianity. In this sense, however, the "ideas" are naturally no longer purely *logical* auxiliary devices, no longer concepts with which reality is compared, but ideals by which it is evaluatively *judged*. Here it is no longer a matter of the purely theoretical procedure of treating empirical reality with respect to values but of *value-judgments* which are integrated into the concept of "*Christianity*." Because the ideal type claims empirical *validity* here, it penetrates into the realm of the evaluative *interpretation* of Christianity. The sphere of empirical science has been left behind and we are confronted with a profession of faith, not an ideal-typical construct. As fundamental as this distinction is in principle, the confusion of these two basically different meanings of the term "idea" appears with extraordinary frequency in historical writings. It is always close at hand whenever the descriptive historian begins to develop his "conception" of a personality of an epoch. [...] In contrast with this, the *elementary duty of scientific self-control* and the only way to avoid serious and foolish blunders requires a sharp, precise distinction between the logically *comparative* analysis of reality by ideal *types* in the logical sense and the *value-judgment* of reality *on the basis of ideals*. An "ideal type" in our sense, to repeat once more, has no connection at all with *value-judgments*, and it has nothing to do with any type of perfection other than a purely *logical* one. There are ideal types of brothels as well as of religions; there are also ideal types of those kinds of brothels which are technically "expedient" from the point of view of police ethics as well as those of which the exact opposite is the case. [...]

We are now at the end of this discussion, the only purpose of which was to trace the course of the hair-line which separates science from faith and to make explicit the *meaning* of the quest for social and economic knowledge. The *objective* validity of all empirical knowledge rests exclusively upon the ordering of the given reality according to categories which are *subjective* in a specific sense, namely, in that they present the *presuppositions* of our knowledge and are based on the presupposition of the *value* of those *truths* which empirical knowledge alone is able to give us. The means available to our science offer nothing to those persons to whom this truth is of no value. It should be remembered that the belief in the value of scientific truth is the product of certain cultures and is not a product of man's original nature. Those for whom scientific truth is of no value will seek in vain for some other truth to take the place of science in just those respects in which it is unique, namely, in the provision of concepts and judgments which are neither empirical reality nor reproductions of it but which facilitate its analytical ordering in a valid manner. In the empirical social sciences, as we have seen, the possibility of meaningful knowledge of what is essential for us in the infinite richness of events is bound up with the unremitting application of viewpoints of a specifically particularized character, which, in the last analysis, are oriented on the basis of evaluative ideas. These evaluative ideas are for their part empirically discoverable and analyzable as elements of meaningful human conduct, but their validity can *not* be deduced from empirical data as such. The "objectivity" of the social sciences depends rather on the fact that the empirical data are always related to those evaluative ideas which alone make them worth knowing and the significance of the empirical data is derived from these evaluative ideas. But these data can never become the foundation for the empirically impossible proof of the validity of the evaluative ideas. The belief which we all have in some form or other, in the meta-empirical validity of ultimate and final values, in which the meaning of our existence is rooted, is not incompatible with the incessant changefulness of the concrete viewpoints, from which empirical reality gets its significance. Both these views are, on the contrary, in harmony with each other. Life with its irrational reality and its store of possible meanings is inexhaustible. The *concrete* form in which value-relevance occurs remains perpetually in flux, ever subject to change in the dimly seen future of human culture. The light which emanates from those highest evaluative ideas always falls on an ever changing finite segment of the vast chaotic stream of events, which flows away through time.

Now all this should not be misunderstood to mean that the proper task of the social sciences should be the continual chase for new viewpoints and new analytical constructs. *On the contrary*: nothing should be more sharply emphasized than the proposition that the knowledge of the *cultural significance* of *concrete historical events and patterns* is exclusively and solely the final end which, among other means, concept-construction and the criticism of constructs also seek to serve.

There are, to use the words of F. Th. Vischer, "subject matter specialists" and "interpretative specialists." The fact-greedy gullet of the former can be filled only with legal documents, statistical worksheets and questionnaires, but he is insensitive to the refinement of a new idea. The gourmandise of the latter dulls his taste for facts by ever new intellectual subtleties. That genuine artistry which, among the historians, Ranke possessed in such a grand measure, manifests itself through its ability to produce new knowledge by interpreting already *known* facts according to known viewpoints.

All research in the cultural sciences in an age of specialization, once it is oriented towards a given subject matter through particular settings of problems and has established its methodological principles, will consider the analysis of the data as an end in itself. It will discontinue assessing the value of the individual facts in terms of their relationships to ultimate value-ideas. Indeed, it will lose its awareness of its ultimate rootedness in the value-ideas in general. And it is well that should be so. But there comes a moment when the atmosphere changes. The significance of the unreflectively utilized viewpoints becomes uncertain and the road is lost in the twilight. The light of the great cultural problems moves on. Then science too prepares to change its standpoint and its analytical apparatus and to view the streams of events from the heights of thought. It follows those stars which alone are able to give meaning and direction to its labors:

> "...... der neue Trieb erwacht,
> Ich eile fort, ihr ewiges Licht zu trinken,
> Vor mir den Tag und hinter mir die Nacht,
> Den Himmel über mir und unter mir die Wellen."[1]

NOTE

1   *Faust*: Act I, Scene II. (Translated by Bayard-Taylor)

> "The newborn impulse fires my mind,
> I hasten on, his beams eternal drinking,
> The Day before me and the Night behind,
> Above me Heaven unfurled, the floor of waves beneath me."

Part V

The Sociological Theory of Max Weber

Introduction to Part V
19 "Objectivity" in Social Science
20 Basic Sociological Terms
21 The Protestant Ethic and the Spirit of Capitalism
22 The Distribution of Power within the Political Community: Class, Status, Party
23 The Types of Legitimate Domination
24 Bureaucracy

Introduction to Part V

This section is devoted to the work of Max Weber (1864–1920). Along with Marx and Durkheim, Weber stands as one of the central figures of classical sociological theory. Weber and Durkheim were both part of the same generation of turn-of-the-century European academics and both worked to found sociology as a serious, and scientific, endeavor. Weber was only a few years younger than his French counterpart, but he was a very different theorist in both style and substance.

Compared with Marx and Durkheim, Weber's approach was more individualist in method and it was more cultural in orientation. Weber's individualism was particularly striking in his methodological essays. Weber insisted that the object of sociological analysis should be the action of individuals, insofar as it is oriented towards others. Weber certainly did not ignore collective actors or institutions, but his analysis of these social formations was linked to the behavior of the individuals that come under their influence. This set him apart particularly from Durkheim, who argued for the social collective as the unit of analysis. Weber was also profoundly interested in the cultural orientations of social actors. For Weber, ideas and value orientations – religious, political, economic, and aesthetic – were important because they motivate action. Although ideas may be shaped by material conditions, Weber held that the reverse might also be true. This differentiated Weber most clearly from Karl Marx, especially in Marx's more programmatic statements on historical materialism.

Classical Sociological Theory, Third Edition. Edited by Craig Calhoun, Joseph Gerteis, James Moody, Steven Pfaff, and Indermohan Virk. Editorial material and organization © 2012 John Wiley & Sons, Ltd. Published 2012 by John Wiley & Sons, Ltd.

Weber's Life and Work

Max Weber grew up in the suburbs of Berlin in a comfortably upper-middle-class family, the son of Helene and Max, Sr., a city councilor and politician. Skinny and somewhat sickly as a child, Weber pursued his own intellectual interests rather than social or athletic ones. He studied history and philosophy in his free time and in class secretly read through a forty-volume edition of Goethe under his desk. At eighteen, Weber enrolled at the University of Heidelberg where he immersed himself in the social life of the bourgeois university student. After serving his year of military service, Weber resumed his studies at the University of Berlin in a more ascetic manner. He studied for a law degree while working as a junior barrister in the courts, and simultaneously completed his qualifications for an academic career. Though trained as a lawyer and a historian, Weber became drawn to the social sciences. He gained a professorship first in economics and later in political science.

Max Weber quickly became an influential scholar, but his work stopped suddenly three years after his first academic appointment. In 1897, Weber descended into a crippling depression that completely curtailed his research. When his capacity for work returned after several years, he channeled it in a different direction. Before his breakdown, Weber's studies were primarily in the fields of economic and legal history. His doctoral dissertation was a study of trading companies in the Middle Ages. This was followed by a second thesis on the agrarian economics of the Roman Empire and by a massive survey of the conditions of agricultural workers in eastern Germany. Virtually all of Weber's work that is read widely by sociologists today dates from after his breakdown, when he began to grapple with the fundamental theoretical issues of the social sciences. It was at this point that he laid out his vision of the field of sociology.

Despite the fact that Weber never again felt well enough to take on full-time duties as a professor, he made up for lost time in his scholarship. In 1903, Weber began work on *The Protestant Ethic and the Spirit of Capitalism*. He also began to edit a journal, the *Archiv für Sozialwissenschaft und Sozialpolitik*, where he published many of his essays and lectures in the following years. He was completing the massive *Economy and Society* when he died. Weber also made up for lost time in his public life. With his wife, Marianne, he remained part of an active social group of intellectuals that included Georg Simmel. He was also drawn to practical political action, although he was adamant in his belief that political beliefs should not cloud scholarship. Weber was a supporter of German nationalism, but remained devoted to the moderate left. He criticized the parties of the extreme left and right for what he saw as their inability to accept political realities. Weber's public role expanded during the course of the First World War. He helped to found the German Democratic Party and had a hand in the construction of the Treaty of Versailles and the Weimar Constitution. Max Weber died in 1920, following a bout of pneumonia.

Social Theory and Social Science

Weber's approach to sociology was directly tied to the intellectual context of German philosophy and social science. Particularly important was his position in relation to the *methodenstreit* – the German debate about the proper method for the social sciences. On one side of the debate stood those who felt that the social sciences should emulate the natural sciences by searching for general laws that govern human behavior. On the other side were those who argued that accounts of social action had to be rooted in historical context. These different goals were tied to different methods. The first group emphasized causal explanations of objective social conditions. The second group sought descriptive accounts of the subjective motivations of actors in particular situations. Weber wanted to overcome this divide. He insisted that social science should seek causal arguments that generalize past any particular case, even if it was not possible to build universal laws of human society. At the same time, Weber was very closely tied to the second position (known as the "historicist school") by training and by temperament. He stressed that the proper object of analysis was social action. Because the meaning of any particular action resides in the head of the actor, sociology must pay attention to the context in which an action happens, and it must involve "*verstehen*" – an interpretive understanding of subjective motivations.

Weber applied his method to his incredibly broad empirical interests, which included religion, politics, organizations, the economy, stratification, and law. There were two consistent themes that connected Weber's sociological work together. One was an interest in the connection between forms of social action (especially relations of power) and patterns of social order. For Weber, bureaucracies, states, and world religions were examples of social institutions that supported certain forms of power relations among people. At the same time, Weber also argued that social action motivated by one kind of social order could lead to a fundamental transformation in other domains. For example, religion could foster changes in economic interactions and ultimately in entire economic systems. A second consistent theme in Weber's theory had to do with the gradual expansion of rationality in social life. Weber argued that the social action of individuals was directed more and more by conscious cost/benefit calculation in all spheres of life. The growth of rationality was marked by the reorganization and formalization of social institutions such as states and corporations to increase efficiency, accountability, and fairness. This had a profound advantage – people were no longer bound by traditional social guidelines – but it also could entail a loss of deeper meaning in people's lives.

The readings in this section give an indication of the breadth of Weber's work, as well as its unifying elements. The readings break roughly into three parts. The first exemplifies Weber's writing on methodology – that is, how to do social science. The essay "'Objectivity' in Social Science," falls into this category, as does "Basic Sociological Terms." The second, represented by "The Protestant Ethic and the Spirit of Capitalism," shows Weber's interest in rationality, and the way that it relates to religion and the economy. The third includes "Class, Status, Party," "Bureaucracy," and "The Types of Legitimate Domination" as examples of Weber's work on political and legal systems.

In the methodological essays, "'Objectivity' in Social Science" is a treatise on the use of what Weber terms "ideal type" constructs (he also calls these "pure types"). Weber takes a position that is very different from Durkheim's social realism and from Marx's materialism. Weber claims that the only way to escape from the subjectivity of the researcher is through the use of ideal types, which are concepts designed to capture the essential characteristics of a particular phenomenon. According to Weber, social researchers have to be able to understand that the terms they use to describe relevant aspects of the social world – capitalism or democracy, for example – are concepts, not historical realities. This does not mean that these concepts are unimportant, but it does mean that researchers in the social sciences have to be very explicit about what they mean when they rely on such terms. There is a more subtle argument about objectivity in this essay as well. Weber argues that the ideal types that social scientists use in objective explanations of social action should be concerned with the ideas that subjectively motivate action. Ideal types were thus Weber's way of connecting large-scale institutions and ideas to the social action of individuals.

The second methodological reading, "Basic Sociological Terms," provides Weber's view of sociology as a part of the social sciences. Weber here explicitly builds on the argument in "'Objectivity'" by defining sociology as the study of social action, a definition that stresses understanding (*verstehen*) of subjective motives rather than the building of law-like relationships. Still, Weber insists on the importance of generalization through the use of ideal-type concepts. Toward this end, Weber establishes a basic ideal-type scheme in outlining four types of social action. Since social action is the core of the field for Weber, the types of social action are a clear starting place. These basic types of action provide the foundation for much of the rest of his work. The two most important categories are instrumentally rational action (defined by the use of cost/benefit calculation) and traditional action (based on habit rather than calculation). In the readings that follow, Weber argues that instrumental rationality is gradually replacing traditional action in many aspects of modern life.

"The Protestant Ethic and the Spirit of Capitalism" is excerpted from Weber's famous book of the same name. Although the bulk of the text was completed in 1905, it was published only near the end of his life. The work develops Weber's interest in the link between religious ideas and economic institutions. Weber argues that a particular form of ascetic Protestantism fostered a "spirit" of modern capitalism, marked by a ceaseless obligation to earn money and to reinvest for profit. It is important to realize that Weber used the terms "Protestant ethic" and "spirit of capitalism" as ideal types and not as collective realities in Durkheim's sense. It is also important to recognize Weber's critique of Marxist historical materialism. The emergence of Protestantism in Europe was partially related to economic factors,

Weber argued, but this could not explain the relationship between ascetic Protestantism and capitalism in the "backwoods" of early America. "To speak *here* of a 'reflection' of 'material' conditions in the 'ideal superstructure' would be complete nonsense." In this case, a religious idea motivating the actions of individuals had a major world-historical effect on the economic structure.

The remaining essays, all from *Economy and Society*, focus in one way or another on the distribution of power and influence. "Class, Status, Party" provides a very different model of stratification from Marxist materialism. Most important is Weber's distinction between class (determined by market position) and status groups (based on social honor). "Bureaucracy" and "The Types of Legitimate Domination" are both concerned with the role of rationality in political and economic institutions. "Bureaucracy" establishes an ideal-typical outline of the functions of modern bureaucracies. Bureaucracies are important because they are both the result and cause of the growth of instrumental rationality in political, economic, and legal institutions. In "The Types of Legitimate Domination," Weber argues that people obey authority when they view it as legitimate. Claims to legitimacy may be based on rational grounds rooted in laws, traditional grounds, or charismatic grounds. Weber suggests a historical trend from traditional to rational types of authority. Movements based on the charismatic authority of political or religious reformers can bring about the end of traditional social orders, but they are also slippery. Because charismatic leadership is not easily passed on to a successor, such movements tend to slip back to traditionalism or become more bureaucratic and hence provide a bridge to a rational social order.

Weber's Legacy in Sociology

The work of Max Weber stands second only to that of Marx in having become classic for historians, philosophers, and political scientists as well as for sociologists. Weber's work continues to have both methodological and substantive resonance. Substantively, the wide range of topics Weber covered has made his work required reading in political sociology, economic sociology, legal sociology, and stratification. Equally important, Weber's method and style allow his work to inform many of the problems at the center of modern debates, including the agency/structure linkage, the nature of causality, and the tension between abstract, general theory and interpretive analysis of particular contexts.

Probably the best way to illustrate the enduring importance of Weber's work is to see how it relates to the more recent work in the second volume of this reader *Contemporary Sociological Theory*. Weber's focus on the growth of rationality and his studies of political, economic, and legal structures clearly influenced much modern work included there. The influence is especially pronounced in Powell and Dimaggio's "The Iron Cage Revisited," the title of which refers to the famous phrase at the end of *The Protestant Ethic*. A renewed interest in action as both reflecting and influencing existing structures has clear Weberian roots and is most visible in the work of Anthony Giddens and Pierre Bourdieu. In a more indirect way, Weber's work provided a model for at least some of the discussions of modernity and postmodernity. Weber, of course, was not alone in grappling with the emergence of modernity. But Weber was the classical theorist who most clearly identified pervasive rationality as the ultimate condition of modernity. He also was the classical theorist to most clearly demonstrate the emergence of modernity as a process rather than a decisive break from traditionalism.

SELECTED BIBLIOGRAPHY

Bendix, Reinhard. 1997. *Max Weber: An Intellectual Portrait.* Berkeley, CA: University of California Press. (A very thorough introduction to Weber's work. One of its most important features is that instead of treating broad themes, it covers the entire range of Weber's work in detail.)

Camic, Charles, Philip S. Gorski, and David M. Trubek (eds.). 2005. *Max Weber's Economy and Society: A Critical Companion.* Stanford, CA: Stanford University Press. (A discussion of the major ideas in Weber's multi-volume opus. Weber's text has been a central source of theoretical insight, but it is usually read in sections by different groups of sociologists interested in particular areas, such as religion or politics.)

Kalberg, Stephen. 1994. *Max Weber's Comparative-Historical Sociology.* Chicago, IL: University of Chicago Press. (A discussion of the way Weber's work answers some of the recurring problems in historical and comparative sociology.)

Käsler, Dirk. 1998. *Max Weber: An Introduction to His Life and Work.* Translated by Philippa Hurd. Chicago, IL: University of Chicago Press. (An excellent advanced introduction to Weber and his work.)

Mitzman, Arthur. 1970. *The Iron Cage: An Historical Interpretation of Max Weber.* New York: Alfred A. Knopf. (Connects the developments of Weber's ideas to his biography. This book corrects some of the biases in Helene Weber's biography.)

Mommsen, Wolfgang H. and Jürgen Osterhammel (eds.). 1987. *Weber and His Contemporaries.* Boston, MA: Allen & Unwin. (Puts Weber into the context of his intellectual contemporaries in politics, social science, and other fields.)

Turner, Bryan S. 1992. *Max Weber: From History to Modernity.* New York: Routledge. (A treatment of the theme of modernity in Weber's work and the way that Weber's work has itself contributed to current discussions of modernity).

Turner, Stephen P. (ed.). 2000. *The Cambridge Companion to Max Weber.* New York: Cambridge University Press. (This volume presents an overview of Weber's thought, but also shows the legacy of Weber's work in the social sciences. It is especially useful as a guide through some of the intellectual debates about Weber's work.)

Weber, Marianne. 1988. *Max Weber: A Biography.* Translated by Harry Zohn. Introduction by Guenther Roth. New Brunswick, NJ: Transaction Books. (The most thorough biography of Weber, written by his wife. It is an excellent source especially on the personal and political context of his work.)

Chapter 20

Basic Sociological Terms [1914]

Max Weber

1 The Definition of Sociology and of Social Action

Sociology (in the sense in which this highly ambiguous word is used here) is a science concerning itself with the interpretive understanding of social action and thereby with a causal explanation of its course and consequences. We shall speak of "action" insofar as the acting individual attaches a subjective meaning to his behavior – be it overt or covert, omission or acquiescence. Action is "social" insofar as its subjective meaning takes account of the behavior of others and is thereby oriented in its course.

(A) Methodological foundations

1   "Meaning" may be of two kinds. The term may refer first to the actual existing meaning in the given concrete case of a particular actor, or to the average or approximate meaning attributable to a given plurality of actors; or secondly to the theoretically conceived *pure type* of subjective meaning attributed to the hypothetical actor or actors in a given type of action. In no case does it refer to an objectively "correct" meaning or one which is "true" in some metaphysical sense. It is this which distinguishes the empirical sciences of action, such as sociology and history, from the dogmatic disciplines in that area, such as jurisprudence, logic, ethics, and

Weber, Max, "Basic Sociological Terms," pp.88–103, 107–117 from Max Weber, *The Theory of Social and Economic Organization*, ed. Talcott Parsons, trans. A. M. Henderson and Talcott Parsons. New York: Simon & Schuster, Inc., The Free Press, 1947. Copyright © 1947. Copyright © renewed 1975 by Talcott Parsons. Reprinted and edited with the permission of The Free Press, A Division of Simon & Schuster Adult Publishing Group. All rights reserved.

Classical Sociological Theory, Third Edition. Edited by Craig Calhoun, Joseph Gerteis, James Moody, Steven Pfaff, and Indermohan Virk. Editorial material and organization © 2012 John Wiley & Sons, Ltd. Published 2012 by John Wiley & Sons, Ltd.

esthetics, which seem to ascertain the "true" and "valid" meanings associated with the objects of their investigation.

2   The line between meaningful action and merely reactive behavior to which no subjective meaning is attached, cannot be sharply drawn empirically. A very considerable part of all sociologically relevant behavior, especially purely traditional behavior, is marginal between the two. In the case of some psychophysical processes, meaningful, i.e., subjectively understandable, action is not to be found at all; in others it is discernible only by the psychologist. Many mystical experiences which cannot be adequately communicated in words are, for a person who is not susceptible to such experiences, not fully understandable. At the same time the ability to perform a similar action is not a necessary prerequisite to understanding; "one need not have been Caeser in order to understand Caesar." "Recapturing an experience" is important for accurate understanding, but not an absolute precondition for its interpretation. Understandable and non-understandable components of a process are often intermingled and bound up together.

3   All interpretation of meaning, like all scientific observations, strives for clarity and verifiable accuracy of insight and comprehension (*Evidenz*). The basis for certainty in understanding can be either rational, which can be further subdivided into logical and mathematical, or it can be of an emotionally empathic or artistically appreciative quality. Action is rationally evident chiefly when we attain a completely clear intellectual grasp of the action-elements in their intended context of meaning. Empathic or appreciative accuracy is attained when, through sympathetic participation, we can adequately grasp the emotional context in which the action took place. The highest degree of rational understanding is attained in cases involving the meanings of logically or mathematically related propositions; their meaning may be immediately and unambiguously intelligible. […]

For the purposes of a typological scientific analysis it is convenient to treat all irrational, affectually determined elements of behavior as factors of deviation from a conceptually pure type of rational action. For example a panic on the stock exchange can be most conveniently analyzed by attempting to determine first what the course of action would have been if it had not been influenced by irrational affects; it is then possible to introduce the irrational components as accounting for the observed deviations from this hypothetical course. Similarly, in analyzing a political or military campaign it is convenient to determine in the first place what would have been a rational course, given the ends of the participants and adequate knowledge of all the circumstances. Only in this way is it possible to assess the causal significance of irrational factors as accounting for the deviations from this type. The construction of a purely rational course of action in such cases serves the sociologist as a type (ideal type) which has the merit of clear understandability and lack of ambiguity. By comparison with this it is possible to understand the ways in which actual action is influenced by irrational factors of all sorts, such as affects and errors, in that they account for the deviation from the line of conduct which would be expected on the hypothesis that the action were purely rational.

Only in this respect and for these reasons of methodological convenience is the method of sociology "rationalistic." It is naturally not legitimate to interpret this procedure as involving a rationalistic bias of sociology, but only as a methodological device. It certainly does not involve a belief in the actual predominance of rational elements in human life, for on the question of how far this predominance does or does not exist, nothing whatever has been said. That there is, however, a danger of rationalistic interpretations where they are out of place cannot be denied. All experience unfortunately confirms the existence of this danger.

4   In all the sciences of human action, account must be taken of processes and phenomena which are devoid of subjective meaning, in the role of stimuli, results, favoring or hindering circumstances. To be devoid of meaning is not identical with being lifeless or non-human; every artifact, such as for example a machine, can be understood only in terms of the meaning which its production and use have had or were intended to have; a meaning which may derive from a relation to exceedingly various purposes. Without reference to this meaning such an object remains wholly unintelligible. ...

5   Understanding may be of two kinds: the first is the direct observational understanding of the subjective meaning of a given act as such, including verbal utterances. We thus understand by direct observation, in this case, the meaning of the proposition $2 \times 2 = 4$ when we hear or read it. This is a case of the direct rational understanding of ideas. We also understand an outbreak of anger as manifested by facial expression, exclamations or irrational movements. This is direct observational understanding of irrational emotional reactions. We can understand in a similar observational way the action of a woodcutter or of somebody who reaches for the knob to shut a door or who aims a gun at an animal. This is rational observational understanding of actions.

Understanding may, however, be of another sort, namely explanatory understanding. Thus we understand in terms of *motive* the meaning an actor attaches to the proposition twice two equals four, when he states it or writes it down, in that we understand what makes him do this at precisely this moment and in these circumstances. Understanding in this sense is attained if we know that he is engaged in balancing a ledger or in making a scientific demonstration, or is engaged in some other task of which this particular act would be an appropriate part. This is rational understanding of motivation, which consists in placing the act in an intelligible and more inclusive context of meaning. Thus we understand the chopping of wood or aiming of a gun in terms of motive in addition to direct observation if we know that the woodchopper is working for a wage or is chopping a supply of firewood for his own use or possibly is doing it for recreation. But he might also be working off a fit of rage, an irrational case. Thus for a science which is concerned with the subjective meaning of action, explanation requires a grasp of the complex of meaning in which an actual course of understandable action thus interpreted belongs. In all such cases, even where the processes are largely affectual, the subjective meaning of the action, including that also of the relevant meaning complexes, will be called the intended meaning. (This involves a departure from ordinary usage, which speaks of intention in this sense only in the case of rationally purposive action.)

6 In all these cases understanding involves the interpretive grasp of the meaning present in one of the following contexts: (a) as in the historical approach, the actually intended meaning for concrete individual action; or (b) as in cases of sociological mass phenomena, the average of, or an approximation to, the actually intended meaning; or (c) the meaning appropriate to a scientifically formulated pure type (an ideal type) of a common phenomenon. [...]

Every interpretation attempts to attain clarity and certainty, but no matter how clear an interpretation as such appears to be from the point of view of meaning, it cannot on this account claim to be the causally valid interpretation. On this level it must remain only a peculiarly plausible hypothesis. ...

More generally, verification of subjective interpretation by comparison with the concrete course of events is, as in the case of all hypotheses, indispensable. Unfortunately this type of verification is feasible with relative accuracy only in the few very special cases susceptible of psychological experimentation. In very different degrees of approximation, such verification is also feasible in the limited number of cases of mass phenomena which can be statistically described and unambiguously interpreted. For the rest there remains only the possibility of comparing the largest possible number of historical or contemporary processes which, while otherwise similar, differ in the one decisive point of their relation to the particular motive or factor the role of which is being investigated. This is a fundamental task of comparative sociology. Often, unfortunately, there is available only the uncertain procedure of the "imaginary experiment" which consists in thinking away certain elements of a chain of motivation and working out the course of action which would then probably ensue, thus arriving at a causal judgment. [...]

7 A motive is a complex of subjective meaning which seems to the actor himself or to the observer an adequate ground for the conduct in question. The interpretation of a coherent course of conduct is "subjectively adequate" (or "adequate on the level of meaning"), insofar as, according to our habitual modes of thought and feeling, its component parts taken in their mutual relation are recognized to constitute a "typical" complex of meaning. It is more common to say "correct." The interpretation of a sequence of events will on the other hand be called *causally* adequate insofar as, according to established generalizations from experience, there is a probability that it will always actually occur in the same way. [...]

Statistical uniformities constitute understandable types of action, and thus constitute sociological generalizations, only when they can be regarded as manifestations of the understandable subjective meaning of a course of social action. Conversely, formulations of a rational course of subjectively understandable action constitute sociological types of empirical process only when they can be empirically observed with a significant degree of approximation. By no means is the actual likelihood of the occurrence of a given course of overt action always directly proportional to the clarity of subjective interpretation. Only actual experience can prove whether this is so in a given case. There are statistics of processes devoid of subjective meaning, such as death rates, phenomena of fatigue, the production rate of machines, the amount of rainfall, in exactly the same sense as there are statistics of meaningful phenomena. But only when the phenomena are meaningful do we speak of sociological statistics. Examples are such cases as crime rates, occupational distributions, price statistics, and statistics of crop acreage. Naturally there are many cases where both components are involved, as in crop statistics.

8   Processes and uniformities, which it has here seemed convenient not to designate as sociological phenomena or uniformities because they are not "understandable," are naturally not on that account any the less important. This is true even for sociology in our sense which is restricted to subjectively understandable phenomena – a usage which there is no intention of attempting to impose on anyone else. Such phenomena, however important, are simply treated by a different method from the others; they become conditions, stimuli, furthering or hindering circumstances of action.

9   Action in the sense of subjectively understandable orientation of behavior exists only as the behavior of one or more *individual* human beings. For other cognitive purposes it may be useful or necessary to consider the individual, for instance, as a collection of cells, as a complex of bio-chemical reactions, or to conceive his psychic life as made up of a variety of different elements, however these may be defined. Undoubtedly such procedures yield valuable knowledge of causal relationships. But the behavior of these elements, as expressed in such uniformities, is not subjectively understandable. [...]

For still other cognitive purposes – for instance, juristic ones – or for practical ends, it may on the other hand be convenient or even indispensable to treat social collectivities, such as states, associations, business corporations, foundations, as if they were individual persons. Thus they may be treated as the subjects of rights and duties or as the performers of legally significant actions. But for the subjective interpretation of action in sociological work these collectivities must be treated as *solely* the resultants and modes of organization of the particular acts of individual persons, since these alone can be treated as agents in a course of subjectively understandable action. Nevertheless, the sociologist cannot for his purposes afford to ignore these collective concepts derived from other disciplines. For the subjective interpretation of action has at least three important relations to these concepts. In the first place it is often necessary to employ very similar collective concepts, indeed often using the same terms, in order to obtain an intelligible terminology. Thus both in legal terminology and in everyday speech the term "state" is used both for the legal concept of the state and for the phenomena of social action to which its legal rules are relevant. [...]

Secondly, the subjective interpretation of action must take account of a fundamentally important fact. These concepts of collective entities, which are found both in common sense and in juristic and other technical forms of thought, have a meaning in the minds of individual persons, partly as of something actually existing, partly as something with normative authority. This is true not only of judges and officials, but of ordinary private individuals as well. Actors thus in part orient their action to them, and in this role such ideas have a powerful, often a decisive, causal influence on the course of action of real individuals. [...]

Thirdly, it is the method of the so-called "organic" school of sociology – classical example: Schäffle's brilliant work, *Bau und Leben des sozialen Körpers* – to attempt to understand social interaction by using as a point of departure the "whole" within which the individual acts. His action and behavior are then interpreted somewhat in the way that a physiologist would treat the role of an organ of the body in the "economy" of the organism, that is from the point of view of the survival of the latter. (Compare the famous dictum of a well-known physiologist: "Sec. 10. The spleen. Of the spleen, gentlemen, we know nothing. So much for the spleen." Actually, of course, he knew a good deal about the spleen – its position, size, shape, etc.; but he could say nothing about its function, and it was his inability to do this that he called "ignorance.") How far in other disciplines this type of functional analysis of the relation of "parts" to a "whole" can be regarded as definitive, cannot be discussed here; but it is well known that the bio-chemical and bio-physical modes of analysis of the organism are on principle opposed to stopping there. For purposes of sociological analysis two things can be said. First this functional frame of reference is convenient for purposes of practical illustration and for provisional orientation. In these respects it is not only useful but indispensable. But at the same time if its cognitive value is overestimated and its concepts illegitimately "reified," it can be highly dangerous. Secondly, in certain circumstances this is the only available way of determining just what processes of social action it is important to understand in order to explain a given phenomenon. But this is only the beginning of sociological analysis as here understood. In the case of social collectivities, precisely as distinguished from organisms, we are in a position to go beyond merely demonstrating functional relationships and uniformities. We can accomplish something which is never attainable in the natural sciences, namely the subjective understanding of the action of the component individuals.

It is a tremendous misunderstanding to think that an "individualistic" *method* should involve what is in any conceivable sense an individualistic system of *values*. It is as important to avoid this error as the related one which confuses the unavoidable tendency of sociological concepts to assume a rationalistic character with a belief in the predominance of rational motives, or even a positive valuation of rationalism. Even a socialistic economy would have to be understood sociologically in exactly the same kind of "individualistic" terms; that is, in terms of the action of individuals, the types of officials found in it, as would be the case with a system of free exchange analyzed in terms of the theory of marginal utility or a "better," but in this respect similar, theory. The real empirical sociological investigation begins with the question: What motives determine and lead the individual members and participants in this socialistic community to behave in such a way that the community came into being in the first place and that it continues to exist? Any form of functional analysis which proceeds from the whole to the parts can accomplish only a preliminary preparation for this investigation – a preparation, the utility and indispensability of which, if properly carried out, is naturally beyond question.

10 It is customary to designate various sociological generalizations, as for example "Gresham's Law," as "laws." These are in fact typical probabilities confirmed by observation to the effect that under certain given conditions an expected course of social action will occur, which is understandable in terms of the typical motives and typical subjective intentions of the actors. These generalizations are both understandable and definite in the highest degree insofar as the typically observed course of action can be understood in terms of the purely rational pursuit of an end, or where for reasons of methodological convenience such a theoretical type can be heuristically employed. In such cases the relations of means and end will be clearly understandable on grounds of experience, particularly where the choice of means was "inevitable." In such cases it is legitimate to assert that insofar as the action was rigorously rational it could not have taken any other course because for technical reasons, given their clearly defined ends, no other means were available to the actors. This very case demonstrates how erroneous it is to regard any kind of psychology as the ultimate foundation of the sociological interpretation of action. [...]

11 We have taken for granted that sociology seeks to formulate type concepts and generalized uniformities of empirical process. This distinguishes it from history, which is oriented to the causal analysis and explanation of individual actions, structures, and personalities possessing cultural significance. The empirical material which underlies the concepts of sociology consists to a very large extent, though by no means exclusively, of the same concrete processes of action which are dealt with by historians. An important consideration in the formulation of sociological concepts and generalizations is the contribution that sociology can make toward the causal explanation of some historically and culturally important phenomenon. As in the case of every generalizing science the abstract character of the concepts of sociology is responsible for the fact that, compared with actual historical reality, they are relatively lacking in fullness of concrete content. To compensate for this disadvantage, sociological analysis can offer a greater precision of concepts. This

precision is obtained by striving for the highest possible degree of adequacy on the level of meaning. It has already been repeatedly stressed that this aim can be realized in a particularly high degree in the case of concepts and generalizations which formulate rational processes. But sociological investigation attempts to include in its scope various irrational phenomena, such as prophetic, mystic, and affectual modes of action, formulated in terms of theoretical concepts which are adequate on the level of meaning. In *all* cases, rational or irrational, sociological analysis both abstracts from reality and at the same time helps us to understand it, in that it shows with what degree of approximation a concrete historical phenomenon can be subsumed under one or more of these concepts. For example, the same historical phenomenon may be in one aspect feudal, in another patrimonial, in another bureaucratic, and in still another charismatic. In order to give a precise meaning to these terms, it is necessary for the sociologist to formulate pure ideal types of the corresponding forms of action which in each case involve the highest possible degree of logical integration by virtue of their complete adequacy on the level of meaning. But precisely because this is true, it is probably seldom if ever that a real phenomenon can be found which corresponds exactly to one of these ideally constructed pure types. [...]

The theoretical concepts of sociology are ideal types not only from the objective point of view, but also in their application to subjective processes. In the great majority of cases actual action goes on in a state of inarticulate half-consciousness or actual unconsciousness of its subjective meaning. The actor is more likely to "be aware" of it in a vague sense than he is to "know" what he is doing or be explicitly self-conscious about it. In most cases his action is governed by impulse or habit. Only occasionally and, in the uniform action of large numbers, often only in the case of a few individuals, is the subjective meaning of the action, whether rational or irrational, brought clearly into consciousness.

(B) Social action

1   Social action, which includes both failure to act and passive acquiescence, may be oriented to the past, present, or expected future behavior of others. Thus it may be motivated by revenge for a past attack, defense against present, or measures of defense against future aggression. The "others" may be individual persons, and may be known to the actor as such, or may constitute an indefinite plurality and may be entirely unknown as individuals. (Thus, money is a means of exchange which the actor accepts in payment because he orients his action to the expectation that a large but unknown number of individuals he is personally unacquainted with will be ready to accept it in exchange on some future occasion.)

2   Not every kind of action, even of overt action, is "social" in the sense of the present discussion. Overt action is non-social if it is oriented solely to the behavior of inanimate objects. Subjective attitudes constitute social action only so far as

they are oriented to the behavior of others. For example, religious behavior is not social if it is simply a matter of contemplation or of solitary prayer. The economic activity of an individual is social only if it takes account of the behavior of someone else. Thus very generally it becomes social insofar as the actor assumes that others will respect his actual control over economic goods. Concretely it is social, for instance, if in relation to the actor's own consumption the future wants of others are taken into account and this becomes one consideration affecting the actor's own saving. Or, in another connexion, production may be oriented to the future wants of other people.

3   Not every type of contact of human beings has a social character; this is rather confined to cases where the actor's behavior is meaningfully oriented to that of others. For example, a mere collision of two cyclists may be compared to a natural event. On the other hand, their attempt to avoid hitting each other, or whatever insults, blows, or friendly discussion might follow the collision, would constitute "social action."

4   Social action is not identical either with the similar actions of many persons or with every action influenced by other persons. Thus, if at the beginning of a shower a number of people on the street put up their umbrellas at the same time, this would not ordinarily be a case of action mutually oriented to that of each other, but rather of all reacting in the same way to the like need of protection from the rain. It is well known that the actions of the individual are strongly influenced by the mere fact that he is a member of a crowd confined within a limited space. Thus, the subject matter of studies of "crowd psychology," such as those of Le Bon, will be called "action conditioned by crowds." It is also possible for large numbers, though dispersed, to be influenced simultaneously or successively by a source of influence operating similarly on all the individuals, as by means of the press.... But for this to happen there need not, at least in many cases, be any meaningful relation between the behavior of the individual and the fact that he is a member of a crowd. It is not proposed in the present sense to call action "social" when it is merely a result of the effect on the individual of the existence of a crowd as such and the action is not oriented to that fact on the level of meaning. At the same time the borderline is naturally highly indefinite. In such cases as that of the influence of the demagogue, there may be a wide variation in the extent to which his mass clientele is affected by a meaningful reaction to the fact of its large numbers; and whatever this relation may be, it is open to varying interpretations.

But furthermore, mere "imitation" of the action of others, such as that on which Tarde has rightly laid emphasis, will not be considered a case of specifically social action if it is purely reactive so that there is no meaningful orientation to the actor imitated. The borderline is, however, so indefinite that it is often hardly possible to discriminate.... On the other hand, if the action of others is imitated because it is fashionable or traditional or exemplary, or lends social distinction, or on similar grounds, it is meaningfully oriented either to the behavior of the source of imitation or of third persons or of both....

2 Types of Social Action

Social action, like all action, may be oriented in four ways. It may be:

(1) *instrumentally rational* (*zweckrational*), that is, determined by expectations as to the behavior of objects in the environment and of other human beings; these expectations are used as "conditions" or "means" for the attainment of the actor's own rationally pursued and calculated ends;
(2) *value-rational* (*wertrational*), that is, determined by a conscious belief in the value for its own sake of some ethical, aesthetic, religious, or other form of behavior, independently of its prospects of success;
(3) *affectual* (especially emotional), that is, determined by the actor's specific affects and feeling states;
(4) *traditional*, that is, determined by ingrained habituation.

1   Strictly traditional behavior, like the reactive type of imitation discussed above, lies very close to the borderline of what can justifiably be called meaningfully oriented action, and indeed often on the other side. For it is very often a matter of almost automatic reaction to habitual stimuli which guide behavior in a course which has been repeatedly followed. The great bulk of all everyday action to which people have become habitually accustomed approaches this type. Hence, its place in a systematic classification is not merely that of a limiting case because, as will be shown later, attachment to habitual forms can be upheld with varying degrees of self-consciousness and in a variety of senses. In this case the type may shade over into value rationality (*Wertrationalität*).
  2   Purely affectual behavior also stands on the borderline of what can be considered "meaningfully" oriented, and often it, too, goes over the line. It may, for instance, consist in an uncontrolled reaction to some exceptional stimulus. It is a case of sublimation when affectually determined action occurs in the form of conscious release of emotional tension. When this happens it is usually well on the road to rationalization in one or the other or both of the above senses.
  3   The orientation of value-rational action is distinguished from the affectual type by its clearly self-conscious formulation of the ultimate values governing the action and the consistently planned orientation of its detailed course to these values. At the same time the two types have a common element, namely that the meaning of the action does not lie in the achievement of a result ulterior to it, but in carrying out the specific type of action for its own sake. Action is affectual if it satisfies a need for revenge, sensual gratification, devotion, contemplative bliss, or for working off emotional tensions (irrespective of the level of sublimation).

Examples of pure value-rational orientation would be the actions of persons who, regardless of possible cost to themselves, act to put into practice their convictions of what seems to them to be required by duty, honor, the pursuit of beauty, a religious call, personal loyalty, or the importance of some "cause" no matter in what it consists. In our terminology, value-rational action always involves "commands" or "demands" which, in the actor's opinion, are binding on him. [...]

4   Action is instrumentally rational (*zweckrational*) when the end, the means, and the secondary results are all rationally taken into account and weighed. This involves rational consideration of alternative means to the end, of the relations of the end to the secondary consequences, and finally of the relative importance of different possible ends. Determination of action either in affectual or in traditional terms is thus incompatible with this type. Choice between alternative and conflicting ends and results may well be determined in a value-rational manner. In that case, action is instrumentally rational only in respect to the choice of means. On the other hand, the actor may, instead of deciding between alternative and conflicting ends in terms of a rational orientation to a system of values, simply take them as given subjective wants and arrange them in a scale of consciously assessed relative urgency. He may then orient his action to this scale in such a way that they are satisfied as far as possible in order of urgency, as formulated in the principle of "marginal utility." Value-rational action may thus have various different relations to the instrumentally rational action. From the latter point of view, however, value-rationality is always irrational. [...]

5   It would be very unusual to find concrete cases of action, especially of social action, which were oriented *only* in one or another of these ways. Furthermore, this classification of the modes of orientation of action is in no sense meant to exhaust the possibilities of the field, but only to formulate in conceptually pure form certain sociologically important types to which actual action is more or less closely approximated or, in much the more common case, which constitute its elements. The usefulness of the classification for the purposes of this investigation can only be judged in terms of its results.

Chapter 21

The Protestant Ethic and the Spirit of Capitalism [1930]

Max Weber

Religious Affiliation and Social Stratification

A glance at the occupational statistics for any country in which several religions coexist is revealing. They indicate that people who own capital, employers, more highly educated skilled workers, and more highly trained technical or business personnel in modern companies tend to be, with striking frequency, overwhelmingly *Protestant*. The variation in this regard between Catholics and Protestants has often been discussed, in a lively fashion, in Catholic newspapers and journals in Germany, as well as at congresses of the Catholic Church.

According to the statistics, this variation between Catholics and Protestants is prominent where differences in religious belief and in nationality – and hence differences in the extent of cultural development – are found in the same region. Germans and Poles in eastern Germany come to mind. Yet the numbers demonstrate as well that differences are equally apparent in nearly all areas where capitalism, in the period of its great expansion [in the eighteenth and nineteenth centuries], possessed a free hand to reorganize, according to its requirements, a population socially and to order it by occupations. Differences according to religious belief became all the more striking to the extent that these changes occurred.

Of course the disproportionately high percentage of Protestants among the owners of capital, the more highly educated skilled workers, and those employed

---

Weber, Max, "The Protestant Ethic and the Spirit of Capitalism," from Max Weber, *Protestant Ethic and the Spirit of Capitalism With Other Writings on the Rise of the West* 4th edn, translated by Stephen Kalberg (2010) pp. 61–65, 69–79, 86, 151–159, published by Oxford University Press. Reprinted with permission of Oxford University Press.

Classical Sociological Theory, Third Edition. Edited by Craig Calhoun, Joseph Gerteis, James Moody, Steven Pfaff, and Indermohan Virk. Editorial material and organization © 2012 John Wiley & Sons, Ltd. Published 2012 by John Wiley & Sons, Ltd.

in large industrial and commercial companies can in part be traced back to historical forces from the distant past. Moreover, religious affiliation may not appear to be the *cause* of economic activity; rather, differences in religious belief may seem, to a certain extent, to be the *result* of economic factors. After all, participation in certain economic activities assumes in part some ownership of capital to begin with, in part a costly education, and in part – most frequently – both. Today this participation is tied to ownership of inherited wealth or at least to a certain material affluence. It must also be noted that, in the old German Empire, a large number of the richest and most economically developed areas – favored by nature or a geographical location that facilitated trade and commerce – turned Protestant in the sixteenth century. This held especially for the majority of the wealthy cities. The effects of this wealth benefit Protestants in the economic struggle for existence even today.

The historical question then arises, however: What reasons explain the particularly strong predilection in the most economically developed regions toward a revolution in the Catholic Church [in the sixteenth century]? The answer is by no means as simple as one might at first believe.

Certainly the shedding of the old economic traditionalism would seem essentially to support both the tendency to doubt, even religious belief, and the resistance to traditional authorities. Nevertheless, that which is today so often forgotten must be noted here: the Reformation of the sixteenth century not only involved the *elimination* of the Catholic Church's domination over the believer's life in its entirety, but also the substitution of one form of control by *another*. A highly agreeable domination that had become a mere formality, one that was scarcely felt in a practical manner, was replaced by an infinitely burdensome and severe regimentation of the entire organization of the believer's life. Religion now penetrated all private and public spheres in the most comprehensive sense imaginable.

A classic adage succinctly characterizes the Catholic Church's domination as it was earlier even more than today: "The heretic must be punished, but the sinner must be treated leniently." This view was upheld at the beginning of the fifteenth century in the richest, most economically developed regions on earth, and it is upheld even now by groups of people with thoroughly modern orientations to economic activity. In contrast, the domination of Calvinism as it existed in the sixteenth century in Geneva and Scotland, at the end of the sixteenth and beginning of the seventeenth centuries in large parts of Holland, in the seventeenth century in New England, and even in England from time to time, would constitute for us today the most absolutely unbearable form of control by the church over the individual. Large segments of the old commercial aristocracy at that time experienced Calvinism in just this way. Yet the religious activists of the Reformation period, who arose in the most economically developed nations, complained that religion and the church exercised too little domination over life rather than too much.

How then did it happen that precisely the most economically developed nations of that period, and (as will become apparent) specifically their upwardly mobile middle classes, not only allowed this heretofore unknown Puritan tyranny to encompass them; rather they even developed a heroic defense of it? *Middle* classes *as such* had only rarely submitted to religious tyranny of this degree prior to the sixteenth and seventeenth centuries, and they have never done so since then. Not without reason, [the Scottish writer and historian Thomas] Carlyle [1795–1881] referred to this defense as "the last of our heroisms."

But let us proceed. Could it be, as noted, that the greater ownership of capital by Protestants and their more frequent participation at the top levels of the modern economy are to be understood today in part as a consequence of their historical possession of substantial wealth and their success in passing it on to succeeding generations? Further observations, only a few of which can be mentioned here, indicate that the causal relationship surely *cannot* be formulated in this manner.

First, as is clearly demonstrable, Catholic parents in [the German states of] Baden and Bavaria, as well as in Hungary, for example, enroll their children in different *types* of programs and curricula from those chosen by Protestant parents. The percentage of Catholic students enrolled in the "accelerated" tracks and schools, and then graduating, remains significantly below the percentage of Catholics in the population as a whole. Of course, one is inclined to explain this difference largely by reference to the greater transfer of wealth by Protestants across generations.

This line of reasoning, however, fails to offer an adequate explanation for a second observation. *Within* the group of Catholic graduates enrolled in the accelerated tracks and schools, the percentage of students who decided to take courses in preparation for university study in technical fields or for careers in commerce and industry (or other middle-class ways of making a living in business) lagged *far* behind the percentage of Protestant graduates who decided to do so. Catholics preferred courses of instruction that emphasized languages, philosophy, and history. Reference to varying levels of inherited wealth will not account for these differences in respect to schooling. Indeed, they must be acknowledged in any explanation for the lower rates of entry into business by Catholics.

Third, an even more remarkable observation helps us to understand the lesser representation of Catholics among skilled *workers* in modern, large industrial concerns. It is well-known that the factory takes its skilled laborers to a large degree from the younger generation of handicraft workers. Thus, the factory leaves the training of its labor force to the crafts. Once skills have been acquired, the factory pulls workers – or "journeymen" – away from the crafts. This situation holds much more for Protestant than for Catholic journeymen. That is, Catholic journeymen demonstrate a much stronger inclination to remain in their crafts and thus more often become master craftsmen. In contrast, Protestants stream into the factory at a comparatively higher rate and then acquire positions as high-level skilled workers and industrial managers. In these cases the causal relationship is undoubtedly one in which a *learned inner quality* decides a person's choice of occupation and further course of occupational development. And this inner quality is influenced by the direction of one's upbringing, which in turn is influenced by the religious climate in one's native town and one's parental home.

The less frequent participation of Catholics in modern business life in Germany is indeed all the more striking because it opposes an age-old (as well as present-day) empirical rule of thumb: ethnic or religious minorities, as "dominated" groups standing opposite a "dominant" group, and *as a consequence of* their voluntary or involuntary exclusion from influential political positions, have been driven to an especially strong degree into the arena of business. Hence, in Germany the most talented among the minority, who might, if not oppressed, hope for the highly sought-after positions at the top levels of the state civil service, instead seek to satisfy their ambitions in the realm of business. Unmistakably, this situation holds for the undoubtedly economically advancing Poles in Russia and eastern Prussia, where, as Catholics, they were a minority (in contrast to their situation in the province of Galicia in Poland, where they were the majority population). It also holds for earlier groupings: the Huguenots in France under Louis XIV, the Nonconformists and Quakers in England, and, last but not least, the Jews for two thousand years. Catholics in Germany, however, do not today follow this pattern. There seems to be no evidence (or at least no clear evidence) of a movement of this minority into large-scale industry, commerce, and business in general. In the past as well, in Holland and England and in both periods of toleration as well as those of persecution of Catholics, in contrast to Protestants, evidence for any particular *economic* development among Catholics cannot be found.

A different situation existed for Protestants. *Both* as ruling *and* ruled strata and *both* as majority *and* minority, Protestants (especially the denominations to be discussed later [in this study]) have demonstrated a specific tendency toward *economic rationalism*. This tendency has not been observed in the same way in the present or the past among Catholics, regardless of whether they were the dominant or dominated stratum *or* constituted a majority or minority. Therefore, the cause of the different behavior must be mainly sought in the enduring inner quality of these religions and *not* only in their respective historical-political, external situations. Our first task will be to investigate which of the elements in the characteristic features of each religion had, and to some extent still have, the effects described above.

On the basis of a superficial consideration of the matter and from the vantage point of certain modern impressions, one could attempt to formulate the contrast as one in which Catholicism's greater "estrangement from the world" – the ascetic features proclaimed by its highest ideals – had to socialize believers to be more indifferent to material and consumer goods. In fact, this explanation corresponds to the familiar mode of evaluating these differences popular in Germany in both religions [at the turn into the twentieth century]. German Protestants employ this view in order to criticize every (real or presumed) ascetic ideal in the Catholic way of organizing life. Catholics answer by reproaching Protestants for the "materialism" that has arisen from a secularization of the very meaning of life, holding Protestantism responsible for this development. A modern writer has attempted to capture the contrasting behavior of German Protestants and Catholics in regard to ways of making a living:

The Catholic … is more calm and endowed with a weaker motivation to become engaged in business, retains as cautious and risk-averse an approach to life's journey as possible, and prefers to get by on a smaller income rather than to become engaged in more dangerous and challenging activities – even if they may lead to greater honor and wealth. It is evident, in light of a popular and humorous maxim in Germany – 'one can either eat well or sleep peacefully' – that the Lutheran gladly eats well. On the other hand, the Catholic prefers to sleep undisturbed.

This "wish to eat well" may indeed correctly sum up the motivation of those Protestants in *Germany today* who remain rather indifferent believers – at least in part and even though it remains incomplete as an explanation. Matters were quite different in the past, however. As was commonly acknowledged, precisely the opposite of a natural and uncomplicated "enjoyment of life's pleasures" characterized the English, Dutch, and American Puritans. And, as will become evident, this approach to life is one of their traits of most importance to us. Moreover, French Protestantism, for example, for centuries and to a certain extent even today, has retained the stamp imposed upon the Calvinist churches generally – although chiefly upon those "under the cross" in the epoch of the religious struggles – namely, a certain severity rather than a natural enjoyment of life. Yet Protestantism was one of the most important carriers of industrial and capitalist development in France, as is well-known. This has remained so even if, owing to persecution, only on a small scale. Was this severity related to Protestantism's important role in capitalist development? This will be our query later.

[…]

That being said, and even if we succeed in demarcating the case we are attempting here to analyze and explain historically, our concern now cannot be to offer a conceptual definition. Instead, our focus at the beginning should be only to provide a provisional *illustration* of the activity implied here by the term *spirit of capitalism*. Indeed, such an illustration is indispensable in order to attain our aim now of simply understanding the object of our investigation. On behalf of this purpose we turn to a document that contains the spirit of concern to us in near classical purity, and simultaneously offers the advantage of being detached from *all* direct connection to religious belief–hence, for our theme, of being "free of presuppositions."

> Remember, that *time* is *money*. He that can earn ten shillings a day by his labour, and goes abroad, or sits idle one half of that day, though he spends but sixpence during his diversion or idleness, ought not to reckon that the only expense; he has really spent or rather thrown away five shillings besides.
> Remember, that *credit* is *money*. If a man lets his money lie in my hands after it is due, he gives me the interest, or so much as I can make of it during that time. This amounts to a considerable sum where a man has good and large credit, and makes good use of it.
> Remember, that money is of the *prolific, generating nature*. Money can beget money, and its offspring can beget more, and so on. Five shillings turned is six, turned again it is seven and threepence, and so on, till it becomes a hundred pounds. The more there is of it, the more it produces every turning, so that the profits rise quicker and

quicker. He that kills a breeding-sow, destroys all her offspring to the thousandth generation. He that murders a crown, *destroys* all that it might have produced, even scores of pounds. ...

Remember this saying: The good *paymaster* is lord of another man's purse. He that is known to pay punctually and exactly to the time he promises, may at any time, and on any occasion, raise all the money his friends can spare.

This is sometimes of great use. After industry and frugality, nothing contributes more to the *raising* of a young man in the world than punctuality and justice in all his dealings; therefore never keep borrowed money an hour beyond the time you promised, lest a disappointment shut up your friend's purse for ever.

The most trifling actions that affect a man's *credit* are to be regarded. The sound of your hammer at five in the morning, or nine at night, heard by a creditor, makes him easy six months longer; but if he sees you at a billiard-table, or hears your voice at a tavern, when you should be at work, he sends for his money the next day; ... [he] demands it before you are able to pay.

It shows, besides, that you are mindful of what you owe; it makes you *appear* a careful as well as an *honest man*, and that still increases your *credit*.

Beware of thinking that you own all that you possess, and of living accordingly. It is a mistake that many people who have credit fall into. To prevent this, keep an exact account both of your expenses and your income. If you make an effort to attend to particular expenses, it will have this good effect: you will discover how wonderfully small, trifling expenses mount up to large sums, and will discern what might have been, and may for the future be saved, without occasioning any great inconvenience.

For six pounds a year you may have the use of one hundred pounds if you are a man of known prudence and honesty.

He that spends a groat a day idly, spends idly above six pounds a year, which is the price of using one hundred pounds.

He that wastes idly a groat's worth of his time per day, one day with another, wastes the privilege of using one hundred pounds each year.

He that idly loses five shillings' worth of time, loses five shillings and might as prudently throw five shillings into the sea.

He that loses five shillings not only loses that sum, but all the advantage that might be made by turning it in dealing, which by the time that a young man becomes old, amounts to a comfortable bag of money.

It is *Benjamin Franklin*[2] [1706–90] who preaches to us in these sentences. As the supposed catechism of a Yankee, Ferdinand Kürnberger satirizes these axioms in his brilliantly clever and venomous *Picture of American Culture*. That the spirit of capitalism is here manifest in Franklin's words, even in a characteristic manner, no one will doubt. It will not be argued here, however, that *all aspects* of what can be understood by this spirit are contained in them.

Let us dwell a moment upon a passage, the worldly wisdom of which is summarized thusly by Kürnberger: "They make tallow for candles out of cattle and money out of men." Remarkably, the real peculiarity in the "philosophy of avarice" contained in this maxim is the ideal of the *credit-worthy* man of honor and, above all, the idea of the *duty* of the individual to increase his wealth, which is assumed to be a self-defined interest in itself. Indeed, rather than simply a common-sense approach to life, a peculiar "ethic" is preached here: its violation is treated not simply as foolishness but as a sort of forgetfulness of *duty*. Above all, this distinction stands at the center of the matter. "Business savvy," which is found commonly enough, is here not *alone* taught; rather, an *ethos* is expressed in this maxim. Just *this* quality is of interest to us in this investigation.

A retired business partner of Jakob Fugger, [1459–1525, an extremely wealthy German financier, export merchant, and philanthropist], once sought to convince him to retire. Yet his colleague's argument – that he had accumulated enough wealth and should allow others their chance – was rebuked by Fugger as "contemptible timidity." He "viewed matters differently," Fugger answered, and "wanted simply to make money as long as he could."

Obviously, the spirit of this statement must be *distinguished* from Franklin's. Fugger's entrepreneurial daring and personal, morally indifferent proclivities now take on the character, in Franklin, of an *ethically*-oriented maxim for the organization of life. The expression *spirit of capitalism* will be used here in just this specific manners – naturally the spirit of *modern* capitalism. That is, in light of the formulation of our theme, it must be evident that the Western European and American capitalism of the last few centuries constitutes our concern rather than the "capitalism" that has appeared in China, India, Babylon, the ancient world, and the Middle Ages. As we will see, *just that peculiar ethic was missing in all these cases*.

Nevertheless, all of Franklin's moral admonishments are applied in a utilitarian fashion: Honesty is *useful* because it leads to the availability of credit. Punctuality, industry, and frugality are also useful, and are *therefore* virtues. It would follow from this that, for example, the *appearance* of honesty, wherever it accomplishes the same end, would suffice. Moreover, in Franklin's eyes an unnecessary surplus of this virtue must be seen as unproductive wastefulness. Indeed, whoever reads in his autobiography the story of his "conversion" to these virtues, or the complete discussions on the usefulness of a strict preservation of the *appearance* of modesty and the intentional minimizing of one's own accomplishments in order to attain a general approval, will necessarily come to the conclusion that all virtues, according to Franklin, become virtues *only to the extent* that they are useful to the individual. The surrogate of virtue – namely, its appearance only – is fully adequate wherever the same purpose is achieved. Indeed, this inseparability of motive and appearance is the inescapable consequence of all strict utilitarianism. The common German tendency to perceive the American virtues as "hypocrisy" appears here confirmed beyond a doubt.

[...]

The complexity of this issue is above all apparent in the *summum bonum* ["supreme good"] of this "ethic": namely, the acquisition of money, and more and more money, takes place here simultaneously with the strictest avoidance of all spontaneous enjoyment of it. The pursuit of riches is fully stripped of all pleasurable (*eudämonistischen*), and surely all hedonistic, aspects. Accordingly, this striving becomes understood completely as an end in itself – to such an extent that it appears as fully outside the normal course of affairs and simply irrational, at least when viewed from the perspective of the "happiness" or "utility" of the single individual. Here, people are oriented to acquisition as the purpose of life; acquisition is no longer viewed as a means to the end of satisfying the substantive needs of life. Those people in possession of spontaneous, fun-loving dispositions experience this situation as an absolutely meaningless reversal of a "natural" condition (as we would say today). Yet this reversal constitutes just as surely a guiding principle of [modern] capitalism as incomprehension of this new situation characterizes all who remain untouched by [modern] capitalism's tentacles.

This reversal implies an internal line of development that comes into close contact with certain religious ideas. One can ask why then "money ought to be made out of persons." In his autobiography, and although he is himself a bland Deist, Franklin answers with a maxim from the Bible that, as he says, his strict Calvinist father again and again drilled into him in his youth: "Seest thou a man vigorous in his vocational calling (*Beruf*)? He shall stand before kings" (Prov. 22:29). As long as it is carried out in a legal manner, the acquisition of money in the modern economic order is the result and manifestation of competence and proficiency in a *vocational calling. This competence and proficiency* is the actual alpha and omega of Franklin's morality, as now can be easily recognized. It presents itself to us both in the passages cited above and, without exception, in all his writings.

In fact, this peculiar idea of a *duty to have a vocational calling,* so familiar to us today but actually not at all self-evident, is the idea that is characteristic of the "social ethic" of modern capitalist culture. In a certain sense, it is even of constitutive significance for it. It implies a notion of duty that individuals ought to experience, and do, vis-à-vis the content of their "vocational" activity. This notion appears regardless of the particular nature of the activity and regardless, especially, of whether this activity seems to involve (as it does for people with a spontaneous, fun-loving disposition) nothing more than a simple utilization of their capacity for labor or their treatment of it as only a material possession (as "capital").

[...]

We can address the idea of naive historical materialism – that such "ideas" arise as a "reflection" or "superstructure" of economic situations – in more detail only later. It must suffice adequately for our purpose at this point to call attention to the fact that the capitalist spirit (according to our definition here) without a doubt existed *before* "capitalist development" in the colony (Massachusetts) where Benjamin Franklin was born. (In contrast to other regions in America, one complained in New England as early as 1632 about specific appearances of a particularly calculating type of profit seeking.) Moreover, for example, in the neighboring colonies that were later to become the southern states of the union, this capitalist spirit remained distinctly less developed despite the fact that the southern states were called into being by large-scale capitalists for *business* purposes. In contrast, the New England colonies were called into existence for *religious* reasons by ministers and seminary graduates, together with small-scale merchants, craftsmen, and farmers. Thus, in *this* case at any rate, the causal relationship between ideas and economic situations lies in the direction opposite from that which would be postulated by the "materialist" argument.

But the youth of these ideas – the capitalist spirit – is altogether more thorny than was assumed by the "superstructure" theorists, and its unfolding does not proceed in the manner of the blossoming of a flower. The capitalist spirit, according to the meaning of this concept thus far acquired, became prominent only after a difficult struggle against a world of hostile powers. The frame of mind (*Gesinnung*) apparent in the cited passages from Benjamin Franklin that met with the approval of an entire people would have been proscribed in the ancient world, as well as in the Middle Ages, for it would have been viewed as an expression of filthy greed and a completely undignified character. Indeed, antagonism to this frame of mind is found even today, particularly (and on a regular basis) in those social groups least integrated into or adapted to the modern capitalist economy. This was the case not because "the acquisitive instinct" in precapitalist epochs was perhaps less well-known or developed, as is so often said, or because the *auri sacra fames* [craving for gold] was then, or is even today, *smaller* outside modern, middle-class capitalism, as is depicted in the illusions of modern-day romantic thinkers. Such arguments will not isolate the distinction between the capitalist and precapitalist spirit: the *greed* of the mandarins in China, of the aristocrats in ancient Rome, and of the modern peasant is second to none. And as anyone can experience for himself, the *auri sacra fames* of the Naples cab driver, or *barcajuolo* [Venetian gondolier], representatives in Asia of similar trades, and craftsmen in southern Europe and Asia is even unusually *more intense*, and especially more unscrupulous, than that of, for example, an Englishman in the same situation.

The universal sway of *absolute* unscrupulousness in establishing one's own self-interest as the legitimate operating assumption for the pursuit of money has been specifically characteristic of precisely those countries where the development of a middle-class capitalism – measured against the standards of modern Western capitalist development – has remained "backward." The absence of *coscienziosità* [conscientiousness] among [wage] workers in such nations (such as Italy in comparison to Germany) has been, and to a certain extent still is, the major obstacle to the unfolding of modern capitalism, as every factory employer knows. Modern capitalism has as little use for *liberum arbitrium* [easygoing] persons as laborers as it has for the businessman fully without scruples in the running of his company, as we already have learned from Franklin. Hence, because its strength has varied, an "instinct" to pursue money cannot be the decisive issue.

The *auri sacra fames* is as old as the history of humanity known to us. We shall see that those who without reservation surrendered themselves to it as an *instinct* – the Dutch captain, for example, who "would sail through hell for profit, even if he burned his sails" – were *in no way* representatives of that frame of mind from which the specifically modern capitalist spirit burst forth as *a mass phenomenon*. That is what matters here. Acquisition unrestrained by internally binding norms has existed in all periods of history; indeed, it has existed wherever its expression was not circumscribed. In relationships across tribes and among peoples fundamentally unknown to each other, as well as in warfare and piracy, trade unbounded by norms has been the rule. A double standard prevailed in such situations: practices considered taboo "among brothers" were permitted with "outsiders."

As an "adventure," capitalist acquisition has found a place in all those economies that have known valuable objects as quasi-money forms of exchange and offered the chance to utilize them for profit. These economies have been based on, for example, *commenda*, tax farming, state-guaranteed loans, and the financing of wars, state functionaries, and the courts of princes. Coexisting everywhere with these external modes of economic organization were persons with an adventurous frame of mind – who mocked all ethical restrictions on action. An absolute and willfully ruthless striving for profit often stood hard and fast alongside a strict adherence to age-old traditions. Then, as these traditions began to disintegrate, a more or less broad-ranging expansion of an unrestrained quest for gain took place. In some situations, it intruded even into the core of social groups.

Hence, adventure capitalism did not imply an ethical affirmation and shaping of this new situation. Rather, the intrusion of an unrestrained quest for gain was only *tolerated* as a new reality; it was treated with ethical indifference or as a disagreeable but unavoidable presence. This was the normal position taken by all ethical teachings. Moreover, and of more essential importance, this view characterized the practical behavior of the average person in the epoch prior to modern capitalism, namely, before a rational use of capital in a managed manner and a systematic capitalist organization *of work* became the dominant forces determining the orientation of economic activity. This toleration of the unrestrained quest for gain, however, constituted everywhere one of the strongest inner barriers against the adaptation of persons to the preconditions of an organized, middle-class capitalist economy.

In the sense of a certain norm-bound style of life that has crystallized in the guise of an "ethic," the spirit of capitalism has had to struggle primarily against a specific opponent: that type of experiencing, perceiving, and ordering of the world that we can denote [*economic*] traditionalism. Every attempt to offer a final "definition," however, must be postponed. Instead, and of course only in a provisional manner, we will attempt a clear rendering of this term by reference to a few special cases. The workers first capture our attention.

One of the technical means used by the modern employer to achieve the highest possible productivity from "his" workers, and to increase the intensity of work, is the *piece-rate* method of payment. People are paid according to the fruits of their labor. In agriculture, for example, the harvesting of the crops requires the highest possible intensity of labor field by field. This requirement is common not least because, owing to the unpredictability of the weather, extraordinarily large profits and losses depend upon the greatest conceivable acceleration of the harvesting. Accordingly, the piece-rate method is customarily employed. Wherever the size of the harvest and the intensity of the company's work rhythms increase, so does the employer's interest in accelerated harvesting. Thus, employers have repeatedly attempted to interest workers in increasing their productivity by increasing the piece rate. Indeed, in doing so employers believed they were offering workers an opportunity to earn, in very short periods of time, what appeared to them an extraordinary wage.

Just at this point, however, peculiar difficulties became apparent. Remarkably, increasing the piece rate often led to less productivity in the same period of time rather than more. This decline occurred because workers responded to the increase by decreasing their daily productivity. For example, a man has been accustomed to harvesting 2½ acres per day and to receiving one German mark for every acre of grain harvested. He thus earns 2½ marks every day. If the piece rate is raised to 1¼ marks per acre, he needs to harvest only 2 acres per day in order to earn the same amount as before, and this, according to the biblical passage, "allows enough for him." Yet the employer's hope of increasing productivity by increasing the piece-rate has been disappointed (if the worker had harvested 3 acres, he would have earned 3¾ marks).

The opportunity of earning more appealed to him less than the idea of working less. He did not ask: "If I produce as much as possible, how much money will I earn each day?" Rather, he formulated the question differently: "How long must I work in order to earn the amount of money – 2½ marks – I have earned until now and that has fulfilled my *traditional* economic needs?"

This example illustrates the type of behavior that should be called economic "traditionalism." People do not wish "by nature" to earn more and more money. Instead, they wish simply to live, and to live as they have been accustomed and to earn as much as is required to do so. Wherever modern capitalism began its task of increasing the "productivity" of human work by increasing its intensity, it confronted, in the precapitalist economy, an infinitely obdurate barrier in the form of this definition of work. Even today modern capitalism everywhere encounters economic traditionalism the more "backward" (from the perspective of modern capitalism) are the very laborers it depends on.

But let us again return to our illustration. Owing to the incapacity of the higher piece-rate to appeal to the "acquisitive sense," it would appear altogether plausible to attempt to do so by utilizing the opposite strategy: by *decreasing* piece-rates, to force workers to produce *more* in order to maintain their accustomed earnings. Moreover, two simple observations seem to have held true in the past, as they do today: a lower wage and higher profit are directly related, and all that is paid out in higher wages must imply a corresponding reduction of profits. Capitalism has been guided by this axiom repeatedly, and even from its beginning, and it has been an article of faith for centuries that lower wages are "productive." In other words, lower wages were believed to enhance worker productivity. As Pieter de la Court, [1618–85, Dutch textile manufacturer and strong proponent of fully unregulated trade and competition], contended (completely in accord in this respect with the old Calvinism, as we will see), people work only because, and only so long as, they are poor.

Nevertheless, the effectiveness of this presumably tried and proven strategy has limitations. Capitalism surely required, for its development, the presence of population surpluses that kept the market costs of labor low. Indeed, under certain circumstances an overly large "reserve army" of workers facilitates capitalism's quantitative expansion. It slows down, however, its qualitative development, especially with respect to the transition to work in organizations that require intensive labor. A lower wage is in no way identical with cheaper labor. Even when scrutinized in reference to purely quantitative considerations, the productivity of work can be seen to sink, under all circumstances, when wages are too low to sustain good health. If retained in the long run, such a wage often leads plainly to a "selection of the least fit." The average farmer from Silesia harvests today, when he exerts himself fully, little more than two-thirds of the land in the same amount of time as the better paid and better nourished farmer from Pomerania or Mecklenburg. Compared to the Germans, the Poles' capacity for physical work declines more and more the farther to the east their homeland.

Even considered purely from the business point of view, lower wages fail, as a pillar of modern capitalist development, in all those situations where goods are produced that require any type of skilled labor, where expensive and easily damaged machines are used, and in general where a significant degree of focused concentration and initiative is demanded. In these circumstances the lower wage does not prove economically feasible, and its effects lead to the opposite of all that was originally intended. This holds in these situations for the simple reason that a developed sense of responsibility is absolutely indispensable. In addition, it is necessary to have a *frame of mind* that emancipates the worker, at least *during* the workday, from a constant question: With a maximum of ease and comfort and a minimum of productivity, how is the accustomed wage nonetheless to be maintained? This frame of mind, if it manages to uproot the worker from this concern, motivates labor as if labor were an absolute end in itself, or a "calling."

Yet such a frame of mind is not inherently given in the nature of the species. Nor can it be directly called forth by high or low wages. Rather, it is the product of a long and continuous process of socialization. Today, sitting triumphantly dominant, modern capitalism is able to recruit its workers in all industrial nations and in all the branches of industry in these nations relatively easily. Yet in the past recruitment was everywhere an extremely difficult problem. Even today, without the assistance of a powerful ally, modern capitalism does not always reach the goals that, as we will further note below, accompanied it in the period of its early development.

An illustration will again offer clarity. A portrait of the older traditional approach to work is very frequently provided [in the early twentieth century] by *female* workers, above all by those who are unmarried.

An almost universal complaint among employers concerns the absolute incapacity and unwillingness of women workers to give up customary and once-mastered modes of work in favor of other, more practical work techniques, and their inability to adapt to new forms of labor, to learn, and to focus the mind's reasoning capacities, or even to use it. This view holds in particular for German young women. Efforts to organize work in a simpler and, especially, more productive manner come up against complete incomprehension. Increases in the piece-rate [designed to raise production] strike against the wall of habit without the least effect.

The situation is often different only with young women from a specific religious background, namely for women from Pietist homes (not an unimportant point for our reflections). One hears often, and it is confirmed by occasional statistical studies, that by far the most favorable prospects for socialization into the rhythms of the workplace exist among young women in this category. The capacity to focus one's thoughts in addition to an absolutely central element – the capacity to feel an "internal dedication to the work" – are found here unusually frequently. Indeed, these qualities combine with an organized approach to economic activity that, on the one hand, *calculates* earnings and their maximum potential and, on the other hand, is characterized by a dispassionate self-control and moderation – all of which increase productive capacities to an unusual degree.

The foundation for perceiving work as an end in itself, or a "calling," as modern capitalism requires, is here developed in a most propitious manner. And the prospect for shattering the leisurely rhythm of economic traditionalism as a *consequence* of a religious socialization is at its highest.

[...]

How then does it come about that activity which, in the most favorable case, is barely morally tolerable becomes a "calling" in the manner practiced by Benjamin Franklin? How is it to be explained historically that in Florence, the center of capitalist development in the fourteenth and fifteenth centuries and the marketplace for money and capital for all of the great political powers, striving for profit was viewed as either morally questionable or at best tolerated? Yet in the business relationships found in small companies in rural Pennsylvania, where scarcely a trace of large-scale commerce could be found, where only the beginning stages of a banking system were evident, and where the economy was continuously threatened with collapse into sheer barter (as a result of a simple lack of money), the same striving for profit became viewed as legitimate. Indeed, it became understood as the essence of a morally acceptable, even praiseworthy, way of organizing and directing life.

To speak *here* of a "reflection" of "material" conditions in the "ideal superstructure" would be complete nonsense. Hence, our question: What set of ideas gave birth to the ordering of activity oriented purely to profit under the category of a "calling," to which the person felt an *obligation*? Just this set of ideas provided the ethical substructure and backbone for the "new style" employer's organized life. [...]

Asceticism and the Spirit of Capitalism

Let us summarize the above. On the one hand, this-worldly Protestant asceticism fought with fury against the spontaneous *enjoyment* of possessions and constricted *consumption*, especially of luxury goods. On the other hand, it had the psychological effect of *freeing* the *acquisition of goods* from the constraints of the traditional economic ethic. In the process, ascetic Protestantism shattered the bonds restricting all striving for gain – not only by legalizing profit but also by perceiving it as desired by God (in the manner portrayed here). The struggle against the desires of the flesh and the attachment to external goods was *not*, as the Puritans explicitly attest (and also the great Quaker apologist, Barclay), a struggle against rational *acquisition*; rather, it challenged the irrational use of possessions. That which remained so familiar to feudal sensibilities – a high regard for the *external* display of luxury consumption – was condemned by the Puritans as a deification of human wants and desires. According to them, God wanted a rational and utilitarian use of wealth on behalf of the basic needs of the person and the community.

Hence, this-worldly asceticism did *not* wish to impose *self-castigation* upon the wealthy. Instead, it wanted that wealth to be used for necessary, *practical*, and *useful* endeavors. The notion of "comfort", typically for the Puritans, encompasses the realm of the ethically permissible use of goods. Thus, it is naturally not by chance that one observes the development of the style of life attached to this notion, earliest and most clearly, precisely in those most consistent representatives of the Puritan life outlook: the Quakers. In opposition to the glitter and pretense of feudalism's pomp and display, which rests upon an unstable economic foundation and prefers a tattered elegance to low-key simplicity, the Puritans placed the ideal of the clean and solid comfort of the middle-class "home."

In terms of capitalism's *production* of wealth, asceticism struggled against greed. It did so in order to confront both the danger it presented to social order and its *impulsive* character. The Puritans condemned all "covetousness" and "mammonism," for both implied the striving for wealth – becoming rich – as an end in itself. Wealth as such constituted a temptation.

The nature of asceticism again becomes clear at this point. Its methodical-rational organization of life was the power "that perpetually wanted good and perpetually cheated evil," namely, evil in the manner conceived by asceticism: wealth and its temptations. For asceticism (together with the Old Testament and completely parallel to the ethical valuation of "good works") defined the pursuit of riches, if viewed as an *end* in itself, as the peak of reprehensibility. At the same time, it also viewed the acquisition of wealth, when it was the *fruit* of work in a vocational calling, as God's blessing. Even more important for this investigation, the religious value set on tireless, continuous, and systematic work in a vocational calling was defined as absolutely the highest of all ascetic means for believers to testify to their elect status, as well as simultaneously the most certain and most visible means of doing so. Indeed, the Puritan's sincerity of belief must have been the most powerful lever conceivable working to expand the life outlook that we are here designating as the spirit of capitalism.

Moreover, if we now combine the strictures against consumption with this unchaining of the striving for wealth, a certain external result [that is, one with an impact outside the realm of religion] now becomes visible: *the formation of capital* through *asceticism's compulsive saving*. The restrictions that opposed the consumption of wealth indeed had their productive use, for profit and gain became used as *investment* capital.

[...]

Of course, these Puritan ideals of life failed to meet the challenge whenever the test – the "temptations" of wealth (which were well known even to the Puritans themselves) – became too great. We find the most sincere followers of the Puritan spirit very frequently among those in the middle class who operated small businesses, among farmers and the *beati possidentes* [those in possession of salvation] – all of whom must be understood as having been at the beginning of an *upwardly mobile* journey. Yet we find that many in these groups were prepared quite frequently to betray the old ideals. Such betrayal eyen occurred among the Quakers. The predecessor of this-worldly asceticism, the monastic asceticism of the Middle Ages, repeatedly fell victim to this same fate. Whenever the rational organization of the economy had fully developed its productive powers in the cloister milieu, which was characterized by a strict regulation of life as a whole and limited consumption, then the accumulated wealth was either used to acquire land and noble status (as occurred in the era before the Reformation) or it threatened the dissolution of monastic discipline. One of the numerous "reform movements" in monasticism had to intervene if this occurred. In a certain sense, the entire history of the religious orders reveals a constantly renewed struggles with the problem of the secularizing effects of wealth.

On a larger scale, the same is true for Puritanism's this-worldly asceticism. The powerful "revival" of Methodism, which preceded the flowering of English industrialism near the end of the eighteenth century, can be appropriately compared with the "reform movements" in the monastic orders. A passage from John Wesley himself can be noted now, for it is well suited to stand as a motto for all that has been stated here. It indicates how the main figures in the ascetic movements were themselves completely aware of the apparently so paradoxical relationships presented here and understood these connections fully.

> I fear, wherever riches have increased, the essence of religion has decreased in the same proportion. Therefore I do not see how it is possible, in the nature of things, for any revival of true religion to continue long. For religion must necessarily produce both industry and frugality, and these cannot but produce riches. But as riches increase, so will pride, anger, and love of the world in all its branches. [...] Is there no way to prevent this continual decay of pure religion? We ought not to prevent people from being diligent and frugal; *we must exhort all Christians to gain all they can, and to save all they can; that is, in effect, to grow rich.* [Weber's emphasis]

(There follows the admonition that those who have "acquired all they can and saved all they can" should also "give all they can" – in order to grow in grace and to assemble a fortune in heaven.) In this passage from Wesley one sees the connection, in all its details, illuminated in the analysis above.

Exactly as Wesley noted here, the significance for economic development of the powerful early religious movements was to be found mainly in the ascetic effects of their *socialization*. To him, their full *economic* impact developed, as a rule, only after the peak of their *pure* religious enthusiasm. As the paroxysms of the search for God's kingdom gradually dissolved into the dispassionate virtues of the vocational calling and the religious roots of the movement slowly withered, a utilitarian orientation to the world took hold. In the popular imagination, if we follow [the Irish scholar of English and French literature Edward] Dowden [1843–1913], "Robinson Crusoe" – the *isolated economic man* (who is engaged in missionary activities in his spare time) – now took the place of Bunyan's "pilgrims" scurrying through the "amusement park of vanity" on their solitary spiritual quest for God's kingdom. If subsequently the basic principle "to make the best of *both* worlds" came to prevail, then, finally, as Dowden also observed, the clear conscience came to be ordered among the series of possessions comprising the comfortable, middle-class life (as is so beautifully expressed in the German adage about the "soft pillow").

That which the religiously lively epoch of the seventeenth century bequeathed to its utilitarian heirs was above all a startlingly clear conscience – we can say without hesitation, *pharisaically* good – as concerns the acquisition of money. Wherever lacking, the making of money was directed exclusively by laws and conventions. Now, with Puritanism, every residual of the medieval proverb *deo placere vix potest* [the merchant cannot be pleasing to God] has disappeared.

A specifically *middle-class vocational ethos* (*Berufsethos*) arose. Now the middle-class employer became conscious of himself as standing in the full grace of God and as visibly blessed by Him. If he stayed within the bounds of formal correctness, if his moral conduct remained blameless, and if the use he made of his wealth was not offensive, this person was now allowed to follow his interest in economic gain – and indeed *should* do so. Moreover, the power of religious asceticism made available to the businessperson dispassionate and conscientious workers. Unusually capable of working, these employees attached themselves to their work, for they understood it as bestowing a purpose on life that was desired by God.

In addition, religious asceticism gave to the employer the soothing assurance that the unequal distribution of the world's material goods resulted from the special design of God's providence. In making such distinctions as well as in deciding who should be among the chosen few, God pursued mysterious aims unknown to terrestrial mortals. Calvin had argued early on (in a passage frequently cited) that the "people" – the overwhelming majority of skilled and unskilled workers – would continue to obey God only if kept poor. The Dutch (Pieter de la Court and others) "secularized" this statement; to them, most persons *worked* only if driven to do so by necessity. In turn, this formulation of a key idea regarding the functioning of the capitalist economy then merged into the plethora of theories on the "productivity" of low wages. Here again, and in full conformity with the developmental pattern we have repeatedly observed, as the religious roots of an idea died out a utilitarian tone then surreptitiously shoved itself under the idea and carried it further.

[…]

Now let us turn away from the Puritan employer and briefly toward the other side, namely, the perspective of the worker. Zinzendorf's branch of Pietism, for example, glorified workers who were loyal to their callings, lived in accord with the ideals of the apostles, and never strove for gain – hence, workers endowed with the charisma of Christ's disciples. Similar views were widespread, in an even more radical form, among the baptizing congregations in their early stages.

Of course, the entire corpus of literature on asceticism, which is drawn from almost *all* religions [East and West], is permeated with the point of view that loyal work is highly pleasing to God, even if performed for low wages by people at a great disadvantage in life and without other opportunities. *Here* Protestant asceticism added nothing new as such. It dramatically deepened, however, this point of view. In addition, it created the norm on which its impact *exclusively depended*: the psychological *motivation* that arose out of the conception of work as a *calling* and as the means best suited (and in the end often as the *sole* means) for the devout to become certain of their state of salvation. Furthermore on the other hand, in interpreting the employer's acquisition of money also as a "calling," Protestant asceticism formally ratified the exploitation of this particular willingness to work.

It is obvious how powerfully the *exclusive* striving for the kingdom of God – through fulfillment of the duty to work in a vocational calling and through strict asceticism, which church discipline naturally imposed in particular upon the propertyless classes – must have promoted the "productivity" of work in the capitalist sense of the word. For the modern worker, the view of work as a "vocational calling" became just as characteristic as the view of gain as a "vocational calling" became for the modern employer. New at the time, this situation was reflected in the keen observations on Dutch economic power of the seventeenth century by the insightful Englishman Sir William Petty. He traced its growth back to the especially numerous "Dissenters" (Calvinists and Baptists) in Holland, who viewed "*work and the industrious pursuit of a trade as their duty to God.*"

[...]

Our analysis should have demonstrated that one of the constitutive components of the modern capitalist spirit and, moreover, generally of modern civilization, was the rational organization of life on the basis of the *idea of the calling*. It was born out of the spirit of *Christian asceticism*. If we now read again the passages from Benjamin Franklin cited at the beginning of this essay, we will see that the essential elements of the frame of mind described as the "spirit of capitalism" are just those that we have conveyed above as the content of Puritan vocational asceticism. In Franklin, however, this "spirit" exists without the religious foundation, which had already died out.

The idea that modern work in a vocational calling supposedly carries with it an *ascetic* imprint is, of course, also not new. The limitation of persons to specialized work, which necessitates their renunciation of the Faustian multi-dimensionality of the human species, is in our world today the precondition for doing anything of value at all – that is, the "specialized task" and "foresaking" of multidimensionality irredeemably presuppose and mutually condition one another. *Goethe*, at the peak of his wisdom in his *Wilhelm Meister's Years of Travel* [1829] and in his depiction of Faust's final stage of life [1808], tried to teach us just this: the middle-class way of ordering life, if it wishes to be guided at all rather than to be devoid of continuity, contains a basic component of asceticism. This realization for Goethe implied a resigned farewell to an era of full and beautiful humanity – and a renunciation of it. For such an era will repeat itself, in the course of our civilizational development, with as little likelihood as a reappearance of the epoch in which Athens bloomed.

The Puritan *wanted* to be a person with a vocational calling; we *must* be. For to the extent that asceticism moved out of the monastic cell and was carried over into the life of work in a vocational calling, and then commenced to rule over this-worldly morality, it helped to do its part to build the mighty cosmos of the modern economic order – namely, an economy bound to the technical and economic conditions of mechanized, machine-based production. This cosmos today determines the style of life of all individuals born into this grinding mechanism, and *not* only those directly engaged in economically productive activity. It does so with overwhelming force – and perhaps it will continue to do so until the last ton of fossil fuel has burnt to ashes. The concern for material goods, according to Baxter, should lie on the shoulders of his saints like "a lightweight coat that one can throw off at any time." Yet fate allowed this coat to become a steel-hard casing (*stahlhartes Gehäuse*). To the extent that asceticism undertook to transform and influence the world, the world's material goods acquired an increasing and, in the end, inescapable power over people – as never before in history.

Today the spirit of asceticism has fled from this casing, whether with finality who knows? Victorious capitalism, in any case, ever since it came to rest on a mechanical foundation, no longer needs asceticism as a supporting pillar. Even the optimistic temperament of the Enlightenment, asceticism's joyful heir, appears finally to be fading. And the idea of an "obligation to search for and then accept a vocational calling" now wanders around in our lives as the ghost of beliefs no longer anchored in the substance of religion. The person of today usually rejects entirely all attempts to make sense of a "fulfillment of one's calling" wherever this notion cannot be directly aligned with the highest spiritual and cultural values, or wherever, conversely, it must not be experienced subjectively simply as economic coercion. Then the person of today rejects entirely all attempts to make sense of it at all. The pursuit of gain, in the region where it has become most completely unchained and stripped of its religious-ethical meaning, the United States, tends to be associated with purely competitive passions. Not infrequently, these passions directly imprint this pursuit with the character of a sports event.

No one any longer knows who will live in this casing and whether entirely new prophets or a mighty rebirth of ancient ideas and ideals will stand at the end of this prodigious development. *Or*, however, if neither, whether a mechanized ossification, embellished with a sort of rigidly compelled sense of self-importance, will arise. Then, indeed, if ossification appears, the saying might be true for the "last humans" in this long civilizational development:

> narrow specialists without minds, pleasure-seekers without heart; in its conceit, this nothingness imagines it has climbed to a level of humanity never before attained.

[...]

This study has attempted, of course, merely to trace ascetic Protestantism's influence, and the particular *nature* of this influence, back to ascetic Protestantism's motives in regard to one, however important, point. The way in which Protestant asceticism was in turn influenced in its development and characteristic uniqueness by the entirety of societal-cultural conditions, and especially *economic* conditions, must also have its day. For sure, even with the best will, the modern person seems generally unable to imagine *how* large a significance those components of our consciousness rooted in religious beliefs have actually had upon culture, national character, and the organization of life. Nevertheless, of course it can not be the intention here to set a one-sided spiritualistic analysis of the causes of culture and history in place of an equally one-sided "materialistic" analysis. *Both* are *equally possible*. Historical truth, however, is served equally little if either of these analyses claims to be the conclusion of an investigation rather than its preparatory stage.

Chapter 22

The Distribution of Power within the Political Community: Class, Status, Party [1914]

Max Weber

A. Economically Determined Power and the Status Order

The structure of every legal order directly influences the distribution of power, economic or otherwise, within its respective community. This is true of all legal orders and not only that of the state. In general, we understand by "power" the chance of a man or a number of men to realize their own will in a social action even against the resistance of others who are participating in the action.

"Economically conditioned" power is not, of course, identical with "power" as such. On the contrary, the emergence of economic power may be the consequence of power existing on other grounds. Man does not strive for power only in order to enrich himself economically. Power, including economic power, may be valued for its own sake. Very frequently the striving for power is also conditioned by the social honor it entails. Not all power, however, entails social honor: The typical American Boss, as well as the typical big speculator, deliberately relinquishes social honor. Quite generally, "mere economic" power, and especially "naked" money power, is by no means a recognized basis of social honor. Nor is power the only basis of social honor. Indeed, social honor, or prestige, may even be the basis of economic power, and very frequently has been. Power, as well as honor, may be guaranteed by the legal

Weber, Max, "The Distribution of Power Within the Political Community: Class, Status, Party," pp. 180–195 from Max Weber, 'The Distribution of Power Within the Political Community: Class, Status, Party,' Politics Journal, 1949.

Classical Sociological Theory, Third Edition. Edited by Craig Calhoun, Joseph Gerteis, James Moody, Steven Pfaff, and Indermohan Virk. Editorial material and organization © 2012 John Wiley & Sons, Ltd. Published 2012 by John Wiley & Sons, Ltd.

order, but, at least normally, it is not their primary source. The legal order is rather an additional factor that enhances the chance to hold power or honor; but it can not always secure them.

The way in which social honor is distributed in a community between typical groups participating in this distribution we call the "status order." The social order and the economic order are related in a similar manner to the legal order. However, the economic order merely defines the way in which economic goods and services are distributed and used. Of course, the status order is strongly influenced by it, and in turn reacts upon it.

Now: "classes," "status groups," and "parties" are phenomena of the distribution of power within a community.

B. Determination of Class Situation by Market Situation

In our terminology, "classes" are not communities; they merely represent possible, and frequent, bases for social action. We may speak of a "class" when (1) a number of people have in common a specific causal component of their life chances, insofar as (2) this component is represented exclusively by economic interests in the possession of goods and opportunities for income, and (3) is represented under the conditions of the commodity or labor markets. This is "class situation."

It is the most elemental economic fact that the way in which the disposition over material property is distributed among a plurality of people, meeting competitively in the market for the purpose of exchange, in itself creates specific life chances. The mode of distribution, in accord with the law of marginal utility, excludes the non-wealthy from competing for highly valued goods; it favors the owners and, in fact, gives to them a monopoly to acquire such goods. Other things being equal, the mode of distribution monopolizes the opportunities for profitable deals for all those who, provided with goods, do not necessarily have to exchange them. It increases, at least generally, their power in the price struggle with those who, being propertyless, have nothing to offer but their labor or the resulting products, and who are compelled to get rid of these products in order to subsist at all. The mode of distribution gives to the propertied a monopoly on the possibility of transferring property from the sphere of use as "wealth" to the sphere of "capital," that is, it gives them the entrepreneurial function and all chances to share directly or indirectly in returns on capital. All this holds true within the area in which pure market conditions prevail. "Property" and "lack of property" are, therefore, the basic categories of all class situations. It does not matter whether these two categories become effective in the competitive struggles of the consumers or of the producers.

Within these categories, however, class situations are further differentiated: on the one hand, according to the kind of property that is usable for returns; and, on the other hand, according to the kind of services that can be offered in the market. Ownership of dwellings; workshops; warehouses; stores; agriculturally usable land in large or small holdings – a quantitative difference with possibly qualitative consequences; ownership of mines; cattle; men (slaves); disposition over mobile instruments of production, or capital goods of all sorts, especially money or objects that can easily be exchanged for money; disposition over products of one's own labor or of others' labor differing according to their various distances from consumability; disposition over transferable monopolies of any kind – all these distinctions differentiate the class situations of the propertied just as does the "meaning" which they can give to the use of property, especially to property which has money equivalence. Accordingly, the propertied, for instance, may belong to the class of rentiers or to the class of entrepreneurs.

Those who have no property but who offer services are differentiated just as much according to their kinds of services as according to the way in which they make use of these services, in a continuous or discontinuous relation to a recipient. But always this is the generic connotation of the concept of class: that kind of chance in the *market* is the decisive moment which presents a common condition for the individual's fate. Class situation is, in this sense, ultimately market situation. The effect of naked possession *per se*, which among cattle breeders gives the non-owning slave or serf into the power of the cattle owner, is only a fore-runner of real "class" formation. However, in the cattle loan and in the naked severity of the law of debts in such communities for the first time mere "possession" as such emerges as decisive for the fate of the individual; this is much in contrast to crop-raising communities, which are based on labor. The creditor–debtor relation becomes the basis of "class situations" first in the cities, where a "credit market," however primitive, with rates of interest increasing according to the extent of dearth and factual monopolization of lending in the hands of a plutocracy could develop. Therewith "class struggles" begin.

Those men whose fate is not determined by the chance of using goods or services for themselves on the market, e.g., slaves, are not, however, a class in the technical sense of the term. They are, rather, a status group.

C. Social Action Flowing from Class Interest

According to our terminology, the factor that creates "class" is unambiguously economic interest, and indeed, only those interests involved in the existence of the market. Nevertheless, the concept of class-interest is an ambiguous one: even as an empirical concept it is ambiguous as soon as one understands it by something other than the factual direction of interests following with a certain probability from the class situation for a certain average of those people subjected to the class situation. The class situation and other circumstances remaining the same, the direction in which the individual worker, for instance, is likely to pursue his interests may vary widely, according to whether he is constitutionally qualified for the task at hand to a high, to an average, or to a low degree. In the same way, the direction of interests may vary according to whether or not social action of a larger of smaller portion of those commonly affected by the class situation, or even an association among them, e.g., a trade union, has grown out of the class situation, from which the individual may expect promising results for himself. The emergence of an association or even of mere social action from a common class situation is by no means a universal phenomenon.

The class situation may be restricted in its efforts to the generation of essentially *similar* reactions, that is to say, within our terminology, of "mass behavior." However, it may not even have this result. Furthermore, often merely amorphous social action emerges. For example, the "grumbling" of workers known in ancient Oriental ethics: The moral disapproval of the work-master's conduct, which in its practical significance was probably equivalent to an increasingly typical phenomenon of precisely the latest industrial development, namely, the slowdown of laborers by virtue of tacit agreement. The degree in which "social action" and possibly associations emerge from the mass behavior of the members of a class is linked to general cultural conditions, especially to those of an intellectual sort. It is also linked to the extent of the contrasts that have already evolved, and is especially linked to the transparency of the connections between the causes and the consequences of the class situation. For however different life chances may be, this fact in itself, according to all experience, by no means gives birth to "class action" (social action by the members of a class). For that, the real conditions and the results of the class situation must be distinctly recognizable. For only then the contrast of life chances can be felt not as an absolutely given fact to be accepted, but as a resultant from either (1) the given distribution of property, or (2) the structure of the concrete economic order. It is only then that people may react against the class structure not only through acts of intermittent and irrational protest, but in the form of rational association. There have been "class situations" of the first category (1), of a specifically naked and transparent sort, in the urban centers of Antiquity and during the Middle Ages; especially then when great fortunes were accumulated by factually monopolized trading in local industrial products or in foodstuffs; furthermore, under certain conditions, in the rural economy of the most diverse periods, when agriculture was increasingly exploited in a profit-making manner. The most important historical example of the second category (2) is the class situation of the modern proletariat.

D. Types of Class Struggle

Thus every class may be the carrier of any one of the innumerable possible forms of class action, but this is not necessarily so. In any case, a class does not in itself constitute a group (*Gemeinschaft*). To treat "class" conceptually as being equivalent to "group" leads to distortion. That men in the same class situation regularly react in mass actions to such tangible situations as economic ones in the direction of those interests that are most adequate to their average number is an important and after all simple fact for the understanding of historical events. However, this fact must not lead to that kind of pseudo-scientific operation with the concepts of class and class interests which is so frequent these days and which has found its most classic expression in the statement of a talented author, that the individual may be in error concerning his interests but that the class is infallible about its interests.

If classes as such are not groups, nevertheless class situations emerge only on the basis of social action. However, social action that brings forth class situations is not basically action among members of the identical class; it is an action among members of different classes. Social actions that directly determine the class situation of the worker and the entrepreneur are: the labor market, the commodities market, and the capitalistic enterprise. But, in its turn, the existence of a capitalistic enterprise presupposes that a very specific kind of social action exists to protect the possession of goods *per se*, and especially the power of individuals to dispose, in principle freely, over the means of production: a certain kind of legal order. Each kind of class situation, and above all when it rests upon the power of property *per se*, will become most clearly efficacious when all other determinants of reciprocal relations are, as far as possible, eliminated in their significance. It is in this way that the use of the power of property in the market obtains its most sovereign importance.

Now status groups hinder the strict carrying through of the sheer market principle. In the present context they are of interest only from this one point of view. Before we briefly consider them, note that not much of a general nature can be said about the more specific kinds of antagonism between classes (in our meaning of the term). The great shift, which has been going on continuously in the past, and up to our times, may be summarized, although at a cost of some precision: the struggle in which class situations are effective has progressively shifted from consumption credit toward, first, competitive struggles in the commodity market and then toward wage disputes on the labor market. The class struggles of Antiquity – to the extent that they were genuine class struggles and not struggles between status groups – were initially carried on by peasants and perhaps also artisans threatened by debt bondage and struggling against urban creditors. [...]

E. Status Honor

In contrast to classes, *Stände* (*status groups*) are normally groups. They are, however, often of an amorphous kind. In contrast to the purely economically determined "class situation," we wish to designate as *status situation* every typical component of the life of men that is determined by a specific, positive or negative, social estimation of *honor*. This honor may be connected with any quality shared by a plurality, and, of course, it can be knit to a class situation: class distinctions are linked in the most varied ways with status distinctions. Property as such is not always recognized as a status qualification, but in the long run it is, and with extraordinary regularity. In the subsistence economy of neighborhood associations, it is often simply the richest who is the "chieftain." However, this often is only an honorific preference. For example, in the so-called pure modern democracy, that is, one devoid of any expressly ordered status privileges for individuals, it may be that only the families coming under approximately the same tax class dance with one another. This example is reported of certain smaller Swiss cities. But status honor need not necessarily be linked with a class situation. On the contrary, it normally stands in sharp opposition to the pretensions of sheer property.

Both propertied and propertyless people can belong to the same status group, and frequently they do with very tangible consequences. This equality of social esteem may, however, in the long run become quite precarious. The equality of status among American gentlemen, for instance, is expressed by the fact that outside the subordination determined by the different functions of business, it would be considered strictly repugnant – wherever the old tradition still prevails – if even the richest boss, while playing billiards or cards in his club would not treat his clerk as in every sense fully his equal in birthright, but would bestow upon him the condescending status-conscious "benevolence" which the German boss can never dissever from his attitude. This is one of the most important reasons why in America the German clubs have never been able to attain the attraction that the American clubs have.

In content, status honor is normally expressed by the fact that above all else a specific *style of life* is expected from all those who wish to belong to the circle. Linked with this expectation are restrictions on social intercourse (that is, intercourse which is not subservient to economic or any other purposes). These restrictions may confine normal marriages to within the status circle and may lead to complete endogamous closure. Whenever this is not a mere individual and socially irrelevant imitation of another style of life, but consensual action of this closing character, the status development is under way.

In its characteristic form, stratification by status groups on the basis of conventional styles of life evolves at the present time in the United States out of the traditional democracy. For example, only the resident of a certain street ("the Street") is considered as belonging to "society," is qualified for social intercourse, and is visited and invited. Above all, this differentiation evolves in such a way as to make for strict submission to the fashion that is dominant at a given time in society. This submission to fashion also exists among men in America to a degree unknown in Germany; it appears as an indication of the fact that a given man puts forward a *claim* to qualify as a gentleman. This submission decides, at least *prima facie*, that he will be treated as such. And this recognition becomes just as important for his employment chances in swank establishments, and above all, for social intercourse and marriage with "esteemed" families, as the qualification for dueling among Germans. As for the rest, status honor is usurped by certain families resident for a long time, and, of course, correspondingly wealthy (e.g. F.F.V., the First Families of Virginia), or by the actual or alleged descendants of the "Indian Princess" Pocahontas, of the Pilgrim fathers, or of the Knickerbockers, the members of almost inaccessible sects and all sorts of circles setting themselves apart by means of any other characteristics and badges. In this case stratification is purely conventional and rests largely on usurpation (as does almost all status honor in its beginning). But the road to legal privilege, positive or negative, is easily traveled as soon as a certain stratification of the social order has in fact been "lived in" and has achieved stability by virtue of a stable distribution of economic power.

F. Ethnic Segregation and Caste

Where the consequences have been realized to their full extent, the status group evolves into a closed caste. Status distinctions are then guaranteed not merely by conventions and laws, but also by religious sanctions. This occurs in such a way that every physical contact with a member of any caste that is considered to be lower by the members of a higher caste is considered as making for a ritualistic impurity and a stigma which must be expiated by a religious act. In addition, individual castes develop quite distinct cults and gods.

In general, however, the status structure reaches such extreme consequences only where there are underlying differences which are held to be "ethnic." The caste is, indeed, the normal form in which ethnic communities that believe in blood relationship and exclude exogamous marriage and social intercourse usually associate with one another. As mentioned before, such a caste situation is part of the phenomenon of pariah peoples and is found all over the world. These people form communities, acquire specific occupational traditions of handicrafts or of other arts, and cultivate a belief in their ethnic community. They live in a diaspora strictly segregated from all personal intercourse, except that of an unavoidable sort, and their situation is legally precarious. Yet, by virtue of their economic indispensability, they are tolerated, indeed frequently privileged, and they live interspersed in the political communities. The Jews are the most impressive historical example.

A status segregation grown into a caste differs in its structure from a mere ethnic segregation: the caste structure transforms the horizontal and unconnected coexistences of ethnically segregated groups into a vertical social system of super- and subordination. Correctly formulated: a comprehensive association integrates the ethnically divided communities into one political unit. They differ precisely in this way: ethnic coexistence, based on mutual repulsion and disdain, allows each ethnic community to consider its own honor as the highest one; the caste structure brings about a social subordination and an acknowledgement of "more honor" in favor of the privileged caste and status groups. This is due to the fact that in the caste structure ethnic distinctions as such have become "functional" distinctions within the political association (warriors, priests, artisans that are politically important for war and for building, and so on). But even pariah peoples who are most despised (for example, the Jews) are usually apt to continue cultivating the belief in their own specific "honor," a belief that is equally peculiar to ethnic and to status groups. [...]

G. Status Privileges

For all practical purposes, stratification by status goes hand in hand with a monopolization of ideal and material goods or opportunities, in a manner we have come to know as typical. Besides the specific status honor, which always rests upon distance and exclusiveness, honorific preferences may consist of the privilege of wearing special costumes, of eating special dishes taboo to others, of carrying arms – which is most obvious in its consequences – the right to be a dilettante, for example, to play certain musical instruments. However, material monopolies provide the most effective motives for the exclusiveness of a status group; although, in themselves, they are rarely sufficient, almost always they come into play to some extent. Within a status circle there is the question of intermarriage: the interest of the families in the monopolization of potential bridegrooms is at least of equal importance and is parallel to the interest in the monopolization of daughters. The daughters of the members must be provided for. With an increased closure of the status group, the conventional preferential opportunities for special employment grow into a legal monopoly of special offices for the members. Certain goods become objects for monopolization by status groups, typically, entailed estates, and frequently also the possession of serfs or bondsmen and, finally, special trades. This monopolization occurs positively when the status group is exclusively entitled to own and to manage them; and negatively when, in order to maintain its specific way of life, the status group must *not* own and manage them. For the decisive role of a style of life in status honor means that status groups are the specific bearers of all conventions. In whatever way it may be manifest, all stylization of life either originates in status groups or is at least conserved by them. Even if the principles of status conventions differ greatly, they reveal certain typical traits, especially among the most privileged strata. Quite generally, among privileged status groups there is a status disqualification that operates against the performance of common physical labor. This disqualification is now "setting in" in America against the old tradition of esteem for labor. Very frequently every rational economic pursuit, and especially entrepreneurial activity, is looked upon as a disqualification of status. Artistic and literary activity is also considered degrading work as soon as it is exploited for income, or at least when it is connected with hard physical exertion. An example is the sculptor working like a mason in his dusty smock as over against the painter in his salon-like studio and those forms of musical practice that are acceptable to the status group.

H. Economic Conditions and Effects of Status Stratification

The frequent disqualification of the gainfully employed as such is a direct result of the principle of status stratification, and of course, of this principle's opposition to a distribution of power which is regulated exclusively through the market. These two factors operate along with various individual ones, which will be touched upon below.

We have seen above that the market and its processes knows no personal distinctions: "functional" interests dominate it. It knows nothing of honor. The status order means precisely the reverse: stratification in terms of honor and styles of life peculiar to status groups as such. The status order would be threatened at its very root if mere economic acquisition and naked economic power still bearing the stigma of its extra-status origin could bestow upon anyone who has won them the same or even greater honor as the vested interests claim for themselves. [...]

As to the general economic conditions making for the predominance of stratification by status, only the following can be said. When the bases of the acquisition and distribution of goods are relatively stable, stratification by status is favored. Every technological repercussion and economic transformation threatens stratification by status and pushes the class situation into the foreground. Epochs and countries in which the naked class situation is of predominant significance are regularly the periods of technical and economic transformations. And every slowing down of the change in economic stratification leads, in due course, to the growth of status structures and makes for a resuscitation of the important role of social honor.

I. Parties

Whereas the genuine place of classes is within the economic order, the place of status groups is within the social order, that is, within the sphere of the distribution of honor. From within these spheres, classes and status groups influence one another and the legal order and are in turn influenced by it. "*Parties*" reside in the sphere of power. Their action is oriented toward the acquisition of social power, that is to say, toward influencing social action no matter what its content may be. In principle, parties may exist in a social club as well as in a state. As over against the actions of classes and status groups, for which this is not necessarily the case, party-oriented social action always involves association. For it is always directed toward a goal which is striven for in a planned manner. This goal may be a cause (the party may aim at realizing a program for ideal or material purposes), or the goal may be personal (sinecures, power, and from these, honor for the leader and the followers of the party). Usually the party aims at all these simultaneously. Parties are, therefore, only possible within groups that have an associational character, that is, some rational order and a staff of persons available who are ready to enforce it. For parties aim precisely at influencing this staff, and if possible, to recruit from it party members.

In any individual case, parties may represent interests determined through class situation or status situation, and they may recruit their following respectively from one or the other. But they need be neither purely class nor purely status parties; in fact, they are more likely to be mixed types, and sometimes they are neither. They may represent ephemeral or enduring structures. Their means of attaining power may be quite varied, ranging from naked violence of any sort to canvassing for votes with coarse or subtle means: money, social influence, the force of speech, suggestion, clumsy hoax, and so on to the rougher or more artful tactics of obstruction in parliamentary bodies.

The sociological structure of parties differs in a basic way according to the kind of social action which they struggle to influence; that means, they differ according to whether or not the community is stratified by status or by classes. Above all else, they vary according to the structure of domination. For their leaders normally deal with its conquest. In our general terminology, parties are not only products of modern forms of domination. We shall also designate as parties the ancient and medieval ones, despite the fact that they differ basically from modern parties. Since a party always struggles for political control (*Herrschaft*), its organization too is frequently strict and "authoritarian."

Chapter 23

The Types of Legitimate Domination [1914]

Max Weber

The Basis of Legitimacy

Domination was defined as the probability that certain specific commands (or all commands) will be obeyed by a given group of persons. It thus does not include every mode of exercising "power" or "influence" over other persons. Domination ("authority") in this sense may be based on the most diverse motives of compliance: all the way from simple habituation to the most purely rational calculation of advantage. Hence every genuine form of domination implies a minimum of voluntary compliance, that is, an *interest* (based on ulterior motives or genuine acceptance) in obedience.

Not every case of domination makes use of economic means; still less does it always have economic objectives. However, normally the rule over a considerable number of persons requires a staff, that is, a *special* group which can normally be trusted to execute the general policy as well as the specific commands. The members of the administrative staff may be bound to obedience to their superior (or superiors) by custom, by affectual ties, by a purely material complex of interests, or by ideal (*wertrationale*) motives. The quality of these motives largely determines the type of domination. *Purely* material interests and calculations of advantages as the basis of

Weber, Max, "The Types of Legitimate Domination" pp. 324–325, 328–330, 333–334, 341–343, 358–364, 367, 369–370 from Max Weber, *The Theory of Social and Economic Organization*, ed. Talcott Parsons, trans. A.M. Henderson and Talcott Parsons. New York: Simon & Schuster, Inc., The Free Press, 1947. Copyright © 1947. Copyright © renewed 1975 by Talcott Parsons. Reprinted and edited with the permission of The Free Press, A Division of Simon & Schuster Adult Publishing Group. All rights reserved.

Classical Sociological Theory, Third Edition. Edited by Craig Calhoun, Joseph Gerteis, James Moody, Steven Pfaff, and Indermohan Virk. Editorial material and organization © 2012 John Wiley & Sons, Ltd. Published 2012 by John Wiley & Sons, Ltd.

solidarity between the chief and his administrative staff result, in this as in other connexions, in a relatively unstable situation. Normally other elements, affectual and ideal, supplement such interests. In certain exceptional cases the former alone may be decisive. In everyday life these relationships, like others, are governed by custom and material calculation of advantage. But custom, personal advantage, purely affectual or ideal motives of solidarity, do not form a sufficiently reliable basis for a given domination. In addition there is normally a further element, the belief in *legitimacy*.

Experience shows that in no instance does domination voluntarily limit itself to the appeal to material or affectual or ideal motives as a basis for its continuance. In addition every such system attempts to establish and to cultivate the belief in its legitimacy. But according to the kind of legitimacy which is claimed, the type of obedience, the kind of administrative staff developed to guarantee it, and the mode of exercising authority, will all differ fundamentally. Equally fundamental is the variation in effect. Hence, it is useful to classify the types of domination according to the kind of claim to legitimacy typically made by each. In doing this, it is best to start from modern and therefore more familiar examples. [...]

There are three pure types of legitimate domination. The validity of the claims to legitimacy may be based on:

(1) Rational grounds – resting on a belief in the legality of enacted rules and the right of those elevated to authority under such rules to issue commands (legal authority).
(2) Traditional grounds – resting on an established belief in the sanctity of immemorial traditions and the legitimacy of those exercising authority under them (traditional authority); or finally,
(3) Charismatic grounds – resting on devotion to the exceptional sanctity, heroism or exemplary character of an individual person, and of the normative patterns or order revealed or ordained by him (charismatic authority).

In the case of legal authority, obedience is owed to the legally established impersonal order. It extends to the persons exercising the authority of office under it by virtue of the formal legality of their commands and only within the scope of authority of the office. In the case of traditional authority, obedience is owed to the *person* of the chief who occupies the traditionally sanctioned position of authority and who is (within its sphere) bound by tradition. But here the obligation of obedience is a matter of personal loyalty within the area of accustomed obligations. In the case of charismatic authority, it is the charismatically qualified leader as such who is obeyed by virtue of personal trust in his revelation, his heroism or his exemplary qualities so far as they fall within the scope of the individual's belief in his charisma. [...]

Legal Authority with a Bureaucratic Administrative Staff

Legal authority rests on the acceptance of the validity of the following mutually inter-dependent ideas.

1   That any given legal norm may be established by agreement or by imposition, on grounds of expediency or value-rationality or both, with a claim to obedience at least on the part of the members of the organization. This is, however, usually extended to include all persons within the sphere of power in question – which in the case of territorial bodies is the territorial area – who stand in certain social relationships or carry out forms of social action which in the order governing the organization have been declared to be relevant.

2   That every body of law consists essentially in a consistent system of abstract rules which have normally been intentionally established. Furthermore, administration of law is held to consist in the application of these rules to particular cases; the administrative process in the rational pursuit of the interests which are specified in the order governing the organization within the limits laid down by legal precepts and following principles which are capable of generalized formulation and are approved in the order governing the group, or at least not disapproved in it.

3   That thus the typical person in authority, the "superior," is himself subject to an impersonal order by orienting his actions to it in his own dispositions and commands. (This is true not only for persons exercising legal authority who are in the usual sense "officials," but, for instance, for the elected president of a state.)

4   That the person who obeys authority does so, as it is usually stated, only in his capacity as a "member" of the organization and what he obeys is only "the law." (He may in this connection be the member of an association, of a community, of a church, or a citizen of a state.)

5   In conformity with point 3, it is held that the members of the organization, insofar as they obey a person in authority, do not owe this obedience to him as an individual, but to the impersonal order. Hence, it follows that there is an obligation to obedience only within the sphere of the rationally delimited jurisdiction which, in terms of the order, has been given to him. [...]

The purest type of exercise of legal authority is that which employs a bureaucratic administrative staff. Only the supreme chief of the organization occupies his position of dominance (*Herrenstellung*) by virtue of appropriation, of election, or of having been designated for the succession. But even *his* authority consists in a sphere of legal "competence." The whole administrative staff under the supreme authority then consists, in the purest type, of individual officials (constituting a "monocracy" as opposed to the "collegial" type, which will be discussed below) who are appointed and function according to the following criteria:

(1) They are personally free and subject to authority only with respect to their impersonal official obligations.
(2) They are organized in a clearly defined hierarchy of offices.
(3) Each office has a clearly defined sphere of competence in the legal sense.
(4) The office is filled by a free contractual relationship. Thus, in principle, there is free selection.

(5) Candidates are selected on the basis of technical qualifications. In the most rational case, this is tested by examination or guaranteed by diplomas certifying technical training, or both. They are *appointed*, not elected.
(6) They are remunerated by fixed salaries in money, for the most part with a right to pensions. Only under certain circumstances does the employing authority, especially in private organizations, have a right to terminate the appointment, but the official is always free to resign. The salary scale is graded according to rank in the hierarchy; but in addition to this criterion, the responsibility of the position and the requirements of the incumbent's social status may be taken into account.
(7) The office is treated as the sole, or at least the primary, occupation of the incumbent.
(8) It constitutes a career. There is a system of "promotion" according to seniority or to achievement, or both. Promotion is dependent on the judgment of superiors.
(9) The official works entirely separated from ownership of the means of administration and without appropriation of his position.
(10) He is subject to strict and systematic discipline and control in the conduct of the office.

This type of organization is in principle applicable with equal facility to a wide variety of different fields. It may be applied in profit-making business or in charitable organizations, or in any number of other types of private enterprises serving ideal or material ends. It is equally applicable to political and to hierocratic organizations. With the varying degrees of approximation to a pure type, its historical existence can be demonstrated in all these fields. [...]

Traditional Authority

Authority will be called traditional if legitimacy is claimed for it and believed in by virtue of the sanctity of age-old rules and powers. The masters are designated according to traditional rules and are obeyed because of their traditional status (*Eigenwürde*). This type of organized rule is, in the simplest case, primarily based on personal loyalty which results from common upbringing. The person exercising authority is not a "superior," but a personal master, his administrative staff does not consist mainly of officials but of personal retainers, and the ruled are not "members" of an association but are either his traditional "comrades" or his "subjects." Personal loyalty, not the official's impersonal duty, determines the relations of the administrative staff to the master.

Obedience is owed not to enacted rules but to the person who occupies a position of authority by tradition or who has been chosen for it by the traditional master. The commands of such a person are legitimized in one of two ways:

(a) partly in terms of traditions which themselves directly determine the content of the command and are believed to be valid within certain limits that cannot be overstepped without endangering the master's traditional status;

(b) partly in terms of the master's discretion in that sphere which tradition leaves open to him; this traditional prerogative rests primarily on the fact that the obligations of personal obedience tend to be essentially unlimited.

Thus there is a double sphere:

(a) that of action which is bound to specific traditions;
(b) that of action which is free of specific rules.

In the latter sphere, the master is free to do good turns on the basis of his personal pleasure and likes, particularly in return for gifts – the historical sources of dues (*Gebühren*). So far as his action follows principles at all, these are governed by considerations of ethical common sense, of equity or of utilitarian expediency. They are not formal principles, as in the case of legal authority. The exercise of power is oriented toward the consideration of how far master and staff can go in view of the subjects' traditional compliance without arousing their resistance. When resistance occurs, it is directed against the master or his servant personally, the accusation being that he failed to observe the traditional limits of his power. Opposition is not directed against the system as such – it is a case of "traditionalist revolution."

In the pure type of traditional authority it is impossible for law or administrative rule to be deliberately created by legislation. Rules which in fact are innovations can be legitimized only by the claim that they have been "valid of yore," but have only now been recognized by means of "Wisdom" [the *Weistum* of ancient Germanic law]. Legal decisions as "finding of the law" (*Rechtsfindung*) can refer only to documents of tradition, namely to precedents and earlier decisions. […]

In the pure type of traditional rule, the following features of a bureaucratic administrative staff are absent:

(a) a clearly defined sphere of competence subject to impersonal rules,
(b) a rationally established hierarchy,
(c) a regular system of appointment on the basis of free contract, and orderly promotion,
(d) technical training as a regular requirement,
(e) (frequently) fixed salaries, in the type case paid in money. […]

Charismatic Authority

The term "charisma" will be applied to a certain quality of an individual personality by virtue of which he is considered extraordinary and treated as endowed with supernatural, superhuman, or at least specifically exceptional powers or qualities. These are such as are not accessible to the ordinary person, but are regarded as of divine origin or as exemplary, and on the basis of them the individual concerned is treated as a "leader." In primitive circumstances this peculiar kind of quality is thought of as resting on magical powers, whether of prophets, persons with a reputation for therapeutic or legal wisdom, leaders in the hunt, or heroes in war. How the quality in question would be ultimately judged from any ethical, aesthetic, or other such point of view is naturally entirely indifferent for purposes of definition. What is alone important is how the individual is actually regarded by those subject to charismatic authority, by his "followers" or "disciples." [...]

I   It is recognition on the part of those subject to authority which is decisive for the validity of charisma. This recognition is freely given and guaranteed by what is held to be a proof, originally always a miracle, and consists in devotion to the corresponding revelation, hero worship, or absolute trust in the leader. But where charisma is genuine, it is not this which is the basis of the claim to legitimacy. This basis lies rather in the conception that it is the duty of those subject to charismatic authority to recognize its genuineness and to act accordingly. Psychologically this recognition is a matter of complete personal devotion to the possessor of the quality, arising out of enthusiasm, or of despair and hope. [...]

II   If proof and success elude the leader for long, if he appears deserted by his god or his magical or heroic powers, above all, if his leadership fails to benefit his followers, it is likely that his charismatic authority will disappear. This is the genuine meaning of the divine right of kings (*Gottesgnadentum*). [...]

III   An organized group subject to charismatic authority will be called a charismatic community (*Gemeinde*). It is based on an emotional form of communal relationship (*Vergemeinschaftung*). The administrative staff of a charismatic leader does not consist of "officials"; least of all are its members technically trained. It is not chosen on the basis of social privilege nor from the point of view of domestic or personal dependency. It is rather chosen in terms of the charismatic qualities of its members. The prophet has his disciples; the warlord his bodyguard; the leader, generally, his agents (*Vertrauensmänner*). There is no such thing as appointment or dismissal, no career, no promotion. There is only a call at the instance of the leader on the basis of the charismatic qualification of those he summons. There is no hierarchy; the leader merely intervenes in general or in individual cases when he considers the members of his staff lacking in charismatic qualification for a given task. There is no such thing as a bailiwick or definite sphere of competence, and no appropriation of official powers on the basis of social privileges. There may, however, be territorial or functional limits to charismatic powers and to the individual's mission. There is no such thing as a salary or a benefice. [...]

IV   Pure charisma is specifically foreign to economic considerations. Wherever it appears, it constitutes a "call" in the most emphatic sense of the word, a "mission" or a "spiritual duty." In the pure type, it disdains and repudiates economic exploitation of the gifts of grace as a source of income, though, to be sure, this often remains more an ideal than a fact. It is not that charisma always demands a renunciation of property or even of acquisition, as under certain circumstances prophets and their disciples do. The heroic warrior and his followers actively seek booty; the elective ruler or the charismatic party leader requires the material means of power. The former in addition requires a brilliant display of his authority to bolster his prestige. What is despised, so long as the genuinely charismatic type is adhered to, is traditional or rational everyday economizing, the attainment of a regular income by continuous economic activity devoted to this end. [...]

V In traditionalist periods, charisma is *the* great revolutionary force. The likewise revolutionary force of "reason" works from *without*: by altering the situations of life and hence its problems, finally in this way changing men's attitudes toward them; or it intellectualizes the individual. Charisma, on the other hand, *may* effect a subjective or *internal* reorientation born out of suffering, conflicts, or enthusiasm. It may then result in a radical alteration of the central attitudes and directions of action with a completely new orientation of all attitudes toward the different problems of the "world." In prerationalistic periods, tradition and charisma between them have almost exhausted the whole of the orientation of action.

The Routinization of Charisma

In its pure form charismatic authority has a character specifically foreign to everyday routine structures. The social relationships directly involved are strictly personal, based on the validity and practice of charismatic personal qualities. If this is not to remain a purely transitory phenomenon, but to take on the character of a permanent relationship, a "community" of disciples or followers or a party organization or any sort of political or hierocratic organization, it is necessary for the character of charismatic authority to become radically changed. Indeed, in its pure form charismatic authority may be said to exist only *in statu nascendi*. It cannot remain stable, but becomes either traditionalized or rationalized, or a combination of both.

The following are the principal motives underlying this transformation: (a) The ideal and also the material interests of the followers in the continuation and the continual reactivation of the community, (b) the still stronger ideal and also stronger material interests of the members of the administrative staff, the disciples, the party workers, or others in continuing their relationship. Not only this, but they have an interest in continuing it in such a way that both from an ideal and a material point of view, their own position is put on a stable everyday basis. This means, above all, making it possible to participate in normal family relationships or at least to enjoy a secure social position in place of the kind of discipleship which is cut off from ordinary worldly connections, notably in the family and in economic relationships.

These interests generally become conspicuously evident with the disappearance of the personal charismatic leader and with the problem of *succession*. The way in which this problem is met – if it is met at all and the charismatic community continues to exist or now begins to emerge – is of crucial importance for the character of the subsequent social relationships. [...]

Concomitant with the routinization of charisma with a view to insuring adequate succession, go the interests in its routinization on the part of the administrative staff. It is only in the initial stages and so long as the charismatic leader acts in a way which is completely outside everyday social organization, that it is possible for his followers to live communistically in a community of faith and enthusiasm, on gifts, booty, or sporadic acquisition. Only the members of the small group of enthusiastic disciples and followers are prepared to devote their lives purely idealistically to their call. The great majority of disciples and followers will in the long run "make their living" out of their "calling" in a material sense as well. Indeed, this must be the case if the movement is not to disintegrate.

Hence, the routinization of charisma also takes the form of the appropriation of powers and of economic advantages by the followers or disciples, and of regulating recruitment. This process of traditionalization or of legalization, according to whether rational legislation is involved or not, may take any one of a number of typical forms. [...]

For charisma to be transformed into an everyday phenomenon, it is necessary that its anti-economic character should be altered. It must be adapted to some form of fiscal organization to provide for the needs of the group and hence to the economic conditions necessary for raising taxes and contributions. When a charismatic movement develops in the direction of prebendal provision, the "laity" becomes differentiated from the "clergy" – derived from κλῆρος, meaning a "share" – that is, the participating members of the charismatic administrative staff which has now become routinized. These are the priests of the developing "church." Correspondingly, in a developing political body – the "state" in the rational case – vassals, benefice-holders, officials or appointed party officials (instead of voluntary party workers and functionaries) are differentiated from the "tax payers." ...

It follows that, in the course of routinization, the charismatically ruled organization is largely transformed into one of the everyday authorities, the patrimonial form, especially in is estate-type or bureaucratic variant. Its original peculiarities are apt to be retained in the charismatic status honor acquired by heredity or office-holding. This applies to all who participate in the appropriation, the chief himself and the members of his staff. It is thus a matter of the type of prestige enjoyed by ruling groups. A hereditary monarch by "divine right" is not a simple patrimonial chief, patriarch, or sheik; a vassal is not a mere household retainer or official. Further details must be deferred to the analysis of status groups.

As a rule, routinization is not free of conflict. In the early stages personal claims on the charisma of the chief are not easily forgotten and the conflict between the charisma of the office or of hereditary status with personal charisma is a typical process in many historical situations.

Chapter 24

Bureaucracy [1922]

Max Weber

Characteristics of Modern Bureaucracy

Modern officialdom functions in the following manner:

I. There is the principle of official *jurisdictional areas*, which are generally ordered by rules, that is, by laws or administrative regulations. This means:

1   The regular activities required for the purposes of the bureaucratically governed structure are assigned as official duties.
2   The authority to give the commands required for the discharge of these duties is distributed in a stable way and is strictly delimited by rules concerning the coercive means, physical, sacerdotal, or otherwise, which may be placed at the disposal of officials.
3   Methodical provision is made for the regular and continuous fulfillment of these duties and for the exercise of the corresponding rights; only persons who qualify under general rules are employed.

In the sphere of the state these three elements constitute a bureaucratic *agency*, in the sphere of the private economy they constitute a bureaucratic *enterprise*. Bureaucracy, thus understood, is fully developed in political and ecclesiastical communities only

---

Weber, Max, "Bureaucracy," pp. 135–144, 149–158, 163–164, 173–178 from H.H. Gerth and C. Wright Mills, eds. and trans., *From Max Weber: Essays in Sociology*. New York: Oxford University Press, Inc., 1946. Copyright © 1946, 1958 by H. H. Gerth and C. Wright Mills. Used by permission of Oxford University Press.

Classical Sociological Theory, Third Edition. Edited by Craig Calhoun, Joseph Gerteis, James Moody, Steven Pfaff, and Indermohan Virk. Editorial material and organization © 2012 John Wiley & Sons, Ltd. Published 2012 by John Wiley & Sons, Ltd.

in the modern state, and in the private economy only in the most advanced institutions of capitalism. Permanent agencies, with fixed jurisdiction, are not the historical rule but rather the exception. This is even true of large political structures such as those of the ancient Orient, the Germanic and Mongolian empires of conquest, and of many feudal states. In all these cases, the ruler executes the most important measures through personal trustees, table-companions, or court-servants. Their commissions and powers are not precisely delimited and are temporarily called into being for each case.

II. The principles of *office hierarchy* and of channels of appeal (*Instanzenzug*) stipulate a clearly established system of super and subordination in which there is a supervision of the lower offices by the higher ones. Such a system offers the governed the possibility of appealing, in a precisely regulated manner, the decision of a lower office to the corresponding superior authority. With the full development of the bureaucratic type, the office hierarchy is *monocratically* organized. The principle of hierarchical office authority is found in all bureaucratic structures: in state and ecclesiastical structures as well as in large party organizations and private enterprises. It does not matter for the character of bureaucracy whether its authority is called "private" or "public."

When the principle of jurisdictional "competency" is fully carried through, hierarchical subordination – at least in public office – does not mean that the "higher" authority is authorized simply to take over the business of the "lower." Indeed, the opposite is the rule; once an office has been set up, a new incumbent will always be appointed if a vacancy occurs.

III. The management of the modern office is based upon written documents (the "files"), which are preserved in their original or draft form, and upon a staff of subaltern officials and scribes of all sorts. The body of officials working in an agency along with the respective apparatus of material implements and the files makes up a *bureau* (in private enterprises often called the "counting house," *Kontor*).

In principle, the modern organization of the civil service separates the bureau from the private domicile of the official and, in general, segregates official activity from the sphere of private life. Public monies and equipment are divorced from the private property of the official. This condition is everywhere the product of a long development. Nowadays, it is found in public as well as in private enterprises; in the latter, the principle extends even to the entrepreneur at the top. In principle, the *Kontor* (office) is separated from the household, business from private correspondence, and business assets from private wealth. The more consistently the modern type of business management has been carried through, the more are these separations the case. The beginnings of this process are to be found as early as the Middle Ages.

It is the peculiarity of the modern entrepreneur that he conducts himself as the "first official" of his enterprise, in the very same way in which the ruler of a specifically modern bureaucratic state [Frederick II of Prussia] spoke of himself as "the first servant" of the state. The idea that the bureau activities of the state are intrinsically different in character from the management of private offices is a continental European notion and, by way of contrast, is totally foreign to the American way.

IV. Office management, at least all specialized office management – and such management is distinctly modern – usually presupposes thorough training in a field of specialization. This, too, holds increasingly for the modern executive and employee of a private enterprise, just as it does for the state officials.

V. When the office is fully developed, official activity demands the *full working capacity* of the official, irrespective of the fact that the length of his obligatory working hours in the bureau may be limited. In the normal case, this too is only the product of a long development, in the public as well as in the private office. Formerly the normal state of affairs was the reverse: Official business was discharged as a secondary activity.

VI. The management of the office follows *general rules*, which are more or less stable, more or less exhaustive, and which can be learned. Knowledge of these rules represents a special technical expertise which the officials possess. It involves jurisprudence, administrative or business management.

The reduction of modern office management to rules is deeply embedded in its very nature. The theory of modern public administration, for instance, assumes that the authority to order certain matters by decree – which has been legally granted to an agency – does not entitle the agency to regulate the matter by individual commands given for each case, but only to regulate the matter abstractly. This stands in extreme contrast to the regulation of all relationships through individual privileges and bestowals of favor, which, as we shall see, is absolutely dominant in patrimonialism, at least in so far as such relationships are not fixed by sacred tradition.

The Position of the Official within and outside of Bureaucracy

All this results in the following for the internal and external position of the official:

I. Office holding as a vocation

That the office is a "vocation" (*Beruf*) finds expression, first, in the requirement of a prescribed course of training, which demands the entire working capacity for a long period of time, and in generally prescribed special examinations as prerequisites of employment. Furthermore, it finds expression in that the position of the official is in the nature of a "duty" (*Pflicht*). This determines the character of his relations in the following manner: Legally and actually, office holding is not considered ownership of a source of income, to be exploited for rents or emoluments in exchange for the rendering of certain services, as was normally the case during the

Middle Ages and frequently up to the threshold of recent times, nor is office holding considered a common exchange of services, as in the case of free employment contracts. Rather, entrance into an office, including one in the private economy, is considered an acceptance of a specific duty of fealty to the purpose of the office (*Amtstreue*) in return for the grant of a secure existence. It is decisive for the modern loyalty to an office that, in the pure type, it does not establish a relationship to a *person*, like the vassal's or disciple's faith under feudal or patrimonial authority, but rather is devoted to *impersonal* and *functional* purposes. These purposes, of course, frequently gain an ideological halo from cultural values, such as state, church, community, party or enterprise, which appear as surrogates for a this-worldly or other-worldly personal master and which are embodied by a given group.

The political official – at least in the fully developed modern state – is not considered the personal servant of a ruler. Likewise, the bishop, the priest and the preacher are in fact no longer, as in early Christian times, carriers of a purely personal charisma, which offers other-worldly sacred values under the personal mandate of a master, and in principle responsible only to him, to everybody who appears worthy of them and asks for them. In spite of the partial survival of the old theory, they have become officials in the service of a functional purpose, a purpose which in the present-day "church" appears at once impersonalized and ideologically sanctified.

II.   *The social position of the official*

A.   SOCIAL ESTEEM AND STATUS CONVENTION.   Whether he is in a private office or a public bureau, the modern official, too, always strives for and usually attains a distinctly elevated *social esteem* vis-à-vis the governed. His social position is protected by prescription about rank order and, for the political official, by special prohibitions of the criminal code against "insults to the office" and "contempt" of state and church authorities.

The social position of the official is normally highest where, as in old civilized countries, the following conditions prevail: a strong demand for administration by trained experts; a strong and stable social differentiation, where the official predominantly comes from socially and economically privileged strata because of the social distribution of power or the costliness of the required training and of status conventions. [...]

B.   APPOINTMENT VERSUS ELECTION: CONSEQUENCES FOR EXPERTISE.   Typically, the bureaucratic official is appointed by a superior authority. An official elected by the governed is no longer a purely bureaucratic figure. Of course, a formal election may hide an appointment – in politics especially by party bosses. This does not depend upon legal statutes, but upon the way in which the party mechanism functions. Once firmly organized, the parties can turn a formally free election into the mere acclamation of a candidate designated by the party chief, or at least into a contest, conducted according to certain rules, for the election of one of two designated candidates.

In all circumstances, the designation of officials by means of an election modifies the rigidity of hierarchical subordination. In principle, an official who is elected has an autonomous position vis-à-vis his superiors, for he does not derive his position "from above" but "from below," or least not from a superior authority of the official hierarchy but from powerful party men ("bosses"), who also determine his further career. The career of the elected official is not primarily dependent upon his chief in the administration. The official who is not elected, but appointed by a master, normally functions, from a technical point of view, more accurately because it is more likely that purely functional points of consideration and qualities will determine his selection and career. As laymen, the governed can evaluate the expert qualifications of a candidate for office only in terms of experience, and hence only after his service. Moreover, if political parties are involved in any sort of selection of officials by election, they quite naturally tend to give decisive weight not to technical competence but to the services a follower renders to the party boss. This holds for the designation of otherwise freely elected officials by party bosses when they determine the slate of candidates as well as for free appointment of officials by a chief who has himself been elected. The contrast, however, is relative: substantially similar conditions hold where legitimate monarchs and their subordinates appoint officials, except that partisan influences are then less controllable.

Where the demand for administration by trained experts is considerable, and the party faithful have to take into account an intellectually developed, educated, and free "public opinion," the use of unqualified officials redounds upon the party in power at the next election. Naturally, this is more likely to happen when the officials are appointed by the chief. The demand for a trained administration now exists in the United States, but wherever, as in the large cities, immigrant votes are "corralled," there is, of course, no effective public opinion. Therefore, popular election not only of the administrative chief but also of his subordinate officials usually endangers, at least in very large administrative bodies which are difficult to supervise, the expert qualification of the officials as well as the precise functioning of the bureaucratic mechanism, besides weakening the dependence of the officials upon the hierarchy. [...]

C. TENURE AND THE INVERSE RELATIONSHIP BETWEEN JUDICIAL INDEPENDENCE AND SOCIAL PRESTIGE.   Normally, the position of the official is held for life, at least in public bureaucracies, and this is increasingly the case for all similar structures. As a factual rule, *tenure for life* is presupposed even where notice can be given or periodic reappointment occurs. In a private enterprise, the fact of such tenure normally differentiates the official from the worker. Such legal or actual life-tenure, however, is not viewed as a proprietary right of the official to the possession of office as was the case in many structures of authority of the past. Wherever legal guarantees against discretionary dismissal or transfer are developed, as in Germany for all judicial and increasingly also for administrative officials, they merely serve the purpose of guaranteeing a strictly impersonal discharge of specific office duties. [...]

D. RANK AS THE BASIS OF REGULAR SALARY. The official as a rule receives a *monetary* compensation in the form of a *salary*, normally fixed, and the old age security provided by a pension. The salary is not measured like a wage in terms of work done, but according to "status," that is, according to the kind of function (the "rank") and, possibly, according to the length of service. The relatively great security of the official's income, as well as the rewards of social esteem, make the office a sought-after position, especially in countries which no longer provide opportunities for colonial profits. In such countries, this situation permits relatively low salaries for officials.

E. FIXED CAREER LINES AND STATUS RIGIDITY. The official is set for a "career" within the hierarchical order of the public service. He expects to move from the lower, less important and less well paid, to the higher positions. The average official naturally desires a mechanical fixing of the conditions of promotion: if not of the offices, at least of the salary levels. He wants these conditions fixed in terms of "seniority," or possibly according to grades achieved in a system of examinations. Here and there, such grades actually form a *character indelebilis* of the official and have lifelong effects on his career. To this is joined the desire to reinforce the right to office and to increase status group closure and economic security. All of this makes for a tendency to consider the offices as "prebends" of those qualified by educational certificates. The necessity of weighing general personal and intellectual qualifications without concern for the often subaltern character of such patents of specialized education, has brought it about that the highest political offices, especially the "ministerial" positions, are as a rule filled without reference to such certificates. [...]

The Technical Superiority of Bureaucratic Organization over Administration by Notables

The decisive reason for the advance of bureaucratic organization has always been its purely *technical* superiority over any other form of organization. The fully developed bureaucratic apparatus compares with other organizations exactly as does the machine with the non-mechanical modes of production. Precision, speed, unambiguity, knowledge of the files, continuity, discretion, unity, strict subordination, reduction of friction and of material and personal costs – these are raised to the optimum point in the strictly bureaucratic administration, and especially in its monocratic form. As compared with all collegiate, honorific, and avocational forms of administration, trained bureaucracy is superior on all these points. And as far as complicated tasks are concerned, paid bureaucratic work is not only more precise but, in the last analysis, it is often cheaper than even formally unremunerated honorific service. [...]

Today, it is primarily the capitalist market economy which demands that the official business of public administration be discharged precisely, unambiguously, continuously, and with as much speed as possible. Normally, the very large modern capitalist enterprises are themselves unequaled models of strict bureaucratic organization. Business management throughout rests on increasing precision, steadiness, and, above all, speed of operations. This, in turn, is determined by the peculiar nature of the modern means of communication, including, among other things, the news service of the press. The extraordinary increase in the speed by which public announcements, as well as economic and political facts, are transmitted exerts a steady and sharp pressure in the direction of speeding up the tempo of administrative reaction towards various situations. The optimum of such reaction time is normally attained only by a strictly bureaucratic organization. (The fact that the bureaucratic apparatus also can, and indeed does, create certain definite impediments for the discharge of business in a manner best adapted to the individuality of each case does not belong in the present context.)

Bureaucratization offers above all the optimum possibility for carrying through the principle of specializing administrative functions according to purely objective considerations. Individual performances are allocated to functionaries who have specialized training and who by constant practice increase their expertise. "Objective" discharge of business primarily means a discharge of business according to *calculable rules* and "without regard for persons."

"Without regard for person," however, is also the watchword of the market and, in general, of all pursuits of naked economic interests. Consistent bureaucratic domination means the leveling of "status honor." Hence, if the principle of the free market is not at the same time restricted, it means the universal domination of the "class situation." That this consequence of bureaucratic domination has not set in everywhere proportional to the extent of bureaucratization is due to the differences between possible principles by which polities may supply their requirements. However, the second element mentioned, calculable rules, is the most important one for modern bureaucracy. The peculiarity of modern culture, and specifically of its technical and economic basis, demands this very "calculability" of results. When fully developed, bureaucracy also stands, in a specific sense, under the principle of *sine ira ac studio*. Bureaucracy develops the more perfectly, the more it is "dehumanized," the more completely it succeeds in eliminating from official business love, hatred, and all purely personal, irrational, and emotional elements which escape calculation. This is appraised as its special virtue by capitalism. [...]

The Leveling of Social Differences

In spite of its indubitable technical superiority, bureaucracy has everywhere been a relatively late development. A number of obstacles have contributed to this, and only under certain social and political conditions have they definitely receded into the background.

A. *Administrative democratization*

Bureaucratic organization has usually come into power on the basis of a leveling of economic and social differences. This leveling has been at least relative, and has concerned the significance of social and economic differences for the assumption of administrative functions.

Bureaucracy inevitably accompanies modern *mass democracy*, in contrast to the democratic self-government of small homogeneous units. This results from its characteristic principle: the abstract regularity of the exercise of authority, which is a result of the demand for "equality before the law" in the personal and functional sense – hence, of the horror of "privilege," and the principled rejection of doing business "from case to case." Such regularity also follows from the social preconditions of its origin. Any non-bureaucratic administration of a large social structure rests in some way upon the fact that existing social, material, or honorific preferences and ranks are connected with administrative functions and duties. This usually means that an economic or a social exploitation of position, which every sort of administrative activity provides to its bearers, is the compensation for the assumption of administrative functions.

Bureaucratization and democratization within the administration of the state therefore signify an increase of the cash expenditures of the public treasury, in spite of the fact that bureaucratic administration is usually more "economical" in character than other forms. Until recent times – at least from the point of view of the treasury – the cheapest way of satisfying the need for administration was to leave almost the entire local administration and lower judicature to the landlords of Eastern Prussia. The same is true of the administration by justices of the peace in England. Mass democracy which makes a clean sweep of the feudal, patrimonial, and – at least in intent – the plutocratic privileges in administration unavoidably has to put paid professional labor in place of the historically inherited "avocational" administration by notables.

B. Mass parties and the bureaucratic consequences of democratization

This applies not only to the state. For it is no accident that in their own organizations the democratic mass parties have completely broken with traditional rule by notables based upon personal relationships and personal esteem. Such personal structures still persist among many old conservative as well as old liberal parties, but democratic mass parties are bureaucratically organized under the leadership of party officials, professional party and trade union secretaries, etc. In Germany, for instance, this has happened in the Social Democratic party and in the agrarian mass-movement; in England earliest in the caucus democracy of Gladstone and Chamberlain which spread from Birmingham in the 1870s. In the United States, both parties since Jackson's administration have developed bureaucratically. In France, however, attempts to organize disciplined political parties on the basis of an election system that would compel bureaucratic organization have repeatedly failed. The resistance of local circles of notables against the otherwise unavoidable bureaucratization of the parties, which would encompass the entire country and break their influence, could not be overcome. Every advance of simple election techniques based on numbers alone as, for instance, the system of proportional representation, means a strict and inter-local bureaucratic organization of the parties and therewith an increasing domination of party bureaucracy and discipline, as well as the elimination of the local circles of notables – at least this holds for large states.

The progress of bureaucratization within the state administration itself is a phenomenon paralleling the development of democracy, as is quite obvious in France, North America, and now in England. Of course, one must always remember that the term "democratization" can be misleading. The *demos* itself, in the sense of a shapeless mass, never "governs" larger associations, but rather is governed. What changes is only the way in which the executive leaders are selected and the measure of influence which the *demos*, or better, which social circles from its midst are able to exert upon the content and the direction of administrative activities by means of "public opinion." "Democratization," in the sense here intended, does not necessarily mean an increasingly active share of the subjects in government. This may be a result of democratization, but it is not necessarily the case.

We must expressly recall at this point that the political concept of democracy, deduced from the "equal rights" of the governed, includes these further postulates:

(1) prevention of the development of a closed status group of officials in the interest of a universal accessibility of office, and (2) minimization of the authority of officialdom in the interest of expanding the sphere of influence of "public opinion" as far as practicable. Hence, wherever possible, political democracy strives to shorten the term of office through election and recall, and to be relieved from a limitation to candidates with special expert qualifications. Thereby democracy inevitably comes into conflict with the bureaucratic tendencies which have been produced by its very fight against the notables. The loose term "democratization" cannot be used here, in so far as it is understood to mean the minimization of the civil servants' power in favor of the greatest possible "direct" rule of the *demos*, which in practice means the respective party leaders of the *demos*. The decisive aspect here – indeed it is rather exclusively so – is the *leveling of the governed* in face of the governing and bureaucratically articulated group, which in its turn may occupy a quite autocratic position, both in fact and in form. [...]

The Objective and Subjective Bases of Bureaucratic Perpetuity

Once fully established, bureaucracy is among those social structures which are the hardest to destroy. Bureaucracy is *the* means of transforming social action into rationally organized action. Therefore, as an instrument of rationally organizing authority relations, bureaucracy was and is a power instrument of the first order for one who controls the bureaucratic apparatus. Under otherwise equal conditions, rationally organized and directed action (*Gesellschaftshandeln*) is superior to every kind of collective behavior (*Massenhandeln*) and also social action

(*Gemeinschaftshandeln*) opposing it. Where administration has been completely bureaucratized, the resulting system of domination is practically indestructible.

The individual bureaucrat cannot squirm out of the apparatus into which he has been harnessed. In contrast to the "notable" performing administrative tasks as a honorific duty or as a subsidiary occupation (avocation), the professional bureaucrat is chained to his activity in his entire economic and ideological existence. In the great majority of cases he is only a small cog in a ceaselessly moving mechanism which prescribes to him an essentially fixed route of march. The official is entrusted with specialized tasks, and normally the mechanism cannot be put into motion or arrested by him, but only from the very top. The individual bureaucrat is, above all, forged to the common interest of all the functionaries in the perpetuation of the apparatus and the persistence of its rationally organized domination.

The ruled, for their part, cannot dispense with or replace the bureaucratic apparatus once it exists, for it rests upon expert training, a functional specialization of work, and an attitude set on habitual virtuosity in the mastery of single yet methodically integrated functions. If the apparatus stops working, or if its work is interrupted by force, chaos results, which it is difficult to master by improvised replacements from among the governed. This holds for public administration as well as for private economic management. Increasingly the material fate of the masses depends upon the continuous and correct functioning of the ever more bureaucratic organizations of private capitalism, and the idea of eliminating them becomes more and more utopian.

Increasingly, all order in public and private organizations is dependent on the system of files and the discipline of officialdom, that means, its habit of painstaking obedience within its wonted sphere of action. The latter is the more decisive element, however important in practice the files are. The naive idea of Bakuninism of destroying the basis of "acquired rights" together with "domination" by destroying the public documents overlooks that the settled orientation of *man* for observing the accustomed rules and regulations will survive independently of the documents. Every reorganization of defeated or scattered army units, as well as every restoration of an administrative order destroyed by revolts, panics, or other catastrophes, is effected by an appeal to this conditioned orientation, bred both in the officials and in the subjects, of obedient adjustment to such [social and political] orders. If the appeal is successful it brings, as it were, the disturbed mechanism to "snap into gear" again.

The objective indispensability of the once-existing apparatus, in connection with its peculiarly "impersonal" character, means that the mechanism – in contrast to the feudal order based upon personal loyalty – is easily made to work for anybody who knows how to gain control over it. A rationally ordered officialdom continues to function smoothly after the enemy has occupied the territory; he merely needs to change the top officials. It continues to operate because it is to the vital interest of everyone concerned, including above all the enemy. After Bismarck had, during the long course of his years in power, brought his ministerial colleagues into unconditional bureaucratic dependence by eliminating all independent statesmen, he saw to his surprise that upon his resignation they continued to administer their offices unconcernedly and undismayedly, as if it had not been the ingenious lord and very creator of these tools who had left, but merely some individual figure in the bureaucratic machine which had been exchanged for some other figure. In spite of all the changes of masters in France since the time of the First Empire, the power apparatus remained essentially the same.

Such an apparatus makes "revolution," in the sense of the forceful creation of entirely new formations of authority, more and more impossible – technically, because of its control over the modern means of communication (telegraph etc.), and also because of its increasingly rationalized inner structure. The place of "revolutions" is under this process taken by *coups d'état*, as again France demonstrates in the classical manner since all successful transformations there have been of this nature. [...]

Part VI

Self and Society in Sociological Theory

Introduction to Part VI

25 The Self

26 The Stranger

27 Group Expansion and the Development of Individuality

28 The Dyad and the Triad

29 Civilization and its Discontents

30 The Souls of Black Folk

31 The Regulation of the Wishes

Part I

Self and Society in Sociological Theory

Introduction to Part VI

The concept of the "self" at first seems more a psychological construct than a sociological one. Yet as a generation of influential theorists began to understand, the development and expression of the self is deeply social. On the one hand, it is the possession of the individual; it is in fact what makes a person unique from all other people. But at the same time, it is the reflection of the social group. As George Herbert Mead put it, "the self is a social structure."

This concept of "self" makes the work included in this section quite distinct from earlier social theory. In this section, we have gathered work from five influential theorists active at the turn of the century: Georg Simmel, Sigmund Freud, George Herbert Mead, William Edward Burghardt (W.E.B.) Du Bois and William Isaac (W.I.) Thomas. Although there were many differences among these theorists, there were also significant points of comparison in their lives and their theories. Most importantly, each of these authors grappled with the same central issue: the connection between self and the social context.

These authors did not view society as the result of a contract among autonomous individuals, nor did they see social order as driven entirely by relations of power. Sociological understanding of the connection between self and society instead began from the premise that humans are social animals by nature. Society is thus an innate part of human life. An individual human being could physically exist without any form of society, but that person would not be a "person" at all in the sense we normally mean. Such a person would have no *social* identity. But they also wanted to point out that even our individuality – the way we define ourselves as distinct from others – is a social thing, since it involves distinctions made on the basis of socially defined roles.

Classical Sociological Theory, Third Edition. Edited by Craig Calhoun, Joseph Gerteis, James Moody, Steven Pfaff, and Indermohan Virk. Editorial material and organization © 2012 John Wiley & Sons, Ltd. Published 2012 by John Wiley & Sons, Ltd.

As a result of this interest in the connection between self and society, the work in this section claims an important middle ground between Weber's action-centered approach and Durkheim's understanding of society as a reality *sui generis*. There are at least two important methodological ramifications to this fact. First, the authors in this section focus more specifically on the "micro" dimension of individuals as social beings without abandoning an interest in more "macro" social formations. Second, they deal more explicitly with the mental states of individuals.

Lives and Intellectual Contexts

Georg Simmel (1858–1918) and Sigmund Freud (1856–1939) were both German-speaking Europeans, of the same intellectual generation as Max Weber. Both were Jews who experienced the difficulties that their "otherness" entailed. Simmel was born in Berlin to middle-class parents and remained there nearly all his life. Despite his rejection of religious ties, anti-Semitic prejudice hampered his career. After earning his doctorate in 1881, Simmel became a popular teacher at the University of Berlin, but had no regular faculty appointment. He eventually attained a full professorship at the University of Strasbourg in 1914. Throughout his career, Simmel worked out his own conception of sociology in a series of well-known articles and a few longer monographs in which his emphasis on "sociability" as a central trait of humans is evident.

Sigmund Freud grew up in Vienna. Like Simmel, Freud came from a Jewish family and experienced anti-Semitic prejudice despite his lack of religious faith. At the University of Vienna from 1873 to 1881, Freud studied medicine, philosophy, and science. Afterwards, he continued his studies while working as a physician specializing in neurology. During the 1890s, Freud founded the psychoanalytic theory of the mind, and he became an associate professor at the University of Vienna in 1902. Freud's early work helped establish his psychoanalytic movement, while his later works (especially *Civilization and its Discontents*, excerpted here) tie his perspective to more clearly sociological questions. He and his family fled to England in 1938 following the Nazi invasion of Austria. Freud died the following year.

By contrast, George Herbert Mead (1863–1931), W.E.B. Du Bois (1868–1963) and W.I. Thomas (1863–1947) were Americans, and slightly younger than their European counterparts. Mead grew up in Oberlin, Ohio where his father, a Protestant clergyman, was a theology professor. After graduating from Oberlin College in 1883, Mead spent several years working as a teacher, a surveyor, and a laborer. He entered graduate studies at Harvard in 1887, studying philosophy and physiological psychology. Mead eventually abandoned his dissertation, married, and began to teach at the University of Michigan, and later at the University of Chicago where he influenced generations of Chicago sociology students through his popular course in social psychology. Mead published more than 60 articles during his academic career, but never published a longer programmatic discussion of his social thought. After his death, Mead's students published his four books, including *Mind, Self, and Society*, based on his lectures.

Thomas (1863–1947) grew up in Virginia and Tennessee, and began his scholarly career with an interest in classics and languages before shifting to sociology. Like Mead, Thomas spent time at Oberlin College where he taught sociology before moving to the University of Chicago where he finished his dissertation and later became a faculty member. At Chicago, Thomas and Florian Znaniecki published one of the classic studies of immigration, *The Polish Peasant in Europe and America*. Later, Thomas published several studies, including *The Unadjusted Girl*.

Du Bois, a black American, grew up in a middle-class family in Massachusetts. He earned his undergraduate degree at Fisk university and completed his Ph.D. in history at Harvard, becoming the university's first black graduate. After teaching briefly elsewhere, he became a professor of history and economics at Atlanta University until moving to head the National Association for the Advancement of Colored People (NAACP) in 1910, where he also edited NAACP's journal, *The Crisis*. He remained a prolific author of academic articles, speeches, poetry, fiction, and four autobiographies. From 1896 to 1914, Du Bois published at least one book each year based on his research. He remained politically active in Marxist and Pan-African movements until his death in 1963.

Self and Society

The work included in this section develops the relationship between the self and society in several different ways. The first reading is from Mead's discussion of the importance of human communication in the development of the self. While all humans carry the capacity to interpret the "significant symbols" used in communication, it is only by being involved in social life that we learn to do so. Mead bases his distinction between "mind" (the ability to reflectively interpret symbols) and "self" (the experience of ourselves as unique individuals) upon this observation. According to Mead, both mind and self emerge through social interaction and thus must be distinguished from physical being. For Mead, the self is itself a social structure – a thing that both incorporates and helps to reproduce the social world. Mead often used simple examples to generate complex points about the nature of the self. His discussion of children at play, for instance, shows how through such play children learn to take on "the generalized other" and to see themselves and others in specific roles and thereby enter into meaningful social interaction.

Simmel and Du Bois develop the theme of self and society in a different way. In contrast to Mead, both authors discuss the way that aspects of the self are shaped under specific kinds of social circumstances. "Group Expansion and the Development of Individuality" demonstrates Simmel's "formal sociology" and his focus on the size of groups, differentiation within and between groups, and the resulting forms of individuation people experience. Simmel argues that individuality increases as a person's social circle expands, while differentiation within groups also leads to social ties across group boundaries. The social context in which an individual is embedded is thus extremely important for the way that she will define herself. Similarly, the readings on the "dyad" and the "triad" as fundamental sociological units show that social structures shape the character of even our intimate relationships.

"The Stranger" is an example of Simmel's study of social types. Simmel suggests that all relationships have varying amounts of social distance. As a social being, the stranger is created by the individual's place in the social world – he is "both near and far," as Simmel describes it. Drawing on the historical example of Jewish traders in European society, Simmel shows how this combination of physical proximity and social distance leads to a certain freedom of interaction and objectivity in relationships. In a related passage in his 1905 article "How Is Society Possible?", which is not excerpted, Simmel suggested that such distance creates a "veil" of inherent dissimilarity between people. Du Bois used the same metaphor of a veil in his own famous essay to describe social distance between white and black Americans. Black Americans, Du Bois argued, have a "double consciousness" – both black and American – which could prevent the formation of a unified sense of self.

Thomas develops this theme as well. The famous claim in this reading (from *The Unadjusted Girl*, 1923) about the definition of the situation makes this clear. For Thomas, an individual's action depends upon how social situations are defined, a fact that itself is connected to the values and understandings of the community or communities in which the individual is embedded. Thomas pulls examples from different documents – among them interviews, letters, and immigrant newspapers – to show how the actions of individuals reflect and often support the values of the community.

The theme of self and society is developed in a different way in the work of Freud. Like Simmel, Freud was concerned with the forces holding societies together. Freud located these forces in individual and social drives rather than in the formal properties of groups. Freud also emphasized the conflicts that occur between individual drives and social norms. The reading included here, from *Civilization and its Discontents*, was Freud's most sociological work. The opening paragraphs of the excerpt set up Freud's argument. Society – or the process of "civilization," as Freud put it – works to bind people together into sociological units of family, race, nation, and so on. Ties of love and passion are an important element of cohesion, and they help to check what Freud saw as the naturally aggressive instincts of humans. But such ties also lead to feelings of guilt and jealousy, which inevitably come with living in human society. This tension is then manifested as a constant struggle between "ego" and "superego." Although this view differs markedly from Simmel's claim that humans are inherently social beings, it nonetheless speaks to the broad claim made by all the authors that social life is deeply implicated in our experience of the self.

Legacies of the Self

The work of these four authors has had some important ramifications for later sociological theory, much of which is evident in the second volume of this reader. Individually, each of the authors has left their mark. The theoretical legacy of Du

Bois is probably the least clear, in part because his very long public life had so many different facets. Yet Du Bois' work is now having a renaissance of sorts among theorists interested in questions of identity and difference. Simmel's influence can be clearly seen in modern exchange theory and social networks. Peter Blau, once a central figure in exchange theory, also brought aspects of Simmel's formal sociology to his later work on the properties of social structure. Freud's legacy has influenced social theorists who explore how unconscious desires shape individuals' lives and social patterns, including the critical social theorists of the Frankfurt School. French poststructuralist theories and postmodern theories have also employed many of Freud's ideas about the contradictory forces of civilization and individuality. Mead is best known as the founding figure of the school of symbolic interactionism in sociology. Herbert Blumer, for example, developed symbolic interactionism in large part through a dialogue with and interpretation of Thomas' and Mead's ideas. More generally, the central idea that the "self" – or whatever one wishes to call it – is both a personal property and a social structure is a distinctive claim of modern sociology. Although Marx, Weber and Durkheim all hinted at this idea, it was not until the second or third decade of the 20th century that the claim became widely acknowledged.

SELECTED BIBLIOGRAPHY

Aboulafia, Mitchell. 2001. *The Cosmopolitan Self: George Herbert Mead and Continental Philosophy*. Urbana, IL: University of Illinois Press. (A contemporary philosophical work considering the political implications of independence, mind, and self.)

Baldwin, John D. 1986. *George Herbert Mead: A Unifying Theory for Sociology*. Beverly Hills, CA: Sage Publications. (Baldwin summarizes Mead's model of the individual and society as a potentially unifying theory that includes all levels of society.)

Coser, Lewis (ed.). 1965. *Georg Simmel*. Englewood Cliffs, NJ: Prentice-Hall. (This collection includes introductory and biographical information and essays on Simmel's work by his contemporaries including Durkheim, and discusses continuing uses of Simmel's ideas by other theorists.)

Deegan, Mary Jo. 1988. *Jane Addams and the Men of the Chicago School, 1892–1918*. New Brunswick, NJ: Transaction Books. (In a feminist engagement with Mead's ideas, Deegan analyzes how Mead's social activism with Jane Addams of Hull House influenced his theories and why this information is not widely known.)

Frisby, David. 1984. *Georg Simmel*. New York: Tavistock Publications. (Frisby offers a readable yet comprehensive intellectual biography and overview of key issues in Simmel's work.)

Frisby, David. 1992. *Simmel and Since: Essays on Georg Simmel's Social Theory*. London: Routledge. (In this work focusing on modernity, Frisby outlines the historical and cultural context of Simmel's work, and examines his legacy to sociology including links with Weber.)

Gay, Peter. 1988. *Freud: A Life for Our Time*. New York: Norton. (Gay's critical intellectual biography traces Freud's development of ideas in the context of his life history. In a related series, *The Bourgeois Experience: Victoria to Freud*, Gay applies Freud's theory to interpret cultural history.)

Joas, Hans. 1985. *G. H. Mead: A Contemporary Re-examination of his Thought*. Translated by Raymond Meyer. Cambridge, MA: MIT Press. (Joas explores how Mead's ideas related to other pragmatists and how these ideas can be used.)

Jones, Ernest. 1961. *The Life and Work of Sigmund Freud*. Edited and abridged by Lionel Trilling and Steven Marcus. New York: Basic Books. (This is an abridged version of Jones' exhaustive, official biography that focuses on Freud's life and the context of his writings.)

Levine, Donald N. 1980. *Simmel and Parsons: Two Approaches to the Study of Society*. New York: Arno Press. (Levine explores Simmel's and Parsons' work as contrasting perspectives on sociology.)

Lewis, David Levering. 1994. *Du Bois: Biography of a Race, 1868–1919*. New York: Henry Holt. (Lewis' series traces Du Bois' life and thought and discusses their contemporaneous and more recent effects.)

Taylor, Charles. 1989. *Sources of the Self: The Making of the Modern Identity*. Cambridge, MA: Harvard University Press. (An advanced but extremely influential exploration of the social self and its relation to moral deliberations.)

Zamir, Shamoon. 1995. *Dark Voices: W.E.B. Du Bois and American Thought, 1888–1903*. Chicago: University of Chicago Press. (Zamir's study is especially useful for those wishing for a more sustained discussion of Du Bois' early work in its intellectual context.)

Chapter 25

The Self [1934]

George Herbert Mead

In our statement of the development of intelligence we have already suggested that the language process is essential for the development of the self. The self has a character which is different from that of the physiological organism proper. The self is something which has a development; it is not initially there, at birth, but arises in the process of social experience and activity, that is, develops in the given individual as a result of his relations to that process as a whole and to other individuals within that process. The intelligence of the lower forms of animal life, like a great deal of human intelligence, does not involve a self. In our habitual actions, for example, in our moving about in a world that is simply there and to which we are so adjusted that no thinking is involved, there is a certain amount of sensuous experience such as persons have when they are just waking up, a bare thereness of the world. Such characters about us may exist in experience without taking their place in relationship to the self. One must, of course, under those conditions, distinguish between the experience that immediately takes place and our own organization of it into the experience of the self. One says upon analysis that a certain item had its place in his experience, in the experience of his self. We do inevitably tend at a certain level of sophistication to organize all experience into that of a self. We do so intimately identify our experiences, especially our affective experiences, with the self that it takes a moment's abstraction to realize that pain and pleasure can be there without

Mead, George Herbert, "The Self," pp. 135–144, 149–158, 163–164, 173–178 from George Herbert Mead, *Mind, Self and Society: From the Standpoint of a Social Behaviorist*, ed. Charles W. Morris. Chicago: University of Chicago Press, 1934. Copyright © 1934 by University of Chicago Press. Reprinted by permission of The University of Chicago Press.

Classical Sociological Theory, Third Edition. Edited by Craig Calhoun, Joseph Gerteis, James Moody, Steven Pfaff, and Indermohan Virk. Editorial material and organization © 2012 John Wiley & Sons, Ltd. Published 2012 by John Wiley & Sons, Ltd.

being the experience of the self. Similarly, we normally organize our memories upon the string of our self. If we date things we always date them from the point of view of our past experiences. We frequently have memories that we cannot date, that we cannot place. A picture comes before us suddenly and we are at a loss to explain when that experience originally took place. We remember perfectly distinctly the picture, but we do not have it definitely placed, and until we can place it in terms of our past experience we are not satisfied. Nevertheless, I think it is obvious when one comes to consider it that the self is not necessarily involved in the life of the organism, nor involved in what we term our sensuous experience, that is, experience in a world about us for which we have habitual reactions.

We can distinguish very definitely between the self and the body. The body can be there and can operate in a very intelligent fashion without there being a self involved in the experience. The self has the characteristic that it is an object to itself, and that characteristic distinguishes it from other objects and from the body. It is perfectly true that the eye can see the foot, but it does not see the body as a whole. We cannot see our backs; we can feel certain portions of them, if we are agile, but we cannot get an experience of our whole body. There are, of course, experiences which are somewhat vague and difficult of location, but the bodily experiences are for us organized about a self. The foot and hand belong to the self. We can see our feet, especially if we look at them from the wrong end of an opera glass, as strange things which we have difficulty in recognizing as our own. The parts of the body are quite distinguishable from the self. We can lose parts of the body without any serious invasion of the self. The mere ability to experience different parts of the body is not different from the experience of a table. The table presents a different feel from what the hand does when one hand feels another, but it is an experience of something with which we come definitely into contact. The body does not experience itself as a whole, in the sense in which the self in some way enters into the experience of the self.

It is the characteristic of the self as an object to itself that I want to bring out. This characteristic is represented in the word "self," which is a reflexive, and indicates that which can be both subject and object. This type of object is essentially different from other objects, and in the past it has been distinguished as conscious, a term which indicates an experience with, an experience of, one's self. It was assumed that consciousness in some way carried this capacity of being an object to itself. In giving a behavioristic statement of consciousness we have to look for some sort of experience in which the physical organism can become an object to itself.[1]

When one is running to get away from someone who is chasing him, he is entirely occupied in this action, and his experience may be swallowed up in the objects about him, so that he has, at the time being, no consciousness of self at all. We must be, of course, very completely occupied to have that take place, but we can, I think, recognize that sort of a possible experience in which the self does not enter. We can, perhaps, get some light on that situation through those experiences in which in very intense action there appear in the experience of the individual, back of this intense action, memories and anticipations. Tolstoy as an officer in the war gives an account of having pictures of his past experience in the midst of his most intense action. There are also the pictures that flash into a person's mind when he is drowning. In such instances there is a contrast between an experience that is absolutely wound up in outside activity in which the self as an object does not enter, and an activity of memory and imagination in which the self is the principal object. The self is then entirely distinguishable from an organism that is surrounded by things and acts with reference to things, including parts of its own body. These latter may be objects like other objects, but they are just objects out there in the field, and they do not involve a self that is an object to the organism. This is, I think, frequently overlooked. It is that fact which makes our anthropomorphic reconstructions of animal life so fallacious. How can an individual get outside himself (experientially) in such a way as to become an object to himself? This is the essential psychological problem of selfhood or of self-consciousness; and its solution is to be found by referring to the process of social conduct or activity in which the given person or individual is implicated. The apparatus of reason would not be complete unless it swept itself into its own analysis of the field of experience; or unless the individual brought himself into the same experiential field as that of the other individual selves in relation to whom he acts in any given social situation. Reason cannot become impersonal unless it takes an objective, non-affective attitude toward itself; otherwise we have just consciousness, not *self*-consciousness. And it is necessary to rational conduct that the individual should thus take an objective, impersonal attitude toward himself, that he should become an object to himself. For the individual organism is obviously an essential and important fact or constituent element of the empirical situation in which it acts; and without taking objective account of itself as such, it cannot act intelligently, or rationally.

The individual experiences himself as such, not directly, but only indirectly, from the particular standpoints of other individual members of the same social group, or from the generalized standpoint of the social group as a whole to which he belongs. For he enters his own experience as a self or individual, not directly or immediately, not by becoming a subject to himself, but only in so far as he first becomes an object to himself just as other individuals are objects to him or in his experience; and he becomes an object to himself only by taking the attitudes of other individuals toward himself within a social environment or context of experience and behavior in which both he and they are involved.

The importance of what we term "communication" lies in the fact that it provides a form of behavior in which the organism or the individual may become an object to himself. It is that sort of communication which we have been discussing – not communication in the sense of the cluck of the hen to the chickens, or the bark of a wolf to the pack, or the lowing of a cow, but communication in the sense of significant symbols, communication which is directed not only to others but also to the individual himself. So far as that type of communication is a part of behavior it at least introduces a self. Of course, one may hear without listening; one may see things that he does not realize; do things that he is not really aware of. But it is where one does respond to that which he addresses to another and where that response of his own becomes a part of his conduct, where he not only hears himself but responds to himself, talks and replies to himself as truly as the other person replies to him, that we have behavior in which the individuals become objects to themselves.

Such a self is not, I would say, primarily the physiological organism. The physiological organism is essential to it, but we are at least able to think of a self without it. Persons who believe in immortality, or believe in ghosts, or in the possibility of the self leaving the body, assume a self which is quite distinguishable from the body. How successfully they can hold these conceptions is an open question, but we do, as a fact, separate the self and the organism. It is fair to say that the beginning of the self as an object, so far as we can see, is to be found in the experiences of people that lead to the conception of a "double." Primitive people assume that there is a double, located presumably in the diaphragm, that leaves the body temporarily in sleep and completely in death. It can be enticed out of the body of one's enemy and perhaps killed. It is represented in infancy by the imaginary playmates which children set up, and through which they come to control their experiences in their play.

The self, as that which can be an object to itself, is essentially a social structure, and it arises in social experience. After a self has arisen, it in a certain sense provides for itself its social experiences, and so we can conceive of an absolutely solitary self. But it is impossible to conceive of a self arising outside of social experience. When it has arisen we can think of a person in solitary confinement for the rest of his life, but who still has himself as a companion, and is able to think and to converse with himself as he had communicated with others. That process to which I have just referred, of responding to one's self as another responds to it, taking part in one's own conversation with others, being aware of what one is saying and using that awareness of what one is saying to determine what one is going to say thereafter – that is a process with which we are all familiar. We are continually following up our own address to other persons by an understanding of what we are saying, and using that understanding in the direction of our continued speech. We are finding out what we are going to say, what we are going to do, by saying and doing, and in the process we are continually controlling the process itself. In the conversation of gestures what we say calls out a certain response in another and that in turn changes our own action, so that we shift from what we started to do because of the reply the other makes. The conversation of gestures is the beginning of communication. The individual comes to carry on a conversation of gestures with himself. He says something, and that calls out a certain reply in himself which makes him change what he was going to say. One starts to say something, we will presume an unpleasant something, but when he starts to say it he realizes it is cruel. The effect on himself of what he is saying checks him; there is here a conversation of gestures between the individual and himself. We mean by significant speech that the action is one that affects the individual himself, and that the effect upon the individual himself is part of the intelligent carrying-out of the conversation with others. Now we, so to speak, amputate that social phase and dispense with it for the time being, so that one is talking to one's self as one would talk to another person.

This process of abstraction cannot be carried on indefinitely. One inevitably seeks an audience, has to pour himself out to somebody. In reflective intelligence one thinks to act, and to act solely so that this action remains a part of a social process. Thinking becomes preparatory to social action. The very process of thinking is, of course, simply an inner conversation that goes on, but it is a conversation of gestures which in its completion implies the expression of that which one thinks to an audience. One separates the significance of what he is saying to others from the actual speech and gets it ready before saying it. He thinks it out, and perhaps writes it in the form of a book; but it is still a part of social intercourse in which one is addressing other persons and at the same time addressing one's self, and in which one controls the address to other persons by the response made to one's own gesture. That the person should be responding to himself is necessary to the self, and it is this sort of social conduct which provides behavior within which that self appears. I know of no other form of behavior than the linguistic in which the individual is an object to himself, and, so far as I can see, the individual is not a self in the reflexive sense unless he is an object to himself. It is this fact that gives a critical importance to communication, since this is a type of behavior in which the individual does so respond to himself.

We realize in everyday conduct and experience that an individual does not mean a great deal of what he is doing and saying. We frequently say that such an individual is not himself. We come away from an interview with a realization that we have left out important things, that there are parts of the self that did not get into what was said. What determines the amount of the self that gets into communication is the social experience itself. Of course, a good deal of the self does not need to get expression. We carry on a whole series of different relationships to different people. We are one thing to one man and another thing to another. There are parts of the self which exist only for the self in relationship to itself. We divide ourselves up in all sorts of different selves with reference to our acquaintances. We discuss politics with one and religion with another. There are all sorts of different selves answering to all sorts of different social reactions. It is the social process itself that is responsible for the appearance of the self; it is not there as a self apart from this type of experience.

A multiple personality is in a certain sense normal, as I have just pointed out. There is usually an organization of the whole self with reference to the community to which we belong, and the situation in which we find ourselves. What the society is, whether we are living with people of the present, people of our own imaginations, people of the past, varies, of course, with different individuals. Normally, within the sort of community as a whole to which we belong, there is a unified self, but that may be broken up. To a person who is somewhat unstable nervously and in whom there is a line of cleavage, certain activities become impossible, and that set of activities may separate and evolve another self. Two separate "me's" and "I's," two different selves, result, and that is the condition under which there is a tendency to break up the personality. There is an account of a professor of education who disappeared, was lost to the community, and later turned up in a logging camp in the West. He freed himself of his occupation and turned to the woods where he felt, if you like, more at home. The pathological side of it was the forgetting, the leaving out of the rest of the self. This result involved getting rid of certain bodily memories which would identify the individual to himself. We often recognize the lines of cleavage that run through us. We would be glad to forget certain things, get rid of things the self is bound up with in past experiences. What we have here is a situation in which there can be different selves, and it is dependent upon the set of social reactions that is involved as to which self we are going to be. If we can forget everything involved in one set of activities, obviously we relinquish that part of the self. Take a person who is unstable, get him occupied by speech, and at the same time get his eye on something you are writing so that he is carrying on two separate lines of communication, and if you go about it in the right way you can get those two currents going so that they do not run into each other. You can get two entirely different sets of activities going on. You can bring about in that way the dissociation of a person's self. It is a process of setting up two sorts of communication which separate the behavior of the individual. For one individual it is this thing said and heard, and for the other individual there exists only that which he sees written. You must, of course, keep one experience out of the field of the other. Dissociations are apt to take place when an event leads to emotional upheavals. That which is separated goes on in its own way.

The unity and structure of the complete self reflects the unity and structure of the social process as a whole; and each of the elementary selves of which it is composed reflects the unity and structure of one of the various aspects of that process in which the individual is implicated. In other words, the various elementary selves which constitute, or are organized into, a complete self are the various aspects of the structure of that complete self answering to the various aspects of the structure of the social process as a whole; the structure of the complete self is thus a reflection of the complete social process. The organization and unification of a social group is identical with the organization and unification of any one of the selves arising within the social process in which that group is engaged, or which it is carrying on.[2]

The phenomenon of dissociation of personality is caused by a breaking up of the complete, unitary self into the component selves of which it is composed, and which respectively correspond to different aspects of the social process in which the person is involved, and within which his complete or unitary self has arisen; these aspects being the different social groups to which he belongs within that process. …

Another set of background factors in the genesis of the self is represented in the activities of play and the game.

Among primitive people, as I have said, the necessity of distinguishing the self and the organism was recognized in what we term the "double": the individual has a thing-like self that is affected by the individual as it affects other people and which is distinguished from the immediate organism in that it can leave the body and come back to it. This is the basis for the concept of the soul as a separate entity.

We find in children something that answers to this double, namely, the invisible, imaginary companions which a good many children produce in their own experience. They organize in this way the responses which they call out in other persons and call out also in themselves. Of course, this playing with an imaginary companion is only a peculiarly interesting phase of ordinary play. Play in this sense, especially the stage which precedes the organized games, is a play at something. A child plays at being a mother, at being a teacher, at being a policeman; that is, it is taking different rôles, as we say. We have something that suggests this in what we call the play of animals: a cat will play with her kittens, and dogs play with each other. Two dogs playing with each other will attack and defend, in a process which if carried through would amount to an actual fight. There is a combination of responses which checks the depth of the bite. But we do not have in such a situation the dogs taking a definite rôle in the sense that a child deliberately takes the rôle of another. This tendency on the part of the children is what we are working with in the kindergarten where the rôles which the children assume are made the basis for training. When a child does assume a rôle he has in himself the stimuli which call out that particular response or group of responses. He may, of course, run away when he is chased, as the dog does, or he may turn around and strike back just as the dog does in his play. But that is not the same as playing at something. Children get together to "play Indian." This means that the child has a certain set of stimuli which call out in itself the responses that they would call out in others, and which answer to an Indian. In the play period the child utilizes his own responses to these stimuli which he makes use of in building a self. The response which he has a tendency to make to these stimuli organizes them. He plays that he is, for instance, offering himself something, and he buys it; he gives a letter to himself and takes it away; he addresses himself as a parent, as a teacher; he arrests himself as a policeman. He has a set of stimuli which call out in himself the sort of responses they call out in others. He takes this group of responses and organizes them into a certain whole. Such is the simplest form of being another to one's self. It involves a temporal situation. The child says something in one character and responds in another character, and then his responding in another character is a stimulus to himself in the first character, and so the conversation goes on. A certain organized structure arises in him and in his other which replies to it, and these carry on the conversation of gestures between themselves.

If we contrast play with the situation in an organized game, we note the essential difference that the child who plays in a game must be ready to take the attitude of everyone else involved in that game, and that these different rôles must have a definite relationship to each other. Taking a very simple game such as hide-and-seek, everyone with the exception of the one who is hiding is a person who is hunting. A child does not require more than the person who is hunted and the one who is hunting. If a child is playing in the first sense he just goes on playing, but there is no basic organization gained. In that early stage he passes from one rôle to another just as a whim takes him. But in a game where a number of individuals are involved, then the child taking one rôle must be ready to take the rôle of everyone else. If he gets in a ball nine he must have the responses of each position involved in his own position. He must know what everyone else is going to do in order to carry out his own play. He has to take all of these rôles. They do not all have to be present in consciousness at the same time, but at some moments he has to have three or four individuals present in his own attitude, such as the one who is going to throw the ball, the one who is going to catch it, and so on. These responses must be, in some degree, present in his own make-up. In the game, then, there is a set of responses of such others so organized that the attitude of one calls out the appropriate attitudes of the other.

This organization is put in the form of the rules of the game. Children take a great interest in rules. They make rules on the spot in order to help themselves out of difficulties. Part of the enjoyment of the game is to get these rules. Now, the rules are the set of responses which a particular attitude calls out. You can demand a certain response in others if you take a certain attitude. These responses are all in yourself as well. There you get an organized set of such responses as that to which I have referred, which is something more elaborate than the rôles found in play. Here there is just a set of responses that follow on each other indefinitely. At such a stage we speak of a child as not yet having a fully developed self. The child responds in a fairly intelligent fashion to the immediate stimuli that comes to him, but they are not organized. He does not organize his life as we would like to have him do, namely, as a whole. There is just a set of responses of the type of play. The child reacts to a certain stimulus, and the reaction is in himself that is called out in others, but he is not a whole self. In his game he has to have an organization of these rôles; otherwise he cannot play the game. The game represents the passage in the life of the child from taking the rôle of others in play to the organized part that is essential to self-consciousness in the full sense of the term.

We were speaking of the social conditions under which the self arises as an object. In addition to language we found two illustrations, one in play and the other in the game, and I wish to summarize and expand my account on these point. I have spoken of these from the point of view of children. We can, of course, refer also to the attitudes of more primitive people out of which our civilization has arisen. [...]

The fundamental difference between the game and play is that in the latter the child must have the attitude of all the others involved in that game. The attitudes of the other players which the participant assumes organize into a sort of unit, and it is that organization which controls the response of the individual. The illustration used was of a person playing baseball. Each one of his own acts is determined by his assumption of the action of the others who are playing the game. What he does is controlled by his being everyone else on that team, at least in so far as those attitudes affect his own particular response. We get then an "other" which is an organization of the attitudes of those involved in the same process.

The organized community or social group which gives to the individual his unity of self may be called "the generalized other." The attitude of the generalized other is the attitude of the whole community.[3] Thus, for example, in the case of such a social group as a ball team, the team is the generalized other in so far as it enters – as an organized process or social activity – into the experience of any one of the individual members of it.

If the given human individual is to develop a self in the fullest sense, it is not sufficient for him merely to take the attitudes of other human individuals toward himself and toward one another within the human social process, and to bring that social process as a whole into his individual experience merely in these terms: he must also, in the same way that he takes the attitudes of other individuals toward himself and toward one another, take their attitudes toward the various phases or aspects of the common social activity or set of social undertakings in which, as members of an organized society or social group, they are all engaged; and he must then, by generalizing these individual attitudes of that organized society or social group itself, as a whole, act toward different social projects which at any given time it is carrying out, or toward the various larger phases of the general social process which constitutes its life and of which these projects are specific manifestations. This getting of the broad activities of any given social whole or organized society as such within the experiential field of any one of the individuals involved or included in that whole is, in other words, the essential basis and prerequisite of the fullest development of that individual's self: only in so far as he takes the attitudes of the organized social group to which he belongs toward the organized, co-operative social activity or set of such activities in which that group as such is engaged, does he develop a complete self or possess the sort of complete self he has developed. And on the other hand, the complex co-operative processes and activities and institutional functionings of organized human society are also possible only in so far as every individual involved in them or belonging to that society can take the general attitudes of all other such individuals with reference to these processes and activities and institutional functionings, and to the organized social whole of experiential relations and interactions thereby constituted – and can direct his own behavior accordingly.

It is in the form of the generalized other that the social process influences the behavior of the individuals involved in it and carrying it on, i.e., that the community exercises control over the conduct of its individual members; for it is in this form that the social process or community enters as a determining factor into the individual's thinking. In abstract thought the individual takes the attitude of the generalized other toward himself, without reference to its expression in any particular other individuals; and in concrete thought he takes that attitude in so far as it is expressed in the attitudes toward his behavior of those other individuals with whom he is involved in the given social situation or act. But only by taking the attitude of the generalized other toward himself, in one or another of these ways, can he think at all; for only thus can thinking – or the internalized conversation of gestures which constitutes thinking – occur. And only through the taking by individuals of the attitude or attitudes of the generalized other toward themselves is the existence of a universe of discourse, as that system of common or social meanings which thinking presupposes at its context, rendered possible.

The self-conscious human individual, then, takes or assumes the organized social attitudes of the given social group or community (or of some one section thereof) to which he belongs, toward the social problems of various kinds which confront that group or community at any given time, and which arise in connection with the correspondingly different social projects or organized co-operative enterprises in which that group or community as such is engaged; and as an individual participant in these social projects or co-operative enterprises, he governs his own conduct accordingly. In politics, for example, the individual identifies himself with an entire political party and takes the organized attitudes of that entire party toward the rest of the given social community and toward the problems which confront the party within the given social situation; and he consequently reacts or responds in terms of the organized attitudes of the party as a whole. He thus enters into a special set of social relations with all the other individuals who belong to that political party; and in the same way he enters into various other special sets of social relations, with various other classes of individuals respectively, the individuals of each of these classes being the other members of some one of the particular organized subgroups (determined in socially functional terms) of which he himself is a member within the entire given society or social community. In the most highly developed, organized, and complicated human social communities – those evolved by civilized man – these various socially functional classes or subgroups of individuals to which any given individual belongs (and with the other individual members of which he thus enters into a special set of social relations) are of two kinds. Some of them are concrete social classes or subgroups, such as political parties, clubs, corporations, which are all actually functional social units, in terms of which their individual members are directly related to one another. The others are abstract social classes or subgroups, such as the class of debtors and the class of creditors, in terms of which their individual members are related to one another only more or less indirectly, and which only more or less indirectly function as social units, but which afford or represent unlimited possibilities for the widening and ramifying and enriching of the social relations among all the individual members of the given society as an organized and unified whole. The given individual's membership in several of these abstract social classes or subgroups makes possible his entrance into definite social relations (however indirect) with an almost infinite number of other individuals who also belong to or are included within one or another of these abstract social classes or subgroups cutting across functional lines of demarcation which divide different human social communities from one another, and including individual members from several (in some cases from all) such communities. Of these abstract social classes or subgroups of human individuals the one which is most inclusive and extensive is, of course, the one defined by the logical universe of discourse (or system of universally significant symbols) determined by the participation and communicative interaction of individuals; for of all such classes or subgroups, it is the one which claims the largest number of individual members, and which enables the largest conceivable number of human individuals to enter into some sort of social relation, however indirect or abstract it may be, with one another – a relation arising from the universal functioning of gestures as significant symbols in the general human social process of communication.

I have pointed out, then, that there are two general stages in the full development of the self. At the first of these stages, the individual's self is constituted simply by an organization of the particular attitudes of other individuals toward himself and toward one another in the specific social acts in which he participates with them. But at the second stage in the full development of the individual's self that self is constituted not only by an organization of these particular individual attitudes, but also by an organization of the social attitudes of the generalized other or the social group as a whole to which he belongs. These social or group attitudes are brought within the individual's field of direct experience, and are included as elements in the structure or constitution of his self, in the same way that the attitudes of particular other individuals are; and the individual arrives at them, or succeeds in taking them, by means of further organizing, and then generalizing, the attitudes of particular other individuals in terms of their organized social bearings and implications. So the self reaches its full development by organizing these individual attitudes of others into the organized social or group attitudes, and by thus becoming an individual reflection of the general systematic pattern of social or group behavior in which it and the others are all involved – a pattern which enters as a whole into the individual's experience in terms of these organized group attitudes which, through the mechanism of his central nervous system, he takes toward himself, just as he takes the individual attitudes of others. ...

I have so far emphasized what I have called the structures upon which the self is constructed, the framework of the self, as it were. Of course we are not only what is common to all: each one of the selves is different from everyone else; but there has to be such a common structure as I have sketched in order that we may be members of a community at all. We cannot be ourselves unless we are also members in whom there is a community of attitudes which control the attitudes of all. We cannot have rights unless we have common attitudes. That which we have acquired as self-conscious persons makes us such members of society and gives us selves. Selves can only exist in definite relationships to other selves. No hard-and-fast line can be drawn between our own selves and the selves of others, since our own selves exist and enter as such into our experience only in so far as the selves of others exist and enter as such into our experience also. The individual possesses a self only in relation to the selves of the other members of his social group; and the structure of his self expresses or reflects the general behavior pattern of this social group to which he belongs, just as does the structure of the self of every other individual belonging to this social group. [...]

The "I" and the "Me"

We have discussed at length the social foundations of the self, and hinted that the self does not consist simply in the bare organization of social attitudes. We may now explicitly raise the question as to the nature of the "I" which is aware of the social "me." I do not mean to raise the metaphysical question of how a person can be both "I" and "me," but to ask for the significance of this distinction from the point of view of conduct itself. Where in conduct does the "I" come in as over against the "me"? If one determines what his position is in society and feels himself as having a certain function and privilege, these are all defined with reference to an "I," but the "I" is not a "me" and cannot become a "me." We may have a better self and a worse self, but that again is not the "I" as over against the "me," because they are both selves. We approve of one and disapprove of the other, but when we bring up one or the other they are there for such approval as "me's." The "I" does not get into the limelight; we talk to ourselves, but do not see ourselves. The "I" reacts to the self which arises through the taking of the attitudes of others. Though taking those attitudes we have introduced the "me" and we react to it as an "I."

The simplest way of handling the problem would be in terms of memory. I talk to myself, and I remember what I said and perhaps the emotional content that went with it. The "I" of this moment is present in the "me" of the next moment. There again I cannot turn around quick enough to catch myself. I become a "me" in so far as I remember what I said. The "I" can be given, however, this functional relationship. It is because of the "I" that we say that we are never fully aware of what we are, that we surprise ourselves by our own action. It is as we act that we are aware of ourselves. It is in memory that the "I" is constantly present in experience. We can go back directly a few moments in our experience, and then we are dependent upon memory images for the rest. So that the "I" in the memory is there as the spokesman of the self of the second, or minute, or day ago. As given, it is a "me," but it is a "me" which was the "I" at the earlier time. If you ask, then, where directly in your own experience the "I" comes in, the answer is that it comes in as a historical figure. It is what you were a second ago that is the "I" of the "me." It is another "me" that has to take that rôle. You cannot get the immediate response of the "I" in the process. The "I" is in a certain sense that with which we do identify ourselves. The getting of it into experience constitutes one of the problems of most of our conscious experience; it is not directly given in experience.

The "I" is the response of the organism to the attitudes of the others, the "me" is the organized set of attitudes of others which one himself assumes. The attitudes of the others constitute the organized "me," and then one reacts toward that as an "I." I now wish to examine these concepts in greater detail.

There is neither "I" nor "me" in the conversation of gestures; the whole act is not yet carried out, but the preparation takes place in this field of gesture. Now, in so far as the individual arouses in himself the attitudes of the others, there arises an organized group of responses. And it is due to the individual's ability to take the attitudes of these others in so far as they can be organized that he gets self-consciousness. The taking of all of those organized sets of attitudes gives him his "me"; that is the self he is aware of. He can throw the ball to some other member because of the demand made upon him from other members of the team. That is the self that immediately exists for him in his consciousness. He has their attitudes, knows what they want and what the consequence of any act of his will be, and he has assumed responsibility for the situation. Now, it is the presence of those organized sets of attitudes that constitutes that "me" to which he as an "I" is responding. But what that response will be he does not know and nobody else knows. Perhaps he will make a brilliant play or an error. The response to that situation as it appears in his immediate experience is uncertain, and it is that which constitutes the "I."

The "I" is his action over against that social situation within his own conduct, and it gets into his experience only after he has carried out the act. Then he is aware of it. He had to do such a thing and he did it. He fulfills his duty and he may look with pride at the throw which he made. The "me" arises to do that duty – that is the way in which it arises in his experience. He had in him all the attitudes of others, calling for a certain response; that was the "me" of that situation, and his response is the "I."

I want to call attention particularly to the fact that this response of the "I" is something that is more or less uncertain. The attitudes of others which one assumes as affecting his own conduct constitute the "me," and that is something that is there, but the response to it is as yet not given. When one sits down to think anything out, he has certain data that are there. Suppose that it is a social situation which he has to straighten out. He sees himself from the point of view of one individual or another in the group. These individuals, related all together, give him a certain self. Well, what is he going to do? He does not know and nobody else knows. He can get the situation into his experience because he can assume the attitudes of the various individuals involved in it. He knows how they feel about it by the assumption of their attitudes. He says, in effect, "I have done certain things that seem to commit me to a certain course of conduct." Perhaps if he does so act it will place him in a false position with another group. The "I" as a response to this situation, in contrast to the "me" which is involved in the attitudes which he takes, is uncertain. And when the response takes place, then it appears in the field of experience largely as a memory image. [...]

The "I" then, in this relation of the "I" and the "me," is something that is, so to speak, responding to a social situation which is within the experience of the individual. It is the answer which the individual makes to the attitude which others take toward him when he assumes an attitude toward them. Now, the attitudes he is taking toward them are present in his own experience, but his response to them will contain a novel element. The "I" gives the sense of freedom, of initiative. The situation is there for us to act in a self-conscious fashion. We are aware of ourselves, and of what the situation is, but exactly how we will act never gets into experience until after the action takes place.

Such is the basis for the fact that the "I" does not appear in the same sense in experience as does the "me." The "me" represents a definite organization of the community there in our own attitudes, and calling for a response, but the response that takes place is something that just happens. There is no certainty in regard to it. There is a moral necessity but no mechanical necessity for the act. When it does take place then we find what has been done. The above account gives us, I think, the relative position of the "I" and "me" in the situation, and the grounds for the separation of the two in behavior. The two are separated in the process but they belong together in the sense of being parts of a whole. They are separated and yet they belong together. The separation of the "I" and the "me" is not fictitious. They are not identical, for, as I have said, the "I" is something that is never entirely calculable. The "me" does call for a certain sort of an "I" in so far as we meet the obligations that are given in conduct itself, but the "I" is always something different from what the situation itself calls for. So there is always that distinction, if you like, between the "I" and the "me." The "I" both calls out the "me" and responds to it. Taken together they constitute a personality as it appears in social experience. The self is essentially a social process going on with these two distinguishable phases. If it did not have these two phases there could not be conscious responsibility, and there would be nothing novel in experience.

NOTES

1. Man's behavior is such in his social group that he is able to become an object to himself, a fact which constitutes him a more advanced product of evolutionary development than are the lower animals. Fundamentally it is this social fact – and not his alleged possession of a soul or mind with which he, as an individual, has been mysteriously and super-naturally endowed, and with which the lower animals have not been endowed – that differentiates him from them.
2. The unity of the mind is not identical with the unity of the self. The unity of the self is constituted by the unity of the entire relational pattern of social behavior and experience in which the individual is implicated, and which is reflected in the structure of the self; but many of the aspects or features of this entire pattern do not enter into consciousness, so that the unity of the mind is in a sense an abstraction from the more inclusive unity of the self.
3. It is possible for inanimate objects, no less than for other human organisms, to form parts of the generalized and organized – the completely socialized – other for any given human individual, in so far as he responds to such objects socially or in a social fashion (by means of the mechanism of thought, the internalized conversation of gestures).

Chapter 26

The Stranger [1908]

Georg Simmel

If wandering, considered as a state of detachment from every given point in space, is the conceptual opposite of attachment to any point, then the sociological form of "the stranger" presents the synthesis, as it were, of both of these properties. (This is another indication that spatial relations not only are determining conditions of relationships among men, but are also symbolic of those relationships.) The stranger will thus not be considered here in the usual sense of the term, as the wanderer who comes today and goes tomorrow, but rather as the man who comes today and stays tomorrow – the potential wanderer, so to speak, who, although he has gone no further, has not quite got over the freedom of coming and going. He is fixed within a certain spatial circle – or within a group whose boundaries are analogous to spatial boundaries – but his position within it is fundamentally affected by the fact that he does not belong in it initially and that he brings qualities into it that are not, and cannot be, indigenous to it.

In the case of the stranger, the union of closeness and remoteness involved in every human relationship is patterned in a way that may be succinctly formulated as follows: the distance within this relation indicates that one who is close by is remote, but his strangeness indicates that one who is remote is near. The state of being a stranger is of course a completely positive relation; it is a specific form of interaction. The inhabitants of Sirius are not exactly strangers to us, at least not in the sociological sense of the word as we are considering it. In that sense they do not exist for us at all; they are beyond being far and near. The stranger is an element of the group itself, not unlike the poor and sundry "inner enemies" – an element whose membership within the group involves both being outside it and confronting it.

The following statements about the stranger are intended to suggest how factors of repulsion and distance work to create a form of being together, a form of union based on interaction.

In the whole history of economic activity the stranger makes his appearance everywhere as a trader, and the trader makes his as a stranger. As long as production for one's own needs is the general rule, or products are exchanged within a relatively small circle, there is no need for a middleman within the group. A trader is required only for goods produced outside the group. Unless there are people who wander out into foreign lands to buy these necessities, in which case they are themselves "strange" merchants in this other region, the trader *must* be a stranger; there is no opportunity for anyone else to make a living at it.

This position of the stranger stands out more sharply if, instead of leaving the place of his activity, he settles down there. In innumerable cases even this is possible only if he can live by trade as a middleman. Any closed economic group where land and handicrafts have been apportioned in a way that satisfies local demands will still support a livelihood for the trader. For trade alone makes possible unlimited combinations, and through it intelligence is constantly extended and applied in new areas, something that is much harder for the primary producer with his more limited mobility and his dependence on a circle of customers that can be expanded only very slowly. Trade can always absorb more men than can primary production. It is therefore the most suitable activity for the stranger, who intrudes as a supernumerary, so to speak, into a group in which all the economic positions are already occupied. The classic example of this is the history of European Jews. The stranger is by his very nature no owner of land – land not only in the physical sense but also metaphorically as a vital substance which is fixed, if not in space, then at least in an ideal position within the social environment.

Although in the sphere of intimate personal relations the stranger may be attractive and meaningful in many ways, so long as he is regarded as a stranger he is no "landowner" in the eyes of the other. Restriction to intermediary trade and often (as though sublimated from it) to pure finance gives the stranger the specific character of *mobility*. The appearance of this mobility within a bounded group occasions that synthesis of nearness and remoteness which constitutes the formal position of the stranger. The purely mobile person comes incidentally into contact with *every* single element but is not bound up organically, through established ties of kinship, locality, or occupation, with any single one.

Another expression of this constellation is to be found in the objectivity of the stranger. Because he is not bound by roots to the particular constituents and partisan dispositions of the group, he confronts all of these with a distinctly "objective" attitude, an attitude that does not signify mere detachment and nonparticipation, but is a distinct structure composed of remoteness and nearness, indifference and involvement. I refer to my analysis of the dominating positions gained by aliens, in the discussion of superordination and subordination, typified by the practice in certain Italian cities of recruiting their judges from outside, because no native was free from entanglement in family interests and factionalism.

Connected with the characteristic of objectivity is a phenomenon that is found chiefly, though not exclusively, in the stranger who moves on. This is that he often receives the most surprising revelations and confidences, at times reminiscent of a confessional, about matters which are kept carefully hidden from everybody with whom one is close. Objectivity is by no means nonparticipation, a condition that is altogether outside the distinction between subjective and objective orientations. It is rather a positive and definite kind of participation, in the same way that the objectivity of a theoretical observation clearly does not mean that the mind is a passive tabula rasa on which things inscribe their qualities, but rather signifies the full activity of a mind working according to its own laws, under conditions that exclude accidental distortions and emphases whose individual and subjective differences would produce quite different pictures of the same object.

Objectivity can also be defined as freedom. The objective man is not bound by ties which could prejudice his perception, his understanding, and his assessment of data. This freedom, which permits the stranger to experience and treat even his close relationships as though from a bird's-eye view, contains many dangerous possibilities. From earliest times, in uprisings of all sorts the attacked party has claimed that there has been incitement from the outside, by foreign emissaries and agitators. Insofar as this has happened, it represents an exaggeration of the specific role of the stranger: he is the freer man, practically and theoretically; he examines conditions with less prejudice; he assesses them against standards that are more general and more objective; and his actions are not confined to custom, piety, or precedent.[1]

Finally, the proportion of nearness and remoteness which gives the stranger the character of objectivity also finds practical expression in the more *abstract* nature of the relation to him. That is, with the stranger one has only certain *more general* qualities in common, whereas the relation with organically connected persons is based on the similarity of just those specific traits which differentiate them from the merely universal. In fact, all personal relations whatsoever can be analyzed in terms of this scheme. They are not determined only by the existence of certain common characteristics which the individuals share in addition to their individual differences, which either influence the relationship or remain outside of it. Rather, the kind of effect which that commonality has on the relation essentially depends on whether it exists only among the participants themselves, and thus, although general within the relation, is specific and incomparable with respect to all those on the outside, or whether the participants feel that what they have in common is so only because it is common to a group, a type, or mankind in general. In the latter case, the effect of the common features becomes attenuated in proportion to the size of the group bearing the same characteristics. The commonality provides a basis for unifying the members, to be sure; but it does not specifically direct *these* particular persons to one another. A similarity so widely shared could just as easily unite each person with every possible other. This, too, is evidently a way in which a relationship includes both nearness and remoteness simultaneously. To the extent to which the similarities assume a universal nature, the warmth of the connection based on them will acquire an element of coolness, a sense of the contingent nature of precisely *this* relation – the connecting forces have lost their specific, centripetal character.

In relation to the stranger, it seems to me, this constellation assumes an extraordinary preponderance in principle over the individual elements peculiar to the relation in question. The stranger is close to us insofar as we feel between him and ourselves similarities of nationality or social position, of occupation or of general human nature. He is far from us insofar as these similarities extend beyond him and us, and connect us only because they connect a great many people.

A trace of strangeness in this sense easily enters even the most intimate relationships. In the stage of first passion, erotic relations strongly reject any thought of generalization. A love such as this has never existed before; there is nothing to compare either with the person one loves or with our feelings for that person. An estrangement is wont to set in (whether as cause or effect is hard to decide) at the moment when this feeling of uniqueness disappears from the relationship. A skepticism regarding the intrinsic value of the relationship and its value for us adheres to the very thought that in this relation, after all, one is only fulfilling a general human destiny, that one has had an experience that has occurred a thousand times before, and that, if one had not accidentally met this precise person, someone else would have acquired the same meaning for us.

Something of this feeling is probably not absent in any relation, be it ever so close, because that which is common to two is perhaps never common *only* to them but belongs to a general conception which includes much else besides, many *possibilities* of similarities. No matter how few of these possibilities are realized and how often we may forget about them, here and there, nevertheless, they crowd in like shadows between men, like a mist eluding every designation, which must congeal into solid corporeality for it to be called jealousy. Perhaps this is in many cases a more general, at least more insurmountable, strangeness than that due to differences and obscurities. It is strangeness caused by the fact that similarity, harmony, and closeness are accompanied by the feeling that they are actually not the exclusive property of this particular relation, but stem from a more general one – a relation that potentially includes us and an indeterminate number of others, and therefore prevents that relation which alone was experienced from having an inner and exclusive necessity.

On the other hand, there is a sort of "strangeness" in which this very connection on the basis of a general quality embracing the parties is precluded. The relation of the Greeks to the barbarians is a typical example; so are all the cases in which the general characteristics one takes as peculiarly and merely human are disallowed to the other. But here the expression "the stranger" no longer has any positive meaning. The relation with him is a non-relation; he is not what we have been discussing here: the stranger as a member of the group itself.

As such, the stranger is near and far *at the same time*, as in any relationship based on merely universal human similarities. Between these two factors of nearness and distance, however, a peculiar tension arises, since the consciousness of having only the absolutely general in common has exactly the effect of putting a special emphasis on that which is not common. For a stranger to the country, the city, the race, and so on, what is stressed is again nothing individual, but alien origin, a quality which he has, or could have, in common with many other strangers. For this reason strangers are not really perceived as individuals, but as strangers of a certain type. Their remoteness is no less general than their nearness.

This form appears, for example, in so special a case as the tax levied on Jews in Frankfurt and elsewhere during the Middle Ages. Whereas the tax paid by Christian citizens varied according to their wealth at any given time, for every single Jew the tax was fixed once and for all. This amount was fixed because the Jew had his social position as a *Jew*, not as the bearer of certain objective contents. With respect to taxes every other citizen was regarded as possessor of a certain amount of wealth, and his tax could follow the fluctuations of his fortune. But the Jew as taxpayer was first of all a Jew, and thus his fiscal position contained an invariable element. This appears most forcefully, of course, once the differing circumstances of individual Jews are no longer considered, limited though this consideration is by fixed assessments, and all strangers pay exactly the same head tax.

Despite his being inorganically appended to it, the stranger is still an organic member of the group. Its unified life includes the specific conditioning of this element. Only we do not know how to designate the characteristic unity of this position otherwise than by saying that it is put together of certain amounts of nearness and of remoteness. Although both these qualities are found to some extent in all relationships, a special proportion and reciprocal tension between them produce the specific form of the relation to the "stranger."

NOTE

1 Where the attacked parties make such an assertion falsely, they do so because those in higher positions tend to exculpate inferiors who previously have been in a close, solidary relationship with them. By introducing the fiction that the rebels were not really guilty, but only instigated, so they did not actually start the rebellion, they exonerate themselves by denying that there were any real grounds for the uprising.

Chapter 27

Group Expansion and the Development of Individuality [1908]

Georg Simmel

Group Expansion and the Transformation of Social Bonds

Individuation of personality, on the one hand, and the influences, interests, and relationships that attach the personality to its social circle, on the other hand, show a pattern of interdependent development that appears in the most diverse historical and institutional setting as a typical form. *Individuality in being and action generally increases to the degree that the social circle encompassing the individual expands.*

Of the diverse modalities in which group expansion occurs and gives rise to the correlation just underscored, I will first mention the one that occurs when circles that are isolated from one another become approximately alike. Imagine that there are two social groups, M and N, that are sharply distinguished from one another both in characteristic attributes and in opposing systems of shared belief; and imagine further that each of these groups is composed of homogeneous and tightly cohesive elements. This being so, quantitative expansion will produce an increase in social differentiation. What were once minimal differences in inner predilection, external resources, and actualizations of these will be accentuated by the necessity of competing for a livelihood with more and more people using more and more specialized means. Competition will develop the speciality of the individual in direct ratio to the number of participants.

Simmel, Georg, "Group Expansion and the Development of Individuality," pp. 252–266, 268–274, 290–292 from Georg Simmel, *Georg Simmel: On Individuality and Social Forms*, ed. Donald N. Levine. Chicago: University of Chicago Press, 1971. Copyright © 1971 by University of Chicago Press. Reprinted by permission of The University of Chicago Press.

Classical Sociological Theory, Third Edition. Edited by Craig Calhoun, Joseph Gerteis, James Moody, Steven Pfaff, and Indermohan Virk. Editorial material and organization © 2012 John Wiley & Sons, Ltd. Published 2012 by John Wiley & Sons, Ltd.

Different as its points of origin in M and N may have been, this process will inevitably produce a gradually increasing likeness between the two groups. After all, the number of fundamental human formations upon which a group can build is relatively limited, and it can only slowly be increased. The more of these formations that are present in a group – that is, the greater the dissimilarity of constituent elements in M and N respectively – the greater is the likelihood that an ever increasing number of structures will develop in one group that have equivalents in the other. Deviation in all directions from what had thus far been the prevailing norm in each group complex must necessarily result in a likening – at first a qualitative or ideal equivalence – between parts of the two complexes.

This likening will come about if for no other reason than because even within very diverse groups, the forms of social differentiation are identical or approximately the same. What I have in mind here are such forms as the relational pattern of simple competition, the alliance of many who are weak against one who is strong, the pleonexy of lone individuals, the progression in which relationships among individuals, once initiated, become stabilized, the attraction or repulsion that arises between individuals by virtue of their qualitative differentiation, and so on.

This process, quite apart from all bonds based on shared substantive interests, will often lead to actual relations between the elements of any two – or of many – groups that have been made alike in this way. One observes this, for example, in the international sympathy that aristocrats hold for one another. To an astonishing degree, these feelings of solidarity are independent of the specific character of the individuals concerned, a matter that is otherwise decisive in determining personal attraction and repulsion. In the same way, by specialization within groups that were originally independent of one another, solidarities also develop at the other end of the social scale, as in the internationalism of social democrats and in the sentiments underlying the earlier journeymen's unions.

After the process of social differentiation has led to a separation between high and low, the mere formal fact of occupying a particular social position creates among the similarly characterized members of the most diverse groups a sense of solidarity and, frequently, actual relationships. Accompanying such a differentiation of social groups, there arise a need and an inclination to reach out beyond the original spatial, economic, and mental boundaries of the group and, in connection with the increase in individualization and concomitant mutual repulsion of group elements, to supplement the original centripetal forces of the lone group with a centrifugal tendency that forms bridges with other groups.

For example, the guilds were once ruled by the spirit of strict equality. On the one hand, the individual's production was limited to the level of quality and quantity that all other guild members attained; on the other hand, the guild's norms of sale and exchange sought to protect the individual from being outdone by other members. In the long run, it was impossible to maintain this condition of undifferentiation. The master who became rich under whatever circumstances was not inclined to submit further to regulations stipulating that he might sell only his own products, might maintain no more than one salesplace, might have no more than a very limited number of apprentices, and so forth.

Once the affluent masters had won the right – partly after intense struggle – to ignore these restrictions, a certain duality began to appear. The once homogeneous mass of guild members became differentiated with increasing decisiveness into rich and poor, capitalists and laborers. Once the principle of equality had been broken through to the extent that one member could have another labor for him and that he could select his sales market on the basis of his own personal capacity and energy, his knowledge of the market, and his assessment of its prospects, it was inevitable that just these personal attributes, once given the opportunity to unfold, would continue to develop, leading to an ever increasing specialization and individualization within the fellowship of the guild and, finally, to the dissolution of that fellowship. On the other hand, however, structural change made possible an extension far beyond the confines of previous sales regions. Formerly, producer and merchant had been united in *one* person; once they had been differentiated from one another, the merchant won an incomparable freedom of movement, and previously unattainable commercial relations were established.

Individual freedom and the expansion of commercial enterprise are interdependent. Thus, in the case of the coexistence of guild restrictions and large, factory-style workshops around the beginning of the nineteenth century in Germany, it always proved necessary to let the factories have freedoms of production and trade that could or would have been collectivistically restricted in the circles of smaller and more modest enterprises. In this manner, the development away from narrow, homogeneous guild circles prepared their dissolution along two lines: one led to individualizing differentiation, the other to expansion involving ties across great distances. For this reason, the differentiation of English guild members into merchants and actual workers was exhibited most strikingly by those, such as tanners and textile manufacturers, who produced articles of foreign demand.

A fissioning is inherent in this correlation with group expansion that involves not only the content of labor but also its sociological dimension. Even given a certain technical division of labor, as long as the small, primitive group is self-sufficient, a pervasive equality exists in that each member of the group works for the group itself; every achievement is sociologically centripetal. However, as soon as the boundaries of the group are ruptured and it enters into trade in special products with another group, internal differentiation develops between those who produce for export and those who produce for domestic consumption – two wholly opposed inner modes of being.

The history of the emancipation of the serfs, as for example in Prussia, demonstrates a process that is similar in this regard. As he existed in Prussia until about 1810, the enserfed peasant found himself in a peculiar intermediate position regarding both his lord and his land. The land belonged to the lord, to be sure, but not in such a way that the peasant himself could have no right at all to it. Likewise, the peasant was of course bound to work the lord's fields for him, but close by he also worked the land that had been allotted to him for his own benefit. With the abolition of serfdom, a certain part of the land that the peasant had formerly owned in a limited sense was converted into true, free property. The lord was left to seek wage laborers, whom he recruited for the most part from among the owners of smaller parcels that he had purchased. Thus, whereas the peasant had had within himself the partial attributes of owner and of laborer for another's benefit, a sharp differentiation of these attributes followed the abolition of serfdom: one part became pure owner, the other part pure laborer.

It is obvious how free movement of the person and his involvement in spatially more distant relations emerged from this situation. Not only the eradication of the external bond to the soil was involved, but also the very condition of the laborer as one who receives work first in one place, then in another. On the other hand, alienable property was involved, since it made possible sale and hence commercial relations, resettlement, and so on.

So it is that the observation made at the beginning of this section has its justification: differentiation and individualization loosen the bond of the individual with those who are most near in order to weave in its place a new one – both real and ideal – with those who are more distant. […]

An Englishman who had lived for many years in India once told me that it was impossible for a European to get at all close to the natives where castes existed; but that where caste divisions did not prevail this was very easy. The insularity of the caste – maintained by an internal uniformity no less strict than its exclusion of outsiders – seems to inhibit the development of what one has to call a more universal humanity, which is what makes relationships between racial aliens possible.

Consistent with the above, the broad uneducated masses of one civilized people are more homogeneous internally, and they are separated from the masses of a second people by more distinct characteristics, than is the case either within or between the educated strata of these populations. This same pattern of synthesis and antithesis repeats itself intraculturally. The older German corporate system set out to unite guild *members* tightly in order to keep guild *memberships* strictly separated. The modern voluntary association, on the other hand, restricts its members and imposes uniformity upon them only so far as the strictly circumscribed organizational goal requires. In all other matters, it allows members complete freedom and tolerates every individuality and heterogeneity of their full personalities. But for all that, the modern association gravitates toward an all-embracing union of organizations by virtue of interpenetrating division of labor, leveling that results from equal justice and the cash economy, and solidarity of interests in the national economy.

These examples hint at a relation that will be found everywhere in the course of this inquiry. The nonindividuation of elements in the narrower circle and their differentiation in the wider one are phenomena that are found, synchronically, among coexistent groups and group elements, just as they appear, diachronically, in the sequence of stages through which a single group develops.

The Relation between Personal and Collective Individuality

This basic idea can be generalized to the proposition that in each person, other things being equal, there is, as it were, an unalterable ratio between individual and social factors that changes only its form. The narrower the circle to which we commit ourselves, the less freedom of individuality we possess; however, this narrower circle is itself something individual, and it cuts itself off sharply from all other circles precisely because it is small. Correspondingly, if the circle in which we are active and in which our interests hold sway enlarges, there is more room in it for the development of our individuality; but *as parts of this whole*, we have less uniqueness: the larger whole is less individual as a social group. Thus, the leveling of individual differences corresponds not only to the relative smallness and narrowness of the collectivity, but also – or above all – to its own individualistic coloring.

Expressed in a very terse schema, the elements of a distinctive social circle are undifferentiated, and the elements of a circle that is not distinctive are differentiated. Of course this is not a sociological "natural law," but rather what might be called a phenomenological formula that seeks to conceptualize the regular outcome of regularly coexisting sequences of events. It designates no cause of phenomena; instead, it designates a single phenomenon whose underlying, general structure is represented in each individual case as the effect of very diverse cause, but causes whose combined effect is always to release identical formative energies.

Illustrations of the Formula in Religious and Political Settings

The first aspect of this relationship – lack of differentiation among the members of a differentiated group – is exhibited by the social order of the Quakers, in a form that is based on the deepest motives of its members. As a whole, as a religious principle of the most extreme individualism and subjectivism, Quakerism binds members of the congregation to a style of life and a mode of being that are highly uniform and democratic, seeking to exclude, as far as possible, all individual differences. And in turn, Quakerism lacks all understanding for the higher political union and its goals so that the individuality of the smaller group not only precludes the individuality of the person, but also his commitment to the large group. The specific manifestation of this is as follows: in the affairs of the congregation, in the assemblies of worship, each person may act as preacher and may say whatever he likes whenever he likes. On the other hand, the congregation watches over personal affairs such as marriage, and these cannot occur without the permission of a committee that is appointed to investigate each case. Thus, the Quakers are individual only in collective matters, and in individual matters, they are socially regulated.

Both aspects of the formula are exemplified in the differences between the political structures in the Northern and Southern states in the United States, most clearly so during the period before the Civil War. The New England states in North America had a pronounced local orientation from the very beginning. They developed townships in which the individual was tightly bound by his obligations to the whole, and although this whole was relatively small, it was also self-sufficient. The Southern states, by contrast, were populated to a greater extent by lone adventurers who were not particularly predisposed to local self-government. The South very early developed extensive counties as units of administration. Indeed, for the Southerner, the state as a whole is the site of true political significance, whereas in New England, the state is more a combination of towns. The more abstract, less colorful general political structure corresponds to the more independent – to the point of anarchistic inclinations – Southern personalities that were included in it, whereas the more strictly regulated Northern personalities were inclined toward narrower municipal structures that each, as wholes, possessed strongly individual coloring and autonomous characters.

The Basic Relation as a Dualistic Drive

With all the above qualifications in mind, one could speak of a particular quantum of the tendency toward individualization and of the tendency toward nondifferentiation. This quantum is determined by personal, historical, and social circumstances; and it remains constant, whether it applies to purely psychological configurations or to the social community to which the personality belongs.

We lead, as it were, a doubled, or if one will, a halved existence. We live as an individual within a social circle, with tangible separation from its other members, but also as a member of this circle, with separation from everything that does not belong to it. If now there is a need within us both for individuation and for its opposite, then this need can be realized on either side of our existence. The differentiation drive receives satisfaction from the contrast of one's particular personality with one's fellow members, but this plus corresponds to a minus in the satisfaction that the same person, as a purely social being, derives from oneness with his fellows. That is to say: intensified individualization within the group is accompanied by decreased individualization of the group itself, and vice versa, whenever a certain portion of the drive is satiated.

A Frenchman has made the following observation about the mania for clubs in Germany: "It is this that accustoms the German, on the one hand, not to count solely on the state; on the other hand, not to count solely on himself. It keeps him from locking himself up in his particular interests, and from relying on the state in all matters of general interest." Thus, in this negative mode of expression it is argued that a tendency to the most individual and one to the most general are present, but that they cannot both be satisfied in radically separated special structures; rather, the club is said to constitute an intermediate structure that satiates the dualistic drive quantum in a certain fusion.

The Differentiation Drive as a Heuristic Principle

If one uses this notion as a heuristic principle (i.e., not as designating the actual causality of phenomena, but merely as maintaining that phenomena occur *as if* they were governed by such a dual drive whose manifestations on the two sides of our existence balance one another), then what we have here is a most universal norm that is particularly salient when differences in group size are involved, but one that also applies to other arrangements. For example, in certain circles, and perhaps even in certain peoples, where extravagance, nervous enthusiasm, and moody impulsiveness predominate, we notice nonetheless a decidedly slavish preoccupation with fashion. One person perpetrates some madness, and it is aped by all the others as though they were automatons. In contrast, there are other circles whose life style is of a more sober and soldierly cut, hardly as colorful as the former, but whose members have a far stronger individuality drive, and distinguish themselves much more sharply and concisely within their uniform and simple life style than do those others in their bright and transitory way. So in one case, the totality has a very individual character, but its parts are very much alike; in the other, the totality is less colorful and less modeled on an extreme, but its parts are strikingly differentiated from one another.

Fashion, in and of itself, as a form of social life, is a preeminent case of this correlation. The adornment and accentuation that it lends to the personality is accorded to it only as the member of a class that is collectively distinguishing itself from other classes by adopting the new fashion. (As soon as a fashion has diffused into the other classes, it is abandoned and replaced with another.) The adoption of a fashion represents an internal leveling of the class and its self-exaltation above all other classes.

For the moment, however, our principal concern is with the correlation that involves the *extent* of social circles, the one that generally relates the freedom of the group to the restriction of the individual. A good example of this is the coexistence of communal restrictions and political freedom as found in the Russian governmental system during the preczarist period. Especially in the period of the Mongol wars, Russia had a large number of territorial units, principalities, cities, and village communes that were not held together by any kind of unifying political bond; and thus on the whole they enjoyed great political freedom. For all that, however, the restriction of the individual in commune society was the narrowest imaginable, so much so that there was absolutely no private ownership of land, which only the commune possessed. This narrow confinement in the circle of the commune, which deprived the individual of personal property and often of freedom of movement as well, is the counterpart of the lack of all binding relations with a wider political circle.

Bismarck once said that there was a much more narrow-minded small-town provincialism in a French city of 200,000 than in a German city of 10,000, and he explained this by the fact that Germany was composed of a large number of smaller states. Apparently the very large state allows the local community to have a certain mental self-sufficiency and insularity; and if even a relatively small community views itself as a whole, it will exhibit that cherishing of minutiae which constitutes smalltown provincialism. In a smaller state, the community can view itself more as a part of the whole; it is not so much thrown back upon itself. Because the community does not have so much individuality, it can dispense with that internal, coercive leveling of individuals which, because of our psychological sensitivity to differences, must produce a heightened awareness of the smallest and most petty events and interests.

In a narrow circle, one can preserve one's individuality, as a rule, in only two ways. Either one leads the circle (it is for this reason that strong personalities sometimes like to be "number one in the village"), or one exists in it only externally, being independent of it in all essential matters. The latter alternative is possible only through great stability of character or through eccentricity – both traits that are conspicuous most often in small towns.

Stages of Social Commitment

We are surrounded by concentric circles of special interests. The more narrowly they enclose us, the smaller they must be. However, a person is never merely a collective being, just as he is never merely an individual being. For that reason we are naturally speaking here only in terms of more or less, of single aspects and determinants of human existence in which we can see the development away from an excess of one and into an excess of the other.

This development can go through stages in which memberships in both the small and the larger social circle coincide in characteristic sequences. Thus, although commitment to a narrower circle is generally less conducive to the strength of individuality as such than it is in the most general realm possible, it is still psychologically significant that in a very large cultural community, belonging to a family promotes individuation. The lone individual cannot save himself from the totality: only by surrendering a part of his absolute ego to a few others, joining himself in with them, can he preserve his sense of individuality and still avoid excessive isolation, bitterness, and idiosyncrasy. And by extending his personality and his interests around those of a set of other persons, the individual opposes himself in the broader mass, as it were, to the remaining whole. To be sure, individuality in the sense of eccentricity and every kind of abnormality is given broader scope by life without a family in a wider social circle; but for the differentiation that also benefits the greatest whole, for the sort that derives from strength, not from succumbing to one-sided drives – for this, belonging to a narrower circle within the widest is often useful, frequently, to be sure, only as preparation or transition.

The family's significance is at first political and real; then with the growth of culture, it is more and more psychological and ideal. The family as a collective individual offers its members a preliminary differentiation that at least prepares them for differentiation in the sense of absolute individuality; on the other hand, the family offers members a shelter behind which that absolute individuality can develop until it has the strength to stand up against the greatest universality. Belonging to a family in a more advanced culture, where the rights of individuality and of the widest circle developed simultaneously, represents a mixture of the characteristic significance of the narrow and of the expanded circle.

The same observation has been made with respect to the animal kingdom. The tendencies to the creation of families and to the creation of large groups are inversely related. Monogamous and even polygamous relations have something so exclusive about them, and concern for the progeny demands so much from the parents, that a more extensive socialization suffers among such animals. Hence, organized groups are relatively rare among birds, whereas among wild dogs, to name an example in which complete sexual promiscuity and mutual indifference after the act are the rule, the animals live mostly in tightly cohesive packs.

Among the mammals that have both familial and social drives, we invariably notice that during those periods in which the former predominate, that is, during the period of pairing off and mating, the latter decline significantly. The union of parents and offspring is also tighter if the number of young is smaller. I will cite only one distinctive example: within the class of fishes, those whose offspring are left entirely on their own lay countless millions of eggs, whereas among the brooding and nesting fish, where the beginnings of a familial cohesion are found, few eggs are produced.

It is in this sense that it has been argued that social relations among the animals originated not in conjugal or filial ties, but rather in sibling ties alone, since the latter allow much greater freedom to the individual than do the former; hence, they make the individual more inclined to attach itself closely to the larger circle, which certainly first proffers itself in the individual's siblings. Being confined in an animal family has thus been viewed as the greatest hindrance to becoming involved in a larger animal society.

The Sociological Duality of the Family

The family has a peculiar sociological double role. On the one hand, it is an extension of one's own personality; it is a unit through which one feels one's own blood coursing, one which arises in being closed to all other social units and in enclosing us as a part of itself. On the other hand, the family also constitutes a complex within which the individual distinguishes himself from all others and in which, in opposition to other members, he develops a selfhood and an antithesis. This double role unavoidably results in the sociological ambiguity of the family: it appears sometimes as a unitary structure that acts as an individual, thereby assuming a characteristic position in larger and in the largest circles; and sometimes it appears as an intermediate circle that intervenes between the individual and the larger circle that encloses both family and individual.

The developmental history of the family, at least as it still seems to be recognizable from a series of points, recapitulates this schema. The family appears first as the embracing circle that entirely encloses the life horizons of the individual, while it is itself largely independent and exclusive. Then it contracts into a narrower structure and thereby becomes adapted to playing the role of an individual in a social circle that has expanded considerably beyond the boundaries of the previous one. After the matriarchal family had been displaced by the rise of masculine force, at first it was much less the fact of procreation by the father that established a family as *one* than it was the domination that he exercised over a particular number of people. Under his unitary authority, he held together not only his offspring, but also his followers, those whom he had bought, those whom he had married and their entire families, and so on. From this primal patriarchal family, the more recent family of mere blood relationship differentiated itself, a family in which parents and their children constitute an autonomous household. This one was naturally far smaller and more individual in character than the embracing patriarchal family had been. That older group had been self-sufficient in all matters, in gaining a livelihood as in carrying out warlike activity; but once it had individualized itself into small families, it became possible and necessary for these to be amalgamated into a newly expanded group, the superfamilial community of the state. The Platonic Ideal State merely extended this line of development by dissolving the family altogether, setting in place of this intermediate structure only individuals, on the one hand, and the state, on the other.

Methodological Implications

Incidentally, there is a typical epistemological difficulty in sociology that finds its clearest example in the double role of the family: when instead of having simply a larger and a smaller group standing opposed to one another so that the position of the individual in them can readily be compared, one has several continuously expanding, superimposed circles, this relation can seem to shift, since a circle can be the narrower one in relation to a second, but it can be the wider one in relation to a third. Short of the largest circle around us that is still effective, all circles included therein have a double meaning: on the one hand, they function as entities with an individual character, often directly as sociological individualities; while on the other hand, depending on their makeup, they function as higher-order complexes that may also include complexes of lower order in addition to their individual members.

It is always precisely the *intermediate* structure that exhibits the pattern in question – internal cohesion, external repulsion – when contrasted with a more general higher structure and a more individual lower structure. The latter is a *relative individual* in relation to the former, regardless of whether in relation to still others it is a collective structure. Thus, wherever one seeks, as we do here, the normal correlation between three levels that are distinguished by their magnitudes – between the primarily individual element, and the narrower and the wider circle – there one will find that under different circumstances one and the same complex can play all three roles, depending on the relationships into which it enters. This hardly diminishes the theoretical value of the statement of this correlation; on the contrary, it proves that the correlation has a formal character that is open to every determinate content.

The Individuation of Collectivities

There are naturally more than enough sociological constellations in which the value of individuality and the need for it focus exclusively on the individual person, where in comparison to him, every complex of several persons emerges under all circumstances as the essentially other level. But on the other hand, it has already been demonstrated that the meaning and the motive power of individuality do not always stop at the boundaries of individual personality, that this is something more general and more formal that can affect the group as a whole and the individual as its element as soon as something is present that is more inclusive, antithetical; over against this something, the (now relatively individual) collective structure can gain its conscious particularity, its character of uniqueness of indivisibility.

Given this formulation, we can explain phenomena that would seem to disconfirm the correlation at issue here, one of which is the following from the history of the United States. The Anti-Federalist party, which first called itself the Republicans, then the Whigs, then the Democrats, defended the autonomy and the sovereignty of the states at the expense of centralization and of national authority – but always with an appeal to the principle of individual freedom, of noninterference by the totality in the affairs of the individual. On no account does this contradict the relationship of individual freedom to just the relatively *large* circle, for here the sense of individuality has permeated the *narrower* circle enclosing many individual persons, and thus the narrower circle serves here the same sociological function as the discrete individual would otherwise. [...]

Freedom and Individuality

The meanings of freedom

The relatively most individual and the relatively most extensive configurations relate to one another over the head of the intermediate one, as it were. And at this point we have arrived at the basis of a fact that figures prominently in the foregoing discussion as well as in what now follows: the larger circle encourages individual freedom, the smaller one restricts it.

As it is used here, the concept of individual freedom covers various meanings that are differentiated according to the diversity of our provinces of interest. They range, say, from freedom in choosing a spouse to freedom in economic initiative. I will cite one example each for just these two.

During periods of strict group separation by clans, families, occupational and hereditary estates, castes, and so on, the circle within which a man or woman can marry tends to be a relatively narrow one – narrow, that is, relative to advanced or liberal conditions. But so far as we can survey this state of affairs, and so far as we can judge by certain contemporary analogies, selecting a partner from among the available individuals was not at all difficult. The lesser differentiation of persons and of marital relations had its counterpart in the fact that the individual male could take almost any girl from the appropriate circle, choosing on the basis of external attractiveness, since there were no highly specific internal impulses or aloof reservations to be considered by either side.

Culture as it has matured has now displaced this earlier condition in two directions. The circle of possible marriage partners has been vastly expanded by the mixing of status groups, the elimination of religious barriers, the decline of parental authority, free mobility in both the geographic and the social sense, and so forth. But for all that, individual selection is far more stern, a fact and a right of wholly personal inclination. The conviction that out of all mankind, two and only two people are "meant" for each other has now reached a stage of development that was still unheard of by the bourgeoisie of the eighteenth century.

A more profound meaning of freedom emerges here: individual freedom is freedom that is limited by individuality. Out of the uniqueness of the individual's being, there arises a corresponding uniqueness of that which can complement and free him, a specificity of needs whose correlate is the availability of the largest possible circle of possible selections, since as one's wishes and inner drives become more individual, it becomes that much less likely that they will find satisfaction in a narrowly bounded domain. In the earlier condition, conversely, there was far less restriction by the rigidity of personalities: *from the standpoint of his own concerns*, the individual was much more free in making a choice, since instead of a compelling differentiation of choice objects, there was an approximate equivalence of all those that might come under consideration. For this reason, there was no need for the circle of choice objects to be significantly more extensive. So the relatively undeveloped condition certainly imposed a social constraint on the individual; however, this was linked to the negative freedom of nondifferentiation, to the *liberum arbitrium* that was provided by the mere identical worth of objects. In the more advanced state, on the other hand, social possibilities are much enlarged, but now they are restricted by the positive meaning of freedom in which every choice is – or at least ideally should be – the unambiguously determined expression of an unalterable kind of personality.

Now in the general, societal meaning of freedom, I would say that feudalism generated nothing but narrow circles that bound individual to individual and restricted each by his obligation to the other. For this reason, within the feudal system there was room neither for national enthusiasm or public spirit, nor for the spirit of individual enterprise and private energy. The same restrictions that prevented the emergence of conceptions of a higher social union also prevented, at the lower level, the actualization of individual freedom. For just this reason, it is especially pertinent and profound that during the feudal period, the "freeman" is defined as a man who is subject to the law of the realm; bound and unfree is the man who is party to a feudal tie, that is, whose law derives from this narrower circle to the exclusion of the wider one.

If freedom swings to extremes; if the largest group, as I indicated above, affords greater play to extreme formations and malformations of individualism, to misanthropic detachment, to baroque and moody life styles, to crass egoism – then all this is merely the consequence of the wider group's requiring less of us, of its being less concerned with us, and thus of its lesser hindering of the full development even of perverse impulses. The size of the circle has a negative influence here, and it is more a matter, so to speak, of developments outside rather than inside the group, developments in which the large circle gives its members more opportunity to get involved than does the smaller one.

The meanings of individuality

The meaning of individuality in general can be separated into two more specific meanings. One has been emphasized in the above, namely, individuality in the sense of the freedom and the responsibility for oneself that comes from a broad and fluid social environment, whereas the smaller group is "narrower" in a dual sense: not only with regard to its extent, but also with regard to the restraints it imposes upon the individual, the control it exercises over him, the trifling radius of the prospects and the kinds of impetus it allows him. The other meaning of individuality is qualitative: it means that the single human being distinguishes himself from all others; that his being and conduct – in form, content, or both – suit him alone; and that being different has a positive meaning and value for his life.

The elaborations that the principle or ideal of individualism has undergone in the modern era differ according to the accentuation given to the first or the second of these meanings. On the whole, the eighteenth century sought individuality in the form of freedom, the lack of every kind of restraint on personal powers, regardless whether this restraint came from the estates or from the church, whether it was political or economic. But at the same time, the assumption prevailed that once men had been freed from all sociohistorical fetters, they would show themselves to be essentially equal; that "man in general," along with all the goodness and perfection of his nature, was inherent in every personality, needing only to be emancipated from those distorting and diverting bonds. That once men had freedom, they would use it to differentiate themselves; to rule or to become enslaved; to be better or worse than others; in short, to unfold the full diversity of their individual powers – this fact escaped the kind of individualism for which "freedom and equality" were two peacefully coexisting – indeed, two mutually necessary – values.

It should be obvious how this kind of individualism was involved in blowing apart every narrow and narrowing accommodation; partly, this was its historical, real effect, and at least partly, it was involved as a yearning and a demand. In the French Revolution, even the workers were forbidden to join into unions for better working conditions: such a federation would limit the freedom of individual members! So it is that the correlate of this kind of individualism is a wholly "cosmopolitan" disposition; even national integration recedes behind the idea of "mankind." The particularistic rights of status groups and of circles are replaced in principle by the rights of the individual, and these, quite significantly, are called "human rights"; that is, they are the rights that derive from belonging to the widest conceivable circle.

It was the other meaning of individuality that was developed by the nineteenth century, and its contradiction of the meaning just described was not seen on the whole by the eighteenth. This other meaning found its preeminent theoretical expression in Romanticism and its practical expression in the ascendancy of the division of labor. Here individualism means that the person assumes and should assume a position that he and no one else can fill; that this position awaits him, as it were, in the organization of the whole, and that he should search until he finds it; that the personal and social, the psychological and metaphysical meaning of human existence is realized in this immutability of being, this intensified differentiation of performance. This ideal image of individualism seems to have nothing at all to do with the earlier notion of "the generally human," with the idea of a uniform human nature that is present in everyone and that only requires freedom for its emergence. Indeed, the second meaning fundamentally contradicts the first. In the first, the value emphasis is on what men have in common; in the second, it is on what separates them. But with regard to the correlation I am seeking to verify, they coincide.

The enlargement of the circle that is associated with the first conception of individuality also promotes the emergence of the second. Although the second conception does not look to the totality of mankind; although it makes individuals mutually complementary and dependent instead of atomizing society into uniform and absolutely "free" individuals; although historically it promotes nationalism and a certain illiberalism instead of free cosmopolitanism – nevertheless, it too requires a group of relatively considerable size for its origination and survival. One need only refer to the manner in which the mere expansion of the economic circle, the increase in population, or the geographic boundlessness of competition has directly compelled a specialization of performance.

It is no different for mental differentiation, especially since this usually originates in the meeting of latent mental abilities with objectively preexisting mental products. The unmediated interaction of subjectivities or the purely inner energy of a human being rarely elicits all the mental distinctiveness that one possesses; rather, this seems to be associated with the extent of what has been called "objective mind," that is, the traditions and the experiences of one's group, set down in thousands of forms; the art and learning that are present in tangible structures; all the cultural materials that the historical group possesses as something super-subjective and yet available to everyone. The peculiarity of this generally accessible Mind that crystallizes itself in objective structures is that it provides both the material and the impetus for the development of a distinct personal mental type. It is the essence of "being cultured" that our purely personal dispositions are sometimes realized as the *form* of what is given as a content of objective culture [*Geist*], sometimes as the *content* of what is given as a form in objective culture. Only in this synthesis does our mental life attain its full idiom and personality; only thereby do its unique and wholly individual attributes become tangibly incarnated.

This, then, is the connection that links mental differentiation to the size of the circle in which objective mind originates. The circle may be a social, real one, or it may be of a more abstract, literary, historical sort: as that circle enlarges, so too do the possibilities of developing our inner lives; as its cultural offerings increase, regardless of how objective or abstract they may be, so too do the chances of developing the distinctiveness, the uniqueness, the sufficiency of existence of our inner lives and their intellectual, aesthetic, and practical productivity.

The individualism of equality is not, from the very beginning, a *contradictio in adjecto* only if one takes it to mean the freedom and self-sufficiency that are not limited by narrower social bonds. The individualism of inequality is a consequence of that freedom, given the infinite variability of human capacities, and therefore it is incompatible with equality. In the fundamental antithesis of these two forms of individualism, there is one point at which they coincide: each of them has a potential for development to the degree that quantitative expansion of the circle that encloses the individual provides the necessary room, impetus, and material. [...]

Group Expansion and Consciousness of the Ego

Beyond the significance that expansion of the circle has for the differentiation of the determinants of will, one sees its significance for the emergence of the *sensation* of a personal ego. Surely no one can fail to recognize that the style of modern life – precisely because of its mass character, its rushing diversity, its unboundable equalizaion of countless previously conserved idiosyncrasies – has led to unprecedented levelings of the personality form of life. But neither should one fail to recognize the countertendencies, much as these may be diverted and paralyzed in the joint effect that ultimately appears.

Life in a wider circle and interaction with it develop, in and of themselves, more consciousness of personality than arises in a narrower circle; this is so above all because it is precisely through the *alternation* of sensations, thoughts, and activities that personality documents itself. The more uniformly and unwaveringly life progresses, and the less the extremes of sensate experience depart from an average level, the less strongly does the sensation of personality arise; but the farther apart they stretch, and the more energetically they erupt, the more intensely does a human being sense himself as a personality. Just as duration can be determined only in the presence of alternation, and just as it is only the alternation of nonessential properties that throws constancy of substance into bold relief, so too the ego is apparently perceived as the one constant in all the alternation of psychological contents, especially when these contents provide a particularly rich opportunity.

Personality is *not* a single immediate state, not a single quality or single destiny, unique as this last may be; rather it is something that we sense beyond these singularities, something grown into consciousness out of their experienced reality. This is so even if this retroactively generated personality, as it were, is only the sign, the *ratio cognoscendi* of a more deeply unitary individuality that lies at the determinative root of the diverse singularities, an individuality that we cannot become aware of directly, but only as the gradual experience of these multiple contents and variations.

As long as psychic stimulations, especially the stimulations of sensation, occur only in small number, the ego is fused with them and stays latently embedded in them; it rises above them only to the degree that, precisely via a fullness of dissimilarity, it becomes clear to our awareness that the ego itself is common to all this variation. This is just the same as when a general concept cannot be abstracted out of single phenomena if we are familiar with only one or a few of their elaborations, but only if we know very many of them; and its abstractness and purity are all the greater as dissimilarity contrasts more distinctly with the generality. Now this alternation of the contents of the ego, which is what actually first poses the ego to consciousness as the stable pole in the play of psychic phenomena, is extraordinarily more lively within a large circle than it is for life in a narrower group. Stimulations of sensation, which are especially important for subjective ego consciousness, occur most where a highly differentiated individual stands amid other highly differentiated individuals, and where comparisons, frictions, and specialized relations release a profusion of reactions that remain latent in a narrower undifferentiated circle, but which in the larger circle, by virtue of their abundance and diversity, elicit the sensation of the ego as that which is absolutely "one's own."

Chapter 28

The Dyad and the Triad [1908]

Georg Simmel

The Isolated Individual

The numerically simplest structures which can still be designated as social interactions occur between two elements. Nevertheless, there is an externally even simpler phenomenon that belongs among sociological categories, however paradoxical and in fact contradictory this may seem – namely, the isolated individual. […], isolation, insofar as it is important to the individual, refers by no means only to the absence of society. On the contrary, the idea involves the somehow imagined, but then rejected, existence of society. Isolation attains its unequivocal, positive significance only as society's effect at a distance – whether as lingering-on of past relations, as anticipation of future contacts, as nostalgia, or as an intentional turning away from society. The isolated man does not suggest a being that has been the only inhabitant of the globe from the beginning. For his condition, too, is determined by sociation, even though negatively. The whole joy and the whole bitterness of isolation are only different reactions to socially experienced influences. Isolation is interaction between two parties, one of which leaves, after exerting certain influences. The isolated individual is isolated only in reality, however; for ideally, in the mind of the other party, he continues to live and act.

A well-known psychological fact is very relevant here. The feeling of isolation is rarely as decisive and intense when one actually finds oneself physically alone, as

Simmel, Georg, "The Dyad and the Triad," pp. 118–119, 122–127, 135–136, 138–139, 141–142, 145, 146–147, 148–149, 154–157, 159, 161–162, 167–169 from Kurt H. Wolff (trans/ed.), *The Sociology of Georg Simmel*. New York: The Free Press, 1950.

Classical Sociological Theory, Third Edition. Edited by Craig Calhoun, Joseph Gerteis, James Moody, Steven Pfaff, and Indermohan Virk. Editorial material and organization © 2012 John Wiley & Sons, Ltd. Published 2012 by John Wiley & Sons, Ltd.

when one is a stranger, without relations, among many physically close persons, at a "party," on a train, or in the traffic of a large city. [...]

3. Isolation

Isolation thus is a relation which is lodged within an individual but which exists between him and a certain group or group life in general. But it is sociologically significant in still another way: it may also be an interruption or periodic occurrence in a given relationship between two or more persons. As such, it is especially important in those relations whose very nature is the denial of isolation. This applies, above all, to monogamous marriage. [...]

4. The Dyad

We see that such phenomena as isolation and freedom actually exist as forms of sociological relations, although they often do so only by means of complex and indirect connections. In view of this fact, the simplest sociological formation, methodologically speaking, remains that which operates between two elements. It contains the scheme, germ, and material of innumerable more complex forms. Its sociological significance, however, by no means rests on its extensions and multiplications only. It itself is a sociation. Not only are many general forms of sociation realized in it in a very pure and characteristic fashion; what is more, the limitation to two members is a condition under which alone several forms of relationship exist. Their typically sociological nature is suggested by two facts. One is that the greatest variation of individualities and unifying motives does not alter the identity of these forms. The other is that occasionally these forms exist as much between two groups – families, states, and organizations of various kinds – as between two individuals.

Everyday experiences show the specific character that a relationship attains by the fact that only two elements participate in it. A common fate or enterprise, an agreement or secret between two persons, ties each of them in a very different manner than if even only three have a part in it. This is perhaps most characteristic of the secret. General experience seems to indicate that this minimum of two, with which the secret ceases to be the property of the one individual, is at the same time the maximum at which its preservation is relatively secure. [...] More generally speaking, the difference between the dyad[1] and larger groups consists in the fact that the dyad has a different relation to each of its two elements than have larger groups to *their* members. Although, for the outsider, the group consisting of two may function as an autonomous, super-individual unit, it usually does not do so for its participants. Rather, each of the two feels himself confronted only by the other, not by a collectivity above him. The social structure here rests immediately on the one and on the other of the two, and the secession of either would destroy the whole. The dyad, therefore, does not attain that super-personal life which the individual feels to be independent of himself. As soon, however, as there is a sociation of three, a group continues to exist even in case one of the members drops out.

This dependence of the dyad upon its two individual members causes the thought of its existence to be accompanied by the thought of its termination much more closely and impressively than in any other group, where every member knows that even after his retirement or death, the group can continue to exist. Both the lives of the individual and that of the sociation are somehow colored by the imagination of their respective deaths. And "imagination" does not refer here only to theoretical, conscious thought, but to a part or a modification of existence itself. Death stands before us, not like a fate that will strike at a certain moment but, prior to that moment, exists only as an idea or prophecy, as fear or hope, and without interfering with the reality of this life. Rather, the fact that we shall die is a quality inherent in life from the beginning. In all our living reality, there is something which merely finds its last phase or revelation in our death: we are, from birth on, beings that will die. We are this, of course, in different ways. The manner in which we conceive this nature of ours and its final effect, and in which we react to this conception, varies greatly. So does the way in which this element of our existence is interwoven with its other elements. But the same observations can be made in regard to groups. Ideally, any large group can be immortal. This fact gives each of its members, no matter what may be his personal reaction to death, a very specific sociological feeling.[2] A dyad, however, depends on each of its two elements alone – in its death, though not in its life: for its life, it needs *both*, but for its death, only one. This fact is bound to influence the inner attitude of the individual toward the dyad, even though not always consciously nor in the same way. It makes the dyad into a group that feels itself both endangered and irreplaceable, and thus into the real locus not only of authentic sociological tragedy, but also of sentimentalism and elegiac problems.

This feeling tone appears wherever the end of the union has become an organic part of its structure. Not long ago, there came news from a city in northern France regarding a strange "Association of the Broken Dish." Years ago, some industrialists met for dinner. During the meal, a dish fell on the floor and broke. One of the diners noted that the number of pieces was identical with that of those present. One of them considered this an omen, and, in consequence of it, they founded a society of friends who owed one another service and help. Each of them took a part of the dish home with him. If one of them dies, his piece is sent to the president, who glues the fragments he receives together. The last survivor will fit the last piece, whereupon the reconstituted dish is to be interred. The "Society of the Broken Dish" will thus dissolve and disappear. The feeling within that society, as well as in regard to it, would no doubt be different if new members were admitted and the life of the group thereby perpetuated indefinitely. The fact that from the beginning it is defined as one that will die gives it a peculiar stamp – which the dyad, because of the numerical condition of its structure, has always.

5. *Characteristics of the Dyad*

[a] Triviality

It is for the same structural reason that in reality dyads alone are susceptible to the peculiar coloration or discoloration which we call triviality. [...] "Triviality" connotes a certain measure of frequency, of the consciousness that a content of life is repeated, while the value of this content depends on its very opposite – a certain measure of rarity. In regard to the life of a super-individual societal unit and the relation of the individual to such a unit, this question seems not to emerge. Here, where the content of the relation transcends individuality, individuality in the sense of uniqueness or rarity seems to play no role, and its non-existence, therefore, seems not to have the effect of triviality. But in dyadic relations – love, marriage, friendship – and in larger groupings (often, for instance, "social parties") which do *not* result in higher units, the tone of triviality frequently becomes desperate and fatal. This phenomenon indicates the sociological character of the dyad: the dyad is inseparable from the immediacy of interaction; for neither of its two elements is it the super-individual unit which elsewhere confronts the individual, while at the same time it makes him participate in it.

[b]   Intimacy

In the dyad, the sociological process remains, in principle, within personal interdependence and does not result in a structure that grows beyond its elements. This also is the basis of "intimacy." The "intimate" character of certain relations seems to me to derive from the individual's inclination to consider that which distinguishes him from others, that which is individual in a qualitative sense, as the core, value, and chief matter of his existence. The inclination is by no means always justifiable; in many people, the very opposite – that which is typical, which they share with many – is the essence and the substantial value of their personality. The same phenomenon can be noted in regard to groups. They, too, easily make their specific content, that is shared only by the members, not by outsiders, their center and real fulfillment. Here we have the form of intimacy.

In probably each relation, there is a mixture of ingredients that its participants contribute to it alone and to no other, and of other ingredients that are not characteristic of it exclusively, but in the same or similar fashion are shared by its members with other persons as well. The peculiar color of intimacy exists if the ingredients of the first type, or more briefly, if the "internal" side of the relation, is felt to be essential; if its whole affective structure is based on what each of the two participants gives or shows only to the one other person and to nobody else. In other words, intimacy is not based on the *content* of the relationship. Two relationships may have an identical mixture of the two types of ingredients, of individual-exclusive and expansive contents. But only that is intimate in which the former function as the vehicle or the axis of the relation itself. Inversely, certain external situations or moods may move us to make very personal statements and confessions, usually reserved for our closest friends only, to relatively strange people. But in such cases we nevertheless feel that this "intimate" *content* does not yet make the relation an intimate one. For in its basic significance, the whole relation to these people is based only on its general, un-individual ingredients. That "intimate" content, although we have perhaps never revealed it before and thus limit it entirely to this particular relationship, does nevertheless not become the basis of its form, and thus leaves it outside the sphere of intimacy.

It is this nature of intimacy which so often makes it a danger to close unions between two persons, most commonly perhaps to marriage. The spouses share the indifferent "intimacies" of the day, the amiable and the unpleasant features of every hour, and the weaknesses that remain carefully hidden from all others. This easily causes them to place the accent and the substance of their relationship upon these wholly individual but objectively irrelevant matters. It leads them to consider what they share with others and what perhaps is the most important part of their personalities – objective, intellectual, generally interesting, generous features – as lying outside the marital relation; and thus they gradually eliminate it from their marriage.

[...]

6. The Expansion of the Dyad

[a] The Triad vs. the Dyad

This peculiar closeness between two is most clearly revealed if the dyad is contrasted with the triad.[3] For among three elements, each one operates as an intermediary between the other two, exhibiting the twofold function of such an organ, which is to unite and to separate. Where three elements, A, B, C, constitute a group, there is, in addition to the direct relationship between A and B, for instance, their indirect one, which is derived from their common relation to C. The fact that two elements are each connected not only by a straight line – the shortest – but also by a broken line, as it were, is an enrichment from a formal-sociological standpoint. Points that cannot be contacted by the straight line are connected by the third element, which offers a different side to each of the other two, and yet fuses these different sides in the unity of its own personality. Discords between two parties which they themselves cannot remedy, are accommodated by the third or by absorption in a comprehensive whole.

Yet the indirect relation does not only strengthen the direct one. It may also disturb it. No matter how close a triad may be, there is always the occasion on which two of the three members regard the third an intruder. The reason may be the mere fact that he shares in certain moods which can unfold in all their intensity and tenderness only when two can meet without distraction: the sensitive union of two is always irritated by the spectator. It may also be noted how extraordinarily difficult and rare it is for three people to attain a really uniform mood – when visiting a museum, for instance, or looking at a landscape – and how much more easily such a mood emerges between two. A and B may stress and harmoniously feel their m, because the n which A does not share with B, and the x which B does not share with A, are at once spontaneously conceded to be individual prerogatives located, as it were, on another plane. If, however, C joins the company, who shares n with A and x with B, the result is that (even under this scheme, which is the one most favorable to the unity of the whole) harmony of feeling is made completely impossible. Two may actually be *one* party, or may stand entirely beyond any question of party. But it is usual for just such finely tuned combinations of three at once to result in three parties of two persons each, and thus to destroy the unequivocal character of the relations between each two of them.

The sociological structure of the dyad is characterized by two phenomena that are absent from it. One is the intensification of relation by a third element, or by a social framework that transcends both members of the dyad. The other is any disturbance and distraction of pure and immediate reciprocity. In some cases it is precisely this absence which makes the dyadic relationship more intensive and strong. For, many otherwise undeveloped, unifying forces that derive from more remote psychical reservoirs come to life in the feeling of exclusive dependence upon one another and of hopelessness that cohesion might come from anywhere but immediate interaction. Likewise, they carefully avoid many disturbances and dangers into which confidence in a third party and in the triad itself might lead the two. This intimacy, which is the tendency of relations between two persons, is the reason why the dyad constitutes the chief seat of jealousy.

[...]

[c] Dyads, Triads, and Larger Groups

Dyads thus have very specific features. This is shown not only by the fact that the addition of a third person completely changes them, but also, and even more so, by the common observation that the further expansion to four or more by no means correspondingly modifies the group any further. For instance, a marriage with one child has a character which is completely different from that of a childless marriage, but it is not significantly different from a marriage with two or more children. To be sure, the difference resulting from the advent of the second child is again much more considerable than is that which results from the third. But this really follows from the norm mentioned: in many respects, the marriage with one child is a relation consisting of two elements – on the one hand, the parental unit, and on the other, the child. The second child is not only a fourth member of a relation but, sociologically speaking, also a third, with the peculiar effects of the third member. For, as soon as infancy has passed, it is much more often the parents who form a functional unit within the family than it is the totality of the children.

In an analogous way, in regard to marriage forms, the decisive difference is between monogamy and bigamy, whereas the third or twentieth wife is relatively unimportant for the marriage structure. The transition to a second wife is more consequential, at least in one sense, than is that to an even larger number. For it is precisely the duality of wives that can give rise to the sharpest conflicts and deepest disturbances in the husband's life, while they do not arise in the case of a greater plurality. The reason is that a larger number than two entails a de-classing and de-individualizing of the wives, a decisive reduction of the relationship to its sensuous basis (since a more intellectual relationship also is always more individualized). In general, therefore, the husband's deeper disturbances that characteristically and exclusively flow from a double relationship cannot come up.

[...]

In short, the sociological situation between the superordinate and the subordinate is completely changed as soon as a third element is added. Party formation is suggested instead of solidarity; that which separates servant and master is stressed instead of what binds them, because now common features are sought in the comrade and, of course, are found in their common contrast to the superordinate of them both. But this transformation of a numerical into a qualitative difference is no less fundamental if viewed from the master's standpoint. It is easier to keep two rather than one at a desired distance; in their jealousy and competition the master has a tool for keeping them down and making them obedient, while there is no equivalent tool in the case of *one* servant. This is expressed, in formally the same sense, in an old proverb: "He who has one child is his slave; he who has more is their master." It is seen in all these cases that the triad is a structure completely different from the dyad but not, on the other hand, specifically distinguished from groups of four or more members.

Before discussing particular types of triads, we must emphasize the variety of group characteristics that results from the subdivision of the group into two or into three chief parties. Periods of excitement generally place the whole of public life under the slogan, "Who is not for me is against me." The consequence of this is a division of elements into two parties. All interests, convictions, and impulses which put us into a positive or negative relation with others at all, are distinguished from one another by the question of how aptly this alternative applies to them. They may be arranged along a continuum. At the one pole is the radical exclusion of all mediation and impartiality; at the other, tolerance of the opponent's standpoint as legitimate as one's own. Between these extremes lies a whole range of standpoints that concur more or less with one's own position. A point on the continuum is occupied by every decision concerning immediate or remote groups that we have contact with; by every decision defining our positions within these groups; by every decision involving intimate or superficial cooperation, benevolence, or toleration, our increased prestige, or a danger to us. Every decision traces an ideal line around us. This line may definitely include or exclude everybody else; or it may have gaps where the question of inclusion and exclusion does not even arise; or it may permit mere contact, or only a partial inclusion and a partial exclusion. Whether the question of for-or-against-me is raised, and if so how emphatically, is determined not only by the logical rigor of the content of this question, nor only by the passion with which this content is insisted upon, but also by my relation to my social circle. The closer and more solidary this relation is; the more difficult it is for the individual to live with others that are not in complete harmony with him; and the more some ideal claim unites their totality, the more uncompromising is the question for each of them. The radicalism with which Jesus formulated this very decision derives from an infinitely strong feeling of the fundamental unity among all those who had received his message. In regard to it, there can be not only acceptance or rejection but what is more, only acceptance or outright fight against it. This fact is the strongest expression of the unconditional unity of all who belong to Jesus and of the unconditional exclusion of all who do not. For, the fight against the message, the being-against-me, is still an important relation, an inner, though perverted, unity; and this is stronger than any indifferent standing-by or half-hearted fence straddling.

[...]

The Triad

1. The Sociological Significance of the Third Element

What has been said indicates to a great extent the role of the third element, as well as the configurations that operate among *three* social elements. The dyad represents both the first social synthesis and unification, and the first separation and antithesis. The appearance of the third party indicates transition, conciliation, and abandonment of absolute contrast (although, on occasion, it introduces contrast). The triad as such seems to me to result in three kinds of typical group formations. All of them are impossible if there are only two elements; and, on the other hand, if there are more than three, they are either equally impossible or only expand in quantity but do not change their formal type.

2. The Non-Partisan and the Mediator

[...]

When the third element functions as a non-partisan, we have a different variety of mediation. The non-partisan either produces the concord of two colliding parties, whereby he withdraws after making the effort of creating direct contact between the unconnected or quarreling elements; or he functions as an arbiter who balances, as it were, their contradictory claims against one another and eliminates what is incompatible in them. Differences between labor and management, especially in England, have developed both forms of unification. There are boards of conciliation where the parties negotiate their conflicts under the presidency of a non-partisan. The mediator, of course, can achieve reconciliation in this form only if each party believes that the proportion between the reasons for the hostility, in short, the objective situation justifies the reconciliation and makes peace advantageous. The very great opportunity that non-partisan mediation has to produce this belief lies not only in the obvious elimination of misunderstandings or in appeals to good will, etc. It may also be analyzed as follows. The non-partisan shows each party the claims and arguments of the other; they thus lose the tone of subjective passion which usually provokes the same tone on the part of the adversary. What is so often regrettable here appears as something wholesome, namely, that the feeling which accompanies a psychological content when one individual has it, usually weakens greatly when it is transferred to a second. This fact explains why recommendations and testimonies that have to pass several mediating persons before reaching the deciding individual, are so often ineffective, even if their objective content arrives at its destination without any change. In the course of these transfers, affective imponderables get lost; and these not only supplement insufficient objective qualifications, but, in practice, they alone cause sufficient ones to be acted upon.

[...]

It is important for the analysis of social life to realize clearly that the constellation thus characterized constantly emerges in all groups of more than two elements. To be sure, the mediator may not be specifically chosen, nor be known or designated as such. But the triad here serves merely as a type or scheme; ultimately all cases of mediation can be reduced to this form. From the conversation among three persons that lasts only an hour, to the permanent family of three, there is no triad in which a dissent between any two elements does not occur from time to time – a dissent of a more harmless or more pointed, more momentary or more lasting, more theoretical or more practical nature – and in which the third member does not play a mediating role. This happens innumerable times in a very rudimentary and inarticulate manner, mixed with other actions and interactions, from which the purely mediating function cannot be isolated. Such mediations do not even have to he performed by means of words. A gesture, a way of listening, the mood that radiates from a particular person, are enough to change the difference between two individuals so that they can seek understanding, are enough to make them feel their essential commonness which is concealed under their acutely differing opinions, and to bring this divergence into the shape in which it can be ironed out the most easily. The situation does not have to involve a real conflict or fight. It is rather the thousand insignificant differences of opinion, the allusions to an antagonism of personalities, the emergence of quite momentary contrasts of interest or feeling, which continuously color the fluctuating forms of all living together; and this social life is constantly determined in its course by the presence of the third person, who almost inevitably exercises the function of mediation. This function makes the round among the three elements, since the ebb and flow of social life realizes the form of conflict in every possible combination of two members.

[...]

3. *The* Tertius Gaudens[4]

In the combinations thus far considered, the impartiality of the third element either served or harmed the group as a whole. Both the mediator and the arbitrator wish to save the group unity from the danger of splitting up. But, evidently, the non-partisan may also use his relatively superior position for purely egoistic interests. While in the cases discussed, he behaved as a means to the ends of the group, he may also, inversely, make the interaction that takes place between the parties and between himself and them, a means for his own purposes. In the social life of well consolidated groups, this may happen merely as one event among others. But often the relation between the parties and the non-partisan emerges as a new relationship: elements that have never before formed an interactional unit may come into conflict; a third non-partisan element, which before was equally unconnected with either, may spontaneously seize upon the chances that this quarrel gives him; and thus an entirely unstable interaction may result which can have an animation and wealth of forms, for each of the elements engaged in it, which are out of all proportion to its brief life.

[...]

The formations that are more essential here emerge whenever the *tertius* makes his own indirect or direct gain by turning toward one of the two conflicting parties – but not intellectually and objectively, like the arbitrator, but practically, supporting or granting. This general type has two main variants: either two parties are hostile toward one another and therefore compete for the favor of a third element, or they compete for the favor of the third element and therefore are hostile toward one another. This difference is important particularly for the further development of the threefold constellation. For where an already existing hostility urges each party to seek the favor of a third, the outcome of this competition – the fact that the third party joins one of the two, rather than the other – marks the real beginning of the fight. Inversely, two elements may curry favor with a third independently of one another. If so, this very fact may be the reason for their hostility, for their becoming parties. The eventual granting of the favor is thus the object, not the means of the conflict and, therefore, usually ends the quarrel. The decision is made, and further hostilities become practically pointless.

In both cases, the advantage of impartiality, which was the *tertius*' original attitude toward the two, consists in his possibility of making his decision depend on certain conditions. Where he is denied this possibility, for whatever reason, he cannot fully exploit the situation. This applies to one of the most common cases of the second type, namely, the competition between two persons of the same sex for the favor of one of the opposite sex. Here the decision of the third element does not depend on his or her will in the same sense as does that of a buyer who is confronted with two competing offers, or that of a ruler who grants privileges to one of two competing supplicants. The decision, rather, comes from already existing feelings which cannot be determined by any will, and which therefore do not even permit the will to be brought into a situation of choice. In these cases, therefore, we only exceptionally find offers intended to be decided by choice; and, although we genuinely have a situation of *tertius gaudens*, its thorough exploitation is, in general, not possible.

On the largest scale, the *tertius gaudens* is represented by the buying public in an economy with free competition. The fight among the producers for the buyer makes the buyer almost completely independent of the individual supplier. He is, however, completely dependent on their totality; and their coalition would, in fact, at once invert the relationship. But as it is, the buyer can base his purchase almost wholly on his appraisal of quality and price of the merchandise. His position even has the added advantage that the producers must try to anticipate the conditions described: they must guess the consumer's unverbalized or unconscious wishes, and they must suggest wishes that do not exist at all, and train him for them. These situations of *tertius gaudens* may be arranged along a continuum. At the one end, perhaps, there is the above-mentioned case of the woman between two suitors. Here the decision depends on the two men's natures, rather than on any of their activities. The chooser, therefore, usually makes no conditions and thus does not fully exploit the situation. At the other end, there is the situation which gives the *tertius gaudens* his extreme advantage. It is found in modern market economy with its complete exclusion of the personal element: here the advantage of the chooser reaches a point where the parties even relieve him of the maximum intensification of his own bargaining condition.

Let us come back to the other formation. In its beginning, a dispute is not related whatever to a third element. But then it forces its parties to compete for help from such a third element. Ordinarily an example is provided by the history of every federation, whether it be between states or between members of a family. The very simple, typical course of the process, however, gains a particular sociological interest through the following modification. The power the *tertius* must expend in order to attain his advantageous position does not have to be great in comparison with the power of each of the two parties, since the quantity of his power is determined exclusively by the strength which each of them has relative to the other. For evidently, the only important thing is that his superadded power give one of them superiority. If, therefore, the power quanta are approximately equal, a minimum accretion is often sufficient definitely to decide in one direction. This explains the frequent influence of small parliamentary parties: they can never gain it through their own significance but only because the great parties keep one another in approximate balance. Wherever majorities decide, that is, where everything depends on one single vote, as it often does, it is possible for entirely insignificant parties to make the severest conditions for their support. Something similar may occur in the relations of small to large states which find themselves in conflict. What alone is important is that the forces of two antagonistic elements paralyze one another and thus actually give unlimited power to the intrinsically extremely weak position of a third element not yet engaged in the issue. Of course, intrinsically strong third elements profit no less from such a situation.

[...]

Thus the advantage accruing to the *tertius* derives from the fact that he has an equal, equally independent, and for this very reason decisive, relation to two others. The advantage, however, does not exclusively depend on the hostility of the two. A certain general differentiation, mutual strangeness, or qualitative dualism may be sufficient. This, in fact, is the basic formula of the type, and the hostility of the elements is merely a specific case of it, even if it is the most common. The following favorite position of the *tertius*, for instance, is very characteristic, and it results from mere dualism. If B is obligated to a particular duty toward A, and if he delegates this duty to C and D among whom it is to be distributed, then A is greatly tempted to impose on each of them, if possible, a little more than half; from both together, therefore, he profits more than he would have earlier, when the duty was in the hand of only one person. In 1751, the government had to issue an explicit decree in regard to the breaking up of peasant holdings in Bohemia. The law was to the effect that if a holding was divided by the manorial lord, each of its parts could not be burdened with more than its portion, in correspondence with its size, of the socage that adhered to the whole.

[...]

For the general characterization of the *tertius gaudens*, which applies to all of its particular manifestations alike, a further point must be noted. This is, that among the causes of his prerogative, there is the mere difference of psychological energies which he invests in the relationship, as compared with the others. Earlier, in regard to the non-partisan in general, I mentioned that he represents intellectuality, while the parties in conflict represent feeling and will. If the non-partisan is in the position of *tertius gaudens*, that is, of egoistic exploiter of the situation, this intellectuality gives him a dominating place. It is enthroned, as it were, at an ideal height. The *tertius* fully enjoys that external advantage which every complication bestows upon the party whose feelings are not involved. Certainly, he may scorn the practical exploitation of his less biased grasp of the conjuncture, of his strength, which is not committed one way or another but can always be used for different purposes. But even if he does, his situation gives him at least the feeling of a slight ironical superiority over the parties which stake so much for the sake of what to him is so indifferent.

4. Divide et Impera

The previously discussed combinations of three elements were characterized by an existing or emerging conflict between two, from which the third drew his advantage. One particular variety of this combination must now be considered separately, although in reality it is not always clearly delimited against other types. The distinguishing nuance consists in the fact that the third element intentionally produces the conflict in order to gain a dominating position. Here too, however, we must preface the treatment of this constellation by pointing out that the number three is merely the minimum number of elements that are necessary for this formation, and that it may thus serve as the simplest schema. Its outline is that initially two elements are united or mutually dependent in regard to a third, and that this third element knows how to put the forces combined against *him* into action against *one another*. The outcome is that the two either keep each other balanced so that he, who is not interfered with by either, can pursue his advantages; or that they so weaken one another that neither of them can stand up against his superiority.

[...]

Where the purpose of the third party is directed, not toward an object, but toward the immediate domination of the other two elements, two sociological considerations are essential. (1) Certain elements are formed in such a way that they can be fought successfully only by similar elements. The wish to subdue them finds no immediate point of attack. It is, therefore, necessary to divide them within themselves, as it were, and to continue a fight among the parts which they can wage with homogeneous weapons until they are sufficiently weakened to fall to the third element. It has been said of England that she could gain India only by means of India. Already Xerxes had recognized that Greeks were best to fight Greece. It is precisely those whose similarity of interests makes them depend upon one another who best know their mutual weaknesses and vulnerable points. The principle of *similia similibus*, of eliminating a condition by producing a similar one, therefore applies here on the largest scale.

[...]

(2) Where it is not possible for the suppressor to have his victims alone do his business, where, that is, he himself must take a hand in the fight, the schema is very simple: he supports one of them long enough for the other to be suppressed, whereupon the first is an easy prey for him. The most expedient manner is to support the one who is the stronger to begin with. This may take on the more negative form that, within a complex of elements intended for suppression, the more powerful is merely spared. When subjugating Greece, Rome was remarkably considerate in her treatment of Athens and Sparta. This procedure is bound to produce resentment and jealousy in the one camp, and haughtiness and blind confidence in the other – a split which makes the prey easily available for the suppressor. It is a technique employed by many rulers: he protects the stronger of two, both of whom are actually interested in his own downfall, until he has ruined the weaker; then he changes fronts and advances against the one now left in isolation, and subjugates him. This technique is no less popular in the founding of world empires than in the brawls of street urchins. It is employed by governments in the manipulation of political parties as it is in competitive struggles in which three elements confront one another – perhaps a very powerful financier or industrialist and two less important competitors whose powers, though different from one another, are yet both a nuisance to him. In this case, the first, in order to prevent the two others from joining up, will make a price agreement or production arrangement with the stronger of the two, who draws considerable advantages from it, while the weaker is destroyed by the arrangement. Once he is, the second can be shaken off, for until then he was the ally of the first, but now he has no more backing and is being ruined by means of underselling or other methods.

NOTES

1 Never Simmel's term, but shorter and more convenient than his, which here, for instance, is "*Zweierverbindung*" ("union of two"). – Tr.
2 Cf. the more detailed discussion of this point in the chapter on the persistence of groups. [Not contained in Classical Sociological Theory.]

3 Again not Simmel's term, but again more convenient than "*Verbindung zu dreien*" (association of three) and the like. – Tr.
4 Literally, "the third who enjoys," that is, the third party which in some fashion or another draws advantage from the quarrel of two others. – Tr.

Chapter 29

Civilization and its Discontents [1929]

Sigmund Freud

In all that follows I adopt the standpoint that the inclination to aggression is an original, self-subsisting instinctual disposition in man, and I return to my view that it constitutes the greatest impediment to civilization. At one point in the course of this inquiry I was led to the idea that civilization was a special process which mankind undergoes, and I am still under the influence of that idea. I may now add that civilization is a process in the service of Eros, whose purpose is to combine single human individuals, and after that families, then races, peoples and nations, into one great unity, the unity of mankind. Why this has to happen, we do not know; the work of Eros is precisely this. These collections of men are to be libidinally bound to one another. Necessity alone, the advantages of work in common, will not hold them together. But man's natural aggressive instinct, the hostility of each against all and of all against each, opposes this program of civilization. This aggressive instinct is the derivative and the main representative of the death instinct which we have found alongside of Eros and which shares world-dominion with it. And now, I think, the meaning of the evolution of civilization is no longer obscure to us. It must present the struggle between Eros and Death, between the instinct of life and the instinct of destruction, as it works itself out in the human species. This struggle is what all life essentially consists of, and the evolution of civilization may therefore be simply

---

Freud, Sigmund, "Civilization and its Discontents." From Sigmund Freud, *Civilization and its Discontents*, trans. James Strachey. New York: W.W. Norton & Company, Inc., 1961. Copyright © 1961 by James Strachey, renewed 1989 by Alix Strachey. Used by permission of W.W. Norton & Company, Inc. Sigmund Freud © Copyrights, The Institute of Psychoanalysis and The Hogarth Press for permission to quote from *The Standard Edition of the Complete Psychological Works of Sigmund Freud*. Reprinted by permission of The Random House Group Ltd.

Classical Sociological Theory, Third Edition. Edited by Craig Calhoun, Joseph Gerteis, James Moody, Steven Pfaff, and Indermohan Virk. Editorial material and organization © 2012 John Wiley & Sons, Ltd. Published 2012 by John Wiley & Sons, Ltd.

described as the struggle for life of the human species. And it is this battle of the giants that our nurse-maids try to appease with their lullaby about Heaven.[1] [...]

Another question concerns us more nearly. What means does civilization employ in order to inhibit the aggressiveness which opposes it, to make it harmless, to get rid of it, perhaps? We have already become acquainted with a few of these methods, but not yet with the one that appears to be the most important. This we can study in the history of the development of the individual. What happens in him to render his desire for aggression innocuous? Something very remarkable, which we should never have guessed and which is nevertheless quite obvious. His aggressiveness is introjected, internalized; it is, in point of fact, sent back to where it came from – that is, it is directed towards his own ego. There it is taken over by a portion of the ego, which sets itself over against the rest of the ego as super-ego, and which now, in the form of "conscience," is ready to put into action against the ego the same harsh aggressiveness that the ego would have liked to satisfy upon other, extraneous individuals. The tension between the harsh super-ego and the ego that is subjected to it, is called by us the sense of guilt; it expresses itself as a need for punishment. Civilization, therefore, obtains mastery over the individual's dangerous desire for aggression by weakening and disarming it and by setting up an agency within him to watch over it, like a garrison in a conquered city.

As to the origin of the sense of guilt, the analyst has different views from other psychologists; but even he does not find it easy to give an account of it. To begin with, if we ask how a person comes to have a sense of guilt, we arrive at an answer which cannot be disputed: a person feels guilty (devout people would say "sinful") when he has done something which he knows to be "bad." But then we notice how little this answer tells us. Perhaps, after some hesitation, we shall add that even when a person has not actually *done* the bad thing but has only recognized in himself an *intention* to do it, he may regard himself as guilty; and the question then arises of why the intention is regarded as equal to the deed. Both cases, however, presuppose that one had already recognized that what is bad is reprehensible, is something that must not be carried out. How is this judgment arrived at? We may reject the existence of an original, as it were natural, capacity to distinguish good from bad. What is bad is often not at all what is injurious or dangerous to the ego; on the contrary, it may be something which is desirable and enjoyable to the ego. Here, therefore, there is an extraneous influence at work, and it is this that decides what is to be called good or bad. Since a person's own feelings would not have led him along this path, he must have had a motive for submitting to this extraneous influence. Such a motive is easily discovered in his helplessness and his dependence on other people, and it can best be designated as fear of loss of love. If he loses the love of another person upon whom he is dependent, he also ceases to be protected from a variety of dangers. Above all, he is exposed to the danger that this stronger person will show his superiority in the form of punishment. At the beginning, therefore, what is bad is whatever causes one to be threatened with loss of love. For fear of that loss, one must avoid it. This, too, is the reason why it makes little difference whether one has already done the bad thing or only intends to do it.

In either case the danger only sets in if and when the authority discovers it, and in either case the authority would behave in the same way.

This state of mind is called a "bad conscience;" but actually it does not deserve this name, for at this stage the sense of guilt is clearly only a fear of loss of love, "social" anxiety. In small children it can never be anything else, but in many adults, too, it has only changed to the extent that the place of the father or the two parents is taken by the larger human community. Consequently, such people habitually allow themselves to do any bad thing which promises them enjoyment, so long as they are sure that the authority will not know anything about it or cannot blame them for it; they are afraid only of being found out. Present-day society has to reckon in general with this state of mind.

A great change takes place only when the authority is internalized through the establishment of a super-ego. The phenomena of conscience then reach a higher stage. Actually, it is not until now that we should speak of conscience or a sense of guilt. At this point, too, the fear of being found out comes to an end; the distinction, moreover, between doing something bad and wishing to do it disappears entirely, since nothing can be hidden from the super-ego, not even thoughts. It is true that the seriousness of the situation from a real point of view has passed away, for the new authority, the super-ego, has no motive that we know of for ill-treating the ego, with which it is intimately bound up; but genetic influence, which leads to the survival of what is past and has been surmounted, makes itself felt in the fact that fundamentally things remain as they were at the beginning. The superego torments the sinful ego with the same feeling of anxiety and is on the watch for opportunities of getting it punished by the external world. [...]

Thus we know of two origins of the sense of guilt: one arising from fear of an authority, and the other, later on, arising from fear of the super-ego. The first insists upon a renunciation of instinctual satisfactions; the second, as well as doing this, presses for punishment, since the continuance of the forbidden wishes cannot be concealed from the super-ego. We have also learned how the severity of the super-ego – the demands of conscience – is to be understood. It is simply a continuation of the severity of the external authority, to which it has succeeded and which it has in part replaced. We now see in what relationship the renunciation of instincts stands to the sense of guilt. Originally, renunciation of instinct was the result of fear of an external authority: one renounced one's satisfactions in order not to lose its love. If one has carried out this renunciation, one is, as it were, quits with the authority and no sense of guilt should remain. But with fear of the super-ego the case is different. Here, instinctual renunciation is not enough, for the wish persists and cannot be concealed from the super-ego. Thus, in spite of the renunciation that has been made, a sense of guilt comes about. This constitutes a great economic disadvantage in the erection of a super-ego, or, as we may put it, in the formation of a conscience. Instinctual renunciation now no longer has a completely liberating effect; virtuous continence is no longer rewarded with the assurance of love. A threatened external unhappiness – loss of love and punishment on the part of the external authority – has been exchanged for a permanent internal unhappiness, for the tension of the sense of guilt. [...]

Now, I think, we can at last grasp two things perfectly clearly: the part played by love in the origin of conscience and the fatal inevitability of the sense of guilt. Whether one has killed one's father or has abstained from doing so is not really the decisive thing. One is bound to feel guilty in either case, for the sense of guilt is an expression of the conflict due to ambivalence, of the external struggle between Eros and the instinct of destruction or death. This conflict is set going as soon as men are faced with the task of living together. So long as the community assumes no other form than that of the family, the conflict is bound to express itself in the Oedipus complex, to establish the conscience and to create the first sense of guilt. When an attempt is made to widen the community, the same conflict is continued in forms which are dependent on the past; and it is strengthened and results in a further intensification of the sense of guilt. Since civilization obeys an internal erotic impulsion which causes human beings to unite in a closely-knit group, it can only achieve this aim through an ever-increasing reinforcement of the sense of guilt. What began in relation to the father is completed in relation to the group. If civilization is a necessary course of development from the family to humanity as a whole, then – as a result of the inborn conflict arising from ambivalence, of the eternal struggle between the trends of love and death – there is inextricably bound up with it an increase of the sense of guilt, which will perhaps reach heights that the individual finds hard to tolerate. [...]

When we look at the relation between the process of human civilization and the developmental or educative process of individual human beings, we shall conclude without much hesitation that the two are very similar in nature, if not the very same process applied to different kinds of object. The process of the civilization of the human species is, of course, an abstraction of a higher order than is the development of the individual and it is therefore harder to apprehend in concrete terms, nor should we pursue analogies to an obsessional extreme; but in view of the similarity between the aims of the two processes – in the one case the integration of a separate individual into a human group, and in the other case the creation of a unified group out of many individuals – we cannot be surprised at the similarity between the means employed and the resultant phenomena.

In view of its exceptional importance, we must not long postpone the mention of one feature which distinguishes between the two processes. In the developmental process of the individual, the program of the pleasure principle, which consists in finding the satisfaction of happiness, is retained as the main aim. Integration in, or adaptation to, a human community appears as a scarcely avoidable condition which must be fulfilled before this aim of happiness can be achieved. If it could be done without that condition, it would perhaps be preferable. To put it in other words, the development of the individual seems to us to be a product of the interaction between two urges, the urge towards happiness, which we usually call "egoistic," and the urge towards union with others in the community, which we call "altruistic." Neither of these descriptions goes much below the surface. In the process of individual development, as we have said, the main accent falls mostly on the egoistic urge (or the urge towards happiness); while the other urge, which may be described as a "cultural" one, is usually content with the role of imposing restrictions. But in the process of civilization things are different. Here by far the most important thing is the aim of creating a unity out of the individual human beings. It is true that the aim of happiness is still there, but it is pushed into the background. It almost seems as if the creation of a great human community would be most successful if no attention had to be paid to the happiness of the individual. The developmental process of the individual can thus be expected to have special features of its own which are not reproduced in the process of human civilization. It is only in so far as the first of these processes has union with the community as its aim that it need coincide with the second process.

Just as a planet revolves around a central body as well as rotating on its own axis, so the human individual takes part in the course of development of mankind at the same time as he pursues his own path in life. But to our dull eyes the play of forces in the heavens seems fixed in a never-changing order; in the field of organic life we can still see how the forces contend with one another, and how the effects of the conflict are continually changing. So, also, the two urges, the one towards personal happiness and the other towards union with other human beings must struggle with each other in every individual; and so, also, the two processes of individual and of cultural development must stand in hostile opposition to each other and mutually dispute the ground. But this struggle between the individual and society is not a derivative of the contradiction – probably an irreconcilable one – between the primal instincts of Eros and death. It is a dispute within the economics of the libido, comparable to the contest concerning the distribution of libido between ego and objects; and it does admit of an eventual accommodation in the individual, as, it may be hoped, it will also do in the future of civilization, however much that civilization may oppress the life of the individual to-day.

The analogy between the process of civilization and the path of individual development may be extended in an important respect. It can be asserted that the community, too, evolves a super-ego under whose influence cultural development proceeds. It would be a tempting task for anyone who has a knowledge of human civilizations to follow out this analogy in detail. I will confine myself to bringing forward a few striking points. The super-ego of an epoch of civilization has an origin similar to that of an individual. It is based on the impression left behind by the personalities of great leaders – men of overwhelming force of mind or men in whom one of the human impulsions has found its strongest and purest, and therefore often its most one-sided, expression. In many instances the analogy goes still further, in that during their lifetime these figures were – often enough, even if not always – mocked and maltreated by others and even despatched in a cruel fashion. In the same way, indeed, the primal father did not attain divinity until long after he had met his death by violence. The most arresting example of this fateful conjunction is to be seen in the figure of Jesus Christ – if, indeed, that figure is not a part of mythology, which called it into being from an obscure memory of that primal event. Another point of agreement between the cultural and the individual super-ego is that the former, just like the latter, sets up strict ideal demands, disobedience to which is visited with "fear of conscience." Here, indeed, we come across the remarkable circumstance that the mental processes concerned are actually more familiar to us and more accessible to consciousness as they are seen in the group than they can be in the individual man. In him, when tension arises, it is only the aggressiveness of the super-ego which, in the form of reproaches, makes itself noisily heard; its actual demands often remain unconscious in the background. If we bring them to conscious knowledge, we find that they coincide with the precepts of the prevailing cultural super-ego. At this point the two processes, that of the cultural development of the group and that of the cultural development of the individual, are, as it were, always interlocked. For that reason some of the manifestations and properties of the super-ego can be more easily detected in its behaviour in the cultural community than in the separate individual.

The cultural super-ego has developed its ideals and set up its demands. Among the latter, those which deal with the relations of human beings to one another are comprised under the heading of ethics. People have at all times set the greatest value on ethics, as though they expected that it in particular would produce especially important results. And it does in fact deal with a subject which can easily be recognized as the sorest spot in every civilization. Ethics is thus to be regarded as a therapeutic attempt – as an endeavour to achieve, by means of a command of the super-ego, something which has so far not been achieved by means of any other cultural activities. As we already know, the problem before us is how to get rid of the greatest hindrance to civilization – namely, the constitutional inclination of human beings to be aggressive towards one another; and for that very reason we are especially interested in what is probably the most recent of the cultural commands of the super-ego, the commandment to love one's neighbour as oneself. In our research into, and therapy of, a neurosis, we are led to make two reproaches against the super-ego of the individual. In the severity of its commands and prohibitions it troubles itself too little about the happiness of the ego, in that it takes insufficient account of the resistances against obeying them – of the instinctual strength of the id (in the first place), and of the difficulties presented by the real external environment (in the second). Consequently we are very often obliged, for therapeutic purposes, to oppose the super-ego, and we endeavour to lower its demands. Exactly the same objections can be made against the ethical demands of the cultural super-ego. It, too, does not trouble itself enough about the facts of the mental constitution of human beings. It issues a command and does not ask whether it is possible for people to obey it. On the contrary, it assumes that a man's ego is psychologically capable of anything that is required of it, that his ego has unlimited mastery over his id. This is a mistake; and even in what are known as normal people the id cannot be controlled beyond certain limits. If more is demanded of a man, a revolt will be produced in him or a neurosis, or he will be made unhappy. The commandment, "Love thy neighbour as thyself," is the strongest defence against human aggressiveness and an excellent example of the unpsychological proceedings of the cultural super-ego. The commandment is impossible to fulfil; such an enormous inflation of love can only lower its value, not get rid of the difficulty. Civilization pays no attention to all this; it merely admonishes us that the harder it is to obey the precept, the more meritorious it is to do so. But anyone who follows such a precept in present-day civilization only puts himself at a disadvantage *vis-à-vis* the person who disregards it. What a potent obstacle to civilization aggressiveness must be, if the defence against it can cause as much unhappiness as aggressiveness itself! "Natural" ethics, as it is called, has nothing to offer here except the narcissistic satisfaction of being able to think oneself better than others. At this point the ethics based on religion introduces its promises of a better afterlife. But so long as virtue is not rewarded here on earth, ethics will, I fancy, preach in vain. I too think it quite certain that a real change in the relations of human beings to possessions would be of more help in this direction than any ethical commands; but the recognition of this fact among socialists has been obscured and made useless for practical purposes by a fresh idealistic misconception of human nature.

I believe the line of thought which seeks to trace in the phenomena of cultural development the part played by a super-ego promises still further discoveries. I hasten to come to a close. But there is one question which I can hardly evade. If the development of civilization has such a far-reaching similarity to the development of the individual and if it employs the same methods, may we not be justified in reaching the diagnosis that, under the influence of cultural urges, some civilizations, or some epochs of civilization – possibly the whole of mankind – have become "neurotic"? An analytic dissection of such neuroses might lead to therapeutic recommendations which could lay claim to great practical interest. I would not say that an attempt of this kind to carry psycho-analysis over to the cultural community was absurd or doomed to be fruitless. But we should have to be very cautious and not forget that, after all, we are only dealing with analogies and that it is dangerous, not only with men but also with concepts, to tear them from the sphere in which they have originated and been evolved. Moreover, the diagnosis of communal neuroses is faced with a special difficulty. In an individual neurosis we take as our starting-point the contrast that distinguishes the patient from his environment, which is assumed to be "normal." For a group all of whose members are affected by one and the same disorder no such background could exist; it would have to be found elsewhere. And as regards the therapeutic application of our knowledge, what would be the use of the most correct analysis of social neuroses, since no one possesses authority to impose such a therapy upon the group? But in spite of all these difficulties, we may expect that one day someone will venture to embark upon a pathology of cultural communities.

For a wide variety of reasons, it is very far from my intention to express an opinion upon the value of human civilization. I have endeavoured to guard myself against the enthusiastic prejudice which holds that our civilization is the most precious thing that we possess or could acquire and that its path will necessarily lead to heights of unimagined perfection. I can at least listen without indignation to the critic who is of the opinion that when one surveys the aims of cultural endeavour and the means it employs, one is bound to come to the conclusion that the whole effort is not worth the trouble, and that the outcome of it can only be a state of affairs which the individual will be unable to tolerate. My impartiality is made all the easier to me by my knowing very little about all these things. One thing only do I know for certain and that is that man's judgements of value follow directly his wishes for happiness – that, accordingly, they are an attempt to support his illusions with arguments. I should find it very understandable if someone were to point out the obligatory nature of the course of human civilization and were to say, for instance, that the tendencies to a restriction of sexual life or to the institution of a humanitarian ideal at the expense of natural selection were developmental trends which cannot be averted or turned aside and to which it is best for us to yield as though they were necessities of nature. I know, too, the objection that can be made against this, to the effect that in the history of mankind, trends such as these, which were considered unsurmountable, have often been thrown aside and replaced by other trends. Thus I have not the courage to rise up before my fellow-men as a prophet, and I bow to their reproach that I can offer them no consolation: for at bottom that is what they are all demanding – the wildest revolutionaries no less passionately than the most virtuous believers.

The fateful question for the human species seems to me to be whether and to what extent their cultural development will succeed in mastering the disturbance of their communal life by the human instinct of aggression and self-destruction. It may be that in this respect precisely the present time deserves a special interest. Men have gained control over the forces of nature to such an extent that with their help they would have no difficulty in exterminating one another to the last man. They know this, and hence comes a large part of their current unrest, their unhappiness and their mood of anxiety. And now it is to be expected that the other of the two "Heavenly Powers," eternal Eros, will make an effort to assert himself in the struggle with his equally immortal adversary. But who can foresee with what success and with what result?[2]

NOTES

1 ("*Eiapopeia vom Himmel.*" A quotation from Heine's poem *Deutschland*, Caput 1.)
2 (The final sentence was added in 1931 – when the menace of Hitler was already beginning to be apparent.)

Chapter 30

The Souls of Black Folk [1903]

W. E. B. Du Bois

Of Our Spiritual Strivings

> O water, voice of my heart, crying in the sand,
>   All night long crying with a mournful cry,
> As I lie and listen, and cannot understand
>   The voice of my heart in my side or the voice of the sea,
>   O water, crying for rest, is it I, is it I?
>   All night long the water is crying to me.
> Unresting water, there shall never be rest
>   Till the last moon droop and the last tide fail,
> And the fire of the end begin to burn in the west;
>   And the heart shall be weary and wonder and cry like the sea,
>   All life long crying without avail,
>   As the water all night long is crying to me.
>
> ARTHUR SYMONS

Between me and the other world there is ever an unasked question: unasked by some through feeling of delicacy; by others through the difficulty of rightly framing it. All,

---

Du Bois, W.E.B, "The Souls of Black Folk." From W.E.B. Du Bois, *The Souls of Black Folk*. New York: Bantam Books, 1–9, 1989.

Classical Sociological Theory, Third Edition. Edited by Craig Calhoun, Joseph Gerteis, James Moody, Steven Pfaff, and Indermohan Virk. Editorial material and organization © 2012 John Wiley & Sons, Ltd. Published 2012 by John Wiley & Sons, Ltd.

nevertheless, flutter round it. They approach me in a half-hesitant sort of way, eye me curiously or compassionately, and then, instead of saying directly, How does it feel to be a problem? they say, I know an excellent colored man in my town; or, I fought at Mechanicsville; or, Do not these Southern outrages make your blood boil? At these I smile, or am interested, or reduce the boiling to a simmer, as the occasion may require. To the real question, How does it feel to be a problem? I answer seldom a word.

And yet, being a problem is a strange experience, – peculiar even for one who has never been anything else, save perhaps in babyhood and in Europe. It is in the early days of rollicking boyhood that the revelation first bursts upon one, all in a day, as it were. I remember well when the shadow swept across me. I was a little thing, away up in the hills of New England, where the dark Housatonic winds between Hoosac and Taghkanic to the sea. In a wee wooden schoolhouse, something put it into the boys' and girls' heads to buy gorgeous visiting-cards – ten cents a package – and exchange. The exchange was merry, till one girl, a tall newcomer, refused my card, – refused it peremptorily, with a glance. Then it dawned upon me with a certain suddenness that I was different from the others; or like, mayhap, in heart and life and longing, but shut out from their world by a vast veil. I had thereafter no desire to tear down that veil, to creep through; I held all beyond it in common contempt, and lived above it in a region of blue sky and great wandering shadows. That sky was bluest when I could beat my mates at examination-time, or beat them at a foot-race, or even beat their stringy heads. Alas, with the years all this fine contempt began to fade; for the words I longed for, and all their dazzling opportunities, were theirs, not mine. But they should not keep these prizes, I said; some, all, I would wrest from them. Just how I would do it I could never decide: by reading law, by healing the sick, by telling the wonderful tales that swam in my head, – some way. With other black boys the strife was not so fiercely sunny: their youth shrunk into tasteless sycophancy, or into silent hatred of the pale world about them and mocking distrust of everything white; or wasted itself in a bitter cry, Why did God make me an outcast and a stranger in mine own house? The shades of the prison-house closed round about us all: walls strait and stubborn to the whitest, but relentlessly narrow, tall, and unscalable to sons of night who must plod darkly on in resignation, or beat unavailing palms against the stone, or steadily, half hopelessly, watch the streak of blue above.

After the Egyptian and Indian, the Greek and Roman, the Teuton and Mongolian, the Negro is a sort of seventh son, born with a veil, and gifted with second-sight in this American world – a world which yields him no true self-consciousness, but only lets him see himself through the revelation of the other world. It is a peculiar sensation, this double-consciousness, this sense of always looking at one's self through the eyes of others, of measuring one's soul by the tape of a world that looks on in amused contempt and pity. One ever feels his twoness – an American, a Negro; two souls, two thoughts, two unreconciled strivings; two warring ideals in one dark body, whose dogged strength alone keeps it from being torn asunder.

The history of the American Negro is the history of this strife, – this longing to attain self-conscious manhood, to merge his double self into a better and truer self. In this merging he wishes neither of the older selves to be lost. He would not Africanize America, for America has too much to teach the world and Africa. He would not bleach his Negro soul in a flood of white Americanism, for he knows that Negro blood has a message for the world. He simply wishes to make it possible for a man to be both a Negro and an American, without being cursed and spit upon by his fellows, without having the doors of Opportunity closed roughly in his face.

This, then, is the end of his striving: to be a co-worker in the kingdom of culture, to escape both death and isolation, to husband and use his best powers and his latent genius. These powers of body and mind have in the past been strangely wasted, dispersed, or forgotten. The shadow of a mighty Negro past flits through the tale of Ethiopia the Shadowy and of Egypt the Sphinx. Through history, the powers of single black men flash here and there like falling stars, and die sometimes before the world has rightly gauged their brightness. Here in America, in the few days since Emancipation, the black man's turning hither and thither in hesitant and doubtful striving has often made his very strength to lose effectiveness, to seem like absence of power, like weakness. And yet it is not weakness – it is the contradiction of double aims. The double-aimed struggle of the black artisan – on the one hand to escape white contempt for a nation of mere hewers of wood and drawers of water, and on the other hand to plough and nail and dig for a poverty-stricken horde – could only result in making him a poor craftsman, for he had but half a heart in either cause. By the poverty and ignorance of his people, the Negro minister or doctor was tempted toward quackery and demagogy; and by the criticism of the other world, toward ideals that made him ashamed of his lowly tasks. The would-be black *savant* was confronted by the paradox that the knowledge his people needed was a twice-told tale to his white neighbors, while the knowledge which would teach the white world was Greek to his own flesh and blood. The innate love of harmony and beauty that set the ruder souls of his people a-dancing and a-singing raised but confusion and doubt in the soul of the black artist; for the beauty revealed to him was the soul-beauty of a race which his larger audience despised, and he could not articulate the message of another people. This waste of double aims, this seeking to satisfy two unreconciled ideals, has wrought sad havoc with the courage and faith and deeds of ten thousand people, – has sent them often wooing false gods and invoking false means of salvation, and at times has even seemed about to make them ashamed of themselves.

Away back in the days of bondage they thought to see in one divine event the end of all doubt and disappointment; few men ever worshipped Freedom with half such unquestioning faith as did the American Negro for two centuries. To him, so far as he thought and dreamed, slavery was indeed the sum of all villainies, the cause of all sorrow, the root of all prejudice; Emancipation was the key to a promised land of sweeter beauty than ever stretched before the eyes of wearied Israelites. In song and exhortation swelled one refrain – Liberty; in his tears and curses the God he implored had Freedom in his right hand. At last it came, – suddenly, fearfully, like a dream. With one wild carnival of blood and passion came the message in his own plaintive cadences: –

> "Shout, O children!
> Shout, you're free!
> For God has bought your liberty!"

Years have passed away since then, – ten, twenty, forty; forty years of national life, forty years of renewal and development, and yet the swarthy specter sits in its accustomed seat at the Nation's feast. In vain do we cry to this our vastest social problem: –

> "Take any shape but that, and my firm nerves
> Shall never tremble!"

The Nation has not yet found peace from its sins; the freedman has not yet found in freedom his promised land. Whatever of good may have come in these years of change, the shadow of a deep disappointment rests upon the Negro people, – a disappointment all the more bitter because the unattained ideal was unbounded save by the simple ignorance of a lowly people.

The first decade was merely a prolongation of the vain search for freedom, the boon that seemed ever barely to elude their grasp, – like a tantalizing will-o'-the-wisp, maddening and misleading the headless host. The holocaust of war, the terrors of the Ku-Klux Klan, the lies of carpet-baggers, the disorganization of industry, and the contradictory advice of friends and foes, left the bewildered serf with no new watchword beyond the old cry for freedom. As the time flew, however, he began to grasp a new idea. The idea of liberty demanded for its attainment powerful means, and these the Fifteenth Amendment gave him. The ballot, which before he had looked upon as a visible sign of freedom, he now regarded as the chief means of gaining and perfecting the liberty with which war had partially endowed him. And why not? Had not votes made war and emancipated millions? Had not votes enfranchised the freedmen? Was anything impossible to a power that had done all this? A million black men started with renewed zeal to vote themselves into the kingdom. So the decade flew away, the revolution of 1876 came, and left the half-free serf weary, wondering, but still inspired. Slowly but steadily, in the following years, a new vision began gradually to replace the dream of political power, – a powerful movement, the rise of another ideal to guide the unguided, another pillar of fire by night after a clouded day. It was the ideal of "book-learning"; the curiosity, born of compulsory ignorance, to know and test the power of the cabalistic letters of the white man, the longing to know. Here at last seemed to have been discovered the mountain path to Canaan; longer than the highway of Emancipation and law, steep and rugged, but straight, leading to heights high enough to overlook life.

Up the new path the advance guard toiled, slowly, heavily, doggedly; only those who have watched and guided the faltering feet, the misty minds, the dull understandings, of the dark pupils of these schools know how faithfully, how piteously, this people strove to learn. It was weary work. The cold statistician wrote down the inches of progress here and there, noted also where here and there a foot had slipped or some one had fallen. To the tired climbers, the horizon was ever dark, the mists were often cold, the Canaan was always dim and far away. If, however, the vistas disclosed as yet no goal, no resting-place, little but flattery and criticism, the journey at least gave leisure for reflection and self-examination; it changed the child of Emancipation to the youth with dawning self-consciousness, self-realization, self-respect. In those somber forests of his striving his own soul rose before him, and he saw himself, – darkly as through a veil; and yet he saw in himself some faint revelation of his power, of his mission. He began to have a dim feeling that, to attain his place in the world, he must be himself, and not another. For the first time he sought to analyze the burden he bore upon his back, that deadweight of social degradation partially masked behind a half-named Negro problem. He felt his poverty; without a cent, without a home, without land, tools, or savings, he had entered into competition with rich, landed, skilled neighbors. To be a poor man is hard, but to be a poor race in a land of dollars is the very bottom of hardships. He felt the weight of his ignorance, – not simply of letters, but of life, of business, of the humanities; the accumulated sloth and shirking and awkwardness of decades and centuries shackled his hands and feet. Nor was his burden all poverty and ignorance. The red stain of bastardy, which two centuries of systematic legal defilement of Negro women had stamped upon his race, meant not only the loss of ancient African chastity, but also the hereditary weight of a mass of corruption from white adulterers, threatening almost the obliteration of the Negro home.

A people thus handicapped ought not to be asked to race with the world, but rather allowed to give all its time and thought to its own social problems. But alas! while sociologists gleefully count his bastards and his prostitutes, the very soul of the toiling, sweating black man is darkened by the shadow of a vast despair. Men call the shadow prejudice, and learnedly explain it as the natural defense of culture against barbarism, learning against ignorance, purity against crime, the "higher" against the "lower" races. To which the Negro cries Amen! and swears that to so much of this strange prejudice as is founded on just homage to civilization, culture, righteousness, and progress, he humbly bows and meekly does obeisance. But before that nameless prejudice that leaps beyond all this he stands helpless, dismayed, and well-nigh speechless; before that personal disrespect and mockery, the ridicule and systematic humiliation, the distortion of fact and wanton license of fancy, the cynical ignoring of the better and the boisterous welcoming of the worse, the all-pervading desire to inculcate disdain for everything black, from Toussaint to the devil, – before this there rises a sickening despair that would disarm and discourage any nation save that black host to whom "discouragement" is an unwritten word.

But the facing of so vast a prejudice could not but bring the inevitable self-questioning, self-disparagement, and lowering of ideals which ever accompany repression and breed in an atmosphere of contempt and hate. Whisperings and portents came borne upon the four winds: Lo! we are diseased and dying, cried the dark hosts; we cannot write, our voting is vain; what need of education, since we must always cook and serve? And the Nation echoed and enforced this self-criticism, saying: Be content to be servants, and nothing more; what need of higher culture for halfmen? Away with the black man's ballot, by force or fraud, – and behold the suicide of a race! Nevertheless, out of the evil came something of good, – the more careful adjustment of education to real life, the clearer perception of the Negroes' social responsibilities, and the sobering realization of the meaning of progress.

So dawned the time of *Sturm und Drang*: storm and stress to-day rocks our little boat on the mad waters of the world-sea; there is within and without the sound of conflict, the burning of body and rending of soul; inspiration strives with doubt, and faith with vain questionings. The bright ideals of the past, – physical freedom, political power, the training of brains and the training of hands, – all these in turn have waxed and waned, until even the last grows dim and overcast. Are they all wrong, – all false? No, not that, but each alone was over-simple and incomplete, – the dreams of a credulous race-childhood, or the fond imaginings of the other world which does not know and does not want to know our power. To be really true, all these ideals must be melted and welded into one. The training of the schools we need to-day more than ever, – the training of deft hands, quick eyes and ears, and above all the broader, deeper, higher culture of gifted minds and pure hearts. The power of the ballot we need in sheer self-defense, – else what shall save us from a second slavery? Freedom, too, the long-sought, we still seek, – the freedom of life and limb, and freedom to work and think, the freedom to love and aspire. Work, culture, liberty, – all these we need, not singly but together, not successively but together, each growing and aiding each, and all striving toward that vaster ideal that swims before the Negro people, the ideal of human brotherhood, gained through the unifying ideal of Race; the ideal of fostering and developing the traits and talents of the Negro, not in opposition to or contempt for other races, but rather in large conformity to the greater ideals of the American Republic, in order that some day on American soil two world-races may give each to each those characteristics both so sadly lack. We the darker ones come even now not altogether empty-handed: there are to-day no truer exponents of the pure human spirit of the Declaration of Independence than the American Negroes; there is no true American music but the wild sweet melodies of the Negro slave; the American fairy tales and folklore are Indian and African; and, all in all, we black men seem the sole oasis of simple faith and reverence in a dusty desert of dollars and smartness. Will America be poorer if she replace her brutal dyspeptic blundering with light-hearted but determined Negro humility? or her coarse and cruel wit with loving jovial good-humor? or her vulgar music with the soul of the Sorrow Songs?

Merely a concrete test of the underlying principles of the great republic is the Negro Problem, and the spiritual striving of the freedmen's sons is the travail of souls whose burden is almost beyond the measure of their strength, but who bear it in the name of an historic race, in the name of this the land of their fathers' fathers, and in the name of human opportunity.

Chapter 31

The Regulation of the Wishes [1931]

William I. Thomas

One of the most important powers gained during the evolution of animal life is the ability to make decisions from within instead of having them imposed from without. Very low forms of life do not make decisions, as we understand this term, but are pushed and pulled by chemical substances, heat, light, etc., much as iron filings are attracted or repelled by a magnet. They do tend to behave properly in given conditions – a group of small crustaceans will flee as in a panic if a bit of strychnia is placed in the basin containing them and will rush toward a drop of beef juice like hogs crowding around swill – but they do this as an expression of organic affinity for the one substance and repugnance for the other, and not as an expression of choice or "free will." There are, so to speak, rules of behavior but these represent a sort of fortunate mechanistic adjustment of the organism to typically recurring situations, and the organism cannot change the rule.

On the other hand, the higher animals, and above all man, have the power of refusing to obey a stimulation which they followed at an earlier time. Response to the earlier stimulation may have had painful consequences and so the rule or habit in this situation is changed. We call this ability the power of inhibition, and it is dependent on the fact that the nervous system carries memories or records of past experiences. At this point the determination of action no longer comes exclusively from outside sources but is located within the organism itself.

Preliminary to any self-determined act of behavior there is always a stage of examination and deliberation which we may call *the definition of the situation*. And

---

Thomas, William I., "Definition of the Situation," pp. 41–46, 48–50, 54–57, 62, 64–66, 68–69 from William I Thomas, *The Unadjusted Girl*. Boston: Little, Brown, and Company, 1931.

Classical Sociological Theory, Third Edition. Edited by Craig Calhoun, Joseph Gerteis, James Moody, Steven Pfaff, and Indermohan Virk. Editorial material and organization © 2012 John Wiley & Sons, Ltd. Published 2012 by John Wiley & Sons, Ltd.

actually not only concrete acts are dependent on the definition of the situation, but gradually a whole life-policy and the personality of the individual himself follow from a series of such definitions.

But the child is always born into a group of people among whom all the general types of situation which may arise have already been defined and corresponding rules of conduct developed, and where he has not the slightest chance of making his definitions and following his wishes without interference. Men have always lived together in groups. Whether mankind has a true herd instinct or whether groups are held together because this has worked out to advantage is of no importance. Certainly the wishes in general are such that they can be satisfied only in a society. But we have only to refer to the criminal code to appreciate the variety of ways in which the wishes of the individual may conflict with the wishes of society. And the criminal code takes no account of the many unsanctioned expressions of the wishes which society attempts to regulate by persuasion and gossip.

There is therefore always a rivalry between the spontaneous definitions of the situation made by the member of an organized society and the definitions which his society has provided for him. The individual tends to a hedonistic selection of activity, pleasure first; and society to a utilitarian selection, safety first. Society wishes its member to be laborious, dependable, regular, sober, orderly, self-sacrificing; while the individual wishes less of this and more of new experience. And organized society seeks also to regulate the conflict and competition inevitable between its members in the pursuit of their wishes. The desire to have wealth, for example, or any other socially sanctioned wish, may not be accomplished at the expense of another member of the society, – by murder, theft, lying, swindling, blackmail, etc.

It is in this connection that a moral code arises, which is a set of rules or behavior norms, regulating the expression of the wishes, and which is built up by successive definitions of the situation. In practice the abuse arises first and the rule is made to prevent its recurrence. Morality is thus the generally accepted definition of the situation, whether expressed in public opinion and the unwritten law, in a formal legal code, or in religious commandments and prohibitions.

The family is the smallest social unit and the primary defining agency. As soon as the child has free motion and begins to pull, tear, pry, meddle, and prowl, the parents begin to define the situation through speech and other signs and pressures: "Be quiet," "Sit up straight," "Blow your nose," "Wash your face," "Mind your mother," "Be kind to sister," etc. This is the real significance of Wordsworth's phrase, "Shades of the prison house begin to close upon the growing child." His wishes and activities begin to be inhibited, and gradually, by definitions within the family, by playmates, in the school, in the Sunday school, in the community, through reading, by formal instruction, by informal signs of approval and disapproval, the growing member learns the code of his society.

In addition to the family we have the community as a defining agency. At present the community is so weak and vague that it gives us no idea of the former power of the local group in regulating behavior. Originally the community was practically the whole world of its members. It was composed of families related by blood and marriage and was not so large that all the members could not come together; it was a face-to-face group. I asked a Polish peasant what was the extent of an *"okolica"* or neighborhood – how far if reached. "It reaches," he said, "as far as the report of a man reaches – as far as a man is talked about." And it was in communities of this kind that the moral code which we now recognize as valid originated. The customs of the community are "folkways," and both state and church have in their more formal codes mainly recognized and incorporated these folkways.

The typical community is vanishing and it would be neither possible nor desirable to restore it in its old form. It does not correspond with the present direction of social evolution and it would now be a distressing condition in which to live. But in the immediacy of relationships and the participation of everybody in everything, it represents an element which we have lost and which we shall probably have to restore in some form of cooperation in order to secure a balanced and normal society, – some arrangement corresponding with human nature.

Very elemental examples of the definition of the situation by the community as a whole, corresponding to mob action as we know it and to our trial by jury, are found among European peasants. The documents following, all relating to the Russian community or *mir*, give some idea of the conditions under which a whole community, a public, formerly defined a situation.

25. We who are unacquainted with peasant speech, manners and method of expressing thought – mimicry – if we should be present at a division of land or some settlement among the peasants, would never understand anything. Hearing fragmentary, disconnected exclamations, endless quarreling, with repetition of some single word; hearing this racket of a seemingly senseless, noisy crowd that counts up or measures off something, we should conclude that they would not get together, or arrive at any result in an age. ... Yet wait until the end and you will see that the division has been made with mathematical accuracy – that the measure, the quality of the soil, the slope of the field, the distance from the village – everything in short has been taken into account, that the reckoning has been correctly done and, what is most important, that every one of those present who were interested in the division is certain of the correctness of the division or settlement. The cry, the noise, the racket do not subside until every one is satisfied and no doubter is left.

The same thing is true concerning the discussion of some question by the *mir*. There are no speeches, no debates, no votes. They shout, they abuse each other, they seem on the point of coming to blows. Apparently they riot in the most senseless manner. Some one preserves silence, silence, and then suddenly puts in a word, one word, or an ejaculation, and by this word, this ejaculation, he turns the whole thing upside down. In the end, you look into it and find that an admirable decision has been formed and, what is most important, a unanimous decision.[1]

26. As I approached the village, there hung over it such a mixed, varied violent shouting, that no well brought-up parliament would agree to recognize itself, even in the abstract, as analogous to this gathering of peasant deputies. It was clearly a full meeting today. ... At other more quiet village meetings I had been able to make out very little, but this was a real lesson to me. I felt only a continuous, indistinguishable roaring in my ears, sometimes pierced by a particularly violent phrase that broke out

from the general roar. I saw in front of me the "immediate" man, in all his beauty. What struck me first of all was his remarkable frankness; the more "immediate" he is, the less able is he to mask his thoughts and feelings; once he is stirred up the emotion seizes him quickly and he flares up then and there, and does not quiet down till he has poured out before you all the substance of his soul. He does not feel embarrassment before anybody; there are no indications here of diplomacy. Further, he opens up his whole soul, and he will tell everything that he may ever have known about you, and not only about you, but about your father, grandfather, and great-grandfather. Here everything is clear water, as the peasants say, and everything stands out plainly. If any one, out of smallness of soul, or for some ulterior motive, thinks to get out of something by keeping silent, they force him out into clear water without pity. And there are very few such small-souled persons at important village meetings. I have seen the most peaceable, irresponsible peasants, who at other times would not have thought of saying a word against any one, absolutely changed at these meetings, at these moments of general excitement. They believed in the saying, "On people even death is beautiful," and they got up so much courage that they were able to answer back the peasants commonly recognized as audacious. At the moment of its height the meeting becomes simply an open mutual confessional and mutual disclosure, the display of the widest publicity. At these moments when, it would seem, the private interests of each reach the highest tension, public interests and justice in turn reach the highest degree of control.[2]

[...]

The essential point in reaching a communal decision, just as in the case of our jury system, is unanimity. In some cases the whole community mobilizes around a stubborn individual to conform him to the general wish.

> 28. It sometimes happens that all except one may agree but the motion is never carried if that one refuses to agree to it. In such cases all endeavor to talk over and persuade the stiff-necked one. Often they even call to their aid his wife, his children, his relatives, his father-in-law, and his mother, that they may prevail upon him to say yes. Then all assail him, and say to him from time to time: "Come now, God help you, agree with us too, that this may take place as we wish it, that the house may not be cast into disorder, that we may not be talked about by the people, that the neighbors may not hear of it, that the world may not make sport of us!" It seldom occurs in such cases that unanimity is not attained.[3]

A less formal but not less powerful means of defining the situation employed by the community is gossip. The Polish peasant's statement that a community reaches as far as a man is talked about was significant, for the community regulates the behavior of its members largely by talking about them. Gossip has a bad name because it is sometimes malicious and false and designed to improve the status of the gossiper and degrade its object, but gossip is in the main true and is an organizing force. It is a mode of defining the situation in a given case and of attaching praise or blame. It is one of the means by which the status of the individual and of his family is fixed.

The community also, particularly in connection with gossip, knows how to attach opprobrium to persons and actions by using epithets which are at the same time brief and emotional definitions of the situation. "Bastard," "whore," "traitor," "coward," "skunk," "scab," "snob," "kike," etc., are such epithets. In "Faust" the community said of Margaret, "She stinks." The people are here employing a device known in psychology as the "conditioned reflex." If, for example, you place before a child (say six months old) an agreeable object, a kitten, and at the same time pinch the child, and if this is repeated several times, the child will immediately cry at the sight of the kitten without being pinched; or if a dead rat were always served beside a man's plate of soup he would eventually have a disgust for soup when served separately. If the word "stinks" is associated on people's tongues with Margaret, Margaret will never again smell sweet. Many evil consequences, as the psychoanalysts claim, have resulted from making the whole of sex life a "dirty" subject, but the device has worked in a powerful, sometimes a paralyzing way on the sexual behavior of women.

Winks, shrugs, nudges, laughter, sneers, haughtiness, coldness, "giving the once over" are also language defining the situation and painfully felt as unfavorable recognition. The sneer, for example, is incipient vomiting, meaning, "you make me sick."

And eventually the violation of the code even in an act of no intrinsic importance, as in carrying food to the mouth with the knife, provokes condemnation and disgust. The fork is not a better instrument for conveying food than the knife, at least it has no moral superiority, but the situation has been defined in favor of the fork. To smack with the lips in eating is bad manners with us, but the Indian has more logically defined the situation in the opposite way; with him smacking is acompliment to the host.

In this whole connection fear is used by the group to produce the desired attitudes in its member. Praise is used also but more sparingly, And the whole body of habits and emotions is so much a community and family product that disapproval or separation is almost unbearable. [...]

As far as possible the family regulates its affairs within itself without appealing to the community and thus subjecting itself to gossip. Situations arising within the family where members are not in agreement, where a conflict of wishes is involved, are defined through argument, ordering and forbidding, remonstrance, reproof, entreaty, sulking, tears, and beatings. But as a last resort a member of a family may provoke gossip, appeal to the community. In case No. 32 the woman defines the situation to her deserting husband publicly. She does it very tactfully. She uses every art, reminder, and appreciation to influence his return. She wishes to avoid a public scandal, reminds him of the noble professions he has always made as man and father, pictures the children as grieving and herself as ashamed to let them know, and believes that he is fundamentally a fine man who has had a moment of weakness or suffered a temporary madness – so she says. In addition the powerful newspaper through which she seeks publicity will define the situation to the erring husband. Presumably he will return.

32. I come to you with the request that you will write a few words to my husband. He has a high opinion of the answers that you give in *Bintel Brief* and I hope that some

words from you will have a good effect on him so that we shall be able to avoid a public scandal. In the meantime I am containing my troubles but if matters get worse I shall have to turn to people for help. I will say that my husband and I always lived a good life together. He always condemned in the strongest terms those fathers who leave their children to God's mercy. "Children," he said, "are innocent and we must take care not to make them unhappy" – that was the way he always talked. And now he has himself done what he always condemned and regarded as the greatest meanness.

The last night before he went away my husband kissed our youngest daughter so much that she is now sick from longing for him. The older girl is continually asking, "When will father come?" I am frightfully upset by the unexpected misfortune which has struck me.

Dear editor, I have the greatest confidence in the goodness of my husband. Perhaps he has lost his reason for a time, but he is not corrupt. I am almost sure that when he reads my letter he will come back to his senses and will behave as a man and as a decent person should behave. I beg you to print my letter as soon as possible and help to restore a broken family.[4]

Contrary to this we have the device of public confession, a definition of the situation in terms of self-condemnation. The following is a public apology which gives the injured husband favorable public recognition and seeks a reconciliation.

33. I myself drove out my good and true husband in a shameful manner and placed the guilt at his door, and although he is angry he is decent enough not to say anything to anybody. He takes the blame on himself. All my friends and acquaintances think that he is really the guilty one.

I have been married for the last eleven years and up to two years ago I thought that somehow I should end my life peacefully, although I have caused many a quarrel. … My tongue is sharp and burning. … My husband always forgave me. Many times he cried and a week or two would pass by quietly. And then again I could not be quiet. Quite often I would start to fire away at the table and he would get up, leave the house, and go to a restaurant. When he returned he had some more. And according to my behavior my husband began to treat me roughly. …

At this time we tried business for ourselves … and owing to numerous reasons my husband had everything in my name; I was the owner of everything that we had. After that I began to rule over him still more, and when he saw that he could do nothing with me he stopped speaking to me.

I have tried everything to dirty his name. Oh, now my conscience troubles me when I see three live orphans wandering about. Would it not be better if the community had forbidden me to marry in order to avoid such a family-tragedy.

I am a snake by nature and this is not my fault; that's how I am. My friends meet him and they tell me that he does not say a word about our tragedy. He says: "I am doing the best that I can and when I am able to give a home to my children, then I will worry about them." And I am afraid that some day he will take away the children from me and then I shall be left alone like a stone.[5]

The priests in Poland say that if all the influences of the community are active – the family, the priest, the friends, and neighbors – there are few necessarily bad men.

They say also that communities tend to be all good or all bad, and that this is determined largely by majorities. If a community is good the priest thunders from the chancel against any symptom of badness; if it is already bad he praises and encourages any little manifestation of goodness. In examining the letters between immigrants in America and their home communities I have noticed that the great solicitude of the family and community is that the absent member shall not change. Absence and the resulting outside influence are dreaded as affecting the solidarity of the group. And the typical immigrant letter is an assurance and reminder that the writer, though absent, is still a member of the community. [...]

The following passages picture the life of a young American girl of the middle of the last century where the whole community is coöperating with the family to standardize her. Her parents are dead but the influences are complete without them. She is met at every turn with definitions of the situation which in this case are rigid but of the most genial and affectionate character. She does not lose her personality because that is in her nature; she is alert and witty, like her grandmother. If there were no disturbance of the situation she would become such an old woman as her grandmother is. The outside world is, however, beginning to press in. The situation has already been defined to her in terms of "woman's rights."

36. *November 21, 1852.* – I am ten years old today, and I will write a journal and tell who I am and what I am doing. I have lived with my Grandfather and Grandmother Beals ever since I was seven years old, and Anna, too, since she was four. [...]
Sunday. – I almost forgot that it was Sunday this morning and talked and laughed just as I do week days. Grandmother told me to write down this verse before I went to church so I would remember it: "Keep thy foot when thou goest to the house of God, and be more ready to hear than to offer the sacrifice of fools." I will remember it now, sure. My feet are all right anyway with my new patten leather shoes on, but I shall have to look out for my head. Mr. Thomas Howell read a sermon today as Mr. Daggett is out of town. Grandmother always comes upstairs to get the candle and tuck us in before she goes to bed herself, and some nights we are sound asleep and do not hear her, but last night we only pretended to be asleep. She kneeled down by the bed and prayed aloud for us, that we might be good children and that she might have strength given her from on high to guide us in the straight and narrow path which leads to life eternal. Those were her very words. After she had gone down-stairs we sat up in bed and talked about it and promised each other to be good, and crossed our hearts and "hoped to die," if we broke our promise. Then Anna was afraid we would die, but I told her I didn't believe we would be as good as that, so we kissed each other and went to sleep.
Sunday. – Rev. Mr. Tousley preached today to the children and told us how many steps it took to be bad. I think he said lying was first, then disobedience to parents, breaking the Sabbath, swearing, stealing, drunkenness. I don't remember just the order they came. It was very interesting, for he told lots of stories and we sang a great many times. I should think Eddy Tousley would be an awful good boy with his father in the house with him all the while, but probably he has to be away part of the time preaching to other children.

December 20, 1855. – Susan B. Anthony is in town and spoke in Bemis Hall this afternoon. She made a special request that all the seminary girls should come to hear her as well as all the women and girls in town. She had a large audience and she talked very plainly about our rights and how we ought to stand up for them, and said the world would never go right until the women had just as much right to vote and rule as the men. She asked us all to come up and sign our names who would promise to do all in our power to bring about that glad day when equal rights would be the law of the land. A whole lot of us went up and signed the paper. When I told Grandmother about it she said she guessed Susan B. Anthony had forgotten that St. Paul said the women should keep silence. I told her no, she didn't, for she spoke particularly about St. Paul and said if he had lived in these times, instead of eighteen hundred years ago, he would have been as anxious to have the women at the head of the government as she was. I could not make Grandmother agree with her at all and she said we might better all of us stayed at home. [...]

May, 1856. – We were invited to Bessie Seymour's party last night and Grandmother said we could go. The girls all told us at school that they were going to wear low neck and short sleeves. We have caps on the sleeves of our best dresses and we tried to get the sleeves out, so we could go bare arms, but we couldn't get them out. We had a very nice time, though, at the party. Some of the Academy boys were there and they asked us to dance but of course we couldn't do that. We promenaded around the rooms and went out to supper with them. Eugene Stone and Tom Eddy asked to go home with us but Grandmother sent our two girls for us, Bridget Flynn and Hannah White, so they couldn't. We were quite disappointed, but perhaps she won't send for us next time.[7]

At the best no society has ever succeeded in regulating the behavior of all its members satisfactorily all the time. There are crimes of passion, of avarice, of revenge, even in face-to-face communities where the control is most perfect. In the Hebrew code there were ten offenses for which the punishment was death by stoning. One of the examples cited above from the Russian *mir* was concerned with horse stealing. And the sexual passions have never been completely contained within the framework of marriage. But communities have been so powerful that all members have acknowledged the code and have been ready to repent and be forgiven. And forgiveness has been one of the functions of the community, sometimes more particularly the function of the God of the community. A dying reprobate (the anecdote is attached to Rabelais) has been represented as saying, "*Dieu me pardonnera. C'est son métier.*" The community usually wishes to forgive and restore the offending member. It wants no breach in its solidarity and morale. And as long as the offender wishes to be forgiven and restored the code is working. The code is failing only if the sinner does not recognize it and does not repent. And when crime and prostitution appear as professions they are the last and most radical expressions of loss of family and community organization.

NOTES

1   A. N. Engelgardt: "Iz Derevni: 12 Pisem" ("From the Country; 12 Letters"), p. 315.
2   N. N. Zlatovratsky: "Ocherki Krestyanskoy Obshchiny" ("Sketches of the Peasant Commune"), p. 127.

3 F. S. Krauss: "Sitte und Brauch der Südslaven," p. 103.
4 *Forward*, July 9, 1920.
5 *Forward*, February 6, 1914.
6 *Forward*, November 26, 1920.
7 Caroline C. Richards: "Village Life in America," pp. 21–188, *passim*. New York, Henry Holt and Company. Reprinted by permission. Quoted by R. E. Park and E. W. Burgess: "Introduction to the Science of Sociology," p. 305.

Chapter 32

Traditional and Critical Theory [1937]

Max Horkheimer

What is "theory"? The question seems a rather easy one for contemporary science. Theory for most researchers is the sum-total of propositions about a subject, the propositions being so linked with each other that a few are basic and the rest derive from these. The smaller the number of primary principles in comparison with the derivations, the more perfect the theory. The real validity of the theory depends on the derived propositions being consonant with the actual facts. If experience and theory contradict each other, one of the two must be reexamined. Either the scientist has failed to observe correctly or something is wrong with the principles of the theory. [...]

The derivation as usually practiced in mathematics is to be applied to all science. The order in the world is captured by a deductive chain of thought.

> Those long chains of deductive reasoning, simple and easy as they are, of which geometricians make use in order to arrive at the most difficult demonstrations, had caused me to imagine that all those things which fall under the cognizance of men might very likely be mutually related in the same fashion; and that, provided only that we abstain from receiving anything as true which is not so, and always retain the order which is necessary in order to deduce the one conclusion from the other, there can be nothing so remote that we cannot reach to it, nor so recondite that we cannot discover it.[1]

Horkheimer, Max, "Traditional and Critical Theory," pp.188–243 from Max Horkheimer, *Critical Theory: Selected Essays*. New York: Herder and Herder, Inc., 1972. English translation copyright © 1972 by Herder & Herder. Reprinted by permission of The Copyright Clearance Center on behalf of The Continuum Publishing Group.

Classical Sociological Theory, Third Edition. Edited by Craig Calhoun, Joseph Gerteis, James Moody, Steven Pfaff, and Indermohan Virk. Editorial material and organization © 2012 John Wiley & Sons, Ltd. Published 2012 by John Wiley & Sons, Ltd.

Depending on the logician's own general philosophical outlook, the most universal propositions from which the deduction begins are themselves regarded as experiential judgments, as inductions (as with John Stuart Mill), as evident insights (as in rationalist and phenomenological schools), or as arbitrary postulates (as in the modern axiomatic approach). In the most advanced logic of the present time, as represented by Husserl's *Logische Untersuchungen*, theory is defined "as an enclosed system of propositions for a science as a whole."[2] Theory in the fullest sense is "a systematically linked set of propositions, taking the form of a systematically unified deduction."[3] Science is "a certain totality of propositions ..., emerging in one or other manner from theoretical work, in the systematic order of which propositions a certain totality of objects acquires definition."[4] The basic requirement which any theoretical system must satisfy is that all the parts should intermesh thoroughly and without friction. Harmony, which includes lack of contradictions, and the absence of superfluous, purely dogmatic elements which have no influence on the observable phenomena, are necessary conditions, according to Weyl.[5]

In so far as this traditional conception of theory shows a tendency, it is towards a purely mathematical system of symbols. As elements of the theory, as components of the propositions and conclusions, there are ever fewer names of experiential objects and ever more numerous mathematical symbols. Even the logical operations themselves have already been so rationalized that, in large areas of natural science at least, theory formation has become a matter of mathematical construction.

The sciences of man and society have attempted to follow the lead of the natural sciences with their great successes. The difference between those schools of social science which are more oriented to the investigation of facts and those which concentrate more on principles has nothing directly to do with the concept of theory as such. The assiduous collecting of facts in all the disciplines dealing with social life, the gathering of great masses of detail in connection with problems, the empirical inquiries, through careful questionnaires and other means, which are a major part of scholarly activity, especially in the Anglo-Saxon universities since Spencer's time – all this adds up to a pattern which is, outwardly, much like the rest of life in a society dominated by industrial production techniques. [...]

There can be no doubt, in fact, that the various schools of sociology have an identical conception of theory and that it is the same as theory in the natural sciences. Empirically oriented sociologists have the same idea of what a fully elaborated theory should be as their theoretically oriented brethren. The former, indeed, are persuaded that in view of the complexity of social problems and the present state of science any concern with general principles must be regarded as indolent and idle. If theoretical work is to be done, it must be done with an eye unwaveringly on the facts; there can be no thought in the foreseeable future of comprehensive theoretical statements. These scholars are much enamored of the methods of exact formulation and, in particular, of mathematical procedures, which are especially congenial to the conception of theory described above. [...] There is always, on the one hand, the conceptually formulated knowledge and, on the other, the facts to be subsumed under it. Such a subsumption or establishing of a relation between the simple perception or verification of a fact and the conceptual structure of our knowing is called its theoretical explanation.

[...] For Weber, the historian's explanations, like those of the expert in criminal law, rest not on the fullest possible enumeration of all pertinent circumstances but on the establishment of a connection between those elements of an event which are significant for historical continuity, and particular, determinative happenings. This connection, for example the judgment that a war resulted from the policies of a statesman who knew what he was about, logically supposes that, had such a policy not existed, some other effect would have followed. If one maintains a particular causal nexus between historical events, one is necessarily implying that had the nexus not existed, then in accordance with the rules that govern our experience another effect would have followed in the given circumstances. The rules of experience here are nothing but the formulations of our knowledge concerning economic, social, and psychological interconnections. With the help of these we reconstruct the probable course of events, going beyond the event itself to what will serve as explanation.[6] We are thus working with conditional propositions as applied to a given situation. If circumstances a, b, c, and d are given, then event q must be expected; if d is lacking, event r; if g is added, event s, and so on. This kind of calculation is a logical tool of history as it is of science. It is in this fashion that theory in the traditional sense is actually elaborated.

What scientists in various fields regard as the essence of theory thus corresponds, in fact, to the immediate tasks they set for themselves. The manipulation of physical nature and of specific economic and social mechanisms demand alike the amassing of a body of knowledge such as is supplied in an ordered set of hypotheses. The technological advances of the bourgeois period are inseparably linked to this function of the pursuit of science. On the one hand, it made the facts fruitful for the kind of scientific knowledge that would have practical application in the circumstances, and, on the other, it made possible the application of knowledge already possessed. Beyond doubt, such work is a moment in the continuous transformation and development of the material foundations of that society. But the conception of theory was absolutized, as though it were grounded in the inner nature of knowledge as such or justified in some other ahistorical way, and thus it became a reified, ideological category.

As a matter of fact, the fruitfulness of newly discovered factual connections for the renewal of existent knowledge, and the application of such knowledge to the facts, do not derive from purely logical or methodological sources but can rather be understood only in the context of real social processes. When a discovery occasions the restructuring of current ideas, this is not due exclusively to logical considerations or, more particularly, to the contradiction between the discovery and particular elements in current views. If this were the only real issue, one could always think up further hypotheses by which one could avoid changing the theory as a whole. That new views in fact win out is due to concrete historical circumstances, even if the scientist himself may be determined to change his views only by immanent motives.

Modern theoreticians of knowledge do not deny the importance of historical circumstance, even if among the most influential nonscientific factors they assign more importance to genius and accident than to social conditions. [...]

The traditional idea of theory is based on scientific activity as carried on within the division of labor at a particular stage in the latter's development. It corresponds to the activity of the scholar which takes place alongside all the other activities of a society but in no immediately clear connection with them. In this view of theory, therefore, the real social function of science is not made manifest; it speaks not of what theory means in human life, but only of what it means in the isolated sphere in which for historical reasons it comes into existence. Yet as a matter of fact the life of society is the result of all the work done in the various sectors of production. Even if therefore the division of labor in the capitalist system functions but poorly, its branches, including science, do not become for that reason self-sufficient and independent. They are particular instances of the way in which society comes to grips with nature and maintains its own inherited form. They are moments in the social process of production, even if they be almost or entirely unproductive in the narrower sense. Neither the structures of industrial and agrarian production nor the separation of the so-called guiding and executory functions, services, and works, or of intellectual and manual operations are eternal or natural states of affairs. They emerge rather from the mode of production practiced in particular forms of society. The seeming self-sufficiency enjoyed by work processes whose course is supposedly determined by the very nature of the object corresponds to the seeming freedom of the economic subject in bourgeois society. The latter believe they are acting according to personal determinations, whereas in fact even in their most complicated calculations they but exemplify the working of an incalculable social mechanism. [...]

The whole perceptible world as present to a member of bourgeois society and as interpreted within a traditional worldview which is in continuous interaction with that given world, is seen by the perceiver as a sum-total of facts; it is there and must be accepted. The classificatory thinking of each individual is one of those social reactions by which men try to adapt to reality in a way that best meets their needs. But there is at this point an essential difference between the individual and society. The world which is given to the individual and which he must accept and take into account is, in its present and continuing form, a product of the activity of society as a whole. The objects we perceive in our surroundings – cities, villages, fields, and woods – bear the mark of having been worked on by man. It is not only in clothing and appearance, in outward form and emotional make-up that men are the product of history. Even the way they see and hear is inseparable from the social life-process as it has evolved over the millennia. The facts which our senses present to us are socially preformed in two ways: through the historical character of the object perceived and through the historical character of the perceiving organ. Both are not simply natural; they are shaped by human activity, and yet the individual perceives himself as receptive and passive in the act of perception. The opposition of passivity and activity, which appears in knowledge theory as a dualism of sense-perception and understanding, does not hold for society, however, in the same measure as for the individual. The individual sees himself as passive and dependent, but society, though made up of individuals, is an active subject, even if a nonconscious one and, to that extent, a subject only in an improper sense. This difference in the existence of man and society is an expression of the cleavage which has up to now affected the historical forms of social life. The existence of society has either been founded directly on oppression or been the blind outcome of conflicting forces, but in any event not the result of conscious spontaneity on the part of free individuals. Therefore the meaning of "activity" and "passivity" changes according as these concepts are applied to society or to individual. In the bourgeois economic mode the activity of society is blind and concrete, that of individuals abstract and conscious.

Human production also always has an element of planning to it. To the extent then that the facts which the individual and his theory encounter are socially produced, there must be rationality in them, even if in a restricted sense. But social action always involves, in addition, available knowledge and its application. The perceived fact is therefore co-determined by human ideas and concepts, even before its conscious theoretical elaboration by the knowing individual. Nor are we to think here only of experiments in natural science. The so-called purity of objective event to be achieved by the experimental procedure is, of course, obviously connected with technological conditions, and the connection of these in turn with the material process of production is evident. But it is easy here to confuse two questions: the question of the mediation of the factual through the activity of society as a whole, and the question of the influence of the measuring instrument, that is, of a particular action, upon the object being observed. The latter problem, which continually plagues physics, is no more closely connected with the problem that concerns us here than is the problem of perception generally, including perception in everyday life. Man's physiological apparatus for sensation itself largely anticipates the order followed in physical experiment. As man reflectively records reality, he separates and rejoins pieces of it, and concentrates on some particulars while failing to notice others. This process is just as much a result of the modern mode of production, as the perception of a man in a tribe of primitive hunters and fishers is the result of the conditions of his existence (as well, of course, as of the object of perception). [...]

At least Kant understood that behind the discrepancy between fact and theory which the scholar experiences in his professional work, there lies a deeper unity, namely, the general subjectivity upon which individual knowledge depends. The activity of society thus appears to be a transcendental power, that is, the sum-total of spiritual factors. However, Kant's claim that its reality is sunk in obscurity, that is, that it is irrational despite all its rationality, is not without its kernel of truth. The bourgeois type of economy, despite all the ingenuity of the competing individuals within it, is not governed by any plan; it is not consciously directed to a general goal; the life of society as a whole proceeds from this economy only at the cost of excessive friction, in a stunted form, and almost, as it were, accidentally. The internal difficulties in the supreme concepts of Kantian philosophy, especially the ego of transcendental subjectivity, pure or original apperception, and consciousness-in-itself, show the depth and honesty of his thinking. The two-sidedness of these Kantian concepts, that is, their supreme unity and purposefulness, on the one hand, and their obscurity, unknownness, and impenetrability, on the other, reflects exactly the contradiction-filled form of human activity in the modern period. The collaboration of men in society is the mode of existence which reason urges upon them, and so they do apply their powers and thus confirm their own rationality. But at the same time their work and its results are alienated from them, and the whole process with all its waste of work-power and human life, and with its wars and all its senseless wretchedness, seems to be an unchangeable force of nature, a fate beyond man's control. [...]

We must go on now to add that there is a human activity which has society itself for its object.[7] The aim of this activity is not simply to eliminate one or other abuse, for it regards such abuses as necessarily connected with the way in which the social structure is organized. Although it itself emerges from the social structure, its purpose is not, either in its conscious intention or in its objective significance, the better functioning of any element in the structure. On the contrary, it is suspicious of the very categories of better, useful, appropriate, productive, and valuable, as these are understood in the present order, and refuses to take them as nonscientific presuppositions about which one can do nothing. The individual as a rule must simply accept the basic conditions of his existence as given and strive to fulfill them; he finds his satisfaction and praise in accomplishing as well as he can the tasks connected with his place in society and in courageously doing his duty despite all the sharp criticism he may choose to exercise in particular matters. But the critical attitude of which we are speaking is wholly distrustful of the rules of conduct with which society as presently constituted provides each of its members. The separation between individual and society in virtue of which the individual accepts as natural the limits prescribed for his activity is relativized in critical theory. The latter considers the overall framework which is conditioned by the blind interaction of individual activities (that is, the existent division of labor and the class distinctions) to be a function which originates in human action and therefore is a possible object of planful decision and rational determination of goals.

The two-sided character of the social totality in its present form becomes, for men who adopt the critical attitude, a conscious opposition. In recognizing the present form of economy and the whole culture which it generates to be the product of human work as well as the organization which mankind was capable of and has provided for itself in the present era, these men identify themselves with this totality and conceive it as will and reason. It is their own world. At the same time, however, they experience the fact that society is comparable to nonhuman natural processes, to pure mechanisms, because cultural forms which are supported by war and oppression are not the creations of a unified, self-conscious will. That world is not their own but the world of capital.

Previous history thus cannot really be understood; only the individuals and specific groups in it are intelligible, and even these not totally, since their internal dependence on an inhuman society means that even in their conscious action such individuals and groups are still in good measure mechanical functions. The identification, then, of men of critical mind with their society is marked by tension, and the tension characterizes all the concepts of the critical way of thinking. Thus, such thinkers interpret the economic categories of work, value, and productivity exactly as they are interpreted in the existing order, and they regard any other interpretation as pure idealism. But at the same time they consider it rank dishonesty simply to accept the interpretation; the critical acceptance of the categories which rule social life contains simultaneously their condemnation. This dialectical character of the self-interpretation of contemporary man is what, in the last analysis, also causes the obscurity of the Kantian critique of reason. Reason cannot become transparent to itself as long as men act as members of an organism which lacks reason. Organism as a naturally developing and declining unity cannot be a sort of model for society, but only a form of deadened existence from which society must emancipate itself. An attitude which aims at such an emancipation and at an alteration of society as a whole might well be of service in theoretical work carried on within reality as presently ordered. But it lacks the pragmatic character which attaches to traditional thought as a socially useful professional activity.

In traditional theoretical thinking, the genesis of particular objective facts, the practical application of the conceptual systems by which it grasps the facts, and the role of such systems in action, are all taken to be external to the theoretical thinking itself. This alienation, which finds expression in philosophical terminology as the separation of value and research, knowledge and action, and other polarities, protects the savant from the tensions we have indicated and provides an assured framework for his activity. Yet a kind of thinking which does not accept this framework seems to have the ground taken out from under it. [...]

... Its opposition to the traditional concept of theory springs in general from a difference not so much of objects as of subjects. For men of the critical mind, the facts, as they emerge from the work of society, are not extrinsic in the same degree as they are for the savant or for members of other professions who all think like little savants. The latter look towards a new kind of organization of work. But in so far as the objective realities given in perception are conceived as products which in principle should be under human control and, in the future at least, will in fact come under it, these realities lose the character of pure factuality.

The scholarly specialist "as" scientist regards social reality and its products as extrinsic to him, and "as" citizen exercises his interest in them through political articles, membership in political parties or social service organizations, and participation in elections. But he does not unify these two activities, and his other activities as well, except, at best, by psychological interpretation. Critical thinking, on the contrary, is motivated today by the effort really to transcend the tension and to abolish the opposition between the individual's purposefulness, spontaneity, and rationality, and those work-process relationships on which society is built. Critical thought has a concept of man as in conflict with himself until this opposition is removed. If activity governed by reason is proper to man, then existent social practice, which forms the individual's life down to its least details, is inhuman, and this inhumanity affects everything that goes on in the society. There will always be something that is extrinsic to man's intellectual and material activity, namely nature as the totality of as yet unmastered elements with which society must deal. But when situations which really depend on man alone, the relationships of men in their work, and the course of man's own history are also accounted part of "nature," the resultant extrinsicality is not only not a suprahistorical eternal category (even pure nature in the sense described is not that), but it is a sign of contemptible weakness. To surrender to such weakness is nonhuman and irrational. [...]

Critical thought and its theory are opposed to both the types of thinking just described. Critical thinking is the function neither of the isolated individual nor of a sum-total of individuals. Its subject is rather a definite individual in his real relation to other individuals and groups, in his conflict with a particular class, and, finally, in the resultant web of relationships with the social totality and with nature. [...]

How is critical thought related to experience? One might maintain that if such thought were not simply to classify but also to determine for itself the goals which classification serves, in other words its own fundamental direction, it would remain locked up within itself, as happened to idealist philosophy. If it did not take refuge in utopian fantasy, it would be reduced to the formalistic fighting of sham battles. The attempt legitimately to determine practical goals by thinking must always fail. If thought were not content with the role given to it in existent society, if it were not to engage in theory in the traditional sense of the word, it would necessarily have to return to illusions long since laid bare.

The fault in such reflections as these on the role of thought is that thinking is understood in a detachedly departmentalized and therefore spiritualist way, as it is today under existing conditions of the division of labor. ... Now, inasmuch as every individual in modern times has been required to make his own the purposes of society as a whole and to recognize these in society, there is the possibility that men would become aware of and concentrate their attention upon the path which the social work process has taken without any definite theory behind it, as a result of disparate forces interacting, and with the despair of the masses acting as a decisive factor at major turning points. Thought does not spin such a possibility out of itself but rather becomes aware of its own proper function. In the course of history men have come to know their own activity and thus to recognize the contradiction that marks their existence. [...]

Yet, as far as the role of experience is concerned, there is a difference between traditional and critical theory. The viewpoints which the latter derives from historical analysis as the goals of human activity, especially the idea of a reasonable organization of society that will meet the needs of the whole community, are immanent in human work but are not correctly grasped by individuals or by the common mind. A certain concern is also required if these tendencies are to be perceived and expressed. According to Marx and Engels such a concern is necessarily generated in the proletariat. [...]

But it must be added that even the situation of the proletariat is, in this society, no guarantee of correct knowledge. The proletariat may indeed have experience of meaninglessness in the form of continuing and increasing wretchedness and injustice in its own life. Yet this awareness is prevented from becoming a social force by the differentiation of social structure which is still imposed on the proletariat from above and by the opposition between personal class interests which is transcended only at very special moments. Even to the proletariat the world superficially seems quite different than it really is. Even an outlook which could grasp that no opposition really exists between the proletariat's own true interests and those of society as a whole, and would therefore derive its principles of action from the thoughts and feelings of the masses, would fall into slavish dependence on the status quo. The intellectual is satisfied to proclaim with reverent admiration the creative strength of the proletariat and finds satisfaction in adapting himself to it and in canonizing it. He fails to see that such an evasion of theoretical effort (which the passivity of his own thinking spares him) and of temporary opposition to the masses (which active theoretical effort on his part might force upon him) only makes the masses blinder and weaker than they need be. His own thinking should in fact be a critical, promotive factor in the development of the masses. [...]

If critical theory consisted essentially in formulations of the feelings and ideas of one class at any given moment, it would not be structurally different from the special branches of science. It would be engaged in describing the psychological contents typical of certain social groups; it would be social psychology. The relation of being to consciousness is different in different classes of society. If we take seriously the ideas by which the bourgeoisie explains its own order – free exchange, free competition, harmony of interests, and so on – and if we follow them to their logical conclusion, they manifest their inner contradiction and therewith their real opposition to the bourgeois order. The simple description of bourgeois self-awareness thus does not give us the truth about this class of men. Similarly, a systematic presentation of the contents of proletarian consciousness cannot provide a true picture of proletarian existence and interests. [...]

If, however, the theoretician and his specific object are seen as forming a dynamic unity with the oppressed class, so that his presentation of societal contradictions is not merely an expression of the concrete historical situation but also a force within it to stimulate change, then his real function emerges. The course of the conflict between the advanced sectors of the class and the individuals who speak out the truth concerning it, as well as of the conflict between the most advanced sectors with their theoreticians and the rest of the class, is to be understood as a process of interactions in which awareness comes to flower along with its liberating but also its aggressive forces which incite while also requiring discipline. The sharpness of the conflict shows in the ever present possibility of tension between the theoretician and the class which his thinking is to serve. The unity of the social forces which promise liberation is at the same time their distinction (in Hegel's sense); it exists only as a conflict which continually threatens the subjects caught up in it. This truth becomes clearly evident in the person of the theoretician; he exercises an aggressive critique not only against the conscious defenders of the status quo but also against distracting, conformist, or utopian tendencies within his own household. [...]

One thing which this way of thinking has in common with fantasy is that an image of the future which springs indeed from a deep understanding of the present determines men's thoughts and actions even in periods when the course of events seems to be leading far away from such a future and seems to justify every reaction except belief in fulfillment. It is not the arbitrariness and supposed independence of fantasy that is the common bond here, but its obstinacy. Within the most advanced group it is the theoretician who must have this obstinacy. The theoretician of the ruling class, perhaps after difficult beginnings, may reach a relatively assured position, but, on the other hand, the theoretician is also at times an enemy and criminal, at times a solitary utopian; even after his death the question of what he really was is not decided. The historical significance of his work is not self-evident; it rather depends on men speaking and acting in such a way as to justify it. It is not a finished and fixed historical creation. [...]

Our consideration of the various functions of traditional and critical theory brings to light the difference in their logical structure. The primary propositions of traditional theory define universal concepts under which all facts in the field in question are to be subsumed; for example, the concept of a physical process in physics or an organic process in biology. [...]

The critical theory of society also begins with abstract determinations; in dealing with the present era it begins with the characterization of an economy based on exchange.[8] The concepts Marx uses, such as commodity, value, and money, can function as genera when, for example, concrete social relations are judged to be relations of exchange and when there is question of the commodity character of goods. But the theory is not satisfied to relate concepts of reality by way of hypotheses. The theory begins with an outline of the mechanism by which bourgeois society, after dismantling feudal regulations, the guild system, and vassalage, did not immediately fall apart under the pressure of its own anarchic principle but managed to survive. The regulatory effects of exchange are brought out on which bourgeois economy is founded. The conception of the interaction of society and nature, which is already exercising its influence here, as well as the idea of a unified period of society, of its self-preservation, and so on, spring from a radical analysis, guided by concern for the future, of the historical process. The relation of the primary conceptual interconnections to the world of facts is not essentially a relation of classes to instances. It is because of its inner dynamism that the exchange relationship, which the theory outlines, dominates social reality, as, for example, the assimilation of food largely dominates the organic life of plant and brute beast. [...]

Thus the critical theory of society begins with the idea of the simple exchange of commodities and defines the idea with the help of relatively universal concepts. It then moves further, using all knowledge available and taking suitable material from the research of others as well as from specialized research. Without denying its own principles as established by the special discipline of political economy, the theory shows how an exchange economy, given the condition of men (which, of course, changes under the very influence of such an economy), must necessarily lead to a heightening of those social tensions which in the present historical era lead in turn to wars and revolutions.

The necessity just mentioned, as well as the abstractness of the concepts, are both like and unlike the same phenomena in traditional theory. In both types of theory there is a strict deduction if the claim of validity for general definitions is shown to include a claim that certain factual relations will occur. For example, if you are dealing with electricity, such and such an event must occur because such and such characteristics belong to the very concept of electricity. To the extent that the critical theory of society deduces present conditions from the concept of simple exchange, it includes this kind of necessity, although it is relatively unimportant that the hypothetical form of statement be used. That is, the stress is not on the idea that wherever a society based on simple exchange prevails, capitalism must develop – although this is true. The stress is rather on the fact that the existent capitalist society, which has spread all over the world from Europe and for which the theory is declared valid, derives from the basic relation of exchange. Even the classificatory judgments of specialized science have a fundamentally hypothetical character, and existential judgments are allowed, if at all, only in certain areas, namely the descriptive and practical parts of the discipline.[9] But the critical theory of society is, in its totality, the unfolding of a single existential judgment. To put it in broad terms, the theory says that the basic form of the historically given commodity economy on which modern history rests contains in itself the internal and external tensions of the modern era; it generates these tensions over and over again in an increasingly heightened form; and after a period of progress, development of human powers, and emancipation for the individual, after an enormous extension of human control over nature, it finally hinders further development and drives humanity into a new barbarism. ...

Even the critical theory, which stands in opposition to other theories, derives its statements about real relationships from basic universal concepts, as we have indicated, and therefore presents the relationships as necessary. Thus both kinds of theoretical structure are alike when it comes to logical necessity. But there is a difference as soon as we turn from logical to real necessity, the necessity involved in factual sequences. The biologist's statement that internal processes cause a plant to wither or that certain processes in the human organism lead to its destruction leaves untouched the question whether any influences can alter the character of these processes or change them totally. Even when an illness is said to be curable, the fact that the necessary curative measures are actually taken is regarded as purely extrinsic to the curability, a matter of technology and therefore nonessential as far as the theory as such is concerned. The necessity which rules society can be regarded as biological in the sense described, and the unique character of critical theory can therefore be called in question on the grounds that in biology as in other natural sciences particular sequences of events can be theoretically constructed just as they are in the critical theory of society. The development of society, in this view, would simply be a particular series of events, for the presentation of which conclusions from various other areas of research are used, just as a doctor in the course of an illness or a geologist dealing with the earth's prehistory has to apply various other disciplines. Society here would be the individual reality which is evaluated on the basis of theories in the special sciences.

However many valid analogies there may be between these different intellectual endeavors, there is nonetheless a decisive difference when it comes to the relation of subject and object and therefore to the necessity of the event being judged. The object with which the scientific specialist deals is not affected at all by his own theory. Subject and object are kept strictly apart. Even if it turns out that at a later point in time the objective event is influenced by human intervention, to science this is just another fact. The objective occurrence is independent of the theory, and this independence is part of its necessity: the observer as such can effect no change in the object. A consciously critical attitude, however, is part of the development of society: the construing of the course of history as the necessary product of an economic mechanism simultaneously contains both a protest against this order of things, a protest generated by the order itself, and the idea of self-determination for the human race, that is the idea of a state of affairs in which man's actions no longer flow from a mechanism but from his own decision. The judgment passed on the necessity inherent in the previous course of events implies here a struggle to change it from a blind to a meaningful necessity. If we think of the object of the theory in separation from the theory, we falsify it and fall into quietism or conformism. Every part of the theory presupposes the critique of the existing order and the struggle against it along lines determined by the theory itself.

The theoreticians of knowledge who started with physics had reason, even if they were not wholly right, to condemn the confusion of cause and operation of forces and to substitute the idea of condition or function for the idea of cause. For the kind of thinking which simply registers facts there are always only series of phenomena, never forces and counterforces; but this, of course, says something about this kind of thinking, not about nature. If such a method is applied to society, the result is statistics and descriptive sociology, and these can be important for many purposes, even for critical theory.

For traditional science either everything is necessary or nothing is necessary, according as necessity means the independence of event from observer or the possibility of absolutely certain prediction. But to the extent that the subject does not totally isolate himself, even as thinker, from the social struggles of which he is a part and to the extent that he does not think of knowledge and action as distinct concepts, necessity acquires another meaning for him. If he encounters necessity which is not mastered by man, it takes shape either as that realm of nature which despite the far-reaching conquests still to come will never wholly vanish, or as the weakness of the society of previous ages in carrying on the struggle with nature in a consciously and purposefully organized way. Here we do have forces and counterforces. Both elements in this concept of necessity – the power of nature and the weakness of society – are interconnected and are based on the experienced effort of man to emancipate himself from coercion by nature and from those forms of social life and of the juridical, political, and cultural orders which have become a strait-jacket for him. The struggle on two fronts, against nature and against society's weakness, is part of the effective striving for a future condition of things in which whatever man wills is also necessary and in which the necessity of the object becomes the necessity of a rationally mastered event. [...]

Critical theory does not have one doctrinal substance today, another tomorrow. The changes in it do not mean a shift to a wholly new outlook, as long as the age itself does not radically change. The stability of the theory is due to the fact that amid all change in society the basic economic structure, the class relationship in its simplest form, and therefore the idea of the supercession of these two remain identical. The decisive substantive elements in the theory are conditioned by these unchanging factors and they themselves therefore cannot change until there has been a historical transformation of society. On the other hand, however, history does not stand still until such a point of transformation has been reached. The historical development of the conflicts in which the critical theory is involved leads to a reassignment of degrees of relative importance to individual elements of the theory, forces further concretizations, and determines which results of specialized science are to be significant for critical theory and practice at any given time.

In order to explain more fully what is meant, we shall use the concept of the social class which disposes of the means of production. In the liberalist period economic predominance was in great measure connected with legal ownership of the means of production. The large class of private property owners exercised leadership in the society, and the whole culture of the age bears the impress of this fact. Industry was still broken up into a large number of independent enterprises which were small by modern standards. The directors of factories, as was suitable for this stage of technological development, were either one or more of the owners or their direct appointees. Once, however, the development of technology in the last century had led to a rapidly increasing concentration and centralization of capital, the legal owners were largely excluded from the management of the huge combines which absorbed their small factories, and management became something quite distinct from ownership before the law. Industrial magnates, the leaders of the economy, came into being.

... Once the legal owners are cut off from the real productive process and lose their influence, their horizon narrows; they become increasingly unfitted for important social positions, and finally the share which they still have in industry due to ownership and which they have done nothing to augment comes to seem socially useless and morally dubious. These and other changes are accompanied by the rise of ideologies centering on the great personality and the distinction between productive and parasitic capitalists. The idea of a right with a fixed content and independent of society at large loses its importance. The very same sector of society which brutally maintains its private power to dispose of the means of production (and this power is at the heart of the prevailing social order) sponsors political doctrines which claim that unproductive property and parasitic incomes must disappear. The circle of really powerful men grows narrower, but the possibility increases of deliberately constructing ideologies, of establishing a double standard of truth (knowledge for insiders, a cooked-up story for the people), and of cynicism about truth and thought generally. The end result of the process is a society dominated no longer by independent owners but by cliques of industrial and political leaders.

Such changes do not leave the structure of the critical theory untouched. It does not indeed fall victim to the illusion that property and profit no longer play a key role, an illusion carefully fostered in the social sciences. On the one hand, even earlier it had regarded juridical relations not as the substance but as the surface of what was really going on in society. It knows that the disposition of men and things remains in the hands of a particular social group which is in competition with other economic power groups, less so at home but all the more fiercely at the international level. Profit continues to come from the same social sources and must in the last analysis be increased by the same means as before. On the other hand, in the judgment of the critical theorist the loss of all rights with a determined content, a loss conditioned by the concentration of economic power and given its fullest form in the authoritarian state, has brought with it the disappearance not only of an ideology but also of a cultural factor which has a positive value and not simply a negative one.

When the theory takes into account these changes in the inner structure of the entrepreneurial class, it is led to differentiate others of its concepts as well. The dependence of culture on social relationships must change as the latter change, even in details, if society indeed be a single whole. Even in the liberalist period political and moral interpretations of individuals could be derived from their economic situation. Admiration for nobility of character, fidelity to one's word, independence of judgment, and so forth, are traits of a society of relatively independent economic subjects who enter into contractual relationships with each other. But this cultural dependence was in good measure psychologically mediated, and morality itself acquired a kind of stability because of its function in the individual. (The truth that dependence on the economy thoroughly pervaded even this morality was brought home when in the recent threat to the economic position of the liberalist bourgeoisie the attitude of freedom and independence began to disintegrate.) Under the conditions of monopolistic capitalism, however, even such a relative individual independence is a thing of the past. The individual no longer has any ideas of his own. The content of mass belief, in which no one really believes, is an immediate product of the ruling economic and political bureaucracies, and its disciples secretly follow their own atomistic and therefore untrue interests; they act as mere functions of the economic machine.

The concept of the dependence of the cultural on the economic has thus changed. ... This influence of social development on the structure of the theory is part of the theory's doctrinal content. Thus new contents are not just mechanically added to already existent parts. Since the theory is a unified whole which has its proper meaning only in relation to the contemporary situation, the theory as a whole is caught up in an evolution. The evolution does not change the theory's foundations, of course, any more than recent changes essentially alter the object which the theory reflects, namely contemporary society. Yet even the apparently more remote concepts of the theory are drawn into the evolution. The logical difficulties which understanding meets in every thought that attempts to reflect a living totality are due chiefly to this fact. [...]

There are no general criteria for judging the critical theory as a whole, for it is always based on the recurrence of events and thus on a self-reproducing totality. Nor is there a social class by whose acceptance of the theory one could be guided. It is possible for the consciousness of every social stratum today to be limited and corrupted by ideology, however much, for its circumstances, it may be bent on truth. For all its insight into the individual steps in social change and for all the agreement of its elements with the most advanced traditional theories, the critical theory has no specific influence on its side, except concern for the abolition of social injustice. This negative formulation, if we wish to express it abstractly, is the materialist content of the idealist concept of reason.

In a historical period like the present true theory is more critical than affirmative, just as the society that corresponds to it cannot be called "productive." The future of humanity depends on the existence today of the critical attitude, which of course contains within it elements from traditional theories and from our declining culture generally. Mankind has already been abandoned by a science which in its imaginary self-sufficiency thinks of the shaping of practice, which it serves and to which it belongs, simply as something lying outside its borders and is content with this separation of thought and action. Yet the characteristic mark of the thinker's activity is to determine for itself what it is to accomplish and serve, and this not in fragmentary fashion but totally. Its own nature, therefore, turns it towards a changing of history and the establishment of justice among men. Behind the loud calls for "social spirit" and "national community," the opposition between individual and society grows ever greater. The self-definition of science grows ever more abstract. But conformism in thought and the insistence that thinking is a fixed vocation, a self-enclosed realm within society as a whole, betrays the very essence of thought.

NOTES

1 Descartes, *Discourse on Method*, in *The Philosophical Works of Descartes*, tr. by Elizabeth S. Haldane and G. R. T. Ross (Cambridge: Cambridge University Press, 1931), volume 1, p. 92.
2 Edmund Husserl, *Formale und transzendentale Logik* (Halle, 1929), p. 89.
3 Ibid., p. 79.
4 Ibid., p. 91.
5 Hermann Weyl, *Philosophie der Naturwissenschaft*, in *Handbuch der Philosophie*, Part 2 (Munich, 1927), pp. 118ff.
6 Max Weber, "Critical Studies in the Logic of the Cultural Sciences I: A Critique of Eduard Meyer's Methodological Views," in *Max Weber on the Methodology of the Social Sciences*, ed. and tr. by Edward A. Shils and Henry A. Finch (Glencoe, IL: Free Press, 1949), pp. 113–63.

7   In the following pages this activity is called "critical" activity. The term is used here less in the sense it has in the idealist critique of pure reason than in the sense it has in the dialectical critique of political economy. It points to an essential aspect of the dialectical theory of society.

8   On the logical structure of the critique of political economy, cf. the essay "Zum Problem der Wahrheit," in Horkheimer, *Kritische Theorie*, vol. 1 (Frankfurt, 1968), pp. 265ff.

9   There are connections between the forms of judgment and the historical periods. A brief indication will show what is meant. The classificatory judgment is typical of prebourgeois society: this is the way it is, and men can do nothing about it. The hypothetical and disjunctive forms belong especially to the bourgeois world: under certain circumstances this effect can take place; it is either thus or so. Critical theory maintains: it need not be so; man can change reality, and the necessary conditions for such change already exist.

Part VII

Critical Theory and the Sociology of Knowledge

Introduction to Part VII

32 Traditional and Critical Theory

33 The Work of Art in the Age of Mechanical Reproduction

34 The Culture Industry

35 One-dimensional Man

Introduction to Part VII

The sociology of knowledge and the related academic movement known as critical theory grew out of the fertile, if contentious, dialogue between German idealism, the radical critique of society and culture associated with Marxism, and Freudian theory and the nascent science of psychoanalysis. It sought to understand the social foundation of ideas, the sociological conditions that shaped them, and the role of knowledge in the maintenance and reproduction of a class-divided society. As Horkeimer announced in his programmatic essay on "Traditional and Critical Theory" (excerpted below), critical theory would break with the conventions of both social philosophy and positivistic social science to offer a social analysis based on the negation of existing knowledge.

The chief figures in this movement were associated with the so-called Frankfurt School of Critical Theory established at the Institute for Social Research in Frankfurt. The School, founded in Germany but forced into exile in the United States in 1933 (to return again after German defeat), involved such prominent figures in German philosophy as Max Horkheimer, Theodor W. Adorno, Herbert Marcuse, and later Jürgen Habermas. Frankfurt School critical theory combined the thought of Marx, Weber, and Freud. Unlike traditional philosophers, the Frankfurt School theorists wished to engage the problems of the day by making critical interventions in the spheres of politics, social policy, and the arts. The School's project led to a sustained program of theoretically oriented sociological research that critically analyzed, among other things, the development of socialism, the eclipse of the labor movement, the rise of fascism, characteristics of authoritarian personality, and the emergence of mass consumer culture.

Classical Sociological Theory, Third Edition. Edited by Craig Calhoun, Joseph Gerteis, James Moody, Steven Pfaff, and Indermohan Virk. Editorial material and organization © 2012 John Wiley & Sons, Ltd. Published 2012 by John Wiley & Sons, Ltd.

The Critical Theory of Society

This new sociology of knowledge was concerned particularly with the role of intellectuals in a society fraught with conflict. Could knowledge still be understood as the disinterested search for truth in accordance with Enlightenment ideals? Or was knowledge merely a serviceable good to be put to use in legitimating or opposing unequal social relations?

Confidence in the capacity of science and understanding to improve the human condition was shaken by the mounting difficulties of the European democracies and the global economic disaster of the 1930s. In Germany, where the modern sociology of knowledge had developed, the triumph of Nazism, and with it the establishment of a racist dictatorship enjoying broad popular support, cemented a crisis in Western Marxism already divided by disappointment with the authoritarian police state erected by the Bolsheviks in the Soviet Union. For many intellectuals, the rise of totalitarianism signaled both the eclipse of the European Enlightenment and the decline of the working class as a revolutionary subject. Confidence in the power of knowledge to emancipate was replaced with a pessimistic appraisal of culture and society that drew upon Freudian theory. Theorists painted a picture of a pathological modernity in which the pathological desire of the masses to be dominated promoted a masochistic longing for strong leaders and a taste for political violence. Fascism was thus understood as a reaction to the deep-seated alienation and frustrated desires of a modern world fractured by capitalism and aggression. In arriving at this understanding, Weber's account of capitalist modernity as the progressive rationalization of society was also influential (see Part V). For Weber, modernity was a process that inevitably entailed the decline of the religious worldview and the disenchantment of everyday life. For the Frankfurt School theorists this aspect of capitalism – the triumph of instrumental rationality at the expense of substantive values, authentic experience, and the ethic of emancipation – became a chief concern, evident especially in Max Horkheimer and Theodor Adorno's *The Dialectic of Englightenment* (1944).

The Frankfurt School theorists shared a profound pessimism concerning the question of critical consciousness and effective political agency in an age of bureaucratic control and the mass media. In Marcuse's indictment of "One-Dimensional Man," human capacities for autonomy and authentic self-expression had been smothered under the weight of techniques of domination – ranging from propaganda, advertisement, and mass marketing to "scientific" management techniques – that anchored the capitalist system. If the Enlightenment ideal, expressed so clearly in Kant's political ethics, had been one of universal education and a liberated citizenship, it had been surrendered in the face of a "culture industry" that practiced mass deception and manipulation. In Adorno's "Cultural Criticism and Society," excerpted below, both artistic originality and aesthetic transcendence have been obliterated by the requirements of a professionalized culture industry. Indeed, Adorno's ringing indictment of the commercialization of culture and the unfulfilled promise of information and communications technology has taken on new meaning in light of the proliferation of new media and the contemporary obsession with popular culture.

The radical critique that the Frankfurt School reached in portraying a drift towards totalitarianism in liberal capitalist society was clearly colored by its preoccupation with explaining the disaster of European fascism and the decline of European high culture. However, critical theory's fundamental insight into the irrationality of an overly rationalized, bureaucratic society that threatened to suffocate individual personality and self-expression and its unmasking of the techniques of deception and manipulation that suffused a mass culture based on consumption remain remarkably relevant today.

A central, though often underappreciated, figure in the development of the sociology of knowledge and the Frankfurt School of Critical Theory was Max Weber. Weber's theories concerning the role of cultural change in the transition to modernity suggested how a revolution in consciousness might contribute to social revolutions. This contrasted with the common Marxian understanding of ideas as little more than after-the-fact justifications for material and social inequalities. For Marx and his followers, the realm of ideas reflected the material interests of rulers, to be dispelled only through the proper, historical-materialist understanding of objective conditions based on the concrete standpoint of a universal subject (i.e. the industrial proletariat). Weber's history of ideas, on the other hand, was hostile to the notion of a trans-historical subject and recognized a more independent role for culture and ideas in social development.

The Legacy of Critical Theory

Critical theory remains an important tradition in linking the contemporary sociology of knowledge to diverse strands of Marxism, feminism, and cultural studies. Its basic critique of social inequality and the corrosion of culture as well as its vigilant criticism of the forces that undermine a genuine democratic citizenship continue to inspire criticism and research. Concepts drawn from critical theory are essential to understanding the capacity of actors in society to communicate and act collectively on the basis of common understandings and interests. The problem of the standpoint of knowledge, explored by Mannheim and the Frankfurt School theorists in the sociology of knowledge, has become an important part of the theoretical arsenal of feminism and critical ethnic studies. By raising the issue of epistemological standpoint, the biases and theoretical lacunae of traditional social sciences can be revealed and false claims to universalism can be unseated. Perhaps most importantly, the legacy of critical theory has been to defend the liberating potential of knowledge in the face of new and continuing threats from ideology and inequality.

SELECTED BIBLIOGRAPHY

Adorno, Theodor W., et al. 1950. *The Authoritarian Personality*. New York: W.W. Norton & Company. (An influential analysis shaped by Frankfurt School thinking to engage in a sustained empirical research project aimed at exploring the cultural and psychological conditions that support fascism. Famous for its development of an index to measure attitudinal and psychological attributes that make individuals susceptible to authoritarian control.)

Adorno, Theodor W. 1973. *Negative Dialectics*. New York: Seabury Press. (Adorno's most important philosophical writing, which extends the dialectical tradition from its roots in Hegel and Marx.)

Adorno, Theodor W. 1967. *Prisms*. Translated by Samuel Weber and Shierry Weber. London: Spearman Press. (A set of wide-ranging essays on aesthetics and the sociology of culture that reflect the critical brilliance of Adorno's style.)

Horkheimer, Max and Theodor W. Adorno. 1972. *The Dialectic of Enlightenment*. John Cumming, translator. New York: Herder and Herder. (A devastating critique of modernity and of the triumph of instrumental reason over the ethical principles of the Enlightenment. Explores how mass culture and consumer capitalism are crippling the capacity for mankind's self-liberation from domination and unreason.)

Mannheim, Karl. 1936. *Ideology and Utopia*. New York: Harcourt, Brace & Company.

_____.1940. *Man and Society in an Age of Reconstruction*. London: K. Paul, Trench, Trubner & Company. (Mannheim was a founding figure in the sociology of knowledge. In these works he reveals the role intellectuals play in propagating ideology and the potential for the reconstruction of reason by ethically committed intellectuals.)

Marcuse, Herbert. 1964. *One-Dimensional Man*. Boston: Beacon Press. (Marcuse's book helped to inspire the student radicals of the 1960s with its indictment of a society preoccupied with consumption and conformity [see the influential cable TV series *Mad Men* for a sense of the times] and its call for a rebellion against apparent contentment and complacency.)

Jay, Martin. 1973. *The Dialectical Imagination*. Boston: Little, Brown. (This is the standard intellectual history of the Frankfurt School from its inception through the 1950s.)

Wiggershaus, Rolf. 1994. *The Frankfurt School: Its History, Theories, and Political Significance*. Cambridge, MA: MIT Press. (A brilliant history of the institution, personalities, and ideas of the Frankfurt School from its founding generation through present practitioners.)

Chapter 33

The Work of Art in the Age of Mechanical Reproduction [1936]

Walter Benjamin

Our fine arts were developed, their types and uses were established, in times very different from the present, by men whose power of action upon things was insignificant in comparison with ours. But the amazing growth of our techniques, the adaptability and precision they have attained, the ideas and habits they are creating, make it a certainty that profound changes are impending in the ancient craft of the Beautiful. In all the arts there is a physical component which can no longer be considered or treated as it used to be, which cannot remain unaffected by our modern knowledge and power. For the last twenty years neither matter nor space nor time has been what it was from time immemorial. We must expect great innovations to transform the entire technique of the arts, thereby affecting artistic invention itself and perhaps even bringing about an amazing change in our very notion of art.[1]

Paul Valéry, "La Conquête de l'ubiquité" (Paris)

Preface

When Marx undertook his critique of the capitalistic mode of production, this mode was in its infancy. Marx directed his efforts in such a way as to give them prognostic value. He went back to the basic conditions underlying capitalistic production and through his presentation showed what could be expected of

Benjamin, Walter, "The Work of Art in the Age of Mechanical Reproduction," pp. 217–251 from Walter Benjamin, *Illuminations*, ed. Hannah Arendt, trans. Harry Zohn. New York: Schocken Books, 1969. Copyright © 1955 by Suhrkamp Verlag, Frankfurt a. M., English translation by Harry Zohn copyright © 1968 and renewed 1996 by Harcourt, Inc., reprinted by permission by Harcourt, Inc., and The Random House Group Ltd.

Classical Sociological Theory, Third Edition. Edited by Craig Calhoun, Joseph Gerteis, James Moody, Steven Pfaff, and Indermohan Virk. Editorial material and organization © 2012 John Wiley & Sons, Ltd. Published 2012 by John Wiley & Sons, Ltd.

capitalism in the future. The result was that one could expect it not only to exploit the proletariat with increasing intensity, but ultimately to create conditions which would make it possible to abolish capitalism itself.

The transformation of the superstructure, which takes place far more slowly than that of the substructure, has taken more than half a century to manifest in all areas of culture the change in the conditions of production. Only today can it be indicated what form this has taken. Certain prognostic requirements should be met by these statements. However, theses about the art of the proletariat after its assumption of power or about the art of a classless society would have less bearing on these demands than theses about the developmental tendencies of art under present conditions of production. Their dialectic is no less noticeable in the superstructure than in the economy. It would therefore be wrong to underestimate the value of such theses as a weapon. They brush aside a number of outmoded concepts, such as creativity and genius, eternal value and mystery – concepts whose uncontrolled (and at present almost uncontrollable) application would lead to a processing of data in the Fascist sense. The concepts which are introduced into the theory of art in what follows differ from the more familiar terms in that they are completely useless for the purposes of Fascism. They are, on the other hand, useful for the formulation of revolutionary demands in the politics of art.

I

In principle a work of art has always been reproducible. Man-made artifacts could always be imitated by men. Replicas were made by pupils in practice of their craft, by masters for diffusing their works, and, finally, by third parties in the pursuit of gain. Mechanical reproduction of a work of art, however, represents something new. Historically, it advanced intermittently and in leaps at long intervals, but with accelerated intensity. The Greeks knew only two procedures of technically reproducing works of art: founding and stamping. Bronzes, terra cottas, and coins were the only art works which they could produce in quantity. All others were unique and could not be mechanically reproduced. With the woodcut graphic art became mechanically reproducible for the first time, long before script became reproducible by print. The enormous changes which printing, the mechanical reproduction of writing, has brought about in literature are a familiar story. However, within the phenomenon which we are here examining from the perspective of world history, print is merely a special, though particularly important, case. During the Middle Ages engraving and etching were added to the woodcut; at the beginning of the nineteenth century lithography made its appearance.

With lithography the technique of reproduction reached an essentially new stage. This much more direct process was distinguished by the tracing of the design on a stone rather than its incision on a block of wood or its etching on a copperplate and permitted graphic art for the first time to put its products on the market, not only in large numbers as hitherto, but also in daily changing forms. Lithography enabled graphic art to illustrate everyday life, and it began to keep pace with printing. But only a few decades after its invention, lithography was surpassed by photography. For the first time in the process of pictorial reproduction, photography freed the hand of the most important artistic functions which henceforth devolved only upon the eye looking into a lens. Since the eye perceives more swiftly than the hand can draw, the process of pictorial reproduction was accelerated so enormously that it could keep pace with speech. A film operator shooting a scene in the studio captures the images at the speed of an actor's speech. Just as lithography virtually implied the illustrated newspaper, so did photography foreshadow the sound film. The technical reproduction of sound was tackled at the end of the last century. These convergent endeavors made predictable a situation which Paul Valéry pointed up in this sentence: "Just as water, gas, and electricity are brought into our house from far off to satisfy our needs in response to a minimal effort, so we shall be supplied with visual or auditory images, which will appear and disappear at a simple movement of the hand, hardly more than a sign" (op. cit., p. 226). Around 1900 technical reproduction had reached a standard that not only permitted it to reproduce all transmitted works of art and thus to cause the most profound change in their impact upon the public; it also had captured a place of its own among the artistic processes. For the study of this standard nothing is more revealing than the nature of the repercussions that these two different manifestations – the reproduction of works of art and the art of the film – have had on art in its traditional form.

II

Even the most perfect reproduction of a work of art is lacking in one element: its presence in time and space, its unique existence at the place where it happens to be. This unique existence of the work of art determined the history to which it was subject throughout the time of its existence. This includes the changes which it may have suffered in physical condition over the years as well as the various changes in its ownership.[2] The traces of the first can be revealed only by chemical or physical analyses which it is impossible to perform on a reproduction; changes of ownership are subject to a tradition which must be traced from the situation of the original.

The presence of the original is the prerequisite to the concept of authenticity. Chemical analyses of the patina of a bronze can help to establish this, as does the proof that a given manuscript of the Middle Ages stems from an archive of the fifteenth century. The whole sphere of authenticity is outside technical – and, of course, not only technical – reproducibility.[3] Confronted with its manual reproduction, which was usually branded as a forgery, the original preserved all its authority; not so *vis à vis* technical reproduction. The reason is twofold. First, process reproduction is more independent for the original than manual reproduction. For example, in photography, process reproduction can bring out those aspects of the original that are unattainable to the naked eye yet accessible to the lens, which is adjustable and chooses its angle at will. And photographic reproduction, with the aid of certain processes, such as enlargement or slow motion, can capture images which escape natural vision. Secondly, technical reproduction can put the copy of the original into situations which would be out of reach for the original itself. Above all, it enables the original to meet the beholder halfway, be it in the form of a photography or a phonograph record. The cathedral leaves its locale to be received in the studio of a lover of art; the choral production, performed in an auditorium or in the open air, resounds in the drawing room.

The situations into which the product of mechanical reproduction can be brought may not touch the actual work of art, yet the quality of its presence is always depreciated. This holds not only for the art work but also, for instance, for a landscape which passes in review before the spectator in a movie. In the case of the art object, a most sensitive nucleus – namely, its authenticity – is interfered with whereas no natural object is vulnerable on that score. The authenticity of a thing is the essence of all that is transmissible from its beginning, ranging from its substantive duration to its testimony to the history which it has experienced. Since the historical testimony rests on the authenticity, the former, too, is jeopardized by reproduction when substantive duration ceases to matter. And what is really jeopardized when the historical testimony is affected is the authority of the object.[4]

One might subsume the eliminated element in the term "aura" and go on to say: that which withers in the age of mechanical reproduction is the aura of the work of art. This is a symptomatic process whose significance points beyond the realm of art. One might generalize by saying: the technique of reproduction detaches the reproduced object from the domain of tradition. By making many reproductions it substitutes a plurality of copies for a unique existence. And in permitting the reproduction to meet the beholder or listener in his own particular situation, it reactivates the object reproduced. These two processes lead to a tremendous shattering of tradition which is the obverse of the contemporary crisis and renewal of mankind. Both processes are intimately connected with the contemporary mass movements. Their most powerful agent is the film. Its social significance, particularly in its most positive form, is inconceivable without its destructive, cathartic aspect, that is, the liquidation of the traditional value of the cultural heritage. This phenomenon is most palpable in the great historical films. It extends to ever new positions. In 1927 Abel Gance exclaimed enthusiastically: "Shakespeare, Rembrandt, Beethoven will make films ... all legends, all mythologies and all myths, all founders of religion, and the very religions ... await their exposed resurrection, and the heroes crowd each other at the gate."[5] Presumably without intending it, he issued an invitation to a far-reaching liquidation.

III

During long periods of history, the mode of human sense perception changes with humanity's entire mode of existence. The manner in which human sense perception is organized, the medium in which it is accomplished, is determined not only by nature but by historical circumstances as well. The fifth century, with its great shifts of population, saw the birth of the late Roman art industry and the Vienna Genesis, and there developed not only an art different from that of antiquity but also a new kind of perception. The scholars of the Viennese school, Riegl and Wickhoff, who resisted the weight of classical tradition under which these later art forms had been buried, were the first to draw conclusions from them concerning the organization of perception at the time. However far-reaching their insight, these scholars limited themselves to showing the significant, formal hallmark which characterized perception in late Roman times. They did not attempt – and, perhaps, saw no way – to show the social transformations expressed by these changes of perception. The conditions for an analogous insight are more favorable in the present. And if changes in the medium of contemporary perception can be comprehended as decay of the aura, it is possible to show its social causes.

The concept of aura which was proposed above with reference to historical objects may usefully be illustrated with reference to the aura of natural ones. We define the aura of the latter as the unique phenomenon of a distance, however close it may be. If, while resting on a summer afternoon, you follow with your eyes a mountain range on the horizon or a branch which casts its shadow over you, you experience the aura of those mountains, of that branch. This image makes it easy to comprehend the social bases of the contemporary decay of the aura. It rests on two circumstances, both of which are related to the increasing significance of the masses in contemporary life. Namely, the desire of contemporary masses to bring things "closer" spatially and humanly, which is just as ardent as their bent toward overcoming the uniqueness of every reality by accepting its reproduction.[6] Every day the urge grows stronger to get hold of an object at very close range by way of its likeness, its reproduction. Unmistakably, reproduction as offered by picture magazines and newsreels differs from the image seen by the unarmed eye. Uniqueness and permanence are as closely linked in the latter as are transitoriness and reproducibility in the former. To pry an object from its shell, to destroy its aura, is the mark of a perception whose "sense of the universal equality of things" has increased to such a degree that it extracts it even from a unique object by means of reproduction. Thus is manifested in the field of perception what in the theoretical sphere is noticeable in the increasing importance of statistics. The adjustment of reality to the masses and of the masses to reality is a process of unlimited scope, as much for thinking as for perception.

IV

The uniqueness of a work of art is inseparable from its being imbedded in the fabric of tradition. This tradition itself is thoroughly alive and extremely changeable. An ancient statue of Venus, for example, stood in a different traditional context with the Greeks, who made it an object of veneration, than with the clerics of the Middle Ages, who viewed it as an ominous idol. Both of them, however, were equally confronted with its uniqueness, that is, its aura. Originally the contextual integration of art in tradition found its expression in the cult. We know that the earliest art works originated in the service of a ritual – first the magical, then the religious kind. It is significant that the existence of the work of art with reference to its aura is never entirely separated from its ritual function.[7] In other words, the unique value of the "authentic" work of art has its basis in ritual, the location of its original use value. This ritualistic basis, however remote, is still recognizable as secularized ritual even in the most profane forms of the cult of beauty.[8] The secular cult of beauty, developed during the Renaissance and prevailing for three centuries, clearly showed that ritualistic basis in its decline and the first deep crisis which befell it. With the advent of the first truly revolutionary means of reproduction, photography, simultaneously with the rise of socialism, art sensed the approaching crisis which has become evident a century later. At the time, art reacted with the doctrine of *l'art pour l'art*, that is, with a theology of art. This gave rise to what might be called a negative theology in the form of the idea of "pure" art, which not only denied any social function of art but also any categorizing by subject matter. (In poetry, Mallarmé was the first to take this position.)

An analysis of art in the age of mechanical reproduction must do justice to these relationships, for they lead us to an all-important insight: for the first time in world history, mechanical reproduction emancipates the work of art from its parasitical dependence on ritual. To an ever greater degree the work of art reproduced becomes the work of art designed for reproducibility.[9] From a photographic negative, for example, one can make any number of prints; to ask for the "authentic" print makes no sense. But the instant the criterion of authenticity ceases to be applicable to artistic production, the total function of art is reversed. Instead of being based on ritual, it begins to be based on another practice – politics.

V

Works of art are received and valued on different planes. Two polar types stand out: with one, the accent is on the cult value; with the other, on the exhibition value of the work.[10] Artistic production begins with ceremonial objects destined to serve in a cult. One may assume that what mattered was their existence, not their being on view. The elk portrayed by the man of the Stone Age on the walls of his cave was an instrument of magic. He did expose it to his fellow men, but in the main it was meant for the spirits. Today the cult value would seem to demand that the work of art remain hidden. Certain statues of gods are accessible only to the priest in the cella; certain Madonnas remain covered nearly all year round; certain sculptures on medieval cathedrals are invisible to the spectator on ground level. With the emancipation of the various art practices from ritual go increasing opportunities for the exhibition of their products. It is easier to exhibit a portrait bust that can be sent here and there than to exhibit the statue of a divinity that has its fixed place in the interior of a temple. The same holds for the painting as against the mosaic or fresco that preceded it. And even though the public presentability of a mass originally may have been just as great as that of a symphony, the latter originated at the moment when its public presentability promised to surpass that of the mass.

With the different methods of technical reproduction of a work of art, its fitness for exhibition increased to such an extent that the quantitative shift between its two poles turned into a qualitative transformation of its nature. This is comparable to the situation of the work of art in prehistoric times when, by the absolute emphasis on its cult value, it was, first and foremost, an instrument of magic. Only later did it come to be recognized as a work of art. In the same way today, by the absolute emphasis on its exhibition value the work of art becomes a creation with entirely new functions, among which the one we are conscious of, the artistic function, later may be recognized as incidental.[11] This much is certain: today photography and the film are the most serviceable exemplifications of this new function.

VI

In photography, exhibition value begins to displace cult value all along the line. But cult value does not give way without resistance. It retires into an ultimate retrenchment: the human countenance. It is no accident that the portrait was the focal point of early photography. The cult of remembrance of loved ones, absent or dead, offers a last refuge for the cult value of the picture. For the last time the aura emanates from the early photographs in the fleeting expression of a human face. This is what constitutes their melancholy, incomparable beauty. But as man withdraws from the photographic images, the exhibition value for the first time shows its superiority to the ritual value. To have pinpointed this new stage constitutes the incomparable significance of Atget, who, around 1900, took photographs of deserted Paris streets. It has quite justly been said of him that he photographed them like scenes of crime. The scene of a crime, too, is deserted; it is photographed for the purpose of establishing evidence. With Atget, photographs become standard evidence for historical occurrences, and acquire a hidden political significance. They demand a specific kind of approach; free-floating contemplation is not appropriate to them. They stir the viewer; he feels challenged by them in a new way. At the same time picture magazines begin to put up signposts for him, right ones or wrong ones, no matter. For the first time, captions have become obligatory. And it is clear that they have an altogether different character than the title of a painting. The directives which the captions give to those looking at pictures in illustrated magazines soon become even more explicit and more imperative in the film where the meaning of each single picture appears to be prescribed by the sequence of all preceding ones.

VII

The nineteenth-century dispute as to the artistic value of painting versus photography today seems devious and confused. This does not diminish its importance, however; if anything, it underlines it. The dispute was in fact the symptom of a historical transformation the universal impact of which was not realized by either of the rivals. When the age of mechanical reproduction separated art from its basis in cult, the semblance of its autonomy disappeared forever. The resulting change in the function of art transcended the perspective of the century; for a long time it even escaped that of the twentieth century, which experienced the development of the film.

Earlier much futile thought had been devoted to the question of whether photography is an art. The primary question – whether the very invention of photography had not transformed the entire nature of art – was not raised. Soon the film theoreticians asked the same ill-considered question with regard to the film. But the difficulties which photography caused traditional aesthetics were mere child's play as compared to those raised by the film. Whence the insensitive and forced character of early theories of the film. Abel Gance, for instance, compares the film with hieroglyphs: "Here, by a remarkable regression, we have come back to the level of expression of the Egyptians. ... Pictorial language has not yet matured because our eyes have not yet adjusted to it. There is as yet insufficient respect for, insufficient cult of, what it expresses."[12] Or, in the words of Séverin-Mars: "What art has been granted a dream more poetical and more real at the same time! Approached in this fashion the film might represent an incomparable means of expression. Only the most high-minded persons, in the most perfect and mysterious moments of their lives, should be allowed to enter its ambience."[13] Alexandre Arnoux concludes his fantasy about the silent film with the question: "Do not all the bold descriptions we have given amount to the definition of prayer?"[14] It is instructive to note how their desire to class the film among the "arts" forces these theoreticians to read ritual elements into it – with a striking lack of discretion. Yet when these speculations were published, films like *L'Opinion publique* and *The Gold Rush* had already appeared. This, however, did not keep Abel Gance from adducing hieroglyphs for purposes of comparison, nor Séverin-Mars from speaking of the film as one might speak of paintings by Fra Angelico. Characteristically, even today ultrareactionary authors give the film a similar contextual significance – if not an outright sacred one, then at least a supernatural one. Commenting on Max Reinhardt's film version of *A Midsummer Night's Dream,* Werfel states that undoubtedly it was the sterile copying of the exterior world with its streets, interiors, railroad stations, restaurants, motorcars, and beaches which until now had obstructed the elevation of the film to the realm of art. "The film has not yet realized its true meaning, its real possibilities ... these consist in its unique faculty to express by natural means and with incomparable persuasiveness all that is fairylike, marvelous, supernatural."[15]

VIII

The artistic performance of a stage actor is definitely presented to the public by the actor in person; that of the screen actor, however, is presented by a camera, with a twofold consequence. The camera that presents the performance of the film actor to the public need not respect the performance as an integral whole. Guided by the cameraman, the camera continually changes its position with respect to the performance. The sequence of positional views which the editor composes from the material supplied him constitutes the completed film. It comprises certain factors of movement which are in reality those of the camera, not to mention special camera angles, close-ups, etc. Hence, the performance of the actor is subjected to a series of optical tests. This is the first consequence of the fact that the actor's performance is presented by means of a camera. Also, the film actor lacks the opportunity of the stage actor to adjust to the audience during his performance, since he does not present his performance to the audience in person. This permits the audience to take the position of a critic, without experiencing any personal contact with the actor. The audience's identification with the actor is really an identification with the camera. Consequently the audience takes the position of the camera; its approach is that of testing.[16] This is not the approach to which cult values may be exposed.

IX

For the film, what matters primarily is that the actor represents himself to the public before the camera, rather than representing someone else. One of the first to sense the actor's metamorphosis by this form of testing was Pirandello. Though his remarks on the subject in his novel *Si Gira* were limited to the negative aspects of the question and to the silent film only, this hardly impairs their validity. For in this respect, the sound film did not change anything essential. What matters is that the part is acted not for an audience but for a mechanical contrivance – in the case of the sound film, for two of them. "The film actor," wrote Pirandello, "feels as if in exile – exiled not only from the stage but also from himself. With a vague sense of discomfort he feels inexplicable emptiness: his body loses its corporeality, it evaporates, it is deprived of reality, life, voice, and the noises caused by his moving about, in order to be changed into a mute image, flickering an instant on the screen, then vanishing into silence. ... The projector will play with his shadow before the public, and he himself must be content to play before the camera."[17] This situation might also be characterized as follows: for the first time – and this is the effect of the film – man has to operate with his whole living person, yet forgoing its aura. For aura is tied to his presence; there can be no replica of it. The aura which, on the stage, emanates from Macbeth, cannot be separated for the spectators from that of the actor. However, the singularity of the shot in the studio is that the camera is substituted for the public. Consequently, the aura that envelops the actor vanishes, and with it the aura of the figure he portrays.

It is not surprising that it should be a dramatist such as Pirandello who, in characterizing the film, inadvertently touches on the very crisis in which we see the theater. Any thorough study proves that there is indeed no greater contrast than that of the stage play to a work of art that is completely subject to or, like the film, founded in, mechanical reproduction. Experts have long recognized that in the film "the greatest effects are almost always obtained by 'acting' as little as possible. [...]" In 1932 Rudolf Arnheim saw "the latest trend ... in treating the actor as a stage prop chosen for its characteristics and ... inserted at the proper place."[18] With this idea something else is closely connected. The stage actor identifies himself with the character of his role. The film actor very often is denied this opportunity. His creation is by no means all of a piece; it is composed of many separate performances. Besides certain fortuitous considerations, such as cost of studio, availability of fellow players, décor, etc., there are elementary necessities of equipment that split the actor's work into a series of mountable episodes. In particular, lighting and its installation require the presentation of an event that, on the screen, unfolds as a rapid and unified scene, in a sequence of separate shootings which may take hours at the studio; not to mention more obvious montage. Thus a jump from the window can be shot in the studio as a jump from a scaffold, and the ensuing flight, if need be, can be shot weeks later when outdoor scenes are taken. Far more paradoxical cases can easily be construed. Let us assume that an actor is supposed to be startled by a knock at the door. If his reaction is not satisfactory, the director can resort to an expedient: when the actor happens to be at the studio again he has a shot fired behind him without his being forewarned of it. The frightened reaction can be shot now and be cut into the screen version. Nothing more strikingly shows that art has left the realm of the "beautiful semblance" which, so far, had been taken to be the only sphere where art could thrive.

X

The feeling of strangeness that overcomes the actor before the camera, as Pirandello describes it, is basically of the same kind as the estrangement felt before one's own image in the mirror. But now the reflected image has become separable, transportable. And where is it transported? Before the public.[19] Never for a moment does the screen actor cease to be conscious of this fact. While facing the camera he knows that ultimately he will face the public, the consumers who constitute the market. This market, where he offers not only his labor but also his whole self, his heart and soul, is beyond his reach. During the shooting he has as little contact with it as any article made in a factory. This may contribute to that oppression, that new anxiety which, according to Pirandello, grips the actor before the camera. The film responds to the shriveling of the aura with an artificial build-up of the "personality" outside the studio. The cult of the movie star, fostered by the money of the film industry, preserves not the unique aura of the person but the "spell of the personality," the phony spell of a commodity. So long as the movie-makers' capital sets the fashion, as a rule no other revolutionary merit can be accredited to today's film than the promotion of a revolutionary criticism of traditional concepts of art. We do not deny that in some cases today's films can also promote revolutionary criticism of social conditions, even of the distribution of property. However, our present study is no more specifically concerned with this than is the film production of Western Europe.

It is inherent in the technique of the film as well as that of sports that everybody who witnesses its accomplishments is somewhat of an expert. This is obvious to anyone listening to a group of newspaper boys leaning on their bicycles and discussing the outcome of a bicycle race. It is not for nothing that newspaper publishers arrange races for their delivery boys. These arouse great interest among the participants, for the victor has an opportunity to rise from delivery boy to professional racer. Similarly, the newsreel offers everyone the opportunity to rise from passer-by to movie extra. In this way any man might even find himself part of a work of art, as witness Vertoff's *Three Songs About Lenin* or Ivens' *Borinage*. Any man today can lay claim to being filmed. This claim can best be elucidated by a comparative look at the historical situation of contemporary literature.

For centuries a small number of writers were confronted by many thousands of readers. This changed toward the end of the last century. With the increasing extension of the press, which kept placing new political, religious, scientific, professional, and local organs before the readers, an increasing number of readers became writers – at first, occasional ones. It began with the daily press opening to its readers space for "letters to the editor." And today there is hardly a gainfully employed European who could not, in principle, find an opportunity to publish somewhere or other comments on his work, grievances, documentary reports, or that sort of thing. Thus, the distinction between author and public is about to lose its basic character. The difference becomes merely functional; it may vary from case to case. At any moment the reader is ready to turn into a writer. As expert, which he had to become willy-nilly in an extremely specialized work process, even if only in some minor respect, the reader gains access to authorship. In the Soviet Union work itself is given a voice. To present it verbally is part of a man's ability to perform the work. Literary license is now founded on polytechnic rather than specialized training and thus becomes common property.[20]

All this can easily be applied to the film, where transitions that in literature took centuries have come about in a decade. In cinematic practice, particularly in Russia, this change-over has partially become established reality. Some of the players whom we meet in Russian films are not actors in our sense but people who portray *themselves* – and primarily in their own work process. In Western Europe the capitalistic exploitation of the film denies consideration to modern man's legitimate claim to being reproduced. Under these circumstances the film industry is trying hard to spur the interest of the masses through illusion-promoting spectacles and dubious speculations.

XI

The shooting of a film, especially of a sound film, affords a spectacle unimaginable anywhere at any time before this. It presents a process in which it is impossible to assign to a spectator a viewpoint which would exclude from the actual scene such extraneous accessories as camera equipment, lighting machinery, staff assistants, etc. – unless his eye were on a line parallel with the lens. This circumstance, more than any other, renders superficial and insignificant any possible similarity between a scene in the studio and one on the stage. In the theater one is well aware of the place from which the play cannot immediately be detected as illusionary. There is no such place for the movie scene that is being shot. Its illusionary nature is that of the second degree, the result of cutting. That is to say, in the studio the mechanical equipment has penetrated so deeply into reality that its pure aspect freed from the foreign substance of equipment is the result of a special procedure, namely, the shooting by the specially adjusted camera and the mounting of the shot together with other similar ones. The equipment-free aspect of reality here has become the height of artifice; the sight of immediate reality has become an orchid in the land of technology.

Even more revealing is the comparison of these circumstances, which differ so much from those of the theater, with the situation in painting. Here the question is: How does the cameraman compare with the painter? To answer this we take recourse to an analogy with a surgical operation. The surgeon represents the polar opposite of the magician. The magician heals a sick person by the laying on of hands; the surgeon cuts into the patient's body. The magician maintains the natural distance between the patient and himself; though he reduces it very slightly by the laying on of hands, he greatly increases it by virtue of his authority. The surgeon does exactly the reverse; he greatly diminishes the distance between himself and the patient by penetrating into the patient's body, and increases it but little by the caution with which his hand moves among the organs. In short, in contrast to the magician – who is still hidden in the medical practitioner – the surgeon at the decisive moment abstains from facing the patient man to man; rather, it is through the operation that he penetrates into him.

Magician and surgeon compare to painter and cameraman. The painter maintains in his work a natural distance from reality, the cameraman penetrates deeply into its web.[21] There is a tremendous difference between the pictures they obtain. That of the painter is a total one, that of the cameraman consists of multiple fragments which are assembled under a new law. Thus, for contemporary man the representation of reality by the film is incomparably more significant than that of the painter, since it offers, precisely because of the thoroughgoing permeation of reality with mechanical equipment, an aspect of reality which is free of all equipment. And that is what one is entitled to ask from a work of art.

XII

Mechanical reproduction of art changes the reaction of the masses toward art. The reactionary attitude toward a Picasso painting changes into the progressive reaction toward a Chaplin movie. The progressive reaction is characterized by the direct, intimate fusion of visual and emotional enjoyment with the orientation of the expert. Such fusion is of great social significance. The greater the decrease in the social significance of an art form, the sharper the distinction between criticism and enjoyment by the public. The conventional is uncritically enjoyed, and the truly new is criticized with aversion. With regard to the screen, the critical and the receptive attitudes of the public coincide. The decisive reason for this is that individual reactions are predetermined by the mass audience response they are about to produce, and this is nowhere more pronounced than in the film. The moment these responses become manifest they control each other. Again, the comparison with painting is fruitful. A painting has always had an excellent chance to be viewed by one person or by a few. The simultaneous contemplation of paintings by a large public, such as developed in the nineteenth century, is an early symptom of the crisis of painting, a crisis which was by no means occasioned exclusively by photography but rather in a relatively independent manner by the appeal of art works to the masses.

Painting simply is in no position to present an object for simultaneous collective experience, as it was possible for architecture at all times, for the epic poem in the past, and for the movie today. Although this circumstance in itself should not lead one to conclusions about the social role of painting, it does constitute a serious threat as soon as painting, under special conditions and, as it were, against its nature, is confronted directly by the masses. In the churches and monasteries of the Middle Ages and at the princely courts up to the end of the eighteenth century, a collective reception of paintings did not occur simultaneously, but by graduated and hierarchized mediation. The change that has come about is an expression of the particular conflict in which painting was implicated by the mechanical reproducibility of paintings. Although paintings began to be publicly exhibited in galleries and salons, there was no way for the masses to organize and control themselves in their reception.[22] Thus the same public which responds in a progressive manner toward a grotesque film is bound to respond in a reactionary manner to surrealism.

XIII

The characteristics of the film lie not only in the manner in which man presents himself to mechanical equipment but also in the manner in which, by means of this apparatus, man can represent his environment. A glance at occupational psychology illustrates the testing capacity of the equipment. Psychoanalysis illustrates it in a different perspective. The film has enriched our field of perception with methods which can be illustrated by those of Freudian theory. Fifty years ago, a slip of the tongue passed more or less unnoticed. Only exceptionally may such a slip have revealed dimensions of depth in a conversation which had seemed to be taking its course on the surface. Since the *Psychopathology of Everyday Life* things have changed. This book isolated and made analyzable things which had heretofore floated along unnoticed in the broad stream of perception. For the entire spectrum of optical, and now also acoustical, perception the film has brought about a similar deepening of apperception. It is only an obverse of this fact that behavior items shown in a movie can be analyzed much more precisely and from more points of view than those presented on paintings or on the stage. As compared with painting, filmed behavior lends itself more readily to analysis because of its incomparably more precise statements of the situation. In comparison with the stage scene, the filmed behavior item lends itself more readily to analysis because it can be isolated more easily. This circumstance derives its chief importance from its tendency to promote the mutual penetration of art and science. Actually, of a screened behavior item which is neatly brought out in a certain situation, like a muscle of a body, it is difficult to say which is more fascinating, its artistic value or its value for science. To demonstrate the identity of the artistic and scientific uses of photography which heretofore usually were separated will be one of the revolutionary functions of the film.[23]

By close-ups of the things around us, by focusing on hidden details of familiar objects, by exploring commonplace milieus under the ingenious guidance of the camera, the film, on the one hand, extends our comprehension of the necessities which rule our lives; on the other hand, it manages to assure us of an immense and unexpected field of action. Our taverns and our metropolitan streets, our offices and furnished rooms, our railroad stations and our factories appeared to have us locked up hopelessly. Then came the film and burst this prison-world asunder by the dynamite of the tenth of a second, so that now, in the midst of its far-flung ruins and debris, we calmly and adventurously go traveling. With the close-up, space expands; with slow motion, movement is extended. The enlargement of a snapshot does not simply render more precise what in any case was visible, though unclear: it reveals entirely new structural formations of the subject. So, too, slow motion not only presents familiar qualities of movement but reveals in them entirely unknown ones "which, far from looking like retarded rapid movements, give the effect of singularly gliding, floating, supernatural motions."[24] Evidently a different nature opens itself to the camera than opens to the naked eye – if only because an unconsciously penetrated space is substituted for a space consciously explored by man. Even if one has a general knowledge of the way people walk, one knows nothing of a person's posture during the fractional second of a stride. The act of reaching for a lighter or a spoon is familiar routine, yet we hardly know what really goes on between hand and metal, not to mention how this fluctuates with our moods. Here the camera intervenes with the resources of its lowerings and liftings, its interruptions and isolations, its extensions and accelerations, its enlargements and reductions. The camera introduces us to unconscious optics as does psychoanalysis to unconscious impulses.

XIV

One of the foremost tasks of art has always been the creation of a demand which could be fully satisfied only later.[25] The history of every art form shows critical epochs in which a certain art form aspires to effects which could be fully obtained only with a changed technical standard, that is to say, in a new art form. The extravagances and crudities of art which thus appear, particularly in the so-called decadent epochs, actually arise from the nucleus of its richest historical energies. In recent years, such barbarisms were abundant in Dadaism. It is only now that its impulse becomes discernible: Dadaism attempted to create by pictorial – and literary – means the effects which the public today seeks in the film.

Every fundamentally new, pioneering creation of demands will carry beyond its goal. Dadaism did so to the extent that it sacrificed the market values which are so characteristic of the film in favor of higher ambitions – though of course it was not conscious of such intentions as here described. The Dadaists attached much less importance to the sales value of their work than to its uselessness for contemplative immersion. The studied degradation of their material was not the least of their means to achieve this uselessness. Their poems are "word salad" containing obscenities and every imaginable waste product of language. The same is true of their paintings, on which they mounted buttons and tickets. What they intended and achieved was a relentless destruction of the aura of their creations, which they branded as reproductions with the very means of production. Before a painting of Arp's or a poem by August Stramm it is impossible to take time for contemplation and evaluation as one would before a canvas of Derain's or a poem by Rilke. In the decline of middle-class society, contemplation became a school for asocial behavior; it was countered by distraction as a variant of social conduct.[26] Dadaistic activities actually assured a rather vehement distraction by making works of art the center of scandal. One requirement was foremost: to outrage the public.

From an alluring appearance or persuasive structure of sound the work of art of the Dadaists became an instrument of ballistics. It hit the spectator like a bullet, it happened to him, thus acquiring a tactile quality. It promoted a demand for the film, the distracting element of which is also primarily tactile, being based on changes of place and focus which periodically assail the spectator. Let us compare the screen on which a film unfolds with the canvas of a painting. The painting invites the spectator to contemplation; before it the spectator can abandon himself to his associations. Before the movie frame he cannot do so. No sooner has his eye grasped a scene than it is already changed. It cannot be arrested. Duhamel, who detests the film and knows nothing of its significance, though something of its structure, notes this circumstance as follows: "I can no longer think what I want to think. My thoughts have been replaced by moving images."[27] The spectator's process of association in view of these images is indeed interrupted by their constant, sudden change. This constitutes the shock effect of the film, which, like all shocks, should be cushioned by heightened presence of mind.[28] By means of its technical structure, the film has taken the physical shock effect out of the wrappers in which Dadaism had, as it were, kept it inside the moral shock effect.[29]

XV

The mass is a matrix from which all traditional behavior toward works of art issues today in a new form. Quantity has been transmuted into quality. The greatly increased mass of participants has produced a change in the mode of participation.

The fact that the new mode of participation first appeared in a disreputable form must not confuse the spectator. Yet some people have launched spirited attacks against precisely this superficial aspect. Among these, Duhamel has expressed himself in the most radical manner. What he objects to most is the kind of participation which the movie elicits from the masses. Duhamel calls the movie "a pastime for helots, a diversion for uneducated, wretched, worn-out creatures who are consumed by their worries [...], a spectacle which requires no concentration and presupposes no intelligence [...], which kindles no light in the heart and awakens no hope other than the ridiculous one of someday becoming a 'star' in Los Angeles."[30] Clearly, this is at bottom the same ancient lament that the masses seek distraction whereas art demands concentration from the spectator. That is a commonplace. The question remains whether it provides a platform for the analysis of the film. A closer look is needed here. Distraction and concentration form polar opposites which may be stated as follows: A man who concentrates before a work of art is absorbed by it. He enters into this work of art the way legend tells of the Chinese painter when he viewed his finished painting. In contrast, the distracted mass absorbs the work of art. This is most obvious with regard to buildings. Architecture has always represented the prototype of a work of art the reception of which is consummated by a collectivity in a state of distraction. The laws of its reception are most instructive.

Buildings have been man's companions since primeval times. Many art forms have developed and perished. Tragedy begins with the Greeks, is extinguished with them, and after centuries its "rules" only are revived. The epic poem, which had its origin in the youth of nations, expires in Europe at the end of the Renaissance. Panel painting is a creation of the Middle Ages, and nothing guarantees its uninterrupted existence. But the human need for shelter is lasting. Architecture has never been idle. Its history is more ancient than that of any other art, and its claim to being a living force has significance in every attempt to comprehend the relationship of the masses to art. Buildings are appropriated in a twofold manner: by use and by perception – or rather, by touch and sight. Such appropriation cannot be understood in terms of the attentive concentration of a tourist before a famous building. On the tactile side there is no counterpart to contemplation on the optical side. Tactile appropriation is accomplished not so much by attention as by habit. As regards architecture, habit determines to a large extent even optical reception. The latter, too, occurs much less through rapt attention than by noticing the object in incidental fashion. This mode of appropriation, developed with reference to architecture, in certain circumstances acquires canonical value. For the tasks which face the human apparatus of perception at the turning points of history cannot be solved by optical means, that is, by contemplation, alone. They are mastered gradually by habit, under the guidance of tactile appropriation.

The distracted person, too, can form habits. More, the ability to master certain tasks in a state of distraction proves that their solution has become a matter of habit. Distraction as provided by art presents a covert control of the extent to which new tasks have become soluble by apperception. Since, moreover, individuals are tempted to avoid such tasks, art will tackle the most difficult and most important ones where it is able to mobilize the masses. Today it does so in the film. Reception in a state of distraction, which is increasing noticeably in all fields of art and is symptomatic of profound changes in apperception, finds in the film its true means of exercise. The film with its shock effect meets this mode of reception halfway. The film makes the cult value recede into the background not only by putting the public in the position of the critic, but also by the fact that at the movies this position requires no attention. The public is an examiner, but an absent-minded one.

Epilogue

The growing proletarianization of modern man and the increasing formation of masses are two aspects of the same process. Fascism attempts to organize the newly created proletarian masses without affecting the property structure which the masses strive to eliminate. Fascism sees its salvation in giving these masses not their right, but instead a chance to express themselves.[31] The masses have a right to change property relations; Fascism seeks to give them an expression while preserving property. The logical result of Fascism is the introduction of aesthetics into political life. The violation of the masses, whom Fascism, with its *Führer* cult, forces to their knees, has its counterpart in the violation of an apparatus which is pressed into the production of ritual values.

All efforts to render politics aesthetic culminate in one thing: war. War and war only can set a goal for mass movements on the largest scale while respecting the traditional property system. This is the political formula for the situation. The technological formula may be stated as follows: Only war makes it possible to mobilize all of today's technical resources while maintaining the property system. It goes without saying that the Fascist apotheosis of war does not employ such arguments. Still, Marinetti says in his manifesto on the Ethiopian colonial war: "For twenty-seven years we Futurists have rebelled against the branding of war as antiaesthetic. [...] Accordingly we state: ... War is beautiful because it establishes man's dominion over the subjugated machinery by means of gas masks, terrifying megaphones, flame throwers, and small tanks. War is beautiful because it initiates the dreamt-of metalization of the human body. War is beautiful because it enriches a flowering meadow with the fiery orchids of machine guns. War is beautiful because it combines the gunfire, the cannonades, the cease-fire, the scents, and the stench of putrefaction into a symphony. War is beautiful because it creates new architecture, like that of the big tanks, the geometrical formation flights, the smoke spirals from burning villages, and many others. ... Poets and artists of Futurism! ... remember these principles of an aesthetics of war so that your struggle for a new literature and a new graphic art ... may be illumined by them!"

This manifesto has the virtue of clarity. Its formulations deserve to be accepted by dialecticians. To the latter, the aesthetics of today's war appears as follows: If the natural utilization of productive forces is impeded by the property system, the increase in technical devices, in speed, and in the sources of energy will press for an unnatural utilization, and this is found in war. The destructiveness of war furnishes proof that society has not been mature enough to incorporate technology as its organ, that technology has not been sufficiently developed to cope with the elemental forces of society. The horrible features of imperialistic warfare are attributable to the discrepancy between the tremendous means of production and their inadequate utilization in the process of production – in other words, to unemployment and the lack of markets. Imperialistic war is a rebellion of technology which collects, in the form of "human material," the claims to which society has denied its natural material. Instead of draining rivers, society directs a human stream into a bed of trenches; instead of dropping seeds from airplanes, it drops incendiary bombs over cities; and through gas warfare the aura is abolished in a new way.

"*Fiat ars – pereat mundus*," says Fascism, and, as Marinetti admits, expects war to supply the artistic gratification of a sense perception that has been changed by technology. This is evidently the consummation of "*l'art pour l'art*." Mankind, which in Homer's time was an object of contemplation for the Olympian gods, now is one for itself. Its self-alienation has reached such a degree that it can experience its own destruction as an aesthetic pleasure of the first order. This is the situation of politics which Fascism is rendering aesthetic. Communism responds by politicizing art.

NOTES

1 Quoted from Paul Valéry, *Aesthetics*, "The Conquest of Ubiquity," translated by Ralph Manheim, p. 225. Pantheon Books, Bollingen Series, New York, 1964.
2 Of course, the history of a work of art encompasses more than this. The history of the "Mona Lisa," for instance, encompasses the kind and number of its copies made in the seventeenth, eighteenth, and nineteenth centuries.
3 Precisely because authenticity is not reproducible, the intensive penetration of certain (mechanical) processes of reproduction was instrumental in differentiating and grading authenticity. To develop such differentiations was an important function of the trade in works of art. The invention of the woodcut may be said to have struck at the root of the quality of authenticity even before its late flowering. To be sure, at the time of its origin a medieval picture of the Madonna could not yet be said to be "authentic." It became "authentic" only during the succeeding centuries and perhaps most strikingly so during the last one.
4 The poorest provincial staging of *Faust* is superior to a Faust film in that, ideally, it competes with the first performance at Weimar. Before the screen it is unprofitable to remember traditional contents which might come to mind before the stage – for instance, that Goethe's friend Johann Heinrich Merck is hidden in Mephisto, and the like.
5 Abel Gance, "Le Temps de l'image est venu," *L'Art cinématographique*, Vol. 2, pp. 94 f, Paris, 1927.
6 To satisfy the human interest of the masses may mean to have one's social function removed from the field of vision. Nothing guarantees that a portraitist of today, when painting a famous surgeon at the breakfast table in the midst of his family, depicts his social function more precisely than a painter of the seventeenth century who portrayed his medical doctors as representing this profession, like Rembrandt in his "Anatomy Lesson."

7   The definition of the aura as a "unique phenomenon of a distance however close it may be" represents nothing but the formulation of the cult value of the work of art in categories of space and time perception. Distance is the opposite of closeness. The essentially distant object is the unapproachable one. Unapproachability is indeed a major quality of the cult image. True to its nature, it remains "distant, however close it may be." The closeness which one may gain from its subject matter does not impair the distance which it retains in its appearance.

8   To the extent to which the cult value of the painting is secularized the ideas of its fundamental uniqueness lose distinctness. In the imagination of the beholder the uniqueness of the phenomena which hold sway in the cult image is more and more displaced by the empirical uniqueness of the creator or of his creative achievement. To be sure, never completely so; the concept of authenticity always transcends mere genuineness. (This is particularly apparent in the collector who always retains some traces of the fetishist and who, by owning the work of art, shares in its ritual power.) Nevertheless, the function of the concept of authenticity remains determinate in the evaluation of art; with the secularization of art, authenticity displaces the cult value of the work.

9   In the case of films, mechanical reproduction is not, as with literature and painting, an external condition for mass distribution. Mechanical reproduction is inherent in the very technique of film production. This technique not only permits in the most direct way but virtually causes mass distribution. It enforces distribution because the production of a film is so expensive that an individual who, for instance, might afford to buy a painting no longer can afford to buy a film. In 1927 it was calculated that a major film, in order to pay its way, had to reach an audience of nine million. With the sound film, to be sure, a setback in its international distribution occurred at first: audiences became limited by language barriers. This coincided with the Fascist emphasis on national interests. It is more important to focus on this connection with Fascism than on this setback, which was soon minimized by synchronization. The simultaneity of both phenomena is attributable to the depression. The same disturbances which, on a larger scale, led to an attempt to maintain the existing property structure by sheer force led the endangered film capital to speed up the development of the sound film. The introduction of the sound film brought about a temporary relief, not only because it again brought the masses into the theaters but also because it merged new capital from the electrical industry with that of the film industry. Thus, viewed from the outside, the sound film promoted national interests, but seen from the inside it helped to internationalize film production even more than previously.

10 This polarity cannot come into its own in the aesthetics of Idealism. Its idea of beauty comprises these polar opposites without differentiating between them and consequently excludes their polarity. Yet in Hegel this polarity announces itself as clearly as possible within the limits of Idealism. We quote from his *Philosophy of History*:

> Images were known of old. Piety at an early time required them for worship, but it could do without *beautiful* images. These might even be disturbing. In every beautiful painting there is also something nonspiritual, merely external, but its spirit speaks to man through its beauty. Worshipping, conversely, is concerned with the work as an object, for it is but a spiritless stupor of the soul. ... Fine art has arisen ... in the church ..., although it has already gone beyond its principle as art.

Likewise, the following passage from *The Philosophy of Fine Art* indicates that Hegel sensed a problem here.

> We are beyond the stage of reverence for works of art as divine and objects deserving our worship. The impression they produce is one of a more reflective kind, and the emotions they arouse require a higher test. ... (G. W. F. Hegel, *The Philosophy of Fine Art*, trans., with notes, by F. P. B. Osmaston, Vol. I, p. 12, London, 1920).

The transition from the first kind of artistic reception to the second characterizes the history of artistic reception in general. Apart from that, a certain oscillation between these two polar modes of reception can be demonstrated for each work of art. Take the Sistine Madonna. Since Hubert Grimme's research it has been known that the Madonna originally was painted for the purpose of exhibition. Grimme's research was inspired by the question: What is the purpose of the molding in the foreground of the painting which the two cupids lean upon? How, Grimme asked further, did Raphael come to furnish the sky with two draperies? Research proved that the Madonna had been commissioned for the public lying-in-state of Pope Sixtus. The Popes lay in state in a certain side chapel of St. Peter's. On that occasion Raphael's picture had been fastened in a nichelike background of the chapel, supported by the coffin. In this picture Raphael portrays the Madonna approaching the papal coffin in clouds from the background of the niche, which was demarcated by green drapes. At the obsequies of Sixtus a pre-eminent exhibition value of Raphael's picture was taken advantage of. Some time later it was placed on the high altar in the church of the Black Friars at Piacenza. The reason for this exile is to be found in the Roman rites which forbid the use of paintings exhibited at obsequies as cult objects on the high altar. This regulation devalued Raphael's picture to some degree. In order to obtain an adequate price nevertheless, the Papal See resolved to add to the bargain the tacit toleration of the picture above the high altar. To avoid attention the picture was given to the monks of the far-off provincial town.

11 Bertolt Brecht, on a different level, engaged in analogous reflections: "If the concept of 'work of art' can no longer be applied to the thing that emerges once the work is transformed into a commodity, we have to eliminate this concept with cautious care but without fear, lest we liquidate the function of the very thing as well. For it has to go through this phase without mental reservation, and not as noncommittal deviation from the straight path; rather, what happens here with the work of art will change it fundamentally and erase its past to such an extent that should the old concept be taken up again – and it will, why not? – it will no longer stir any memory of the thing it once designated."

12 Abel Gance, op. cit., pp. 100–1.

13 Séverin-Mars, quoted by Abel Gance, op. cit., p. 100.

14 Alexandre Arnoux, *Cinéma pris*, 1929, p. 28.

15 Franz Werfel, "Ein Sommernachtstraum. Ein Film von Shakespeare und Reinhardt," *Neues Wiener Journal*, cited in *Lu* 15, November, 1935.

16 "The film ... provides – or could provide – useful insight into the details of human actions. ... Character is never used as a source of motivation; the inner life of the persons never supplies the principal cause of the plot and seldom is its main result" (Bertolt Brecht, *Versuche*, "Der Dreigroschenprozess," p. 268). The expansion of the field of the testable which mechanical equipment brings about for the actor corresponds to the extraordinary expansion of the field of the testable brought about for the individual

through economic conditions. Thus, vocational aptitude tests become constantly more important. What matters in these tests are segmental performances of the individual. The film shot and the vocational aptitude test are taken before a committee of experts. The camera director in the studio occupies a place identical with that of the examiner during aptitude tests.

17   Luigi Pirandello, *Si Gira*, quoted by Léon Pierre-Quint, "Signification du cinéma," *L'Art cinématographique*, op. cit., pp. 14–15.

18   Rudolf Arnheim, *Film als Kunst*, Berlin, 1932, pp. 176 f. In this context certain seemingly unimportant details in which the film director deviates from stage practices gain in interest. Such is the attempt to let the actor play without make-up, as made among others by Dreyer in his *Jeanne d'Arc*. Dreyer spent months seeking the forty actors who constitute the Inquisitors" tribunal. The search for these actors resembled that for stage properties that are hard to come by. Dreyer made every effort to avoid resemblances of age, build, and physiognomy. If the actor thus becomes a stage property, this latter, on the other hand, frequently functions as actor. At least it is not unusual for the film to assign a role to the stage property. Instead of choosing at random from a great wealth of examples, let us concentrate on a particularly convincing one. A clock that is working will always be a disturbance on the stage. There it cannot be permitted its function of measuring time. Even in a naturalistic play, astronomical time would clash with theatrical time. Under these circumstances it is highly revealing that the film can, whenever appropriate, use time as measured by a clock. From this more than from many other touches it may clearly be recognized that under certain circumstances each and every prop in a film may assume important functions. From here it is but one step to Pudovkin's statement that "the playing of an actor which is connected with an object and is built around it ... is always one of the strongest methods of cinematic construction" (W. Pudovkin, *Filmregie und Filmmanuskript*, Berlin, 1928, p. 126). The film is the first art form capable of demonstrating how matter plays tricks on man. Hence, films can be an excellent means of materialistic representation.

19   The change noted here in the method of exhibition caused by mechanical reproduction applies to politics as well. The present crisis of the bourgeois democracies comprises a crisis of the conditions which determine the public presentation of the rulers. Democracies exhibit a member of government directly and personally before the nation's representatives. Parliament is his public. Since the innovations of camera and recording equipment make it possible for the orator to become audible and visible to an unlimited number of persons, the presentation of the man of politics before camera and recording equipment becomes paramount. Parliaments, as much as theaters, are deserted. Radio and film not only affect the function of the professional actor but likewise the function of those who also exhibit themselves before this mechanical equipment, those who govern. Though their tasks may be different, the change affects equally the actor and the ruler. The trend is toward establishing controllable and transferrable skills under certain social conditions. This results in a new selection, a selection before the equipment from which the star and the dictator emerge victorious.

20   The privileged character of the respective techniques is lost. Aldous Huxley writes:

> Advances in technology have led ... to vulgarity. ... Process reproduction and the rotary press have made possible the indefinite multiplication of writing and pictures. Universal education and relatively high wages have created an enormous public who know how to read and can afford to buy reading and pictorial matter. A

great industry has been called into existence in order to supply these commodities. Now, artistic talent is a very rare phenomenon; whence it follows ... that, at every epoch and in all countries, most art has been bad. But the proportion of trash in the total artistic output is greater now than at any other period. That it must be so is a matter of simple arithmetic. The population of Western Europe has a little more than doubled during the last century. But the amount of reading – and seeing – matter has increased, I should imagine, at least twenty and possibly fifty or even a hundred times. If there were n men of talent in a population of x millions, there will presumably be 2n men of talent among 2x millions. The situation may be summed up thus. For every page of print and pictures published a century ago, twenty or perhaps even a hundred pages are published today. But for every man of talent then living, there are now only two men of talent. it may be of course that, thanks to universal education, many potential talents which in the past would have been still-born are now enabled to realize themselves. Let us assume, then, that there are now three or even four men of talent to every one of earlier times. it still remains true to say that the consumption of reading – and seeing – matter has far outstripped the natural production of gifted writers and draughtsmen. It is the same with hearing-matter. Prosperity, the gramophone and the radio have created an audience of hearers who consume an amount of hearing-matter that has increased out of all proportion to the increase of population and the consequent natural increase of talented musicians. It follows from all this that in all the arts the output of trash is both absolutely and relatively greater than it was in the past; and that it must remain greater for just so long as the world continues to consume the present inordinate quantities of reading-matter, seeing-matter, and hearing-matter" (Aldous Huxley, *Beyond the Mexique Bay. A Traveller's Journal*, London, 1949, pp. 274 ff. First published in 1934)

This mode of observation is obviously not progressive.

21 The boldness of the cameraman is indeed comparable to that of the surgeon. Luc Durtain lists among specific technical sleights of hand those "which are required in surgery in the case of certain difficult operations. I choose as an example a case from oto-rhinolaryngology; ... the so-called endonasal perspective procedure; or I refer to the acrobatic tricks of larynx surgery which have to be performed following the reversed picture in the laryngoscope. I might also speak of ear surgery which suggests the precision work of watchmakers. What range of the most subtle muscular acrobatics is required from the man who wants to repair or save the human body! We have only to think of the couching of a cataract where there is virtually a debate of steel with nearly fluid tissue, or of the major abdominal operations (laparotomy)" (Luc Durtain, op. cit).

22 This mode of observation may seem crude, but as the great theoretician Leonardo has shown, crude modes of observation may at times be usefully adduced. Leonardo compares painting and music as follows: "Painting is superior to music because, unlike unfortunate music, it does not have to die as soon as it is born. ... Music which is consumed in the very act of its birth is inferior to painting which the use of varnish has rendered eternal" (Trattato I, 29).

23 Renaissance painting offers a revealing analogy to this situation. The incomparable development of this art and its significance rested not least on the integration of a number of new sciences, or at least of new scientific data. Renaissance painting made use of anatomy and perspective, of mathematics, meteorology, and chromatology. Valéry

writes: "What could be further from us than the strange claim of a Leonardo to whom painting was a supreme goal and the ultimate demonstration of knowledge? Leonardo was convinced that painting demanded universal knowledge, and he did not even shrink from a theoretical analysis which to us is stunning because of its very depth and precision. ..." (Paul Valéry, *Pièces sur l'art*, "Autour de Corot," Paris, p. 191).

24   Rudolf Arnheim, loc. cit., p. 138.

25   "The work of art," says André Breton, "is valuable only in so far as it is vibrated by the reflexes of the future." Indeed, every developed art form intersects three lines of development. Technology works toward a certain form of art. Before the advent of the film there were photo booklets with pictures which flitted by the onlooker upon pressure of the thumb, thus portraying a boxing bout or a tennis match. Then there were the slot machines in bazaars; their picture sequences were produced by the turning of a crank.

Secondly, the traditional art forms in certain phases of their development strenuously work toward effects which later are effortlessly attained by the new ones. Before the rise of the movie the Dadaists' performances tried to create an audience reaction which Chaplin later evoked in a more natural way.

Thirdly, unspectacular social changes often promote a change in receptivity which will benefit the new art form. Before the movie had begun to create its public, pictures that were no longer immobile captivated an assembled audience in the so-called *Kaiserpanorama*. Here the public assembled before a screen into which stereoscopes were mounted, one to each beholder. By a mechanical process individual pictures appeared briefly before the stereoscopes, then made way for others. Edison still had to use similar devices in presenting the first movie strip before the film screen and projection were known. This strip was presented to a small public which stared into the apparatus in which the succession of pictures was reeling off. Incidentally, the institution of the *Kaiser-panorama* shows very clearly a dialectic of the development. Shortly before the movie turned the reception of pictures into a collective one, the individual viewing of pictures in these swiftly outmoded establishments came into play once more with an intensity comparable to that of the ancient priest beholding the statue of a divinity in the cella.

26   The theological archetype of this contemplation is the awareness of being alone with one's God. Such awareness, in the heyday of the bourgeoisie, went to strengthen the freedom to shake off clerical tutelage. During the decline of the bourgeoisie this awareness had to take into account the hidden tendency to withdraw from public affairs those forces which the individual draws upon in his communion with God.

27   Georges Duhamel, *Scènes de la vie future*, Paris, 1930, p. 52.

28   The film is the art form that is in keeping with the increased threat to his life which modern man has to face. Man's need to expose himself to shock effects is his adjustment to the dangers threatening him. The film corresponds to profound changes in the apperceptive apparatus – changes that are experienced on an individual scale by the man in the street in big-city traffic, on a historical scale by every present-day citizen.

29   As for Dadaism, insights important for Cubism and Futurism are to be gained from the movie. Both appear as deficient attempts of art to accommodate the pervasion of reality by the apparatus. In contrast to the film, these schools did not try to use the apparatus as such for the artistic presentation of reality, but aimed at some sort of alloy in the joint presentation of reality and apparatus. In Cubism, the premonition that this apparatus will be structurally based on optics plays a dominant part; in Futurism, it is the premonition of the effects of this apparatus which are brought out by the rapid sequence of the film strip.

30 Duhamel, op. cit., p. 58.
31 One technical feature is significant here, especially with regard to newsreels, the propagandist importance of which can hardly be overestimated. Mass reproduction is aided especially by the reproduction of masses. In big parades and monster rallies, in sports events, and in war, all of which nowadays are captured by camera and sound recording, the masses are brought face to face with themselves. This process, whose significance need not be stressed, is intimately connected with the development of the techniques of reproduction and photography. Mass movements are usually discerned more clearly by a camera than by the naked eye. A bird's-eye view best captures gatherings of hundreds of thousands. And even though such a view may be as accessible to the human eye as it is to the camera, the image received by the eye cannot be enlarged the way a negative is enlarged. This means that mass movements, including war, constitute a form of human behavior which particularly favors mechanical equipment.

Chapter 34

The Culture Industry [1944]

Max Horkheimer and Theodor W. Adorno

The Culture Industry: Enlightenment as Mass Deception

[…]

[…] Films and radio no longer need to present themselves as art. The truth that they are nothing but business is used as an ideology to legitimize the trash they intentionally produce. They call themselves industries, and the published figures for their directors' incomes quell any doubts about the social necessity of their finished products.

Interested parties like to explain the culture industry in technological terms. Its millions of participants, they argue, demand reproduction processes which inevitably lead to the use of standard products to meet the same needs at countless locations. The technical antithesis between few production centers and widely dispersed reception necessitates organization and planning by those in control. The standardized forms, it is claimed, were originally derived from the needs of the consumers: that is why they are accepted with so little resistance. In reality, a cycle of manipulation and retroactive need is unifying the system ever more tightly. What is not mentioned is that the basis on which technology is gaining power over society is the power of those whose economic position in society is strongest. Technical rationality today is the rationality of domination. It is the compulsive character of a society alienated from itself.

Horkheimer, Max and W. Adorno, Theodor, "The Culture Industry: Enlightenment as Mass Deception," pp. 95–97, 99–100, 108–113, 115–117, 128–133, 135–136 from *The Dialectic of Enlightenment: Philosophical Fragments*, ed. Gunzelin Schmid Noerr, trans. by Edmund Jephcott. Standford: Stanford University Press, 2002. (c) 1944 by Social Studies Association, NY. New edition (c) S. Fisher Verlag GmbH, Frankfurt am Main 1969. Reprinted with permission of Stanford University Press.

Classical Sociological Theory, Third Edition. Edited by Craig Calhoun, Joseph Gerteis, James Moody, Steven Pfaff, and Indermohan Virk. Editorial material and organization © 2012 John Wiley & Sons, Ltd. Published 2012 by John Wiley & Sons, Ltd.

Automobiles, bombs, and films hold the totality together until their leveling element demonstrates its power against the very system of injustice it served. For the present the technology of the culture industry confines itself to standardization and mass production and sacrifices what once distinguished the logic of the work from that of society. These adverse effects, however, should not be attributed to the internal laws of technology itself but to its function within the economy today. Any need which might escape the central control is repressed by that of individual consciousness. The step from telephone to radio has clearly distinguished the rotes. The former liberally permitted the participant to play the role of subject. The latter democratically makes everyone equally into listeners, in order to expose them in authoritarian fashion to the same programs put out by different stations. No mechanism of reply has been developed, and private transmissions are condemned to unfreedom. They confine themselves to the apocryphal sphere of "amateurs," who, in any case, are organized from above. Any trace of spontaneity in the audience of the official radio is steered and absorbed into a selection of specializations by talent-spotters, performance competitions, and sponsored events of every kind. The talents belong to the operation long before they are put on show; otherwise they would not conform so eagerly. The mentality of the public, which allegedly and actually favors the system of the culture industry, is a part of the system, not an excuse for it. If a branch of art follows the same recipe as one far removed from it in terms of its medium and subject matter; if the dramatic denouement in radio "soap operas" is used as an instructive example of how to solve technical difficulties – which are mastered no less in "jam sessions" than at the highest levels of jazz – or if a movement from Beethoven is loosely "adapted" in the same way as a Tolstoy novel is adapted for film, the pretext of meeting the public's spontaneous wishes is mere hot air. An explanation in terms of the specific interests of the technical apparatus and its personnel would be closer to the truth, provided that apparatus were understood in all its details as a part of the economic mechanism of selection. Added to this is the agreement, or at least the common determination, of the executive powers to produce or let pass nothing which does not conform to their tables, to their concept of the consumer, or, above all, to themselves.

If the objective social tendency of this age is incarnated in the obscure subjective intentions of board chairmen, this is primarily the case in the most powerful sectors of industry: steel, petroleum, electricity, chemicals. Compared to them the culture monopolies are weak and dependent. They have to keep in with the true wielders of power, to ensure that their sphere of mass society, the specific producr of which still has too much of cozy liberalism and Jewish intellectualism abour it, is not subjected to a series of purges. The dependence of the most powerful broadcasting company on the electrical industry, or of film on the banks, characterizes the whole sphere, the individual sectors of which are themselves economically intertwined. Everything is so tightly clustered that the concentration of intellect reaches a level where it overflows the demarcations between company names and technical sectors. The relentless unity of the culture industry bears witness to the emergent unity of politics. Sharp distinctions like those between A and B films, or between short stories published in magazines in differenr price segmenrs, do not so much reflect real differences as assist in the classification, organization, and identification of consumers. Something is provided for everyone so that no one can escape; differences are hammered home and propagated. The hierarchy of serial qualities purveyed to the public serves only to quantify it more completely. Everyone is supposed to behave spontaneously according to a "level" determined by indices and to select the category of mass produce manufactured for their type. On the charts of research organizations, indistinguishable from those of political propaganda, consumers are divided up as statistical material into red, green, and blue areas according to income group.

[...]

The whole world is passed through the filter of the culture industry. The familiar experience of the moviegoer, who perceives the street outside as a continuation of the film he has just left, because the film seeks strictly to reproduce the world of everyday perception, has become the guideline of production. The more densely and completely its techniques duplicate empirical objects, the more easily it creates the illusion that the world outside is a seamless extension of the one which has been revealed in the cinema. Since the abrupt introduction of the sound film, mechanical duplication has become entirely subservient to this objective. According to this tendency, life is to be made indistinguishable from the sound film. Far more strongly than the theatre of illusion, film denies its audience any dimension in which they might roam freely in imagination – contained by the film's framework but unsupervised by its precise actualities – without losing the thread; thus it trains those exposed to it to identify film directly with reality. The withering of imagination and spontaneity in the consumer of culture today need not be traced back to psychological mechanisms. The products themselves, especially the most characteristic, the sound film, cripple those faculties through their objective makeup. They are so constructed that their adequate comprehension requires a quick, observant, knowledgeable cast of mind but positively debars the spectator from thinking, if he is not to miss the fleeting facts. This kind of alertness is so ingrained that it does not even need to be activated in particular cases, while still repressing the powers of imagination. Anyone who is so absorbed by the world of the film, by gesture, image, and word, that he or she is unable to supply that which would have made it a world in the first place, does not need to be entirely transfixed by the special operations of the machinery at the moment of the performance. The required qualities of attention have become so familiar from other films and other culture products already known to him or her that they appear automatically. The power of industrial society is imprinted on people once and for all. The products of the culture industry are such that they can be alertly consumed even in a state of distraction. But each one is a model of the gigantic economic machinery, which, from the first, keeps everyone on their toes, both at work and in the leisure time which resembles it. In any sound film or any radio broadcast something is discernible which cannot be attributed as a social effect to any one of them, but to all together. Each single manifestation of the culture industry inescapably reproduces human beings as what the whole has made them. And all its agents, from the producer to the women's organizations, are on the alert to ensure that the simple reproduction of mind does not lead on to the expansion of mind.

[...]

Nevertheless, the culture industry remains the entertainment business. Its control of consumers is mediated by entertainment, and its hold will not be broken by outright dictate but by the hostility inherent in the principle of entertainment to anything which is more than itself. Since the tendencies of the culture industry are turned into the flesh and blood of the public by the social process as a whole, those tendencies are reinforced by the survival of the market in the industry. Demand has not yet been replaced by simple obedience. The major reorganization of the film industry shortly before the First World War, the material precondition for its expansion, was a deliberate adaptation to needs of the public registered at the ticket office, which were hardly thought worthy of consideration in the pioneering days of the screen. That view is still held by the captains of the film industry, who accept only more or less phenomenal box-office success as evidence and prudently ignore the counterevidence, truth. Their ideology is business. In this they are right to the extent that the power of the culture industry lies in its unity with fabricated need and not in simple antithesis to it – or even in the antithesis between omnipotence and powerlessness. Entertainment is the prolongation of work under late capitalism. It is sought by those who want to escape the mechanized labor process so that they can cope with it again. At the same time, however, mechanization has such power over leisure and its happiness, determines so thoroughly the fabrication of entertainment commodities, that the off-duty worker can experience nothing but after-images of the work process itself. The ostensible content is merely a faded foreground; what is imprinted is the automated sequence of standardized tasks. The only escape from the work process in factory and office is through adaptation to it in leisure time. This is the incurable sickness of all entertainment. Amusement congeals into boredom, since, to be amusement, it must cost no effort and therefore moves strictly along the well-worn grooves of association. The spectator must need no thoughts of his own: the product prescribes each reaction, not through any actual coherence – which collapses once exposed to thought – but through signals. Any logical connection presupposing mental capacity is scrupulously avoided. Developments are to emerge from the direcdy preceding situation, not from the idea of the whole. There is no plot which could withstand the screenwriters' eagerness to extract the maximum effect from the individual scene. Finally, even the schematic formula seems dangerous, since it provides some coherence of meaning, however meager, when only meaninglessness is acceptable. Often the plot is willfully denied the development called for by characters and theme under the old schema. Instead, the next step is determined by what the writers take to be their most effective idea. Obtusely ingenious surprises disrupt the plot. The product's tendency to fall back perniciously on the pure nonsense which, as buffoonery and clowning, was a legitimate part of popular art up to Chaplin and the Marx brothers, emerges most strikingly in the less sophisticated genres. Whereas the films of Greer Garson and Bette Davis can still derive some claim to a coherent plot from the unity of the socio-psychological case represented, the tendency to subvert meaning has taken over completely in the text of novelty songs, suspense films, and cartoons. The idea itself, like objects in comic and horror films, is massacred and mutilated. Novelty songs have always lived on contempt for meaning, which, as both ancestors and descendants of psychoanalysis, they reduce to the monotony of sexual symbolism. In crime and adventure films the spectators are begrudged even the opportunity to witness the resolution. Even in nonironic examples of the genre they must make do with the mere horror of situations connected in only the most perfunctory way.

Cartoon and stunt films were once exponents of fantasy against rationalism. They allowed justice to be done to the animals and things electrified by their technology, by granting the mutilated beings a second life. Today they merely confirm the victory of technological reason over truth. A few years ago they had solid plots which were resolved only in the whirl of pursuit of the final minutes. In this their procedure resembled that of slapstick comedy. But now the temporal relations have shifted. The opening sequences state a plot motif so that destruction can work on it throughout the action: with the audience in gleeful pursuit the protagonist is tossed about like a scrap of litter. The quantity of organized amusement is converted into the quality of organized cruelty. The self-elected censors of the film industry, its accomplices, monitor the duration of the atrocity prolonged into a hunt. The jollity dispels the joy supposedly conferred by the sight of an embrace and postpones satisfaction until the day of the pogrom. To the extent that cartoons do more than accustom the senses to the new tempo, they hammer into every brain the old lesson that continuous attrition, the breaking of all individual resistance, is the condition of life in this society. Donald Duck in the cartoons and the unfortunate victim in real life receive their beatings so that the spectators can accustom themselves to theirs.

The enjoyment of the violence done to the film character turns into violence against the spectator; distraction becomes exertion. No stimulant concocted by the experts may escape the weary eye; in face of the slick presentation no one may appear stupid even for a moment; everyone has to keep up, emulating the smartness displayed and propagated by the production. This makes it doubtful whether the culture industry even still fulfils its self-proclaimed function of distraction. If the majority of radio stations and cinemas were shut down, consumers probably would not feel too much deprived. In stepping from the street into the cinema, they no longer enter the world of dream in any case, and once the use of these institutions was no longer made obligatory by their mere existence, the urge to use them might not be so overwhelming. Shutting them down in this way would not be reactionary machine-wrecking. Those who suffered would not be the film enthusiasts but those who always pay the penalty in any case, the ones who had lagged behind. For the housewife, despite the films which are supposed to integrate her still further, the dark of the cinema grants a refuge in which she can spend a few unsupervised hours, just as once, when there were still dwellings and evening repose, she could sit gazing out of the window. The unemployed of the great centers find freshness in summer and warmth in winter in these places of regulated temperature. Apart from that, and even by the measure of the existing order, the bloated entertainment apparatus does not make life more worthy of human beings. The idea of "exploiting" the given technical possibilities, of fully utilizing the capacities for aesthetic mass consumption, is part of an economic system which refuses to utilize capacities when it is a question of abolishing hunger.

The culture industry endlessly cheats its consumers out of what it endlessly promises. The promissory note of pleasure issued by plot and packaging is indefinitely prolonged: the promise, which actually comprises the entire show, disdainfully intimates that there is nothing more to come, that the diner must be satisfied with reading the menu. The desire inflamed by the glossy names and images is served up finally with a celebration of the daily round it sought to escape. Of course, genuine works of art were not sexual exhibitions either. But by presenting denial as negative, they reversed, as it were, the debasement of the drive and rescued by mediation what had been denied. That is the secret of aesthetic sublimation: to present fulfillment in its brokenness. The culture industry does not sublimate: it suppresses. By constantly exhibiting the object of desire, the breasts beneath the sweater, the naked torso of the sporting hero, it merely goads the unsublimated anticipation of pleasure, which through the habit of denial has long since been mutilated as masochism. There is no erotic situation in which innuendo and incitement are not accompanied by the clear notification that things will never go so far. The Hays Office merely confirms the ritual which the culture industry has staged in any case: that of Tantalus. Works of art are ascetic and shameless; the culture industry is pornographic and prudish. It reduces love to romance. And, once reduced, much is permitted, even libertinage as a marketable specialty, purveyed by quota with the trade description "daring." The mass production of sexuality automatically brings about its repression. Because of his ubiquity, the film star with whom one is supposed to fall in love is, from the start, a copy of himself. Every tenor now sounds like a Caruso record, and the natural faces of Texas girls already resemble those of the established models by which they would be typecast in Hollywood. The mechanical reproduction of beauty – which, admittedly, is made only more inescapable by the reactionary culture zealots with their methodical idolization of individuality – no longer leaves any room for the unconscious idolatry with which the experience of beauty has always been linked. The triumph over beauty is completed by humor, the malicious pleasure elicited by any successful deprivation. There is laughter because there is nothing to laugh about. Laughter, whether reconciled or terrible, always accompanies the moment when a fear is ended. It indicates a release, whether from physical danger or from the grip of logic. Reconciled laughter resounds with the echo of escape from power; wrong laughter copes with fear by defecting to the agencies which inspire it. It echoes the inescapability of power. Fun is a medicinal bath which the entertainment industry never ceases to prescribe. It makes laughter the instrument for cheating happiness. To moments of happiness laughter is foreign; only operettas, and now films, present sex amid peals of merriment. But Baudelaire is as humorless as Hölderlin. In wrong society laughter is a sickness infecting happiness and drawing it into society's worthless totality. Laughter about something is always laughter at it, and the vital force which, according to Bergson, bursts through rigidity in laughter is, in truth, the irruption of barbarity, the self-assertion which, in convivial settings, dares to celebrate its liberation from scruple. The collective of those who laugh parodies humanity. They are monads, each abandoning himself to the pleasure – at the expense of all others and with the majority in support – of being ready to shrink from nothing. Their harmony presents a caricature of solidarity. What is infernal about wrong laughter is that it compellingly parodies what is best, reconciliation. Joy, however, is austere: *res severa verum gaudium*. The ideology of monasteries, that it is not asceticism but the sexual act which marks the renunciation of attainable bliss, is negatively confirmed by the gravity of the lover who presciently pins his whole life to the fleeting moment. The culture industry replaces pain, which is present in ecstasy no less than in asceticism, with jovial denial. Its supreme law is that its consumers shall at no price be given what they desire: and in that very deprivation they must take their laughing satisfaction. In each performance of the culture industry the permanent denial imposed by civilization is once more inflicted on and unmistakably demonstrated to its victims. To offer them something and to withhold it is one and the same. That is what the erotic commotion achieves. Just because it can never take place, everything revolves around the coitus. In film, to allow an illicit relationship without due punishment of the culprits is even more strictly tabooed than it is for the future son-in-law of a millionaire to be active in the workers' movement. Unlike that of the liberal era, industrial no less than nationalist culture can permit itself to inveigh against capitalism, but not to renounce the threat of castration. This threat constitutes its essence. It outlasts the organized relaxation of morals toward the wearers of uniforms, first in the jaunty films produced for them and then in reality. What is decisive today is no longer Puritanism, though it still asserts itself in the form of women's organizations, but the necessity, inherent in the system, of never releasing its grip on the consumer, of not for a moment allowing him or her to suspect that resistance is possible. This principle requires that while all needs should be presented to individuals as capable of fulfillment by the culture industry, they should be so set up in advance that individuals experience themselves through their needs only as eternal consumers, as the culture industry's object. Not only does it persuade them that its fraud is satisfaction; it also gives them to understand that they must make do with what is offered, whatever it may be. The flight from the everyday world, promised by the culture industry in all its branches, is much like the abduction of the daughter in the American cartoon: the father is holding the ladder in the dark. The culture industry presents that same everyday world as paradise. Escape, like elopement, is destined from the first to lead back to its starting point. Entertainment fosters the resignation which seeks to forget itself in entertainment.

[...]

The more strongly the culture industry entrenches itself, the more it can do as it chooses with the needs of consumers – producing, controlling, disciplining them; even withdrawing amusement altogether: here, no limits are set to cultural progress. But the tendency is immanent in the principle of entertainment itself, as a principle of bourgeois enlightenment. If the need for entertainment was largely created by industry, which recommended the work to the masses through its subject matter, the oleograph through the delicate morsel it portrayed and, conversely, the pudding mix through the image of a pudding, entertainment has always borne the trace of commercial brashness, of sales talk, the voice of the fairground buckster. But the original affinity between business and entertainment reveals itself in the meaning of entertainment itself: as society's apologia. To be entertained means to be in agreement. Entertainment makes itself possible only by insulating itself from the totality of the social process, making itself stupid and perversely renouncing from the first the inescapable claim of any work, even the most trivial: in its restrictedness to reflect the whole. Amusement always means putting things out of mind, forgetting suffering, even when it is on display. At its root is powerlessness. It is indeed escape, but not, as it claims, escape from bad reality but from the last thought of resisting that reality. The liberation which amusement promises is from thinking as negation. The shamelessness of the rhetorical question "What do people want?" lies in the fact that it appeals to the very people as thinking subjects whose subjectivity it specifically seeks to annul. Even on those occasions when the public rebels against the pleasure industry it displays the feebleness systematically instilled in it by that industry. Nevertheless, it has become increasingly difficult to keep the public in submission. The advance of stupidity must not lag behind the simultaneous advance of intelligence. In the age of statistics the masses are too astute to identify with the millionaire on the screen and too obtuse to deviate even minutely from the law of large numbers. Ideology hides itself in probability calculations. Fortune will not smile on all – just on the one who draws the winning ticket or, rather, the one designated to do so by a higher powet – usually the entertainment industry itself, which presents itself as ceaselessly in search of talent. Those discovered by the talent scouts and then built up by the studios are ideal types of the new, dependent middle classes. The female starlet is supposed to symbolize the secretary, though in a way which makes her seem predestined, unlike the real secretary, to wear the flowing evening gown. Thus she apprises the female spectator not only of the possibility that she, too, might appear on the screen but still more insistently of the distance between them. Only one can draw the winning lot, only one is prominent, and even though all have mathematically the same chance, it is so minimal for each individual that it is best to write it off at once and rejoice in the good fortune of someone else, who might just as well be oneself but never is. Where the culture industry still invites naïve identification, it immediately denies it. It is no longer possible to lose oneself in others. Once, film spectators saw their own wedding in that of others. Now the happy couple on the screen are specimens of the same species as everyone in the audience, but the sameness posits the insuperable separation of its human elements. The perfected similarity is the absolute difference. The identity of the species prohibits that of the individual cases. The culture industry has sardonically realized man's species being. Everyone amounts only to those qualities by which he or she can replace everyone else: all are fungible, mere specimens. As individuals they are absolutely replaceable, pure nothingness, and are made aware of this as soon as time deprives them of their sameness. This changes the inner composition of the religion of success, which they are sternly required to uphold.

[...]

In the demand for entertainment and relaxation, purpose has finally consumed the realm of the purposeless. But as the demand for the marketability of art becomes total, a shift in the inner economic composition of cultural commodities is becoming apparent. For the use which is made of the work of art in antagonistic society is largely that of confirming the very existence of the useless, which art's total subsumption under usefulness has abolished. In adapting itself entirely to need, the work of art defrauds human beings in advance of the liberation from the principle of utility which it is supposed to bring about. What might be called use value in the reception of cultural assets is being replaced by exchange value; enjoyment is giving way to being thete and being in the know, connoisseurship by enhanced prestige. The consumer becomes the ideology of the amusement industry, whose institutions he or she cannot escape. One has to have seen Mrs. Miniver, just as one must subscribe to *Life* and *Time*. Everything is perceived only from the point of view that it can serve as something else, however vaguely that other thing might be envisaged. Everything has value only in so far as it can be exchanged, not in so far as it is something in itself. For consumers the use value of art, its essence, is a fetish, and the fetish – the social valuation which they mistake for the merit of works of art – becomes its only use value, the only quality they enjoy. In this way the commodity character of art disintegrates just as it is fully realized. Art becomes a species of commodity, worked up and adapted to industrial production, saleable and exchangeable; but art as the species of commodity which exists in order to be sold yet not for sale becomes something hypocritically unsaleable as soon as the business transaction is no longer merely its intention but its sole principle. The Toscanini performance on the radio is, in a sense, unsaleable. One listens to it for nothing, and each note of the symphony is accompanied, as it were, by the sublime advertisement that the symphony is not being interrupted by advertisements – "This concert is brought to you as a public service." The deception takes place indirectly *via* the profit of all the united automobile and soap manufacturers, on whose payments the stations survive, and, of course, *via* the increased sales of the electrical industry as the producer of the receiver sets. Radio, the progressive latecomer to mass culture, is drawing conclusions which film's pseudomarket at present denies that industry. The technical sttucture of the commercial radio system makes it immune to liberal deviations of the kind the film industry can still permit itself in its own preserve. Film is a private enterprise which already represents the sovereign whole, in which respect it has some advantages over the other individual combines. Chesterfield is merely the nation's cigarette, but the radio is its mouthpiece. In the total assimilation of culture products into the commodity sphere radio makes no attempt to purvey its products as commodities. In America it levies no duty from the public. It thereby takes on the deceptive form of a disinterested, impartial authority, which fits fascism like a glove. In fascism radio becomes the universal mouthpiece of the *Führer*; in the loudspeakers on the street his voice merges with the howl of sirens proclaiming panic, from which modern propaganda is hard to distinguish in any case. The National Socialists knew that broadcasting gave their cause stature as the printing press did to the Reformation. The *Führer's* metaphysical charisma, invented by the sociology of religion, turned out finally to be merely the omnipresence of his radio addresses, which demonically parodies that of the divine spirit. The gigantic fact that the speech penetrates everywhere replaces its content, as the benevolent act of the Toscanini broadcast supplants its content, the symphony. No listener can apprehend the symphony's true coherence, while the *Führer's* address is in any case a lie. To posit the human word as absolute, the false commandment, is the immanent tendency of radio. Recommendation becomes command. The promotion of identical commodities under different brand names, the scientifically endorsed praise of the laxative in the slick voice of the announcer between the overtures of *La Traviata* and *Rienzi*, has become untenable if only for its silliness. One day the *Diktat* of production, the specific advertisement, veiled by the semblance of choice, can finally become the *Führer's* overt command. In a society of targe-scale fascistic rackets which agree among themselves on how much of the national product is to be allocated to providing for the needs of the people, to invite the people to use a particular soap powder would, in the end, seem anachronistic. In a more modern, less ceremonious style, the *Führer* directly orders both the holocaust and the supply of trash.

Today works of art, suitably packaged like political slogans, are pressed on a reluctant public at reduced prices by the culture industry; they are opened up for popular enjoyment like parks. However, the erosion of their genuine commodity character does not mean that they would be abolished in the life of a free society but that the last barrier to their debasement as cultural assets has now been removed. The abolition of educational privilege by disposing of culture at bargain prices does not admit the masses to the preserves from which they were formerly excluded but, under the existing social conditions, contributes to the decay of education and the progress of barbaric incoherence. Someone who in the nineteenth or early twentieth century spent money to attend a drama or a concert, paid the performance at least as much respect as the money spent. The citizen who wanted a return for his outlay might occasionally try to establish some connection to the work. The guidebooks to Wagner's music dramas or the commentaries on *Faust* bear witness to this. They form a transition to the biographical glaze applied to works of art and the other practices to which works of art are subjected today. Even when the art business was in the bloom of youth, use value was not dragged along as a mere appendage by exchange value but was developed as a precondition of the latter, to the social benefit of works of art. As long as it was expensive, art kept the citizen within some bounds. That is now over. Art's unbounded proximity to those exposed to it, no longer mediated by money, completes the alienation between work and consumer, which resemble each other in triumphant reification. In the culture industry respect is vanishing along with criticism: the latter gives way to mechanical expertise, the former to the forgetful cult of celebrities. For consumers, nothing is expensive any more. Nevertheless, they are dimly aware that the less something costs, the less it can be a gift to them. The twofold mistrust of traditional culture as ideology mingles with that of industrialized culture as fraud. Reduced to mere adjuncts, the degraded works of art are secretly rejected by their happy recipients along with the junk the medium has made them resemble. The public should rejoice that there is so much to see and hear. And indeed, everything is to be had. The "screenos" and cinema vaudevilles, the competitions in recognizing musical extracts, the free magazines, rewards, and gift articles handed out to the listeners of certain radio programs are not mere accidents, but continue what is happening to the culture products themselves. The symphony is becoming the prize for listening to the radio at all, and if the technology had its way the film would already be delivered to the apartment on the model of the radio. It is moving towards the commercial system. Television points the way to a development which easily enough could push the Warner brothers into the doubtless unwelcome position of little theatre performers and cultural conservatives. However, the pursuit of prizes has already left its imprint on consumer behavior. Because culture presents itself as a bonus, with unquestioned private and social benefits, its reception has become a matter of taking one's chances. The public crowds forward for fear of missing something. What that might be is unclear, but, at any rate, only those who join in have any chance. Fascism, however, hopes to reorganize the gift-receivers trained by the culture industry into its enforced adherents.

Culture is a paradoxical commodity. It is so completely subject to the law of exchange that it is no longer exchanged; it is so blindly equated with use that it can no longer be used. For this reason it merges with the advertisement. The more meaningless the latter appears under monopoly, the more omnipotent culture becomes. Its motives are economic enough. That life could continue without the whole culture industry is too certain; the satiation and apathy it generates among consumers are too great. It can do little to combat this from its own resources. Advertising is its elixir of life. But because its product ceaselessly reduces the pleasure it promises as a commodity to that mere promise, it finally coincides with the advertisement it needs on account of its own inability to please. In the competitive society advertising performed a social service in orienting the buyer in the market, facilitating choice and helping the more efficient but unknown supplier to find customers. It did not merely cost labor time, but saved it. Today, when the free market is coming to an end, those in control of the system are entrenching themselves in advertising. It strengthens the bond which shackles consumers to the big combines. Only those who can keep paying the exorbitant fees charged by the advertising agencies, and most of all by radio itself, that is, those who are already part of the system or are co-opted into it by the decisions of banks and industrial capital, can enter me pseudomarket as sellers. The costs of advertising, which finally flow back into the pockets of the combines, spare them the troublesome task of subduing unwanted outsiders; they guarantee that the wielders of influence remain among their peers, not unlike the resolutions of economic councils which control the establishment and continuation of businesses in the totalitarian state. Advertising today is a negative principle, a blocking device: anything which does not bear its seal of approval is economically suspect. All-pervasive advertising is certainly not needed to acquaint people with the goods on offer, the varieties of which are limited in any case. It benefits the selling of goods only directly. The termination of a familiar advertising campaign by an individual firm represents a loss of prestige, and is indeed an offence against the discipline which the leading clique imposes on its members. In wartime, commodities which can no longer be supplied continue to be advertised merely as a display of industrial power. At such times the subsidizing of the ideological media is more important than the repetition of names. Through their ubiquitous use under the pressure of the system, advertising techniques have invaded the idiom, the "style" of the culture industry. So complete is their triumph that in key positions it is no longer even explicit: the imposing buildings of the big companies, floodlit advertisements in stone, are free of advertising, merely displaying the illuminated company initials on their pinnacles, with no further need of self-congratulation. By contrast, the buildings surviving from the nineteenth century, the architecture of which still shamefully reveals their utility as consumer goods, their function as accommodation, are covered from basement to above roof level with hoardings and banners: the landscape becomes a mere background for signboards and symbols. Advertising becomes simply the art with which Goebbels presciently equated it, *l'art pour l'art*, advertising for advertising's sake, the pure representation of social power. In the influential American magazines *Life* and *Fortune* the images and texts of advertisements are, at a cursory glance, hardly distinguishable from the editorial section. The enthusiastic and unpaid picture story about the living habits and personal grooming of celebrities, which wins them new fans, is editorial, while the advertising pages rely on photographs and data so factual and lifelike that they represent the ideal of information to which the editorial section only aspires. Every film is a preview of the next, which promises yet again to unite the same heroic couple under the same exotic sun: anyone arriving late cannot tell whether he is watching the trailer or the real thing. The montage character of the culture industry, the synthetic, controlled manner in which its products are assembled – factory-like not only in the film studio but also, virtually, in the compilation of the cheap biographies, journalistic novels, and hit songs – predisposes it to advertising: the individual moment, in being detachable, replaceable, estranged even technically from any coherence of meaning, lends itself to purposes outside the work. The special effect, the trick, the isolated and repeatable individual performance have always conspired with the exhibition of commodities for advertising purposes, and today every close-up of a film actress is an advert for her name, every hit song a plug for its tune. Advertising and the culture industry are merging technically no less than economically. In both, the same thing appears in countless places, and the mechanical repetition of the same culture product is already that of the same propaganda slogan. In both, under the dictate of effectiveness, technique is becoming psychotechnique, a procedure for manipulating human beings. In both, the norms of the striking yet familiar, the easy but catchy, the worldly wise but straightforward hold good; everything is directed at overpowering a customer conceived as distracted or resistant.

[…]

[…] Today the culture industry has taken over the civilizing inhertance of the frontier and entrepreneurial democracy, whose receptivity to intellectual deviations was never too highly developed. All are free to dance and amuse themselves, just as, since the historical neutralization of religion, they have been free to join any of the countless sects. But freedom to choose an ideology, which always reflects economic coercion, everywhere proves to be freedom to be the same. The way in which the young girl accepts and performs the obligatory date, the tone of voice used on the telephone and in the most intimate situations, the choice of words in conversation, indeed, the whole inner life compartmentalized according to the categories of vulgarized depth psychology, bears witness to the attempt to turn oneself into an apparatus meeting the requirements of success, an apparatus which, even in its unconscious impulses, conforms to the model presented by the culture industry. The most intimate reactions of human beings have become so entirely reified, even to themselves, that the idea of anything peculiar to them survives only in extreme abstraction: personality means hardly more than dazzling white teeth and freedom from body odor and emotions. That is the triumph of advertising in the culture industry: the compulsive imitation by consumers of cultural commodities which, at the same time, they recognize as false.

Chapter 35

One-Dimensional Man [1964]

Herbert Marcuse

A comfortable, smooth, reasonable, democratic unfreedom prevails in advanced industrial civilization, a token of technical progress. Indeed, what could be more rational than the suppression of individuality in the mechanization of socially necessary but painful performances; the concentration of individual enterprises in more effective, more productive corporations; the regulation of free competition among unequally equipped economic subjects; the curtailment of prerogatives and national sovereignties which impede the international organization of resources. That this technological order also involves a political and intellectual coordination may be a regrettable and yet promising development.

The rights and liberties which were such vital factors in the origins and earlier stages of industrial society yield to a higher stage of this society: they are losing their traditional rationale and content. Freedom of thought, speech, and conscience were – just as free enterprise, which they served to promote and protect – essentially *critical* ideas, designed to replace an obsolescent material and intellectual culture by a more productive and rational one. Once institutionalized, these rights and liberties shared the fate of the society of which they had become an integral part. The achievement cancels the premises. [...]

Contemporary industrial civilization demonstrates that it has reached the stage at which "the free society" can no longer be adequately defined in the traditional terms of economic, political, and intellectual liberties, not because these liberties have become insignificant, but because they are too significant to be confined within the traditional forms. New modes of realization are needed, corresponding to the new capabilities of society.

Such new modes can be indicated only in negative terms because they would amount to the negation of the prevailing modes. Thus economic freedom would mean freedom *from* the economy – from being controlled by economic forces and relationships; freedom from the daily struggle for existence, from earning a living. Political freedom would mean liberation of the individuals *from* politics over which they have no effective control. Similarly, intellectual freedom would mean the restoration of individual thought now absorbed by mass communication and indoctrination, abolition of "public opinion" together with its markers. The unrealistic sound of these propositions is indicative, not of their utopian character, but of the strength of the forces which prevent their realization. The most effective and enduring form of warfare against liberation is the implanting of material and intellectual needs that perpetuate obsolete forms of the struggle for existence.

The intensity, the satisfaction and even the character of human needs, beyond the biological level, have always been preconditioned. Whether or not the possibility of doing or leaving, enjoying or destroying, possessing or rejecting something is seized as a *need* depends on whether or not it can be seen as desirable and necessary for the prevailing societal institutions and interests. In this sense, human needs are historical needs and, to the extent to which the society demands the repressive development of the individual, his needs themselves and their claim for satisfaction are subject to overriding critical standards.

We may distinguish both true and false needs. "False" are those which are superimposed upon the individual by particular social interests in his repression: the needs which perpetuate toil, aggressiveness, misery, and injustice. Their satisfaction might be most gratifying to the individual, but this happiness is not a condition which has to be maintained and protected if it serves to arrest the development of the ability (his own and others,) to recognize the disease of the whole and grasp the chances of curing the disease. The result then is euphoria in unhappiness. Most of the prevailing needs to relax, to have fun, to behave and consume in accordance with the advertisements, to love and hate what others love and hate, belong to this category of false needs.

Such needs have a societal content and function which are determined by external powers over which the individual has no control; the development and satisfaction of these needs is heteronomous. No matter how much such needs may have become the individual's own, reproduced and fortified by the conditions of his existence; no matter how much he identifies himself with them and finds himself in their satisfaction, they continue to be what they were from the beginning – products of a society whose dominant interest demands repression.

The prevalence of repressive needs is an accomplished fact, accepted in ignorance and defeat, but a fact that must be undone in the interest of the happy individual as well as all those whose misery is the price of his satisfaction. The only needs that have an unqualified claim for satisfaction are the vital ones – nourishment, clothing, lodging at the attainable level of culture. The satisfaction of these needs is the prerequisite for the realization of *all* needs, of the unsublimated as well as the sublimated ones. ...

The distinguishing feature of advanced industrial society is its effective suffocation of those needs which demand liberation – liberation also from that which is tolerable and rewarding and comfortable – while it sustains and absolves the destructive power and repressive function of the affluent society. Here, the social controls exact the overwhelming need for the production and consumption of waste; the need for stupefying work where it is no longer a real necessity; the need for modes of relaxation which soothe and prolong this stupefaction; the need for maintaining such deceptive liberties as free competition at administered prices, a free press which censors itself, free choice between brands and gadgets.

Under the rule of a repressive whole, liberty can be made into a powerful instrument of domination. The range of choice open to the individual is not the decisive factor in determining the degree of human freedom, but *what* can be chosen and what *is* chosen by the individual. The criterion for free choice can never be an absolute one, but neither is it entirely relative. Free election of masters does not abolish the masters or the slaves. Free choice among a wide variety of goods and services does not signify freedom if these goods and services sustain social controls over a life of toil and fear – that is, if they sustain alienation. And the spontaneous reproduction of superimposed needs by the individual does not establish autonomy; it only testifies to the efficacy of the controls. [...]

It is a rational universe which, by the mere weight and capabilities of its apparatus, blocks all escape. In its relation to the reality of daily life, the high culture of the past was many things – opposition and adornment, outcry and resignation. But it was also the appearance of the realm of freedom: the refusal to behave. Such refusal cannot be blocked without a compensation which seems more satisfying than the refusal. The conquest and unification of opposites, which finds its ideological glory in the transformation of higher into popular culture, takes place on a material ground of increased satisfaction. This is also the ground which allows a sweeping *desublimation*.

Artistic alienation is sublimation. It creates the images of conditions which are irreconcilable with the established Reality Principle but which, as cultural images, become tolerable, even edifying and useful. Now this imagery is invalidated. Its incorporation into the kitchen, the office, the shop; its commercial release for business and fun is, in a sense, desublimation – replacing mediated by immediate gratification. But it is desublimation practiced from a "position of strength" on the part of society, which can afford to grant more than before because its interests have become the innermost drives of its citizens, and because the joys which it grants promote social cohesion and contentment.

The Pleasure Principle absorbs the Reality Principle; sexuality is liberated (or rather liberalized) in socially constructive forms. This notion implies that there are repressive modes of desublimation,[1] compared with which the sublimated drives and objectives contain more deviation, more freedom, and more refusal to heed the social taboos. It appears that such repressive desublimation is indeed operative in the sexual sphere, and here, as in the desublimation of higher culture, it operates as the by-product of the social controls of technological reality, which extend liberty while intensifying domination. The link between desublimation and technological society can perhaps best be illuminated by discussing the change in the social use of instinctual energy.

In this society, not all the time spent on and with mechanisms is labor time (i.e., unpleasurable but necessary toil), and not all the energy saved by the machine is labor power. Mechanization has also "saved" libido, the energy of the Life Instincts – that is, has barred it from previous modes of realization. This is the kernel of truth in the romantic contrast between the modern traveler and the wandering poet or artisan, between assembly line and handicraft, town and city, factory-produced bread and the home-made loaf, the sailboat and the outboard motor, etc. True, this romantic pre-technical world was permeated with misery, toil, and filth, and these in turn were the background of all pleasure and joy. Still, there was a "landscape," a medium of libidinal experience which no longer exists.

With its disappearance (itself a historical prerequisite of progress), a whole dimension of human activity and passivity have been de-eroticized. The environment from which the individual could obtain pleasure – which he could cathect as gratifying almost as an extended zone of the body – has been rigidly reduced. Consequently, the "universe" of libidinous cathexis is likewise reduced. The effect is a localization and contraction of libido, the reduction of erotic to sexual experience and satisfaction.[2]

For example, compare love-making in a meadow and in an automobile, or a lovers' walk outside the town walls and on a Manhattan street. In the former cases, the environment partakes of and invites libidinal cathexis and tends to be eroticized. Libido transcends beyond the immediate erotogenic zones – a process of nonrepressive sublimation. In contrast, a mechanized environment seems to block such self-transcendence of libido. Impelled in the striving to extend the field of erotic gratification, libido becomes less "polymorphous," less capable of eroticism beyond localized sexuality, and the *latter* is intensified.

Thus diminishing erotic and intensifying sexual energy, the technological reality *limits the scope of sublimation*. It also reduces the *need* for sublimation. In the mental apparatus, the tension between that which is desired and that which is permitted seems considerably lowered, and the Reality Principle no longer seems to require a sweeping and painful transformation of instinctual needs. The individual must adapt himself to a world which does not seem to demand the denial of his innermost needs – a world which is not essentially hostile.

The organism is thus being preconditioned for the spontaneous acceptance of what is offered. Inasmuch as the greater liberty involves a contraction rather than extension and development of instinctual needs, it works *for* rather than *against* the status quo of general repression – one might speak of "institutionalized desublimation." The latter appears to be a vital factor in the making of the authoritarian personality of our time.

It has often been noted that advanced industrial civilization operates with a greater degree of sexual freedom – "operates" in the sense that the latter becomes a market value and a factor of social mores. Without ceasing to be an instrument of labor, the body is allowed to exhibit its sexual features in the everyday work world and in work relations. This is one of the unique achievements of industrial society – rendered possible by the reduction of dirty and heavy physical labor; by the availability of cheap, attractive clothing, beauty culture, and physical hygiene; by the requirements of the advertising industry, etc. The sexy office and sales girls, the handsome, virile junior executive and floor walker are highly marketable commodities, and the possession of suitable mistresses – once the prerogative of kings, princes, and lords – facilitates the career of even the less exalted ranks in the business community.

Functionalism, going artistic, promotes this trend. Shops and offices open themselves through huge glass windows and expose their personnel; inside, high counters and non-transparent partitions are coming down. The corrosion of privacy in massive apartment houses and suburban homes breaks the barrier which formerly separated the individual from the public existence and exposes more easily the attractive qualities of other wives and other husbands.

This socialization is not contradictory but complementary to the de-eroticization of the environment. Sex is integrated into work and public relations and is thus made more susceptible to (controlled) satisfaction. Technical progress and more comfortable living permit the systematic inclusion of libidinal components into the realm of commodity production and exchange. But no matter how controlled the mobilization of instinctual energy may be (it sometimes amounts to a scientific management of libido), no matter how much it may serve as a prop for the status quo – it is also gratifying to the managed individuals, just as racing the outboard motor, pushing the power lawn mower, and speeding the automobile are fun.

This mobilization and administration of libido may account for much of the voluntary compliance, the absence of terror, the pre-established harmony between individual needs and socially-required desires, goals, and aspirations. The technological and political conquest of the transcending factors in human existence, so characteristic of advanced industrial civilization, here asserts itself in the instinctual sphere: satisfaction in a way which generates submission and weakens the rationality of protest.

The range of socially permissible and desirable satisfaction is greatly enlarged, but through this satisfaction, the Pleasure Principle is reduced – deprived of the claims which are irreconcilable with the established society. Pleasure, thus adjusted, generates submission.

In contrast to the pleasures of adjusted desublimation, sublimation preserves the consciousness of the renunciations which the repressive society inflicts upon the individual, and thereby preserves the need for liberation. To be sure, all sublimation is enforced by the power of society, but the unhappy consciousness of this power already breaks through alienation. To be sure, all sublimation accepts the social barrier to instinctual gratification, but it also transgresses this barrier.

The Superego, in censoring the unconscious and in implanting conscience, also censors the censor because the developed conscience registers the forbidden evil act not only in the individual but also in his society. Conversely, loss of conscience due to the satisfactory liberties granted by an unfree society makes for a *happy consciousness* which facilitates acceptance of the misdeeds of this society. It is the token of declining autonomy and comprehension. Sublimation demands a high degree of autonomy and comprehension; it is mediation between the conscious and the unconscious, between the primary and secondary processes, between the intellect and instinct, renunciation and rebellion. In its most accomplished modes, such as in the artistic *oeuvre*, sublimation becomes the cognitive power which defeats suppression while bowing to it.

In the light of the cognitive function of this mode of sublimation, the desublimation rampant in advanced industrial society reveals its truly conformist function. This liberation of sexuality (and of aggressiveness) frees the instinctual drives from much of the unhappiness and discontent that elucidate the repressive power of the established universe of satisfaction. To be sure, there is pervasive unhappiness, and the happy consciousness is shaky enough – a thin surface over fear, frustration, and disgust. This unhappiness lends itself easily to political mobilization; without room for conscious development, it may become the instinctual reservoir for a new fascist way of life and death. But there are many ways in which the unhappiness beneath the happy consciousness may be turned into a source of strength and cohesion for the social order. The conflicts of the unhappy individual now seem far more amenable to cure than those which made for Freud's "discontent in civilization," and they seem more adequately defined in terms of the "neurotic personality of our time" than in terms of the eternal struggle between Eros and Thanatos.

The way in which controlled desublimation may weaken the instinctual revolt against the established Reality Principle may be illuminated by the contrast between the representation of sexuality in classical and romantic literature and in our contemporary literature. If one selects, from among the works which are, in their very substance and inner form, determined by the erotic commitment, such essentially different examples as Racine's *Phèdre*, Goethe's *Wahlverwandtschaften*, Baudelaire's *Les Fleurs du Mal*, Tolstoy's *Anna Karenina*, sexuality consistently appears in a highly sublimated, "mediated," reflective form – but in this form, it is absolute, uncompromising, unconditional. The dominion of Eros is, from the beginning, also that of Thanatos. Fulfillment is destruction, not in a moral or sociological but in an ontological sense. It is beyond good and evil, beyond social morality, and thus it remains beyond the reaches of the established Reality Principle, which this Eros refuses and explodes.

In contrast, desublimated sexuality is rampant in O'Neill's alcoholics and Faulkner's savages, in the *Streetcar Named Desire* and under the *Hot Tin Roof*, in *Lolita*, in all the stories of Hollywood and New York orgies, and the adventures of suburban housewives. This is infinitely more realistic, daring, uninhibited. It is part and parcel of the society in which it happens, but nowhere its negation. What happens is surely wild and obscene, virile and tasty, quite immoral – and, precisely because of that, perfectly harmless.

Freed from the sublimated form which was the very token of its irreconcilable dreams – a form which is the style, the language in which the story is told – sexuality turns into a vehicle for the bestsellers of oppression. It could not be said of any of the sexy women in contemporary literature what Balzac says of the whore Esther: that hers was the tenderness which blossoms only in infinity. This society turns everything it touches into a potential source of progress *and* of exploitation, of drudgery *and* satisfaction, of freedom *and* of oppression. Sexuality is no exception.

The concept of controlled desublimation would imply the possibility of a simultaneous release of repressed sexuality *and* aggressiveness, a possibility which seems incompatible with Freud's notion of the fixed quantum of instinctual energy available for distribution between the two primary drives. According to Freud, strengthening of sexuality (libido) would necessarily involve weakening of aggressiveness, and vice versa. However, if the socially permitted and encouraged release of libido would be that of partial and localized sexuality, it would be tantamount to an actual compression of erotic energy, and this desublimation would be compatible with the growth of unsublimated as well as sublimated forms of aggressiveness. The latter is rampant throughout contemporary industrial society.

Has it attained a degree of normalization where the individuals are getting used to the risk of their own dissolution and disintegration in the course of normal national preparedness? Or is this acquiescence entirely due to their impotence to do much about it? In any case, the risk of avoidable, man-made destruction has become normal equipment in the mental as well as material household of the people, so that it can no longer serve to indict or refute the established social system. Moreover, as part of their daily household, it may even tie them to this system. The economic and political connection between the absolute enemy and the high standard of living (and the desired level of employment!) is transparent enough, but also rational enough to be accepted.

Assuming that the Destruction Instinct (in the last analysis: the Death Instinct) is a large component of the energy which feeds the technical conquest of man and nature, it seems that society's growing capacity to manipulate technical progress also increases its *capacity to manipulate and control this instinct*, i.e., to satisfy it "productively." Then social cohesion would be strengthened at the deepest instinctual roots. The supreme risk, and even the fact of war would meet, not only with helpless acceptance, but also with instinctual approval on the part of the victims. Here too, we would have controlled desublimation.

Institutionalized desublimation thus appears to be an aspect of the "conquest of transcendence" achieved by the one-dimensional society. Just as this society tends to reduce, and even absorb opposition (the qualitative difference!) in the realm of politics and higher culture, so it does in the instinctual sphere. The result is the atrophy of the mental organs for grasping the contradictions and the alternatives and, in the one remaining dimension of technological rationality, the *Happy Consciousness* comes to prevail.

It reflects the belief that the real is rational, and that the established system, in spite of everything, delivers the goods. The people are led to find in the productive apparatus the effective agent of thought and action to which their personal thought and action can and must be surrendered. And in this transfer, the apparatus also assumes the role of a moral agent. Conscience is absolved by reification, by the general necessity of things.

In this general necessity, guilt has no place. One man can give the signal that liquidates hundreds and thousands of people, then declare himself free from all pangs of conscience, and live happily ever after. The antifascist powers who beat fascism on the battlefields reap the benefits of the Nazi scientists, generals, and engineers; they have the historical advantage of the late-comer. What begins as the horror of the concentration camps turns into the practice of training people for abnormal conditions – a subterranean human existence and the daily intake of radioactive nourishment. A Christian minister declares that it does not contradict Christian principles to prevent with all available means your neighbor from entering your bomb shelter. Another Christian minister contradicts his colleague and says it does. Who is right? Again, the neutrality of technological rationality shows forth over and above politics, and again it shows forth as spurious, for in both cases, it serves the politics of domination.

> The world of the concentration camps [...] was not an exceptionally monstrous society. What we saw there was the image, and in a sense the quintessence, of the infernal society into which we are plunged every day.[3]

It seems that even the most hideous transgressions can be repressed in such a manner that, for all practical purposes, they have ceased to be a danger for society. Or, if their eruption leads to functional disturbances in the individual (as in the case of one Hiroshima pilot), it does not disturb the functioning of society. A mental hospital manages the disturbance.

The Happy Consciousness has no limits – it arranges games with death and disfiguration in which fun, team work, and strategic importance mix in rewarding social harmony. [...]

Obviously, in the realm of the Happy Consciousness, guilt feeling has no place, and the calculus takes care of conscience. When the whole is at stake, there is no crime except that of rejecting the whole, or not defending it. Crime, guilt, and guilt feeling become a private affair. Freud revealed in the psyche of the individual the crimes of mankind, in the individual case history the history of the whole. This fatal link is successfully suppressed. Those who identify themselves with the whole, who are installed as the leaders and defenders of the whole can make mistakes, but they cannot do wrong – they are not guilty. They may become guilty again when this identification no longer holds, when they are gone.

NOTES

1 See my book *Eros and Civilization* (Boston: Beacon Press, 1954), esp. Chapter X.
2 In accordance with the terminology used in the later works of Freud: sexuality as "specialized" partial drive; Eros as that of the entire organism.
3 E. Ionesco, in *Nouvelle Revue Française*, July 1956, as quoted in *London Times Literary Supplement*, March 4, 1960.

Part VIII

Structural-Functional Analysis

Introduction to Part VIII

36 The Position of Sociological Theory

37 An Outline of the Social System

38 Manifest and Latent Functions

39 On Sociological Theories of the Middle Range

Introduction to Part VIII

Functionalism (sometimes called "structural-functionalism") refers to a body of theory first developed in the 1930s and 1940s that treats society as a set of interdependent systems. The theory rests on an organic analogy that likens a social system to a physical body, in which each subsystem is necessary to maintain the proper functioning of the entire organism. From a functionalist point of view, the key to understanding a social subsystem is thus to trace its function in the working of the whole.

According to such arguments, there are a number of functional "requisites" necessary to meet the basic needs of any society (see Aberle, et al., 1950). Specific subsystems develop to meet those social needs. Functional theorists generally assumed that these subsystems would tend toward a stable equilibrium, with social change proceeding in a gradual evolutionary manner. For example, the social need for a common form of communication leads to a stable, slowly evolving system of language. The need to control disruptive behavior leads to a relatively stable legal and political system. Perhaps most importantly, every society has some system for assigning people to different social positions and socializing them into the relevant roles, resulting in a relatively stable stratification system. To say that a system is "functional" is thus to say that it serves the needs of the society as a whole, not that it serves the interests of every individual.

The intellectual roots of functionalism stem largely from the organic perspectives of Auguste Comte, Herbert Spencer, and Emile Durkheim and the formal sociology of Georg Simmel. Spencer's work emphasized a social Darwinist position in which societies adapted to their environments through adaptation and natural selection, a position

Classical Sociological Theory, Third Edition. Edited by Craig Calhoun, Joseph Gerteis, James Moody, Steven Pfaff, and Indermohan Virk. Editorial material and organization © 2012 John Wiley & Sons, Ltd. Published 2012 by John Wiley & Sons, Ltd.

used to support laissez faire political perspectives in the late 19th century. Durkheim adopted this organic analogy, focusing on the way that social systems functioned to produce different forms of integration. Durkheim also influenced the later functionalists by noting that the cause of a given phenomenon and its function were separate.

This early work, and especially that of Durkheim, spawned two distinct legacies. In France, it influenced the work of structuralist anthropology, which in turn deeply influenced theorists such as Foucault and Bourdieu (see *Contemporary Sociological Theory*, the sister volume to this reader). In America, it fostered the functionalists. Functionalist ideas were rekindled by the theoretical efforts of Talcott Parsons and his students and colleagues, most notably Robert K. Merton. Substantive work in the functionalist tradition has focused on system-level properties, attempting to identify and understand how various elements of society fit together. Parsons claimed that the study of *social institutions* was the primary business of sociology, and a number of studies focused on how institutions develop and the functions they exercise.

Lives and Intellectual Contexts

Talcott Parsons and Robert Merton are the central figures in the American structural-functionalist tradition. As this introduction will detail below, Parsons and Merton differed in many ways; however, the two figures were immensely important in the development of functionalism as a central mode of inquiry in mid-20th-century American sociology.

Talcott Parsons (1902–79) was born in Colorado Springs, Colorado. He earned his undergraduate degree from Amherst College where he studied both biology and economics. After graduating, he spent a year at the London School of Economics. There, he was introduced to the field of sociology and took two classes with Bronislaw Malinowski, the famous structural anthropologist. After his year in London, Parsons accepted an exchange fellowship at Heidelberg. Max Weber had died several years before Parsons arrived at Heidelberg, but his thinking still held a strong influence there. Traces of Weber's thought are especially evident in Parsons' early work. His focus on the social action as the proper subject for sociology is directly influenced by Weber's definition of the field. In fact, Parsons introduced Weber's work to much of the English-speaking academic world with his translation of the first part of *Economy and Society*. Weber's focus on social action became crucial to Parsons' early theoretical contributions.

Parsons' first academic position was as an instructor in the Harvard economics department. He moved to sociology when Pitirim Sorokin founded the department in 1930. Parsons published his first major work, *The Structure of Social Action*, in 1937. In 1939 he was given tenure at Harvard, and was appointed the chair of the Harvard sociology department in 1944. He went on to found the influential Program in Social Relations in 1946. The Program in Social Relations was Parsons' attempt to realize his vision of an integrated system of social sciences. He died in 1979 while returning to Heidelberg on the fiftieth anniversary of his Ph.D.

Robert K. Merton (1910–2003) was born in Philadelphia to a working-class Jewish immigrant family. After winning a scholarship to Temple University, where he became interested in sociology, he went on to do his graduate work at Harvard with Talcott Parsons and George Sarton. Merton, along with his colleague Paul Lazarsfeld, was largely responsible for making the sociology department at Columbia University famous by focusing attention away from grand theory and toward empirical research. He served as the associate director of Columbia's Bureau of Applied Social Research (1942–71). Merton was University Professor Emeritus at Columbia University when he passed away in 2003.

American Structural-Functionalism

Of Parsons' many books and papers, *The Structure of Social Action* (1937) and *The Social System* (1951) are his most influential. In *The Structure of Social Action*, Parsons turned a critical eye on the work of four classical theorists (Alfred Marshall, Vilfredo Pareto, Emile Durkheim, and Max Weber), showing how each had responded to the inadequacies of simple utilitarian perspectives in social thought. Through careful critique and comparison, Parsons showed that the four theorists converged on a single underlying vision of social order and action. This vision was neither individualistically rational (*utilitarian*) nor normatively determined (*idealistic*), but instead a synthesis that he termed "voluntaristic." Voluntaristic action implies that people make choices in a way that balances normative and self-interested pressures. For order to prevail in a system of such agents, Parsons suggested that some notion of value consensus was needed. Like Durkheim, Parsons did not suggest that a society would or should adopt any particular set of values. Rather, he argued that a society simply needs some common set of values as orienting principles.

Parsons and his colleagues extended the basic elements of the voluntaristic theory of action by introducing what they called *pattern variables*. The five pattern variables are value dimensions that characterize basic dilemmas facing actors, and are represented with labels that define extreme positions of each continuum. The first of the five pattern variables is gratification ↔ discipline, relating to the extent of an actor's emotional involvement. The second is private ↔ collective, depending on whether action relates to the needs of the individual or the needs of a wider population. Universalism ↔ particularism refers to whether action relates to a particular person, such as one's child, or a wider class of generalized others. Fourth, interaction with others can be related to their achievements or their ascribed characteristics (achievement ↔ ascription). And finally, specificity ↔ diffuseness refers to the breadth of possible roles an actor can draw upon in any given interaction.

After his first book, Parsons broadened his focus on action to encompass the larger social context. Parsons argued that society was composed of three interdependent systems: a *cultural* system, consisting of shared symbols (i.e., language, arts, etc.) which serve as modes of expression among actors; a *personality* system, consisting of elements necessary for unique identity; and a *social* system, consisting of modes of interaction among actors. The cultural system becomes connected to the personality system through a process of *internalization* in which actors incorporate cultural factors into their own identities. Understanding the connection between the personality system and the social system involves identifying social roles, which are defined through a process of *socialization*. Finally, Parsons argued that the cultural system and the social system are connected through *social institutions*, which systematize culture within social interaction and roles (see Münch, 1994: 16–30).

Having identified the major systems of society and the relevant features of individual action, Parsons argued that the entire complex was governed by certain functional requirements. Parsons and his colleagues Robert F. Bales and Edward A. Shils described four spheres of activity that any society must accomplish in order to maintain itself. The four functions are usually referred to by their acronym, **AGIL**. The first element is **A**daptation, which refers to how well the social system adapts to its material environment. The economic organization of any society is largely captured under this sphere. The second is **G**oal attainment, or the ability of the group to identify and pursue common goals, even though each member may have contrasting individual goals. Political organization is likely to fall under this sphere. Third, **I**ntegration refers to dimensions of cohesion and solidarity that unite the group. Integration is complicated by the multiple roles that people play in diverse settings (work roles, family roles, etc.), but referred to norms that promote a sense of "we-ness" among the group (Alexander, 1987). Finally, **L**atent pattern maintenance refers to the sphere of general values. While largely subjective, these values tend to be institutionalized within any given society.

While it is impossible to capture in excerpts the full breadth and richness of Parsons' work, the pieces below are intended to cover a wide range of Parsons' thought while focusing on those ideas most influential for later theory development. In "The Position of Sociological Theory" (1948), Parsons presents an early statement of his central ideas. The selection from *Theories of Society* (1961) called "An Outline of the Social System" captures later ideas developed with Bales and Shils.

Merton's writings span multiple sub-fields in sociology. His most consistent empirical focus was on the sociology of knowledge and science – early in his career he published *Science, Technology and Society in Seventeenth Century England* (1938), and he continued to write in the field until his death. But he was also influential in the areas of crime and deviance. His collection of work in *Social Theory and Social Structure* (1949/1957/1968) captures a great deal of this breadth, and provides a useful starting point for reading his work. Of the work not summarized here, "Contributions to the Theory of Reference Group Behavior" and "The Self-fulfilling Prophecy" are among the most widely read. Throughout his work, while maintaining a generally functionalist approach, his strong commitment to understanding phenomena of the "middle range" – those phenomena cast at neither too abstract nor too particularistic a level – contrasts directly with the broad theoretical orientation of Parsons.

The two pieces abstracted below represent Merton's general statements on functionalism and the scope of scientific research. His distinction between manifest and latent functions provides an important answer to the teleological problem of functionalist theory – that is, the problem of conflating the cause of a given phenomenon with its functional ends. Merton argues that a given social action, such as a rain-dance, might be intended for a manifest function (producing rain). Nonetheless, it may also serve another end (building solidarity within the group). This distinction frees functionalists from needing to link the actors' purposes with the functional needs of a society. In contrast to Parsons, Merton argues in "Theories of the Middle Range" that sociologists should develop theories that "lie between the minor but necessary working hypotheses" of research and the "all-inclusive systematic efforts to develop a unified theory" that would explain all social phenomena.

The Legacy of Functionalism

The decline of functionalism was swift, with few decidedly functional theoretical works appearing after the middle 1970s. Functionalism, especially Parsonian functionalism, was challenged on multiple fronts. Critics argued that there was an inherent conservative bias in the Parsonian focus on stability and function, which ignored important tensions within societies. With the rise of the Civil Rights movement and reactions to American action abroad, the harmonious self-balancing system seemed hard to square with direct observation. Aside from the ideological implications, critics charged that Parsonian theory's inability to accommodate dramatic social change and conflict was itself problematic. Additionally, a general critique of functional theory is that it is *teleological*: that the ends of a given phenomenon are sufficient for *causing* the phenomenon. Since such theories reverse the causal order, the underlying logic appeared flawed (but it should be pointed out that Parsons saw this as a misreading of his work). Finally, contemporary theoretic work moved away from the macro level to the individual level with the simultaneous rise of social exchange theory and symbolic interactionism. While exchange theory largely rejected the normative aspects of Parsons in favor of a rational utilitarian perspective, symbolic interactionist approaches claimed a greater creative activity for individuals than the pattern variable scheme would allow, resulting in both approaches being able to explain individual action without need for the overarching Parsonian frame.

Structural-functionalism thus fell deeply out of favor in American sociology by the 1970s. Interestingly, it was particularly Parsons' version, and not Merton's, that was rejected. Merton's work remained relevant for particular sub-fields, such as the sociology of deviance, even while functionalism's dominance waned generally. In part this was also because Merton's middle-range theory seemed more suited to the increasingly individual-level empirical work in the discipline.

But just as this broad historical cycle took structural-functionalism out of favor, so it seemed to be again on the upswing. In the mid 1980s, some aspects of functionalism reappeared, sparked largely through the work of Jeffrey C. Alexander. Alexander has argued that critics of Parsons were correct in many of their aspects, but that a desire to link individual action to wider social norms and a larger systemic view reflects many of the same goals as Parsons. As such, some of the basic systemic elements of a functional perspective provide useful theoretical tools for sociology today. A related body of work on social systems comes from the work of Niklas Luhmann (1995) and incorporates aspects of Parsons' work with that of General Systems Theory (Buckley, 1967).

Ironically, as rational choice theory becomes increasingly dominant in the social sciences, Parsons' emphasis on the contexts and limits of our choices – given by our personality systems, normative environment, and even our biological makeup – provides a necessary reminder of the boundedness of rational action.

SELECTED BIBLIOGRAPHY

Aberle, D.F., A.K. Cohen, A.K. Davis, M.J. Levy Jr., and F.X. Sutton. 1950. "The Functional Prerequisites of a Society." *Ethics* 60(2):100–111. (This piece provides a simple introduction to what the functionalists felt were the necessary elements for making a society work.)

Alexander, Jeffrey C. 1987. *Twenty Lectures: Sociological Theory Since World War II*. New York: Columbia University Press. (Alexander outlines the major currents of social thought during this time in a well-written and clear set of lectures. Most of the early lectures are devoted to Parsons' work.)

Calhoun, Craig. (ed.) 2010. Sociology of Science, Sociology as Science. New York: Columbia University Press. Merton, Robert K. 1968. *Social Theory and Social Structure*. New York: The Free Press. (A collection of Merton's most central work, containing articles on a wide range of theoretical and empirical topics.)

Münch, Richard. 1994. *Sociological Theory: From the 1920s to the 1960s*. Chicago: Nelson-Hall Publishers. (This volume is dedicated almost entirely to Parsons and provides an excellent interpretation and introduction.)

Parsons, Talcott. 1949 (1937). *The Structure of Social Action*. Glencoe, Illinois: The Free Press. (Parsons' major early work on the action frame of reference and its link to social structure.)

Parsons, Talcott. 1951. *The Social System*. New York: The Free Press. (The major work of Parsons' later multi-level theory of the social system.)

Parsons, Talcott. 1977. *The Evolution of Modern Societies*. Edited by Jackson Toby Englewood Cliff, NJ: Prentice-Hall. (A synthetic presentation of a later version of Parsons' theory.)

Ritzer, George. 1992. *Sociological Theory*. New York: McGraw-Hill. (Provides a nice overview of functionalist theory, situating it well within the broader theoretical context of the time.)

Smelser, Neil J. 1963. *Theory of Collective Behavior*. New York: The Free Press. (Chapter 2 is a clear summary of Parsonian theory. Smelser uses this as a basis for his own more specialized theory.)

Chapter 36

The Position of Sociological Theory [1948]

Talcott Parsons

A Few Basic Postulates

It seems possible to lay down a few fundamental propositions which can serve as general guiding lines for the more technical task of building a systematic treatment of sociological theory. I shall try to state these in sufficiently general form to leave room for a variety of different approaches in working out their implications in considerable detail. The following five seem to me the most essential of these basic postulates:

A. Systematic theory itself is of fundamental importance to any science. There is, of course, no intention to deny that work which can be quite legitimately called scientific can develop without systematic theory. Morphologies, classifications and empirical generalizations of various sorts have played very important parts in the development of a variety of sciences. The highest levels of scientific development, however, are not reached without conceptualization on the level of what is ordinarily called that of the theoretical system. The closer social science approaches to realizing this possibility, the more mature will it be considered as a science and the greater the predictive power which it will command.

B. The theoretical system which is basic to sociology must be broader than that of the science of sociology itself. It must be a theory of social systems. There has historically been an important so-called "encyclopedic" view which considered sociology the synthesis of all our knowledge of human social behavior. This has the

Parsons, Talcott, "The Position of Sociological Theory," pp. 156–163 from Talcott Parsons, "The Position of Sociological Theory." *American Sociological Review*, 13, 2. Washington: American Sociological Association, 1948.

Classical Sociological Theory, Third Edition. Edited by Craig Calhoun, Joseph Gerteis, James Moody, Steven Pfaff, and Indermohan Virk. Editorial material and organization © 2012 John Wiley & Sons, Ltd. Published 2012 by John Wiley & Sons, Ltd.

consequence of making economics, political science, etc., branches of sociology, which is not in accord either with current academic reality or with good analytical procedure. We must somehow work out a theoretical scheme which articulates our own field with others which are equally part of the same broader fundamental system.

C. The systematic theory which is most fruitful for our field must conform with the "structural-functional" type, which is current in biological theory, notably physiology. Intrinsically the type of theoretical system best exemplified by analytical mechanics is more desirable, but is not now attainable in our field either as a theoretical system as such or as a useful tool of empirical analysis over a wide range. The most notable attempt to develop such a system was that of Pareto, which with all its merits has not proved very fruitful as a tool in empirical research. The most essential point about a structural-functional theory is that by the use of structural categories it simplifies dynamic problems to the point where a significant proportion of them became empirically manageable with the observational and analytical resources we can hope to command in the near future.

D. The theory must be formulated within what may be called the "action" frame of reference. It cannot, that is, be completely behavioristic in the sense of excluding all reference to the point of view of the actor himself and to what is imputed as belonging to his internal or subjective mental processes. This postulate is essential in order to make it possible to achieve a high degree of articulation with the motivational categories of contemporary psychology which deal with such things as attitudes, sentiments, goals, complexes, and the like.

E. The theoretical system must so far as possible be framed in terms of genuinely operational concepts. The ideal is to have theoretical categories of such a character that the empirical values of the variables concerned are the immediate products of our observational procedures. In relatively few fields of social science is any close approach to this yet possible, but with further development both on the theoretical side and in the invention of new observational and experimental procedures great progress in this direction is to be expected.

Some Methodological Prerequisites of the Formulation of a System

A. *Analysis of the action frame of reference.* In order to be clear about the implications of postulate D above, it is essential to work out some of the major features and implication of the action schema. There are a variety of ways of doing this, but it has seemed on the whole most fruitful in the first instance to distinguish the orientation of the actor on the one hand, and the structure of the situation on the other. Though the situation includes both the physical environment and other persons, the point of view from which it must be analyzed for this purpose is not that of the physical or biological sciences as such, but the various types of significance of situational facts *to the actor*. This means that the analysis of the situation must be fully integrated with the analysis of action itself. Action, in turn, it seems convenient to analyze in terms of three fundamental modes of orientation, which may be called cognitive, goal directed, and affective, respectively. We can, that is, have an adequate analysis of the action of the individual only so far as we understand his action and his situation in terms of his attempts to know it cognitively, in terms of the goals he is striving to achieve, and in terms of his affective attitudes toward these components and toward the situation. This is a very broad and non-commital schema which is, in fundamental respects, in general current use.

B. *The functional prerequisites of the social system.* Somewhat analogous to the spelling out of the action frame of reference is an analysis of the functional prerequisites of the social system; that is, of a system of social action involving a plurality of interacting individuals. If the social system is to be the major unit of reference of the total theoretical schema as a whole, it must be treated in functional terms. It is assumed as a matter of empirical fact that it has either certain given characteristics as a system which differentiate it from other systems and from the non-social situation, or there is a relatively definite empirically observed pattern of change in these characteristics analogous to the pattern of maturation of the young organism. Functional requirements of the maintenance of any such pattern system or pattern line of change can be generalized to a certain degree. In the first place, of course, a social system must somehow provide for the minimum biological and psychological needs of a sufficient proportion of its component members. On a more strictly social level, there seem to be two primary fundamental foci of its functional prerequisites. One lies in the problem of order, in the problem of the coordination of the activities of the various members in such a way that they are prevented from mutually blocking each other's action or destroying one another by actual physical destruction of the organisms, and, on the other hand, they are sufficiently geared in with each other so that they do mutually contribute to the functioning of the system as a whole. The second focus is on adequacy of motivation. The system can only function if a sufficient proportion of its members perform the essential social roles with an adequate degree of effectiveness. If they are not adequately motivated to this minimum level of contribution to the system, the system itself, of course, can not operate. A variety of further elaborations of the problem of functional prerequisites can be worked out from these starting points.

C. *The bases of structure in social systems.* A third fundamental methodological focus is in the nature of the structuring of the social system and the points of reference which must be considered in order to analyze that structuring. A structural category in its significance for a structural-functional system must be treated as a relatively stable patterning of the relationships of the parts, which in this connection may be treated either as component actors or as the roles in terms of which they participate in social relationships. One aspect of the structuring of the system must be what is conveniently called "institutionalization";[1] that is, the organization of action around sufficiently stable patterns so that it may be treated as structured from the point of view of the system. This theoretical function is to enable their assumption as constants for the treatment of limited dynamic problems. There are varying degrees of institutionalization of action in different parts of the total social system.

The second major aspect of the structuring of social systems is differentiation and the patterns according to which differentiation must be studied. This is a very complicated problem, and in general, treatment of it must be conceded to be in a rather unsatisfactory state. It is above all essential, however, that modes of differentiation be treated in terms of a system of categories which make different social structures comparable with each other on the structural level. Without this, any high level of dynamic generalization will prove to be impossible. The most promising lead to solving this problem seems to lie in the demonstration of the existence of certain invariant points of reference about which differentiated structures focus. Some of these may lie in the external non-social situation or action; for instance, it is possible to systematize the comparison of kinship structures by using the fundamental biological facts of relatedness through biological descent as a set of invariant points of reference. Seen in this light, social systems of kinship become as it were variations on the biological theme. In a somewhat comparable way, it is possible to treat certain elements of the structure of action in terms of the pursuit of specific goals and the social relationship complexes which grow out of that pursuit, as another set of invariant points of reference which makes structures in such areas as technology, exchange, property, organization, and the like, fundamentally comparable with each other. This is one aspect of the field which is in need of the most intensive analytical development.

The Main Conceptual Components of the Social System

In the terms most immediately relevant to the sociological level of theoretical analysis, it seems convenient to classify the major conceptual components under the following four categories:

A. The structure of the situation.
B. The cultural tradition.
C. Institutional structure.
D. Motivational forces and mechanisms.

A. The role of the structure of the situation has already been commented on above. Here it is necessary only to say that it is essential to keep continually in mind a distinction of two major levels. The first is the structure of the situation from the point of view of any given individual actor; the second, from the point of view of the functioning of the social system under consideration as a whole. Failure to distinguish these two levels was, for instance, the primary source of the dilemma into which Durkheim fell which was responsible for most of the controversy over the group mind problem. For the most part, the categorization of this area is relatively familiar. It should only be stated that there will be refinements and shifts of emphasis as a result of further development of the more distinctively sociological elements of the total theoretical system.

B. The cultural tradition. In general the usual anthropological definition of culture is applicable in this context.[2] Culture in this sense consists in those patterns relative to behavior and the products of human action which may be transmitted, that is, passed on from generation to generation independently of the biological genes. It is an exceedingly varied and complex entity, and one of the most imperative theoretical tasks is to work out careful and analytical distinctions of the different elements which make it up and of their different relations to the levels of social structure and action. The difference from the usual anthropological usage of the concept culture lies in our interest in the particularly strategic role which is played by those elements in the cultural tradition which define ideal patterns governing the action of individuals. Their strategic significance derives from the fact that these are the patterns of culture which are susceptible of institutionalization, thereby forming components of the main structure of the social system itself. It clarifies discussion of this field, it seems to me, to make clear that there is not a substantive distinction between cultural and institutional patterns, but rather it should be held that all institutional patterns are cultural. However, only some cultural patterns become institutionalized and therefore have the special significance for the social system which institutions have. The distinction is one of functional relationship to the social system.

C. Institutional structure. This is that aspect of the conceptual analysis of the social system which is of closest relevance to the sociologist. Its most generalized role in the social system has been adequately described under C in the preceding section, and will be further elaborated below.

D. Motivational forces and mechanisms. It is here that the psychological theory which is essential to the theory of social systems finds its place. It should be made quite clear that many elements of psychological theory are of only secondary relevance to the theory of social systems. This is true of a great deal of physiological psychology and also of the more idiosyncratic elements of the theory of personality. Fundamentally the basic concern of the theory of social systems is with those elements of motivation which deal with the motivation of typical or expected behavior in social roles, and those tendencies which motivate socially significant deviance. It is important to make clear that the very common statement that psychology provides certain premises or underlying assumptions for the theory of social systems is not correct. This psychological component does not constitute a set of assumptions which lie outside the system, but an indispensable component *of the system itself*. It seems to me that the relation between the psychological theory of motivation of social action and the sociological aspect of the theory of social systems is closely analogous to that between biochemistry and physiology. They are both inextricably interlocked in the same body of analytical thinking in such a way that they are only analytically distinguishable.

Institutions as the Theoretical Focus of Sociological Science

It has been stated above that sociology should not claim to be the encyclopedic science of all human social behavior, but should find a place *among* the various social sciences. In terms of this point of view, institutions constitute the logical focus of sociology. When, for instance, some of the difficulties associated with group mind problems are stripped away, I think this is what is left of Durkheim's emphasis on the study of society as a phenomenon *sui generis*. This point of view should not, however, be interpreted to mean that sociology should be confined to the formal classificatory treatment of the structure of institutions. I should prefer the formula that institutions are the *focus* of its interest and that almost any component of the social system which bears on the functional and dynamic problems of institutions should be defined as sociological. From this point of view, sociological theory would, it seems to me, fall principally into the five following divisions.

A. The systematization of the study of the structural differentiation and integration of institutional patterns on a comparative basis. This includes not simply formal morphology but the theoretical analysis of the relations of structure and structural variation to the functional needs of social systems. However, relatively speaking, this could be called "pure" or "formal" sociology. Its difference from the program of Simmel or von Wiese lies in its relations to the other branches of sociological theory rather than in a difference in specific content. As has been remarked above, it is a grossly undeveloped part of sociological theory, and is much in need of attention. Promising beginnings, however, are to be found.

B. The theory of the dynamic interrelationships of institutions and culture. This is the major point of articulation between sociology and those aspects of anthropology which may be regarded as theoretically distinctive. What may be called the sociology of nonliterate societies cannot be regarded as distinctive of anthropology as a *theoretical* science. It would deal with the selected processes and patterns of the institutionalization of different elements of culture which are not functionally appropriate for institutionalization, such as traditions of science or speculative philosophy or magic. It is within this field that primarily the sociology of knowledge and, for example, the sociology of religion should be placed.

C. The theory of the motivation of institutional behavior. In my opinion, this theory should center about the concept of role, which is the primary name for the focus of the integration of motivation of the individual within the social system. It also would include the sociologically relevant theory of the process of socialization and of what is sometimes called basic personality or character structure. Another important aspect is the theoretical analysis of the structural generalization of goals in institutional behavior. This whole field is, of course, one of the major points of articulation between the theory of social systems and psychology. One may perhaps speak of this and the next category as in a very broad sense constituting either "psychological sociology" or an essential part of social psychology.

D. The theory of the motivation of deviant behavior and the problem of social control. This branch of sociological theory within the general framework of a theory of motivation and institutional behavior would be particularly concerned with the dynamics of the balance between conforming and deviant behavior. It would analyze the sources of the motivation to deviant behavior in terms of their relations to the social status and role of the individuals concerned, and the strains placed upon them in those situations. Conversely, it would analyze the mechanisms of social control by which deviance is kept at a relatively low level. It assumes both knowledge of institutional structure and of the basic motivation of institutional behavior as a starting point.

E. The final branch of sociological theory according to this conception is the dynamic theory of institutional change. It is most important to realize that this from a theoretical point of view would involve a synthesis of all the other branches of the total theoretical system. It is impossible to understand the dynamics of change without a knowledge of the structural base from which any given process of change starts. It is also impossible to understand it without some knowledge of the possibilities of new definitions of the situation which are available in the cultural tradition. Finally, the motivation of any such change requires explicit analysis of the relevant motivational problems. This is above all true of the starting points of the process of change in terms of what, from the point of view of the initial starting point of a process of change, must be defined as deviant behavior. It must include an analysis of the ways in which deviant behavior becomes socially structured and linked with legitimizing cultural patterns. It is unquestionably the culminating synthetic aspect of the theoretical structure of our science, and high levels of achievement in this aspect must depend on the development of the tools in the other branches with which the theorist of dynamic change must work.

NOTES

1 To avoid misunderstanding it should be clearly stated what concept of institutions and correspondingly of institutionalization is being employed in this paper. A pattern governing action in a social system will be called "institutionalized" in so far as it defines the main modes of the *legitimately expected* behavior of the persons acting in the relevant social roles, and in so far as conformity with these expectations is of strategic structural significance to the social system. An institutional pattern is thus a culture pattern (see below) to which a certain structured complex of motivations and social sanctions has become attached. It is an *ideal* pattern, but since conformity is legitimately expected it is not a "utopian" pattern. An institution is a complex of such institutional patterns which it is convenient to treat as a structural unit in the social system.
2 There is, of course, no single standardized definition of culture accepted by all anthropologists. The theme of "social heredity" may, however, be considered the dominant one.

Chapter 37

An Outline of the Social System [1961]

Talcott Parsons

Let us now turn to a more detailed discussion of our conception of a social system. First, the concept of interpenetration implies that, however important *logical* closure may be as a theoretical ideal, *empirically* social systems are conceived as *open* systems, engaged in complicated processes of interchange with environing systems. The environing systems include, in this case, cultural and personality systems, the behavioral and other subsystems of the organism, and, through the organism, the physical environment. The same logic applies internally to social systems, conceived as differentiated and segmented into a plurality of subsystems, each of which must be treated analytically as an open system interchanging with environing subsystems of the larger system.

The concept of an open system interchanging with environing systems also implies *boundaries* and their maintenance. When a set of interdependent phenomena shows sufficiently definite patterning and stability over time, then we can say that it has a "structure" and that it is fruitful to treat it as a "system." A boundary means simply that a theoretically and empirically significant difference between structures and processes internal to the system and those external to it exists and tends to be maintained. In so far as boundaries in this sense do not exist, it is not possible to identify a set of interdependent phenomena as a system; it is merged in some other, more extensive system. It is thus important to distinguish a set of phenomena not meant to constitute a system in the theoretically relevant sense – e.g., a certain type of statistical sample of a population – from a true system.

Parsons, Talcott, "An Outline of the Social System," pp. 36–43, 44–47, 70–72 from Talcott Parsons, Edward A. Shils, Kaspar D. Naegle, Jesse R. Pitts, eds., *Theories of Society*. New York: Simon & Schuster, The Free Press, 1961. Copyright © 1961 by The Free Press. Reprinted with the permission of The Free Press, A Division of Simon & Schuster Adult Publishing Group. All rights reserved.

Classical Sociological Theory, Third Edition. Edited by Craig Calhoun, Joseph Gerteis, James Moody, Steven Pfaff, and Indermohan Virk. Editorial material and organization © 2012 John Wiley & Sons, Ltd. Published 2012 by John Wiley & Sons, Ltd.

Structural and Functional Modes of Analysis. Besides identifying a system in terms of its patterns and boundaries, a social system can and should be analyzed in terms of three logically independent – i.e., cross-cutting – but also interdependent, bases or axes of variability, or as they may be called, bases of selective abstraction.

The first of these is best defined in relation to the distinction between "structural" and "functional" references for analysis. However relative these two concepts may be, the distinction between them is highly important. The concept of structure focuses on those elements of the patterning of the system which may be regarded as independent of the lower-amplitude and shorter time-range fluctuations in the relation of the system to its external situation. It thus designates the features of the system which can, in certain strategic respects, be treated as constants over certain ranges of variation in the behavior of other significant elements of the theoretical problem.

Thus, in a broad sense, the American Constitution has remained a stable reference point over a period of more than a century and a half. During this time, of course, the structure of American society has changed very greatly in certain respects; there have been changes in legal terms, through legislation, through legal interpretations, and through more informal processes. But the federal state, the division between legislative and executive branches of government, the independent judiciary, the separation of church and state, the basic rights of personal liberty, of assembly, and of property, and a variety of other features have for most purposes remained constant.

The functional reference, on the other hand, diverges from the structural in the "dynamic" direction. Its primary theoretical significance is integrative; functional considerations relate to the problem of *mediation* between two fundamental sets of exigencies: those imposed by the relative constancy or "givenness" of a structure, and those imposed by the givenness of the environing situation external to the system. Since only in a theoretically limiting case can these two be assumed to stand in a constant relation to each other, there will necessarily exist a system of dynamic processes and mechanisms.

Concepts like "structure" and "function" can be considered as either concrete or analytical. Our present concern is with their analytical meaning; we wish to state in a preliminary way a fundamental proposition about the structure of social systems that will be enlarged upon later – namely, that their structure as treated within the frame of reference of action *consists* in institutionalized patterns of normative culture. It consists in components of the organisms or personalities of the participating individuals only so far as these "interpenetrate" with the social and cultural systems, i.e., are "internalized" in the personality and organism of the individual. I shall presently discuss the problem of classifying the elements of normative culture that enter into the structure of social systems.

The functional categories of social systems concern, then, those features in terms of which systematically ordered modes of adjustment operate in the changing relations between a given set of patterns of institutionally established structure in the system and a given set of properties of the relevant environing systems.

Historically, the most common model on which this relationship has been based is that of the behaving organism, as used in psychological thinking. From this point of view, the functional problem is that of analyzing the mechanisms which make orderly response to environmental conditions possible. When using this model in analyzing social systems, however, we treat not only the environment but the structure of the system as problematical and subject to change, in a sense which goes farther than the traditional behavioral psychologist has been accustomed to go.

In interpreting this position, one should remember that the immediately environing systems of a social system are not those of the physical environment. They are, rather, the other primary subsystems of the general system of action – i.e., the personalities of its individual members, the behaviorally organized aspects of the organisms underlying those personalities, and the relevant cultural systems in so far as they are not fully institutionalized in the social system but involve components other than "normative patterns of culture" that are institutionalized.

"Dynamic" Modes of Analysis. The importance of the second basis or axis of empirical variability, and hence of theoretical problem formulation, follows directly. A fundamental distinction must be made between two orders of "dynamic" problems relative to a given system. The first of these concerns the processes which go on under the assumption that the structural patterns of institutionalized culture are given, i.e., are assumed to remain constant. This is the area of problems of *equilibrium* as that concept has been used by Pareto, Henderson, and others, and of homeostasis as used by Cannon. The significance of such problems is directly connected with both the concept of system and the ways in which we have defined the relation between structure and function.

The concept of equilibrium is a fundamental reference point for analyzing the processes by which a system either comes to terms with the exigencies imposed by a *changing* environment, without essential change in its own structure, or fails to come to terms and undergoes other processes, such as structural change, dissolution as a boundary-maintaining system (analogous to biological death for the organism), or the consolidation of some impairment leading to the establishment of secondary structures of a "pathological" character. Theoretically, the concept of equilibrium has a normative reference in only one sense. Since the structure of social systems consists in institutionalized normative culture, the "maintenance" of these normative patterns is a basic reference point for analyzing the equilibrium of the system. However, whether this maintenance actually occurs or not, and in what measure, is entirely an empirical question. Furthermore, "disequilibrium" may lead to structural change which, from a higher-order normative point of view, is desirable.

The second set of dynamic problems concerns processes involving change in the structure of the system itself. This involves, above all, problems of interchange with the cultural system, however much these may in turn depend upon the internal state of the social system and its relations to other environing systems. Leaving distinctions within the category of internal adjustive processes aside for the moment, one can say that, with respect to its external interchanges, problems of equilibrium for the social system involve primarily its relations to its individual members as personalities and organisms, and, through these, to the physical environment. Problems of structural change, on the other hand, primarily involve its relations to the cultural systems affecting its patterns of institutionalized normative culture.

However fundamental the distinction between dynamic problems which do and do not involve structural change may be, the great importance of an intermediate or mixed case should be emphasized. This is the problem of change involving the structure of subsystems of the social system, but not the over-all structural pattern. The most important case in this category is that of processes of structural differentiation. Structural differentiation involves genuine *reorganization* of the system and, therefore, fundamental structural change of various subsystems and their relations to each other. Its analysis therefore presents problems of structural change for the relevant subsystems, but not in the same sense for the system as a whole. The problems involved concern the organization of the structural components of social systems, particularly the hierarchical order in which they are placed. Further discussion will have to await clarification of these problems.

The Hierarchy of Relations of Control. The third of the three essential axes of theoretical analysis may be defined as concerning a hierarchy of relations of control. The development of theory in the past generation in both the biological and the behavioral sciences has revealed the primary source of the difficulty underlying the prominent reductionism of so much earlier thought. This was the reductionist tendency to ignore the importance of the ways in which the organization of living systems involved structures and mechanisms that operated as agencies of control – in the cybernetic sense of control – of their metabolic and behavioral processes. The concept of the "behavioral organism" put forward above is that of a cybernetic system located mainly in the central nervous system, which operates through several intermediary mechanisms to control the metabolic processes of the organism and the behavioral use of its physical facilities, such as the motions of limbs.

The basic subsystems of the general system of action constitute a hierarchical series of such agencies of control of the behavior of individuals or organisms. The behavioral organism is the point of articulation of the system of action with the anatomical-physiological features of the physical organism and is its point of contact with the physical environment. The personality system is, in turn, a system of control over the behavioral organism; the social system, over the personalities of its participating members; and the cultural system, a system of control relative to social systems.

It may help if we illustrate the nature of this type of hierarchical relationship by discussing the sense in which the social system "controls" the personality. There are two main empirical points at which this control operates, though the principles involved are the same in both cases. First, the situation in which any given individual acts is, far more than any other set of factors, composed of *other* individuals, not discretely but in ordered sets of relationship to the individual in point. Hence, as the source of his principal facilities of action and of his principal rewards and deprivations, the concrete social system exercises a powerful control over the action of any concrete, adult individual. However, the *patterning* of the motivational system in terms of which he faces this situation also depends upon the social system, because his own personality *structure* has been shaped through the internalization of systems of social objects and of the patterns of institutionalized culture. This point, it should be made clear, is independent of the sense in which individuals are concretely autonomous or creative rather than "passive" or "conforming," for individuality and creativity are, to a considerable extent, phenomena of the institutionalization of expectations. The social system which controls the personality is here conceived analytically, not concretely.

Control Relations within the Social System. The same basic principle of cybernetic hierarchy that applies to the relations between general subsystems of action applies again *within* each of them, notably to social systems, which is of primary concern here. The principle of the order of cybernetic priority, combined with primacy of relevance to the different boundary-interchange exigencies of the system, will be used as the fundamental basis for classifying the components of social systems. The relevance of this hierarchy applies, of course, to all the components distinguished according to the first of our three ranges of variation, to structures, functions, mechanisms, and categories of input and output.

The most strategic starting point for explaining this basic set of classifications is the category of functions, the link between the structural and the dynamic aspects of the system. I have suggested that it is possible to reduce the essential functional imperatives of any system of action, and hence of any social system, to four, which I have called pattern-maintenance, integration, goal-attainment, and adaptation. These are listed in order of significance from the point of view of cybernetic control of action processes in the system type under consideration.

The Function of Pattern-maintenance. The function of pattern-maintenance refers to the imperative of maintaining the stability of the patterns of institutionalized culture defining the structure of the system. There are two distinct aspects of this functional imperative. The first concerns the character of the normative pattern itself; the second concerns its state of "institutionalization." From the point of view of the individual participant in a social system, this may be called his motivational *commitment* to act in accordance with certain normative patterns; this, as we shall see, involves their "internalization" in the structure of his personality.

Accordingly, the focus of pattern-maintenance lies in the structural category of *values*, which will be discussed presently. In this connection, the essential function is maintenance, at the cultural level, of the stability of institutionalized values through the processes which articulate values with the belief system, namely, religious beliefs, ideology, and the like. Values, of course, are subject to change, but whether the empirical tendency be toward stability or not, the potentialities of disruption from this source are very great, and it is essential to look for mechanisms that tend to protect such order – even if it is orderliness in the process of change.

The second aspect of this control function concerns the motivational commitment of the individual – elsewhere called "tension-management." A very central problem is that of the mechanisms of socialization of the individual, i.e., of the processes by which the values of the society are internalized in his personality. But even when values have become internalized, the commitments involved are subject to different kinds of strain. Much insight has recently been gained about the ways in which such mechanisms as ritual, various types of expressive symbolism, the arts, and indeed recreation, operate in this connection. Durkheim's analysis of the functions of religious ritual may be said to constitute the main point of departure here.

Pattern-maintenance in this sense plays a part in the theory of social systems, as of other systems of action, comparable to that of the concept of inertia in mechanics. It serves as the most fundamental reference point to which the analysis of other, more variable factors can be related. Properly conceived and used, it does not imply the empirical predominance of stability over change. However, when we say that, because of this set of functional exigencies, social systems show a *tendency* to maintain their structural patterns, we say essentially two things. First, we provide a reference point for the orderly analysis of a whole range of problems of variation which can be treated as arising from sources *other* than processes of structural change in the system, including, in the latter concept, its dissolution. Second, we make it clear that when we do analyze structural change we are dealing with a different kind of theoretical problem than that involved in equilibration. Hence, there is a direct relation between the function of pattern-maintenance – as distinguished from the other three functional imperatives – and the distinction between problems of equilibrium analysis, on the one hand, and the analysis of structural change on the other. The distinction between these two types of problems comes to focus at this point in the paradigm.

The Function of Goal-attainment. For purposes of exposition it seems best to abandon the order of control set forth above and to concentrate next upon the function of goal-attainment and its relation to adaptation. In contrast to the constancy of institutionalized cultural patterns, we have emphasized the variability of a system's relation to its situation. The functions of goal-attainment and adaptation concern the structures, mechanisms, and processes involved in this relation.

We have compared pattern-maintenance with inertia as used in the theory of mechanics. Goal-attainment then becomes a "problem" in so far as there arises some discrepancy between the inertial tendencies of the system and its "needs" resulting from interchange with the situation. Such needs necessarily arise because the internal system and the environing ones cannot be expected to follow immediately the changing patterns of process.[1] A goal is therefore defined in terms of equilibrium. It is a directional change that tends to reduce the discrepancy between the needs of the system, with respect to input–output interchange, and the conditions in the environing systems that bear upon the "fulfillment" of such needs. Goal-attainment or goal-orientation is thus, by contrast with pattern-maintenance, essentially tied to a specific situation.

A social system with only one goal, defined in relation to a generically crucial situational problem, is conceivable. Most often, however, the situation is complex, with many goals and problems. In such a case two further considerations must be taken into account. First, to protect the integrity of the system, the several goals must be arranged in some scale of relative urgency, a scale sufficiently flexible to allow for variations in the situation. For any complex system, therefore, it is necessary to speak of a system of goals rather than of a single unitary goal, a system, however, which must have some balance between integration as a system and flexible adjustment to changing pressures.

For the social system as such, the focus of its goal-orientation lies in its relation as a system to the personalities of the participating individuals. It concerns, therefore, not commitment to the values of the society, but motivation to contribute what is necessary for the functioning of the system; these "contributions" vary according to particular exigencies. For example, considering American society, one may suggest that, given the main system of values, there has been in the Cold-War period a major problem of motivating large sectors of the population to the level of national effort required to sustain a position of world leadership in a very unstable and rapidly changing situation. I would interpret much of the sense of frustration expressed in isolationism and McCarthyism as manifestations of the strains resulting from this problem.[2]

The Function of Adaptation. The second consequence of plurality of goals, however, concerns the difference between the functions of goal-attainment and adaptation. When there is only one goal, the problem of evaluating the usefulness of facilities is narrowed down to their relevance to attaining this particular goal. With a plurality of goals, however, the problem of "cost" arises. That is, the same scarce facilities will have *alternative* uses within the system of goals, and hence their use for one purpose means sacrificing the gains that would have been derived from their use for another. It is on this basis that an analytical distinction must be made between the function of effective goal-attainment and that of providing disposable facilities independent of their relevance to any particular goal. The adaptive function is defined as the provision of such facilities.

Just as there is a pluralism of lower-order, more concrete goals, there is also a pluralism of relatively concrete facilities. Hence there is a parallel problem of the organization of such facilities in a system. The primary criterion is the provision of flexibility, so far as this is compatible with effectiveness, for the system; this means a maximum of generalized disposability in the processes of allocation between alternative uses. Within the complex type of social system, this disposability of facilities crystallizes about the institutionalization of money and markets. More generally, at the macroscopic social-system level, the function of goal-attainment is the focus of the political organization of societies, while that of adaptation is the focus of economic organization.[3]

The most important kinds of facilities involve control of physical objects, access to the services of human agents, and certain cultural elements. For their mechanisms of control to be at all highly generalized, particular units of such resources must be "alienable," i.e., not bound to specific uses through ascription. The market system is thus a primary focus of the society's organization for adaptation. Comparable features operate in less differentiated societies, and in more differentiated subsystems where markets do not penetrate, such as the family.

Within a given system, goal-attainment is a more important control than adaptation. Facilities subserve the attainment of goals, not vice versa – though of course the provision or "production" of facilities may itself be a goal, with a place within the more general system of goals. There are, however, complications in the implications of this statement.

The Function of Integration. The last of four functional imperatives of a system of action – in our case, a social system – is that of integration. In the control hierarchy, this stands between the functions of pattern-maintenance and goal-attainment. Our recognition of the significance of integration implies that all systems, except for a limiting case, are differentiated and segmented into relatively independent units, i.e., must be treated as boundary-maintaining systems within an environment of other systems, which in this case are other subsystems of the same, more inclusive system. The functional problem of integration concerns the mutual adjustment of these "units" or subsystems from the point of view of their "contributions" to the effective functioning of the system as a whole. This, in turn, concerns their relation to the pattern-maintenance problem, as well as to the external situation through processes of goal-attainment and adaptation.

In a highly differentiated society, the primary focus of the integrative function is found in its system of legal norms and the agencies associated with its management, notably the courts and the legal profession. Legal norms at this level, rather than that of a supreme constitution, govern the *allocation* of rights and obligations, of facilities and rewards, between different units of the complex system; such norms facilitate internal adjustments compatible with the stability of the value system or its orderly change, as well as with adaptation to the shifting demands of the external situation. The institutionalization of money and power are primarily integrative phenomena, like other mechanisms of social control in the narrower sense. These problems will be further discussed in later sections of this essay.

For any given type of system – here, the social – the integrative function is the focus of its most distinctive properties and processes. We contend, therefore, that the problems focusing about the integrative functions of social systems constitute the central core of the concerns of sociological theory. [...]

Categories of Social Structure

Historically, the theoretical preoccupations of sociological theory have emerged from two main points of reference. One concerns the relations of social systems and culture and focuses on the problem of values and norms in the social system. The second concerns the individual as organism and personality and focuses on the individuals' participation in social interaction. Generally, neither of these reference points may be considered more important than the other. However, since the foregoing discussion of functional imperatives has started with pattern-maintenance, which chiefly concerns the institutionalization of normative culture, it may help to balance the picture if we begin our detailed discussion of structure at the other end, with the problem of the interaction of individuals.

Social interaction and roles

For sociology, the essential concept here is that of *role*. I should like to treat this concept as the "bottom" term of a series of structural categories, of which the other terms, in ascending order, are *collectivity*, *norm*, and *value*. (It is interesting, and I think significant, that systematic introduction of the concept of role has been, perhaps, the most distinctively American contribution to the structural aspects of sociological theory.)

The essential starting point is the conception of two (or more) individuals interacting in such a way as to constitute an interdependent system. As personalities, each individual may be considered a system with its own values, goals, etc., facing the others as part of an "environment" that provides certain opportunities for goal-attainment as well as certain limitations and sources of frustration. Though interdependence can be taken into account at this level, this is not equivalent to treating the process of interaction as a social system. True, the action of Alter is an essential part of the conditions bearing on the attainment of Ego's goals, but the vital sociological question concerns the nature and degree of the integration of the *system* of interaction as a social system. Here the question arises of the conditions under which the interaction process can be treated as stable – in the sense, at least, that it does not prove to be so mutually frustrating that dissolution of the system (i.e., for the individual, "leaving the field") seems more likely than its continuation.

The problem of stability introduces considerations of temporal continuity, which immediately brings us to the relevance of normative orientation. It can be shown that, within the action frame of reference, stable interaction implies that acts acquire "meanings" which are interpreted with reference to a common set of normative conceptions. The particularity of specific acts is transcended in terms of the generalization of the normative common culture as well as in the normative component of the expectations that get built into the guiding mechanisms of the process. This means that the response to Alter to an act of Ego may be interpreted as a sanction expressing an evaluation of the past act and serving as a guide to desirable future behavior.

The essentials of the interaction situation can be illustrated by any two-player game, such as chess. Each player is presumed to have some motivation to participate in the game, including a "desire to win." Hence, he has a goal, and, relative to this, some conception of effective "strategies." He may plan an opening gambit but he cannot carry advance planning too far, because the situation is not stable: it is contingent on the moves made both by himself and by his opponent as the game proceeds. The basic facilities at his command consist of his knowledge of the opportunities implicit in the changing situation; his command of these opportunities means performance of the adaptive function. Hence, at the goal-attainment and adaptive levels, goals are defined and facilities are provided, but *specific acts are not prescribed.* The facilities are generalized, and their allocation between the players depends upon each player's capacities to take advantage of opportunities.

In turn, the meaningfulness of the goals and the stability of the generalized pattern of facilities depend on the existence of a well defined set of rules, which forms the center of the integration of the system. The roles, in this case, are not differentiated on a permanent basis; rather, the rules define the consequences of any given move by one player for the situation in which the other must make his next choice. Without such rules the interactive process could not be stable, and the system of adaptive facilities would break down; neither player would know what was expected of him or what the consequences of a given set of moves would be. Finally, the differentiated and contingent rules must be grounded in a set of values which define the nature of a "good game" of this sort, including the value of equality of opportunity for both contestants and the meaningfulness of the goal of "winning."

A stable system of interaction, therefore, orients its participants in terms of mutual expectations which have the dual significance of expressing normative evaluations and stating contingent predictions of overt behavior. This mutuality of expectations implies that the *evaluative* meanings of acts are shared by the interacting units in two ways: what a member does can be categorized in terms meaningful to both; also, they share criteria of behavior, so that there are common standards of evaluation for particular acts.

We can say that even such an elementary two-member system of social interaction has most of the structural essentials of a social system. The essential property is mutuality of orientation, defined in terms of shared patterns of normative culture. Such normative patterns are *values*; the normatively regulated complex of behavior of one of the participants is a *role*; and the system composed by the interaction of the two participants, so far as it shares a common normative culture and is distinguishable from others by the participation of these two and not others, is a *collectivity*.

One further condition, not present in our chess game example, is necessary in order to complete the roster of structural components, namely, differentiation between the roles of the participants. This is to say that, in most social systems, participants do not *do* the same things; their performances may be conceived as *complementary* contributions to the "functioning" of the interaction system. When there are two or more structurally distinct units which perform essentially *the same* function in the system (e.g., nuclear families in a community) we will speak of segmentation as distinguished from differentiation. When differentiation of roles is present, it becomes necessary to distinguish between two components of the normative culture of the system: that of values, which are shared by the members over and above their particular roles, and that of role-expectations, which are differentiated by role and therefore define rights and obligations applicable to one role but not to the other. I propose to use the term *values* for the shared normative component, and the term (differentiated) *norm* for the component that is specific to a given role or, in more complex systems, to other empirical units of the system, i.e., various collectivities such as families, churches, business firms, governmental agencies, universities.

Where roles are differentiated, the sharing of values becomes an essential condition of integration of the system. Only on this assumption can the reactions of Alter to Ego's performances have the character of sanctions regulation Ego action in the interests of the system. However, it should be clear that for Alter to be in a position to evaluate Ego's acts, the acts need not be such that Alter is, by virtue of his role, expected to perform. Thus, in marriage, one of the most important dyadic relationships in all societies, the roles of the partners are differentiated by sex. The mutual evaluation of performance is an essential regulatory mechanism, but to be in a position to evaluate the partner's performance is not to assume his role.

The Concepts of Role and Collectivity. A role may now be defined as the structured, i.e., normatively regulated, participation of a person in a concrete process of social interaction with specified, concrete role-partners. The system of such interaction of a plurality of role-performers is, so far as it is normatively regulated in terms of common values and of norms sanctioned by these common values, a collectivity. Performing a role within a collectivity defines the category of *membership*, i.e., the assumption of obligations of performance in that concrete interaction system. Obligations correlatively imply rights.

Since the normal individual participates in many collectivities, it is a commonplace, though a crucial one, that only in a limiting case does a single role constitute the entire interactive behavior of a concrete individual. The role is rather a *sector* in his behavioral system, and hence of his personality. For most purposes, therefore, it is not the individual, or the person as such, that is a unit of social systems, but rather his role-participation at the boundary directly affecting his personality. It is largely when interpreted as this particular boundary-concept that the concept of role has an important theoretical significance for sociology.

So long as we restrict our illustrations to the dyadic interaction system it may seem that the distinction of four analytical structural components – role, collectivity, norm, and value – is overelaborate. At this level it is still possible to identify values and the collectivity, norms and the role. In more complex social systems, however, there is not just one collectivity but many; and a differentiated norm does not define expectations for just one role but for a class of roles (and also for classes of collectivities). The social systems with which the sociologist normally deals are complex networks of many different types of categories of roles and collectivities on many different levels of organization. It therefore becomes essential to conceptualize values and norms independently of any particular collectivity or role. [...]

The structure of complex systems

Having outlined these essential structural components of a social system and their rank in the general hierarchy of control, we can now outline their main pattern of organization so as to constitute a relatively complex system. What is here presented is necessarily a schematic "ideal type," one that pretends merely to define and distinguish rather broad structural categories; we cannot take into account the immense richness of various concrete social structures.

The main guiding line of the analysis is the concept that a complex social system consists of a network of interdependent and interpenetrating subsystems, each of which, seen at the appropriate level of reference, is a social system in its own right, subject to all the functional exigencies of any such system relative to *its* institutionalized culture and situation and possessing all the essential structural components, organized on the appropriate levels of differentiation and specification.

The Concept of a Society. The starting point must be the concept of a *society*, defined as a collectivity, i.e., a system of concrete interacting human individuals, which is the primary bearer of a distinctive institutionalized culture and which cannot be said to be a differentiated subsystem of a higher-order collectivity oriented to most of the functional exigencies of a social system. It will be noted that this conception is stated in terms that leave the question of the "openness" of a society in various directions to be treated empirically. At the social-system level, however, rather than the cultural,[4] the main criterion is *relative* self-sufficiency.

To approach the structural analysis of the subsystem organization of a society, we must refer to the appropriate functional exigencies of both the societal system itself and its various subsystems. The primary, over-all principle is that of differentiation in relation to functional exigency; this is the master concept for the analysis of social structure. By itself, however, it is not adequate; it must be supplemented by the two principles of specification and segmentation. The first refers primarily to the institutionalized culture components of the structure, the second to the exigencies confronting the concrete behaving units, i.e., to collectivities and roles. It seems preferable to discuss the latter first.

We have noted that, in *one* (but only one) of its aspects, a society is a *single* collectivity with a specifiable, though naturally changing, membership of individuals. This fact is related to three fundamental imperatives. First, there must be, to some degree and on some level, a unitary system of institutionalized values, in this aspect a common culture. In so far as maintenance of a common value system requires the kinds of functions collectivities must perform, the society will have to constitute a single collectivity – what Durkheim called a "moral community." Second, however, since the system is differentiated, the implementation of these values for different units requires a relatively *consistent* system of norms that receive a unitary formulation and interpretation. In highly differentiated societies this system of norms takes the form of an integrated legal system administered by courts. The need for coordinated dealing with the external situation is also relevant, as will be brought out presently.

The Segmentation of Social Units. But if, for one set of reasons, a society must be a single collectivity, other reasons prevent its being only that. These reasons can be summed up in the generalized principles economists refer to as determining the "economies of scale." Beyond certain points, that is to say, "costs" increase as the size of the unit of organization increases, though what the points are varies greatly according to the specific factors involved. Thus, under modern industrial conditions the manufacture of such commodities as automobiles takes place in very large units indeed, whereas there seem to be important reasons which inhibit entrusting the early socialization of children primarily to units with membership much larger than the nuclear family.

Perhaps the most fundamental determinant underlying the segmentation of social systems is the indispensability of the human individual as an agency of performance. But there are essential limits, not only to what a given individual can do, but to the effectiveness with which individuals can co-operate. The problems of communication and other aspects of integration may thus multiply as a result of an increasing scale of organization; in certain respects, therefore, subcollectivities may acquire a distinctive organization, including a special integration or solidarity relative to the larger systems of which they are parts.

By the concept *segmentation* I refer, in discussing the formation of collectivities, to the development of subcollectivities, within a larger collectivity system, in which some of the members of the larger system participate more intimately than in others. In this sense, segmentation is a factor independent of the differentiation of function between the subcollectivities. Thus a large-scale society may comprise millions of nuclear families, all of which perform essentially similar functions in the socialization of children; here the structure is highly segmented but not highly differentiated.

The necessity of segmentation derives largely from the problems of integration resulting from the other exigencies to which units of the system are subject. At the same time, however, it gives rise to new problems of integration: the more units there are, the less likely they will be just "naturally" to co-ordinate their activities in ways compatible with the smooth functioning of the system as a whole. This tends, in more complex systems, to give rise to special mechanisms of integration, which will have to be discussed in due course.

The Specification of Normative Culture. As already noted, there is an important relation between the hierarchy of control and the levels of generality of the components of normative culture. Thus, values were defined as standing at the highest level of generality of "conceptions of the desirable," i.e., without specification of function or situation. In comparison to values, therefore, norms are differentiated on the basis of specification of function of the units or subunits to which they apply. Subcollectivities, in turn, involve further specification on the basis of situation. This is to say that, given its function(s), a collectivity is identified in terms of specified memberships of concrete individuals acting in concrete situations. When the collectivity is treated as a differentiated system, there must be further specifications applicable to the roles of the participating members.

There is, therefore, a hierarchy of generality of the patterns of normative culture institutionalized in a social system, one that corresponds to the general hierarchical relations of its structural components. Each subunit of the society, as collectivity, will have its own institutionalized values, which should be conceived as specifications, at the appropriate level, of the more general values of the society. To cope with its own internal differentiation of function, then, each subunit will have a set of differentiated norms, which should be regarded as specifications both of the subcollectivity values and of the more general norms applicable both to it and to other types of subcollectivity. The principle of specification restricts the generality of the pattern of culture by introducing qualifications arising from specialization of function, on the one hand, and from specificity of situation, on the other.

The last of the three principles of organization of complex systems, functional differentiation, has already been discussed in general terms. In accord with this principle, structured units acquire specialized significance in the functioning of the system. The general scheme of functional categories that we have presented is very simple, being limited to four categories. In using it, however, one must do justice to the empirical complexity of the situation by taking account of the many steps in segmentation and specification, and hence of the compounding of the patterns of differentiation by their repetition for subsystems at each level of segmentation.

Since our general approach has been in terms of the hierarchy of control observed in descending order, a brief account should now be given of the "anchorage" of social systems at the base. This anchorage is in the personalities and behavioral organisms of the individual members and, *through* these, in the lower-order subsystems of the organism and in the physical environment. Concretely, all social interaction is bound to the physical task performance of individuals in a physical environment; it is bound to spatial location in the physical sense. Following the usage of ecologically oriented theory, I have elsewhere referred to this spatial location as the "community" aspect of social structure.[5] It can be broken down most conveniently into four complexes: (1) residential location and the crystallization of social structure around that focus; (2) functional task-performance through occupation, and the attendant locational problems; (3) jurisdictional application of normative order through the specification of categories of persons, and the relevance of this to the spatial locations of their interests and activities; and (4) the physical exigencies of communication and of the movements of persons and commodities. More generally, the category of technology – not only what is usually called "physical production," but all task-performance involving the physical organism in relation to its physical environment – belongs in this area of borderline problems. Technology relates to physical exigencies, but it is also based on *cultural* resources in their significance as facilities for social action. Empirical knowledge of the physical world is an instance of such a cultural resource.

The Integration of Societies as Collectivities. Let us now approach the problem of outlining the structure of a complex society as a social system. As we have said, three different exigencies underlie the fact that a society can always be regarded as a single collectivity, namely, the maintenance of its patterns of institutionalized culture at the value level, the integration of its system of differentiated norms, and the co-ordinated handling of external situations.

The prevalence of fundamental patterns of value and the general commitment of units to common values are so crucial that the problem of the relation of the overall collectivity to values is a universal one. At the other end, however, the problems of jurisdiction and enforcement with reference to normative order are equally crucial; the over-all collectivity structure cannot be divorced from political organization, oriented to maintaining commitments to this order and to the jurisdictional functions associated with it, in relation both to its own population and to other societies. This means that the boundaries of a society tend to coincide with the territorial jurisdiction of the highest-order units of political organization.

The primary area in which the problems of value-commitment are played out is that of religion; for most societies, the paramount over-all collectivity has been at the same time a religious collectivity and a political collectivity, both a "church" and a "state." Law, we may say, has tended to stand in the middle, to be legitimized by religion and enforced by political authority; often the function of interpreting it has been a serious bone of contention.

However, the formula of religio-political-legal unity is not, by itself, adequate as a universal generalization. In the first place, within the over-all collectivity these functions have tended to be differentiated with respect to personnel and subcollectivities. But, in a more radical sense, in the Western world since the Christian era there has been a process of fundamental differentiation of church and state. In interpreting the sociological implications of this, one must consider this process in terms of the relation between social and cultural systems. Even before its Protestant phase, Western Christianity was characterized by a special type of religious "individualism." In the present context, this means that, except on the most general level of over-all societal membership, the individual's religious and social status did not necessarily coincide. The church was an organization of the religious interests and orientations of the population conceived as independent of (but not unrelated to) their secular or temporal orientations, especially at the level of societal value-commitment. It was a "Christian society," but one in which the function of religion was more specialized than in other pre- and non-Christian types.

This I interpret to mean that, in societal as distinguished from cultural terms, the "moral community" aspect shifted from religious organization as such to the area of interpenetration between the religious and the secular. The paramount societal collectivity became the "state," administered by laymen – or when administered, in fact, by priests, not in their special clerical capacity. This differentiation was never fully carried out in medieval Europe – for instance, it was impossible to divest bishops of secular functions that went beyond the administration of ecclesiastical affairs – but it was, nevertheless, the main pattern.

Since the Reformation, this process has gone farther, particularly where the principle of the separation, as distinguished from the differentiation, of church and state has prevailed. As in the United States today, the values are still clearly anchored in theistic religion ("In God We Trust"), but on the level of collectivity organization the "moral community" is clearly the "politically organized community." What has happened, essentially, is that any agency whose orientation is primarily cultural rather than societal has been deprived of legitimate authority to prescribe values and enforce norms for the society; in this sense the society has become "secularized." The religious anchorage of the values is still there, but religion is pluralistically and "privately" organized. Formally, the values are embodied in the Constitution and in the official interpretations of it, above all by judicial and legislative agencies.

The universal association of the over-all collectivity structure with political organization is based on another set of imperatives, involving the special significance of physical force as a sanction. The central point here is that, while there are many limitations on the efficacy of this sanction, control of sufficiently superior socially organized force is almost always a completely effective preventive of any undesired action. Therefore, without the control that includes "neutralization" of organized force, which is inherently territorial in its reference, the guarantee of the binding power of a normative order is not possible.

I conceive of political organization as functionally organized about the attainment of *collective* goals, i.e., the attainment or maintenance of states of interaction between the system and its environing situation that are relatively desirable from the point of view of the system. The maintenance of security against the adverse use of force is a crucial collective goal for every society. Considerations such as these underlie the general tendency of the over-all collectivity to develop an effective monopoly of the internal organization of force through police and military agencies. Such statements are not meant to imply that the control of force is the paramount function of political organization. Force is not the only function that is primarily negative, i.e., "protective" in significance, and, in general, government is a central agency of positive societal goal-attainment. But force is so strategically significant that its control is an indispensable function, a necessary, but not sufficient, condition of social order. Accordingly, in a well-integrated society, most subcollectivities except those specifically concerned with force are almost totally deprived of it.

Because of the problems involved in the use and control of force, the political organization must always be integrated with the legal system, which is concerned with administering the highest order of norms regulating the behavior of units within the society. No society can afford to permit any other normative order to take precedence over that sanctioned by "politically organized society." Indeed, the promulgation of any such alternative order is a revolutionary act, and the agencies responsible for it must assume the responsibility of political organization.

In this context it is of great significance that in a few societies, notably in the modern West, the organization of the legal system has attained a significant degree of independence in the judicial and, to some extent, in the legislative departments. There are two main aspects of this independent collectivity structure: the judiciary, with certain types of insulation from the pressures of "politics"; second, very notable, the development of a legal profession whose members occupy an interstitial status, partly through membership in the bar, functioning as "officers of the court," and partly by dealing privately with clients – indeed, protected from even governmental intervention by such institutions as privileged communication.

Summing up, we may say that the highest over-all collectivity in even a modern society is, to an important degree, necessarily "multifunctional," or functionally "diffuse." At the same time, under certain circumstances the diffuseness characteristic of the more "monolithic" religio-political structures – even of such high development as classical China or late Republican Rome – has tended to differentiate further. The most notable of these differentiations have been the "secularization" of political organization, which has gone through many stages and modes, and the institutionalization of a relatively independent legal function.[6]

The problem of the kind and degree of differentiation likely to occur at this highest level of societal collectivity organization may be described as a function of four primary sets of factors, all variable over considerable ranges. These are: (1) the *type* of societal values which are more or less fully institutionalized in the society (classified in terms of modes of categorizations of the society, at the highest level of generality, as an evaluated object – the appropriate categories seem to be pattern variables); (2) the degree and mode of their institutionalization, including its "security" relative particularly to the religious and cultural foundations of value-commitments in the society (long-range institutionalization of new values implies a relatively low level of such security); (3) the kind and level of structural differentiation of the society, with special reference to the severity and kinds of integrative problems they impose on the society; and (4) the kinds of situational exigencies to which the system is exposed. [...]

The Problem of Structural Change

According to the program laid out above, the last major problem area is the analysis of processes of structural change in social systems. The process of structural change may be considered the obverse of equilibrating process; the distinction is made in terms of boundary-maintenance. Boundary implies both that there is a difference of state between phenomena internal and external to the system; and that the type of process tending to maintain that difference of state is different from the type tending to break it down. In applying this concept to social systems, one must remember that their essential boundaries are those *vis-à-vis* personalities, organisms, and cultural systems, and not those directly *vis-à-vis* the physical environment.

A boundary is thus conceived as a kind of watershed. The control resources of the system are adequate for its maintenance up to a well-defined set of points in one direction: beyond that set of points, there is a tendency for a *cumulative* process of change to begin, producing states progressively farther from the institutionalized patterns. The metaphor of the watershed, however, fails to demonstrate the complexity of the series of control levels and, hence, of the boundaries of subsystems within larger systems. The mechanisms discussed earlier are involved in the dynamic aspects of such a hierarchical series of subboundaries; if a subboundary is broken, resources within the larger system counteract the implicit tendency to structural change. This is most dramatically shown in the capacity of social control mechanisms, in a narrow sense, to reverse cumulative processes of deviance. The conception of the nature of the difference between processes of equilibration and processes of structural change seems inherent in the conception of a social system as a cybernetic system of control over behavior.

As observed, structural change in subsystems is an inevitable part of equilibrating process in larger systems. The individual's life-span is so short that concrete role-units in any social system of societal scope must, through socialization, continually undergo structural change. Closely bound to this is a low-order collectivity like the nuclear family. Though the institutional norms defining "the family" in a society or a social sector may remain stable over long periods, *the family* is never a collectivity; and real families are continually being established by marriages, passing through the "family cycle," and, eventually, disappearing, with the parents' death and the children's dispersion. Similar considerations apply to other types of societal subsystems.

Within this frame of reference, the problem of structural change can be considered under three headings, as follows: (1) the sources of tendencies toward change; (2) the impact of these tendencies on the affected structural components, and the possible consequences; and (3) possible generalizations about trends and patterns of change.

The sources of structural change

The potential sources of structural change are exogenous and endogenous – usually in combination. The foregoing discussion has stressed the instability of the relations between any system of action and its situation, because this is important for defining the concepts of goal and the political function. We were emphasizing *relation*, and a relation's internal sources of instability may derive from external tendencies to change.

Exogenous Sources of Change. The exogenous sources of social structural change consist in endogenous tendencies to change in the organisms, personalities, and cultural systems articulated with the social systems in question. Among such sources are those operating through genetic changes in the constituent human organisms and changes in the distribution of genetic components within populations, which have an impact on behavior as it affects social role-performance, including the social system's capacities for socialization. Changes in the physical environment are mediated most directly either through the organism – e.g., through perception – or through appropriate aspects of the cultural system – e.g., technological knowledge.

One particularly important source of exogenous change is a change originating in other social systems. For the politically organized society, the most important are other politically organized societies. To consider change in this context, it is essential to treat the society of reference as a unit in a more inclusive social system. Even when the system's level of integration is relatively low and chronic conflicts between its subunits continually threaten to break into war, *some* element of more or less institutionalized order always governs their interrelations – otherwise, a concept like "diplomacy" would be meaningless. Of course, exogenous cultural borrowing and diffusion are mediated through interrelations among societies.

Endogenous Sources: "Strains." The most general, commonly used term for an endogenous tendency to change is "strain." *Strain* here refers to a condition in the *relation* between two or more structured units (i.e., subsystems of the system) that constitutes a tendency or pressure toward changing that relation to one incompatible with the equilibrium of the relevant part of the system. If the strain becomes great enough, the mechanisms of control will not be able to maintain that conformity to relevant normative expectations necessary to avoid the breakdown of the structure. A strain is a tendency to disequilibrium in the input-output balance between two or more units of the system.

Strains can be relieved in various ways. For the system's stability, the ideal way is resolution – i.e., restoring full conformity with normative expectations, as in complete recovery from motivated illness. A second relieving mechanism is arrestation or isolation – full conformity is not restored, but some accommodation is made by which less than normal performance by the deficient units is accepted, and other units carry the resulting burden. However, it may be extremely difficult to detect a unit's failure to attain full potentiality, as in the case of handicap contrasted with illness. Completely eliminating the unit from social function is the limiting case here.

Strain may also be relieved by change in the structure itself. Since we have emphasized strain in the *relations* of units (instability internal to the unit itself would be analyzed at the next lower level of system reference), structural change must be defined as alteration in the normative culture defining the expectations governing that relation – thus, at the systemic level, comprising all units standing in strained relations. The total empirical process may also involve change in the structure of typical units; but the essential reference is to *relational pattern*. For example, chronic instability in a typical kind of market might lead to a change in the norms governing that market; but if bargaining units change their tactics in the direction of conforming with the old norms, this would not constitute *structural* change of *this* system. In line with the general concepts of inertia and of the hierarchy of controls, we may say that endogenous change occurs only when the lower-order mechanisms of control fail to contain the factors of strain.

Factors in Change. In introducing our discussion of the factors in structural change, we must establish the essential point that the conception of a system of interdependent variables, on the one hand, and of units or parts, on the other, by its nature implies that there is no necessary order of teleological significance in the sources of change. This applies particularly to such old controversies as economic or interest explanations *versus* explanations in terms of ideas or values. This problem is logically parallel to the problem of the relations between heredity and environment. Of a set of "factors," *any or all may be sources of change*, whose nature will depend on the ways an initial impetus is propagated through the system by the types of dynamic process analyzed above.

To avoid implying a formless eclecticism we must add two other points. First, careful theoretical identifications must be made of the nature of the factors to which an impetus to structural change is imputed. Many factors prominent in the history of social thought are, according to the theory of social systems, exogenous – including factors of geographical environment and biological heredity, and outstanding personalities, as "great men," who are never conceived of simply as products of their societies. This category of exogenous factors also includes cultural explanations, as those in terms of religious ideas. Furthermore, these different exogenous sources are not alike in the nature of their impact on the social system.

Among these exogenous sources of change is the size of the population of any social system. Perhaps the most important relevant discussion of this was Durkheim's, in the *Division of Labor*, where he speaks of the relations between "material" and "dynamic" density. Populations are partially resultants of the processes of social systems, but their size is in turn a determinant.

The second, related point concerns the implications of the hierarchy of control in social systems. It may be difficult to define magnitude of impact; however, given approximate equality of magnitude, the probability of producing structural change is greater in proportion to the position in the order of control at which the impact of its principal disturbing influence occurs. This principle is based on the assumption that stable systems have mechanisms which can absorb considerable internal strains, and thus endogenous or exogenous variabilities impinging at lower levels in the hierarchy of control may be neutralized before extending structural changes to higher levels. It follows that the crucial focus of the problem of change lies in the stability of the value system.

The analytical problems in this area are by no means simple. Difficulties arise because of the complex ways in which societies are composed of interpenetrating subsystems, and because of the ways in which the exogenous factors impinge somehow on every role, collectivity norm, and subvalue. Thus the collectivity component of social structure has been placed, in general analytical terms, only third in the general control hierarchy. Yet every society must be organized as a whole on the collectivity level, integrating goal-attainment, integrative, and pattern-maintenance functions. Hence an important change in the leadership composition of the over-all societal collectivity *may* have a far greater impact on the norms and values of the society generally than would a value change in lower-order subsystems. Hence a naïve use of the formula, the higher in the control hierarchy the greater the impact, is not recommended.

NOTES

1 When we speak of the *pattern* of the system tending to remain constant, we mean this in an analytical sense. The outputs to environing systems need not remain constant in the same sense, and their variations may disturb the relationship to the environing system. Thus scientific investigation may be stably institutionalized in a structural sense but result in a continuing output of new knowledge, which is a dynamic factor in the system's interchanges with its situation.
2 Cf. the paper, Parsons, "McCarthyism and American Social Tension," *Yale Review*, Winter, 1955. Reprinted as Chap. 7, *Structure and Process in Modern Societies*.
3 It should be noted that the above formulation of the function of adaptation carefully avoids any implication that "passive" adjustment is the keynote of adaptation. Adaptation is relative to the values and goals of the system. "Good adaptation" may consist either in passive acceptance of conditions with a minimization of risk or in active mastery of conditions. The inclusion of active mastery in the concept of adaptation is one of the most important tendencies of recent developments in biological theory. An important relation between the two functional categories of goal-attainment and adaptation and the old categories of ends and means should be noted. The basic discrimination of ends and means may be said to be the special case, for the personality system, of the more general discrimination of the functions of goal-attainment and adaptation. In attempting to squeeze analysis of social behavior into this framework, utilitarian theory was guilty both of narrowing it to the personality case (above all, denying the independent analytical

significance of social systems) and of overlooking the independent significance of the functions of pattern-maintenance and of integration of social systems themselves.

4. By this criterion a system such as the Catholic Church is not a society. It clearly transcends and interpenetrates with a number of different societies in which its values are more or less fully institutionalized and its subunits are constituent collectivities. But the Church, primarily a *culturally* oriented social system, is not itself capable of meeting very many of the functional exigencies of a society, especially the political and economic needs. Similarly, even a "world government," should anything approaching that conception come into being, need not itself constitute a "world-society," though its effectiveness would imply a level of normative integration which would make the degree of separateness we have traditionally attributed to "national societies" problematical.

5. Cf. Parsons, "The Principal Structures of Community" in C. J. Friedrich (ed.), *Community*, Nomos, vol. II, Liberal Arts Press, 1959, and in Parsons, *Structure and Process in Modern Societies*, Free Press, 1959, Chap, 8.

6. It may be noted that allowing the institutionalized values to be determined through agencies not fully controlled by the paramount political collectivity involves a certain risk to it. The relatively full institutionalization of anything like the separation of church and state is therefore probably an index of the completeness of institutionalization of values. Modern totalitarian regimes are partly understandable in terms of the insecurity of this institutionalization. Therefore totalitarian parties are functionally equivalent to "churches," though they may put their value focus at a nontranscendental level, which is, e.g., allegedly "economic," which attempts to establish the kind of relation to government typical of a less differentiated state of the paramount collectivity than has existed in the modern West.

Chapter 38

Manifest and Latent Functions [1957]

Robert K. Merton

The distinction between manifest and latent functions was devised to preclude the inadvertent confusion, often found in the sociological literature, between conscious *motivations* for social behavior and its *objective consequences*. Our scrutiny of current vocabularies of functional analysis has shown how easily, and how unfortunately, the sociologist may identify *motives* with *functions*. It was further indicated that the motive and the function vary independently and that the failure to register this fact in an established terminology has contributed to the unwitting tendency among sociologists to confuse the subjective categories of motivation with the objective categories of function. This, then, is the central purpose of our succumbing to the not-always-commendable practice of introducing new terms into the rapidly growing technical vocabulary of sociology, a practice regarded by many laymen as an affront to their intelligence and an offense against common intelligibility.

As will be readily recognized, I have adapted the terms "manifest" and "latent" from their use in another context by Freud (although Francis Bacon had long ago spoken of "latent process" and "latent configuration" in connection with processes which are below the threshold of superficial observation). ...

Since the occasion for making the distinction arises with great frequency, and since the purpose of a conceptual scheme is to direct observations toward salient elements of a situation and to prevent the inadvertent oversight of these elements, it would seem justifiable to designate this distinction by an appropriate set of terms.

This is the rationale for the distinction between manifest functions and latent functions; the first referring to those objective consequences for a specified unit (person, subgroup, social or cultural system) which contribute to its adjustment or adaptation and were so intended; the second referring to unintended and unrecognized consequences of the same order.

There are some indications that the christening of this distinction may serve a heuristic purpose by becoming incorporated into an explicit conceptual apparatus, thus aiding both systematic observation and later analysis. In recent years, for example, the distinction between manifest and latent functions has been utilized in analyses of racial intermarriage,[1] social stratification,[2] affective frustration,[3] Veblen's sociological theories,[4] prevailing American orientations toward Russia,[5] propaganda as a means of social control,[6] Malinowski's anthropological theory,[7] Navajo witchcraft,[8] problems in the sociology of knowledge,[9] fashion,[10] the dynamics of personality,[11] national security meansures,[12] the internal social dynamics of bureaucracy,[13] and a great variety of other sociological problems.

The very diversity of these subject-matters suggests that the theoretic distinction between manifest and latent functions is not bound up with a limited and particular range of human behavior. But there still remains the large task of ferreting out the specific uses to which this distinction can be put, and it is to this large task that we devote the remaining pages of this chapter.

Heuristic Purposes of the Distinction

Clarifies the analysis of seemingly irrational social patterns. In the first place, the distinction aids the sociological interpretation of many social practices which persist even though their manifest purpose is clearly not achieved. The time-worn procedure in such instances has been for diverse, particularly lay, observers to refer to these practices as "superstitions," "irrationalities," "mere inertia of tradition," etc. In other words, when group behavior does not – and, indeed, often cannot – attain its ostensible purpose there is an inclination to attribute its occurrence to lack of intelligence, sheer ignorance, survivals, or so-called inertia. Thus, the Hopi ceremonials designed to produce abundant rainfall may be labeled a superstitious practice of primitive folk and that is assumed to conclude the matter. It should be noted that this in no sense accounts for the group behavior. It is simply a case of name-calling; it substitutes the epithet "superstition" for an analysis of the actual role of this behavior in the life of the group. Given the concept of latent function, however, we are reminded that this behavior *may* perform a function for the group, although this function may be quite remote from the avowed purpose of the behavior.

The concept of latent function extends the observer's attention beyond the question of whether or not the behavior attains its avowed purpose. Temporarily ignoring these explicit purposes, it directs attention *toward* another range of consequences: those bearing, for example, upon the individual personalities of

Hopi involved in the ceremony and upon the persistence and continuity of the larger group. Were one to confine himself to the problem of whether a manifest (purposed) function occurs, it becomes a problem, not for the sociologist, but for the meteorologist. And to be sure, our meteorologists agree that the rain ceremonial does not produce rain; but this is hardly to the point. It is merely to say that the ceremony does not have this technological use; that this purpose of the ceremony and its actual consequences do not coincide. But with the concept of latent function, we continue our inquiry, examining the consequences of the ceremony not for the rain gods or for meteorological phenomena, but for the groups which conduct the ceremony. And here it may be found, as many observers indicate, that the ceremonial does indeed have functions – but functions which are non-purposed or latent.

Ceremonials may fulfill the latent function of reinforcing the group identity by providing a periodic occasion on which the scattered members of a group assemble to engage in a common activity. As Durkheim among others long since indicated, such ceremonials are a means by which collective expression is afforded the sentiments which, in a further analysis, are found to be a basic source of group unity. Through the systematic application of the concept of latent function, therefore, *apparently* irrational behavior may *at times* be found to be positively functional for the group. Operating with the concept of latent function we are not too quick to conclude that if an activity of a group does not achieve its nominal purpose, then its persistence can be described only as an instance of "inertia," "survival," or "manipulation by powerful subgroups in the society."

In point of fact, some conception like that of latent function has very often, almost invariably, been employed by social scientists observing *a standardized practice designed to achieve an objective which one knows from accredited physical science cannot be thus achieved*. This would plainly be the case, for example, with Pueblo rituals dealing with rain or fertility. *But with behavior which is not directed toward a clearly unattainable objective, sociological observers are less likely to examine the collateral or latent functions of the behavior.*

Directs attention to theoretically fruitful fields of inquiry. The distinction between manifest and latent functions serves further to direct the attention of the sociologist to precisely those realms of behavior, attitude and belief where he can most fruitfully apply his special skills. For what is his task if he confines himself to the study of manifest functions? He is then concerned very largely with determining whether a practice instituted for a particular purpose does, in fact, achieve this purpose. He will then inquire, for example, whether a new system of wage-payment achieves its avowed purpose of reducing labor turnover or of increasing output. He will ask whether a propaganda campaign has indeed gained its objective of increasing "willingness to fight" or "willingness to buy war bonds," or "tolerance toward other ethnic groups." Now, these are important, and complex, types of inquiry. But, so long as sociologists *confine* themselves to the study of manifest functions, their inquiry is set for them by practical men of affairs (whether a captain of industry, a trade union leader, or, conceivably, a Navaho chieftain, is for the moment immaterial), rather than by the theoretic problems which are at the core of the discipline. By dealing primarily with the realm of manifest functions, with the key problem of whether deliberately instituted practices or organizations succeed in achieving their objectives, the sociologist becomes converted into an industrious and skilled recorder of the altogether familiar pattern of behavior. *The terms of appraisal are fixed and limited by the question put to him by the non-theoretic men of affairs*, e.g., has the new wage-payment program achieved such-and-such purposes?

But armed with the concept of latent function, the sociologist extends his inquiry in those very directions which promise most for the theoretic development of the discipline. He examines the familiar (or planned) social practice to ascertain the latent, and hence generally unrecognized, functions (as well, of course, as the manifest functions). He considers, for example, the consequences of the new wage plan for, say, the trade union in which the workers are organized or the consequences of a propaganda program, not only for increasing its avowed purpose of stirring up patriotic fervor, but also for making larger numbers of people reluctant to speak their minds when they differ with official policies, etc. In short, it is suggested that the *distinctive* intellectual contributions of the sociologist are found primarily in the study of unintended consequences (among which are latent functions) of social practices, as well as in the study of anticipated consequences (among which are manifest functions).

There is some evidence that it is precisely at the point where the research attention of sociologists has shifted from the plane of manifest to the plane of latent functions that they have made their *distinctive* and major contributions. This can be extensively documented but a few passing illustrations must suffice.

THE HAWTHORNE WESTERN ELECTRIC STUDIES:[14] As is well known, the early stages of this inquiry were concerned with the problem of the relations of "illumination of efficiency" of industrial workers. For some two and a half years, attention was focused on problems such as this: do variations in the intensity of lighting affect production? The initial results showed that within wide limits there was no uniform relation between illumination and output. Production output increased *both* in the experimental group where illumination was increased (or *decreased*) *and* in the control group where no changes in illumination were introduced. In short, the investigators confined themselves wholly to a search for the manifest functions. Lacking a concept of latent social function, no attention whatever was initially paid to the social consequences *of the experiment* for relations among members of the test and control groups or for relations between workers and the test room authorities. In other words, the investigators lacked a sociological frame of reference and operated merely as "engineers" (just as a group of meteorologists might have explored the "effects" upon rainfall of the Hopi ceremonial).

Only after continued investigation did it occur to the research group to explore the consequences of the new "experimental situation" for the self-images and self-conceptions of the workers taking part in the experiment, for the interpersonal relations among members of the group, for the coherence and unity of the group. As Elton Mayo reports it, "the illumination fiasco had made them alert to the need that very careful records should be kept of everything that happened in the room in addition to the obvious engineering and industrial devices. Their observations therefore included not only records of industrial and engineering changes but also records of physiological or medical changes, and, *in a sense*, of social and anthropological. This last took the form of a 'log' that gave as full an account as possible of the actual events of every day…"[15] In short, it was only after a long series of experiments which wholly neglected the latent social functions of the experiment (as a contrived social situation) that this distinctly sociological framework was introduced. "With this realization," the authors write, "the inquiry changed its character. No longer were the investigators interested in testing for the effects of single variables. In the place of a controlled experiment they substituted the notion of a social situation which needed to be described and understood as a system of interdependent elements." Thereafter, as is now widely known, inquiry was directed very largely toward ferreting out the latent functions of standardized practices among the workers, of informal organization developing among workers, of workers' games instituted by "wise administrators," of large programs of worker counseling and interviewing, etc. The new conceptual scheme entirely altered the range and types of date gathered in the ensuing research.

One has only to turn to Thomas and Znaniecki, in their classical work of some thirty years ago,[16] to recognize the correctness of Shils' remark:

> […] indeed the history of the study of primary groups in American sociology is a supreme instance of the *discontinuities of the development of this discipline*: a problem is stressed by one who is an acknowledged founder of the discipline, the problem is left unstudied, then, some years later, it is taken up with enthusiasm as if no one had ever thought of it before.[17]

For Thomas and Znaniecki had repeatedly emphasized the sociological view that, whatever its major purpose, "the association as a concrete group of human personalities unofficially involves many other interests; the social contacts between its members are not limited to their common pursuit. …" In effect, then, it had taken years of experimentation to turn the attention of the Western Electric research team to the latent social functions of primary groups emerging in industrial organizations. It should be made clear that this case is not cited here as an instance of defective experimental design; that is not our immediate concern. It is considered only as an illustration of the pertinence for *sociological* inquiry of the concept of latent function, and the associated concepts of functional analysis. It illustrates how the inclusion of this concept (whether the term is used or not is inconsequential) can sensitize sociological investigators to a range of significant social variables which are otherwise easily overlooked. The explicit ticketing of the concept may perhaps lessen the frequency of such occasions of discontinuity in future sociological research.

The discovery of latent functions represents significant increments in sociological knowledge. There is another respect in which inquiry into latent functions represents a distinctive contribution of the social scientist. It is precisely the latent functions of a practice or belief which are *not* common knowledge, for these are unintended and generally unrecognized social and psychological consequences. As a result, findings concerning latent functions represent a greater increment in knowledge than findings concerning manifest functions. They represent, also, greater departures from "common-sense" knowledge about social life. Inasmuch as the latent functions depart, more or less, from the avowed manifest functions, the research which uncovers latent functions very often produces "paradoxical" results. The seeming paradox arises from the sharp modification of a familiar popular preconception which regards a standardized practice or belief *only* in terms of its manifest functions by indicating some of its subsidiary or collateral latent functions. The introduction of the concept of latent function in social research leads to conclusions which show that "social life is not as simple as it first seems." For as long as people confine themselves to *certain* consequences (e.g., manifest consequences), it is comparatively simple for them to pass moral judgments upon the practice or belief in question. Moral evaluations, generally based on these manifest consequences, tend to be polarized in terms of black or white. But the perception of further (latent) consequences often complicates the picture. Problems of moral evaluation (which are not our immediate concern) and problems of social engineering (which are our concern) both take on the additional complexities usually involved in responsible social decisions. ...

Precludes the substitution of naive moral judgments for sociological analysis. Since moral evaluations in a society tend to be largely in terms of the manifest consequences of a practice or code, we should be prepared to find that analysis in terms of latent functions at times runs counter to prevailing moral evaluations. For it does not follow that the latent functions will operate in the same fashion as the manifest consequences which are ordinarily the basis of these judgments. Thus, in large sectors of the American population, the political machine or the "political racket" are judged as unequivocally "bad" and "undesirable." The grounds for such moral judgment vary somewhat, but they consist substantially in pointing out that political machines violate moral codes: political patronage violates the code of selecting personnel on the basis of impersonal qualifications rather than on grounds of party loyalty or contributions to the party war-chest; bossism violates the code that votes should be based on individual appraisal of the qualifications of candidates and of political issues, and not on abiding loyalty to a feudal leader; bribery, and "honest graft" obviously offend the proprieties of property; "protection" for crime clearly violates the law and the mores; and so on.

In view of the manifold respects in which political machines, in varying degrees, run counter to the mores and at times to the law, it becomes pertinent to inquire how they manage to continue in operation. The familiar "explanations" for the continuance of the political machine are not here in point. To be sure, it may well be that if "respectable citizenry" would live up to their political obligations, if the electorate were to be alert and enlightened; if the number of elective officers were substantially reduced from the dozens, even hundreds, which the average voter is now expected to appraise in the course of town, county, state and national elections; if the electorate were activated by the "wealthy and educated classes without whose participation," as the not-always democratically oriented Bryce put it, "the best-framed government must speedily degenerate"; – if these and a plethora of similar changes in political structure were introduced, perhaps the "evils" of the political machine would indeed be exorcized. But it should be noted that these changes are often not introduced, that political machines have had the phoenix-like quality of arising strong and unspoiled from their ashes, that, in short, this structure has exhibited a notable vitality in many areas of American political life.

Proceeding from the functional view, therefore, that we should *ordinarily* (not invariably) expect persistent social patterns and social structures to perform positive functions *which are at the time not adequately fulfilled by other existing patterns and structures*, the thought occurs that perhaps this publicly maligned organization is, *under present conditions*, satisfying basic latent functions. [...]

NOTES

1. Robert K. Merton, "Intermarriage and the Social Structure," *Psychiatry* 1941, 4: 361–74.
2. Kingsley Davis, "A Conceptual Analysis of Stratification," *American Sociological Review* 1942, 7: 309–21.
3. Isidor Thorner, "Sociological Aspects of Affectional Frustration," *Psychiatry* 1943, 6: 157–73, esp. at 165.
4. A. K. Davis, "Thorstein Veblen's Social Theory," Harvard Ph.D dissertation, 1941 and "Veblen on the Decline of the Protestant Ethic," *Social Forces* 1944, 22: 282–6; Louis Schneider, *The Freudian Psychology and Veblen's Social Theory* (New York: King's Crown Press, 1948), esp. Chapter 2.
5. A. K. Davis, "Some Sources of American Hostility to Russia," *American Journal of Sociology* 1947, 53: 174–83.
6. Talcott Parsons, "Propaganda and Social Control," in his *Essays in Sociological Theory*.
7. Clyde Kluckhohn, "Bronislaw Malinowski, 1884–1942," *Journal of American Folklore* 1943, 56: 208–19.
8. Clyde Kluckhohn, *Navaho Witchcraft*, Papers of the Peabody Museum of American Archaeology and Ethnology, Harvard University, XXII, No. 2, 1944, 47a, esp. at 46–7 ff.
9. Robert K. Merton, "The Sociology of Knowledge," in R. K. Merton, *Social Theory and Social Structure*, 1968, pp. 510–42.
10. Bernard Barber and L. S. Lobel, "'Fashion' in Women's Clothes and the American Social System," *Social Forces* 1952, 31: 124–31.
11. O. H. Mowrer and C. Kluckhohn, "Dynamic Theory of Personality," in J. M. Hunt (ed.), *Personality and the Behavior Disorders* (New York: Ronald Press, 1944), 1, pp. 69–135, esp. at 72.
12. Marie Jahoda and S. W. Cook, "Security Measures and Freedom of Thought: an Exploratory Study of the Impact of Loyalty and Security Programs," *Yale Law Journal* 1952, 61: 296–333.
13. Philip Selznick, *TVA and the Grass Roots* (University of California Press, 1949); A. W. Gouldner, *Patterns of Industrial Bureaucracy* (Glencoe, IL: The Free Press, 1954); P. M. Blau, *The Dynamics of Bureaucracy* (University of Chicago Press, 1955); A. K. Davis, "Bureaucratic Patterns in Navy Officer Corps," *Social Forces* 1948, 27: 142–53.

14 This is cited as a case study of how *an elaborate research was wholly changed in theoretic orientation and in the character of its research findings by the introduction of a concept approximating the concept of latent function.* Selection of the case for this purpose does not, of course, imply full acceptance of the *interpretations* which the authors give their findings. Among the several volumes reporting the Western Electric research, see particularly F. J. Roethlisberger and W. J. Dickson, *Management and the Worker* (Harvard University Press, 1939).

15 Elton Mayo, *The Social Problems of an Industrial Civilization* (Harvard University Press, 1945), p. 70.

16 W. I. Thomas and F. Znaniecki, *The Polish Peasant in Europe and America* (New York: Knopf, 1927).

17 Edward Shils, *The Present State of American Sociology* (Glencoe, IL: The Free Press, 1948), p. 42 [italics supplied].

Chapter 39

On Sociological Theories of the Middle Range [1949]

Robert K. Merton

Like so many words that are bandied about, the word theory threatens to become meaningless. Because its referents are so diverse – including everything from minor working hypotheses, through comprehensive but vague and unordered speculations, to axiomatic systems of thought – use of the word often obscures rather than creates understanding.

The term *sociological theory* refers to logically interconnected sets of propositions from which empirical uniformities can be derived. Throughout we focus on what I have called *theories of the middle range*: theories that lie between the minor but necessary working hypotheses that evolve in abundance during day-to-day research and the all-inclusive systematic efforts to develop a unified theory that will explain all the observed uniformities of social behavior, social organization, and social change.

Middle-range theory is principally used in sociology to guide empirical inquiry. It is intermediate to general theories of social systems which are too remote from particular classes of social behavior, organization, and change to account for what is observed, and to those detailed orderly descriptions of particulars that are not generalized at all. Middle-range theory involves abstractions, of course, but they are close enough to observed data to be incorporated in propositions that permit empirical testing. Middle-range theories deal with delimited aspects of social phenomena, as is indicated by their labels. One speaks of a theory of reference groups, of social mobility, or role-conflict and of the formation of social norms just as one speaks of a theory of prices, a germ theory of disease, or a kinetic theory of gases.

The seminal ideas in such theories are characteristically simple: consider Gilbert on magnetism, Boyle on atmospheric pressure, or Darwin on the formation of coral atolls. Gilbert *begins* with the relatively simple idea that the earth may be conceived as a magnet; Boyle, with the simple idea that the atmosphere may be conceived as a "sea of air"; Darwin, with the idea that one can conceive of the atolls as upward and outward growths of coral over islands that had long since subsided into the sea. Each of these theories provides an image that gives rise to inferences. To take but one case: if the atmosphere is thought of as a sea of air, then, as Pascal inferred, there should be less air pressure on a mountain top than at its base. The initial idea thus suggests specific hypotheses which are tested by seeing whether the inferences from them are empirically confirmed. The idea itself is tested for its fruitfulness by noting the range of theoretical problems and hypotheses that allow one to identify new characteristics of atmospheric pressure.

In much the same fashion, the theory of reference groups and relative deprivation starts with the simple idea, initiated by James, Baldwin, and Mead and developed by Hyman and Stouffer, that people take the standards of significant others as a basis for self-appraisal and evaluation. Some of the inferences drawn from this idea are at odds with common-sense expectations based upon an unexamined set of "self-evident" assumptions. Common sense, for example, would suggest that the greater the actual loss experienced by a family in a mass disaster, the more acutely it will feel deprived. This belief is based on the unexamined assumption that the magnitude of objective loss is related linearly to the subjective appraisal of the loss and that this appraisal is confined to one's own experience. But the theory of relative deprivation leads to quite a different hypothesis – that self-appraisals depend upon people's comparisons of their own situation with that of other people perceived as being comparable to themselves. This theory therefore suggests that, under specifiable conditions, families suffering serious losses will feel *less* deprived than those suffering smaller losses if they are in situations leading them to compare themselves to people suffering even more severe losses. For example, it is people in the area of greatest impact of a disaster who, though substantially deprived themselves, are most apt to see others around them who are even more severely deprived. Empirical inquiry supports the theory of relative deprivation rather than the common-sense assumptions: "the feeling of being relatively *better off* than others *increases with objective loss*" up to the category of highest loss" and only then declines. This pattern is reinforced by the tendency of public communications to focus on "the *most extreme sufferers* [which] tends to fix them as a reference group against which even other sufferers can compare themselves favorably." As the inquiry develops, it is found that these patterns of self-appraisal in turn affect the distribution of morale in the community of survivors and their motivation to help others.[1] Within a particular *class* of behavior, therefore, the theory of relative deprivation directs us to a set of hypotheses that can be empirically tested. The confirmed conclusion can then be put simply enough: when few are hurt to much the same extent, the pain and loss of each seems great; where many are hurt in greatly varying degree, even fairly large losses seem small as they are compared with far larger ones. The probability that comparisons will be made is affected by the differing visibility of losses of greater and less extent.

The specificity of this example should not obscure the more general character of middle-range theory. Obviously, behavior of people confronted with a mass disaster is only one of an indefinitely large array of particular situations to which the theory of reference groups can be instructively applied, just as is the case with the theory of change in social stratification, the theory of authority, the theory of institutional interdependence, or the theory of anomie. But it is equally clear that such middle-range theories have not been logically *derived* from a single all-embracing theory of social systems, though once developed they may be consistent with one. Furthermore, each theory is more than a mere empirical generalization – an isolated proposition summarizing observed uniformities of relationships between two or more variables. A theory comprises a set of assumptions from which empirical generalizations have themselves been derived.

Another case of middle-range theory in sociology may help us to identify its character and uses. The theory of role-sets[2] begins with an image of how social status is organized in the social structure. This image is as simple as Boyle's image of the atmosphere as a sea of air or Gilbert's image of the earth as a magnet. As with all middle-range theories, however, the proof is in the using, not in the immediate response to the originating ideas as obvious or odd, as derived from more general theory or conceived of to deal with a particular class of problems.

Despite the very diverse meanings attached to the concept of *social status*, one sociological tradition consistently uses it to refer to a position in a social system, with its distinctive array of designated rights and obligations. In this tradition, as exemplified by Ralph Linton, the related concept of *social role* refers to the behavior of status-occupants that is oriented toward the patterned expectations of others (who accord the rights and exact the obligations). Linton, like others in this tradition, went on to state the long recognized and basic observation that each person in society inevitably occupies multiple statuses and that each of these statuses has its associated role.

It is at this point that the imagery of the role-set theory departs from this long-established tradition. The difference is initially a small one – some might say so small as to be insignificant – but the shift in the angle of vision leads to successively more fundamental theoretical differences. Role-set theory begins with the concept that each social status involves not a single associated role, but an array of roles. This feature of social structure gives rise to the concept of role-set: that complement of social relationships in which persons are involved simply because they occupy a particular social status. Thus, a person in the status of medical student plays not only the role of student *vis-à-vis* the correlative status of his teachers, but also an array of other roles relating him diversely to others in the system: other students, physicians, nurses, social workers, medical technicians, and the like. Again, the status of school teacher has its distinctive role-set which relates the teacher not only to the correlative status, pupil, but also to colleagues, the school principal and superintendent, the Board of Education, professional associations and, in the United States, local patriotic organizations.

Notice that the role-set differs from what sociologists have long described as "multiple roles." The latter term has traditionally referred not to the complex of roles associated with a single social status but to the various social statuses (often, in different institutional spheres) in which people find themselves – for example, one person might have the diverse statuses of physician, husband, father, professor, church elder, Conservative Party member and army captain. [...]

Up to this point, the concept of role-set is *merely* an image for thinking about a component of the social structure. But this image is a beginning, not an end, for it leads directly to certain analytical problems. The notion of the role-set at once leads to the inference that social structures confront men with the task of articulating the components of countless role-sets – that is, the functional task of managing somehow to organize these so that an appreciable degree of social regularity obtains, sufficient to enable most people most of the time to go about their business without becoming paralyzed by extreme conflicts in their role-sets.

If this relatively simple idea of role-set has theoretical worth, it should generate distinctive problems for sociological inquiry. The concept of role-set does this. It raises the general but definite problem of identifying the social mechanisms – that is, the social processes having designated consequences for designated parts of the social structure – which articulate the expectations of those in the role-set sufficiently to reduce conflicts for the occupant of a status. It generates the further problem of discovering how these mechanisms come into being, so that we can also explain why the mechanisms do not operate effectively or fail to emerge at all in some social systems. Finally, like the theory of atmospheric pressure, the theory of role-set points directly to relevant empirical research. Monographs on the workings of diverse types of formal organization have developed empirically-based theoretical extensions of how role-sets operate in practice.

The theory of role-sets illustrates another aspect of sociological theories of the middle range. They are frequently consistent with a variety of so-called systems of sociological theory. So far as one can tell, the theory of role-sets is not inconsistent with such broad theoretical orientations as Marxist theory, functional analysis, social behaviorism, Sorokin's integral sociology, or Parsons' theory of action. This may be a horrendous observation for those of us who have been trained to believe that systems of sociological thought are logically close-knit and mutually exclusive sets of doctrine. But in fact, as we shall note later in this introduction, comprehensive sociological theories are sufficiently loose-knit, internally diversified, and mutually overlapping that a *given theory of the middle range*, which has a measure of empirical confirmation, can often be subsumed under comprehensive theories which are themselves discrepant in certain respects.

This reasonably unorthodox opinion can be illustrated by reexamining the theory of role-sets as a middle-range theory. We depart from the traditional concept by assuming that a single status in society involves, not a single role, but an array of associated roles, relating the status-occupant to diverse others. Second, we note that this concept of the role-set gives rise to distinctive theoretical problems, hypotheses, and so to empirical inquiry. One basic problem is that of identifying the social mechanisms which articulate the role-set and reduce conflicts among roles. Third, the concept of the role-set directs our attention to the structural problem of identifying the social arrangements which integrate as well as oppose the expectations of various members of the role-set. The concept of multiple roles, on the other hand, confines our attention to a different and no doubt important issue: how do *individual* occupants of statuses happen to deal with the many and sometimes conflicting demands made of them? Fourth, the concept of the role-set directs us to the further question of how these social mechanisms come into being; the answer to this question enables us to account for the many concrete instances in which the role-set operates ineffectively. (This no more assumes that all social mechanisms are functional than the theory of biological evolution involves the comparable assumption that no dysfunctional developments occur.) Finally, the logic of analysis exhibited in this sociological theory of the middle range is developed wholly in terms of the elements of social structure rather than in terms of providing concrete *historical descriptions* of particular social systems. Thus, middle-range theory enables us to transcend the mock problem of a theoretical conflict between the nomothetic and the idiothetic, between the general and the altogether particular, between generalizing sociological theory and historicism.

From all this, it is evident that according to role-set theory there is always a *potential* for differing expectations among those in the role-set as to what is appropriate conduct for a status-occupant. The basic source of this potential for conflict – and it is important to note once again that on this point we are at one with such disparate general theorists as Marx and Spencer, Simmel, Sorokin and Parsons – is found in the structural fact that the other members of a role-set are apt to hold various social positions differing from those of the status-occupant in question. To the extent that members of a role-set are diversely located in the social structure, they are apt to have interests and sentiments, values, and moral expectations, differing from those of the status-occupant himself. This, after all, is one of the principal assumptions of Marxist theory as it is of much other sociological theory: social differentiation generates distinct interests among those variously located in the structure of the society. For example, the members of a school board are often in social and economic strata that differ significantly from the stratum of the school teacher. The interests, values, and expectations of board members are consequently apt to differ from those of the teacher who may thus be subject to conflicting expectations from these and other members of his role-set: professional colleagues, influential members of the school board and, say, the Americanism Committee of the American Legion. An educational essential for one is apt to be judged as an educational frill by another, or as downright subversion, by the third. What holds conspicuously for this one status holds, in identifiable degree, for occupants of other statuses who are structurally related through their role-set to others who themselves occupy differing positions in society.

As a theory of the middle range, then, the theory of role-sets begins with a concept and its associated imagery and generates an array of theoretical problems. Thus, the assumed structural basis for potential disturbance of a role-set gives rise to a double question (which, the record shows, has not been raised in the absence of the theory): which social mechanisms, if any, operate to counteract the theoretically assumed instability of role-sets and, correlatively, under which circumstances do these social mechanisms fail to operate, with resulting inefficiency, confusion, and conflict? Like other questions that have historically stemmed from the general orientation of functional analysis, these do not assume that role-sets invariably operate with substantial efficiency. For this middle-range theory is not concerned with the historical generalization that a degree of social order or conflict prevails in society but with the analytical problem of identifying the social mechanisms which produce a greater degree of order or less conflict than would obtain if these mechanisms were not called into play.

Total Systems of Sociological Theory

The quest for theories of the middle range exacts a distinctly different commitment from the sociologist than does the quest for an all-embracing, unified theory. The pages that follow assume that this search for a total system of sociological theory, in which observations about every aspect of social behavior, organization, and change promptly find their preordained place, has the same exhilarating challenge and the same small promise as those many all-encompassing philosophical systems which have fallen into deserved disuse. The issue must be fairly joined. Some sociologists still write as though they expect, here and now, formulation of *the* general sociological theory broad enough to encompass the vast ranges of precisely observed details of social behavior, organization, and change and fruitful enough to direct the attention of research workers to a flow of problems for empirical research. This I take to be a premature and apocalyptic belief. We are not ready. Not enough preparatory work has been done.

An historical sense of the changing intellectual contexts of sociology should be sufficiently humbling to liberate these optimists from this extravagant hope. For one thing, certain aspects of our historical past are still too much with us. We must remember that early sociology grew up in an intellectual atmosphere in which vastly comprehensive systems of philosophy were being introduced on all sides. Any philosopher of the eighteenth and early nineteenth centuries worth his salt had to develop his own philosophical system – of these, Kant, Fichte, Schelling, Hegel were only the best known. Each system was a personal bid for the definitive overview of the universe of matter, nature and man.

These attempts of philosophers to create total systems became a model for the early sociologists, and so the nineteenth century was a century of sociological systems. Some of the founding fathers, like Comte and Spencer, were imbued with the *esprit de système*, which was expressed in their sociologies as in the rest of their wider-ranging philosophies. Others, such as Gumplowicz, Ward, and Giddings, later tried to provide intellectual legitimacy for this still "new science of a very ancient subject." This required that a general and definitive framework of sociological thought be built rather than developing special theories designed to guide the investigation of specific sociological problems within an evolving and provisional framework.

Within this context, almost all the pioneers in sociology tried to fashion his own system. The multiplicity of systems, each claiming to be the genuine sociology, led naturally enough to the formation of schools, each with its cluster of masters, disciples and epigoni. Sociology not only became differentiated with other disciples, but it became internally differentiated. This differentiation, however, was not in terms of specialization, as in the sciences, but rather, as in philosophy, in terms of total systems, typically held to be mutually exclusive and largely at odds. As Bertrand Russell noted about philosophy, this total sociology did not seize "the advantage, as compared with the [sociologies] of the system-builders, of being able to tackle its problems one at a time, instead of having to invent at one stroke a block theory of the whole [sociological] universe."[3]

Another route has been followed by sociologists in their quest to establish the intellectual legitimacy of their discipline: they have taken as their prototype systems of scientific theory rather than systems of philosophy. This path too has sometimes led to the attempt to create total systems of sociology – a goal that is often based on one or more of three basic misconceptions about the sciences.

The first misinterpretation assumes that systems of thought can be effectively developed before a great mass of basic observations has been accumulated. According to this view, Einstein might follow hard on the heels of Kepler, without the intervening centuries of investigation and systematic thought about the results of investigation that were needed to prepare the terrain. The systems of sociology that stem from this tacit assumption are much like those introduced by the system-makers in medicine over a span of 150 years: the systems of Stahl, Boissier de Sauvages, Broussais, John Brown and Benjamin Rush. Until well into the nineteenth century eminent personages in medicine thought it necessary to develop a theoretical system of disease long before the antecedent empirical inquiry had been adequately developed. These garden-paths have since been closed off in medicine but this sort of effort still turns up in sociology. It is this tendency that led the biochemist and avocational sociologist, L. J. Henderson, to observe:

> A difference between most system-building in the social sciences and systems of thought and classification in the natural sciences is to be seen in their evolution. In the natural sciences both theories and descriptive systems grow by adaptation to the increasing knowledge and experience of the scientists. *In the social sciences, systems often issue fully formed from the mind of one man.* Then they may be much discussed if they attract attention, but *progressive adaptive modification as a result of the concerted efforts of great numbers of men is rare.*[4]

The second misconception about the physical sciences rests on a mistaken assumption of historical contemporaneity – *that all cultural products existing at the same moment of history have the same degree of maturity.* In fact, to perceive differences here would be to achieve a sense of proportion. The fact that the discipline of physics and the discipline of sociology are both identifiable in the mid-twentieth century does not mean that the achievements of the one should be the measure of the other. True, social scientists today live at a time when physics has achieved comparatively great scope and precision of theory and experiment, a great aggregate of tools of investigation, and an abundance of technological by-products. Looking about them, many sociologists take the achievements of physics as the standard for self-appraisal. They want to compare biceps with their bigger brothers. They, too, want to *count*. And when it becomes evident that they neither have the rugged physique nor pack the murderous wallop of their big brothers, some sociologists despair. They begin to ask: is a science of society really possible unless we institute a total system of sociology? But this perspective ignores the fact that between twentieth-century physics and twentieth-century sociology stand billions of man-hours of sustained, disciplined, and cumulative research. Perhaps sociology is not yet ready for its Einstein because it has not yet found its Kepler – to say nothing of its Newton, Laplace, Gibbs, Maxwell or Planck.

Third, sociologists sometimes misread the actual state of theory in the physical sciences. This error is ironic, for physicists agree that they have not achieved an all-encompassing system of theory, and most see little prospect of it in the near future. What characterizes physics is an array of special theories of greater or less scope, coupled with the historically-grounded hope that these will continue to be brought together into families of theory. As one observer puts it: "though most of us hope, it is true, for an all embracive future theory which will unify the various postulates of physics, we do not wait for it before proceeding with the important business of science."[5] More recently, the theoretical physicist, Richard Feynman, reported without dismay that "today our theories of physics, the laws of physics, are a multitude of different parts and pieces that do not fit together very well."[6] But perhaps most telling is the observation by that most comprehensive of theoreticians who devoted the last years of his life to the unrelenting and unsuccessful search "for a unifying theoretical basis for all these single disciplines, consisting of a minimum of concepts and fundamental relationships, from which all the concepts and relationships of the single disciplines might be derived by logical process." Despite his own profound and lonely commitment to this quest, Einstein observed:

> The greater part of physical research is devoted to the development of the various branches in physics, in each of which the object is the theoretical understanding of more or less restricted fields of experience, and in each of which the laws and concepts remain as closely as possible related to experience.[7]

These observations might be pondered by those sociologists who expect a sound general system of sociological theory in our time – or soon after. If the science of physics, with its centuries of enlarged theoretical generalizations, has not managed to develop an all-encompassing theoretical system, then *a fortiori* the science of sociology, which has only begun to accumulate empirically grounded theoretical generalizations of modest scope, would seem well advised to moderate its aspirations for such a system.

Utilitarian Pressures for Total Systems of Sociology

The conviction among some sociologists that we must, here and now, achieve a grand theoretical system not only results from a misplaced comparison with the physical sciences, it is also a response to the ambiguous position of sociology in contemporary society. The very uncertainty about whether the accumulated knowledge of sociology is adequate to meet the large demands now being made of it – by policy-makers, reformers and reactionaries, by business-men and government-men, by college presidents and college sophomores – provokes an overly-zealous and defensive conviction on the part of some sociologists that they must somehow be equal to these demands, however premature and extravagant they may be.

This conviction erroneously assumes that a science must be adequate to meet *all* demands, intelligent or stupid, made of it. This conviction is implicitly based on the sacrilegious and masochistic assumption that one must be omniscient and omnicompetent – to admit to less than total knowledge is to admit to total ignorance. So it often happens that the exponents of a fledgling discipline make extravagant claims to total systems of theory, adequate to the entire range of problems encompassed by the discipline. It is this sort of attitude that Whitehead referred to in the epigraph to this book: "It is characteristic of a science in its earlier stages ... to be both ambitiously profound in its aims and trivial in its handling of details."

Like the sociologists who thoughtlessly compared themselves with contemporary physical scientists because they both are alive at the same instant of history, the general public and its strategic decision-makers often err in making a definitive appraisal of social science on the basis of its ability to solve the urgent problems of society today. The misplaced masochism of the social scientist and the inadvertent sadism of the public both result from the failure to remember that social science, like all science, is continually developing and that there is no providential dispensation providing that at any given moment it will be adequate to the entire array of problems confronting men. In historical perspective this expectation would be equivalent to having forever prejudged the status and promise of medicine in the seventeenth century according to its ability to produce, then and there, a cure or even a preventative for cardiac diseases. If the problem had been widely acknowledged – look at the growing rate of death from coronary thrombosis – its very importance would have obscured the *entirely independent question* of how adequate the medical knowledge of 1650 (or 1850 or 1950) was for solving a wide array of other health problems. Yet it is precisely this illogic that lies behind so many of the practical demands made on the social sciences. Because war and exploitation and poverty and racial discrimination and psychological insecurity plague modern societies, social science must justify itself by providing solutions for all of these problems. Yet social scientists may be no better equipped to solve these urgent problems today than were physicians, such as Harvey or Sydenham, to identify, study, and cure coronary thrombosis in 1655. Yet, as history testifies, the inadequacy of medicine to cope with this particular problem scarcely meant that it lacked powers of development. If everyone backs only the sure thing, who will support the colt yet to come into its own?

My emphasis upon the gap between the practical problems assigned to the sociologist and the state of his accumulated knowledge and skills does not mean, of course, that the sociologist should not seek to develop increasingly comprehensive theory or should not work on research directly relevant to urgent practical problems. Most of all, it does not mean that sociologists should deliberately seek out the pragmatically trivial problem. Different sectors in the spectrum of basic research and theory have different probabilities of being germane to particular practical problems; they have differing potentials of relevance.[8] But it is important to re-establish an historical sense of proportion. The urgency or immensity of a practical social problem does not ensure its immediate solution.[9] At any given moment, men of science are close to the solutions of some problems and remote from others. It must be remembered that necessity is only the mother of invention; socially accumulated knowledge is its father. Unless the two are brought together, necessity remains infertile. She may of course conceive at some future time when she is properly mated. But the mate requires time (and sustenance) if he is to attain the size and vigor needed to meet the demands that will be made upon him.

This book's orientation toward the relationship of current sociology and practical problems of society is much the same as its orientation toward the relationship of sociology and general sociological theory. It is a developmental orientation, rather than one that relies on the sudden mutations of one sociologist that suddenly bring solutions to major social problems or to a single encompassing theory. Though this orientation makes no marvellously dramatic claims, it offers a reasonably realistic assessment of the current condition of sociology and the ways in which it actually develops.

Total Systems of Theory and Theories of the Middle Range

From all this it would seem reasonable to suppose that sociology will advance insofar as its major (but not exclusive) concern is with developing theories of the middle range, and it will be retarded if its primary attention is focused on developing total sociological systems. So it is that in his inaugural address at the London School of Economics, T. H. Marshall put in a plea for sociological "stepping-stones in the middle distance."[10] Our major task today is to develop special theories applicable to limited conceptual ranges – theories, for example, of deviant behavior, the unanticipated consequences of purposive action, social perception, reference groups, social control, the interdependence of social institutions – rather than to seek immediately the total conceptual structure that is adequate to derive these and other theories of the middle range.

Sociological theory, if it is to advance significantly, must proceed on these interconnected planes: (1) by developing special theories from which to derive hypotheses that can be empirically investigated and (2) by evolving, not suddenly revealing, a progressively more general conceptual scheme that is adequate to consolidate groups of special theories.

To concentrate entirely on special theories is to risk emerging with specific hypotheses that account for limited aspects of social behavior, organization, and change but that remain mutually inconsistent.

To concentrate entirely on a master conceptual scheme for deriving all subsidiary theories is to risk producing twentieth-century sociological equivalents of the large philosophical systems of the past, with all their varied suggestiveness, their architectonic splendor, and their scientific sterility. The sociological theorist who is *exclusively* committed to the exploration of a total system with its utmost abstractions runs the risk that, as with modern décor, the furniture of his mind will be bare and uncomfortable.

The road to effective general schemes in sociology will only become clogged if, as in the early days of sociology, each charismatic sociologist tries to develop his own general system of theory. The persistence of this practice can only make for the balkanization of sociology, with each principality governed by its own theoretical system. Though this process has periodically marked the development of other sciences – conspicuously, chemistry, geology, and medicine – it need not be reproduced in sociology if we learn from the history of science. We sociologists can look instead toward progressively comprehensive sociological theory which, instead of proceeding from the head of one man, gradually consolidates theories of the middle range, so that these become special cases of more general formulations.

Developments in sociological theory suggest that emphasis on this orientation is needed. Note how few, how scattered, and how unimpressive are the specific sociological hypotheses which are *derived* from a master conceptual scheme. The proposals for an all-embracing theory run so far ahead of confirmed special theories as to remain unrealized programs rather than *consolidations* of theories that at first seemed discrete. Of course, as Talcott Parsons and Pitirim Sorokin (in his *Sociological Theories of Today*) have indicated, significant progress has recently been made. The gradual convergence of streams of theory in sociology, social psychology and anthropology records large theoretical gains and promises even more. Nonetheless, a large part of what is now described as sociological theory consists of *general orientations toward data, suggesting types of variables which theories must somehow take into account, rather than clearly formulated, verifiable statements of relationships between specified variables*. We have many concepts but fewer confirmed theories; many points of view, but few theorems; many "approaches" but few arrivals. Perhaps some further changes in emphasis would be all to the good.

Consciously or unconsciously, men allocate their scant resources as much in the production of sociological theory as they do in the production of plumbing supplies, and their allocations reflect their underlying assumptions. Our discussion of middle-range theory in sociology is intended to make explicit a policy decision faced by all sociological theorists. Which shall have the greater share of our collective energies and resources: the search for confirmed theories of the middle range or the search for an all-inclusive conceptual scheme? I believe – and beliefs are of course notoriously subject to error – that theories of the middle range hold the largest promise, *provided that* the search for them is coupled with a pervasive concern with consolidating special theories into more general sets of concepts and mutually consistent propositions. Even so, we must adopt the provisional outlook of our big brothers and of Tennyson:

> Our little systems have their day;
> They have their day and cease to be.

NOTES

1 Allen Barton, *Social Organization Under Stress: A Sociological Review of Disaster Studies* (Washington, DC: National Academy of Sciences – National Research Council, 1963).
2 Robert K. Merton, 1957, "The Role Set: Problems in Sociological Theory," *The British Journal of Sociology* 8: 106–20.
3 Bertrand Russell, *A History of Western Philosophy* (New York: Simon and Schuster, 1945), p. 834.
4 Lawrence J. Henderson, *The Study of Man* (Philadelphia: University of Pennsylvania Press, 1941), pp. 19–20, italics supplied; for that matter, the entire book can be read with profit by most of us sociologists.
5 Henry Margenau, "The Basis of Theory in Physics," unpublished MS., 1949, pp. 5–6.
6 Richard Feynman, *The Character of Physical Law* (London: Cox & Wyman, 1965), p. 30.
7 Albert Einstein, "The Fundamentals of Theoretical Physics," in L. Hamalian and E. L. Volpe (eds.), *Great Essays by Nobel Prize Winners* (New York: Noonday Press, 1960), pp. 219–30 at 220.
8 This conception is developed in R. K. Merton, "Basic Research and Potentials of Relevance," *American Behavioral Scientist* May 1963, VI: 86–90 on the basis of my earlier discussion, "The Role of Applied Social Science in the Formation of Policy," *Philosophy of Science* 1949, 16: 161–81.
9 As can be seen in detail in such works as the following: Paul F. Lazarsfeld, William Sewell and Harold Wilensky (eds.), *The Uses of Sociology* (New York: Basic Books, 1967); Alvin W. Gouldner and S. M. Miller, *Applied Sociology: Opportunities and Problems* (New York: The Free Press, 1965); Bernard Rosenberg, Israel Gerver and F. William Howton, *Mass Society in Crisis: Social Problems and Social Pathology* (New York: Macmillan, 1964); Barbara Wootton, *Social Science and Social Pathology* (New York: Macmillan, 1959).
10 The inaugural lecture was delivered 21 February 1946. It is printed in T. H. Marshall, *Sociology at the Crossroads* (London: Heinemann, 1963), pp. 3–24.

Index

References in *italic* type are to works extracted in this text.

action
   distinguished from social action, 287–8
   imitative, 288, 289
   instrumentally rational, 290
   meaningful, 281
   rational and irrational, 281–2
   of social collectivities, 284–5
   sociological interpretation of, 284–5
   see also action frame of reference; social action
action frame of reference, 496–8
actors, 448–50
Adam, 39
adaptation, 492, 508–9
admiration (of the rich), 78–1
Adorno, Theodore, 13, 422, *465–77*
advertising, 474, 475–6
affectual behavior, 289
African-Americans, 131–2, 405–6
   emancipation, 407–8
   prejudice against, 408–9
aggression, 396–7, 402
   guilt as inhibitor, 397–8
   see also violence; war

AGIL, 492
agriculture, 57, 220, 300–2
Alexander, Jeffrey C., 493–4
alienation, 41, 44, 47–8
   artistic, 480–1
   between art and consumer, 474–5
   people from nature, 26
   see also estrangement
ambition, 78–80
America, 32
   see also United States
American Revolution, 128
amiable virtue, 74–5
Amtstreue, 331
anger, 75
animals, 61, 143, 151, 255–6, 374
anomic suicide, 264
anomie, 240–1, 261
   division of labor, 238–41
   suicide and, 264
apologies, 415
approval (of another), 72–3
architecture, 456

Classical Sociological Theory, Third Edition. Edited by Craig Calhoun, Joseph Gerteis, James Moody, Steven Pfaff, and Indermohan Virk. Editorial material and organization © 2012 John Wiley & Sons, Ltd. Published 2012 by John Wiley & Sons, Ltd.

aristocracy, 96–7, 367
    individualism and, 106–7
    pre-Revolutionary France, 101
    singular individuals within, 111
    see also bourgeoisie; ruling class
Aristotle, 39
Arnheim, Rudolf, 450
art
    as advertising, 476
    aura, 444, 445
    authenticity, 443–4
    commodification, 473
    criticism, 446–7
    Dadaism, 454–5
    democratization, 455–7
    desublimation, 482–3
    devaluation, 468–9, 475
    as distraction, 456–7
    vs. entertainment, 471–2
    function, 454–5
    human perception and, 444–5, 453–4
    nature of, 448
    as opposed to culture industry, 470
    public reaction to, 452–3
    reproduction, 442–3, 452–3
    uniqueness, 445–6
    see also culture industry; literature; stage acting; writers
arts, 76–7
Arunta people, 250
asceticism, 294, 303–4, 471
    see also Puritanism
Association of the Broken Dish, 384
associations see civil associations
Atget, Eugène, 447
aura, 444, 445, 449
auri sacra fames, 299
authenticity, 443–4
authority, 320–1
    charismatic, 321, 324–7
    domination by divide and rule, 394–5
    on legal grounds, 321–3
    legitimate, classification, 321
    traditional, 323–4
    see also despotism

Bachofen, Johann, 245–6
Bacon, Francis, 23, 523

Bakuninism, 337
Balboa, Nunez, 47
Bales, Robert F., 492
Baraka, Amiri, 1
Bau und Leben des sozialen Krpers, 285
Bavaria, 263
de Beaumont, Gustave, 86
beauty cult, 446
beggars, 62, 68
behavior regulation, 416–17
Belgium, 263
birds, 374
Bismarck, Otto von, 337–8, 372–3
black Americans see African-Americans
Blake, William, 7–8
Bohemia, 393
Bonaparte, Louis, 87, 179, 180–1
    1851 coup, 174–5
Bonaparte, Napoleon, 85
bourgeoisie, 100, 136, 157
    abolition of bourgeois property, 166–8
    definition, 171
    development, 157–8
    effects on world economy, 158–9
    ideologists, 163
    see also capitalism; middle classes
Boutroux, Émile, 196
Boyle, Robert, 532
brothels, 278
buildings, 456
bureaucracy, 12, 322–3
    advantages, 334
    characteristics, 328–30
    office management, 329–30
    position of officials, 331–3
    social equality and, 334–6
    stability, 336–8
Burke, Edmund, 95

Caligula, 39
capital, 164–5, 166, 189
    distribution of, 311–12
    growth, 185–6
Capital (Marx), 137
capitalism, 8–9, 28–9, 161–2
    choice and, 12
    greed and, 299–300
    productive vs. parasitic, 437–8

Protestant asceticism and, 303–7
  spirit of, 295–6, 298–9, 303–4
    asceticism and, 307–8
  see also markets
capitalists, 185–6
career paths, bureaucrats, 333
cartoon films, 469
castes, 316
  India, 369
Catholicism, 292
  education and, 293
  participation in business, 294
ceremony, 253, 525
  see also ritual
change, 519–20
charismatic authority, 321, 324–6
  routinization, 326–7
charismatic community, 325–6
Charles I, 80
chemistry, 2–3
chess, 410–11, 510
Chesterfield cigarettes, 473–4
children, 206, 352–3, 411, 416–17, 513
  see also education
Chiliasts, 175
China, 2, 237
Christianity, 7–8, 75, 169–70, 211, 250, 516
  ideal types, 277
  social thought, 7–8
  see also asceticism; Catholicism;
    Methodism; Protestantism;
    Puritanism; religion
civic associations, 89–90, 110–13
  newspapers and, 113–15
  political organizations and, 115–19
Civil Rights movement, 493
civil service, 329
  see also bureaucracy
civil society, 8, 21–2, 104, 130–1
civilization, 402–3
class see social class
class consciousness, 162–3
  critical theory and, 433
class situation, 311–12
Class, Status, Party, 271
class struggle, 156–8, 313–14
clergymen, 52–3, 245
  see also religion

clubs, in Germany, 371
collective consciousness, 225–9, 233
  see also class consciousness
collective entities, 284–5
collective representations, 199, 217, 247
collectivities, 511–12
  family considered as, 518–19
  normative culture, 514–15
  segmentation, 514
  societies as, 515–16
  society considered as, 513
commitment, 373–4
commodities, 183–4
  pricing, 184–5
  see also markets
commonwealth, 22, 26, 28–9, 34–5
  institution, 36–7
communication, 349
communication technology, 236
Communism, 156
  abolition of the family, 167–8
  abolition of property, 165–7
  measures proposed in manifesto, 170–1
  proletariat and, 165–71
  women and, 168–9
Communist League, 136
Communist Manifesto, 136, 139, 156–71
community action, 412–13, 416–17
community behavior regulation, 416–17
competition, 31, 147, 184, 187–8, 366, 392
Comte, August, 14, 21, 196, 210, 238, 536
concentration camps, 485
The Condition of the Working Class in England in 1844, 138
conquest, 42
conscience collective, 198–9
consciousness, 143–4
consumer culture, 474–5
contracts, 231, 238–9
control relations, 505–6
Cooley, Charles Horton, 12
coronary thrombosis, 539–40
de Coulanges, Fustel, 196
coups d'etat, 174–5
  1851 France, see also French
    Revolution (1848)

covenant, 36–7
credit, 296, 312
crime, 224, 225–6
   see also law; punishment
critical theory, 13, 421–3, 430–7
   continuity of thought, 437
   criticism, 439
   dependence of cultural on economic factors, 438–9
   economic basis, 434–5
critical thinking, 432
critique (Kantian), 27, 431
crowd psychology, 288
cult value, 447
cultural tradition, 498–9
culture, 438–9
   commodification see culture industry
   see also art
culture industry, 465–6, 470
   advertising and, 476
   dependence on commercial interests, 466–7
   distortion of public perception, 467–9
   ideological hegemony, 473–4
   as opposed to art, 470
   passivization of consumer, 471
   see also art
custom, 206–7, 222
cybernetic priority, 506

Dadaism, 455
day-laborers, 60
de Tocqueville, Alexis see Tocqueville, Alexis de
Death Instinct, 484
decision-making, 410
   by gossip, 413–14
   definition of situation, 410–11
   Russian peasants, 412–13
deductive reasoning, 425–6
demagogues, 288
democracy
   bureaucracy and, 335–7
   extension to black Americans, 407
   relation to 'the people', 22
   threats to, 130–1
   as tyranny of the majority, 124–6, 128–31

   in United States, 122–4, 128–30
      dangers, 130–1
   see also despotism
Democracy in America, 11, 86, 88, *103–21*, *122–32*
democratic states, 88–9
   equality and, 105
   individualism, 106–7
Descartes, Rene, 23, 243–4
desires, 256
despotism, 42–3, 107–8, 127
   see also authority; sovereign power
Destruction Instinct, 484
desublimation, 483, 484–5
deviant behavior, 500–1
dialectic method, 137–8
differentiation, 497, 497–8, 500, 508, 511, 515
   see also division of labor; social stratification
differentiation drive, 372–3
diffidence, 31
Dissenters, 307
dissociation, 207
distraction, 456–7, 467–8
divide and rule, 393–4
division of labor, 9, 55–61, 112, 144, 161, 220–1, 428
   anomic, 238–41
   bureaucratic, 334
   causes, 233–8
      population density, 234–5
   commercial, 368
   as consequence of competition, 187–8
   function of, 221–5
   machinery and, 58–9
   social density and, 237–8
   social solidarity and, 233
   underlying principles, 61–3
   see also differentiation; protectionism
The Division of Labor in Society, 197–8, 198–9, 510, 520
dogs, 61
domination see authority
domination, liberty as instrument of, 480
double, the, 352–3
Dowden, Edward, 305–6

Dreyfus affair, 197–8
Du Bois, W. E. B., 342, 343, *344–5, 404–9*
dues, 324
Durkheim, Emile, 14, 92, *201–64*, 489–90, 491, 520, 521
  influence, 195, 199–200, 489–90
  life, 195–8
  work, 198–9
duty, 330
dyads, 383–5, 511
  characteristics, 385
  termination, 384
  triads and, 386–7
dynamic analysis, 504–5

École Normale Supérieure, 196
economic disaster, 259–60
  suicide and, 262–3
economic materialism, 262
economic power, 310–11
economic traditionalism, 301
education, 168, 204, 206, 411–12
  Catholic *vs.* Protestant, 293
ego, 357–8, 380–1
egotism, 106
18th Century thinkers, 97–100
The Eighteenth Brumaire of Louis Bonaparte, 138
Einstein, Albert, 538–9
elections, 108
The Elementary Forms of the Religious Life, 199
elites *see* aristocracy; ruling class
emancipation, 131, 407–8
  serfs, 368–9
empathy, 67–8
empirical knowledge and research, 3–4, 247
  dependence on ideal types, 278
  theoretical development and, 537–8
endogenous, 519–20
Engels, Friedrich, 136, 137, *142–5, 156–71*, 432
England, 57, 98, 111
  class structure, 190
  democracy, 125
English Revolution, 80, 173

Enlightenment (historical period), 23–9, 97–8, 308
enlightenment (Kantian concept), 50–1, 53–4
entertainment business *see* culture industry
epistemology, 248–9, 436
equal rights, 336
equality, 26–7, 90, 105, 258–9
  of ability, 30–1
  America, 103–4
  bureaucracy and, 334–6
  de Tocqueville on, 103–4
  democracy and, 107
  individualism and, 379–80
  of opportunity, 31
  pre-revolutionary France, 95–6
  of status, 315
  United States, 109, 123–4, 315
equilibrium, 504
erotic relations *see* sexuality
estranged labor, 150
estrangement, 150–1
  see also alienation
ethics, 401
ethnicity, 316
ethnology, 245–6
Europe, 10–11
evil, 250
evolutionary theory, 3
exogenous change, 519
explanatory understanding, 2
exploration, 10–11

factories, 220–1
facts *see* social facts
family, 5, 38–9, 211, 411
  abolition of, 168
  considered as collectivity, 518–19
  dual social role, 374–5
  individualism and, 373–4
  social regulation, 414–15
  see also kinship structures
Fascism, 457–8, 473–4, 485
fashion, 372
Ferguson, Adam, 28
feudalism, 100–1, 157, 160, 377
  see also monarchy

Feynman, Richard, 538
film, 443, 449–50
    cartoon and stunt, 469
    changes in perception of art, 453–4
    effect on perception of the world, 467–8
    as entertainment, 468–9
    as perceptual filter, 467
    post WWI, 468
    shooting process, 451–2
    trailers, 476
    violence, 469–70
fish, 374
Florence, 303
Fortune magazine, 476
founding, 442
France, 105–6
    agriculture, 57
    aristocracy, 96–7
    bourgeois republic, 177–8
    1851 coup d'etat, 174–5
        first phase, 176
    social structure pre-revolution, 91, 95–7
    suicide rate, 263
    18th century intellectual culture, 97–100
    see also French Revolution
Frankfurt School, 13, 140, 345, 421
Franklin, Benjamin, 296, 297, 298
Frederick II, 330
freedom, 26–7, 54, 104–5, 478–9
    of association, 115–18
    enlightenment and, 51–2
    equality and, 104–6
    of the individual, 368, 376–7
    individual *vs.* social group, 372–3
    Kant on, 51
    as natural state of humankind, 38–9
    of the press, 118–19
    societal, 377–8
    of strangers to society, 363
    see also emancipation
freemen, 378, 407
French Revolution (1789), 87, 91, 94–5, 95, 172–3, 378–9
    aims, 94–5
    causes, 95–7, 100–2

    effects, 95
    inevitability, 100–2
    see also France, 1851 coup d'etat; revolution
French Revolution (1848), 176–7
Freud, Sigmund, 12, 342, 344, *396–405*, 484, 485
friendship, 71
Fugger, Jakob, 297
functional analysis
    adaptation, 508–9
    differentiation, 515
    distinction between latent and manifest function, 523–4
        heuristic purpose, 524–9
    goal-attainment, 507–8
    pattern maintenance, 506–7
    see also structural-functionalism
functional integration, 13
functionalism (architectural), 482
functionalism (sociological) *see* structural-functionalism
Futurism, 457

games, 352–4, 510–11
Gance, Abel, 444, 448
Gedankenausdruck, 274
Gedankenbilder, 274
German Democratic Party, 268
German Ideology, 137–8
Germany, 371–2
gestures, 358
Gilbert, William, 532
glory, 31
goal attainment, 492, 507–8
God, 35
Goethe, Johann Wolfgang von, 307–8
gossip, 413–14
governments, 8, 21–3, 34–5, 111–12, 112, 211, 261–2
    limits of power, 112–13
    mixed, 125
    see also authority; democracy; monarchy; sovereign power
Greece, 259, 364, 442
greed, 78–9, 147, 299
grief, 69, 72

Grotius, Hugo, 39, 40, 43
guardianship, 224
guilds, 367–8, 368
guilt, 397–8, 485
Guizot, Franois, 180

Halbwachs, Maurice, 199
happy consciousness, 483, 485–6
Harvard University, 490
Hawthorne Western Electric Studies, 526–7
Hegel, Georg Wilhelm, 137, 138–9, 172
Henderson, L. J., 537
heredity, 258–9
heresy, 292
hide-and-seek, 353–4
historicism, 269
history, 143, 286, 427
Hobbes, Thomas, 7, 25, 25–6, 30–8
   Natural Law, 33–4
home markets, 63–4
honesty, 297
hope, 256–7
Horkheimer, Max, 425–40, 465–77
'How is Society Possible?', 344
human property, 155
humankind
   distinguished from animals, 61, 61–2, 143
   estrangement from nature, 150
   innate religiosity, 217
   life activity, 151–2
   wellbeing, 256
Hume, David, 28
humor, 470
hunting, 1, 62
Husserl, Edmund, 426

I, the, 357–60
   see also ego; self; super-ego
ideal type constructs, 270, 273–4
   capitalist culture, 274
   distinguished from moral ideals, 277–8
   relationship to ideas, 276–7
   religion, 276–7
   role in structuring empirical knowledge, 278
   use in empirical research, 274–5
idealization, 251–2

ideas, 276–7
identity, 351–2
   see also self
ideology, 143–4
imitation, 288–9
immorality, 226–7
   see also morality
India, 369
individualism, 6–8, 88, 378–9
   democratic states, 106–7
   individuals considered in isolation, 382–3
   as limit on individual freedom, 377
   personal and collective, 370
   principle of interest and, 119–21
   see also individuals
Individualism and Intellectuals, 197
individualist sociology, 285–6
individuals, 214
   development, 399–401
   freedom, and commercial enterprise, 368
   see also dyads; ego
industrialization, 159–60
industry, 64–5, 157, 220–1
   division of labor, 59–61
   see also manufacturing
inheritance, 258–9
inhibitive movements, 215
Institute for Social Research, 13
institutions, 202, 499–500, 499–501
integration, 492, 509
intellectuals see writers
interest rightly understood, 119–21
intimacy, 385–6
invisible companions, 352–3
irrationality, 281, 524–5
isolation, 383
Italy, 263

James II, 80
jealousy, 79
Jefferson, Thomas, 131
Jesus Christ, 401
Jews, 237, 294, 316, 365
   as strangers, 362, 365
Jones, LeRoi, 1
journeymen, 293
joy, 69, 471

June insurrection, 177
jurisdictional areas, 328
justice
    de Tocqueville on, 124–5
    Hobbes on, 33
    judicial tenure, 332–3
    restitutory, 224–5, 229–30
    in a state of war, 33
    see also crime; law

Kant, Immanuel, 27, 28, 50–54, 429, 431
kings, 47–8, 79–80, 126
    divine right of, 123
    see also monarchy; sovereign power
kinship structures, 498
    see also family
knowledge, 248–9
Krünberger, Ferdinand, 296

labor, 147–9
    as commodity, 182–3
    Communism and, 166–7
    division of see division of labor
    estranged, 150, 154–5
    price of, 188, 301–2
        see also wages
    see also proletariat; workers
latent function, 492–3, 523–4
    avoidance of naive moral judgment, 528–9
    irrational behaviour, 524–5
    ritual, 527–8
latent pattern maintenance, 492
laughter, 470–1
law, 124, 221–2, 231
    as arbitrator between individuals, 231
    authority under and obedience to, 321–3
    norms, 509
    relation to social solidarity, 223–4
    repressive, 227
    sanctions, 224–5
    see also authority; crime; justice; punishment
laws (of Nature), 33–4
    see also scientific theory
laws (sociological), 286
    see also sociological theory

legal authority, 321–3
Lehon, Countess, 180
Lex Naturalis see Natural Law
liberalism, 136
liberty, 41
libido, 400, 481–2, 482
life activity, 151
Life magazine, 476
lithography, 442–3
living standards see standard of living
locally-focused collective action, 89
Locke, John, 7, 10–11
loss, 532
Louis IX, 41
Louis XVIII, 173
Louis Phillipe I, 177
love, 71
Luhmann, Niklas, 494
Luther, Martin, 172

machinery, 58–9, 186
magicians, 452
majority opinion, 126–8
mammals, 374
man see humankind
manifest function, 523–4
    irrational behaviour, 525
Manifesto of the Communist Party see Communist Manifesto
Mannheim, Karl, 12
manufacturing, 55–7, 220–1
    use of machinery, 58–9
    see also division of labor; industry
Marcuse, Herbert, 422, *478–86*
marginal utility, 290
Marinetti, Fillipo, 457
markets, 28, 392, 508–9
    protectionism, 63–6
    see also capitalism
marriage, 376–7, 383, 415
    bigamy, 387–9
Marshall, Alfred, 491
Marx, Karl, 15, 135, *142–92*, 432, 434, 441–2
    influence on social theory, 140–1
    life, 135–7

Massachusetts, 298–9
materialism, 142–4, 434
mathematics, 425
Mauss, Marcel, 199
Mayo, Elton, 527
Mead, George Herbert, 12, 342, *347–60*
　social theory, 343
meaning, 280–1
　in action, 281
mediation, 389–91
medicine, 99, 539
men (humankind) *see* humankind
Merton, Robert K., 4, 199, 491, 492–3, *523–42*
methodenstreit, 269
Methodism, 305
Middle Ages, 22, 365, 442, 443
middle class, 163, 305
　vocational ethos, 306
　work ethic, 307–8
　see also bourgeoisie
middle-range theory, 531–2
Mill, John Stuart, 220
mixed government, 125
mobility (physical), 362
　see also social mobility
modern states *see* nation states
Molire, 127
monarchy, 47–8, 105–6, 123, 126–7, 127–8, 177
　absolute, 127–8
　see also feudalism; sovereign power
money, 287
　see also capital
monocratic organization, 329
de Montaigne, Michel, 120
Montesquieu, 10
morality, 438
　community, 415–16, 513
　moral codes, 411
　moral judgment, 72–4
　　in sociological analysis, 528–9
　moral sentiment, 80–1
　utilitarian, 297
de Morny, Charles, 180
morphological social facts, 209–10
motivational forces, 499

motives, 283
Motley, Marie, 87–8
mystical experience, 281

Napoleon Bonaparte, 85
nation states, 6, 8
　relationship to church, 516
nationalism, 216
Natural Law, 33–4
nature, humanity's estrangement from, 150–1
Nature (Hobbesian state), 32
Nazism, 422, 474, 485
needs, 479–80
neighborhood, 412
neurosis, 402
New England states, 371
newspapers, 113–15
　press liberty, 118–19
Newton, Isaac, 23–4
nobility *see* aristocracy
normative behaviour, 204, 509, 514–15

objectivity, 363
Objectivity in Social Science, 270
office hierarchy, 329, 330–1
office management, 329–30
officials
　elected and appointed, 331–2
　social position, 331–3
　social status, 331–3
　see also bureaucracy
The Old Regime and the French Revolution, 87, 88, 90, *93–102*
opinions, 73
organicism, 197, 285

pain, 77–8
Paine, Thomas, 24
painting, 447–8, 456
　contrasted with film, 452
Pareto, Vilfredo, 491
Parsons, Talcott, 11–12, 199, 490–1, 493, *495–522*, 541
　work, 491
parties *see* political parties and organizations

Party of Order, 178
passions, 69
patriotism, 109–10
   United States, 129–30
pattern maintenance, 506, 506–7
pattern variables, 491
pay *see* wages
peasants, 412–16
   see also serfdom
pedagogy *see* education
Pennsylvania, 303
personality, 381
photography, 446, 447
   painting and, 447–8
   see also arts; culture industry; film
physical sciences *see* science
Picture of American Culture, 296
piece-rate working, 300–1
Pietism, 306–7
pin-makers, 56
Pirandello, Luigi, 449–50
play, 352–3
pleasure principle, 399–400, 480–1, 482
Poland, 57, 301–2, 415–16
   peasantry, 412–16
political economy, 146–7
political parties and organizations, 115–17, 318–19
   bureaucratic democratization and, 335–6
   civil associations and, 115–19
   latent purpose, 528–9
   United States, 376
   see also democracy
politics, 457–8
polygamy, 387–8
Popper, Karl, 3
population density, 234–5
   division of labor and, 237–8
poverty, 408
power, 310–11
prejudice, 408–9
press *see* newspapers
press freedom, 118–19
pricing
   commodities, 184–5
   labor, 184
primitive societies, 235–6, 245, 250

division of labor, 62–3
principle of interest rightly understood, 119–21
private property, 153–4, 154–5
   abolition, 165–7
   relation to human property, 155
private↔collective, 491
production, 143–4, 147–8, 428–9
   costs, 186–7
   ownership of, 152–3
   see also industry; manufacturing
profit, 186–7
profit motive, 301
Program in Social Relations, 490
progress, 25
proletariat, 161, 177
   class consciousness, 433–4
   Communism and, 165–71
   condition of, 163–4
   development of, 162
   organization of, 162–3
   supremacy, 169–70
   see also workers
property, 46–8, 78–9, 146–7, 153–4, 311–12
   abolition of, 165–8
   as basis for class division, 311–12, 437–8
   human, 155–6
   status groups and, 316–17
propositions, 4
propriety, 76
   economic effects on judgment, 77–8
prostitution, 168, 169
protectionism, 63–6
Protestant Reformation, 7, 292, 516
Protestantism, 291–2
   asceticism, 303–4
   economic rationalism, 294
      accumulation of capital, 297–8
      work ethic, 295–6
   education and, 293
   greed and, 299
   work ethic, *see also* asceticism; vocation
   see also Christianity; Methodism; Puritanism
The Protestant Ethic and the Spirit of Capitalism, 268, 270–1
provincialism, 372–3

prudence, 30
Prussia, 263, 294
psychology, 218, 226
Psychopathology of Everyday Life, 453
public associations *see* civil associations
public conscience, 204
public opinion, 125–6, 126–8
   science, 539–40
   social mobility and, 257–8
publishing, 451
Pueblo people, 525
punishment, 224–5, 226
   purpose, 228
   see also crime
Puritanism, 295, 303–7
Putnam, Robert, 92–3

Quakers, 131, 304, 305, 370

race politics, 405–9
racism, 408–9
Radcliffe-Brown, Alfred, 199
radio, 473–4
rationality, 281–2, 289
   economic, 294
reason, 51–2, 431
Recollections, 88
reference group theory, 532
Reformation, 7, 292, 516
Region Western Philosophy School French
   spiritualism
relations of control, 505
relationships, 5, 361
relative deprivation, 532
religion, 217, 243–5, 269, 275, 415–16
   dependence on social conditions,
      250–1
   development, 244
   enlightenment and, 52–3
   evil in, 250
   as expression of collective ideal, 251–2
   future development, 252–3
   general definition, 244–5
   ideal type constructs, 276–7
   idols, 446–7
   individualism and, 7
   personal and collective individuality, 370

primitive, 245–6, 250
   relation to society, 249–50
   secularization, 4
   social thought, 7–8
   value-commitment, 516
   see also clergymen
Renouvier, Charles, 196
reproducibility, 442–3
   authenticity and, 443–4
   response to art and, 452–3
resentment, 71, 72, 75
respectable virtue, 74–5
restitutary sanction *see* restorative justice
restorative justice, 224–5, 229
revolution, 8, 145, 163–4, 172–3
   bourgeois *vs.* proletarian, 174–5
   de Tocqueville on, 93
   proposed Communist, 170
   see also American Revolution; coups
      d'etat; English revolution; French
      Revolution
Rhode Island, 131
rights, 24, 36–7
   development of concept, 24
   of Nature, 33–4
   of property, 46–8
   slavery and, 42
   of sovereigns by institutions, 35–6
   of the strong to power, 39–40
   to kill, 42
ritual, 524, 527–8
   art and, 446
   see also ceremony; tradition
role-sets, 533–5
roles, 510–11, 511–12
Roman civilization, 224, 235, 259, 37
Roman Republic, 173
Romanticism, 379
Rousseau, Jean-Jacques, 7, 26, *38–49*
The Rules, 198
ruling class, 144–6
Russell, Bertrand, 537
Russia, 11, 237, 294
   peasantry, 412–13

salary, 333
   see also wages

Satan, 250
saving, 304
Saxony, 263
science, 2–3, 23–4, 30, 436–7
   theory, 427, 495, 537–9
   see also empirical research
scientific revolution, 2
sects, 275
secularization, 4
segmentary constitution, 234, 236, 241
segmentation, 513–14
self, 341
   considered as object, 348–9
   development, 347, 356–7
   distinguished from body, 348
   personality, 381
   relation of the subjective to the socially constructed, 357–60
   self-consciousness, 355–6
   as social construct, 350–1
      multiple identity, 351–2
   see also ego; super-ego
self-interest, 62
selfishness, 67–8
sense perception, 444–5
sentiments, 73
serfdom, 164, 368–9
   see also peasants; slavery
sexuality, 364, 396–7, 400, 481–2, 482–4
shears, 60
Shils, Edward A., 492, 527
significant speech, 350–1
Simmel, Georg, 13, 342, 344, *361–95*
slavery, 39, 40–2, 86
   in America, 406–7
   illegitimacy, 42
   see also emancipation; serfdom
Smith, Adam, 9, 28, *55–66, 67–82*, 220
social action, 270
   class interest as cause, 312–13
   classification, 289–90
   criteria for, 287–8
   determining class situation, 314
   instrumentally rational, 290
   motivation, 287
   relation to mass action, 288
social capital, 89
social class, 190–1, 257–8, 437–8
   bureaucratic leveling, 334–5
   determination by economic situation, 311–12, 437
   interests engendering social action, 312–13
   stratification, 190
   see also aristocracy; bourgeoisie; class consciousness; class situation; proletariat; ruling class; social groups; status groups
social commitment, 373–4
social consciousness, 225
social contract, 7, 43–4, 44–6
social criticism, 138
social currents, 205
social facts, 201–2, 203–10, 223
   anatomical, 208–9
   causation, 218
   class distinction, 257–8
   definition, 204–5
   intentionality and, 283–4
   morphological, 209–10
   rules for explanation, 210–18
social function, 213
social groups
   differentiation within, 367, 370–1, 372–3
   expansion, 366–9, 372–3
      individuality and, 379
   the individual and multiple, 373–4
   multiple overlapping, 375–6
   sense of self and, 354–6
   see also dyads; family; triads
social institutions, 202
social mobility, 257–8
   economic crises and, 260
   see also social class
social order, 38
   as restraint upon individual desire, 259–60
social solidarity, 221–3, 238
   arising from the division of labor, 229–33
   crime and, 226–7
   division of labor and, 233
   mechanical, 225–9
   organic, 238
   regulatory rules, 238–40
   relation to law, 223–4
social status, 533–4

capital and, 166–7
social systems, 497
   basis of structure, 497–8
   boundaries, 502–3
   categories, 509–10
   conceptual components, 498–9
   considered as organism, 503–4
   control relations within, 506
   cultural tradition, 498–9
   equilibrium, 504
   functional prerequisites, 497
   sources of structural change, 519–21
   structural analysis *see* structural analysis
The Social System, 491
Socialism: Utopian and Scientific, 137
society, 513
   concept of, 21–3
   definition, 6
   integration as collectivities, 515–16
   as moderator of individual desire, 257
   primitive *see* primitive societies
   see also civil society; commonwealth
sociological theory *see* theory
sociology, 202–3, 208, 223, 278–9, 426
   definition, 1–2
   distinguished from history, 286–7
   history, 1–2, 4–14
   individualist, 285–6
   institutions as focus, 499–501
   laws, 286
   organicist, 197, 285
   origins, 14
   psychological standpoint, 218
   relation to historical fact, 286–7
   as study of groups, 216
   theory *see* theory
   total theory, 539–40
   understanding of action, 283–5
   Weberan definition, 280–7
   see also social facts; structural-functionalism; theory
solidarity *see* social solidarity
Sorokin, Pitirim, 541
sorrow, sympathy with, 77–8
sound reproduction, 443
sovereign power, 26, 35, 44–6, 125–6
   divine right, 123
   enlightened, 53–4
   institutional rights, 36–7
   rights of property and, 46–8
   Rousseau on, 47–8
   see also authority; despotism; government
Soviet Union, 451
Spanish Inquisition, 128
specificity↔diffuseness, 491
Spencer, Herbert, 10, 197, 210, 234–5, 236, 489, 536
Spinoza, Baruch, 23, 226
spleen, 285
stage acting, 448–9
stamping, 442
standard of living, 259–60
state power, 44–6
state, the, 224
statistics, 284
status groups, 314–15
   effect of stratification, 317–18
   ethnicity and caste, 316
   officials, 331–3
   privilege, 316–17
   see also social class
strain, 519–20
stranger, the
   freedom, 363
   objective attitude, 362–3
   trade and, 361–2
strength, 39–40
structural change, 520–1
structural-functionalism, 489–90, 491–3, 496
   dynamic analysis, 504
   functional analysis
      adaptation, 508–9
      goal-attainment, 507–8
      integration, 509
      pattern maintenance, 506–7
   hierarchy of relations of control, 505
   legacy, 493–4
   main components, 498–9
   structural vs. functional analysis, 503
structure, 502

The Structure of Social Action, 491
stunt films, 469
Suicide, 198

suicide
  by nationality and occupation, 262–4
  economic conditions and, 262–3
  rates, 263
super-ego, 400–1, 483
surgery, 452
Switzerland, 263
sympathy, 68–70
  friendship and, 71–2
  judgment and, 72–4
  pleasure of mutual, 70–2
  with sorrow, 77–8
  virtue and, 75

Tarde, Gabriel, 229
taxation, 52, 365
technology, 466
  see also film; industry
temperance, 113
Tennyson, Alfred, 542
tension-management, 506
tenure, 332–3
tertius gaudens, 390–3
theory, 4–5, 425–7, 495–6
  dependence on empirical data, 537
  of knowledge see epistemology
  limits, 15
  middle-range, 531–2
    consistency with overarching theory, 534
  necessary criteria, 6
  purpose, 4–5
  scientific, 427, 495
  total systems, 536–9
  traditional *vs.* critical, 430–1, 432–3, 434–5
  underlying consensus, 429–30
  see also critical theory; sociology; structural-functionalism
things, 201–2
Thomas, W. I., 342, 343, 344, *410–18*
de Tocqueville, Alexis, 11, 15, *94–102, 103–21, 122–32*
  influence, 92–3
  life, 85–8
  social theory, 88–92
Tolstoy, Leo, 348–9
total theory, 536–9

pressure toward, 539–40
towns, 235–6
trade, 62
  strangers, 362
  traders, 362
Trades Unions, 162
tradition, 289
  authority under, 323–4
  see also ritual
training, 184
triads
  divide and rule, 393–4
  dyads and, 386–7
  non-partisan third party, 389–90
  role of third party, 390–3
Trier, 135
triviality, 385

understanding, 282–3
United States, 11–12, 89
  black experience see African-Americans
  civic associations, 110–13
  constitution, 22, 503
  Declaration of Independence, 24
  democracy, 122–4
  equality, 103–4, 109, 123–4
  free institutions, 107–10
  national character, 128–30
  New England states, 370–1
  patriotism, 129–30
  political parties, 376
  principle of interest rightly understood, 120–3
  separation of church and state, 516
  slavery, 406–7
  status equality, 315
  system of government, 122–3
  see also African-Americans; America (for pre US references); civil associations
universalism↔particularism, 491
University of Chicago, 342
University of Heidelberg, 268
upper classes see aristocracy
urbanization, 235–6

Valry, Paul, 441, 443
value-rational action, 289–90

values, 506, 511
  universal collectivity and, 515–16
  see also ethics; morality
Vienna school, 445
violence
  in entertainment, 469
  see also aggression; war
virtues, 119–20, 296–7, 297
  amiable and respectable, 74–7
Vischer, Friedrich Theodore, 279
vocation, 298, 307
  ethos, 306, 308
  officialdom as, 330–3

wage minimum, 185
wages, 166–7, 182–3
  bureaucrats, 333
  effect of competition, 188
  levels of, 184–5
  piece-rate, 300–1, 301–2
  property and, 154
wandering, 361
war, 41–2
  aesthetics, 457
  causes, 32–3
  justice and, 33
  see also competition; World War I; World War II
The Wealth of Nations, 9, 28

weavers, 183
Weber, Max, 14–15, 140, 267–338, 422, 423, 427, 491
  legacy, 271–2
  life, 268
  social theory, 269
Wertrationalitt, 289
will of all, 26
Wollstonecraft, Mary, 24
women, 24, 168–9, 302–3
Wordsworth, William, 411
workers
  devaluation of value, 188
  interests opposed to capital, 185–6
  piece-rate, 300–1
  relation to the products of labor, 148–9
  relationship to production, 147–9
  wages, 182–3
  see also division of labor; labor; proletariat
working classes *see* proletariat
World War I, 11, 197–8
World War II, 13
writers, 97–100, 127, 127–8, 451
Wundt, Wilhelm, 197
Wurttemberg, 263

Xerxes, 394

zweckrational action, 289, 290